James Morton is the author of the hugely
successful Gangland series. He has long experience as a solicitor specialising in criminal
work and was editor-in-chief of NEW LAW
JOURNAL for many years.

'An essential addition to the library shelf'
Time Out

'Written by a lawyer who knows his subject at
first hand, it is not only enjoyable as a read but
valuable as a reference' *Irish Independent*

'Every police officer who thinks "it would never
happen at my nick" will learn from reading it'
Police Review

'Faithfully factual, gripping . . . prescribed
reading' *Evening Standard*

'The tales are told with a flourish in a fascinating, useful and lively history' *The Times*

Supergrasses & Informers and
Bent Coppers Omnibus

SUPERGRASSES AND INFORMERS

BENT COPPERS

JAMES MORTON

A *Time Warner* Paperback

This omnibus edition first published in Great Britain by
Time Warner Paperbacks in 2002
Supergrasses & Informers and Bent Coppers Omnibus
Copyright © James Morton 2002

Previously published separately:
Supergrasses & Informers first published in Great Britain by
Little, Brown in 1995
Published by Warner Books in 1996
Reprinted 1999
Copyright © James Morton 1995

Bent Coppers first published in Great Britain by
Little, Brown in 1993
Published by Warner Books in 1994
Reprinted 1994, 1995, 1996, 1998, 1999, 2001
Copyright © James Morton 1993

A CIP catalogue record for this book
is available from the British Library.

ISBN 0 7515 3293 2

Printed and bound in Great Britain by
Clays Ltd, St Ives plc

Time Warner Paperbacks
An imprint of
Time Warner Books UK
Brettenham House
Lancaster Place
London WC2E 7EN

www.TimeWarnerBooks.co.uk

SUPERGRASSES AND INFORMERS

Contents

Early on one Monday morning
In his dreary prison cell
British soldiers tortured Barry
Just because he would not tell
The names of his companions
And other things they wished to know.
'Turn informer or we'll kill you.'
Kevin Barry answered, 'No!'

Prologue

'Justice was blindfolded,' said Lord Justice Winn, giving the judgment of the Court of Appeal in *Macro and others* on 9 February 1969. 'Let us hope to God it does not happen again.' Cedric Macro, Melvyn Colman and Richard Cork had all appealed against their convictions for robbery with aggravation together with a man unknown. They had all pleaded guilty; they had received four years apiece, and the court substituted a sentence which meant they could be released that day.[1]

Macro and Co. had taken part in what, on the face of it, was a typical raid on a sub-post office. Appearances were deceptive, however. Cork had driven the car to the sub-post office and the fourth man, Raymond Scrutton, entered the building.

> As was now known, although not revealed to the judge, he spoke to the sub-postmaster and confirmed the sub-postmaster had already received a warning from the police that a raid would take place that afternoon, with the assurance that he would not be hurt and the police would protect him.

What Lord Justice Winn described as 'the charade' began. A

1 *The Times*, 10 February 1969.

police officer was in an inner room on the premises. Scrutton called out, 'Be quiet or you'll get yourself hurt.' He tied the hands and feet of the sub-postmaster, put tissues in his mouth, and put him behind the counter. Macro and Colman took postal orders to the value of some £700. Macro was stopped by the police outside the shop; Colman managed to make it to the car but he and Cork were arrested later. Scrutton was given two rewards; one from the police and the other from the Post Office. Macro and the others made statements saying they had been talked into it by Scrutton, whom they did not name.

Lord Justice Winn laid about him: 'It is a horrible experience for any judge to find that justice had been perverted in this fashion even though the degree of blame has not yet been allocated.' An inquiry had been instituted but the whole circumstances had still to be revealed: 'Fortunately very rarely could such a situation have arisen, and it is to be hoped that very rarely indeed would it arise in the future.'

In fact it had already happened, for on 19 May 1969 Frank Alexander Birtles left the Court of Appeal in London a slightly happier man than he had entered it. On 7 February 1968, at what was then West Riding Quarter Sessions, he had pleaded guilty to burglary and carrying an imitation firearm for which he had received a total of five years' imprisonment. His arrest had been preordained.

Birtles had spent a good deal of a previous prison sentence dreaming up an elaborate plan to rob a post office on his release. Once out of prison, he was approached by an informer who in turn introduced him to one of London's 'top' criminals, in fact a police officer. Cars and an imitation firearm were provided for the hapless man, who on his appeal at least had his sentence reduced from five to three years.[2] Lord Parker, the Lord Chief Justice, added:

Before leaving this case, the court would like to say a

2 *Birtles* [1969] 2 All E.R. 1131.

word about the use which, as the cases coming before the court reveal, is being made of informers. The court, of course, recognises that, disagreeable as it may seem to some people, the police must be able in certain cases to make use of informers and further – and this is really a corollary – that within certain limits such informers should be protected. At the same time, unless the use made of informers is kept within strict limits, grave injustice may result. In the first place the court of trial should not be misled.

Secondly, it is vitally important to ensure so far as possible that the informer does not create an offence, that is to say, incite others to commit an offence which those others would not otherwise have committed.

It is one thing for the police to make use of information concerning an offence that is already laid on. In such a case the police are clearly entitled, indeed it is their duty to mitigate the consequences of the proposed offence, for example to protect the proposed victim, and to that end it may be perfectly proper for them to encourage the informer to take part in the offence or indeed for the police officer himself to do so. But it is quite another thing, and something of which this court thoroughly disapproves, to use an informer to encourage another to commit an offence or indeed an offence of a more serious character which he would not otherwise commit, still more so if the police themselves take part in carrying it out.

After Macro the Home Secretary announced that H. M. Inspectors of Constabulary had been asked to inquire into the current practice where information had been received from informers, and to review what was happening to that information. The material was duly obtained and guidance was given but never published on the ground that it related to 'an operational police matter'. It did, however, take account of the following points:

If society is to be protected from criminals, the police must be able to make use of informants in appropriate circumstances, Informants, appropriately employed, are essential to criminal investigations and, within limits, ought to be protected. The police must not embark on a course which will constrain them to withhold information from or mislead a court in order to protect an informant.

What follows is an account of what has happened in the courts in England and America, both before and after Frank Birtles and James Macro made their small piece of British legal history. Not only the role of the informer and super-informer (the grass and supergrass) will come under scrutiny, but also the inextricably linked behaviour of the police and private detectives in infiltrating criminal enterprises.

The police do not regard all people who give information to the police as informants. The other three groups are what they describe as public-spirited citizens, eccentric or nuisance individuals, and contacts. People in the first category are, of course, to be encouraged, whilst those in the second category generally fall into two sub-categories: eccentrics who are suffering from some mental aberration or delusion short of certifiable insanity; or inquisitive busybodies who imagine that offences of a certain type are being committed. Their information is regarded as being usually completely unreliable and valueless. Many confess to crimes they could not have possibly committed. Officers are enjoined to treat them with caution and tolerance and not to dismiss their claims out of hand.

The urge to confess is an interesting one. In the case of the killing of Elizabeth Short, the 'Black Dahlia', who was literally cut in half in Los Angeles in 1947, over forty people, both men and women, confessed to being her murderer. The spate of confessions was not unexpected. Dr J. Paul de River, the psychiatrist working on the case on behalf of the Los Angeles police, said that those who confessed did not do so out of a desire for publicity but rather this would spring from masochism, exhibitionism or a guilt complex engendered by some forgotten incident of childhood.[3]

The third category, of contacts, comprises individuals – such as bank managers, caretakers or DSS investigators – who whilst supplying information of value and expecting protection do so without thought of payment. It is envisaged that contacts may develop into informants, and they are divided into four categories:

(i) the informant who gives information about crime and criminal associates either for money or the kudos; (ii) the participating informant; (iii) an individual who has been registered as a police informant on the authority of an officer of the rank of Assistant Chief Constable or above, in the knowledge that he may play a part in a crime or its preparation; (iv) a resident informant who has been an active participant in serious crime and who after arrest or conviction is willing to give evidence against his former colleagues. Serious crime is defined as one which on conviction would generate a prison sentence of ten or more years.

The last category is the overlapping protected informant: someone who informs on associates who participate in crime, and who subsequently becomes known, thus placing him in danger. Generally people in this category, which includes participating informants, will not be prosecuted. It is on the stories of people in the last three categories as well as the so-called undercover agent – a police officer who adopts a false identity or cover story to enter into an existing conspiracy with individuals involved in criminals acts, and whose purpose is to facilitate the arrest of the individual as well as to recover money, stolen goods or drugs – that this book is based. It is in these roles that the definitions have become blurred.

Nowadays police surveillance and infiltration has become an industry in itself, with high-technology gadgetry employed for electronic eavesdropping and intelligence systems. I propose,

3 The unsolved case of the 'Black Dahlia' is examined in detail by Richard and Molly Whittington-Egan in *The Bedside Book of Murder*, pp. 91–118.

however, to concentrate on the men and women on the ground who are, so to speak, at the coal-face. They may now have gadgetry at their disposal if things go wrong and, to use a police expression, the wheels come off. Twenty years ago – and even less – they certainly did not. This is the history of the infiltrator and the undercover agent who operated, and still largely does, alone and with little in the way of day-to-day protection. Primarily, however, it is the story of the use of the informer by the authorities, and of the authorities by the informer.

I have endeavoured to limit the book to the role of the informer, *agent provocateur* and undercover agent in the criminal field rather than the political one. Profit, not politics, is again the key word. Of course, matters overlap and it is not entirely possible to separate them completely. At the beginning of the chapter on informers I have therefore put together a very brief history of the use made of these men in the political field. Those who wish to look at that other side of the fence more closely may care to turn to Bernard Porter's double bill of *Plots and Paranoia* and *The Origins of the Vigilant State*, as well as Philip Knightley's *The Second Oldest Profession*. I have deliberately avoided a discussion and history of the use of the supergrass in Italy. Those who are particularly interested in the work of the informer there may care to read *The Dishonoured Society* by John Follain.

Given the use of the rise and fall of the supergrass system in Ireland, I have also included an account of their troubled history there. I accept, of course, that this is almost wholly politics and not profit, but since it largely runs parallel with the use in criminal cases *per se* in England I thought it appropriate to include it.

There is a variety of colourful words and definitions, both English and American, for informants, all denoting the opprobrium of society. None can be seen as a synonym for a hero. In alphabetical order they include *Bertie Smalls*, from the first of the modern British supergrasses; *canary* (from singing); *fink* (originally a police officer); *grass, nark* and the less derogatory term *nose* (both Victorian or earlier), *peacher, snitch, squawker, squeaker, squealer, stag* and *stoolie* and *supergrass* itself.

The derivation of the usually British term *grass* is obscure. In America it usually means lettuce, the straight hair typical of Caucasians and marijuana. Here it most likely comes from the rhyming slang *grasshopper* = copper. Another version of its derivation is that grass whispers in a wind and the phrase was popular in the 1930s following Fred Fisher's song *Whispering Grass* popularised by The Inkspots. Recently I came across the phrase *in the grass* meaning to be on the run from the police or prison. Perhaps this is the real derivation of grass – the person who informs on a person on the run. It has some logic to it. A *nark*, often used as copper's nark, is Victorian and comes from the Romany *nak* meaning nose; in fact, in the eighteenth century a *nose* was a term for an informer. Copper itself comes from to cop or to catch, and dates from around 1700. In American slang, a *copper* can mean not only a police officer but also an informer. To *peach* derives from Shakespearian times, and one of the informers in John Gay's *The Beggar's Opera* was Polly Peachum. Although *snitch* dates back to the beginning of the eighteenth century, it is now more common in American slang than in British. Originally it referred to a cardsharper who, when his colleagues had refused to share their winnings with him, went to tell the victim of the crooked game how it had been worked against him. In Scottish slang, *snitchers* were also handcuffs.

Squeaker comes from the end of the seventeenth century and certainly lasted until the middle of this one, when Edgar Wallace wrote his successful novel *The Squeaker*. It has largely faded from use in the last seventy years.

The American word *squealer* probably derives from the noise made by a pig, which is said to resemble that of an informant. Another version of the origin of the term is that an old-time thief was caught when villagers heard the squeals of a pig he was abducting. Certainly, the squealer or informant had been regarded on a par with the child molester in criminal and particularly prison society.

A relatively early American criticism of the behaviour of a squealer comes from the Kansas newspaper *Kinsley Graphic* in the 1870s, when four train robbers were convicted on the testimony of the fifth, Dave Rudabaugh. With a fine command of journalese the newspaper editorialized:

> Rudabaugh testified that he was promised entire immunity from punishment if he would 'squeal', therefore he squole. Someone has said there is a kind of honour among thieves. Rudabaugh don't think so.[4]

Squawker, originally meaning a protester, first shows up as an informer in American slang in the latter half of the nineteenth century when *to play baby* was also common. A *squawker* was also a burglar alarm. A *stag* was originally an enemy, but by the middle of the eighteenth century it had come to mean an informer, and the term was used in mid-nineteenth-century America. *Stoolie* or *stool pigeon* was originally a man made use of by criminals, but by the end of the nineteenth century in America it referred to a man who had been turned by the police to betray his colleagues; the derivation is from a decoy duck. *Stool pigeon* was also an uncommon term for the moon; no doubt because it betrayed a criminal's whereabouts. More often it was used in the same way as *shill*, meaning a person in the pay of a gambling house who attracted players to a faro table.

All the words indicate a dislike and distrust of the informer and the concept behind it. Of course, no police force can function without it, however. From an early age a police officer learns that informers are useful. In a questionnaire devised by one American force, one question read:

4 Carl Sifakis, *An Encyclopedia of American Crime*, p. 680.

The best arrests are made:

(a) As a result of hard work and intelligent dedication to duty
(b) As a result of good information from an informer
(c) Coming from the 'coop' (a police resting place on duty such as a café).

Out of a total sample of 186, 44 per cent thought the correct answer was (b), a figure which rose to 52 per cent in patrolmen of 2–12 years' standing and remained at 50 per cent for patrolmen with up to 19 years' service. 47 per cent of detectives thought that (b) was the correct answer.[5]

Here is the District Attorney of New York County making a pitch for the good guy and misunderstood grass before the New York Grand Jury Association in February 1947:

> . . . we appear to have developed a public morality which condemns – rather than praises – any private citizen that we – as members of a free society – have called into being.
>
> We want the laws enforced and to this end we hire men at good salaries to secure obedience to the law, to preserve order, and to protect our persons and property. They, by declining to co-operate and, indeed, by bringing social pressure against those who would co-operate we make it difficult, if not impossible, for those men to serve us effectively. They would fight our enemies, but we refuse to point them out. We make a sort of game of it, between law enforcement officials and criminals, and sit complacently quite ready to applaud a brilliant stroke on either side.

Seven years later J. Edgar Hoover had this to say in further bolstering the low self-esteem of the informer:

5 Arthur Niederhoffer, *Behind the Shield*, p. 218.

Experience demonstrates that the cooperation of individuals who can readily furnish accurate information is essential if law enforcement is to discharge its obligations.

The objective of the investigator must be to ferret out the truth. It is fundamental that the search includes the most logical source of information – those persons with immediate access to necessary facts who are willing to cooperate in the interest of the common good. Their disservices contribute greatly to the ultimate goal of justice convicting the guilty and clearing the innocent. Necessarily unheralded in their daily efforts, they not only uncover crimes but furnish the intelligence data so vital in preventing serious violations of law and national security.

There can be no doubt that the use of informants in law enforcement is justified. The public interest and the personal safety of those helpful citizens demand the zealous protection of their confidence. Unlike the totalitarian practice, the informant in America serves of his own free will, fulfilling one of the citizenship obligations of our democratic form of government.

The criminal and subversive underworld has long sought to destroy our effective informant system.[6]

What must be remembered is that because it is essentially a secretive subject and because the lives of their officers are at risk, the police are naturally and rightly reluctant to say how much undercover work is going on at any one time. 'Very much more than you think,' says a London solicitor with a major criminal practice. Whether this is deep cover work or, more likely, short in-and-out assignments such as playing the role of a hit-man and conducting negotiations with a sulky wife or husband, is impossible to say. Even awards made to undercover officers are done privately, and no mention is made in official police papers.

6 *Law Enforcement Bulletin*, June 1955.

Throughout the text there are numerous quotations and I have endeavoured to give an attribution to them. This does not mean in any way at all that the words quoted were actually spoken. Many of the recollections have been written years after the incident was supposedly recorded verbatim. In recent years, however, more efforts have been made to ensure that there is a good deal of accuracy in what criminals in particular have to say. Gone (or nearly gone) are the days of the sensational reportage of, say, the Jack Spot autobiography. For example, before the autobiography of the Mafia hit-man, the ferocious Donald 'Tony the Greek' Frankos, the tapes of his voice were analysed by a voice-stress analyst who thought that the confessions were 'free of mendacious stress'. Similarly other writers have begun to triangulate the stories told to them by major criminals by checking with lawyers, newspapers and court papers. Nevertheless, in the case of criminals there have been scores to settle and debts to be paid, let alone memories genuinely impaired. It is impossible to guarantee that what they say is the whole truth or in some cases even a great percentage of it.

The quotations from Robert Fleming and Hugh Miller's *Scotland Yard* are made with the permission of the Peters Fraser and Dunlop Group Ltd.

My thanks are due to Al Alschuler, Michael Bailey, J.P. Bean, Rowan Bosworth-Davies, Andrew Boyd, Dave Critchley, Oliver Cyriax, Clifford and Marie Elmer who tracked down countless books for me, Sean Enright, Jeremy Fordham, Frank Fraser, Dominique Harvie, Brian Hilliard, Gabriel Jewel, Jennifer Kavanagh, John Kaye, Joan Lock, Cal McCrystal, David Martin-Sperry, Jean Maund, Adrian Neale, Clive Norris, Bill Pizzi, Nipper Read, John Rigbey, Jack Slipper, Edda Tasiemka, Graham Tutthill, Alice Wood and many others on both sides of the fence who have asked not to be named.

As is always the case, the book could not have been written without the endless patience of, and help from, Dock Bateson.

1

There's Always an Excuse

There is a belief amongst police officers that all but the most
staunch villains are capable of being turned into grasses. In
Crime Inc. Martin Short points out how, when it suited them,
the major crime figures, Lucky Luciano and Meyer Lansky,
were quite capable of telling the police something which might
get them off a temporary hook.[1] In England, members of one
major London gang of the 1960s were reputed to be protected
at Assistant Commissioner level because of the quality of
information supplied by them.

An ex-detective sergeant (Flying Squad) says:

> They will all do it, from the biggest professional villain
> down to the kid just starting out on the back streets –
> it's just a question of catching them right. They do it
> for all sorts of reasons but money is always the big
> draw and if the reward is high enough, there's always
> someone . . .

1 Luciano admitted his convictions, for running a gambling house in 1930 and
for narcotics in 1916. He claimed he had never touched dope again but Dewey
(Thomas E. Dewey, the special prosecutor) proved he had been caught selling
drugs in 1923 when police had found morphine and heroin at his home. Luciano
told them that at 163 Mulberry Street there was a trunk full of narcotics. Thirteen
years later Dewey revealed his treachery, showing that even the great Luciano
would turn stool pigeon when it suited him. Martin Short, *Crime Inc.*, p. 153.

Repentance and rehabilitation, at least a sufficient amount to dollop before the court and jury, are necessary requirements of any self-respecting supergrass's confession.

> I have been in police custody since Sunday 18 May 1980 during which time I have been asked by Detective Chief Inspector Peters about jobs I have done with Tony Fiori, Christopher Wren and others. I have had time to consider all these matters and I had the opportunity of speaking to my wife. I now want to admit all these matters and to completely wipe my slate clean, because I have decided to finish my life of crime and start a new life with my family. I should like to tell you today about a burglary . . .[2]

Indeed one of the least palatable excuses of the defendant in general and the informer in particular is that he has found religion. It is as old as the hills, but two examples may be picked from more modern times. In America in the trial of Big Bill Haywood, Pettibone and Moyer in 1907, the assassin Harry Orchard, who had been put on death row for a ten-day period, was seen by the Pinkerton agent James McParland and hectored on the benefits of repentance and with tales from the Bible. Eventually sufficient seeds had been sown in the mind of the man who, quite apart from blowing up fourteen non-union miners and later the ex-Governor, had

> begun his career of crime by short-weighting the farmers who brought milk to his Canadian cheese factory; who burned down the factory to collect the insurance; who abandoned his wife and six-months-old daughter to run away with another man's wife; who married a third

2 Michael Gervaise (1 July 1980), beginning one of his many statements, this time against a man who was acquitted. Gervaise subsequently retracted this statement.

woman without bothering to divorce his first wife, spent
the money she had inherited from her husband and
deserted her when she had become so destitute that she
had to take in washing; who had stolen from his miner
roommate the possessions of his truck; who had robbed
mines for their ore; who had burned down a saloon for a
hundred dollars so the owner could collect his insurance;
who had plotted to kidnap the child of a former partner
to rob streetcar conductors, to sweat gold coins; a man
who for years had roamed the West, living off the kit of
burglars' tools found in his truck . . .

Now:

I am ready to make a full confession. I am asking no
leniency. My lonely imprisonment will drive me crazy
if I do not confess. My conscience will not permit me
to keep the guilty secrets. If ever a man suffered the
torments of hell, I am that man, I can only hope that
God in his infinite mercy will heed my prayers. I have
been a wicked man. I want to tell.[3]

In his piece about the killing of his daughter, Dominique,
and the subsequent character assassination by her killer,
her boyfriend John Sweeney, the novelist Dominick Dunne
comments acidly on Sweeney's new-found state of grace:

It is the fashion among the criminal fraternity to find God,
and Sweeney, the killer, was no exception. He arrived
daily in the courtroom clutching a Bible, looking like a
sacristan. The Bible was a prop; Sweeney never read it, he
rested his folded hands on it. He also wept regularly. One
day the court had to be recessed because he claimed the

3 Irving Stone, *Clarence Darrow for the Defense*, pp. 199–200.

other prisoners had been harassing him before he entered
and he needed time to cry in private.[4]

On 24 May 1992 thirty-eight-year-old George Woodhatch was
shot twice in the head and twice in the chest as he was using
the telephone at the Royal Free Hospital, Hampstead, where he
was recovering from an operation for piles. It was a contract
killing and although his business partners, Paul Tubbs and
Keith Bridges, were charged with his murder, initially the
magistrates found there was no case to answer and they were
discharged.

The prosecution's case was that Woodhatch had swindled them out of £50,000 in their roofing business. Despite
a lifestyle which included a Porsche and a Japanese-style
house in Hertfordshire, he was in serious financial trouble,
owing £400,000 in tax and having substantial business debts.
Woodhatch was also becoming increasingly irrational and at
the time of his death was on bail for threatening to kill
his secretary. A twenty-seven-year-old Maori woman, Ti
Rangimara Ngarimu, was hired by Tubbs and Bridges for a
fee of £7,000. She had met Bridges, another New Zealander,
when she was working as a barmaid in London in the late
1980s. At first when Bridges put the proposition to her she
thought he was joking, but almost immediately agreed.

The plan was that she would shoot Woodhatch while he was
in hospital and then immediately fly out to New Zealand. On
her first effort she could not find the ward and, now wearing a
baseball cap, tracksuit and gloves, returned the next day. This
time she shot him from a distance of three feet. Bridges, she
said, had told her, 'Shoot him twice in the head and twice in
the body to be sure of death.' She then caught the 4.30 flight
from Gatwick, leaving the clothes and gun at Bridges' flat in
Camden Town to be disposed of.

4 Sweeney was acquitted of first degree murder and sentenced to six and a
half years' imprisonment for voluntary manslaughter. Dominick Dunne, *Fatal
Charms*, p. 24.

It seems that, at first, it was thought that Woodhatch had died from a brain haemorrhage and it was not until five hours later, in the mortuary, that the bullet wounds were discovered. After the killing, Tubbs telephoned a friend and asked him to meet Bridges to help in getting rid of the holdall. The friend looked inside and threw the holdall in a pond, later helping the police retrieve it.

In early 1994 Ngarimu returned to England. She had been contacted by the police but at first told them, 'I couldn't kill a chicken. I am a vegetarian.' Over the years, however, she had embraced religion and after at first fighting extradition procedures she voluntarily returned to England as she wished to clear her conscience. Bridges and Tubbs were re-arrested and were convicted largely on her evidence. They had already pleaded guilty to conspiracy to pervert the course of justice by disposing of the gun and clothes she had worn. Bridges and Tubbs were sent to prison for life, with a recommendation they serve fifteen and sixteen years' imprisonment respectively. The trial judge added that he thought the Home Secretary should consider making each man serve a further third of the sentence. 'In my view it is necessary to protect the public from serious harm from each of you,' said Sir Lawrence Verney, the Recorder of London. Ngarimu was sentenced to life imprisonment.

The case has two interesting features. The first is that this appears to be the first use of a female hit-man in this country. The second is that during the trial, which began in May 1994, Bridges was shot in the chest and leg while walking in Ruislip, Middlesex. No arrest was made over that attack.

The motives of the first of the so-called Mafia informers, Joe Valachi, were described by narcotics agent James P. Flynn who eventually gained his confidence.

Revenge was a large part of it, but it was also a cold calculated move for survival. Don't think for a moment that this was a repentant sinner. He was a killer capable of extreme violence. He was devious, rebellious against all constituted authority and he lived in a world of fear and suspicion. Fear especially marked him. Fear of what he was doing and at the same time fear that nobody would believe him.[5]

In general, though, in common with many supergrasses, Valachi believed that nothing was his fault at all. James Flynn's view was that:

Joe thought everybody was responsible for Joe. He only took up crime, for instance, because he never had a chance as a kid. It was the prison administration's fault that he had to kill a man he didn't even know. He doesn't consider himself a traitor to the Cosa Nostra; in his mind Vito Genovese was the real traitor.[6]

Sometimes the reasons can be personal. Former Ghost Squad officer John Gosling recalls an instance where a small-time thief informed on his daughter's boyfriend in order to break up the relationship.

Norris and Dunnighan found in their survey that one informer was a father who informed on his son and collected money, whilst another was a man who was having an affair with his neighbour's wife and found that, first, it was a good method by which to keep the husband away and, secondly, that it provided money for the relationship.[7] A senior officer recalls an early informant:

I was on the desk one Friday when a call came through giving me details of a potential drug bust. The caller wouldn't say who he was and when I checked out the address it was not known so I did nothing further. The

5 Peter Maas, *The Valachi Papers*, p. 34.
6 *Ibid.* p. 38.
7 For further details of the findings of the survey, see chapter 11: *The Police*.

same thing happened the next Friday. The man recognised my voice, asked why I'd done nothing and gave even more details. I checked out the address again. Nothing was known about it and I still waited. Third Friday the call comes again so this time I acted. It was the best bust I had that month. As I was in the front room a middle-aged man comes in and looks at me. He's the father-in-law. I thought, 'Hello, I know where those calls have been coming from.'

Others would inform on their wives, mothers, and assorted relations if it suited them. An ex-Flying Squad officer recalls one instance:

Another man who worked for me was called Pat. He lived out Woodford with his wife and several grown-up kids and was totally without scruple. He had worked for various Flying Squad and divisional officers for years and, although he was rather lazy, when he could be motivated there was no better grass in London.

Once, when he had been a bit backward in coming forward, we met him in a pub in Loughton and told him he'd better pull his socks up. He protested the usual story of there 'not being much about, Guv', but after a while and his fourth pint he perked up and said, 'Tell you what – you can have the old woman if you like.' We fell about at the double meaning but we were completely speechless when we heard what he really meant. His wife had, he said, recently purchased a television stolen from one of the TV rental firms, and Pat was suggesting we turn over his own house and charge her with receiving. There wasn't going to be much money in it, £20 if he was lucky, but as far as he was concerned that was £20 he wouldn't have had otherwise. He also complained that she did nothing but watch *Coronation Street* and he never got a chance to have a sensible conversation.

Oddly, when we nicked her, his wife did not have much to say at all. She pleaded guilty and was fined a fiver or something nominal. Pat sat in the back of the court and later got his £20. As far as I know she never ever sussed him.

Pat fell neatly into the category described by John Gosling.

The category of informants who give the most trouble are the ones who do it strictly for the money. These are usually the real toe-rags or slags – the dregs of the criminal fraternity – and they can cause you endless problems. If a job doesn't come off we call it a blow-out. With an informant who works for money, you can expect seven or eight blow-outs from ten pieces of information. You're doing the work, getting the warrants, setting up the searches, making yourself look an idiot if it does blow out. They're gambling on a few tips coming off, so they can scrape together £20 or £25 out of the information fund to carry them through one more day or have one more booze-up. I've always avoided that kind of informant whenever I can, but it's very easy to get trapped until you get to know the ropes.[8]

Informants could, occasionally, be used to recruit other informants.

Some time later Pat set us onto a stolen car parked up outside a block of flats in West Ham. 'The ice cream,'[9] said Pat, 'lives in the flats and he's driving the motor every day. When you nick 'im, be a bit shrewd – 'e'll be shit scared and you can get him on the firm.' We had to sit outside the flats for less than an hour: the ice cream came

8 Jack Slipper, *Slipper of the Yard*, p. 33.
9 Ice cream freezer = geezer.

out, got in the vehicle and promptly had his collar felt. Pat's assessment of his character was completely accurate. After an hour in the nick he was bending backwards to tell us anything and everything he knew. All he wanted in exchange was bail and a bit of help in court. Within three weeks we had a very good receiver in Bow from him, a conspiracy to forge fifty-pence pieces, an escapee from prison who'd been on the run for years, and we passed on a couple of nice hashish jobs to the Drugs Squad.

I don't remember if he got a discharge or a fine but he was compromised. Even if he'd wanted to walk away he couldn't and we teamed him up with Pat. Many policemen go all their service without contact with one effective working grass and to those who have never experienced it, two working together is akin to having two ferrets working a seemingly inexhaustible rabbit warren.

Some men become informers because they simply cannot handle being in a police station. This was the situation of one thief recalled by a major London player:

Golly became an informer after the Silver Bullion Raid at Mountnessing. Funnily he didn't grass everyone. Instead he named four out of the eight men, and two were just buyers.

I'd had a row with him over some dough back in the 1960s and in 1972 as I was walking along the landing at Brixton who was there but Golly. I said, 'Forget about the argument. We were in it all together.' He showed me his body and it was black and blue. He'd been caught running across the fields. He was a man who'd been at it for years. He'd been arrested for loitering and he'd done approved school but he'd never been tested. That's why he'd named names but he wouldn't go in the box to give evidence.

Years later I was in a restaurant in Romford and called

a cab to go home. Who was the driver but Golly? I didn't recognise him at first but then he said who he was and I replied, 'Do me a favour. Stop the cab. I'm getting out.' He said he hadn't really been a grass and if he'd wanted he could just about have got me life. I said, 'For old times' sake what I'm going to do if I bump into any of the others I'm going to have to tell them where you're working, so turn the job in.' In the end I never ever mentioned it but he quit the job.

Some informers turned, or at any rate said they did, because they thought that they were likely to be killed by their employers. Cecil Kirby, a Canadian former member of the Satan Choice motorcycle gang who became a hit-man for the Toronto-based Commisso gang, was convinced that they were plotting to do away with him. He had found them unreliable employers in the first place, welshing on deals and undercutting his payments for arson, beatings and murder plots on the pretext either that they hadn't been paid or that he had not completed the work satisfactorily. Now, in 1979, he was sure that his health required a change in occupation. They had, he claimed, suggested he go on a mission for them to Calabria to kill Girolamo 'Momo' Piromalli – then a powerful, if not the most powerful, Calabrian boss in Southern Italy. They would, they said, arrange for his travel there and back and pay him 10,000 Canadian dollars. He was afraid that all that would be paid was his fare to Italy, and that he would become part of a foreign field that was for ever Canada.

Kirby is also honest enough to admit that he was due to face a long sentence for a substantial breaking and entering offence: 'My choice was doing a long stretch in jail and probably being killed there by one of the Commissos' people or being done by the Commissos outside prison walls.'

He also had problems knowing to whom to turn. The previous year he had tried to work with an officer in the Ontario Provincial Police – assisting, he says, in saving his life by tipping him off that the Vagabonds, a particularly unpleasant Toronto motorcycle gang, had put out a contract on him. He had expected some tangible assistance from him with future court cases, but received none. Now out of the blue he called the Royal Canadian Mounted Police National Crime Intelligence Section and found safety if not redemption.[10]

Thank God for the telephone! Small-time thief Vito Zaccagnini was unable to pay the juice or interest on his loan. By 1963 he owed more than $22,000 to Cosa Nostra money-lenders, with total weekly repayments running at $1,500. Now he found himself in Winnebago County Jail at Rockford near Chicago. He arranged for a bondsman to obtain his release and was, he says, given a message by Pete Cappelletti, the bondsman, that there was a contract out on him. On 14 March 1964, on his way back to the wing, he saw a way out.

> I knew I couldn't pass up that telephone. If I didn't grab it then, I never would. So I called the FBI office in Chicago. I'd hardly started to talk when I froze with fear. I'd never done anything like that before. I knew what the code was. And I knew what would happen to me if I broke the code and they [the mobsters] got to me.
>
> They'd capture me to torture me, that was what I was afraid of. They kill you slow. I know what happened to Jackson [William Jackson, murdered in 1960]. They hung him on a hook and left him there. It took him a couple of days to die.[11]

One man who knew, or should have known, how the Mafia worked was Donald 'Tony the Greek' Frankos who at the end of a long career as a contract killer, during which time he had worked for both the Italians and the Westies, eventually decided discretion was the better part of valour. He was

10 Thomas C. Renner and C. Kirby, *Mafia Enforcer*, pp. 3–13.
11 Sandy Smith, 'How an informer traded mob secrets for his life', in A. Halper, *The Chicago Crime Book*, p. 455.

arrested on 15 October 1981 in Jilly's nightclub (named after
Frank Sinatra's then bodyguard) and identified as one of the
killers of Clarence Jones, a former basketball star and then
drug-dealer, who had been shot to death outside his apartment
in the Bronx, one of the few hits of the time with which Frankos
actually denies involvement. Convicted, he was sentenced to
25-years-to-life. Whilst in prison he negotiated a contract for
himself to dispose of another prisoner who was to be a witness
in a major drugs trial. He then discovered that his potential
employer had decided to extend the number of people who
were to be hit, and these included the prosecuting attorney and
the arresting officer. Frankos decided to look after himself. In
a touching passage, this killer describes his feelings:

> I hated the idea of being a rat. I know everybody says
> that, but I believe my entire life points to this truth: the
> main satisfaction I obtained as a criminal came from being
> acknowledged as a tough guy, a hitter, an individual who
> knew the consequences and accepted them . . . and if I
> went to the cops I'd become a pariah.
>   The thought wouldn't leave my head, though I tried to
> banish it, order it to go away. It made my stomach churn,
> and I cursed myself repeatedly, calling myself every name
> in the book. I became physically sick, retching in the toilet
> bowl, but the thought wouldn't go away.

Eventually he heard a prison guard joke that 'the walls have
ears' and in his paranoid state decided that the plot had been
uncovered: 'A few days later I whispered in a guard's ear, I
want to talk to the U.S. Attorney.'

What he would not do, however, was to give evidence, and
as time went on he came to realise that unless he did the
protection he was being offered under the Witness Protection
Program extended only to being kept safe in prison. A return to
the street was not available. He testified before a grand jury and
then thought better of it. He was returned to the general prison

population in Attica, where he lasted only a short period before being badly beaten and shanked. Frankos agreed to return to the Witness Protection Program but apparently has consistently refused to give evidence. He is continually shifted from prison to prison for his own protection.[12]

Becoming a supergrass is not confined to the lower echelons of criminal society. The best can become one. Warwick Reid, the head of Hong Kong Legal Department's Commercial Crime Bureau went down the grassy path. He admitted accepting $1.6 million in bribes to fix fraud cases, but his original eight-year sentence was reduced in return for his testimony against his accomplices. He served four years and eight months and was released in November 1994. The Hong Kong Government hopes to recover about half the bribe money by selling Reid's home and fruit orchards in New Zealand. He said the rest of the money had been spent in an effort to flee Hong Kong justice. He had disguised himself as the adopted Caucasian son of a Chinese fishing family, and had so managed to slip into China. He then made his way to the Philippines where he was traced in Manila.

On his release he said he would not go into the Witness Protection Program and had been offered consultancy work throughout Eastern Asia. 'I have a very, very deep sense of regret about many things,' he told the press. 'I regret that I betrayed my office and took money in the first place.'

Of course, even a temporary intention to 'go straight' may be sufficient self-justification for an informer. As Jack Slipper says:

> I was less impressed, though, by the reasons O'Mahoney[13] gave me for wanting to become a supergrass. He told me he was sick of crime and wanted to make a complete break from it. If he grassed on everyone, he said, no one would ever invite him into another team, and that way he

12 Donald Frankos, *Contract Killer*, Ch. 21.
13 For the career of Mr O'Mahoney, see pp. 65–73.

wouldn't be tempted back into the criminal world. But supergrasses need excuses – excuses they can make to themselves – more than they need reasons.[14]

There are some who become informers simply because they are getting old. Men who in their youth would have been the lions of – and been lionised in – the prison, in middle age no longer hold that same position. No matter how many repetitions are done in the prison gymnasium, no matter how many pounds are lifted on the Nautilus equipment, the reactions and the ability to inflict, and more importantly to receive, punishment are not the same. The once king of the prison is now relegated to a role where, instead of ruling and protecting, he is ruled and often needs to be protected.

Others do it because, having grown old, they cannot keep at their old trade. In the nineteenth century the Pinkerton agency was particularly good at recruiting old American burglars. One was the sixty-one-year-old William Forrester, who had been a prime suspect in the killing of millionaire Benjamin Nathan.

At 6 a.m. on 28 July 1870, Washington Nathan went downstairs in his home at 12 West 23rd Street, New York, to get a glass of water. Passing by his father's bedroom he looked in. On the floor lay Benjamin Nathan, said by some, almost certainly inaccurately, to be the richest man in the world. At least when his death was announced the flag over the New York Stock Exchange was flown at half-mast. He had been hit over the head a number of times with a carpenter's tool. There were signs of a struggle and a safe in the room had been opened. It appeared that the killer had washed his hands in a basin in the room but had not bothered to remove a handprint from the bedroom wall. The science of fingerprints was, however, unknown in America at the time.

Young Nathan was known to have been in financial trouble and to have quarrelled with his father over money. He had,

14 Jack Slipper, *Slipper of the Yard*, p. 114.

however, an alibi for most of the time-of-death bracket, provided in part by what the newspapers coyly described as a 'lass of the pavements'.

Nathan was not the only son of the family under suspicion. His brother Frederick was also in the house, as was William Kelly, the son of the housekeeper, a man with at least a passing acquaintanceship with the Underworld. Curiously, neither of them appears to have heard anything of what must have been a violent incident.

As is often the case in a high-profile murder, over the months and years a number of people confessed. One man, John T. Irving, was brought from California but was unable to persuade the authorities of his guilt. A prisoner in Sing Sing later implicated a burglar, William Forrester; he said he had heard that Forrester had intended merely to rob the house, but was surprised by Nathan and killed him. Forrester denied, almost certainly falsely, that he was in New York that night, but there was no hard evidence against him except that of the squealer and he was never charged. One puzzle was the question of the street door. Everyone in the house said it had been locked up for the night, but when Washington Nathan went down to get his glass of water he found it unlocked.

In 1879 Washington was shot in the neck by a former girlfriend, Fanny Barrett. The Chief of the New York Police then had the ingenious idea that whilst Nathan was recovering from the anaesthetic he would be questioned about his father's murder. Unfortunately the scheme came to nothing when the bullet worked its way out of its own accord. He remained under a cloud for the rest of his life, finally leaving America to live in Europe, where he died in 1892 at the age of forty-two. His hair was said to have turned prematurely white.

Now William Forrester, down on his luck, became a poacher turned gamekeeper. He dressed in old clothes and, staying in rooming houses in Toledo and Canton, became a mine of information. His street (or should that be hotel) credibility was, of course, first class.

Other Pinkerton informants included John C. Archer who, after a none too successful career as a pickpocket and burglar, opened a rooming house in Dayton, Ohio, along with his wife, herself a rather more successful pickpocket.

Archer, writing under the engaging name of Birdstone (it had previously been Brimstone), reported to his supervisor, Seymour Beutler, on the growing menace of the Yegg, or safebreaker:

> I don't know what connections you've got in Toledo, but if you're interested in Yegg work throughout the country that's your town. There are now about three mobs in there, one of whom came in about three months ago $10,000 strong, and they frequent only three places, Bill Downey's on Erie St., Johnnie Henry's, also Bill Herbert's place. If you've got a hot Yegg kick take Toledo for it and win.[15]

Archer kept his cover by coming out of retirement to execute raids on his own behalf. There was honour amongst thieves, and an informer could rely on at least tacit help from his employers. In December 1903 Archer was arrested in Indianapolis and put on an identification parade attended by a Pinkerton superintendent, Irle, who helpfully failed to pick him out. Seven years later, when he was charged with a bank robbery, the agency gave no effective evidence against him.

Some inducements to turn informer may not receive the hoped-for response.

In the spring of 1992 the Tokyo police offered a reha- bilitation programme for Yakuza gangsters who wished

15 Quoted in Frank Morn, *The Eye that Never Sleeps*, p. 146. The derivation of Yegg is interesting. In this context it almost certainly refers to John Yegg, said to be the first safe-blower to use nitro-glycerine. There are, however, alternative suggestions on offer. One is that the word was used for a professional killer employed by Chinese Tongs. Another is that it comes from the German *Jaeger*, meaning hunter, and yet another that it meant a beggar.

to retire and cross over to the paths of righteousness, that is the Tokyo police. One of the problems is the disconcerting habit of self-mutilation to be performed ritually if, in any way, a junior member has offended a senior. Off comes the top joint of the little finger (and for repeated offences other joints and other fingers). This makes the former Yakuza easily identifiable, and the police offered a package which involved reconstruction with toes substituting for the missing joints. It was not a success.

On the other hand, some do.

Later in the year the Italian police devised a package offering informers a new name, home and nose. Special telephone lines were installed so that viewers of teletext p.166 who dialled Rome 33170804 could ring in. In the first nine months of the operation some 280 *penititi* telephoned, a substantial increase on the dozen who had grassed in the previous forty years.[16]

The use of informants has long been regarded as good control policing. Commenting on corruption in the Metropolitan Police, a PC with twenty-two years' service said:

Prior to the Mark era, it was getting to such a state that particular squads just ran London. But it kept a lot of the villainy down. Now they're not keeping it down. They're not allowed out drinking so they don't get their informants in pubs.[17]

Says John Gosling:

Some did it for the excitement which, in cases where

16 O. Cyriax, *Crime*, p. 444.
17 Roger Graeff, *Talking Blues*, p. 326.

the snout had ceased to be a crook, compensated for the loss of thieving's thrill. Minor snouts worked for you for a variety of reasons: from motives of spite, envy or jealousy, or to try to evade the worst consequences of their crimes. A few did it to enjoy the thought that they were in a sense private detectives.[18]

One of the other problems for the police is how to keep their charges happy in isolation from the prison population as a whole. The technique does not seem to have changed over the last century. In the Haywood trial of 1907 it was thoroughly desirable to find someone who would back up Orchard's confession. He had implicated a Steve Adams and that man had promptly been arrested. At first he was placed in a cell with Orchard, who worked on him for five days to warn him of the dangers of non-cooperation and recount the good things which would follow if he helped out. Adams was then introduced to the Pinkerton agent McParland and signed a confession corroborating Orchard on a number of crimes against property.

He was instantly taken out of his cell 'and placed in a sunny room in the hospital'. His wife and children were brought from Oregon and the family was set up in a bungalow outside the penitentiary walls. Three meals a day were brought in from the guards' table.

Unfortunately Adams did not appreciate all the blessings which were being heaped upon him as an informer and State witness. He retracted his statement and was immediately arrested and taken three hundred miles north to Wallace where he was charged with murder.[19]

When Bertie Smalls decided to become the first real supergrass

18 John Gosling, *The Ghost Squad*, p. 39.
19 Irving Stone, *Clarence Darrow for the Defense*, p. 214. Defended by Darrow, Adams was acquitted after two jury disagreements.

in 1971, he received numerous benefits such as a suite in a Wembley hotel and then a series of safe houses. Others, such as Maurice O'Mahoney and Billy Williams, were lodged in Chiswick police station where they had colour television, games of snooker, rounds of golf and walks in the countryside and, according to O'Mahoney, drink and visits from his girl-friend who conceived a child in the cell. The cell conception was something he denied at a subsequent trial, but there is a picture of Billy Williams in a policeman's hat holding a bottle of champagne.

As Jack Slipper recalls:

Billy Williams was not a likeable sort of man. He was only too pleased to bite the hand that fed him. He was getting more extra facilities than he ever dreamed of, but he still saw fit to bite the hand that fed him and have photographs taken of him wearing a policeman's helmet.

When the *News of the World* photographs were pub-lished I expected to be called in to explain how it could have happened. I was quite pleased to find my immediate superiors accepted this could happen when you had a man like this.

Informers had to be treated with kid gloves. Once they had received their five-year sentence they could, and sometimes did, decide to have little more to do with the case.

Even with regular exercise O'Mahoney went into his shell and wouldn't talk with anyone. I spent a fair bit of time with him, not necessarily coaxing him to pull him out of his depression but to find out what interests he could safely be allowed to have put into operation.

One of the better-class North London villains, John Moriarty, also ended as a supergrass. By this time he was, however, heavily into drugs. He introduced smack to one of his partners, Tony 'Carrots' McLean, the son of Ginger Dennis from the

Spot slashing and cousin of the street fighter, Lenny 'Mean Machine' McLean. As one old face recalls, 'Carrots always said to me, "If only I could go back in time I would kill that bastard stone dead or anyone else who gets kids on drugs."'

By then the supergrass system was becoming more and more complicated. There now seemed to be competing teams of supergrasses: those who gave evidence under Scotland Yard detective Lundy's aegis and those, such as John Moriarty, who gave evidence against Lundy's friend Garner. Moriarty had twice been shot by rivals and had served periods of imprisonment. Now he decided to give evidence and to implicate Roy Garner.

'I never knew why he did it,' says former local police officer, Dave Brady. 'After all I was the officer called to The Favourite, the pub in Hornsey Rise where he'd been kneecapped. I asked what had happened and all he said was, "I fell down the fucking stairs, didn't I?"'

In the early 1970s Garner, together with a friend Kenny Ross, had purchased premises in Upper Street and then tried to evict the tenants. When this failed the premises were fired. Now, after the two shootings, Moriarty was prepared to name them in his statement as the organisers of the arson attacks.

Often the most loyal of supporters was a hidden blade of grass. One ex-CID officer recalls the double career of Charlie Clark, highly thought of by the Kray twins. It shows how easy it is for a police officer to lean on a villain.

Some time in 1967 when I was stationed at Walthamstow I got some information that a man living near Walthamstow dog track was an active receiver. With another officer I obtained a search warrant and called to see the man, who I had been told was named Charlie Clark. He lived in a bungalow off the main road and as soon as I saw him I knew that he was not the normal, run-of-the-mill denizen of East London's suburbia. Aged over fifty and a widower, he looked ill and gaunt, and I concluded that he had either 'prison pallor' or the type of complexion which results from too many late and very heavy nights on the tiles. The bungalow was clean and tidy in a bachelor sort of way and as we meticulously searched the house I became more and more aware that something was amiss, but for the life of me I could not put my finger on it. Charlie Clark was the perfect gentleman: wearing a smart cardigan and suit trousers, he showed us round and was almost too happy to co-operate fully and answer any questions we put to him. He didn't work, he said, he was 'on the panel', and did a bit of gambling.

We found no stolen property, and as Clark pressed a cup of tea on us the niggle in my mind suddenly resolved itself. Leaving him and my colleague in the small kitchen I had another look round the little bungalow, and sure enough I was right: there were two beds made up – one in a bedroom which was certainly that of Charlie Clark, and another single bed in a front room. Also in this room was a clothing rail of the type used by dress and clothing shops, and hanging from this in plastic covers were eight or nine expensive-looking men's suits. The suits weren't stolen; they were obviously in current use. I pointed this out to Clark and after some prevarication he said: 'They're Ronnie's, aren't they? He stays here on and off, when he feels like it.' 'Ronnie', it turned out, was Ronnie Kray and on being taxed further about his association with the Twins, Clark said he did a bit of driving for them, a bit of this and a bit of that – all in all a general factotum. I should point out at this stage that this was at a time after the Twins had been acquitted of the McCowan fiasco, and as far as the run of the mill CID officers were concerned no major inquiry into their activities was current.[20]

At that time, though, we knew that the Krays had

20 The Krays had been charged with blackmailing Huw McCowan, and after considerable shenanigans and a retrial had been acquitted. For a full account of the case, see L. Read, *Nipper*.

interests in premises in Hoe Street, Walthamstow and that a well-known Walthamstow hardman Tommy 'The Bear' Brown was believed to be a close associate, so we were not too surprised at the revelations. Clark, though, looked very sheepish and was foolish enough to say that it would not go down too well with the Krays if they knew that his house had been 'turned over' and that in addition to having incurred their wrath by having been stupid enough to draw police attention to the address, he would also lose considerable income as they would certainly ditch him.

From his point of view this, of course, was the worst thing he could have said. Within a few minutes he had been left in no doubt whatsoever that unless he was prepared to 'help' me with information, no matter what about, the Krays would certainly get to hear from one source or another that the bungalow had been visited and further that Ronnie's temporary digs had been noted. We left the bungalow with Clark's assurances that reliable information would be forthcoming ringing in our ears. We had, of course, no intention of ever 'leaking' what had taken place to anyone at all, let alone the Krays. We had played 'the game' with Clark and if he was fooled and went along with it, all well and good, but to be honest I had little hope.

Much to my amazement Clark was in touch by telephone within a few days and thereafter on a fairly regular basis. Obviously it would never have been a very good idea to call at the bungalow and as far as I can recall I never actually saw Clark in person again. His information, though, was always one hundred per cent reliable: there were several small receivers, a couple of stolen cars – all that sort of thing, but nothing about the Krays, which I suppose was very much on the cards. From time to time I would ask him what 'the Firm' were up to, where they were drinking and who they were annoying, but he never seemed to know anything apart from what was common knowledge.

Then, after a few months something very odd happened. One morning the Walthamstow Detective Inspector Frank Nichols called me into his office and told me I had been summoned to the Yard to see a Chief Superintendent named 'Fergie' Walker. Nichols said he had no idea what it was about but I had to go and that was all there was about it.

I arrived at the Yard to see Walker with no small feeling of apprehension: the man was a senior officer in C.1 department, which amongst many other things dealt with discipline and complaints against police at that time. I knew it was odd to be summoned in person but just the same I was concerned. As it turned out, my fears were misplaced and I knew there were no problems as soon as I went into Walker's office and he called me 'Sarge'. He had become aware, he told me, that I had an informant named Charlie Clark who was closely associated with the Krays. I had done very well to cultivate such a snout, he said, and he was just wondering if Clark had ever had much to say about what the Twins were up to. I told him that he had not, but assured him that if he ever did I would contact Walker or his sergeant immediately.

Driving back to Walthamstow, I thought over what had happened. No one knew that Clark was working for me – with the exception of the DC who had accompanied me on the original search of the bungalow – so how had Walker found out? There could only be one explanation: Walker had a telephone intercept on Clark and had therefore overheard all of our mutual conversations. A year or so later, after the arrest of the Twins by Nipper Read and Henry Mooney, and when I knew that Fergie Walker had started off the second major investigation into their activities, this was confirmed to me.

Over the months, he faded out and I did not pressurise

him. I had drawn his criminal record file and noted that
he had a few minor convictions years before both in the
name of Clark and Bateman, but apart from that there
was nothing of any interest at all.

During the whole period of our association, he told me
only a few small pieces of information relative to the Firm
and these, I imagined, were pretty common knowledge
in any event. He told me that Ronnie was intent on
becoming some sort of country squire and was spending
most weekends in Suffolk, and told me that the Twins had
persuaded the writer, John Pearson, to do their biography.
He stressed that this was to be in the manner they saw
fit and, very tongue-in-cheek, he told us that they were
well on the way to convincing Mr Pearson that they were
some sort of Saviours and Benefactors of the East End
Poor and Needy as well as the Well Known Sporting and
Philanthropic Twins they encouraged the press to refer to
them as, and that suggestions that they were engaged in
criminal activities – let alone gangsterism – were wicked
lies. Years later Nipper Read told me that after the arrest
of the Krays and on their first appearance at Bow Street
magistrates' court Pearson had offered to bail them. 'You
just sit here for a couple of weeks, Mr Pearson, and listen
to what's going to be said,' Nipper told him, 'and then
come and tell me if you want to bail them.' Needless to
say, the offer was not repeated!

Clark also told me of Ronnie's predilection for homosexual activities, which at that time came as something
of a surprise to me, although according to Clark's
informant this was well-known amongst London's criminal fraternity.

In his book *Villains We Have Known*, Reggie Kray
refers to Charlie Clark as being some sort of King of
the Cat Burglars – a master climber. I never saw any
evidence of this and there was nothing in his criminal
file to give even the slightest indication that he was any

sort of a villain at all. Kray also alludes to how loyal to the Firm Clark was, how fond he was of Ronnie and that he was a dependable and unswerving associate. Countless CID officers over the years have maintained that there is no such beast as a criminal who will not give information if needs must; the Krays, perhaps, should have borne this in mind![21]

The informer can expect a hard time in prison with much, if not all, his sentence served on Rule 43.[22] Some were reasonably fortunate:

There were four men, Johnny R., Billy T., Kenny Baker,[23] he's dead now, and another old-time villain from Manchester were arrested up there over a set-up by a man who was very well respected, Billy E.

   During their sentence when they got a lot of bird he turns up in Ford. I'm in there as well. Billy T went over to Billy E and said something. The man went white and went over to the screw in charge. That was at midday. He was taken to the security room and by 1.30 he was

21 In the early hours of 10 March 1989 Charlie Clark, now known as Bateman, was found stabbed to death at his home in Beaufoy Terrace, Dover. He was then seventy-one and after having had a leg amputated, spent most of his time sitting looking out of the window of his home. In July 1990 nineteen-year-old Shane Keeler was sentenced to life imprisonment for his murder. Keeler, who had been in care since the age of five and was suffering from an abnormality of the mind, had pleaded guilty to manslaughter on the grounds of diminished responsibility, but the plea had not been accepted. He had broken into Clark's home and, when discovered, had stabbed him in the neck. He made off with £5, which he spent at the docks on video games and a cup of tea. Clark's neighbours challenged the prosecution's description of him as a 'likeable old man'. They referred to the court case the previous year and some said they had been obliged to move because of his behaviour.
22 Rule 43 allows the separation of certain categories of prisoners from the main congregation. These include men who are convicted of sex offences and those who are informers, as well as convicted police and prison officers. The governor of a prison may also order a disruptive man to be detained under Rule 43 for the good order of the prison.
23 On 27 November 1990 Baker was shot dead by the police when he and three members of the South-London-based Arif family were cornered after they had ambushed a Securicor van at a filling station in Reigate, Surrey.

in a van on his way out of Ford. No one knew where they took him.

Some were not so fortunate:

> So one day when this grass was at work in the bag shop one of the chaps asked the screw if he could fall out to go to the recess, having got permission he went into the recess; had a shit in his handkerchief, holding it behind his back he went up behind the grass (who was bisily sewing away at a mailbag, and he was not expecting anything to happen to him) and emptied the contence of his handkerchief into this unsuspecting geezers bin, and then just walked away as inocent as you like, sat down in his place and carried on with his work. After a while the grass put his hand in his bin for something or other, and was horryfied at what he found, he went and showed the screw what someone had done, but the screw began to raw with laughter, at this every one began to laugh untill the whole place was in an upraw. [*sic*]24

Some had it even worse.

> In 1967 I nearly took Joe Cannon's eye out in Pentonville. I was back there for visits and now Joey was doing his seven for armed robbery and he had a name as a grass in prison.
> I got this great big, long needle which was used for sewing mailbags. When he came in and was locked up, I crept up to his cell. He said, 'Who is it?' I said, 'It's me, look through the spy-hole,' and as he did I stabbed it through. He screamed out and immediately rung his cell bell. I just drifted away. He told the authorities it was me, but there was nothing they could do because by the time

24 F. Norman, *Bang to Rights*, p. 85.

they got to me the needle was long gone and I was back in my cell. It was his word or mine, and the screws weren't going to act just on his word. He was immediately taken to the hospital and then transferred out of the prison.[25]

Many informers both in history and in more recent times have found that they could not manage to bear the burden they had brought on themselves and the damage they had done. In modern times Richard Piggott, who sold forged letters to try to implicate Parnell in the Phoenix Park murders, gassed himself in Madrid. In June 1927 a man named Johnstone – who had, it seems, been the paid spy of Scotland Yard, keeping them informed on the National Unemployed Workers' Movement – committed suicide on a beach at Southend by drinking a bottle of disinfectant. David Smith, the robber, now planning to repeat his career as a supergrass, changed his mind and hanged himself in his cell shortly after his birthday.

25 F. Fraser, *Mad Frank*, pp. 112–113.

2

Grasses – The Early Days

It is not given to everyone to leave his name in the English language. Lord Cardigan did; so did the Duke of Wellington. Leotard, who invented the art of the flying trapeze at the Cirque d'Hiver in Paris, also fashioned a body-suit. The Earl of Sandwich left his name as a type of food, and a poker-playing man named Reuben had his given to a variety of that food. Opera singers and ballet dancers have given their names to meringues, puddings and toast. The early 1970s introduced a new word – supergrass – into the English language. It also gave a new phrase to criminal slang – *to do a Bertie*, or inform to the police. Even Capone and the American gangsters of the twenties and thirties did not reach that height of acclaim, neither did Jack Spot, Billy Hill or the Krays. Now Bertie Smalls of Edmonton, North London, reached the pinnacle of fame. The phrase quickly passed into more general usage; schoolchildren in London used the phrase of others who had sneaked to their teacher. It had taken centuries for a criminal to attain that position of fashion-making.

There is no thing new under the sun, said Ecclesiastes, and informers themselves are as old as history. Although, in English law, strictly speaking he was probably an ordinary person acting under duress rather than an informer, one of

the first recorded uses of the confidential informant seems to
be found in the Old Testament:

> *24:*And the spies saw a man come forth out of the city, and
> they said unto him, Shew us, we pray thee, the entrance
> into the city, and we will show thee mercy.
> *25:*And when he shewed them the entrance into the city,
> they smote the city with the edge of the sword; but they
> let go the man and all his family.[1]

In around 200 BC, Scipio Africanus had his soldiers dress up
as slaves in order to spy on the Carthaginians. A problem
arose when one of the 'slaves' was recognised as having been
at the same school as a Numidian general. In about 100 BC
Quintus Servius offered to spy on the Teutons who were then
threatening Roman Gaul. His idea was to put on Celtic dress
and acquire 'the commonest expressions of that language for
such conversations as might be necessary'. His undercover
mission seems to have been successful; he 'mingled with the
barbarians, and after seeing or hearing what was necessary,
came back'.[2]

These were rare examples, however, and quite clearly
military and political. More germane, in Ancient Greece
there were sycophants or fig-blabbers who informed the
authorities on those who were exporting figs illegally. In
the Roman Empire the fire-brigade was used for the purposes
of the secret police:

> A soldier, dressed like a civilian, sits down by your side,
> and begins to speak ill of Caesar, and then you do too,
> just as though you had received from him some guarantee
> of good faith in the fact he began the abuse, tell likewise
> everything you think, and the next thing is – you are led
> off to prison in chains.[3]

1 Judges 1 24–25.
2 J. Haswell, *Spys and Spymasters*, p. 12.
3 Chester G. Starr, *Civilisation and the Caesars*, p. 141.

In sixteenth-century India scavengers, refuse collectors, merchants and pedlars were employed as police spies, and in Arabian countries eunuchs often headed networks of secret police. England long had a political spy system going back at least to Harold, and this reached a relatively early apotheosis in Francis Walsingham and his spy system for Elizabeth I.

Historically, in England, the individual was required in law to inform on a man whom he knew to have committed a felony – an offence which, on conviction, could lead to the forfeiture of possessions to the Crown. If he did not, then he could be prosecuted for the offence of misprison of that felony and in turn could himself be fined or imprisoned.[4] There was therefore a large body of people who were quite prepared to inform on their neighbours and friends. In Walsingham's case he was prepared to take the matter a stage further and pay for the information.

There was also the related concept of the hue and cry. A person witnessing a felony had a duty to sound a general alarm, calling, 'Out! Out!' Those hearing the call then, under pain of fines and imprisonment, had a duty to turn out with bows, arrows and knives to chase down the felon. This was the *posse comitatus*. There was also an obligation to take part in a night watch.

There is now some doubt amongst legal writers as to whether the obligation still exists. If it does, it now exists more in its breach than its observance. It has certainly persisted in the requirement that a citizen should go to the assistance of a police constable in uniform who calls for help. However, in a recent case in 1993, although a prosecution was brought against a man who had declined to assist a police officer trying to catch a burglar, it was abandoned. Possibly this was due to the fact that, the previous week, a man who had done

4 Felonies were the serious crimes such as murder, rape, robbery. In mediaeval times they carried not only the death penalty but also the forfeiture to the Crown of the felon's property. Other crimes were called misdemeanours and did not carry forfeiture. The difference between a felony and a misdemeanour was abolished by the Criminal Justice Act 1967.

just that had been shot and killed. In any event the prospect
of a conviction seemed unlikely.

Given there was no such animal as a police force as we
know it in England and Wales until 1829, one of the ways
of controlling crime was the use of the dedicated common
informer. He was described by Radzinowicz as:

> a person who brought certain transgressions to the notice
> of the authorities and instituted proceedings not because
> he, personally, had been aggrieved or wished to see justice
> done, but because under law he was entitled to a part of a
> fine which might be imposed.[5]

By the end of the seventeenth century, with the rise of the
highwayman, the coiner and other serious criminals, the
reward for apprehending felons was a judge's certificate
which exempted the holder from any obligation to put in
a spell of duty as a part-time parish constable. It soon came
to be known as blood-money or a Tyburn Ticket, and could
change hands at auction for up to £300 although between
£10 and £50 was a more usual price. The proceeds of sale
would be divided between the informer and the arresting
constable. One result was that small-time criminals had a
virtual licence to commit crime in the hope that they would
graduate from misdemeanours to felonies and so make their
arrest financially worthwhile to the informer. A second was
that anyone of substance and intelligence, if not integrity,
could buy a lifelong exemption from duty. As a result many
of the parish constables were illiterate or foolish and very
often both.

By the beginning of the nineteenth century a common
informer, as now, could make a good living from receiving part
of the penalty imposed. The awards for bringing to the notice
of the authorities 'offences leading to corruption of morals'

5 L.Radzinowicz, *A History of the English Criminal Law*, vol ii, p. 138.

could range from 1s 8d (8p) to the much more worthwhile
£200. A publican who was found to have allowed his licensed
premises to be used for gaming by 'journeymen, labourers,
servants or apprentices' could expect to pay the informer
10s (50p) for the first offence and £2. 10s on subsequent
occasions.[6]

Common informers could not expect to be popular and
indeed they were not.

> . . . popular prejudice has attached odium to the common
> informer not because the thing itself is wrong since the
> law has made it necessary but because many dissolute
> characters have taken up this state, seldom with a view
> to benefit the public . . . Informers are indispensibly
> necessary to the execution of the law.[7]

Certainly in London the common informer, as a legal entity,
faded from view shortly after Peel's New Police marched
into the streets in 1829. By the end of the next decade
the magistrates had power to reduce the part of the penalty
which was paid to the informer or deny him the right to any
payment, and as they imposed this practice more and more
often the sport became less profitable. As it took longer
to establish police forces throughout England and Wales,
so it took rather longer for the practice to die out in the
provinces.

On the other hand the decision of the supergrass, as
opposed to the common or garden informer, to assist the
police has almost invariably been taken at a moment when his
professional life, for one reason or another – very often because

6 *Ibid.* p. 142.
7 P. Colquhoon, *A Treatise on the Functions and Duties of a Constable etc.*, p.
57. Colquhoon was a metropolitan stipendiary magistrate who was obsessed with
the idea of establishing a proper police force to replace the often inefficient and
corrupt Bow Street Runners who operated at the time. By 1800 his *Treatise on
the Metropolitan Police* had reached its sixth edition.

he has been arrested and finds that death, transportation or more recently a long term of imprisonment is looming large – has become impossible, so as to cut himself a better deal. It also happens when he finds that his life on the outside is similarly threatened by his employers or former friends.

Possibly the first of the British supergrasses was a professional housebreaker, John Smith. On 5 December 1705 he appeared at the Old Bailey on four indictments including the theft of fifty pairs of men's shoes, 900 yards of cloth, 400 lb of China silk and 128 pairs of gloves. Ironically in the case of the shoes an accomplice gave evidence against him to the effect that they had been stealing as a team for some six years. There was accomplice evidence in the second case (the cloth), which was dismissed, and he was acquitted over the matter of the silk. There was nothing much he could do about the matter of the shoes, since he was caught in the shop with the goods packed up neatly awaiting disposal. Since, at the time, conviction for any offence of theft where the value of the goods was more than five shillings carried the death penalty, he was sentenced to be hanged.[8]

Smith appeared at Tyburn on 12 December, having travelled west from Newgate prison, a journey which coined the expression 'to go West' well before either Mae West or the American newspaper proprietor, Horace Greely, put their names to the phrase. There he was hanged, or rather half-hanged because while he had been swinging on the

---

8 The practice was for a merciful jury to return a verdict that the prisoner had stolen goods value 4s 11d and so avert the death penalty. Even if they did not do so, there were still a number of ways in which the prisoner could escape the gallows. There was the Oath of Clergy under which if verses of the Bible could be read (or memorised) then the prisoner went free. There was also branding which, as the years went by, was often done with a cold iron.

From 1706 onwards Smith appeared on an infrequent basis in the London courts until in 1720 he was sentenced to transportation. At the age of sixty-six he had been found trying to break into a warehouse. There is a full account of the activities of John Smith in James Bland, *Crime, Strange but True*, pp. 183 *et seq.*

gibbet for between seven and fifteen minutes, his reprieve was announced. He was cut down and resuscitated.[9]

A reprieve then was not necessarily a complete escape for a prisoner. It was more in the way of a stay of execution. Many would be subsequently pardoned, and a good few not. Smith was fortunate; and it may be that fortune favours those who help themselves because on 20 February he received an unconditional pardon. By 3 March he had informed on 350 pickpockets and housebreakers who had joined the Army to avoid detection. In the November of that year he named two sergeants and six soldiers in the Second Regiment of Footguards in which he had served. The men were acquitted.

One of those who was not so fortunate in obtaining a pardon was John Poulter, otherwise known as Baxter. In one of those gallows repentance books which were so popular, and which were the ancestors of the 'true crime' books of today, Mr Poulter was condemned to hang for robbery and then in Ivelchester jail purportedly wrote an account of his life and crimes:[10] 'I have followed Gambling and Defrauding these five years passed, and lived on the Spoil of other Men's Substance.'

He had met John Brown, alias Dawson, Mary Brown and Mary Davies at Lichfield in Staffordshire on a fair day and

after some ceremony we all agreed to go and drink a glass of wine; accordingly we went to Mr Wm Brook's at the George Inn, in the said town, and were shown up stairs; we had not been there long before Mary Brown espied a large chest, and said here is a chance, the lid being loose, and her hand but small, she pulled out of the said chest

9 Failed executions were not all that uncommon. In November 1740 the seventeen-year-old William Duell had hung for half an hour before he was cut down from Tyburn and resuscitated. He was later transported. In 1782 John Hayes was revived after his hanging and was later given a passage to America paid for by a surgeon from Gough Square, London. Douglas Hay *et al, Albion's Fatal Tree*, p. 104.
10 John Poulter, *The Discoveries of John Poulter, alias Baxter*.

one yellow silk flowered damask gown, one green silk
ditto, one brown silk ditto, and one black flowered silk
capuchin, which Mary Brown carried out of the said house
in her apron, to the place where our horses were . . .

and off they went for a rip-roaring five years spent in theft and
robbery in Britain and Ireland.[11]

It ended in tears, of course, after the robbery of a Dr
Hancock of Salisbury, and, in an effort to save himself
from the scragsman, Poulter turned informer naming some
thirty-one of his friends and accomplices to the justices at
Taunton. Perhaps because there was no great success in
apprehending these villains, who included his old friend John
Brown, no reprieve was forthcoming.

The author of the postscript to the book certainly believes
Poulter was unlucky:

This unfortunate man, after having made important discoveries of great use to the public and for much less
than which many a man has not only receiv'd pardon
for capital offences, but also rewards, had the fate by a
series of unlucky incidents & circumstances, to be brought
to suffer, after having entertained the most allured and
flattering hopes to the contrary. When he first made his
informations against his accomplices, which was soon
after he was taken up, he desired they might be kept very
secret; and particularly he gave a charge to the officer
who was sent to Bath to apprehend his accomplices, not
to divulge his errand at his arrival to any one person there

11 Mary Brown had a splendid career. In the previous 4½ years she had been
tried six times all over the country. The first was in Westmorland, where she
was acquitted and her then husband Peter executed. After that she appeared in
Ruthen, Derbyshire, with Brown, alias Dawson, and then in Staffordshire and
the Fen country mostly for pickpocketing. She was transported in 1746 but had
effected her illegal return. After the death of her husband she seems to have
teamed up with Rosey Brown, who himself was transported in 1750 but also
returned before the expiration of his sentence.

except the mayor; because there were several persons who lived in good credit in the eye of the world, that yet had intelligence with his gang.

The charge did no good to Poulter or the officer. Within an hour of the man's arrival the gossip was all over town and, it seems, the names of the wanted men and women appeared in a printed broadsheet. Unsurprisingly, the birds flew.

Dr Hancock seems to have played the market both ways. In return for the confession, the return of some of his property and the information, it seems he told Poulter he would be 'very favourable to him in the prosecution'. Not so, writes the author. 'The doctor behaved against him with the greatest inveteracy, and used all his interest to prevent the judge from granting him any respite from execution.' In return for his information and the details of how transported felons could get back into the country unapprehended . . .

. . . just before they go on board a ship, their friends or acquaintances purchase their freedom from the captain, for about 10l sterling. Then the friend of the convict gets a note from the captain that the person is free to go where they please, unmolested, when the ship arrives between the Capes of Virginia.

There is also advice to retailers how to detect and prevent thefts:

The counter being covered with goods, one of the two shall look over the goods, whilst the other shall plant a piece under the rest, not opened, altho' one or more persons be behind the counter, who shall not see them, because they will open a piece of stuff and hold it up between the owner and their partner, who sits with her petticoats half up, ready for the word napp it; she puts it

> between her carriers (that is her thighs), gets up & lets
> her cloaths drop agreeing and paying for what they like,
> and so go off, and can walk very well without putting
> her hands to hold it; then going into a yard or entry, the
> partner takes it from them.

Respites were given and indeed there was some feeling
amongst members of the community that Poulter was worth
preserving. The fairly disingenuous argument was that his
accomplices, who were now believed to be abroad, would
never feel able to return to England because he knew their
haunts and would be able to inform on them again.

Unfortunately those members did not include the local
gaoler who refused to allow Poulter a bed. A campaign
was begun to ensure that the repentant man was given
some comfort, but it seems this may have rebounded with
the authorities. Poulter was sentenced to hang in March 1752.
All his good intentions and protestations came to nothing
when, after forcing a window with an iron bar from his
cell, he escaped on 17 February along with a debtor who
was lodged in the prison. Poulter was obliged to walk in his
irons, resulting in a very badly chafed leg. The intention was
to make for Wales, but when they arrived in Wookey they
thought they were near Axbridge. Poulter went to bed and
then it was a case of the informer informed upon. He was
captured by some workmen and returned to Ivelchester where
the gaoler, smarting from the escape and the bedding incident,
successfully petitioned that Poulter be hanged immediately.

Poulter received the news and spent the day in prayer.
However, he still had one last card to play. In his book he
had named a man 'F' as being involved in the robberies and
having melted plate for him. On the scaffold he denounced 'F'
whom he saw in the crowd.

> F denied this with bitter imprecations, Poulter affirmed
> that, as he was going to appear before his great judge and

hoped to receive mercy from him, what he had said was true: He then desired the spectators to take warning by his sad end, and to avoid ill company, acknowledging that he deserved to die, but most of his accomplices more so.

There is no record of what, if anything, then happened to 'F'.

Between this pair and under the licence of the trading justice the celebrated criminal 'thief-taker' Jonathan Wild operated with marked success. Wild, who carried a silver-mounted staff as an emblem of his self-styled rank, was a broker for stolen goods and an informer. Provided no questions were asked and there were adequate rewards, the goods were returned to the warehouses from which he had often arranged their theft. Indeed he seems to have provided a role-model for some policemen to the present day.[12]

His career was an interesting one. Born in Wolverhampton in 1683, he was apprenticed to a buckle-maker. He married and left his wife. In 1708 he was imprisoned for debt and was discharged four years later when he set up house in Drury Lane with his mistress Mary Milliner, a prostitute whom he had met in prison. Initially he was what was called a twang, the pickpocket who would take the wallets of Milliner's clients. In those days intercourse with prostitutes was almost invariably undertaken vertically. He began his criminal apprenticeship proper with a Charles Hitchin, a City Marshal, who taught him the trade of receiver which Wild was to perfect.

From then on he set up a loose association of thieves, pickpockets and highwaymen. He was described in the *Newgate Calendar* as The Prince of Robbers. He also set himself up as a thief-taker and opened an office near the Old Bailey where he acted as agent between thief and victim, often later

12 For a full account of Wild's life, see *The Thief Takers* by Patrick Pringle. The character MacHeath in John Gay's *The Beggar's Opera* was based on Wild.

arresting the former.[13] If anyone threatened to expose him he brought a capital charge against the man, fabricating a felony charge. At the time no convicted felon could give evidence against anyone else. It is difficult, at this distance in time, to understand why anyone at all went near him, but for twelve years he was able to maintain such a successful double life that by 1723 he petitioned to be made a freeman of the City. By 1718 he had already designated himself as 'Thief Catcher General of Great Britain and Ireland' and had issued himself with his silver staff.

It was not as though the authorities were unaware of the dangers of the receiver-cum-thief-taker. In 1691 anti-pawnshop legislation had driven the receiver underground and in 1718 Hitchin, now suffering from the predations of his protégé, had published a pamphlet, *A True Discovery of the Conduct of Receivers and Thief Takers, In and about the City of London*, denouncing Wild. A bill – later known as the Jonathan Wild Act – sponsored by Sir William Thompson, Recorder of London and Solicitor-General, was passed, making it a felony to receive rewards under the pretence of retrieving stolen goods. In the debate over the bill Wild was denounced again but, for the moment, he was adroit enough to circumvent trouble.

13 An earlier example of thief-recoverer was Mary Frith, known as Moll Cutpurse and celebrated in *The Roaring Girle*, by Middleton and Dekker. She was probably born in 1584, the daughter of a shoemaker in Barbican and 'particular care was bestowed on her education'. It did her no good. Her anonymous biographer quoted in the *Dictionary of National Biography* says of her, 'A very tomrig or rumpscutttle she was and delighted and sported only in boy's play, not minding or companying with the girls.' When she was grown to a 'lusty and servicable wench' she was put out to service but she disliked housework of any kind and 'had a natural abhorrence to the tending of children'. An accomplished pickpocket, who dressed like a man, drank heavily and smoked a pipe, she was said to be scrupulously honest in her dealings with robber and robbed alike. Accompanied by her dog, she also seems to have been a highway robber. On one occasion, the story goes, she held up General Fairfax on Hounslow Heath, shooting him (in the arm) and both his horses. Her own horse failed her at Turnham Green and she was caught. Amazingly she bought herself out of prison with a payment of the immense sum of £2,000 to the aggrieved General. If the story is correct she was sixty at the time. She died of dropsy and in her will she left £20 for the celebration of the return of the monarchy. She was buried on 10 August 1659.

In an early example of international crime, stolen goods, particularly English watches which were highly prized on the continent, were shipped to Holland and kept in a warehouse in Flushing. The proceeds of sale were translated into dutiable goods which were then smuggled back to England. In 1723 Wild was still sufficiently confident of his invulnerability that he made his petition to the Lord Mayor and Aldermen for the freedom of the City of London 'in return for his services to justice'. He had, he said, sent sixty men to the gallows. By now he had a 'branch office' in the care of a manager, had become a successful slum landlord and owned a country house tended by a butler and a footman.

That year he survived an assassination attempt by Joseph Blake, known as Blueskin, a highwayman, who cut his throat in court. He and Blake had at one time been associates, and Blake expected some help in arranging his release. When it was not forthcoming Blake attacked him. Blueskin did not survive; he was hanged, to be commemorated by Dean Swift in the elegy *Blueskin's Ballad*.

Wild's end came when he was indicted under his own Act, so to speak, for receiving ten guineas as a reward for helping a Mrs Steham to recover stolen lace, the theft of which he had arranged. Convicted, he was hanged on 24 May 1725 despite another petition to the Lord Mayor of London. He tried to commit suicide, taking an overdose of laudanum the night before his execution and, still drowsy, was pelted by the mob on the way to Tyburn.

On Monday about the usual Time, Jonathan Wild was executed at Tyburn. Never was there seen so prodigious a Concourse of People before, not even upon the most popular Occasion of that Nature. The famous Jack Sheppard had a tolerable Number to attend his Exit; but no more to be compared to the present, than a Regiment to an Army, and, which is very remarkable, in all that innumerable Crowd, there was not one Pitying Eye to

be seen, nor one Compassionate Word to be heard; but
on the contrary, whenever he came, there was nothing
but Hollering and Huzzas, as if it had been upon a
Triumph.[14]

His body was saved from the Tyburn surgeons but one of the
Newgate chaplains betrayed his burial place and it was dug up.
Several generations later it was donated to the Royal College of
Surgeons. He was survived by both Mary Milliner and Charles
Hitchin. Ms Milliner, whose ear had been sliced off by Wild
in a temper, had been paid a pension by him to the date of his
death. Hitchin remained a City Under-Marshal for a further
three years when he was tried for sodomy. Acquitted of the
capital offence but convicted of a kindred misdemeanour, he
was sentenced to a term in the pillory, as well as six months'
imprisonment, and fined £20.

However, not everyone was pleased with the death of this
celebrated informer:

14 *Applebee's Journal*, 29 May 1725, quoted in William Robert Irwin, *The Making
of Jonathan Wild: A Study of the Literary Method of Henry Fielding*. As for
Jack Sheppard, he was born in 1702 and apprenticed to a cane-chair maker.
He fell into the company of Bess Lyon, better known as Edgeworth Bess, who
together with Poll Maggott incited him to larceny. His first recorded offence
is the theft of silver spoons from the Rummer Tavern, Charing Cross, but his
fame lies in his brilliant and daring escapes from prison. He rescued Bess from
St Giles' Round House and she returned the compliment when in April 1724
he was betrayed by his brother-in-law and sent to the New prison, from which
he escaped on 25 May by getting rid of his irons, cutting through a double grille
of oak and iron bars and scaling a 25-foot wall with a man on his back. Wild
caught him on 23 July 1724, but Sheppard escaped again on 31 August and was
at liberty for eleven days, working as a highwayman. After his capture and now
in Newgate prison, he was chained to two iron staples from which he escaped
on 13 September. He remained at large for a fortnight, burgling throughout the
City happily, and was caught after he drank himself insensible in the Maypole
Tavern near Clare Market. He was hanged on 16 November 1724 and buried in
St Martin in the Fields' churchyard. He is described by Horace Bleakley in *The
Hangmen of England* (p. 45) as having '. . . a cheery and impudent humour that
appealed to the common folk, whose love for him grew fonder when they saw
that he was always merry when everything seemed most black. Sharp of tongue
and quick of wit, he was a typical specimen of the Cockney guttersnipe, and as
such the great city of London took him to its heart. Jack's physique was also
a help to his renown. A dapper fellow such as he, subtle as a panther and with
muscles of steel, was naturally the ideal hero of his particular feats of skill. In
popular fancy he became the will-o'-the-wisp of crime.'

Tis remarkable that since the Dissolution of Jonathan Wild, not one Felon has been convicted capitally, which by some is attributed to a Reform amongst the Rogues and by others to the Want of a proper Person to detect them.[15]

Since the Death of Jonathan Wild has been so much lamented for Want of his useful Intelligence, this is to inform the Publick, that his ghost gives constant Attendance every Night at a certain House in Bury Street; where he resolves all Sorts of Questions, As his former Business was to discover Robberies committed, he has now the Gift of Revealing Rogueries intended.[16]

Horace Bleackley is another champion of Wild.

Nature intended Jonathan Wild for a sleuth, and had he been born two centuries later it is probable that he would have won a responsible position at Scotland Yard. For ten years at least, from 1715 until he died, he was by far the most efficient thief-taker in England. Fear was unknown to him. He was as tenacious as a bull-dog. Whenever he had resolved to clasp hands on a mill-ken or a bridle-cull – as burglar and highwayman were termed in his jargon – he ran his quarry to earth at whatever hazard. Scores of times this intrepid man arrested some armed desparado single-handed or rounded up a dangerous gang with a couple of his henchmen.[17]

Thief-taking did not, however, end with Wild. Four men, Stephen McDaniel, John Berry, James Salmon and a man named Egan, were convicted at the Old Bailey in February 1756 of a conspiracy to procure two other persons to commit

15 *Daily Journal*, 5 July 1735.
16 *Daily Post*, 5 February 1726.
17 H. Bleackley, *The Hangmen of England*, p. 47.

a robbery. The four men had, according to the prosecution, been practising as thief-takers for some fifteen or sixteen years. Their tried and tested methods were an example which has lasted until today. They would induce a simpleton to join them in committing crime and then denounce him to a magistrate and collect the reward.

Their come-uppance arrived when they persuaded two young men to take part in a staged robbery in Deptford, scene of the death of the playwright and spy Christopher Marlowe. Salmon was the purported victim and McDaniel came on the scene and arrested the boys. Initially they were convicted at Kent Assizes but Salmon and his friends reckoned without the abilities of a local constable, Joseph Cox, who arrested the entire gang. The truth came out and McDaniel and the members of his gang were sentenced to seven years' imprisonment accompanied by a stand in the pillory. Cox capitalised on his efforts with his treatise *A Faithful Narrative of the Most Wicked and Inhuman Transactions of that Bloody-Minded Gang of Thief-Takers alias Thief Makers*.[18]

When McDaniel and Berry took their turn in Hatton Garden up the road from the Old Bailey, they were nearly lynched by the mob and were rescued by prison warders. Three days later Salmon and Egan went in the pillory in Smithfield and neither was so fortunate. Egan was killed in the ensuing riot and Salmon died of his injuries received after he was rescued and taken back to Newgate prison. There was a story that the men were linked to the Bow Street Court and the magistrate, 'Blind' John Fielding, inserted a notice in the *Public Advertiser* denouncing the men and dissociating himself from their behaviour.[19]

Turning informer – or in legal terminology entering a plea of approvement which translated into turning Queen's Evidence –

18 Joseph Cox, *A Faithful Narrative of the Most Wicked and Inhuman Transactions of that Bloody-Minded Gang of Thief-Takers alias Thief Makers*, pp. 154–74.
19 A. Babington, *A House in Bow Street*, pp. 128–9.

was, however, a reasonable bet to save one's neck and possibly to obtain a pardon even in murder cases.

Some seventy years after the death of John Poulter, the Irish body-snatchers William Burke and William Hare arrived in Scotland to work as navvies on the Union Canal being built between Glasgow and Edinburgh. They met whilst staying in the same lodgings at Tanner's Close, West Port, Edinburgh. These they shared with an army pensioner, 'Old Donald', who died in November 1827 owing Hare £4. Bodies to be used by anatomy students – there were over 500 to be catered for in the city alone – were hard to come by, and the temptation to recoup his losses must have been irresistible to Burke.[20] 'Old Donald' was dug up and sold for £7 10s to the fashionable surgeon Dr Robert Knox of the Anatomy School, who lived at 10 Surgeon's Square, Edinburgh.

After that the enterprise burgeoned even if it did not last a full year. They had two 'wives', Helen McDougal and Maggie Laird respectively, as accomplices to lure people to their lodgings where, having been plied with drink, they were suffocated. The bodies were placed in a tea chest and carried round to Dr Knox to be sold at prices ranging between £8 and £14. On 31 October 1828 Margaret Docherty had the dubious privilege of being the last of their victims. A husband and wife, fellow-lodgers named Grey, found Burke cleaning the room after the murder and saw the corpse. On their way to the police they were met by McDougal and Laird who took them to an inn. In the meantime Knox's assistant, a David Patterson, paid £5 for the body. Eventually the Greys, no doubt fearful for their own safety, went to the police. Hare told all and gave King's Evidence, so saving himself and Maggie Laird. Burke and Helen McDougal were tried with the murders of Margaret Docherty, James Wilson and a prostitute, Mary Patterson. Burke was found guilty, and the Scottish verdict of 'not proven' was returned against Helen

20 Before Warburton's Act of 1830 everybody was required to have a Christian burial, and this prohibited the sale of the dead.

Docherty. In all sixteen people were murdered, but despite their soubriquet of body-snatchers Burke and Hare, in fact, snatched only one man.

Burke was hanged at Liberton's Wynd on 27 January 1829. For a fee of sixpence a time he had allowed himself to be sketched in his condemned cell, ranting that he had been swindled over the price paid for the body of Margaret Docherty. Appropriately his body was dissected at a public lecture by the Professor of Surgery in Edinburgh; his skeleton remains in the Anatomical Museum at the University. Both Helen McDougal and Maggie Laird were attacked by the mob outside the court and were saved only through the intervention of the police. McDougal went to Australia, where she died in 1868. Hare went to London, where he became a beggar in Oxford Street. One story is that on his way south he found work in a lime-kiln and when his fellow workers discovered his identity they blinded him. Dr Knox, hounded from his Edinburgh practice, also travelled south, in his case to Hackney, where he became a general practitioner and died in 1862.

A century later, grassing as such is perhaps the principal method by which the police obtain information which will lead either to the prevention of a crime, or to the arrest of the villains and recovery of stolen property. Any good detective keeps a small, or sometimes large, string of informers who may be active thieves themselves or who may simply hang about on the fringes of the Underworld. In the past they were paid out of a police information fund, or sometimes out of the pocket of the officer who ran them; it was regarded as a good investment towards promotion. Sometimes in the case of a drug bust the informer was given a part of the bust itself as his reward. Sometimes an informer had a licence to commit crimes, short of violence, in a particular area. Sometimes all three applied. One singularly corrupt Flying Squad officer of the 1960s, Alec Eist, is described in admiring terms by a former colleague:

He was the best informed police officer in London. What he took off one criminal he gave back to another. If he got £200 from a villain for giving him bail, Eist would give £195 to cultivate an informant.[21]

And another says of the practice:

You find three pounds of heroin and put only one on the charge sheet. The villains are pleased; less they're found with means less bird, and you give the other two to the informant. The job won't pay the informant so the only way is you give it back.

The grass could also expect help from his runner if he was arrested. This might well take the form of an intercession to prevent a charge being preferred.

Nipper Read, who arrested the Krays, maintains that the first of the modern supergrasses was Leslie Payne, the *consigliere* and financial whizz, if not genius, behind the twins. Payne's was a curious story, one which certainly led to the downfall of the twins. It was also part of the interesting, and extremely rare, example of the wholesale defection by a substantial part of a criminal gang not to another enterprise but into the arms of the police.

Payne had managed the Krays' financial empire and, without doubt, had built a platform from which they could have expanded possibly into the legitimate world. He had both tired of the Krays and been edged out by them as they saw his usefulness diminish. It was Payne who, unknowingly, had contributed to the death of Jack 'The Hat' McVitie. McVitie had been paid £1,500 to shoot Payne and had taken Billy Exley along with him. The expedition was neither well planned nor a

21 Eist, a florid, handsome, black-haired man, was acquitted in one of the trials of police officers and solicitors in the 1970s. Later he had a dress shop: 'It did no good. He was always having fires and burglaries – it was an embarrassment.' Later he owned a public house near Newmarket. He died of a heart attack.

success. They arrived at Payne's home, were told by his wife that he was not in and went away. Unfortunately for McVitie, now into the dangerous – and in his case fatal – combination of drugs and alcohol, he boasted that he had turned over the twins for the money. Naturally, it was not something which appealed to them. McVitie was lured from the Regency Club where he was drinking and stabbed to death by Reggie Kray, urged on by his brother Ronnie.

Initially the Krays were arrested over allegations of fraud, but once they were in custody all manner of their acquaintances came out of the woodwork at the urging of Read and his men. Some, such as Billy Exley and Lennie Dunn who had minded Frank Mitchell after his escape from Dartmoor, had been fearful of reprisals against them. For example, Albert Donaghue maintains he changed sides when he believed that he was being set up to take the rap for the Mitchell murder. Unexpectedly, Charles Mitchell, horse-doper, fraudsman and thieves' ponce, was another to change sides.

> Mitchell was a small, broad-shouldered man with a fresh
> face and a full set of sparkling white teeth; he was also
> completely bald. He ran his bookmaking and money-
> lending business from Fulham's North End Road.[22]

He had been a long-time friend, running long-firm frauds. He went with Charles Kray and some others to Toronto to talk with Don Ceville, a Canadian mafioso, when they were all arrested and deported. Rightly, Charles Kray did not trust him, but his brothers were more accommodating.

For purely pragmatic reasons he was able to tell Read that there was a contract out for both him and Leslie Payne. He, Mitchell, was to bankroll the hiring of an American hitman.

On 25 June, the day of Mitchell's defection, they were

22 Colin Fry and Charles Kray, *Doing the Business*, p. 118.

all sitting there in their usual studiously unconcerned way when Kenneth Jones [prosecuting counsel] asked that Mitchell be allowed to stand down.

'He [Mitchell] has made a complete statement and it has been decided he should be used as a prosecution witness,' he told the Court.

Mitchell walked from the back row as though he was going to collect a prize at a Sunday school. Even then the twins could not believe what was going on. It was only later they realised the full implication of the betrayal and, by then, it was too late for them to show their displeasure in a tangible way.[23]

It is curious that in no other of the gang cases, either before (Richardsons) or afterwards (Tibbs, Dixons), was there any such defection from the ranks.

---

23 Leonard Read and James Morton, *Nipper*, pp. 184–5.
   Frequent threats come out of prison, I am told, mostly aimed at the relatives of anyone whom they dislike. Lip-service seems to be paid by the 'faithful', but it is all really dead. An attempt to shoot a well-known figure who had fallen out with them, Charlie Mitchell (of horse-doping fame in the past), was attributed to them by the Press. It was not true: the shooting was the result of an alleged injury much nearer home. No damage was sustained by Mitchell and all simmered down. Since the Krays are rightly credited with many black deeds, it seems only fair to exonerate them on this one! Peta Fordham, *Inside the Underworld*, p. 139.
   Mitchell went on with his double career – including an incident in the Fulham Road when a car window was wound up on his throat and he was dragged for several hundred yards – before going to Spain where he was murdered.

3

Grasses – The Super Days

The Kray case aside, grassing changed gear on to a wholly different level with the arrest in 1970 of Derek Creighton 'Bertie' Smalls. It became the era of the supergrass, the criminal who, to dig himself out of trouble, would inform not just on his colleagues on a particular job but on his associates and their efforts going back years and years. In turn he could expect to receive a minimal sentence compared with that handed out to his former friends. He could also expect, through a nominee, a share of the insurance rewards.

In the late 1960s and early 1970s Bertie Smalls led a highly successful team of armed robbers in a series of attacks on banks, mainly in North and North West London but on occasion as far afield as Lloyds Bank in Bournemouth.

Peter Kelly was a part-time member of the squad. Talking of his time as a villain in the 1960s and 1970s, he recalls:

How did we look out the banks? On a Monday Georgie and I would drive round looking for a bank with a side turning. This was in the days before bandit glass – it was us made them put it in. One of us would go and change a note to see what drawers there were and then we'd go in mob-handed with pick-axe handles. One of us would stay by the door. Sometimes Bertie Smalls used to do that

because he was fat and unfit and I'd jump on the counter
and cause mayhem.

Each time the operational method was almost identical. The
robbers wore balaclavas, possibly with a nylon stocking
underneath, and masks. The raids were in banking hours.
A ladder was used to get over – and a sledge-hammer was
used to smash – the security grilles put up in the 1960s, but
not yet made ceiling to counter. A shotgun would be fired into
the ceiling to concentrate the minds of staff and any customers
there might be in the bank. There would be one or two getaway
cars waiting. The haul was usually substantial.

Smalls' name was 'in the frame' so to speak. He had been
wanted for a robbery on one of the branches of Lloyds
in Bournemouth in September 1970 and his wife, Diane
(sometimes confusingly referred to as Alice), had been arrested
along with others, including a Donald Barrett who had made a
confession naming names. At the trial at Winchester Crown
Court, he pleaded guilty. The only evidence against Diane
Smalls and the other defendants was that of a Stella Robinson
who worked as an *au pair* for the Smalls' children. She missed
the trial, having spent the time in Mablethorpe where Smalls
had a caravan. The trial collapsed and the case against Diane
Smalls and the others was dismissed. For a period the police
were seriously worried that she had been killed and it was
only when Smalls produced her at a solicitor's office that
they were satisfied of her safety and abandoned a potential
murder inquiry. Barrett's reward was a sentence of twelve
years and a card posted from Spain from the others, who had
all been acquitted, reading, 'Wish you were here.' In law, his
confession was no evidence against anyone but himself unless
he chose to give evidence in the witness box. On this occasion
he did not wish to do so.

Now Smalls had also been identified from a photograph in
the 'Rogues Gallery' at Scotland Yard as being involved in
the National Westminster Bank raid at Palmers Green in May

1972. The number-plate of a Jaguar car which had been used in a trial run had been noted by an off-duty police officer, and was traced back to a garage at Tower Bridge in which Smalls was known to have an interest. That was certainly not sufficient to bring a charge. After a robbery at Barclays Bank in Wembley High Road in August 1972 which had netted over £138,000 in old notes, a special unit was formed by the police under the direction of Jim Marshall; it would eventually become the nucleus of the Robbery Squad.

It was not the first time the police had eyed Smalls as a potential informant. One Flying Squad detective recalls the early 1960s:

Living and 'performing' in Wood Green at that time was Derek Creighton 'Bertie' Smalls who years later would make his mark on criminal history by being the first of a long line of supergrasses. No matter how my buck and I tried we could not turn Bertie. There were a couple of occasions when we were very close, though. He kept a few meets in various pubs but to his credit and our chagrin he managed to withstand the pressure we were putting on him. Eventually he drifted off the manor.

This time things were much more serious. Now Smalls was remanded in custody by Harrow Magistrates' Court for committal papers to be prepared. It was when they were served on the defence that Peter Donnelly, the solicitor's managing clerk who had acted for Smalls over the years, noticed a reference in them to 'outers'. Smalls would, so the statement of a police officer read, give names if he had 'outers'.

I went to see him in Brixton and asked, 'Did you say it?' He's hedgy. 'I've got to have guarantees,' he said. I went to see either Marshall or Wilding and asked if it was a serious proposition. 'Yes,' was the reply, 'but we don't believe he'll do it.' 'If he does what will you give us?' I asked, and it's then they start thinking it's possible. I went back to Smalls and said, 'Go and sit tight, keep your trap shut.' Then I got word they were interested.

I went and saw him again and told him he's got to put his cards on the table. They wanted robberies, names and so on, but not unnaturally he was reluctant to go into details at this stage. Finally we got a skeleton of the jobs from him in areas.

Then I arranged a meeting with Marshall and Wilding at Wembley. I went up there with Peter Steggles, the senior partner. They've got a clip-board with a list of names and robberies I could see upside down.

I said that everything on the board they could have plus XYZ additional robberies. That seemed to take them off guard. From then we had the advantage. They were reluctant and thought it would be difficult to have anything in writing. Nothing in writing – no deal. They said they'd take instructions. It was then going to have to go to Deputy Commissioner or Commissioner level.

We then tell them that we will draft heads of agreement as to our conditions and the main concerns were one, the immunity from prosecution, and two, the security. There was no question of a reduced sentence. Another term was that it had to be agreed upon by the DPP. We had two more meetings before they agreed to write a letter which was the final document and was basically word for word our heads of agreement.

It was then lined up that on receipt of that letter Smalls was to be produced at Harrow court. The Bench had been squared to grant him bail – that had been dealt with before we arrived – and he was bailed into police custody and we're taken down to Wembley. We sat down 12–14 hours a day whilst he reminisced.

By this time I had spread the word I was going on holiday, but the day he appeared people were asking what

was happening. Where was he? Where was I? The word
was out. That's why I think the rest of the team had paid
their money.

Diane Smalls was never happy with the whole business.
Donnelly met her on Brixton Hill one afternoon when he
had been to see Bertie in prison and explained things. She
stood by Smalls, but their relationship was effectively over
by this time anyway. One of the reasons was the appearance
of Susan Mattis, attractive and divorced with three children
and who graced the newspapers for some time after the case,
telling how Bertie would leap out of bed in the middle of
the night and how on the day of a raid he would stiffen his
resolve with a quick vodka and grapefruit juice at 6 a.m. She
had been to school with Smalls' sister. Smalls seems to have
had a reasonably pleasant time whilst under guard. *Private
Eye* reported nude swimming with a female police officer who
subsequently retired from the force.

By now Smalls had given so much detail – the statement
ran to 65 pages and covered 11 other suspects and 20 crimes
– the police were starting to look for corroboration and . . .

They heaved in Stella Robinson, got a statement from her
as to how various robbers, including Bertie, descended on
a flop and when they were playing around with one of
the sawn-offs had mistakenly fired it into the floorboards.
They managed to identify the address, took the carpet up
and the damage was still there with the pellets. But they
still needed Diane and I went to her and said if you don't
do it the deal won't be accepted because we didn't know
whether they'd say the evidence was sufficient. I said,
'Do it or it may not go through.'

Very reluctantly she made the statement, but she then
refused to take the oath at court.

One of the final conditions was that if Smalls' statement
wasn't used and he was not to be a witness and immunity

given, then what amounted to a total confession would remain on police files and not be used against him at a trial. But there was such a level of corruption at that time that sooner or later it would have got out and he'd have been dead.

During those three days Smalls stayed at Wembley with an armed guard. On the third day the police had to say 'yes' or 'no'. They said 'yes' and Smalls was then produced at Harrow, granted formal bail and taken to a hotel by Wembley Stadium where he and his family were put in the suite in which David Cassidy had stayed the week before; it seemed to please him. Later he was moved out to a couple of addresses, being guarded by shifts of police officers. The only time Donnelly could see him was at an arranged point which he would be given half an hour beforehand.

I'm sure there was a contract out. Publicity had it that it was £100,000 but I heard from Smalls' friend Jackie O'Connell that it was only £50,000.[1]

The sweep took place in the early hours of 6 April when over a hundred police officers rounded up twenty-seven of Smalls' former colleagues. Then the problem to be faced was whether Smalls, who was drinking heavily, would actually go through with things when it came to it.

The committal proceedings took place in a heavily guarded gymnasium in Wembley and Smalls appeared to give evidence minutes after his formal acquittal at the Old Bailey.

1 Jackie O'Connell, a high class safe-breaker, was another informer. Due to turn Queen's Evidence in the Bank of America safe raid case in which he was a defendant, he was shot on the way to court. It was never exactly clear whether he had organised the hit himself in an effort to put together some mitigation, or whether he wished to have his case put back so that he was tried separately. He was wounded so badly in the leg that it had to be amputated. He committed suicide some years later.

He stood in the witness box, looking towards the magistrate, resting on his elbow. His eyes seemed dead and he almost mumbled his answers, so that a couple of times the magistrate had to ask him to speak up. I was really worried at that point that Bertie might be about to crack but, just in time, there was an incident which completely changed the picture.

One of the prisoners was Danny Allpress, a real comedian and a live wire, who had always run around with Smalls and had virtually been his assistant. Danny kept quiet at first, then suddenly he leaned across the dock and said in a loud whisper, 'Well, Bertie, who's been having Slack Alice while you're away?' The remark got a lot of laughs from the prisoners, but Danny couldn't have made a more serious mistake.

'The remark brought Bertie to life. You could see the determination come into his eyes,' recounts Jack Slipper, who had chased Train Robber Ronnie Biggs to Brazil and was now one of the senior officers in the case.[2]

Diane Smalls was not popular with the rest of the wives. Once, because of friction, she had left a holiday in Torremolinos early and had later chosen to spend her time in Tangier. But was the Slack Alice joke as crucial as Slipper believes? According to Peter Donnelly:

I don't think the Slack Alice joke enamoured them to him, but I don't think it was the end of the world. His attitude was that most of them when pulled in had tried to do exactly the same but he got in first. From that point of view he felt justified. There had also been some trouble earlier when he was on remand for possession of a firearm. He got out but he was skint and one of them was meant to have given Diane money

2 J. Slipper, *Slipper of the Yard*, p. 108.

to look after her. He hadn't, and I think that annoyed him as well.

The men in court clearly had a sense of humour. The *Daily Mirror* printed a press release smuggled from the dock.

Mr Bert Smalls, the famous and solo singer who recently broke away from the Home Counties Choral Society, is about to give up the singing side of his career. Apparently Mr Smalls feels that the singing may affect his throat. On Wednesday Mr Smalls refused to comment.[3]

In July 1974 at the Central Criminal Court, Danny Allpress received a sentence of twenty-one years' imprisonment, reduced on appeal to eighteen. Donald Barrett, who had already had twelve years for the Bournemouth job, received another seventeen, reduced to twelve years on appeal. Others had sentences of up to twenty-one years reduced by the odd couple of years on their appeals.

One of them, Philip Morris, had been involved in a raid in February 1973 on the Unigate Dairies Depot in Ewell, Surrey. Morris had the job of standing guard over a young man, Frank Kidwell, who had just been named 'Milkman of the Year'. The shotgun went off and Kidwell died. The raid netted £148,000. Morris pleaded guilty to Kidwell's manslaughter and received a seventeen-year sentence. For his part in the Wembley raid he received a concurrent sentence of twenty years, reduced by the Court of Appeal to twelve. His appeal against the seventeen-year sentence for manslaughter was dismissed.

There were rumours of contracts on Smalls' life until the *Sun* gleefully reported that, following the making of a series of bankruptcy orders against the defendants in the case in October 1974, there was now not enough money available to pay the killer:

3 *Daily Mirror*, 23 May 1974.

'No one ever made threats to me,' says Smalls. 'Of course
I didn't put myself about and if I went into a pub and saw
someone who was a friend of the others I just left, but no,
overall I had no trouble.'

In any event, Smalls had set the tone for the 1970s. The
opprobrium attached to most supergrasses never seems to
have stuck to him. In a curious way he appears to have been
regarded as an innovator.

Here is John McVicar talking about supergrasses in general
and Smalls in particular:

> Some of them are very strong people. Look at Bert. He
> was a good worker, although there was always something
> odd about him.[4]

What he did have was a sense of humour. After one bank raid
in the Wood Green area a woman witness who was shopping
in the High Road ran more or less slap-bang into the men
escaping after the robbery. She had heard what she thought
was a car backfiring, but when three men wearing stocking
masks rushed past her she knew exactly what had happened.
She backed up against a wall and then started to walk to the
end of the alleyway when a fourth man, also wearing a mask,
loped towards her. Again she backed up, but as he went past
he stopped.

'What a way to earn a fucking living, eh, girl?' said a
sweating Smalls as he disappeared down the alleyway.

After the trial Smalls had an armed guard for some months,
but eventually this was phased out and from then the family
lived more or less normally under another name.

Smalls didn't do as well as he could have from his story.
A book he was planning never came to fruition – due in part,
perhaps, to both his and his ghost's then enthusiasm for vodka.

4 L. Taylor, *In the Underworld*, p. 82.

Later in April 1975 a short series of articles appeared in the *Daily Express* in which he offered a few pearls as to his life and times, saying he reckoned he had squandered between £250,000 and £300,000. The general consensus was that he was correct when he said, 'I did it for my wife and kids.' Well, certainly the kids. Of the present he said:

> I prune the roses and I say good morning to my neighbours. And that's it – nobody knows who I am.

And of the use of guns on the raids:

> I reckoned it was really safer for everybody. If you're only carrying axe handles you have to use 'em haven't you, and people get hurt, plus they might fight back and maybe hurt some of your mob. If you pull a gun they're terrified. The bank clerks don't feel they've got to be heroes in front of the birds, do they? I mean they can always say afterwards, 'Well he was carrying a gun so I couldn't do nothing.'[5]

It was only a matter of time before the defendants went to the Court of Appeal where the presiding judge, Lord Justice Lawton, was not amused.

> The spectacle of the Director of Public Prosecutions recording in writing, at the behest of a criminal like Smalls, his undertaking to give immunity from further prosecution is one which we find distasteful. Nothing of a similar kind must ever happen again. Undertakings of immunity from prosecution may have to be given in the public interest. They should never be given by the police. The Director should give them most sparingly and, in cases involving grave crimes, it would be prudent of

5 *Daily Express*, 3 April 1975.

him to consult the law officers before making any promises.

Nevertheless the appeals were dismissed and off went the defendants to the House of Lords where they fared no better, but this time Lord Justice Lawton had his wrist slapped by Lord Diplock.

> I am wondering to what extent it is right for any court to give directions to the Director as to how he should conduct his business. The Director of Public Prosecutions works under the Attorney General. He does not work under any judges at all and any directions he receives as to the way in which he does his work surely must come from the Attorney General. I would have thought it quite wrong for it to come from any judicial authority at all. He may be condemned for what he has done, but he must not be told what he has to do in the future.

Nor were the police by any means apologetic. Said Roy Yorke, who had nurtured Smalls and obtained his confidence:

> I have no regrets. We were totally justified. We performed a public service. Before the deal with Smalls there were five major armed jobs a week. After the arrests were made possible by Smalls' statement, violent armed robberies went down by sixty per cent. It was the only way to break into the most exclusive and possibly violent robbery organisation ever known in this country.[6]

As for supergrasses generally, there were two spin-offs from Smalls' defection to the angels which caused the authorities some concern. The first was the curious story of Arthur John 'Jimmy' Saunders, a man from a non-criminal and by no means

6 *Daily Mail*, 25 March 1975.

poor family who in his thirties became something of a criminal groupie and who was convicted of a bank robbery in Ilford in February 1970. The only real evidence against him was a confession to the then Superintendent Albert Wickstead. He made a series of ambiguous answers and, asked if he was on the robbery, Saunders was said to have replied, 'There's no point in saying no, is there?' Later he said, 'Whatever I was doing I didn't have a shooter.'

Saunders put up an alibi defence but his witnesses did not come up to proof. His appeal was dismissed in December 1971, but now Smalls said that Saunders had not been on the raid. This presented a problem. How could Smalls be put forward as a witness of truth in one part of the case (since his evidence would, in due course, convict his old friend from the Bournemouth robbery Bobby King), but not in another? His evidence was taken on commission by Lord Justice James and accepted by the court with some reluctance.

The Lord Chief Justice in giving judgment had this to say:

> We have, as I say, approached this question with caution, because the evidence of accomplices can be as dangerous when used for the defence as it can when used for the Crown and we are not unmindful of the fact that it sometimes occurs when criminals are together in prison that they put their heads together and arrange to make statements with a view to exculpating one of them. We do look at evidence of accomplices or alleged accomplices with considerable caution in this context, as in others.

In the end the Court of Appeal quashed the conviction, resolving the dilemma by pointing out in explanation that when Saunders made his confession he had been drinking.

> . . . the appellant had been drinking appreciably before his arrest, and, although a doctor brought in by the police to examine him described him as not in any sense incapable

by drink, the Court thinks that some of the slightly jocular answers which were included in that conversation do have something of the stamp of a man who had had some drink and whose responsibility for the precise language which he used might have been affected by that drink.

And therefore had been foolish in what he had been saying. No blame attached to the police; it was indeed Saunders' own fault.[7]

Another potential embarrassment was averted in April 1978 when John Short was jailed for twenty-one years. He had provided the hideaway in Torremolinos where Bertie and his friends had sunned themselves before and after robberies. At the time of the trial he and Bryan Turner disappeared abroad. Now he was back and, it seemed, Bertie would have to be brought out of retirement to give evidence against him in the Ilford case. What would happen if the jury acquitted Short?

Short had changed his name to McGrath and whilst in Canada along with his friend, Roy Radovan, had been engaged in some horse-trading, selling trotting horses for racing in and around Montreal. Unfortunately the horses either had a touch of the slows or more seriously did not match their pedigrees. The Montreal police received discreet inquiries from 'businessmen' complaining about the horses. No, they did not want to press charges, merely to know the whereabouts of the vendors. Short returned to London where six months later he was arrested. Radovan's body was found in the Hudson river. Short pleaded guilty to other charges and received twenty-one years. Everyone's face was saved when the Ilford robbery charge was allowed to remain on the file.

Twenty-five years later Peter Donnelly, the solicitors' clerk

7 *Saunders*, 58 Cr. App. R.251. The experience did not do Saunders that much good although he received substantial compensation for his time in prison. In 1986 he was back in serious trouble, convicted of an attempted armed robbery in Baker Street. He and the other members of the team were over fifty at the time. He received fifteen years.

who did the deal for Smalls, has serious doubts on the supergrass scheme from his own and a more general point of view:

> Was the principle of supergrasses correct in the first place? Because Bertie Smalls was successful they used it here, there and everywhere. They were adopting the supergrass system in Northern Ireland. Trials collapsed here and then over there where there was a string of acquittals and allowed appeals.
>
> I'm not so sure nowadays that sort of evidence would be encouraged by the courts. The use of supergrasses like Smalls has largely died out.
>
> Actually I think it is an unhealthy basis for a case. It's open to abuse. The incentives are too great. If you have a supergrass who's a pathological liar – and some of them have been – it's extremely dangerous.
>
> So far as I am concerned it damaged the practice and with a large amount of hindsight and many years later, I don't think we should have acted for Bertie. Before he gave evidence there was a good deal of pressure on me to stop him and certainly I had to watch my back for a long time afterwards.

Donald Barrett, himself to become a supergrass not once but twice, put it succinctly. 'They should have put a bullet in the first one's nut,' he says of Smalls. 'That would have stopped it in its tracks.'

The next in line to repent, recant and recount all was a man who did publish his memoirs, designating himself as 'King Squealer', Maurice O'Mahoney. Jack Slipper, in charge of the new supergrass, recalls him:

> O'Mahoney must be one of the cunningest, not necess-arily cleverest individuals I've ever met. My first impres-sion of whether he would be suitable to become a

supergrass was that he had a fantastic memory – and what a liar he was. So much so that after discussing things with my superior officer I suggested he would be suitable because of his memory but, as he put in his book, I spent a long time explaining how detrimental it would be to a whole trial should it be proved he was telling just one lie as the defence would use it to discredit his whole evidence.

As far as I was concerned he kept on the lines I'd insisted.

O'Mahoney's has been a curious story.

On 1 June 1974, a Securicor security van was ambushed in Phoenix Way, Heston, Middlesex. There were at least five, and probably six, attackers, all of whom were masked and carrying weapons including shotguns, a Luger, a revolver and a sledgehammer. The van was rammed, one guard was hit with the sledgehammer; a pistol was fired and a rather disappointing take of a little over £13,000 was stolen. According to O'Mahoney, who was being urged by his girlfriend to give up his life of crime – to which, he said, he had been giving serious thought – the job had been offered around the Underworld by some of his colleagues. One man, George du Burriatte, who had once been an associate, if not an intimate, of some of London's classier criminals, had turned police informer. O'Mahoney believed it was he who first informed on him. He was probably correct.

Du Burriatte named between 100 and 150 criminals and by October 1979 was said to have a contract of £100,000 on his head. His career as a supergrass had ended in the June of that year when his evidence sent Ray Deck down for six and a half years over a £1 million international car fraud. Du Burriatte had been the boss of the underbelly of London Airport when he suddenly changed sides and contacted officers at Chiswick police station. Nevertheless he continued working and, to fool any of his colleagues who might see him, when he went to

contact the officers at the station he would put on a wig or
false moustache or, if the need arose, have his arm twisted
behind his back by an officer so it would appear that he had
been arrested. He never really made it plain why he had crossed
over to the other side, but he was able to give this encomium to
the police:

> The Yard looked after me well while I was working
> for them. They'd hand me out one-ers and two-ers.
> And I picked up £3,000 reward money from banks
> and insurance firms.

And, no doubt, a few shillings from the newspapers to whom
he told his tale.

As for the Securicor robbery itself, in his book, as befits
a man trying to get out of crime, O'Mahoney played a
sympathetic part.

> As I got in through the back doors, I found an elderly
> man. He was obviously another guard, though he looked
> too frail to be doing such dangerous work. 'Please God,
> don't hurt me,' he said. I told him, 'Don't worry, pop,
> no one's going to hurt you.' Then I began throwing out
> boxes of money, and mentally photographing the interior
> again for further use.[8]

The first of the men to be arrested on 11 June were John
Thorne, Joseph Stevens and Angus Smith. O'Mahoney evaded
the swoop and was arrested with his girlfriend, Susan Norville,
at her flat about 4 p.m. the next day.

Despite O'Mahoney's belief that du Burriatte was the
villain of the piece the whisper went around that he was
going to squeal. Susan Norville had made a full statement.
The prosecution would later allege that Thorne, Stevens and

8 M. O'Mahoney, *King Squealer*, pp. 123 et seq.

Smith suspected O'Mahoney of tipping off the police, and that Thorne and Stevens now threatened to gouge out his eyes if he talked. Various girlfriends threatened Susan Norville in an effort to dissuade her from giving evidence. It is also possible that a contract of £2,000 was taken out on her life. In *King Squealer* O'Mahoney says:

> The troubles just mounted up for me. One day I was attacked by several members of my team who threatened to gouge out my eyes with a toothbrush. These savages, some of them weighing 16 stone, were hardened criminals and meant every nasty word they said. I managed to get free from them that time, but I knew they would eventually get me. I certainly didn't want to lose my sight for something I had never done. Later I found out someone had even smuggled a cyanide capsule into the prison and planned to slip it in my tea.

According to Detective Chief Superintendent Jack Slipper, in whose charge O'Mahoney was, this was the turning point for him.

> But before this happened I had decided to take the most momentous decision of my life – to turn squealer.

Despite his fears for his safety from the 16-stone hardened criminals, the twenty-nine-year-old O'Mahoney was no shrinking violet. In his time he had bitten the diamond off the ring of a victim and swallowed it. He was adroit with a hammer and was a kneecap breaker. He was a contract enforcer and had been paid £1,000 (the going rate) for shooting a man in the legs. His book tells of his plots to kidnap Elton John and Elizabeth Taylor (consecutively rather than concurrently). Now he asked a Brixton prison officer to call a high-ranking Flying Squad officer.

'Something like Bertie Smalls, is it?' he asked.

'Bigger,' I said.

Clearly he had to be kept out of the way of his co-accused and the rest of the prison population, and so on 22 June he was moved to Chiswick police station where he had two cells, a colour television, a record player and was allowed domiciliary if not conjugal visits. Both his wife, Maureen, and his girlfriend, Susan, visited him frequently and the latter gave birth on 4 May 1975. He claimed the child as his, but at the trial of his co-accused denied having intercourse with her whilst he was in police custody. Over a period of time he told the police he had been involved in some thirteen robberies, sixty-six burglaries and assorted other crimes of violence. He named about 150 people as being his associates in the crimes.

On 20 September 1974 he pleaded guilty to the Phoenix Way robbery, an attempted robbery and a burglary. He asked for ninety-nine other offences to be taken into consideration. He was helped by the prosecution, who described him as the most guarded man in Britain and said that his assistance to the police had been incalculable. Kenneth Machin, now himself a judge at the Old Bailey, suggested that by his action O'Mahoney 'may have already signed his own death warrant'. The man himself, allowed to address the court, emotionally explained that: 'I know that what I have done in the past is wrong and I believe that what I am doing now is right . . . I want to hit right at the heart of the criminal underworld.'

It all stood him in good stead. He received five years' imprisonment from Sir Carl Aarvold, the Recorder of London, in thanks for the help he was continuing to give to the police and to assist him to realise his protestations about giving up a life of crime. Had he not done so, he could not have complained about a sentence of eighteen to twenty years. O'Mahoney spent a few weeks in prison before he was moved back to the comfort of Chiswick police station.

He began to give evidence in trials early in the New Year. The trials in which he appeared as the principal witness culminated in that of Thorne and the others for the Heston security van robbery, a wages snatch at Greenford and a robbery at the Allied Irish bank in Hammersmith. In the meantime, in other cases eight defendants were acquitted. No one, except Ronald Cook in the Heston trial, was convicted on the unsupported word and evidence of the 'King Squealer'.

After the Heston robbery trial he was given a form of parole and immediately his enthusiasm for giving evidence vanished in a puff of smoke. There were still ten defendants against whom O'Mahoney had made statements. No evidence was offered against them. In the week beginning 11 January 1977, he gave a series of stories to the *Sun* telling of his life and hi-jinks in the police station. Now he told of how he had intercourse with Susan in his cell, the back of his head blocking the Judas window. A police investigation followed before the appeals of the Heston defendants reached the Court of Appeal. It concluded that much was untrue and that O'Mahoney had 'told a colourful and probably, in parts, a lying story to the press for money, adding little to the villainy which was known to the jury'. What was more significant, the court found, was the tendency – as with many a subsequent supergrass – to play down his role in the case. In an earlier instance involving an armed robbery in Greenford, O'Mahoney had said he had been in the getaway car and named the men who went into the firm armed with a gun and a cosh. The Court of Appeal thought it rather more likely that O'Mahoney had been the man with the shotgun.

> This incident shows that when it suited him to do so he was willing to attribute to others serious criminal acts of his own. In this case he did much the same in respect of his part in the Phoenix Way robbery. The evidence showed that he had carried and fired a pistol. He said in evidence that this is what Cook had done.

Cook's conviction was quashed. As for O'Mahoney, once he

refused to co-operate the police dropped their protection. He told the *Guardian*:

> They've dropped me flat, the canary that fell from its cage. They've told me to go out and get a decent job. The only trade I know how is to break into banks. I'm in a terrible state. I could go round the corner and cry.[9]

Happily, however, he picked himself up, put himself back on the perch and was used as a security man by musicians David Bowie and Rick Wakeman who wrote the preface to his book. Then in 1993, sporting a Flying Squad tie, now known as Peter Davies, and charged once more with robbery, he was telling a most amazing story from the witness box.

Following his successful career as a bank robber, and a subsequent equally gratifying one as a supergrass, O'Mahoney kept out of public vision until he was arrested in Reading in 1990 on a charge of shoplifting. He had been found, along with his young son, pushing a shopping trolley out of a store. His defence was that he was on his way to the electrical department to obtain some guarantees before paying. The case was stopped by magistrates at the committal proceedings.

Three years later his defence to the charge of robbery was that it was a snatch carried out on the instructions of the police to incriminate another man. In the witness box he told a strange story. After his acquittal at Reading, when curiously his custody record had disappeared, his cover was blown. He now tried to see a senior officer whose job it had been to protect supergrasses but received no substantial help. In the November he went to see a DI whom he knew at Brixton police station and asked what help he could have. Again there was a negative response, but this time O'Mahoney asked when and where the station's Christmas party would be held. He entered the raffle, which carried the first prize of a ticket to Paris.

9 D. Campbell, *The Underworld*, p. 157.

According to O'Mahoney he was later contacted by the man whom he had seen at Brixton police station, and asked to carry out a small commission for him. What the police wanted, said O'Mahoney, was for him to carry out a smash and grab at a sub-post office in Shepherd's Bush, leave behind the main money and instead take a money-bag containing £250-worth of 20p pieces. The robbery was to take place on 30 June. The idea was that when O'Mahoney handed the bag over to the police they would then plant the money on another man.

O'Mahoney went on to say that, since he had packed in the job of supergrass, or more probably it had packed him in, and he had served his five-year sentence in Chiswick police station, he was a frequent visitor to Briefs wine bar, a popular haunt of villains, barristers, solicitors and the police, not necessarily in that order, which was opposite Inner London Crown Court in Newington Causeway. Briefs had been opened by three former police officers who had subsequently left the Metropolitan Police, along with solicitor Michael Relton who later received twelve years' imprisonment for his part in laundering the money from the Brinks-Mat robbery. O'Mahoney told the court he spent much of his time in Briefs and his function in life was collecting and laundering money and generally helping Relton. The wine bar was one which, from time to time, had been placed off-limits by the Commissioners.

According to O'Mahoney's evidence, he was introduced at the Brixton party to an officer known as 'Basher' who, he said, had acquired the nickname because every time he was drunk he started to fight. It was then the proposition was put to him, and it was suggested he should recruit someone who was clean to carry out the raid with him.

O'Mahoney found a man in Bristol and duly appeared in Shepherd's Bush. A white Ford Escort car was, he said, to be near the shop and a red one for the getaway outside a local public house, the Fox and Hounds. As he looked round the area before the robbery he saw a Rover motor vehicle with three officers in it, as well as two mounted police officers near by. Something, he told the court, was wrong. He had intended to do the snatch himself, but now he sent the other man in; it was completed but the alarm went off, the man got back into O'Mahoney's car and as he did so the police started shooting.

In the car provided by the police, according to O'Mahoney, was a bag of guns – one a starting pistol, a second which had been tampered with – and cartridges which had been sprayed with oil. The effect of this would make them extremely unreliable. He maintained, and there was no evidence to contradict him, that neither he nor his friend ever shot back.

According to the Home Office expert eight shots were fired, all by the police. O'Mahoney never attempted to reach the exchange getaway car. Instead he took to his feet, was caught and taken to Shepherd's Bush police station where DS Fuller, who had looked after him when he was in custody in Chiswick in his supergrass days, arrived. The custody record showed that no one knew who O'Mahoney was and that Fuller took his prints to identify him. According to O'Mahoney, Fuller told him that everything would be sorted out.

In the witness box O'Mahoney listed the officers with whom, he said, he had had dealings both commercial and corrupt, going back as far as the early 1970s. Much of his time seems to have been spent in the company of retired or serving police officers. He had, for example, rewired the house of one of his former bodyguards as well as for Detective Chief Inspector Peter Atkins whose garden lights he had rewired, putting power to his pond. He refuted suggestions that he had turned up uninvited at the Christmas party by producing the voucher for the winning flight from Gatwick to Paris.

It was, wrote Duncan Campbell of his behaviour in the witness-box, '. . . a virtuoso performance. The prosecution dismissed his case as rubbish but the jury acquitted him.'[10]

10 *Guardian*, 16 July 1993.

As Campbell went on to write, this has left O'Mahoney in something of a dilemma and his lawyer, Adrian Neale, wrote to the Home Office and indeed went to see the Home Secretary, Kenneth Baker, asking for a guarantee of his client's safety. He has been given no promises. An inquiry by the Police Complaints Authority carried out before the trial exonerated the officers involved in the Shepherd's Bush case. Late in 1993 O'Mahoney issued a writ against the Commissioner of Police for the Metropolis, claiming damages for malicious prosecution. It is being defended with vigour.

Although the figures floated as to the price may have been exaggerated, there is no doubt that the gangland rumours of contracts out against O'Mahoney after he first gave evidence were correct. Says an East End figure:

I knew some people who missed O'Mahoney in Bayswater. Their card was marked that he'd be in the Monmouth of Westbourne Grove but by the time they got there he'd gone.

It was whilst O'Mahoney was in Chiswick police station that he met another man on his way to becoming a supergrass – Billy Williams, whose conversion to the forces of good apparently came on the road away from a bank robbery at Barclays Bank in St John's Wood, London. PC David Clements was shot at the wheel of the Panda car in which he was chasing Williams and Jimmy and Philip Trusty. Clements survived, but Jimmy Trusty turned against his younger brother when Philip – who fired the shot, and feared a twenty-year sentence if he was found guilty – tried to persuade him to take the blame. Jimmy had virtually nothing in the way of convictions. Philip Trusty had considerably more.

Jimmy also turned informer and received a two-year-nine-month sentence. Philip, on the wrong end of his brother's evidence, received twenty.

There were repercussions from this case which rumbled on

for the next half-dozen years. On 26 September 1974 Peter Wilding was arrested when he became stuck in a traffic jam in Hounslow. He had been grassed by Billy Williams. According to Wilding, Williams visited him in his cell.

One of the problems for Williams and the others was boredom, and there is little doubt that the police and the authorities did what they could to keep their charges amused and in the right frame of mind to give evidence. Williams had had his share of troubles before he pleaded guilty to three armed robberies and asked for a further thirty-three, including more of the same, to be taken into consideration. He received five years from the judge and threats from the prison inmates. Before he was moved he had scalding water thrown over him – the standard, if extra-curricular, punishment meted out by inmates in prison to informers and sex offenders.

Whilst he was in Chiswick he was allowed out of his cell to marry his girlfriend Barbara Stanikowski at the local register office. Back in the police station there was champagne at a reception. Later they took pictures of each other with a smuggled camera, and a story appeared in the *News of the World* together with a picture of Billy Williams wearing a policeman's helmet, which he had borrowed from a peg, and drinking champagne. The report said that Jack Slipper was his best man but the truth is that, in charge of the security for Williams, rather more prosaically he was merely there as a witness.[11]

When it came to it George du Burriatte was a witness in one of the O'Mahoney trials and a number of others.

At that time (1972) he had a little firm robbing banks and post offices and security vehicles. Seven or eight others were with him. They were bringing the money back to George and he was paying them a wage and promising

[11] *News of the World*, 16 May 1976.

to invest their money. He was acquitted and they never saw their money.

Third in line of value was Charlie Lowe, a then fairly well respected East End villain. For a change he was not a Met informer but belonged, if that is the right word, to No. 5 Regional Crime Squad which looked after Essex. The end of that particular period of his criminal career took about a year to stutter to its conclusion – at least that is what the Court of Appeal seemed to have thought, but in all probability it did not know the real facts.

In July 1975 Lowe and another man, both armed with ammonia, were seen by the police as they ran from a garage in Stamford Hill. The other man squirted ammonia at the police but after a chase both were arrested. Lowe was committed for trial at the Old Bailey, but failed to surrender to his bail on 15 January 1976. In the meantime, on 27 September he had been given bail after being stopped in a hire-car overdue for return. He had thrown away a driving licence in the name of Crowe and had been found to have a small amount of cannabis resin in his pocket. He was committed for trial, this time to the Inner London Sessions, but again he failed to appear.

Whilst his luck with crime in general was clearly out – although if you commit crimes on a weekly basis you must expect to be caught fairly frequently – with the courts it was spilling over. In November, now on bail twice, he was seen to put a sack in the boot of an MG parked in East London. When searched by the police it was found to contain a sawn-off shotgun. Lowe said he had been 'set up' and was only selling it on; again he was given bail. Later Lord Justice Roskill sitting in the Court of Appeal remarked wryly: 'We make no comment upon the number of times he appears to have been released on bail.'[12]

On 26 June 1976 he was arrested whilst bathing on the Isle of Sheppey. Now, with the accumulation of cases lined

12 79 Cr. App. R. 122.

up against him, he could see a middle-length prison sentence in prospect and he offered to tell all.

He was kept under wraps until the October when the *Guardian* broke the bad news to his former colleagues. One of the ruses employed to keep him hidden had been to bring him before the local magistrates under a false name. During his time in the relative comfort of Southend police station, where he was allowed female visitors and a television, he made statements admitting his own involvement in ninety-one offences including fifteen robberies, and implicating forty-five different criminals in cases involving over £300,000 cash and valuables in which he admitted he and his friends had used coshes and ammonia, and sawn-off shotguns had been carried – the stock-in-trade of the professional armed robber. £100,000 of drugs were recovered. Thirty-seven people were arrested.

Then came something which must have approached shock-horror to him. After the Court of Appeal's comments on the Smalls' deal, Lowe could not have expected to walk free. However, what he certainly did not expect, on 13 December 1976 when he appeared before Mr Justice Stocker at Chelmsford Crown Court, was a ten-year sentence plus a further eighteen months of a suspended sentence. He was not happy and went to the Court of Appeal where he was duly rewarded.

Lord Justice Roskill said that not enough credit had been given to him for the enormous help he had given to the police both before and after his conviction.

It must be in the public interest that persons who have become involved in gang activities of this kind should be encouraged to give information of this kind to the police in order that others may be brought to justice and that, where such information is given and can be acted upon and, as here, has already been in part successfully acted upon, substantial credit should be given upon pleas of guilty especially in cases where there is no other evidence

against the accused than the accused's own confession,
and be given substantial credit for it.

From then on he gave evidence in a number of successful
prosecutions against his former colleagues until, in February
1978, the Lowe Express was derailed. The defence in the case
of a hi-jacking had managed to learn something of Lowe's
background over and above his life as a blagger. He was not
simply an uncomplicated, decent English criminal, wielding
a pick-axe handle in a post-Marxist attempt to redistribute
wealth; he was, it seems, an international fraudsman as well.
He had, it appeared, been a part of one particular swindle
which had involved millions. His stamping ground had been
Europe and the Middle East, with the Lebanon as a particularly
favourite spot. Why the Lebanon? Because one should always
go where there is a war. It disrupts communications and it is
more difficult to check stolen credit cards. He had, he admitted,
also been involved in what was then a major conspiracy to
import twenty kilos of cannabis from Morocco. It seems that
he had told the investigating officers of this verbally. At least
that is what he told the court, but he had never written it
down because no one had asked him to. When it came to
it, however, in the Court of Appeal's spirit of rapprochement
and the rehabilitation of Charlie Lowe, it is doubtful whether
it would have made that much difference to his sentence. It
was, however, a big stick for the defence to wield.

Now, said prosecuting counsel, Mr John Bloefeld, the credit
card fraud had been 'fully investigated' and the Director of
Public Prosecutions was not prepared to bring further charges.
Judge Peter Greenwood, who had presided over a number of
the Lowe cases, was not pleased. Summing up to the jury, he
called him disgusting, evil and brutal. The defendants were
acquitted.

On his release Lowe paid for his own plastic surgery, but he
could not keep his fingers out of the criminal pie and, within
a year, was back in trouble.

Now with the blessing of the Court of Appeal to guide trial judges, supergrasses could expect a sentence of around five years instead of one of twenty. With time spent on remand counting towards a release date, much of their sentence would have been worked off before they actually appeared in the dock. During this time, and whilst they were giving evidence, they would be kept in police custody and, allowing for remission and parole, released immediately or very soon after the last hearing. They could expect reasonable accommodation visits from their wives and sometimes the opportunity to go out to the local pubs with the detectives guarding them. There would be reward money and a new identity at the end of their sentence. It is hardly surprising that there was now a steady queue of men willing to testify against their former colleagues.

Despite this, some commentators see Charlie Lowe as the beginning of the end of the golden age of the supergrass.

4

The Grass Withers

One of the next up to bat was Leroy Davies. According to his version of events, he was extremely unfortunate to have been caught in the first place. He was arrested for handling money stolen from a security truck robbery at Leverstock Green near Hemel Hempstead, Hertfordshire, in December 1977. It seems that the robbery of £231,000 – carried out with John Gorman, Bruce Frazer, Roy Allen, Tony Knightley and a power-saw – was successful. It was not until his then brother-in-law, Dave Stockwin, wanted to earn some money that things turned sour for him. Davies sold him £500 for £400 and Stockwin passed this straight on to another relative, forgetting to warn him it was stolen money. On his arrest and that of his wife, Christine, Stockwin told the police the money had come from Davies.

Davies really was unfortunate. According to his story, subsequently sold to the *Daily Express*,[1] Davies had been keeping out of harm's way in the Metropolitan Police area by a system of well-placed bribes.

> After a bank robbery in the West End earlier, I was pulled in and told that the 'governor', a Chief Superintendent, wanted bodies.

1 15 July 1980.

In other words, names of the team on the job. In those days there was no way he would get those from me. So I was told it would have to be cash unless I wanted to be nicked. Ten big ones. I did not give it direct to the governor, one of his men, a sergeant took it.

After an attempted robbery in the Mile End Road in 1974 an inspector who knew I had done it demanded £500 for keeping quiet. I paid him after I had pulled another job to finance it.

These were part of regular payments I made to a few officers between 1971 and 1977. Detectives right down to the rank of constable were involved. Some of them were on retainers of £100 to £200 a week.

Now Davies found himself in Hertfordshire well away from the Met where he might have been able to call on a friendly officer for help.

Davies believed that he was about to be fitted up for the murder of a Hatton Garden jeweller near his home in Golders Green.[2] With his then girlfriend Elizabeth agreeing to stand by him despite the attendant risks of being the girlfriend of a grass, Davies began to tell nearly all. As he wrote in the *Daily Express* over his decision to turn supergrass: '. . . she agreed that I should start paying some of my debt to society

---

2 In fact the real killer was one of the oldest surviving armed robbers of recent times, John Hilton, who was jailed for life in 1991. He and Alan Roberts robbed a Hatton Garden jeweller, Leo Grunhut, outside his home in Golders Green. Hilton accidentally shot his partner in the thigh and as the jeweller tried to escape shot him in the back. The proceeds of the raid were £3,000 in cash and £277,000 in diamonds. Hilton managed to get his partner into their getaway car and drove him to a garage in South London where he bled to death. Roberts was buried on a railway embankment at Dartford, Kent. Grunhut died a month later. It was this murder to which Davies was referring.

By the time he reached the Old Bailey in September 1991, Hilton was sixty-two, frail and grey-haired, but he had killed three people during his thirty-year career which had ended in Burlington Gardens, Piccadilly, London, the previous year. In 1963 he had been given a life sentence for the murder of a man in the celebrated raid on the Co-op dairy in Mitcham, South London. He was freed on licence in February 1978 and it was a month later that he shot and killed both Grunhut and his partner. At his 1991 trial he refused to allow his counsel to put forward any mitigation.

and that she would stand by me.'

He had been born in the East End, one of a large family with
an elder brother, Glanford. His father had been a professional
boxer. Colleagues remember that he had 'started screwing
young' and then in the 1960s had become a bank robber. One
man on remand with him recalls:

I was nicked and was in Brixton with Joey Cannon and
George du Burriatte. Joey and Leroy decided to escape and
one Sunday night they tied up a screw in the toilets where
they kept Cat 'A' men. Cannon and Leroy unlocked all the
'A' men but none of us wanted to go. They escaped over
the wall but it was half-baked. I don't think they even had
transport waiting. Meanwhile the prison's running amok
with people smashing the control rooms up. What I really
remember was George du Burriatte being mysteriously
taken off the Escapers list shortly after that.

As a result of Leroy Davics' statements and those of two more
supergrasses, Edward Martin and Roger Dennhardt, *Operation
Kestrel* run by the Hertfordshire police netted twenty-four
villains who were jailed for up to eighteen years. They
included Tony Knightley, who received sixteen years for
another security van robbery. In his tearful recollections to
the *Daily Express*, Davies remembered how he had saved
Knightley's name until last and how it had grieved him finally
to offer him up.

On 24 July 1978 Davies appeared at St Albans Crown
Court and pleaded guilty to seven counts of robbery, one of
conspiracy to rob, seven of having a firearm with intent to
commit an indictable offence, and asked for thirty-three similar
offences to be taken into consideration.

The trial judge, again Mr Justice Stocker who had originally
sentenced Lowe, had apparently not seen the clear signals sent
down by the Court of Appeal and put Davies away for ten
years. Leroy Davies appealed and was represented by the

celebrated silk William Howard QC. His co-defendant, John Michael Gorman, who had pleaded guilty to one robbery and one firearm offence and had received a total of nine years' imprisonment, was also represented by leading counsel.

Davies' sentence was reduced to seven years by the Lord Chief Justice, Lord Widgery. He had, after all, assisted in supplying information which had led to the arrest of what were described as dangerous and violent criminals in over a hundred cases. There was a recommendation that the police should help resettle Davies and his family in another country. This meant that Davies, for all his crimes, would serve rather less than Gorman for his two. Surely this was wrong? No, said the Lord Chief Justice:

> One must necessarily ask oneself: does that matter? It is not contended that Gorman assisted the police. It is not contended that Gorman should receive a sentence reduced on that account. Gorman has received a sentence of nine years, and the argument on behalf of Gorman is that the sentence on Davies should not be reduced for considerations such as I have mentioned in order to provide Davies with a substantial discount if the result is going to be to reduce the sentence on Davies to below that passed on Gorman.
>
> We have considered this argument and we reject it.[3]

Davies also gave statements to *Operation Countryman*, which at that time was investigating allegations of wholesale corruption in the Metropolitan Police, naming the detectives to whom he had been making regular payments. No charges were ever brought against any of them.

It would be pleasant to record that Davies was able to settle down after that with his new family, but it would not be accurate. In April 1982 he appeared at the Old Bailey

3 68 Cr. App. R.321.

charged, along with his elder brother, with a robbery at the French Revolution public house in Putney where he had worked as an under-manager. His brother, Glanford, who pleaded guilty and implicated him, received five years imprisonment.

It was alleged that Leroy Davies, now known as Leslie Newton, had escaped after firing one barrel of a sawn-off shotgun at the police. Davies had told the jury, which took only ninety minutes to acquit him, that he would never have been party to such an inefficient robbery. The trial judge was not so impressed. Mr Justice Lawson invited the jury to stay behind and listen to Glanford's confession which had been excluded from the evidence against Leroy. Davies-Newton stayed behind to hear his brother's counsel say:

> In a mad, reckless, drunken moment he was lured away from his home by the person who is much more evil than he is and who carried the gun on the robbery.

He also heard Mr Justice Lawson add: 'I have no doubt as to the true identity of that gunman.'

Davies jnr had reason to be pleased. Not only had he been acquitted, but the trial judge had made an order prohibiting the publication of any photograph of him. Thereafter he faded from the London scene; he had married into a well-known East End family who were unattracted by his behaviour.

For many supergrasses, the decision to turn squealer came when they heard that one of their former colleagues was about to inform on them. Roger Dennhardt was one. He was serving thirteen years for robbing a security van on its way from the Express Dairy in Hemel Hempstead, and was on trial for conspiracy to pervert the course of justice when he heard that a man – with whom he had taken part in a 1976 robbery at Murphy's, a building company in Islington, during which a security guard had been injured – was about to tell all. 'All' would be that Dennhardt was the man who had pulled the trigger. Dennhardt maintained that the injuries

were an accident and that he had been shooting at a lock, but he
was influenced by a friend who received life for 'accidentally'
shooting a police officer.

His *apologia pro vita sua* to the police makes pretty
nauseating reading.

> During the past three years I have wrestled with a strong
> desire to confess my crimes and to a great extent put right
> the damage I have inflicted on my fellow citizens . . .
>   It is really the only honourable course a man such as
> myself has left to take. I have caused a major schism within
> my family. This act of informing is the most positive
> proof I can give that I have concluded my criminal career
> for ever.

His confession may also not have been completely untinged by
the potential loss of his girlfriend, Melissa, whom he described
(as she did herself) to the *Daily Mirror* as a dog. Recalling his
arrest, Dennhardt spoke movingly of her.

> I could still smell her on my body. I kept thinking, it'll
> be years now before I see her again. Years, mate, bloody
> stinking years.[4]

On 24 January 1980 Dennhardt changed his plea in the
conspiracy-to-pervert trial and made a 1,000-page handwritten
statement. This case involved two solicitors, a young girl clerk
and a licensee. One of Dennhardt's problems had been explaining how he had accumulated substantial sums of money in his
bank account, and the idea had been for the licensee to explain

---

4 *Daily Mirror*, 7 September 1981. As for the 'dog' bit, in general slang terms
'a dog' is used to describe an unattractive woman. Dennhardt used the word
in approbation and Melissa spoke of the privileges of being a robber's dog,
which were denied to the common or garden criminal's wife. These included
the screw turning a blind eye if the man and the dog wished to 'have a bit
of a grope' whilst on a visit.

that this came from business dealings. Within minutes, there was Dennhardt in the witness box alleging that the solicitor had wanted £10,000 to prepare the false defence.

His subsequent evidence cleared up 329 crimes involving £3 million of stolen property. Twenty-nine people were jailed. As a thank-you for his co-operation in *Operation Carter*, he received an eight-year sentence concurrent with his thirteen-year term and was released from prison in 1981 having obtained full remission. He was able to tell the *Daily Mirror*: 'Now there is nobody, absolutely nobody, that a robber can trust.'[5]

His criminal career had started in the 1960s when he had been a member of the so-called English Bonnie and Clyde gang. He escaped from Ashford Remand Centre and, with friends, carried out a four-month orgy of robberies on betting shops, sub-post offices and banks. Scotland Yard appealed to the youths to give themselves up to avoid what they feared was going to be a shoot-out and Dennhardt walked into a police station to give himself up. Whilst on the run he had sent his mother £2,000 to tide her over while he faced what he feared would be a long sentence. In fact he received only five years and three months.

Dennhardt, who always wore black with a black hood to work, had also given his version as to how to carry out a successful raid: 'The mask is not just to hide your features. It has got to be frightening. It has got to be black so that the imprint of blackness is horrible.'

It is something of a shame that Graham Sayer, the detective sergeant who was assigned to be Dennhardt's minder, did not read the paper that morning. Had he done so, his life might have been a happier one. Sayer, who had been involved in the kudos of *Operation Carter* and had twenty-two years' service, fourteen of them as a detective, fell under the spell of Dennhardt's charms.

In November 1986 Sayer found himself in the dock at
Nottingham Crown Court where he was acquitted of a
conspiracy to rob a post office in Aldershot but convicted
of a similar offence at Mansfield. Dennhardt was not with him.
It was claimed he had broken through a police road-block after
the Aldershot raid, and had hidden in a hole in the ground for
two days before slipping out of the country by mingling with
the Liverpool supporters on their way to the Heysel stadium. He
returned and, using Sayer's knowedge of how deliveries were
made to sub-post offices, organised the raid at Mansfield. Sayer
had behaved incredibly foolishly. He had used his mother's car
to rehearse a getaway route, spending so much time on this that
an old lady in the neighbourhood had become suspicious and
noted down the number. On 7 November Sayer received nine
years. Dennhardt was safely in Spain, from where he gave an
interview to a newspaper saying that he denied his involvement
in the raids.

He explained that when he had broken through the road-
block he believed it was a trap organised by vengeful
colleagues. He was certainly the subject of a contract and it
is possible that he survived an attack. In October 1984 Arthur
Farr, a Berkshire haulage contractor, was shot dead. He bore
some physical resemblance to the supergrass and had traded as
Denhardt.

> It was like reading my own obituary. I have feared
> something like this for a long time. There are plenty
> of hardened villains who would shoot me. There are
> a lot of people I know who have sworn to get even
> with me.

Others who should have taken notice of Dennhardt's comment
about the safety of bank robbers included those who worked
with Donald Barrett. His trustworthiness had long been in
question, if not from the time when he had named names in
the Smalls bank robbery case in Bournemouth, then certainly

a decade later when he became a supergrass in 1981. For this
string of offences he received fourteen years, but the Court of
Appeal halved the sentence. When it came to it he served three
years and four months and within a year was at it again. Now in
1988 the reason for his downfall was a mixture of carelessness
and ill-fortune.

In 1985 a young boy had found a home-made remote-control
device in a rubbish sack outside a house in the East End.
Technically minded, he had taken it home and stripped it. It
was similar to one he had in a model racing car and he thought
no more about it. In the rubbish sack there had also been a mask,
hair and glue. Then six months later, watching *Crimewatch* on
television in November, he realised it was a device similar to
those being used by a team of robbers who were strapping
bombs to their victims, to persuade them to hand over gold
bullion and cash. He eventually convinced his mother it was
worth telling the police.

The house outside which the boy had found the device
belonged to David Croke, its maker and leader of the team
of which Barrett was a member. On 11 December 1985, as part
of a robbery at the Armaguard Security Depot in Essex, one of
the security guards had been attacked in his home. His wife
and daughter were handcuffed and threatened, and he agreed
to have what he was told was a remote-control bomb attached
to him as he drove to the security depot from which £500,000
was stolen.

Now the police kept watch on Croke's house, which he had
purchased for £85,000 cash in the February of that year, and
they identified Barrett as one of the visitors.

The police swooped on the motorway as the men set out with
a haul of £280,000 gold bullion from South London which they
had just hi-jacked. Barrett, who on his arrest recognised one of
the officers and gave himself up saying, 'Hello, Phil, nice little
tickle you've had here', once again turned informer implicating
his former colleagues. This time he received sixteen years for
his trouble – a discount of 25 per cent, said Judge Michael

Coombe when sentencing him on 6 May 1988. It was reduced
to twelve years on appeal. There was said to be a contract in the
sum of £250,000 on his head, but he survived to appear in the
Gangland series on BBC television in 1994, commenting on his
life and times. The robberies had been particularly unpleasant
with, on one occasion, a security guard being doused in petrol.
Croke received twenty-three years and Croke's wife's son,
Alan Turne, a security guard on the last robbery, went down
for seven years.

Detective Superintendent MacRae, in charge of the case,
said:

> Imagine Donald Barrett carrying on with criminals, doing
> robberies, when they know he's a supergrass. It's stag-
> gering and astounding. What is clear is that there was a
> body of opinion among criminals that having once been
> a supergrass, he could never, ever, ever, be a supergrass
> again. They felt in this sense he was safer to indulge in
> criminality with than any other criminal.[6]

But one London criminal thinks that Croke was not really at
fault: 'I mean Ronnie Darke recommended him. The man
wasn't really into the scene, so there was no way of him
knowing he was a wrong un.'[7]

Indeed it does seem that the profession as a whole is
careless with whom it associates. An East End criminal now
approaching middle age and father-figurehood finds that young
criminals simply will not listen.

> I know kids who are working with fucking well-known
> grasses. When I tell them, they won't have it. They're

6 Liz Mills, *Crimewatch*, p. 157.
7 On 21 January 1995 a gang tied a 'bomb' to a security guard and told him to
hand over £1,500,000 or be blown up. The gang escaped with the cash and
left him still attached to the bomb and fearful that they would detonate it by
remote control. It was the first time that this method had been used since the
arrest of Croke and Barratt.

making so much money out of grasses they don't want
to know . . .

Tony G. has to have been a grass for fifty years.
His brother was a self-confessed grass. He said so at
Snaresbrook[8] yet P. [a professional and successful] still
goes with him.

I could never prove H.A. was a grass but his solicitor
swore black was blue that he was, yet everybody has it
with him in the East End.

He covers his tracks. When I was done in 1976 I thought
I was going for good. They had more evidence against
him than they did me but he was never even charged or
questioned. I've never had it with him since. If anyone
asked me for a recommendation I'd just tell them to be
careful.

Were people more careful in the good old days? Frank Fraser
recalls those golden times.

In my days you never knew for sure who was a grass. Street
bookmakers would be informers to ensure they were only
nicked from time to time, same with the brasses in the West
End, so instead of being nicked four days a week they would
only be nicked once a week. In those days there was hardly
any crime. The population was 10 or 12 m lower than it is
now; maybe even more. People could go into the Army or
Navy for a career and now those avenues are closed to them.
Then there was an open door for them.

You would get a whisper who was a grass so who could
be left out. Those who didn't take that course would be
the informers or people who bought themselves out. The
police didn't shop their informers. Their word was God.
He could swear he'd seen you climbing up a drainpipe and
had a monkey with you and you'd given the jewellery to
the monkey and he would be believed. It was one in a

8 A Crown Court in East London.

million where the policeman was not believed. He was believed automatically.

In the upper echelons of crime, however, he believes the thief or robber had innate protection from the informer:

In those days it was impossible for it to happen to us. Everyone we knew. You could trace their history back. Not even that. You automatically knew it. No stranger could ever infiltrate that circle. In 1949–50 I would say if there were twenty people in London doing the type of crime we were doing that was about it. At the very most thirty and that's topping it up.

Then when three people were arrested for a bank, wages, etc. the three were always together. The only ones who went to Parkhurst were those with health problems. In cases like Lewes 1938 when they were convicted [after the racecourse fight] they were split up. In the 1948 airport robbery when they were convicted they went to local prisons. Jimmy Woods to Exeter, Teddy Hughes to Bristol. In our case, the Spot case [the slashing of a London villain] we were all split up.

The beginning of the end was the dispersal. Now you couldn't trust your cellmate. With the drugs which is the thing today, what they do with the informers is have a load of drugs through – really big – the informer sells it and customs get their cut. That's part of the deal. They may do this two or three times and then the informer is allowed to slip out. All nicked. I'm allowed out. It's part of the deal.

Police would consider it demeaning to give the grass money. He would be allowed not to get nicked. The police would take a larger slice.

Last year the police arrested an old-timer – man was in his late seventies – and put a deal where he'd get £500 a week if he fed them information. The man more or less spat in their face and promptly told everybody.

Not all reprisals against grasses and supergrasses were violent and illegal. In giving evidence at the trial of George Ernest Turner in March 1978 at the Chelmsford Crown Court, for a robbery committed in Southgate in January 1974, Colin Saggs had admitted his part in the affair. During the trial leading counsel for the Crown had said that Saggs was giving evidence at some personal risk because although the Director of Public Prosecutions had undertaken not to prosecute him if Saggs gave evidence, he was still not safe from a private prosecution. Two months into his seven-year prison sentence in May 1978, George Turner decided to do just that. He took out a summons in the Tottenham Magistrates' Court.

The DPP stepped in immediately to protect his little lamb and wrote to Turner's solicitors saying that in accordance with his powers under the Prosecution of Offences Acts and Regulations, he proposed to intervene in the prosecution and offer no evidence. Turner was not unnaturally upset and challenged the decision, contending that it was unlawful. The Director then applied to strike out the action as being vexatious. Turner was particularly aggrieved, as well he might have been, that he was convicted on Saggs' evidence, the truth of which had apparently been bolstered by counsel's remark on his exposure to a private prosecution. Mr Justice Mars-Jones was having nothing of the argument. Apart from the harm done to Saggs by bringing a prosecution,

> the Director of Public Prosecutions had to take into consideration the possible effects of such a private prosecution being allowed to proceed upon current and future criminal inquiries and proceedings.

Quite clearly, if witness could then be prosecuted on their own admissions when giving evidence for the Crown, the supply would soon dry up.[9]

9 79 Cr.App. R.70.

The Director was not going to allow any further mistakes and misunderstandings to occur. In the same year the Right Honourable Jeremy Thorpe, the former leader of the Liberal Party, was charged with conspiracy and incitement to murder Norman Scott who had claimed to have had a homosexual relationship with Thorpe. Proceedings were also brought against David Holmes, John Le Mesurier, a carpet dealer, and George Deakin who was alleged to have recruited a former airline pilot, Andrew Gino Newton, to carry out the £10,000 contract. It was alleged that Newton had driven Norman Scott and his Great Dane, Rinka, to a hilltop near Porlock on the Devon moors in October 1975, when the dog had been shot. Now the Director wished to have as one of his principal witnesses a Peter Bessell, then living in California. The undertaking was clear that there would be no prosecution against him by the police or anyone else, and 'in the event of the private prosecution of Mr Bessell in respect of any such matter, the Director will assume responsibility for the conduct of those proceedings and offer no evidence against Mr Bessell.' In the event Thorpe, Le Mesurier and Holmes did not give evidence and Deakin said that it was a conspiracy to frighten and not to kill. Bessell stood to gain £50,000 from the *Sunday Telegraph* if there was a conviction, and only half that if there was an acquittal of Thorpe. There was an acquittal of Thorpe and all the other defendants.[10]

But whatever successes Marshall and Slipper had had with Smalls and O'Mahoney, it was nothing to the success which would come to a rising star in the Met, Tony Lundy. In May 1977 Detective Chief Inspector Tony Lundy rejoined the Flying Squad, soon to be reorganised in part as the Robbery Squad with its headquarters at Finchley. It was Lundy who developed the supergrass into a whole business of its own.

10 According to an article in the *New Statesman*, at least one juror apparently thought this half-price deal destroyed Bessell's credibility. This interview with a juror led to the unsuccessful prosecution of the *New Statesman* and the subsequent passing of the Contempt of Court Act 1981 in which s.8 prevents any research into, or publication of, a jury's findings.

Within six months he had his first major success with David Smith, arrested for an attack in September 1977 on two elderly men who collected their company's wages near The Thatched Barn, a restaurant at Borehamwood in Hertfordshire. The money was snatched but then one of the team, Alf Berkley, tore off the glasses of one of the men and squirted ammonia in his eyes. The man was almost completely blinded.

Smith turned supergrass, confessing to over sixty armed robberies. He was kept at Finchley police station for over fifteen months, at the end of which, as a result of his efforts, sixty-nine people were charged, of whom 90 per cent pleaded guilty. Two of the other robbers in the Thatched Barn team were also allowed to become supergrasses. One of them, George Williams, who had been offered the supergrass deal before Smith had rolled over but had initially held out, also received five years for a total of eighty robberies.

His evidence was necessary because there was a small problem with Smith. He had actually killed a man, and the DPP's policy was to require a plea of guilty to a murder – which carried a mandatory life sentence – and so he could not be considered a credible witness. Smith had coshed Kurt Hess, an elderly factory owner, during a robbery in Shoreditch. Hess had died three weeks later. However, Smith's luck was in. A statement was obtained from a pathologist which showed that Hess' poor health had contributed to his death. A charge of manslaughter was sufficient and so Smith could be reinstated as a prosecution witness.[11] Later the rules were relaxed and supergrasses who had pleaded guilty to murder were allowed to give evidence for the Crown, in one case with fairly disastrous results.

In fact George Williams' hands were none too clean either. In 1967 he and Smith had kidnapped the manager of a North London supermarket, Walter Price, to get the keys from his

---

11 Smith was also reputed to have killed a bookmaker, Harry Barham, found shot in the back of the head in his car in Hackney. £40,000 had been stolen from him. There was no hard evidence against Smith and he was never charged. In fairness, many a name was put up for the Barham killing including that of the ubiquitous West Ham hardman, Teddy Machin.

safe. The 16-stone Williams, known as 'Fat George', coshed Price, who died eight weeks later from heart failure. Price had staggered home with a lump on his head described by his widow as 'as big as an egg'. Judge Michael Argyle, his hands tied by public policy, commented that he considered Smith and Williams as 'two of the most dangerous criminals in British history', adding that whilst he accepted they were telling the truth: '. . . it was nauseating to hear these hypocrites and that as a matter of policy they have only been sentenced to five years each.'

But Smith did not last long on the outside. Throughout his adult life he had been an unsuccessful career criminal and he spent only short periods out of prison. On 29 September 1986 he was caught in a raid on a Securicor vehicle in Golders Green along with another former supergrass, Ron Simpson. Smith again turned supergrass, but this time he did not live long enough to testify. In a cell which had been hung with balloons for his birthday five days earlier, Smith cut his throat with a razor-blade on Monday 13 October. Simpson was gaoled for twenty-one years.

Recruit followed recruit through the Lundy supergrass factory, some thirty of them defended by Roland Pelly, a Bishops Stortford solicitor who had been the DPP's agent in Hertfordshire in the early 1970s when the DPP used to send cases to local firms of solicitors.

One of Lundy's least successful supergrasses was Londoner Billy Amies. Given the sobriquet 'The Snake', Amies served only two years in prison, but although he had named fifty-eight criminals it seems he was responsible for the conviction of only five.

But, so far as the police were concerned, the most serious incident had involved the Flying Squad's Detective Sergeant Bernard Craven who suffered brain damage in an attack on him whilst guarding Billy Amies in Liverpool. Versions of what exactly happened and how vary.

Amies was one of the more unpleasant of armed robbers. Amongst his other roles, while dressed as a policeman he had threatened his victim in a robbery with castration, and had the man's daughter stripped to her underwear asking, 'How would you like to see your daughter raped?' He had also been at work on Merseyside. In the first of his three cases there, a middle-aged woman had been repeatedly punched in the face; in the second another middle-aged woman, her Down's Syndrome daughter and her son had all been tied up; the latter had also been threatened with castration. In the third incident a garage owner and his family had been tied up and the owner had had his testicles bitten to persuade him to open his safe.

Lundy described him as follows:

> In some ways Billy was a nutter. He was also known as Billy the Queer because he's a raving homosexual. A big hard man, over six foot, a real animal, a compulsive armed robber who was really feared, but clever too.

Amies was in serious difficulties. He was caught out of his territory and had been arrested with one of Liverpool's real hardmen, John Tremarco. Lundy was told by another supergrass, David Smith, that Amies wanted help because he feared a corrupt Liverpool police officer, John Keating, was trying to lighten Tremarco's load by placing it on Amies' shoulders. It appears that Amies was being pressured into pleading guilty. Lundy went incognito to Walton jail and saw Amies who, once he had read Smith's statements involving him, decided that the path to safety was for him to turn supergrass. Much to the fury of the Merseyside police, Amies was transferred to Brixton on Rule 43 (see Ch.1, fn. 22) and then to Acton police station. There he told his version of his life of crime, implicating Tremarco and also Keating.

In October 1977, he went back to Liverpool to plead guilty. His statement was then shown to the solicitors for the other defendants who, as soon as Amies walked into the witness box, in turn were forced to put their hands up. The public gallery howled revenge, and the case was adjourned until the Monday for the sentencing of everyone including Amies.

The new and reformed supergrass was, unsurprisingly, unhappy about staying in the North West for the weekend; he wanted to do the round trip to the safety of London. It was agreed he should be returned on the Sunday night, to be lodged overnight in a Liverpool police station. So far so good, except that on the Sunday night the London sergeants who had custody of Amies could not find him a home; nor could they manage to contact the local Serious Crimes Officers. They therefore turned up with Amies in tow at the hotel in Liverpool where Lundy was staying. Further efforts to find Amies a bed in a cell failed, and so he was booked into the hotel along with his guarding officers Craven and O'Rourke. On a toss of the coin it was decided that Craven should sleep in the room with Amies, and O'Rourke outside.

Unfortunately, Amies thought it would be a good idea to go out for a last drink. This was by no means an uncommon situation with supergrasses, and the officer agreed. Off he and Craven went to a pub in the docks called the Crow's Nest. Even more unfortunately, it was the haunt of Tremarco's friends. Lundy seems to have been full of admiration for his protégé:

> Typical of the fearless animal he is, off goes Amies with Craven into the lions' den. But as soon as they walk in, they're set upon! Amies, big strong beast, fights his way out and escapes, but Bernie Craven gets an almighty kicking. He's almost kicked to death but he manages to stagger out of the pub, he's found in the front garden of a nearby house and he's rushed to hospital.[12]

12 The quotations are from M. Short's *Lundy*, pp. 51–2. There is a full account of Amies' career in Chapter 4 of the book. An alternative view is expressed in A. Jennings and others, *Scotland Yard's Cocaine Connection*. They point out that apart from the two men in Liverpool, Amies' evidence served to convict only three more people.

Amies was badly cut and had a broken arm by the time he returned to the safety of the hotel. Craven was not so fortunate, suffering severe concussion, a broken nose and a fractured cheekbone. He never really recovered, and retired from the force on health grounds. The next morning Lundy managed to have Amies' case remitted to London, where he could be sentenced for all his offences. Tremarco received fifteen years; back in London Amies served only two. Two years later, Keating was convicted of attempting to extort half the money an insurance company had paid to a police informer. He received two and a half years.

The story in the Underworld was that Amies had been punished in the pub by a Liverpool hardman, Billy Grimwood, assisted by two London brothers from a well-known and influential family. The mystery remains as to why Amies chose the Crow's Nest, of all Liverpool pubs, in which to drink.

Amies, an only child, had grown up in the East End with his father George and mother Rosie. They lived at Carr Street, Stepney. He grew up a thief and graduated into robbery. In 1964 he was arrested for tying up a woman in a robbery along with Thomas 'Golly' Sillett – who was later arrested for the Mountnessing Silver Bullion Robbery in which he named a number of names but would not give evidence against them at the trial – and Joe Flynn. Amies was convicted – the others were acquitted – and was sentenced to four years' imprisonment. Whilst in Maidstone prison he developed a relationship with another prisoner and, when that man was upset by another inmate, Amies attacked the third person, as a result of which he received a further eighteen months. On his release he resumed his occupation. He was well respected amongst the heavy London set and was attacked by Albert Donoghue, who thought he was being kidnapped when he got in a car with him after the Kray trial. In 1970 Amies was arrested and sentenced to seven years for a robbery in Portsmouth.

As has been said, the interesting thing about supergrasses is not the people whom they name but the ones they do not. In one instance Amies named a George Almond but then proceeded to give evidence in mitigation for him saying how he, Amies, had led Almond astray and onto the particular job.

Another East End figure recalls his dealings with Amies:

He could have put me away four or five times but he didn't. I don't know why. Joey was questioned about a robbery put up by Amies and he was never on it. I fucking know because I was. I think it was because Joey had had a row with Amies over one of his boyfriends. He never ever worked with Amies but he was put up on this robbery.

He was a very dangerous man. They may have called him Billy the Queen but I would never have underestimated him. Even when he was in the police station he was blagging people. 'If you don't pull up 10 or 20 grand you'll go down for a robbery.' Someone would be put in a cell with him and he'd get everything out of the bloke and give it back to the police.

The only thing I can think of why he didn't put me in was something that happened in about 1968 or 1969 and it happened with Golly S.[13] Golly, me and Amies were looking at a robbery and then we decided to leave it alone for a month. One day I went round to the lock-up and looked in and there was nothing there – no cars, no nothing. I went round to see Golly S and he said he hadn't done nothing and we should see Amies.

It was winter and when Amies opened the door to his flat he was wearing a check dressing gown and had his hand in his pocket. I could see the shape of the gun. 'What do you fucking want?' he asked. Golly said he'd been round and the stuff was gone. 'Of course, it's fucking gone. You've had it.' He said this to Golly. He never muddled me up.

I said, 'Why did you let that pouf cunt talk to you like

---

13 Golly S obtained his nickname because of his shock of hair.

that?' and he said he'd had a gun. I said he'd never have used it. I saw Billy Amies about a month later and he said, 'You do know that he was on it.' I said, 'I don't know, but you was out of order coming out of your house with a gun.' He said, 'That was for him.' I said, 'You should have sat down and talked it over.' Amies then told me the names of all the people on the robbery, and they included Golly S.

I gave him £500 and, although I never worked with him again, a bit later, after the Donoghue business when he was arrested on the Embankment with guns and a mask in his car, I did all the business for him and he got out on bail. I think that was his way of saying thank you.

Mind you, I wasn't the only one. I can name a dozen people Billy Amies could have put away and didn't. There again he put Ritchie Smith, a cousin of the Twins, away. He got fifteen years and he was innocent.

Amies served his sentence and, according to an East Ender, died outside London some two or three years ago 'of natural causes'.

But in many ways, the seemingly prize catch was nothing to do with Lundy. It was Maxwell Thomas Piggott who was to turn what the police thought would be the major supergrass of the decade, and would give evidence against Ronnie Knight who was thought, perhaps with some justification, to be one of the top figures in London's Underworld.

Bradshaw, as Piggott became known, had a long and interesting criminal career. His father had a slot-machine business in cafés and clubs from the Oval to Brixton, and was well respected by people such as 'Whippo' Brindle of the powerful South London family. Bradshaw junior was educated at the same school as Commander David Powis of the Metropolitan Police. In September 1965 he was charged with housebreaking, and in November of the same year with throwing acid at the police, for which he was sentenced to seven years' imprisonment. He escaped from Wormwood Scrubs in

1968 and went to live in Putney. He set up an antiques business, but this went into decline and following a wages snatch to restore the family fortunes, he moved to the South Coast and the next year he popped up in Brighton running a long-firm fraud[14] for which he received six years at Lewes Assizes. He then lived a chequered life running a fish restaurant with Micky Hennessy of the well-known South London family and Alfie Gerard, the notorious hit-man, as well as the more lucrative business of being an armed robber, arsonist and armourer. In 1977 he was arrested for robbery and was offered the chance to become a supergrass. Initially he declined, but it was whilst he was serving the ten-year sentence he received that he decided to turn. He. had already managed to have a substantial slice shaved off what should have been a much longer sentence by disclosing to the police part of his cache of guns. Now a year or so into his sentence, and still in contact with his arresting officer, he put up the deal under which he would bring down Ronnie Knight, former owner of the A & R Club, then husband of actress Barbara Windsor and a celebrated London family figure. Initially Bradshaw tried to bargain – protection for his family, which was obviously granted; immunity from prosecution which, following the Smalls' decision, wasn't; and being taken into protective police custody.

After serving only twenty months of his sentence, he was moved from Wormwood Scrubs to Twickenham police station to begin his detailed account of his association with the top brass of London's Underworld.

On 17 January 1980 he pleaded guilty before Mr Justice Comyn to his part in the Zomparelli murder, arson of the Directors Club in Drummond Street, a shooting in Woolwich

---

14 A long-firm fraud in its simplest form involves buying goods in ever increasing quantities on credit, and when a substantial line of goodwill has been established, buying the maximum possible amount. The goods are then sold to the public at a knock-down price and the managers of the business decamp. In its more sophisticated form the long-firm involves numerous linked companies with references being given between them and the international market being tapped.

and two armed robberies. As was the practice, he was praised for his courage in naming 105 criminals in a long confession. He was then gaoled for life but without the recommendation of a minimum term. This was his, as with other murderers, *quid pro quo*. If he played his cards correctly he could expect to be released in about five years, during which time he would be kept under wraps.

The authorities thought this was to be the start of another major breakthrough in the war against professional crime. In true supergrass fashion it was not Bradshaw who had fired the fatal shot which killed Zomparelli as he played 'Wild Life' on the pin-table in the Golden Goose in Old Compton Street, but Nicky Gerard, Alf's son. The contract had, he said, been set up by Ronnie Knight as a result of a quarrel which had involved his brother David, who had been stabbed to death by Zomparelli in the Underworld hang-out Tolaini's Latin Quarter. However, when both Gerard junior and Ronnie Knight were acquitted of the Zomparelli murder, plans to use Bradshaw in other trials were quickly shelved and he was returned to prison, going to the Rule 43 unit in Wakefield prison. He eventually served ten years for the murder before his release.[15]

Perhaps 1979 was the high-watermark for the use of supergrasses. At least twenty leading villains had queued up for their day or, more likely, weeks, in the witness box. Scotland Yard believed that serious crime had tumbled from its 1977 all-time high when it had netted £166 million. Part of the success of the crack-down on crime was the sheer ineptitude of many criminals. A new recruit to the ranks of baby supergrass was James George Gallant, who had been

15 Bradshaw had alleged that Ronnie Knight had paid him to kill Zomparelli after the man received what was seen to be the extremely lenient sentence of four years for stabbing David Knight, Ronnie's brother. This in turn stemmed from a fight in North London. The police, however, claimed that the death of David Knight had resulted from a protection racket. In January 1995 Ronnie Knight, who had returned from his home on the Costa del Sol to stand trial for dishonestly handling proceeds from the Security Express robbery at Easter 1983, received seven years' imprisonment. The Crown accepted his plea of not guilty to the robbery itself. See J. Morton, *Gangland*.

found with his share of a £4,600 robbery in his packet of cornflakes. He informed on twenty-one criminals and there was a further 'break-through' when former seaman Norman Jones, together with Raymond Fowles and Peter Rose, put their hands up to a string of burglaries and robberies. All were said by Mr Brian Leary, QC for Jones, to have the shadow of death or serious injury over the rest of their lives. It was, said Assistant Commissioner David Powis, a year when 'London's criminal fraternity is experiencing its lowest ebb ever.'[16] Statistics can mean different things to different people. In 1972 armed robberies in England and Wales had totalled 539. In 1977 they had risen to 1,234. It is true that over that period bank robberies in London had fallen from 65 to 41, but this must be viewed against the more stringent security measures adopted by the banks.

On 24 March 1980 a robbery went off which surpassed the Great Train Robbers' caper. It was also one which would have the greatest repercussions on the credibility of Scotland Yard and, in particular, Tony Lundy. Three hundred and twenty-one silver ingots of bullion, worth £3.4 million, were stolen from a lorry on its way from London to Tilbury Docks when a gang of bogus traffic officials, together with a man wearing a police uniform, flagged down the lorry into a lay-by and held up the crew at gunpoint.

The instigator of the enterprise was Michael Gervaise, six-foot tall, a fluent linguist and a skilled burglar-alarm engineer, described as a 'balding figure with the mild air of a retail tobacconist', another man who would become a supergrass. He had received eighteen months for his part in the 1975 Bank of America robbery, but otherwise had no record worth speaking of. Together with an old friend, Micky Sewell, who had been given bail on a charge of armed robbery so that he too could act as an informant, Gervaise put together a team which included Lennie Gibson, Rudolpho Aguda, and Aguda's

16 *Daily Telegraph*, 29 November 1979.

nephew, Renaldo 'Ron' Aguda. Ron's specialities included the ability to uncouple trailers from their tractor units at speed.

If not actually working on the pavement, Gervaise had on his team a number of bent police officers who were paid to over-look his activities. One, Terence Donovan, who later served a prison sentence, was employed as a 'security adviser' after his retirement from the force. His job was to advise Gervaise of suitable places to burgle. Another bribed by Gervaise was the notorious Alec Eist.

The lorry was stopped by Gervaise, flagging it down wearing his policeman's uniform – supplied by a sergeant in the Met to Billy Young, who had passed it and some others to Lennie Gibson – and directing it into a lay-by for a bogus traffic census. The guards were threatened that their kneecaps would be blown off if they did not co-operate, and off went Gervaise and Co with the silver to store it in a 'slaughter', a rented lock-up garage, near Oakwood tube station at the northern end of the Piccadilly line. Gibson and Aguda senior were the only ones to hold keys to it and they had these on them when arrested.

Sewell was on bail at the time for a £200,000 wages snatch, and was being used as a snout by the then DCI Bill Peters of the Flying Squad. His mission for Peters was to infiltrate another robbery team headed by Ronnie Johnson, and his information led to the arrest of that team hours after they had shot a guard in a robbery at a bank in East Finchley. One of the men soon accepted Lundy's offer to turn supergrass and he named Tony Fiori, an Islington thief, who graduated from grass to supergrass with some facility. In turn, he named Gervaise.

It was only a matter of time before Gervaise joined the supergrass circuit – and it was only a matter of time before someone claimed the £300,000 reward being put up by the insurers. The claimant would be Lundy's protégé Roy Garner, part-owner of a thoroughly disreputable nightclub, Eltons, which more or less backed on to Tottenham police station. He had turned down an approach to do the silver bullion job.

The important thing was the recovery of the silver. Gibson,

when arrested, held out for some time as to its whereabouts until he had spoken with Aguda senior. Quite clearly there was much to be discussed because then Gibson had a two-hour private meeting with Lundy.

On the night of 4 June 1980, the police went to the lock-up at Oakwood, kicked in the door and recovered the silver – all but twelve bars worth £120,000. No one has ever been able to establish where they went to, but there again no one has ever seemed to worry too much about it. Nor has anyone ever satisfactorily explained why it was necessary to kick the door down; after all, Aguda and Gibson had been arrested with their keys to the 'slaughter' on them. Gibson and the Agudas received ten years each on pleas of guilty, rather more than the seven they had been half promised. Micky Sewell had long disappeared – tipped off by a police officer – and Gervaise had his five years. 'Dave Granger' – a pseudonym for Roy Garner – received the £300,000 reward. Garner also submitted claims through Lundy for payment for information from a Brinks-Mat security van hold-up in Hampstead in December 1979 and a fraudulent insurance claim based on a faked armed robbery, the reward for which was £75,000. After much haggling Garner received £178,000. Over the years he is believed to have accumulated more than £500,000 through rewards recommended by Lundy.

By then the supergrass system was becoming more and more complicated. There now seemed to be competing teams of supergrasses: those who gave evidence under Lundy's aegis and those, such as John Moriarty, who gave evidence against Lundy's friend Garner. Moriarty had twice been shot by rivals and had served periods of imprisonment. Now he decided to give evidence and to implicate Roy Garner.

'I never knew why he did it,' says former police officer, Dave Brady. 'After all, I was the officer called to The Favourite, the pub in Hornsey Rise where he'd been kneecapped. I asked what had happened and all he said was, "I fell down the fucking stairs, didn't I?"'

Presumably he did it because he was tired of being beaten up and shot at.

In the early 1970s Garner, together with a friend, Kenny Ross, had purchased premises in Upper Street, Islington, and then tried to evict the tenants. When this failed the premises were fired. Now Moriarty was prepared to name them in his statement as the organisers of the arson attacks.

Yet another series of supergrasses was being run from Reading by No. 5 Regional Crime Squad under the name *Operation Carter*. In 1977 a security van at Hemel Hempstead in Hertfordshire had been taken for £34,000, and three years later a North London robber, Freddie Sinfield, was arrested. The name he put in the frame was Billy Young, Gervaise's police uniform supplier.

By now there was no great problem in allowing murderers to become the main prosecution witness. On 27 June 1979, John Henry 'Bruce' Childs was arrested in Hertfordshire following the hijacking of a Security Express armoured van seven days earlier. In his turn he had been grassed by one of the others involved. Now he admitted his involvement with Henry MacKenny in six murders and, instead of his usual role of getaway driver, became the chief prosecution witness in a bizarre trial. They had put together a small version of Murder Incorporated – hiring themselves out as killers, on one occasion, said Childs, on hire-purchase terms.

He was arrested through his own carelessness in what had otherwise been a well-planned and executed robbery. The robbers had cleared £500,000 by impersonating Security Express employees. After the robbery they changed out of their uniforms in a public lavatory, leaving the clothing behind, but in the pocket of one of the overalls were the keys to a BMW and it was not difficult for the police to trace the vehicle to its owner, an East End greengrocer. In a deal for a light sentence, he returned the money which had been left in his care and then implicated both John Childs and MacKenny as part of the robbery team.

The case was initially investigated by Tony Lundy, then a Detective Inspector. He rightly supposed that this was not the first raid the team had carried out and interviewed each member with a view to getting confessions of other jobs. One of the team was even more forthcoming and named Childs and MacKenny as being involved in the killings of Ronnie Andrews, Terence Eve and the Bretts.[17]

Lundy's initial inclination was to laugh at him, but as he recalls the conversation went on:

'There's going to be another murder shortly – and you know the victim.'

'What are you talking about?'

'Do you know a police officer called Treen?'

I said 'Yeh' because John Treen had been one of my inspectors on the Flying Squad in 1977, so I knew him well. Treen had arrested MacKenny and Terry Pinfold in December 1976, but then the Director of Public Prosecutions dropped the case against MacKenny.

He said, 'MacKenny is going to murder Treen and Butcher,' who was the sergeant on the same case.

Lundy recalled that MacKenny had been arrested in December 1976 over two bank robberies at Romford and Woodford. He was then placed on a total of eight identification parades but was not picked out. Nevertheless, he was detained on the basis of witnesses' remarks of a big man – he stood 6 foot 6 inches. He was an associate of Terence Pinfold and, so the detectives investigating the case said, he had made verbal admissions. MacKenny denied these verbals and wrote out a statement giving a detailed notice of alibi.

17 George Brett, a haulage contractor, and his ten-year-old son Terence had disappeared in January 1975. Robert 'White Angel' Brown – a part-time professional wrestler who worked with MacKenny – and Ronnie Andrews, a close friend, had also disappeared. For a full account of their disappearances and the subsequent trial, see James Morton, *Gangland*, pp. 281–7.

The case against him had been dropped in the July of the next year, whilst Pinfold was gaoled for ten years. When the allegations were dismissed he shouted threats at Treen, the officer in charge of the case. Later MacKenny had endeavoured to interest the media in a number of cases in which he said miscarriages of justice had occurred.

In turn Lundy had difficulties in getting senior officers to accept that the stories told by his informant were credible, and it took him some time to persuade Commander Arthur Howard that the matter should be investigated further.

In December 1979 Childs became the first serial murderer in modern times to confess and give evidence against his accomplices. He had a hard time in the witness box, saying that he was drinking a bottle of whisky a day to try to obliterate the memory of killing Terence Brett. He did admit that he had thought about writing a book on the killing but denied the potential title 'East End Butcher'.

The juries' verdicts were curious. As to the murder of their partner Terence Eve, Pinfold was convicted and MacKenny acquitted. Both were acquitted of the murder of Robert Brown. MacKenny was charged with the murder of Brett and his son, along with Leonard Thompson. MacKenny was convicted and Thompson acquitted to leave court without a stain on his character, as did Paul Morton-Thurtle who was acquitted in the case of Sherwood, the nursing-home owner. MacKenny was convicted in that case, as he was over the killing of Ronnie Andrews. All received life sentences, in MacKenny's case with a recommendation that he serve not less than twenty-five years.

He was not happy, shouting that he had never killed anybody but that through his life-saving jacket he had saved plenty. 'Straight people need protection from you,' he told Mr Justice May, 'and from mongols and mugs like you,' he added to the jury before the court was cleared.

But where did all the bodies go? Although there had been considerable forensic evidence of bloodstains and traces of hair which went to corroborate Childs' story, there was no trace of any of the six who had disappeared. Again, according to Childs, initially the idea had been to cut up the bodies using a butcher's mincing machine. This had proved too blunt to deal with Eve and the idea was abandoned.

The next suggested method was simplicity in itself and extremely efficient. The bodies were cut up and then burned in a standard-size fireplace with an anthracite fire augmented by a gas burner. Bones which did not dissolve could be pounded on the hearth. The ashes were then emptied on waste ground. The disposal of a complete body took about 24 hours.

Professor James Cameron, the pathologist, was asked whether it would be possible to cremate a body in this way and tests were carried out. The carcass of an 11-stone male pig, calculated as being the equivalent of a fully developed average-sized man, was taken to Childs' home. Cameron, using brute force, sawed up the carcass, taking just over five minutes. He described it as, 'Perfectly simple, requiring no anatomical knowledge.'

The police and the pathologist then sat down to burn the body. Later Cameron told Philip Paul:

The temperature in the fire reached over 1,000 degrees but the room never went above 75. It was all properly measured, logged and photographed. But when we put the intestines on the fire it almost went out. Because, as soon as it burnt through, the fluid ran. Later on we were told that MacKenny had washed out and dried the intestines before they were burnt.

The total burning of the pig took thirteen hours. We ended up with remains of ash, bone and whatnot which filled two large plastic bags. We then went over it twice with a hammer, as we were told MacKenny had done, and eventually finished up with a small plastic bag of ash with not a remnant of teeth or bone visible to the naked eye.

Repeated checks had been made outside the building during

the burning, but no smell of roasting pork or other odour had been detected.

Childs' reward was that he received no minimum sentence in his term of life imprisonment.

In the meantime, Roy Garner's life as a double agent continued happily. He was informing on his colleagues to the police, unaware that the customs had him in their sights.

On 19 June 1987, one of the potentially greatest of supergrasses, the forty-four-year-old German-born Nikolaus Chrastny, was arrested in a spectacular raid by armed officers as he left his flat in Baker Street. Two days later cocaine valued at £14 million was found cached in a flat in nearby Harley Street. Here was a man who could not only blow the whistle on major drug importers, but could also do the same for corrupt London police officers.

Chrastny was caught through a complicated deal which had been struck in the United States with a jewel thief, Jimmy Tullevere, and one of Chrastny's colleagues Roy Whitehorne. Now Tullevere was allowed out of prison and used as an infiltrator. He went to Whitehorne's jewellery store in Fort Lauderdale and over a period of time recorded 125 hours of tapes. In October 1986 Whitehorne was arrested and pleaded guilty to conspiracy to distribute drugs. He turned informer, in return for which he was not imprisoned but instead received ten years' probation. Now he worked with the Department of Law Enforcement. He was given total immunity from the British customs officers to whom the Bertie Smalls no immunity rule did not apply.

To keep things nicely symmetrical, it was appropriate that Chrastny named his partner as none other than Roy Garner. Garner was arrested on 23 June 1987.

Chrastny, who also went under the name of Charles Flynn, was short, fat and bald, an expert marksman, fluent in five languages and with a former policewoman for a wife. At the time of his arrest he was wanted in Munich for an armed robbery which had netted him 1 million deutschmarks' worth of jewellery; in fact he had been wanted for that escapade since 1973. His capture was a triumph for the police and the customs.

Chrastny did a deal: his admissions and help in nailing others would let his wife out of the net. He was remanded into the custody of customs officers who wanted him to sing well away from London in case the melody came to the ears of Scotland Yard officers. He was handed over to the South Yorkshire police and taken to Rotherham. Chrastny was not only a robber and drug-dealer, he was a man of considerable charm and, within days, had exerted that charm on his keepers. He was moved from the protection of the South Yorkshire force to that of West Yorkshire and into Dewsbury.

The instructions given to the force were that customs officers who wished to question him must be given access on a twenty-four-hour basis, but that apart from them his whereabouts were to be secret. His life was thought to be in danger. He was placed in a cell normally reserved for women prisoners, which had a barred gate on the outside of the door that opened on to a corridor.

As befits a high-quality supergrass, Chrastny was supplied with all sorts of goodies: cigars, chutney, books, paints and model-making equipment. He was also given a television set but, because there was no power in his cell, he was allowed to keep his door open – the gate was in place – and a power-lead extension was run through from the doctor's room across the hall. He also acquired two files – alleged to have been smuggled in by his wife in the spine of a copy of *The Hound of the Baskervilles*.

He put his files and model-making equipment to good use. Without anyone being any the wiser, by working late at night and with his television full on to conceal the noise, he filed through the three-quarter-inch bars of the cell gate which opened on to the cell block. The day he was due to be taken down to London for a remand hearing he completed his task, went through a window in the doctor's room and was, so it is thought, driven off in a waiting car. He left a note behind which read:

> Gentlemen, I have not taken this step lightly. I have been planning it for several weeks. The tools have been in my wash-kit for several years in preparation for such an occasion. Greetings, Nick.

After the escape, as might be expected, everybody blamed everybody else. Mrs Chrastny was charged with assisting in the escape of her husband and defended by Timothy Cassells QC. Suggestions as to various other organisers were bandied about at her trial:

> Cassells: Chrastny had also given evidence about corruption in the police: who was involved?
> Customs officer: Lundy and Garner.
> Cassells: A number of people would have an interest in Chrastny's escape?
> C.O: Yes.
> Cassels: New Scotland Yard, for instance?
> C.O.: I cannot comment on that.

Mrs Chrastny was acquitted but, sadly for her, with her husband out of the way such immunity as she had vanished with him; she received seven years' imprisonment for the cocaine conspiracy. The inquiry into Chrastny's escape was not all that revealing. No collusion between him and either the customs or the police was proved. Two senior officers were given formal warnings, one received counselling, there were harsh words about the muddle as to who was actually in charge of guarding the prisoner, and finally it was decided that Dewsbury police station was unsuitable for housing a man who required a high level of security. This last was unsurprising; shortly before Chrastny took up residence, three men had escaped from the station.

And what of the potential supergrass? J. P. Bean records that he has been seen in Costa Rica, but there are other reports that he is dead.[18]

One of the great problems for the police in high-profile cases has been the power the grass has to get the officer who is running him to protect him. Nipper Read found this to his cost shortly before the arrest of the Krays. He decided to charge Alan Bruce Cooper who, he believed, had instructed a Paul Elvery to collect dynamite from Scotland to be used in an assassination attempt on the Maltese Club owner George Caruana. Elvery had been arrested and implicated Cooper in, amongst other things, another attempt to kill a man in the lobby at the Old Bailey by using a suitcase with a concealed hypodermic syringe and, when that failed, a crossbow.

> . . . Cooper was brought to me at Tintagel House and the interview did not begin well. He was stuttering in his fright and told me he knew nothing about either the dynamite or Elvery.
>
> 'Fine,' I said. 'Then I'm going to charge you with conspiracy to murder and that's all there is to it.'
>
> He then protested and asked to see John du Rose [a superior officer]. I told him I was running the show and asked him why. What he said came as a tremendous shock.
>
> 'If you contact John du Rose,' he said in his stuttering American drawl, 'he will tell you I am his informant.' He had, he said, been John du Rose's informant and spy for up to two years.
>
> I simply didn't believe it and asked du Rose to come and see me. He did so almost immediately and I asked him if Cooper was telling the truth and that he, du Rose, was running him.
>
> He accepted that they had been in contact for some

18 J. P. Bean, *Over the Wall*, pp. 273–7.

time, but he was, he said, not really running him as an
informant as such, and had really received no information
worth passing on: 'If there had been, I'd have let you
know, Nipper.' At the time I was furious and du Rose
knew it.[19]

Meanwhile Tony Lundy was endeavouring to protect – as far
as possible – his informant, Roy Garner.

Lundy has been the subject of much speculation and gossip.
His great defender, Martin Short, has suggested that it 'is worse
than perverse to blame Scotland Yard' for Chrastny's escape,
pointing out that his whereabouts were a closely guarded secret
and that if officers had been involved Mrs Chrastny would
have used them as a bargaining point to get a reduction on
her seven-year sentence. On the other hand, J. P. Bean regards
the sentence as by no means out of the way for an involvement
with £2.6 million of drugs. Short believes that Scotland Yard
could not have found out the supergrass's whereabouts and
that Lundy's telephone was being tapped. Bean points out that
it is not difficult to find the resting place of a prisoner. When,
in 1991 amidst great secrecy, Roy Garner was transferred to
Attercliffe police station in Sheffield when he was making
allegations against Lundy, it was not long before the local
paper had the news on its front page.

The allegations came to nothing. Lundy had been suspended
from duty for four years before Garner began to speak to police
officers. He retired in 1988 on an ill-health pension, suffering
from stress. Finally his problems came to an end in October
1994, when it was announced that the Crown Prosecution
Service had found no evidence to justify a prosecution against
Lundy. He told the *Police Review*:

> During the eight years this investigation has lasted, not a
> single officer has tried to interview me, although they've
> interviewed dozens of people who have never met me.

19 L. Read, *Nipper*, p. 162.

Throughout the earlier investigations, I co-operated 100 per cent with the officers making the inquiries, making my bank accounts, and my family's bank accounts, available for inspection.[20]

In 1993 the *Police Review* estimated that the investigations into his conduct would cost £5 million.

There was a brief postscript to the Chrastny affair. In May 1992 the Home Office issued guidelines to all forces regarding the supervision and handling of what were coyly referred to as 'resident informers'. Supergrasses must now be held in a special suite away from other cells and be protected by three uniformed officers, who should not be connected with the case, on a twenty-four-hour basis. They could have fifteen-minute visits from friends and family, but no conjugal visits and no alcohol. O'Mahoney and Williams would have hated the regime.

In recent times supergrasses have not had it all their own way.

Supergrass trials have fallen into disrepute and super-grasses aren't used quite as much. But what they did was present to your stock gangland criminal a real threat. Gangs haven't stayed together because of that risk. The risk of being supergrassed got very high about seven or eight years ago. Then jurors started to acquit because supergrasses were being offered immunity or extremely low sentences, money was being offered or facilities in custody, so they died off.[21]

Even so, many made substantial profits from it. A former East London friend of the family recalls the story of one successful grass:

20 *Police Review*, 28 October 1994.
21 Michael Mansfield QC in D. Campbell, *That was Business, This is Personal*, p. 135.

There was a North London family called Smith*. There was George, Phillip and Frankie who died of a heart attack in the reception wing at Brixton. Phillip and Tony Fiske were done for two lorryloads of goods at Herbert's smallholding. The law charged his mother and father and the deal was that they'd drop the charges if Fiske and him will put their hands up to the handling. Smith said no. His mother and father got three years each, Tony Fiske got a five and Herbert got an eight. He got something off on appeal but when he comes out he becomes a police informer. He went into partnership with another grass from South London, George F. He started then to frequent South London. I had my card marked by a copper and I gave both Phillip and George Smith a bashing in the Log Cabin Club which was owned by George Walker and Tommy McCarthy in Soho.

In 1971 Herbert and George F were convicted of receiving a lorryload of goods and got two and a half years apiece. By now Herbert was a well-known informer and he'd got very friendly with a Dave Bailey from Islington. This was about the time when the Sewell shooting took place. Dave's brother-in-law was a Greek who got done for hiding Sewell. The only person apart from Bailey and the brother-in-law to know where Sewell was being hid was Phillip Smith. After Sewell was caught, Smith went back to the Court of Appeal and was given a suspended sentence.

After that he changed his name. A friend of mine comes into a pub and says he's just met him. I told him not to trust him and my friend went and marked Billy Tobin's card but he wouldn't have it. Tobin and Cook and some others were caught with a mechanical digger doing a security van in Dulwich. They were all nicked and Herbert got £80,000 reward money. There was a rumpus about that. He said it

* a pseudonym.

wasn't enough. It was pretty amazing; the solicitor who defended Tobin acted for Herbert in getting the reward money. He took up with Harry's wife and went off to Australia. She died of cancer over there. I don't think he ever came back.

As for F he was involved in the drugs case in which Eddie Watkins shot and killed the customs officer. F was acquitted after a re-trial. A bit after that he was shot in the shoulder in his pub in Kent. It was a motorcycle job and F turned his head at the crucial moment.[22]

It does not appear that, as is so often the case, the Underworld had learned either of F's treachery or had learned their lesson. The same source continues the story:

In about 1984 he went to Freddy Brazil and sets up a meeting in Ronnie Scott's to discuss a load of Old Masters, etchings and other antiques. Freddy agreed to place the stuff and another meet is arranged at the Heston Service Station when Freddy takes along some people with him. When they got there it was a set-up with the police. They fought the case and it came out then that F had been an informer for years. Freddy got four years.

Quite apart from the well-known supergrasses such as Smalls

22 On 23 August 1971 Frederick Sewell shot and killed Superintendent Gerald Richardson, head of the Blackpool Borough Police, in an armed robbery at The Strand in Blackpool. Sewell and four other Londoners undertook what was considered to be a simple snatch which would net them £100,000. Instead one of the staff set off an alarm and a police officer arriving on the scene saw the men escaping. Richardson gave chase and when he caught up with Sewell he was shot twice at point-blank range. The *Daily Mirror* offered a reward of £10,000 for Sewell's capture.

On 20 October 1979 Peter Bennett became the first customs officer to be killed on duty for nearly two hundred years during surveillance of an importation of £2.5 million-worth of cannabis. He was shot in the stomach by Lennie Watkins, who later killed himself in Long Lartin prison whilst serving a life sentence.

For a full account of the Sewell case see C. Borrell and B. Cashinella, *Crime in Britain Today*. For an account of the Watkins case, see J. Morton, *Gangland*, p. 302 *et seq*.

and O'Mahoney, there has been a whole second division whispering away around the countryside. In 1987 a whole lawn was in Bedford prison. Members included Clifford Barnes, who received ten years for theft but informed on robbers and swindlers in the Midlands, and David Medin, who was said to have a £1-million Mafia contract on his head. Medin had been a high-class drugs-dealer and computer genius who had been sent from Detroit to Britain to establish a cocaine distribution centre which, had it been successful, would have flooded the market. When Drugs Squad detectives arrested him he gave the police a 100-page statement which included details of the East London gang recruited by him to distribute the drugs. In Wales John Davies, who received twelve years for armed robbery, informed on at least seventy of his former colleagues. He was said to be the 'biggest leek' in Welsh history. Steven Henry, serving nine years, was another who would disprove the theory that blood was thicker than prison. Henry, who received nine years for his part in some thirty-six armed robberies on sub-post offices, informed on his brother-in-law as well as another five of the gang. From Manchester came Fred Scott who, serving ten years for armed robberies, had named twenty-five of his friends and detailed their involvement in crime.

In more recent times, even though the killing of British supergrasses is still rare, life has become more dangerous for them than in the days of Bertie Smalls.

In February 1989 informer Alan 'Chalky' White disappeared. He was last seen walking to the off-licence in Minchington, Gloucestershire to get some lager. Three months later his body, wrapped in a blue tarpaulin, was spotted by a family at the Cotswold Water Park near Cirencester. Forensic tests showed that he had been stabbed in the heart.

White, who had several minor convictions, was due to give evidence against a Danny Gardiner with whom, so White said, he had robbed a petrol station in Stroud netting £4,800 in 1986. White, who had a drug problem, had declined the police offer of a new identity and instead was given a 'panic button' to use if he felt threatened. Most nights, however, he could be found in the local Crown public house. With the death of White, the case against Danny Gardiner collapsed and he went abroad.

With the help of Interpol the police conducted inquiries in Egypt – where Mr Gardiner was wrongly reported to have died in Cairo – France, Spain, Morocco and Israel. On 4 January 1991 Mr Gardiner flew back voluntarily from Tel Aviv. He had been found there working in a tourist hotel, having apparently entered the country under a false name. He was later convicted of White's murder.

In 1990 yet another informer was killed. He had previously told the police of a planned contract killing resulting in the arrest of the hit-man. Before the trial, the judge accepted the argument of the defence that it needed access to police information. This would have meant a disclosure of the identity of the informant and the trial was abandoned by the prosecution. At the time of his death the man had been resettled in Germany – the cost of relocating an informer, names, passports and driving licences for him and his family, is around £100,000 – and he was murdered shortly afterwards.

A second killing occurred in Amsterdam and involved a man who had given police information about a gang of drug traffickers. The third, early in 1993, was in Ireland, where it seems the link to the identification of the informant had come about through the withdrawal of the case by the prosecution.

In May 1993 the trial began of four men whom the prosecution alleged had brought over hired killers from Northern Ireland to dispose of supergrass David Norris, shot dead in July 1992 by a motorcycle-riding killer in the driveway of his home at Belvedere, Kent. Norris' death had been just another in the series where the prosecution had inadvertently blown their man's cover by dropping a case. Worse than simply being a grass:

He used to set people up on jobs that he had done himself. He would carry out a warehouse job, tell somebody there was still stuff to be taken and then tip the police off.

The police won't say he's a grass because being bumped off is not a terrific advert for a career in grassing. He was on Rule 43 inside which tells its own story.[23]

After nearly six weeks the trial, which had cost almost £1 million, was halted when the Recorder of London, Judge Lawrence Verney, ruled that the evidence of the two main prosecution witnesses, Renwick Dennison and Stuart Warne, was unsafe for the jury to rely on. Patrick Doherty, George McMahon – both from South London – Terence McCrory from Belfast and John Green from Falkirk were all acquitted.

The prosecution had outlined a curious but ultimately unconvincing story of hitmen hired through Northern Ireland drug-dealers who were promised cheap cannabis in return for the completion of the contracts. Two men who were never arrested were said by the prosecution to have helped organise the murder squad. One of these men, so the prosecution said, had come to London from Belfast after he had been shot for supplying Catholics with drugs.[24]

At an earlier trial Warne, the link between the English drug-dealers and the Irish, and Dennison, one of the hit-men, had been sentenced to life imprisonment after admitting conspiracy to murder. Warne had told the jury that he had been met in a South London public house by a man who had whistled up £20,000 in half an hour by using his mobile phone. This was, he said, the price for the unsuccessful attempted killing

23 D. Campbell, 'Gangland Britain', in *Weekend Guardian*, 14–15 December 1991. Rule 43 is protected accommodation away from the mainstream of the prison and is used to house sex offenders and informers along with convicted police officers.

24 This man seems to have had a chequered and eventful life. According to evidence given in the case he had been active in the Belfast Loyalist underworld since the middle 1970s as both a drug-dealer and the recruiter of Protestant hit-men. At one time he was on the run and thought to be in Spain after he had been shot in a car outside a social club in the Shankhill Road area. The IRA had indicated that he was under sentence of death. He had been lucky to survive for so long for he was thought to have had contacts with the IRA and INLA. A relative was killed by the UDA in 1992.

of a second man, John Dale, 'the object of dislike and hatred apparently because he was in the habit of ripping people off in drug deals', said Timothy Langdale QC for the prosecution. Dennison took over the contract and shot him in the back outside his London home in April 1991, and then missed at point-blank range when he shot at his head. So far as Norris was concerned, the forty-five-year-old informer was shot as he begged for mercy with his wife watching helpless.

Perhaps fortunately, America is still several steps ahead in certain aspects of criminal behaviour. The recent tale of Washington's First Street Crew gang makes for unhappy reading.

In the autumn of 1992 the uncle of Arvell 'Pork Chop' Williams was murdered. Williams, a former associate of the First Street Crew, believed gang members had information on the killing which they would not share with him and, more prosaically, that he was himself about to be prosecuted for trading in narcotics. He went to the vice unit of the 3rd Police District. On 6 October he was sitting in a car on Second Street when two gunmen shot him eighteen times. A witness identified Crew members Antone White and Ronald Hughes as the killers.

According to police officers, the intimidation of witnesses began before Williams' body was taken from the white sedan. White stood watching the proceedings eating a bag of potato crisps, noting who was in the area.

On 26 October 'Chinese' Gregg Ingram was shot dead near the White House shortly after a police officer interviewed him about the Williams killing. A week later three Crew members were shot dead; the police had been hoping to question them and two had told their lawyers they were thinking about co-operating. White, Hughes and two others were arrested two weeks later. For a time the killings stopped.

Then on 19 October 1993 a homicide detective Joseph Schwartz gave evidence in the trial, careful to identify witnesses only as W-1 etc. He gave no age, no sex or address. The aim was to ensure that Crew members in the public gallery could not make any identification. His efforts were not successful. Two days later Janellen Jones was shot in the mouth, a symbol – the police say – to warn off potential witnesses. A fifty-three-year-old man who was with her at the time was also shot. In all nine people were shot, and the police believed that seven were killed because the Crew members thought they had turned informer. White and Hughes were convicted of racketeering and were sentenced to life in prison without parole. The jury could not reach a verdict on the murder charge.[25]

Revenge is, after all, a dish best eaten cold. Retribution could come many years later and was often delivered at the most timely opportunity. Edward J. O'Hare, who had been Al Capone's silent partner in greyhound racing, must have known that something was wrong shortly before his death. He had informed Frank Williams that the jury in Capone's 1931 income tax case had been tampered with and a re-trial had been ordered. By so doing he had, in effect, ordered his own death sentence.

It was long stayed. Just before Capone was released from prison O'Hare took to carrying a pistol for protection. It did him little good. On November 8 1942, a bare week before Capone left prison, O'Hare was shot dead in his car whilst driving along Ogden Avenue, Chicago. He was the only government witness in the tax case who was killed but he had, after all, played a conspicuous part in sabotaging Capone's chances of an acquittal.

Nor, if they survive, do informers always get what they see as their proper rewards. Anna Sage was one of these. Her real name was Ana Cumpanas and she was a brothel-keeper in Chicago. A Romanian by birth, she had operated brothels in Gary, Indiana, and East Chicago, acquiring convictions for

25 *Washington Post*, 31 July 1994.

running a disorderly house in both locations. In 1934 she was convicted a third time and steps were being taken to deport her as an undesirable alien. Now at the age of forty-two she was sharing rooms with a twenty-six-year-old waitress Polly Hamilton, whose boyfriend was Jimmy Lawrence, rather better known as John Dillinger.[26] It seems possible that Hamilton did not know Dillinger's real identity and also that Sage – who, from listening to his stories and tales, did – would have not gone to her contacts in the East Chicago police had only the FBI reward of $10,000 been on offer. Sage was able to negotiate a rather better deal: the deportation proceedings against her would be dropped. An arrangement was approved by Melvin Purvis, then the star of Hoover's Bureau.

On 22 July 1934, Dillinger and the women were to go to the cinema. Sage called in to the police to say that she was not sure which film of two they would attend and both houses were staked out. To help identification, she would wear a red dress. As they left the Biograph Theater where Dillinger and the women had been watching Clark Gable in *Manhattan*

26 John Herbert Dillinger was born in Pennsylvania in 1903 and became the superstar of the gangster world as well as achieving top spot on Hoover's Public Enemy list. His bank robberies were carried out with precision. Like many another, both in the United States and England, he had learned from Baron Lamm. Dillinger was the object of a number of daring prison rescues, the last being from the so-called escape-proof jail in Crown Point, Indiana. As with so many folk heroes, many members of the public refused to accept that it was Dillinger who had been shot and believed that, in fact, a substitute fall-guy had been provided. The crime writer J. Robert Nash developed this theory in *Dillinger: Dead or Alive?*, in which he argues that the Agency was duped and had to have a cover-up to avoid the appalling embarrassment. If this is true, then it must be asked what did happen to Dillinger for the rest of his life? Or had he actually died earlier?

There is also a theory that Dillinger was shot by a policeman acting as a hit-man for the local branch of the Mafia (G. Russell Giradin with William J. Helmer, *Dillinger: the Untold Story*).

As for Dillinger's mentor, Herman K. Lamm (?1890–1930), a German officer cashiered for cheating at cards, has been described as America's most brilliant bank robber. From the end of World War 1 until the 1930s Herman K. 'Baron' Lamm's men were the most efficient in the business. Lamm's career came to an end when a tyre blew on the getaway car. They seized another which by mischance had a governor fitted by a well-meaning son to prevent his elderly father from driving too fast. They were overtaken and Lamm died in the ensuing shoot-out.

Melodrama, Purvis saw Sage and according to some versions of the story called on Dillinger to halt. The girls had either vanished or simply gone on ahead by the time he reached for a gun. Two women passers-by were shot as the FBI agents opened fire on Dillinger. One bullet passed through his left side, another went into his back and, again according to some reports, he was shot in the eye.

As for Sage, she and Polly Hamilton were taken to Detroit by federal agents to ensure their silence. Two weeks later Sage went to California where she was paid $5,000 for her part in the killing of Dillinger. On 29 April 1936, despite her complaints and protestations, she was deported.

Nevertheless some still think it is worthwhile to exchange twenty-two years inside for a lifetime of looking over their shoulders. Lawrence Cain, known as 'The Snake', and said, a trifle optimistically given the going rate, to have a £250,000 contract on him, was one of them when, in 1991, he received just seven years for armed robbery. He had given 'valuable help' to the police after admitting taking part in twenty-seven raids in South East London over an eight-year period. The money had gone on foreign travel and a £300-a-day heroin habit. Amongst those who went down as a result of his evidence were his former partner Alan Condon, who drew twenty-one years, Cain's best man when he married a Thai girl who collected sixteen, and William Harding, who netted a year less. Cain's counsel told the court that he had turned informer for the highly praiseworthy reason of divorcing himself from the criminal community. 'No one will come near me unless it is to kill me,' said Cain whilst giving evidence.

Other people discovered that being around grasses is none too safe either. Paul Olson, in the American Government Witness Protection Program, had met with federal prosecutors in Chicago in early September 1994 and was due to testify in a cocaine-trafficking case when the plane on which he was travelling nose-dived when approaching Pittsburgh International Airport. All 132 people aboard were killed. Olson had been a

Chicago bank president who, after his conviction in a financial scam, entered the Witness Protection Program in 1989.

In 1994 another threat came to the grass – exposure by television. The case involved not only an informer but also a police undercover operation. The informer and the police had combined to bring down a man who had, the police believed, been a thorn in their flesh for some time. Richard Green told the court that he had borrowed £20,000 from the man, to be repaid with interest at £500 a week. He had managed to repay the 'nut' but not the 'vig'. He claimed that the man would remit the interest if he would sell on some heroin at £28,000 a kilo. Green, a long-term informer, once more went to the police, who infiltrated the moneylender's offices with Lucy, a secretary, in reality an undercover policewoman. In December 1992 the man was convicted and received fourteen years. In December 1994 his conviction was quashed and a retrial ordered.

Meanwhile in the summer of 1994 the BBC programme *Panorama* threatened to reveal Green's new identity and show photographs. He said:

I am angry and scared, not only about my own security but for the safety of my family, not all of whom had a new identity provided. This programme would endanger my life and make a mockery of the witness protection system.

One of the problems the police in Great Britain have faced over the last two decades has been the steady growth of ethnic minority crime. In particular the Triad operations from Hong Kong have been particularly secretive. In 1992 they must have thought their Sundays had come at once when Triad hit-man, George Wai Hen Cheung became the first Triad supergrass. 'Who better to tell you what happened than the man trusted by the Triads to pull the trigger?' said Martin Heslop for the Crown. Cheung had been ordered to shoot Lam Ying-kit in the spine, Lam's crime having been to come from Hong Kong to wrest control of British Triad crime from the Wo On Lok. The prize of control was the revenue from prostitution, gambling, extortion and loan-sharking. Lam had been shot four times and was crippled as a result of the attack.

In September 1991, after several abortive attempts at assassination, Cheung had stepped behind his target in a crowded Soho restaurant and shot him. Lam, showing considerable courage, had wrestled with Cheung, grabbed the .22 gun and forced him to drop the weapon. Cheung had fled to a waiting car. He was rounded up along with other Triad leaders within a matter of hours of the shooting. As the evidence against Cheung became clearer, he changed sides and decided to help the police.

Cheung did not seem to fit the accepted pattern of hit-man, however. Born in Leicester, where his parents owned a take-away Chinese restaurant, he resented his brother and sisters and his parents had disowned him. Only 5 foot 4 inches in height, with thick spectacles for which he was known as 'Specky', he spoke better English than Cantonese. In a letter from prison he wrote:

All my life I have been stuck in between the English and the Chinese. The Chinese treated me as English. The English treated me as Chinese. I haven't much chance of recognition in England, getting an English job and getting on.

In court it also emerged that because of his acne and generally scruffy appearance he had failed to attract women and had resorted to prostitutes as well as smoking cannabis and taking LSD. His only companion appears to have been his dog, Rambo, which befriended him whilst homeless. 'All I want in life is some love and respect,' said Cheung.

He said he had been the bodyguard of a prominent Triad, and so had enjoyed status and respect. The unsocial activities in which he had engaged included extortion and drug-trafficking as well as violence. On one occasion he had slashed a man with a double-bladed knife. Now he was at the Old Bailey giving evidence against men whom he said were former colleagues from the Sui Fong, also known in Britain as the Wo On Lok group involved in the attempted murder of Lam. Meanwhile he had been held in a special security unit. A £100,000 contract was said to be on his head.

The defence was clear that Cheung was protecting the real villains and blaming his enemies whilst currying favour with the police. One, actor Tang Wai-ming who had been the leading stuntman for film star Jackie Chan, claimed that Cheung had framed him because he was jealous of Tang's success with a Hong Kong girl. Five of the defendants were acquitted. The jury could not agree in the case of Tang Wai-ming and the court ordered the count to be left on the file. All other charges including supplying drugs, blackmail, and arson against the men – and which relied on the evidence of Cheung – were also left on the court file. The police are still some way from a successful infiltration into the workings of the Triads in the United Kingdom.[27]

27 *South China Morning Post*, 6 December 1992.

5

The Supergrass in America

From the point of view of justice and social order in the 1930s perhaps the most important of informers was Abe Reles, referred to after his death as 'the canary who could not fly', whose testimony led to the destruction, by Detective Lieutenant Jack Osnato, of the so-called Murder Inc., the professional hit squad, a gang of professional killers from Brooklyn who were made available by the conglomerate (formed during Prohibition) of Charles 'Lucky' Luciano, Meyer Lansky and the Irish interests of O'Bannion and others. The executions were only carried out for business reasons and, because of the bad publicity which would have ensued, never against politicians and journalists.

The leaders of Murder Inc. were Albert Anastasia and Louis Lepke although it seems that the 400 plus contract killings had to be approved by a council which would include Luciano, Lansky, Joe Adonis and Frank Costello. Concurrence was required or, at the very least, no committed opposition.[1] Next in the hierarchical structure came Louis Capone, no relation of the more famous Al, who ran Chicago rather than New York, Emmanuel 'Mendy'

---

1 The attitude is not dissimilar in England. In 1993, professional criminal James Moody, who had escaped from Brixton some twelve years earlier and was thought to be a contract killer, was himself shot dead. The shooting possibly followed a row he had had with a David Brindle and that man's subsequent death in the Bell Public House, Walworth.

'Much as I knew Jim well, I can understand the feelings about David's death and that it was one that had to be done. I suppose if someone who knew it was going off had really pleaded for him it might have made some difference but I doubt it.' Frank Fraser in *Mad Frank*, p. 221.

Weiss and Abe 'Kid Twist' Reles. They provided a buffer between the killers themselves who included Vito 'Chicken Head' Gurino – so-called not from his shape but because of his use of chickens in gun practice – Frank Abbandando, and 'Pittsburgh' Phil Strauss. The killers frequented Midnight Rose's, an all-night café in Brooklyn, awaiting a telephone call to dispatch them country-wide.

One of the most famous victims of Murder Inc. was Arthur Flegenheimer, rather better known as Dutch Schultz, himself a member of the ruling committee. Schultz, under considerable pressure from Thomas E. Dewey, who had been appointed a special prosecutor to investigate organised crime, asked that a contract be taken out against the lawyer. This was not regarded as sensible Mob policy, and when it was refused Schultz indicated that he would have the matter dealt with himself. On 23 October 1935 just after 10 p.m., Schultz was shot in the men's lavatory of the Palace Chop House and Tavern in Newark, New Jersey. Though, true to his metier, he did not name his killers before he died two days later, they were in fact Charles 'The Big' Workman, and Mendy Weiss. They had also shot three men – including Schultz's mathematical genius, Otto 'Abbadabba' Berman – who were sitting at a table waiting for their master to return.[2] In the ensuing panic Weiss and another man abandoned Workman, leaving him to find his own way back to Manhattan.[3]

It was not until five years later that Osnato, through a series

2 Berman's greatest contribution to life in general and Schultz in particular was when he worked out a way to fix the numbers game, a lottery which paid out on the numbers of winning horses at a race meeting, so beloved of both the public and organised crime. He was said to earn $10,000 a week from Schultz.
3 Workman was eventually arraigned for the murder of Schultz. He had not been picked out on an identification parade by eye-witnesses at the Palace Chop House but his alibi was a thin one involving working at a funeral parlour at the time of the killing. Under cross-examination his 'employer' admitted perjury and Workman entered a plea of *non vult* which saved him from the electric chair. He was sentenced to twenty-three years imprisonment and after a life as a model prisoner was released on 10 March 1964. He is said to have been not displeased that Mendy Weiss who had abandoned him was in fact sentenced to death and executed for the killing of Schultz.

of informers, reached the high level of Abe 'Kid Twist' Reles who in turn began to inform on his colleagues and superiors. Although Reles had been arrested some forty-two times over the previous sixteen years, he had served only short prison sentences and his position in society was unknown to the police. Now he was charged with robbery, the possession of narcotics and six further charges linked to murder. He feared, probably correctly, that some of those arrested with him, including Frank Abbandando, might endeavour to arrange a deal by informing on him and, so to speak, he had the first drop on them. The police were able to clear up some forty-nine killings in Brooklyn alone. He named Abbandando and Workman in the killing of Dutch Schultz, and his evidence was in a large part responsible for the conviction of Reles' superior, Louis Lepke Buchalter, and Mendy Weiss for the murder of Joseph Rosen.

For a year Reles – like so many subsequent informers – was held in protective custody. His safe home was the sixth floor of the Half Moon Hotel on Coney Island, New York, where he was kept under constant surveillance by six uniformed police officers. It was from there that he travelled to the New York courts to give his evidence. On 12 November 1941 he fell from the window of his room, landing on the pavement, and was killed. There have been a number of disparate suggestions as to how he came to be 'the canary who could not fly'. One of the more ingenious is that he was playing a practical joke climbing out of the window on knotted bedsheets and then running back upstairs to frighten the guards outside his room. Another is that he committed suicide. To do this he must have lowered himself to the third floor and then jumped; as his body was found twenty feet out into the street, this seems unlikely.

The much more plausible account is that it was a gangland hit. At the time, Reles was due to testify against Albert Anastasia who was on trial for the killing of waterfront labour leader, Peter Panto. After Reles' death the case against Anastasia was dropped, and although it was re-opened in 1951 no progress was made. He was also due to give evidence against 'Bugsy'

Siegel. Charles 'Lucky' Luciano was later to say that the killing had been done by police officers who had thrown Reles from his room and that the contract price had been $50,000. Later, Meyer Lansky said the fee paid had been $100,000. Even so, it was money well spent. There is also some evidence that Reles' confessions were being used not simply to obtain convictions against organised crime figures but to blackmail them.[4]

The first and one of the most successful of great post-war Mafia informers was Joe Valachi. Described in 1964 by the then Attorney General, Robert F.Kennedy, as the 'biggest single intelligence breakthrough yet in combating organised crime and racketeering in the United States', Valachi turned informer not because he feared prison – he was already serving a sentence – but because he feared being killed whilst in prison.

On 22 June 1962 at the US Penitentiary, Atlanta, Georgia, Joseph Michael Valachi, fifty-eight years old, 5 foot 6 tall and weighing 184 lbs and serving concurrent terms of fifteen and twenty years for drug-trafficking, had taken a 2-foot-long piece of piping and, running up behind another prisoner, Joe Saupp, had beaten him to death. Unfortunately he killed the wrong man. He had mistaken Saupp for a Joe Beck or DiPalermo whom he believed, probably correctly, that Vito Genovese – head of the Luciano crime family, who was himself in the same prison serving a sentence for drug-trafficking – had ordered to kill him.

Valachi now had considerable problems. Quite apart from the additional sentence he would face for the murder of Saupp, he

4 On 25 October 1957 Anastasia was shot to death whilst he sat in a barber's chair in the Park Sheraton hotel in New York. No one was charged, but the contract was believed to have been carried out on behalf of Don Vito Genovese. Charles Luciano was deported to Italy on 10 February 1946, from where he continued to exert considerable authority over crime in America. He died of a heart attack at Capodichino airport in Naples on 26 January 1962, having gone there to meet a film producer with a view to making a bio-pic of his life.
  On 20 June 1947 Ben Siegel was shot dead in Beverly Hills at the home of his girlfriend and Mob bag-lady, Virginia Hill. One account, and probably the most likely, of his death is that it was authorised by Luciano and Lansky because Siegel had been stealing from Mob funds. On 15 January 1983, Lansky died following a heart attack at the age of eighty-three.

knew he was targeted by Genovese who had, falsely, been told that Valachi was an informer. Valachi had survived attempts to murder him before.

In American prisons there are basically three inmate methods of killing a prisoner – poisoned food, an attack in the showers, and being provoked into a fight in the prison yard in the confusion of which he would be stabbed. All three had been tried and failed. Valachi had known he was a marked man following a conversation with Genovese, with whom he shared a cell.

> One night in our cell Vito starts saying to me, 'You know, we take a barrel of apples, and in this barrel of apples there might be a bad apple. Well, this apple has to be removed, and if it ain't removed, it would hurt the rest of the apples.'
>
> I tried to interrupt him when he was saying this, but he waved at me to keep quiet. Finally I couldn't stand it no more. 'If I done anything wrong,' I said, 'show it to me and bring me the pills – meaning poison – and I will take them in front of you.'
>
> He said, 'Who said you done anything wrong?'
>
> There wasn't anything I could say.
>
> Then he said to me that we had known each other for a long time, and he wanted to give me a kiss for old times' sake. Okay, I said to myself, two can play this game. So I grabbed Vito and kissed him back.
>
> I went to my bed and Ralph, who was in the next bed, mumbled, 'The kiss of death.' I pretended I didn't hear him and just laid on my bed. But who could sleep?'[5]

Even before he killed Saupp, Valachi had applied to be put in the hole or solitary confinement.[6] It was a request he could

5 Peter Maas, *The Valachi Papers*, p. 26. The phrase 'kiss of death' – which comes from the betraying kiss given to Christ by Judas Iscariot – seems only to have become really popular after the 1950s, possibly following the publication of an American thriller of that name.
6 The English equivalent is known as Rule 43.

make but on which he could not insist. He stopped bathing and did not go for his meals. He made attempts to contact George Gaffney, then Deputy Director of the Bureau of Narcotics, but his messages were never sent. He also tried to get Thomas 'Three Fingers' Lucchese to intervene on his behalf; again his begging letter was never sent but was, apparently, returned to Valachi for re-writing so that the new draft might reveal why he had applied to be put in solitary confinement. Valachi refused to speak and so was returned to the general prison population. It was then that he attacked the unfortunate Saupp, who had no organised crime convictions and was merely serving a sentence for robbery and forgery.

Now he faced the death penalty from the State as well as a death penalty from his former associates. Valachi managed to get a message to Robert Morganthau saying that he wished to co-operate with the Federal Government. On 17 July he pleaded guilty to the non-capital offence of murder in the second degree and left the court with narcotics agent Frank Selvagi to go to Westchester County jail near New York where he was lodged as Joseph DeMarco. He was not immediately co-operative and grateful. He maintained he had been framed on his twenty-year sentence, and that this was the one which had led to his being wrongly identified as a snitch. Nevertheless he had to co-operate to some degree if he did not wish to be returned once more to the prison population where retribution would have been immediate. It must have been clear that by being allowed to make a plea to the lesser offence he was trying to strike – even if he had not actually yet struck – a deal. Such a man was far too dangerous to be allowed to survive.

It is probable, although with the gift of hindsight difficult to believe, that in the pre-Valachi days the American public knew little of the workings of organised crime. Indeed, those who doubt Valachi's testimony use as a stick with which to beat him the scarcely credible (to us) notion that before Valachi no one had heard the phrase *La Cosa Nostra*. Valachi said the term was used in house, so to speak, in preference to the Mafia. Robert Kennedy insisted that Valachi give public testimony for two reasons. The first was to obtain additional legislation – the authority to provide immunity to witnesses in racketeering investigations; and also the reform and revision of the wire-tapping law. The second, and just as important, was the need to drum up public support against organised crime.

> We have yet to exploit properly our most powerful asset in the battle against the rackets: an aroused, informed, and insistent public.[7]

Initially, however, there was public resistance to these measures and civil libertarians' opposition was not overcome until 1968.

Valachi gave lengthy testimony on the structure of organised crime in *La Cosa Nostra* with its family units which then controlled cities including Boston, Buffalo, Chicago, Cleveland, Detroit, Kansas City, Los Angeles, Newark, New Orleans, New York City, Philadelphia, Pittsburgh and San Francisco. He said that 'open cities' were Miami and Las Vegas and pre-Castro Havana. He went on to detail the structure of the Family with its *capo* or boss, the *sub-capo, caporegime* and soldiers, something with which we are now completely familiar since *The Godfather* was released twenty-five years ago. What he also revealed was the so-called Castellammarese War, a power struggle between Italian-American gangs during the early 1930s, ending with the purge by Lucky Luciano of the old brigade of Mustachio Petes. This is another stick with which Valachi has been beaten. He claimed that up to sixty killings had taken place during that nationwide war, but was able to name only a few.[8]

It may be that, in common with many informers, Valachi simply awarded himself a rather higher status in the criminal hierarchy than he actually deserved. After all, there were few

7 US Senate: 1963: 9.
8 Writers who tend to doubt Valachi's version of events include Jay Albanese, *Organised Crime in America*, Alan A. Block, *East Side – West Side: Organising Crime in New York 1930–1950*, and Humbert S. Nelli, *The Business of Crime: Italians and Syndicate Crime*.

at the time who could contradict him over minor details. *La Cosa Nostra* did not exist or, if by some mischance it did, then the persons he named had no part of it. As the years went by, however, and other Mafia supergrasses grew out of the weeds of Brooklyn, they were quick to play down Valachi's position in polite society. 'I'm only a two dollar bum, and Valachi is dirt under *my* feet,' said Jimmy Blue Eyes.[9]

Despite the apparent inconsistencies and lack of corroboration, the Sub-committee accepted Valachi's version of matters.

> The Sub-committee wanted to hear what Valachi told them, and once he had satisfied their desire there was little need to be skeptical or press for additional, independent information. It was a case of the story being true because it sounded like what ought to be heard.[10]

In his autobiography, Joseph Bonanno wrote:

> Valachi gave an interpretation to My Tradition that made it look cheap and totally criminal in operation. Because he never rose very high himself, Valachi mainly came in contact with the dregs of our society, our lowlife . . . Often he described historical events in which he never participated, but nonetheless inserted himself to make himself seem important to his gullible audience.[11]

Once he had completed his testimony before the Sub-committee, Valachi was allowed to write his memoirs with the author Peter Maas. He was eventually moved to La Tuna

9 Hank Messick, 'Gold Coaster filled shoes of Frank Costello' in *Miami Herald*, 20 December 1966. For once, a gangster was being modest. Vincent Alo, known as Jimmy Blue Eyes, was a long-standing high-ranking member of the hierarchy. At one time he was Meyer Lansky's partner in the Riviera Hotel, Havana. Supergrasses did like to boast with varying degree of licence. 'I was the next big-time Judas of the Underworld,' said O'Mahoney, *King Squealer*, p. 132.
10 Dwight C. Smith, *The Mafia Mystique*, p. 234.
11 Joseph Bonanno, *A Man of Honor*, p. 164.

Federal Correctional Institution at El Paso, Texas where he died
on 3 April 1971. Those who believe in conspiracy theories will
be heartened to know that it was widely believed that his death
was a cover-up and, like that of Mark Twain, was 'greatly
exaggerated' so that he could be released and hidden on the
outside. If there was a cover-up then another informer, Vincent
Teresa, was in on it. In his book he gives an account of the death
of the old man, now riddled with cancer and troubled by the cold
although in La Tuna the summer temperature could reach 110
degrees. According to Teresa, Valachi's body was claimed by
a woman to whom he had been writing and was buried in a
cemetery in Niagara Falls. There was no headstone in case it
was desecrated by the Mob.[12]

Regarded as rather more important by criminologists is the
testimony of Jimmy 'The Weasel' Fratianno, who turned
informer at the age of forty-seven. He was born in Italy
but his family went to Cleveland when he was four. He was
credited with at least eleven gangland killings, rising to become
head of the Los Angeles Mafia as a result not of his talent for
murder but because he was a good businessman. After a second
prison sentence imposed in 1970, he became an FBI informer
and sang happily about the skimming of Las Vegas casinos and
the Teamsters Pension Fund. By 1987 he had been instrumental
in the conviction of six bosses and twenty-three lesser-ranked
mobsters. He had a price of $250,000 on his head and was none
too pleased when he was released back into general circulation.
One compensation was the money he received as royalties from
not one but two autobiographies, of which *The Last Mafioso* was
the more successful.

Next to the plate was Vincent 'Fat Vinnie' Teresa. He was
described by his co-author, in what some might see 'as a rubbish
the opposition' passage, as

. . . no ordinary hoodlum. He is no Joseph Valachi, a

12 Vincent Teresa with Thomas C. Renner, *My Life in the Mafia*, p. 272.

low-level soldier in the Mob. He is not a petulant Salvatore Bonanno, son of a crime boss, telling a disingenuous tale of service to crime for his father's sake. Teresa was a top Mafia thief, a mobster and at times a brutal enforcer, and he dealt at the highest levels of organised crime. Had he not been caught, had he not been double-crossed by those he worked with and trusted, he would still be a powerful and successful criminal.

Teresa, in three short years, has become the most single effective and important informer the U.S. Government has ever obtained. His testimony has convinced juries from Florida to Massachusetts. He is responsible for the indictment or conviction of more than fifty organised crime figures including the Mob's biggest money-maker, Meyer Lansky.[13]

Note the clever use of Lansky's name. Certainly, he was indicted for tax evasion on Teresa's testimony but he was acquitted.

By the time of his testimony against Lansky, Teresa was wearing a false beard and moustache to conceal his series of double chins. Again he was likely to overplay his hand for the purpose of his readers. One of his remarks was of London's Colony Club in the mid-60s that, 'You'd see royalty there every night.' In fact it was a club under Kray protection, and in those days at least royalty did not go to such places *every* night. Amongst Teresa's other grandiose suggestions was that he kept a bowl of piranha fish into which he would threaten to push the hands of his debtors. His crucial evidence was that Lansky had met him to receive cash on or about 17 May 1968 in the Dupont Plaza Hotel. David Rosen, Lansky's counsel, who later declined to write his biography, was able to show that Lansky had been booked into a double room at the Sheraton Plaza, Boston, from 7 May to 28 May with his wife, Teddy. There

13 *Ibid.* p. ix.

was a gap from 8 May to 19 May when Lansky was not there, and Mrs Lansky had renegotiated the room rate downwards to reflect his absence. The crucial witness, however, was a Harvard medical professor, Dr Seymour J. Gray, who had been in the theatre in the Peter Bent Brigham Hospital when there was an operation on Lansky on 10 May. He had also seen him a fortnight later when Lansky was weak and scarcely able to walk. It is always interesting to know how a jury votes, and apparently it was split 6–6 on the first ballot but soon swung round in Lansky's favour.

Just how important Teresa was, both as a Mafia figure and as an informer, is difficult to assess. According to his memoirs he was No. 3 in the New England Mafia. Through his evidence some fifty convictions were obtained and the price of $500,000 put on his head was very much more than the paltry $100,000 on that of Valachi. He turned state's witness because, he said, whilst in prison his one-time friends stole his money, failed to support his wife and threatened one of his children.

He was certainly discredited at the Lansky trial, after which he went into the Witness Protection Program under the name of Charles Cantino. Safely installed, he was able to continue with his life of crime, smuggling endangered birds into America and dealing in cocaine. In 1982 under that name he was jailed for five years in Seattle, and about the same time was sentenced to another ten years for mail fraud. He is reported to have died in February 1990.[14]

Since those early days the use of informers and witnesses has grown to that of a well-organised business. In 1970 it was estimated that between twenty-five and fifty witnesses would be inducted each year into the Program. They would be provided with a new birth certificate and social security number, and relocated far from the area in which they had testified. A subsistence allowance would be paid until the

14 *Seattle Times*, 9 August 1981, 23 September 1981 and 12 February 1982. *New York Times*, 25 February 1990. See also Robert Lacey, *Little Man*, pp. 376–8, 382–3.

witness could once more become self-supporting, preferably
without returning or resorting to crime. The annual cost in 1970
was estimated to be $1 million.

This did not work out quite so economically as had been
hoped. By 1983 more than 4,400 witnesses and double that
number of family members had entered the Program. The game
did, however, show satisfactory results. Analysing a sample of
220 cases in the period 1979–1980 in which witnesses who had
entered the Program testified, 75 per cent of the defendants
were found guilty. It is open to discussion whether there was
the same success in subsequently keeping the witnesses out of
the court as defendants. On average they had made 7.2 court
appearances before they became witnesses, over half of which
were for violent crimes, and after their stint their arrest record
fell to an average of 1.8 with fewer than one-third of these
offences being violent.

The problem with this particular statistic is that the witnesses'
pre-Program criminal career averaged ten years, whilst only
three and a half years in the programme was available for
research purposes. There was still plenty of time for them to
rack up more convictions. Recidivism was 21.4 per cent and
the annual cost had risen to $25 million.

Far cheaper was running an informer or having an undercover
police officer, but even this could damage the long term
budget:

Jack is a well-dressed, middle-aged man, who although
short on education is well-spoken. He has a way of
drawing people into his engaging narratives and would
make a perfect companion on a long train ride; he is warm,
and in his own unpolished style, gentle. Jack is also a crook
. . . Some years ago Jack got into a jam and, as he put it,
'made the decision to go with the Bureau'. In FBI parlance
he is an informant, but he prefers to think of himself as a
source. Whatever the title for the relationship, it has been
a mutually beneficial one: he has helped the Bureau solve

some sticky criminal cases, has made some money, and has stayed out of jail.[15]

One of the more interesting undercover agents used by the CIA and the FBI was Herb Itkin, who was known to the CIA under the code-name 'Poron' and as 'Mr Jerry' to the FBI. He was described by a member of the staff of United States Attorney Robert Morgenthau:

[Itkin is] the most valuable informer the FBI has ever had outside the espionage field. He never lies to us. His information has always been accurate.

The FBI said of him: 'He is probably the most important informer ever to come to the surface. He knew the younger up-and-coming characters in the *Cosa Nostra*.'

It is probably also correct that he left a trail of disaster behind him. Born in 1926, the son of working-class Jewish parents, Herbert Itkin was brought up in the Borough Park section of Brooklyn in what was then the middle-class area of 48th Street. His father had a series of small shops and, by accounts, was mild-mannered and ineffectual whilst his mother was the dominant personality. In 1944 he enlisted in the Army and was sent after VJ day to Japan with a field hospital unit. On his return with $2,000 savings he bought a luncheonette in Bush terminal, Brooklyn, and put it about that he had been a paratrooper attached to Army Intelligence. The luncheonette, where his parents worked, was not a success. According to one account, his father tripped and knocked his head on the gas-tap, turning it on. Itkin told a friend that, when his father did not come home from a Saturday late shift, he went to find him and revived the unconscious man just as the police arrived. In another, more heroic, version protection money was demanded by a Mafia enterprise. His father had resisted their blandishments and his

15 Sanford J. Unger, *FBI*, p. 450.

head was held in the gas-oven. Itkin had set out in revenge and confronted the leader, who told his henchmen to leave the boy alone because 'He has spunk.' Whichever version is correct, Itkin senior did not work in the luncheonette again; he spent some time in hospital and was then divorced.

Meanwhile Itkin junior went to law school, working during the day for a local firm Delson, Levin & Gordon, where his mother now had a position as a bookkeeper. He married Diana Kane, one of the firm's secretaries. He qualified in 1953, by which time he had moved to Hicksville, Long Island. He appears to have been worried that his Jewish name would hold him back in his career. Diana Kane recalled:

> Herbie wanted very badly not to marry a Jewish girl. He wanted a shiksa like me. Once he was going to change his name to something less Jewish and I told him, 'Herbie, you can make it wherever you want to go with your real name. Besides, your mother would have a heart attack. You have enough ambition and talent to overcome it.'

It was now that the web of deceit was spun. In 1957, Itkin left Delsons under something of a cloud because of complaints made to the Bar Association over client poaching. He had, he said, begun his CIA career with a retainer in 1954, the year after his marriage. His version of his recruitment is that it was conducted at the highest level, that of CIA Director, Allen Dulles, who had been impressed with information supplied by Itkin to Senator Joe McCarthy in the early 1950s.

This is not a version which was accepted by Federal officials, who place the date as 1962 as a result of a CIA man meeting Itkin by chance in the Madison Avenue offices he rented with other lawyers. Itkin, the official version goes, was recruited on a part-time unpaid basis because of his contacts in the Caribbean and Asia. The lawyer who had made the introduction became his control. There seems little doubt that his life as a spy was at least a two-way traffic, with Itkin trying to use his CIA connections to further his business interests. The Itkins moved out of Hickville and into the more fashionable resort of Oyster Bay. By now he was exhibiting signs of mild paranoia; he would only eat from tins opened by himself, and if hot meals were prepared for him they had to be tasted first. He began to borrow from friends and relations. There is a story that his father-in-law telephoned the CIA to ask if Itkin did work for them. 'If he does, don't believe anything he says,' he added and hung up. By 1969 Itkin was in debt to the tune of $600,000. On the plus side, however, he clearly did have knowledge of the Mafia and the Teamsters Union system of fund operating. He was turned over to the FBI in 1964.

On 18 January 1967 Itkin flew into London with Tony 'Ducks' Corallo and Tommy Mancuso, with a view to the latter buying into British gambling casinos which were starting to take off in a big way. The visit was also in relation to gaming machines which Corallo was placing in Britain with Dick Kaminitsky, known as Dick Duke. Corallo was refused entry to the United Kingdom and the mission aborted.[16]

What he was also doing was getting out of control and making money for himself without accounting to his handler. Worse, from everyone's point of view, he was boasting about his activities. Diana Kane said that: 'Herbie told just about everybody about the CIA and the FBI. He told some fellows he commuted on the train with.'

By the end of his career, Itkin, who had been involved with countless women and had now fallen in love with a divorcée, Scotty Hersch, was a liability. He was pulled off the street and into protective custody along with his first and second wives – Diana Kane had long been replaced – and their families. He was kept at a military post in New York where, said a Government official, he was allowed the use of the recreational facilities and

16 Kaminitsky was later killed. During his life, he had amassed three convictions for murder. It was alleged that the financing of Corallo's machines came from a company which was convicted in 1972 of having assisted Detroit crime figures to gain control of a casino in Las Vegas.

post exchange but was not allowed to buy liquor. In December 1967 he appeared in the first of the trials in which he was to give evidence. This led to the conviction of Tony Corallo, who received four and a half years, and Carmine De Sapio as well as James L. Marcus, the former city commissioner and confidant of Mayor Lindsay. Marcus received fifteen months.[17]

Although a major figure in dozens of pending cases and described by the FBI as 'risking his neck almost every day' and being praised for his 'reckless patriotism', Itkin was not without his critics. Manhattan District Attorney Frank S. Hogan was out for his blood. In the trial of De Sapio, which resulted in a conviction for conspiracy to bribe Marcus and to extort contracts from Consolidated Edison, the court heard that Itkin had kept large sums of money from swindles, bribes and kickbacks. Now Hogan wished to prosecute him. 'They would love to get me on a perjury conviction to destroy me and all my work,' said Itkin.

A representative of Hogan's office asked:

> How could the Federal officials allow an informer to take that kind of money which was admittedly made from criminal deals and keep it? What do they think informers are? Some sort of bounty hunters?

Well, yes, really is the answer to that.

17 Tony 'Ducks' Corallo was a member of the Lucchese family and had a record of grand larceny and robbery dating back to 1929. In the McClellan Committee report into the Teamsters Union, he is said to have embezzled $69,000 by recording false names on the payroll. On 13 January 1987 he was sentenced to 100 years' imprisonment coupled with a fine for participating in co-ordinating coast-to-coast criminal activities.

6

Ireland

Both the history and the literature of Ireland and the Troubles have been studded with the use by the English of informers. The dishonourable tradition goes back to 1641 when Owen O'Connally informed on the Irish rebels, Lord Maguire and Colonel McMahon, who were taken to London and hanged on Tyburn Hill. O'Connally's reward was cash and an annuity, but he does not seem to have lived long enough to gain much benefit and was killed two years later. He was but the first in a long line of informers. The next crop grew up at the time of the Irish Rebellion of 1798 – Captain Armstrong (who over a period of sixty years as an informer was paid some £30,000 by the government), Frederick Dutton, Leonard McNally (who wrote *Sweet Lass of Richmond Hill* and was said to be the meanest and most mercenary of the tribe), Thomas Reynolds (who was said to be totally despicable and to have robbed his own mother) and Samuel Turner are the better-known ones, but there were others including Dr Conlan of Dundalk, James Hughes in Belfast and Edward Newell of Downpatrick. As a result of their efforts:

> The prisons were crowded with persons denounced by those infamous informers, Armstrong and Reynolds, Dutton and Newell, with a list of subordinate villains acting under the direction of police agents, themselves

steeped deeper in iniquity than the perjured wretches they suborned . . . Numbers, innocent in most cases, through the instrumentality of those bad men, were brought hourly to the scaffold.[1]

It is often assumed that the most damage to the cause was done by Leonard McNally, but in *Secret Service under Pitt*, W. J. Fitzpatrick suggests that a lawyer from Newry, Samuel Turner, was the most dangerous and treacherous. Financed by Pitt, he kept the British government well informed on the activities of the Republican leaders. It is thought that he was responsible for the execution of Father Quigley, arrested at Maidstone on his way to France. The priest was said to be carrying incriminating documents and was offered the opportunity to save himself by turning informer, but he declined the privilege and was hanged at Peneden Heath on 7 June 1798.

Turner seems to have managed to live his double life unsuspected by the United Irishmen. He was killed in a duel in the Isle of Man in 1821 after living in his house, Turner's Glen, quite happily for the period following the rebellion. Edward Newell was apparently responsible for the arrest of nearly 230 men, and for another 300 being obliged to flee from their homes.

The stories of the early use of informers in Ireland follow the pattern of many in England and the United States. A person with an unpleasant, even trifling, secret is caught and is leaned on sufficiently heavily to persuade him to turn against his colleagues. One such was John Joseph Corydon, who was born in Liverpool's dockland and became 'the most fatal and dangerous enemy of the Fenians'. It seems he had been caught with a prostitute and allowed to go free provided he turned informer.

Sometimes the efforts to buy witnesses and informers failed;

1 W. H. Maxwell, *History of the Irish Rebellion of 1798*.

bluffs were called and exposed. Richard Piggott, a journalist, sold (for the sum of £500) forged letters to *The Times* purporting to link Charles Parnell, the Irish statesman, to the Phoenix Park murders. It was part of a plot to defeat the growing campaign for Home Rule. *The Times* sent agents to the United States offering Fenians money to come to London to testify against Parnell. An allegation that one agent offered a Patrick Sheridan £20,000 to return to England, and that Sheridan agreed to do so only to expose the plot when he arrived, was the subject of a libel action by the officer and was settled out of court. The Parnell Commission inquiry into the allegations by *The Times* followed.

The murders of Lord Frederick Cavendish and the Under-Secretary Thomas Burke took place in Phoenix Park, Dublin, on 6 May 1882. Whilst out for an evening stroll at about 6 p.m. they were attacked by four men, led by Joseph Brady, wielding long knives. The attack was witnessed by a number of people, but few were forthcoming to give evidence. Their tongues were loosened by the Severe Crimes Act 1882, which enabled magistrates to hold secret inquiries, and it transpired that the assassination had been carried out by a recently formed group, the Invincibles. It appears there was an overall commander and a council of four including James Carey, a member of the Dublin City Corporation.

Informers also abounded in the case. The police had been helped by a man called Lamie who had led them to a taxi-driver, Kavanagh, who in turn became an informer and told how he had driven Joseph Brady, Timothy Kelly and Patrick Delaney to Phoenix Park, where Carey was waiting and gave the signal for the attack by waving a white handkerchief. The men were then driven back to Dublin.

At the preliminary proceedings on 15 February 1883 Carey, who would appear to have been the ringleader, turned Queen's Evidence to save himself. He was held in custody in Kilmainham Jail, Dublin, until after the trial in April, and then in the July was sent to South Africa to join his family.

He did not survive the journey and was shot by a passenger, O'Donnell, as the ship was nearing Capetown. It is not clear whether he had followed Carey from Ireland or had simply heard that the informer was on board; it may be that he was shot in a personal quarrel. O'Donnell was returned to England and was hanged later that year.

The conspirators were hanged at various times during May and June 1883 at Kilmainham Jail by William Marwood who travelled to Dublin to execute them.[2]

Long-term undercover agents seem to have abounded. Apart from the lawyer Samuel Turner there was also Major Henri le Caron (also known as Thomas Beach), a French doctor with apparently Republican sympathies. A witness to *The Times* inquiry, he was the doctor to a number of Fenians who used him to carry messages to London, Paris and Dublin. These reached their destination, but copies also reached London. It was the good doctor who was able to give both the British and Canadian governments details of the plot to invade Canada. It does not seem to have been a particularly well-thought-out plot, since at the time the Fenians had only one field gun which the doctor was himself able to spike. For his efforts he received £50 from the British Government and the rather more substantial tribute of £500 from the Canadian one.

On Tuesday morning the 5th February 1889, the curtain was rung up, and throwing aside the mask for ever, I

2 When Marwood died suddenly on 4 September 1883 it was rumoured, but never substantiated, that he had been poisoned as retribution for his work as the executioner of the Invincibles and other Irishmen.

On 8 July 1882 Allan Pinkerton, head of the American detective agency, wrote to Gladstone after the Phoenix Park murders recommending him to do away with informers and to eschew rewards 'as I consider them as incentives to crime'. [HO 144/1537/4.] It was an attitude shared by the detectives of the day. 'I have to confess,' wrote John Littlechild in his memoirs (p. 96), 'that the "nark" is very apt to drift into an agent provocateur in his anxiety to secure a conviction, and therefore he requires to be carefully watched.' With a deal of chauvinism George Greenham in his memoirs (p. 61) was also aware of the problem, writing how easy it was for a detective to be deceived by a 'voluntary informer', especially foreigners with shady surroundings.

stepped into the witness box and came out in my true
colours, as an Englishman, proud of his country, and in
no sense ashamed of his record in her service.[3]

He was given a house and an annuity by *The Times* and is
an early example of the witness protection scheme. After his
revelations he was guarded day and night and moved about the
country until he died on 1 April 1894. He was then fifty-two,
and had apparently been living in terror of being poisoned for
the past five years. As with so many deaths of this type, there
were rumours that he had simply been spirited away by the
authorities to go to live abroad. The date of his death may
have had something to do with the story. On the other hand,
Reynold's Newspaper on 8 April 1894 suggested 'the famous
spy is now on his way to one of the most distant colonies'. The
next year the same paper reported on 23 June that he had been
seen 'in the halfpenny omnibus that plies between the Strand
and Waterloo'.

The rise of the modern informer in Irish political and
criminal history can be dated fairly accurately. It began with
the escalation in sectarian street violence in the late 1960s,
and escalated throughout the next few years until in August
1971 internment was added by Stormont to the list of penalties
and sanctions open to courts and police. Six months later, with
the British Government attempting to take direct control of the
situation, Lord Diplock was invited to chair an inquiry into
'whether changes should be made in the administration of
justice in order to deal more effectively with terrorism without
using internment'. Two years later his recommendations were
the substance of the Northern Ireland (Emergency Provisions)
Act 1973. The Act withdrew the right of jury trial, establishing
in its place single judge courts, extended the rights of the police
and the army over stop and search and placed emphasis on
accepting confession evidence. By 1975 internment had been

3 'Henri le Caron', *Twenty-five years in the Secret Service: The Recollections of
a Spy.*

phased out and in its place came pressure on the police to obtain confessions of crime from suspects. The result was not unexpected; a steady stream of complaints about the physical abuse of detainees followed. Eventually the practices were exposed by Amnesty International and, four years later, the Bennett Inquiry indicated that there should be rights of access to a solicitor and a closed-circuit television system to monitor interviews as well as notice of his rights given to a suspect.

At this time there was a series of appalling sectarian murders in the Shankhill Road area, where a gang known as the Shankhill Butchers operated and where at least twenty-four people, almost all Roman Catholics, were hacked to death in north and west Belfast.

As the police in purely criminal matters have found since the implementation of the Police and Criminal Evidence Act 1984, with a monitoring of the interview and access to a solicitor the suspect tends to confess rather less frequently. By the early 1980s a supergrass system was in place. Not only would informers – 'converted terrorists' as they were described by Sir John Hermon, the Chief Constable of the RUC – be used as intelligence gatherers, they would also be used to give evidence in high profile trials, particularly against Republicans. In the two years from November 1981 seven (and possibly more) Loyalist and eighteen Republican supergrasses were used in the arrest of nearly 600 suspects in Northern Ireland.

> It is arguable that this was a direct result of the difficulty which the police encountered in obtaining confessions after the introduction of the Bennett reforms in interrogation procedures. This has resulted in large numbers of IRA and INLA suspects being held on remand, many as a result of the short-circuiting of the normal committal procedures by reliance on the *ex parte* procedure for initiating an indictment.[4]

4 Tom Hadden, a lecturer in law at Queen's University, Belfast, in *Submission to the Review of Northern Ireland (Emergency Provisions) Act 1978*.

Essentially the rules under which the supergrass had to play were twofold. Immunity would only apply to offences to which the supergrass had admitted, but would not be granted to the actual killer.

The statistics of what happened next make for interesting reading. Fifteen of the supergrasses sooner or later retracted their evidence and in the case of a UDA informer, James Williamson, charges were withdrawn against all but two who had been unfortunate enough to make confessions. In the ten trials which did take place, 120 out of 217 defendants (55 per cent) pleaded guilty or were convicted. In five cases appeals were lodged and in them, 67 out of 74 convictions were quashed. The overall conviction rate, confirmed on appeal, stands at 44 per cent.

At first, as with the English courts in purely criminal cases, there was a high conviction rate. Whether this was bolstered by the absence of a jury is difficult to tell; after all, it was juries who convicted in the English cases. Up until November 1983 supergrasses were in the ascendant and, with Joseph Bennett, Christopher Black and Kevin McGrady on the stand on behalf of the Crown, 88 per cent of the accused were convicted – 61 per cent on the uncorroborated evidence of the grass. Things went downhill for the authorities after that, however. The Jackie Grimley case was perhaps the turning point and in the trials which featured him, John Moran, Robert Quigley, Raymond Gilmour, James Crockard, William 'Budgie' Allen and Harry Kirkpatrick, only in the Quigley and Kirkpatrick cases were there convictions on the uncorroborated word of the supergrass.

It would appear at first that the judges who heard the supergrass cases were prepared to accept the word of the sinner who had repented. In the Christopher Black case Mr Justice Kelly returned a verdict of guilty when Black had admitted perjury in a case previously before Kelly.

In December 1982 the trial began of thirty-eight defendants, including five women of whom one was a seventy-one-year-old widow. The 184 counts in the indictment included allegations of murder, attempted murder, possession of firearms and membership of the Provisional IRA. It ran until the following August, occupying 117 days of court time. Some 550 witnesses were called, amongst them – indeed the principal one – Christopher Black.

Black was himself a member of the Provisional IRA which he had joined in 1975. That year he was caught in a robbery, and the following March sentenced to ten years' imprisonment. On his release at the end of 1980 he rejoined the Ardoyne-Oldpark division. He did not last long on the outside, being caught as a member of a road-block set up by the IRA as a publicity stunt the following November.

As with so many informers, Black was terrified by the thought of another long stretch in prison. Now he had a young family and he was vulnerable. When he approached the RUC to offer his services, they were quite happy. If he gave evidence, he was to have immunity from prosecution for crimes to which he had confessed, a new identity and a safe home for himself and family in an English-speaking country of his choice.

He was an impressive witness, standing up to rigorous cross-examination. Judge Kelly was impressed, saying Black was one of the most convincing witnesses he had heard. Thirty-five of the thirty-eight were found guilty. Black was reported to have been given £127,000 and re-settled abroad, where the IRA was said to be conducting an active search for him.

As with non-political supergrasses, a dose of Christianity helps the political ones as well. Kevin McGrady became a born-again Christian and decided his conscience required him to assist the RUC. His background was slightly different from that of his fellow informers. For a start, before he joined the IRA and while working as an apprentice butcher, he had no criminal record. His brothers, Sean and Michael, had been interned without trial and this, said McGrady, was a principal reason for joining the IRA. When he gave evidence at the trial of John Gibney and nine others in September 1983, he stated that he had been the driver when George Rodger Duff was shot in the legs in July 1975. He had been arrested over the murder of Ernest Dowds two months later, but there was no evidence against him and he only received three months for assaulting a police officer. After his release he had worked for eighteen months as a butcher in London and had then drifted to Amsterdam, where he became involved in two fundamental Christian organisations, Youth with a Mission and Salvation for the People. It was now that he became a born-again Christian. He had, he said, been told by his spiritual adviser, Floyd McClung, that he could only clear his conscience by returning to Northern Ireland and making a clean breast of things. This he did in January 1982. His spiritual redemption earned him a life sentence for the murders in which he had taken part and, from his cell in the informers' annexe of the Crumlin Road prison, he became a Crown witness. Despite the fact that McGrady's evidence was described by the trial judge, Lord Lowry, as being 'contradictory, bizarre and in some respects incredible', not all the charges against Gibney were dismissed. Seventeen were but he was, however, found guilty of wounding and being a member of the IRA. He was sentenced to twelve years in prison.

One of the other reasons McGrady gave for his return to Northern Ireland was his desire to clear the name of his brother, Sean, whom had he said been wrongly convicted of the murder of Ernest Dowds. The Court of Appeal, however, was having none of it. The appeal was dismissed on 6 April 1984, with Kevin McGrady's evidence being described as 'quite unpersuasive and incredible'.

Meanwhile, in January 1982, the Provisional IRA had offered an amnesty to all informers who, within two weeks, were prepared to reveal what arrangements they had had with the RUC. They also had to undertake to sever their contacts. A pamphlet put out by Sinn Fein claimed that the RUC was now offering informers 'protective custody, huge sums of money and immunity from prosecution'.

It was about that time that Thomas Charles McCormick,

a detective-sergeant in the Special Branch of the RUC, fell foul of Anthony O'Doherty, an informer whom he had been handling for several years. They drank and ate together, travelled over County Antrim in unmarked police cars, and O'Doherty was provided with money and clothes. This was, believed McCormick, part of the handler's job. It must have been repulsive to him to have to spend so much time in the close company of a man who at the age of seventeen had been convicted of housebreaking, and by the time he appeared in court on 29 October 1981 pleaded guilty to forty-seven charges, including three attempts to murder policemen, and a number of attempts to blackmail bank managers, one of whom under a death threat had travelled to Cushendall to hand over £8,000. He now informed on his handler.

McCormick had met O'Doherty in August 1969 when he was selling the Republican newspaper the *United Irishman* and McCormick was there to pick up information. O'Doherty was arrested in an internment round-up and by then, if not before, he had become an RUC agent. For the next two years he was in weekly contact with the RUC, who appear to have provided him with survival training and, according to his evidence, with a Sten gun, a .303 rifle and a pistol.

The Crown's case was twofold. First, the robberies on banks and post offices about which O'Doherty had grassed and implicated McCormick were carried out because they were short of funds. Second, attacks on the security forces were a blind to deceive the IRA. Sergeant P. J. Campbell, who was killed in February 1977, had been murdered because he knew or suspected McCormick and O'Doherty were responsible for a series of robberies. McCormick's defence was that O'Doherty's evidence was a pack of lies, and that it was being said to discredit the RUC. It was accepted that he was short of money.

Desmond Boal QC, who appeared for McCormick and who described O'Doherty as 'a killer, a liar, a hypocrite, a play-actor, a devious and plausible villain, a maker of bargains with the police and a person of considerable intellectual dexterity which he frequently used to attribute to other people crimes which he himself had committed or in which he had been involved', argued that the man had been schooled in his evidence after dozens of visits by the police during the time he was in custody. The judge accepted that such police action was open to criticism but pronounced himself 'wholly satisfied that no injustice of any kind had resulted from it'. He dismissed all but three of the charges on the basis that he was not satisfied beyond reasonable doubt, and then on the remaining three sentenced McCormick to twenty years on a charge of armed robbery, with lesser sentences for hi-jacking motor cars and possessing a rifle.

The Court of Appeal looked at things in a different way. True, McCormick was tight for cash at the time, but that was not proof that he had helped O'Doherty rob a bank. The fact that a hand grenade had been given by him to O'Doherty did not prove he intended it should be used in bank robberies. Meeting O'Doherty in Portaglenone shortly before the hi-jacking of the motor cars did not prove O'Doherty's allegation that he had been involved. It was thought that the corroborative evidence, without which the trial judge would have acquitted, did not add up to anything. On 12 January 1984 Thomas Charles McCormick had his conviction quashed.

On 22 August 1984 James Prior, then Secretary of State for Northern Ireland, announced that he had recommended the Royal prerogative to remit eight years from the eighteen-year sentence imposed on O'Doherty. This meant that he would be released in 1985. The *Sunday World* suggested that this act of clemency was 'a publicity move aimed at stopping further loss of morale' among informers and ensuring that they knew the government would live up to its side of the bargain.

The virtual collapse of the supergrass system in Northern Ireland came with what was meant to be the evidence of forty-year-old John 'Jackie' Grimley, who was an RUC agent inside the INLA. He seems to have been a minor member of Sinn Fein, from which organisation he was expelled for 'irrational behaviour'. His political activities appear in the main to have been shouting slogans, carrying flags, and the like. His expulsion came after calling a crowd in a Sinn Fein social club in Craigavon 'fucking cunts'. He had also appeared hooded in the Tullygally Tavern in Craigavon and read out a spurious proclamation about theft and sexual violence in the area. After his expulsion he joined the INLA, where his role seems to have been slightly more important. He was deputed to perform robberies, hi-jacking a bus – including shooting the driver in the face when he tried to resist – knee-cappings and to murder a sergeant in the UDR or his brother, a politician. In the event no opportunity presented itself. He informed on twenty-one men and one girl who appeared in the Belfast Crown Court on 9 November 1983. The charges were possessing firearms, murder, and being members of the INLA. A diary of the trial reads:

Thursday 10 November: An application by Grimley to have his identity concealed and to be referred to as Witness A. The defence lawyers continued to call him Grimley. Grimley said he was a truthful person and had committed no other crimes except those with which he had been charged.

Friday 11 November: Desmond Boal QC leading for the defence forced him to admit to crimes which he had not mentioned the day before and to being an exhibitionist, a perjurer, a habitual drinker, given to acts of violence, having spent six months in a psychiatric hospital and manipulating people. The trial was adjourned.

Monday 14 November: Grimley admitted that he had the facility to make people (those in authority over him) believe his lies when he had to get out of an unacceptable situation. For example, he faked suicide twice to get out of the army and succeeded both times. Grimley also told the judge, 'I'm telling some lies, I admit' and admitted that, had he been brought to court for INLA membership before, he would have perjured himself to avoid jail. 'How is the court to know whether you are again perjuring yourself in return for immunity from prosecution?' asked Boal.

Tuesday 15 November: The trial was adjourned because Grimley said he was 'very tired, physically and mentally tired'.

Tuesday 22 November: The trial resumed. Grimley said that the RUC had given him a 'free hand' to carry out crimes and he acknowledged that they had put names to him, including those of a number of people in the dock on his uncorroborated evidence, who they believed were active in the INLA and wanted to implicate in terrorist activities.

Wednesday 23 November: Judge Gibson threw out all the charges against those who were on trial on Grimley's uncorroborated evidence.[5]

Grimley had also admitted being paid £25 for each nugget of information he supplied to the RUC. When such information was scarce, he had invented it. He had a record of more than forty criminal offences including fraud, perjury and theft. He said that Special Branch men were blackmailing him over a sexual offence he had committed in the bushes near the Tullygally tavern.

From 1983 to 1987 only two new supergrasses surfaced, and they did not last long. Eamonn Collins withdrew his evidence in March 1985, and the Director of Public Prosecutions dropped the charges of those implicated by Angela Whorisky. This did not mean there was no accomplice evidence, but in the years 1983–1985 it was used in only 12 per cent of the Diplock court cases.

The system had its critics. Father Denis Faul and Father Raymond Murray, two Catholic priests who have monitored

5 Sean Delaney, 'Ups and Downs for RUC's Perjurer Strategy' in *Iris*, p. 15. I am indebted to Dominque Harvie for her permission to quote extensively from her unpublished MA thesis, *The Use of Supergrasses in Northern Ireland*.

political trials in Northern Ireland, added their weight to the criticism directed against supergrass evidence.

> [informers] . . . have a unique opportunity to pay off old scores . . . they can name persons they have fought with . . . persons whose businesses they covet or wish to ruin . . . with whose wife they have had an affair or wish to have an affair . . . they are held incommunicado from relatives and friends and can be carefully rehearsed for many months to make their evidence more credible.[6]

In *The Informers*, his analysis of the supergrass trials in Northern Ireland, Andrew Boyd looks at the methods of their recruitment by the RUC. Quoting sources of a number of priests, such as Father Pat Buckley of Kileel, he says that there was a good deal of harassment of young people in that area, while Father Denis Faul told the *Irish Times* that the police trawled the prisons for likely informers, picking on men who appeared to be weak and vulnerable. There were also allegations that, apart from pressure, regular payments were made for young people to act as spies for the RUC.

The life of a supergrass in Northern Ireland was, however, much more dangerous that that of his English counterpart. Proof was not necessarily required for a suspected informer to be killed. When Thomas McGeary was blown up in his Mercedes on 29 April 1984, an organisation called the Irish Freedom Fighters said he had been killed because he was collaborating with the RUC. No further proof was deemed necessary, nor was it forthcoming. Brian McNally died some two months later, his body being found on the road near the border of the Republic and South Armagh. He was said to have become an informer for the RUC after being detained in Gough Barracks, Armagh. It seems he had benefited from the amnesty offered. He was de-briefed and all was forgiven if not forgotten

6 A. Boyd, *The Informers*, p. 31.

but, it was said, he had informed once more which had led to an arrest and the capture of an arms dump. He had received £25 a week and the offer of a free holiday in Spain before he was killed.

The life of a supergrass seems to have been much the same as it was in England: hotels, a home provided and a good allowance for expenses. Captive supergrasses were provided with saunas, squash-courts, alcohol, and facilities for sex sessions with visiting girlfriends.[7]

From around 1983, apart from the lack of new supergrasses there was a marked reluctance for informers to go through with giving evidence based on their confessions. By 1984 the judges – who had been accepting the evidence of supergrasses as something approaching gospel, even if they were caught out – began to have serious doubts.[8] In August 1984 Lord Lowry dismissed the evidence of supergrass Raymond Gilmour as 'entirely unworthy of belief' and stopped the trial against the accused, saying it would be an 'abuse of the criminal process'. On 24 December 1984 the appeals were allowed of all those convicted on Joseph Bennett's evidence.

But even if there had been a considerable running-down in the use of the supergrass since the great days of the early 1980s, perhaps he still had a useful role to perform for the authorities. On 22 December 1994 five Ulster Loyalists were jailed for life for the sectarian murder of a Catholic mother of two who had her throat slashed open to the spine. Thought to be an informer, she had been lured from a local football supporters' club to the bedroom of Samuel Cooke's home in East Belfast. Three of the five men were recommended to serve at least twenty-five years and as they were sentenced shouted to the judge that he had convicted innocent men on the word of a supergrass.[9]

7 *Sunday World*, 16 October 1983.
8 One example of a witness caught out was Robert Quigley, who substituted the name Terence Kelly instead of Michael Doherty as the man who had accompanied him on his unlawful expeditions. (Northern Irish barrister Philip McGee, speaking at the Forum Hotel in a meeting with the clergy, 3 April 1994.) It made no difference – the men were convicted.
9 *Scottish Daily Record*, 23 December 1994.

With what it is to be hoped is the end of the conflict in Northern Ireland, it is unlikely that the supergrass system will flourish there in political trials in the foreseeable future. There is, however, a new scenario. It is reported that former Provos and IRA soldiers are now turning to organised crime *per se*. No doubt if the trend is confirmed we may see the rise of the purely criminal supergrass in Northern Ireland. It may be, however, that some lessons over their use have been learned.

7

A Cautionary Tale

The story of Paul Fisher, a medium- to high-grade northern criminal, is a good example of how the supergrass system in England has worked in theory but not necessarily in practice and of the wheeling and dealing which took place, hindered from time to time by the judicial system.

In December 1982 a burglary was reported to the South Yorkshire police. It was one in which over £1.2 million of ferro alloys were stolen from a specialist steel manufacturing firm at Stocksbridge. The report developed into a huge and complicated inquiry into a massive fraud on Napier Steel, an Oughtibridge subsidiary of Sheffield Twist Drill, which lost over £1.7 million. As a result of the investigation over fifty people, including senior management personnel of both Yorkshire-based and international companies, were arrested and eighteen charged with a variety of offences ranging from conspiracy, corruption, arson and burglary to fraud. Two people were also shot.

The first shooting, which actually occurred in November 1981 before the burglary, was in the Derbyshire police force area, when a man named Elkington was attacked. He was a company official who had been bringing – or at least, trying to bring – some pressure to bear over the alloy frauds which preceded the burglary. The second shooting was of Arthur

Davies, the brother-in-law of a South Yorkshire scrap-metal dealer, which occurred on 9 January 1983, by which time the police were making progress in their metal inquiries. Almost certainly the reason behind the shooting of Mr Davies was either to silence him or as a warning to his friends and associates.

Davies left a public house in the east end of Sheffield and, driving a pick-up truck towards Rotherham, was followed by Fisher and a colleague Barrie Walker. As they drew alongside him Fisher fired a 12-bore shotgun into the cab, missing Davies' head but badly injuring his right hand. So far as the police were concerned it was a question of a round-up of the usual suspects, and Fisher and Walker were pulled in. Both admitted the shooting but neither would say who had contracted them. Now the wheeling and dealing with Fisher began.

On 4 May 1983, whilst he was on remand in Armley prison, Leeds, he was visited by senior officers who were convinced that the shooting of Davies was linked not only to the alloy frauds but also to the attack on Elkington. There was no thought in their minds that he had been involved in the Elkington shooting, but rather that he might now be prepared to give some information. Fisher, quite independently, had himself asked to see the police; it was then that he indicated he could give further information about the shooting of Davies. He also went on to say that he had taken part in a mock burglary of a public house for insurance purposes, and that he could and would name a police officer whom he claimed was corrupt. Now he wanted guarantees and a promise that he would be looked after. In return he said he was prepared to offer a good deal of information about Yorkshire crime and criminals, in particular violent ones.

Not surprisingly, Fisher had heard of what the police delicately called Resident Police Informers and clearly had in mind the possibility of becoming a supergrass. He was, it seems, told that subject to the approval of the Director of Public Prosecutions he might qualify, and that a new identity and address would be provided for him. Not surprisingly, the police wanted to hear something worthwhile before they put his case to the DPP. Matters were left in the air, with Fisher saying that he wished first to speak with his solicitor.

By 10 June when he was seen again, this time with his solicitor present, Fisher was convinced he had been promised immunity and a fresh identity, an idea of which he was swiftly disabused. It was made clear that the only time he would get immunity was with the approval of the DPP and that first he, Fisher, had to decide to supply the information in writing and agree to give evidence. Nor was there any change for Fisher in his suggestion that the *s.* 18 Offences Against the Person Act 1861 charge of wounding Davies (which carried life imprisonment) could be whittled down to a *s.* 20 OAPA offence which attracted a maximum of five years. Some of the police thought he was doing well not to be charged with attempted murder in the first place. Stalemate had been reached and Fisher decided not to proceed with the negotiations.

His trial at Doncaster Crown Court on 15 July was not a successful one from his point of view. Apparently given a short time to reconsider his position before he was sentenced, he failed to take heed and received eight years. Walker went down for five. On 20 July the police were back seeing him again in Leeds prison. Fisher had lodged an appeal and the length of his sentence was sinking in. Would the police help in his appeal if he gave the name of his employer for the Davies' shooting? He was nothing if not a trier. What about residency status? As for the first, the answer was that any help he gave would be mentioned to the Court of Appeal. As for the second, he had really burned his boats. In the experience of the police the Director had only been gracious enough to accord that status to the unconvicted. But there was at least one crumb of comfort still on the table, in that the DPP might agree that any other offence to which Fisher cared to admit might be written off. But he had to commit himself first. He hummed and hawed and eventually named Colin Widdowson as his contractor. He also went on to give at least some details of his own previous criminal activities, but sensibly he would put nothing in writing until he was moved from Leeds. Arrangements were made for him to be transferred to Liverpool in the next few weeks.

Whilst the police were speaking with Fisher, a message came that he had a domestic visit from his girlfriend Jenny.[1] He said that she would co-operate, and after her visit to him the police saw both her and another woman who told them Fisher had indeed said they were to help them. The police took Jenny back to Sheffield and learned that she was seeing Widdowson regularly, and that he had deposited some jewellery worth £5,000 as security for payment of the contract. The jewellery was recovered from the house of a third party. Sadly, Fisher seems to have been short-changed; the jewellery was found to be worth only half the amount he thought.

Now the police encouraged Jenny to continue to see Widdowson, surveilling the meetings and obtaining the money handed over. She was fitted with a tape-recorder. Keeping their part of the agreement, the police went to see a member of the staff of the Director of Public Prosecutions. The outcome was clear. There was to be no residential status for Fisher, but if a statement was taken, although he would not be granted immunity it was more than likely that no further proceedings would be instituted against him – if for no other reason than because of the eight years he was already serving.

In August and September Fisher made lengthy confessions about his involvement with Widdowson and other Yorkshire criminals. It was accepted that without his co-operation and that of his girlfriend there would be no real prospects of a successful prosecution of Widdowson. The police agreed that if the court permitted it an officer would tell the Court of Appeal about his help. It was now that, from everyone's point of view, things started to go wrong. The police wrote to the court and the DPP telling of Fisher's help. Fisher's application to a single judge for leave to appeal against his sentence was refused and, worse, the

1 A pseudonym.

various parties learned of this only through a piece in the local newspaper. The police went to see him to try to reassure him that so far as they were concerned there was no going back on the arrangements; they would, they said, be telling the full Court of Appeal about his assistance.[2] In any event there would be help after his release to re-settle both him and his girlfriend.

Fisher continued to show a measure of good faith. He persuaded another prisoner to turn Queen's Evidence and this man was granted residential status by the DPP, something which rankled badly. Unfortunately, however, Fisher had not come entirely clean, having omitted his involvement (with his brother-in-law and some others) in a nasty robbery in which an elderly lady was tied up and relieved of her possessions. It all came to light and when the matter was put to him specifically, Fisher admitted his part. Once more he was too late. Had he been more frank, this would have qualified for immunity.

The police now seem to have tried to persuade the DPP not to prosecute, but they were unsuccessful. After an inspector had outlined his help, Fisher received four years at the Sheffield Crown Court; this sentence was, however, made concurrent with his longer term. From his point of view there was worse to come. The police were not notified of the renewed application for leave to appeal and it was dismissed in February 1984. Once more the local press seem to have had better connections than the authorities, who learned of the dismissal only by reading the newspapers. Their attempt to have the appeal re-opened was unsuccessful. Fisher was effectively left with the Local Review Committee and the full Parole Board to do something about how long he actually served.

There were now complaints that the police had pushed

2 Generally the procedure is for a convicted person to apply to a single judge for leave to appeal against his conviction. This is done in writing and, if granted, there is a full hearing in which the prisoner is legally represented and legal aid is given. If the single judge refuses the application, the prisoner can renew the application which is almost invariably treated as the appeal itself. He can be legally represented if he has the money to pay for a solicitor and barrister. In these circumstances, however, if the application is again rejected he is at risk of losing some of his remission.

Jenny into helping them with Widdowson, something they vehemently denied. Fisher was also worried that she was having a hard time with the local faces. It was arranged that she should be moved to an address well out of the locality but she declined, suggesting a seaside resort more to her liking. Take it or leave it, she and Fisher were told. There would, however, still be the opportunity for help after his release.

In the end, some eight months before his sentence was due to finish, Fisher was told one morning to collect his clothes from the gate; he was being released. Apart from a payment of £500 and the provision of a new name, few arrangements had been made for any rehabilitation on his release; for some time he wandered about Sheffield, in theory under his new name but in reality mixing with his former friends. He and his girlfriend eventually left the area. Widdowson pleaded guilty and received an eight-year sentence; because he had pleaded guilty there was no need for Fisher to give evidence.

As for the metals case itself William Kelsey, a sixty-four-year-old managing director, was jailed for seven and a half years; Graham Storr, the detective sergeant mentioned by Fisher, received a five-year sentence and Bob Green, described as 'one of the blackest villains in South Yorkshire', received four and a half years for his crimes including a conspiracy to commit arson at a private school.

Mr Justice Glidewell told the jury, 'You must have wondered whether you were hearing about Sheffield or Sicily at times during this trial.'

8

The American Infiltrators

One of the earliest and most remarkable police-cum-private detective infiltrators was the Irish-born James McParland, who in 1873 managed to infiltrate and, effectively single-handedly, destroy the Irish-organised secret society – or terrorist group, say their detractors – the Molly Maguires, who were causing havoc in the coalfields of Eastern Pennsylvania. In a two-year operation he lived in the community, sending weekly messages back to the Pinkerton detective agency for whom he worked.

On 8 September 1867 McParland, an Ulsterman, arrived in America via England where he had worked in a factory in Gateshead. He worked throughout the Midwest as a stevedore, boxer, barman, labourer and bodyguard before signing up with the Chicago police, after which he joined Allan Pinkerton in his detective agency in the early 1870s. He was about 5 foot 7 tall, and weighed just over 10 stone, was a good card player, dancer, singer and one who could drink with the best.

It was through Pinkerton, often regarded as the father of undercover police work, that he was sent to infiltrate the Molly Maguires, who had taken their name from the apocryphal leader of an early Irish Land Reform group.[1]

1 In *The Pinkertons*, Richard Rowan suggests their name derives from their wearing women's clothing when carrying out raids. Trench, in his *Realities of Irish Life*, suggests that the name derives from their other habit of meting out duckings and lashings, traditional punishments for women, to their victims. The Maguires were also known as the Ribbon Men, the White Boys and the Buckshots.

At the time the conditions in the Pennsylvania coalfields under which the mainly Irish immigrants worked were some of the worst in America. Apart from the relatively short period of the Civil War when coal was needed urgently, miners in Pennsylvania rarely worked a full week. Their hours at the pits may have totalled fourteen a day, but they were worked for half a dollar. The general conditions were dreadful with a shack in a 'patch', a 'cluster of a few dozen company houses along a crooked, unpaved street, built within the shadow of a towering colliery'.[2] They were obliged to buy goods, usually on credit, at what was known as a 'pluck me', the company-owned store where goods had a 20 per cent mark-up. Given that many of the miners and their families were illiterate, there was considerable scope for further mark-ups. If a complaint was made, or if a miner declined to deal at the 'pluck me', then he would simply be blacklisted and there would be no work for him in Eastern Pennsylvania. A further torment and insult was the contrast of the clean and well-furnished three-storey home of the mine supervisor – almost invariably a Welshman or Scotsman.

The Molly Maguires, no more than a loose association of interests at first, was probably founded in a bar in Cass Township, Schuykill County, run by a Jeremiah Reilly. One story is that the organisation came about because Reilly's daughter and the local priest were roughed up by Welsh and English (and therefore Protestant) miners as the girl drove the priest through Yorkville home to Pottsville. There were reprisals in the form of a beating for the Protestant miners, and from there the communality of interests spread. By the 1850s the only group prepared, or capable, of taking on the mine-owners was the Molly Maguires. In many ways the structure was the same as in the Irish land troubles of two decades earlier. The mine-owners themselves were absent, as were the English from Ireland. In their place the oppressors were the Scots and the Welsh overseers.

2 Arthur H. Lewis, *A Lament for the Molly Maguires*, p. 7. He uses the spelling McParlan for the infiltrating detective, but the more usual is that given.

From 1862 to 1865 there were some 142 unsolved murders and 212 serious assaults, most of which went unpunished in Schuykill County. The victims were mine superintendents, supervisors, foremen and those known to be disloyal to the Mollies. By 1873 their grip on the six Pennsylvania counties appeared invincible, and it was the Molly-organised so-called Long Strike in 1874–75 which led the owners to determine to destroy them.

One of the people who stood to benefit most from the destruction of the Mollies was Franklin B. Gowen, a lawyer and former district attorney in Schuykill County. He was also President of the Philadelphia and Reading Railroad Company and, as such, was hostile to labour organisation – equating, not always incorrectly, crime with labour leadership. Coleman sees the double thrust by Gowen of the destruction of the Maguires and a blow to organised labour as a way of redeeming himself in the eyes of his stockholders, whose shares were not performing well.[3] Gowen is described as being:

> Forceful, courageous, and daring with a personal magnetism that proved well-nigh irresistible even when his arguments were obviously preposterous; his greatest weakness was an incorrigible optimism and an apparent unwillingness to conform his larger projects to the practical necessities of the moment.[4]

Probably he recognised that the vast majority of the coalface workers were browbeaten and down-trodden, unable and unwilling to improve their lot. His wrath was reserved for those who sought to do so.

> I say here, willingly and gladly that the great majority – I believe ninety-five out of every one hundred – of

3 J. Walter Coleman, *The Molly Maguire Riots*, p. 71.
4 Jules I. Bogen, *The Anthracite Railroads*, p. 51.

the men employed about the mines in the coal region
are decent, orderly, law-abiding, respectable men; but
there is among them a class of agitators . . . brought
here for no other purpose than to create confusion, to
undermine confidence, and to stir up dissension between
the employer and the employed.

I have printed for your use a statement . . . of the
outrages in the coal region . . . These outrages are
perpetrated for no other purpose than to intimidate the
workingmen themselves and to prevent them from going
to work.[5]

Those men were the Molly Maguires, of whom their undoubted
leader at the time was John 'Black Jack' Kehoe. Gowen
recognised only too well that the collection of evidence
sufficient to secure a conviction in the coalfield counties
would be difficult, and he consulted Allan Pinkerton.[6] In
Rowan's *The Pinkertons* there is a dramatic account of the
meeting between Franklin B. Gowen and Allan Pinkerton, the
head of the agency, which establishes the ground rules for an
undercover agent. A high-flown passage sets out the qualities
required of such a man:

He'll have to be Irish born, of course, and a Catholic

5 F. B. Gowen, *Argument before the Pennsylvania Legislative Committee*,
pp. 78–86.
6 Allan Pinkerton was the founder of the celebrated detective agency. Born in
Scotland in 1819, ironically he had fled to America in 1842 to avoid arrest
for his part in labour reform agitations. An ardent abolitionist, he had helped to
organise the underground railroad which smuggled runaway slaves to Canada.
He joined the Chicago Police and, after destroying a gang of counterfeiters, had
set up the agency. He continued to take part in the railroad movement and at
one time sheltered John Brown and eleven runaway slaves. He saved Lincoln
from an assassination plot he had uncovered, and during the Civil War was in
charge of the Union secret service operations. After the war he was involved in an
abortive effort to capture the James gang. After a Pinkerton agent was killed, the
agency led a posse to the gang's hideout and killed James' eight-year-old brother.
Pinkerton died in 1884 and the agency was carried on by his sons, William and
Robert. The agency became increasingly active in anti-labour activities, and
obtained a poor reputation following a number of unsavoury episodes including
the breaking of the strike of Texas and Pacific Railroad in 1888. Once more,
spies were used to infiltrate the strikers.

– brave, cool-headed, just about as smart a lad as ever came over the seas. He'll need to work as a miner, and that takes a strong constitution. And he must have his eye peeled every minute to keep from betraying his purpose to the cunning rascals he's sent out to get.

Pinkerton continues:

When the time comes for public prosecution, my operative must not be expected to give testimony in court – unless present circumstances are greatly altered . . . And since we've no idea who's who in the Molly Society I urge you, sir, to guard against spies. So many people are deathly afraid of these ruffians, someone might turn informer to curry favour with them.

Keep no record of this meeting, or of any future dealings with me or the Agency. Avoid everything that even suggests 'detective' – for at least one man's life, and the whole outcome of our enterprise, will be staked upon absolute secrecy. Whether my organisation is kept on the job a week, a month, or a year or more, this sort of caution must be maintained by us all to the end.[7]

Cover appears to have been arranged in the agency. The story was put about that McParland was going abroad to England, both for health reasons and to try to break a forgery ring. Instead he went to Philadelphia, where he hung around the dock area acclimatising himself until on Monday 27 October 1873, now using the name James McKenna, he took a train to Port Clinton, Pennsylvania. It was from there that he was directed to Tamaqua and Mahanoy City which was where most of the state's coal was being produced. At a boarding-house where he lodged, he was apparently warned to keep away

7 Richard W. Rowan, *The Pinkertons*, pp. 203–4.

from Pat Dormer's bar; Dormer, it was said, was 'captain of the Sleepers'. McParland appears to have made straight for the tavern where by his account he first danced and then played cards, caught one of the men cheating, took part in a bare-knuckle fight which he won in short order, and by using the phrase 'Here's to the power that makes English landlords tremble' indicated that he had been a Ribbon man back home and would like to re-join in America. It seems that when he was questioned about the Ancient Order of Hibernians, some of whose lodges were in the control of the Maguires – and about which, if genuine, he should know – he feigned drunkenness and slumped on a bench so putting an end to the questioning.

He was advised by Dormer, who seems to have been completely taken in by McParland, to travel to Shenandoah to see the powerful Mike Lawler. He made his way there in stages only to find Lawler had gone to Pottsville. It was 21 January 1874 before he met the bodymaster of the Shenandoah Lodge. His supply of cash was something to be explained and he gave out that he was peddling counterfeit Confederate money. His explanation brought him entry to the Lawler household, with whom he lodged from the next month, and he began work in the mines late in February.

In the first week of March he crushed his hand in an accident and was transferred to a shovelling job. Here he met Frank McAndrew, a man whom he admired and who was a rival of Lawler for the position of bodymaster. By the end of March 1874 men were being laid off and McParland was advised to go to Wilkes-Barre. He told Lawler, and was persuaded to stay on the promise of election into the Maguires in return for his support in Lawler's re-election campaign. McParland was also adroit at training fighting-cocks and was in charge of Lawler's stable. On 14 April 1874 he was initiated into the Ancient Order of Hibernians.

Quite apart from the initiation oath, the Order had all the trappings beloved by a secret society. A personal recognition was made by putting the tip of the right-hand little finger to the outer corner of the right eye. The response was made by catching the right lapel of the vest or coat with the little finger and thumb of the right hand. If the sign was obscured, then an elaborate drinking toast was proposed: 'The Emperor of France and Don Carlos of Spain'. This must have served anonymity well in miners' bars in deepest Pennsylvania. The response was: 'May unite together and the people's rights maintain'. There were also passwords to be used when entering a division, and a bond phrase to prevent members who did not realise they were arguing with their own from actually coming to blows. 'Your temper is high' was to be answered with 'I have good reason'. It is amazing that they thought non-members would not realise something was up.[8]

McParland must have been a genuinely ingratiating man because when the election came up in July and was won by McAndrew, McParland became secretary to the illiterate bodymaster. It had taken him just over nine months since leaving Philadelphia to obtain this position of power. It appears that McAndrew was not the forceful person hoped for, and there was a campaign for McParland himself to become bodymaster. Before he achieved that dubious honour he would certainly have had to carry out a beating, if not an actual killing. He continued his pretence that he was unreliable in drink, indulging so much that he broke his health with bad liquor; his hair fell out and he bought a wig. Now he was excluded from every decent hotel and bar. Later his eyesight began to fail.

On 18 November 1874 six people were killed as the Maguires stepped up their campaign of intimidation and took reprisals against strike-breaking miners. Throughout the winter McParland appears to have done what he could to dissuade the leaders from this escalating campaign of violence and in April 1875, on the pretext of attending his sister's wedding, he returned to Chicago to see Pinkerton. Now more men were sent to the Pennsylvania coalfields, not as undercover men but

8 The phrases are from the testimony of James McParland reported in *The Pottsville Miner's Journal*, 9 May 1876.

as recruits to the Coal and Iron Police. One of them, Captain Robert Linden, claimed to be an old friend of McParland from Buffalo, now promoted to be in charge of the Shenandoah division of the Mollies, and was used as a go-between.

Part of McParland's undoubted charm seems to have been towards women and he had genuinely become involved with Mary Ann Higgins, whom he met at a Polish wedding. She was the sister-in-law of James Kerrigan, the Mollies' bodymaster at Tamaqua. In the summer of 1875 McParland's difficulties were compounded when Kerrigan ambushed and killed a policeman, Benjamin Yost, as he lit a street-lamp. McParland was also coming under increasing pressure to arrange the assassination of Gomer James, a Welsh miner who was believed to have killed an Irishman. McParland maintained that he sent messages of warning to James and delayed nominating a killer, together with a time and place, by pretending to be drunk.

On 2 June the striking miners paraded and marched towards those collieries still open. These shut down, not re-opening until August. On 14 August the men received their first pay and James was shot and killed. The real killer left the state, but the reward money of $10 paid for the murder was claimed by Thomas Hurley, a Shenandoahan.

In early 1876 matters came to a head. On 18 January two Mollies, Michael J. Doyle and Edward Kelly, were indicted with the killing of a John P. Jones, a manager who had treated one of the Mollies badly. Supervising the killing had been Kerrigan, who now elected to turn States' evidence. His line was that he had been something of a reluctant bystander drawn into the brotherhood, and afraid for his wife and family if he should try to leave. No, he had never taken part in any killing. As Doyle's trial proceeded to a 'guilty' verdict, Kerrigan began to sing loudly to the authorities; his statement ran to 210 pages.

On 5 February seven Mollies were arrested and charged with complicity in the murder of John P. Jones and that of patrolman Benjamin Yost.

The life of Williams *(private collection)*

Ducking and diving - The life of O'Mahoney
(Enterprise News)

The four faces of Chrastney
("PA" Photo Library)

Nothing but the truth -
Joe Valachi testifies
(Camera Press Ltd)

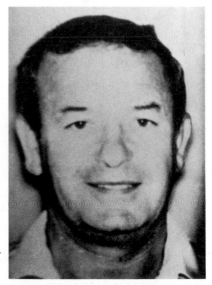

South Londoner, Roy Garner
("PA" Photo Library)

Well it's actually Leroy Davis
(Express Newspapers)

Fat Vinney
(Associated Press)

The Kray Consiglieri - Leslie Payne
(private collection)

At last Roger Dennhardt is happy
with things
(Syndication International)

Nipper Read brought the Krays to justice
(Popperfoto)

Keeping stumm
(S&G Press Agency)

Birth of a legend - Derek 'Bertie' Smalls flanked by
detectives *(London News Service)*

D.C.S. Jack Slipper and D.I. Peter Jones
return from Brazil - without Ronald Biggs
(Syndication International)

Still smiling -
Ronald Biggs in Brazil
(Syndication International)

According to Rowan,[9] Pinkerton had published lists of members of the Molly Maguires in local newspapers and rumour of a spy abounded in the organisation. Now was the time for McParland to be protected; his real identity was in danger of being revealed and he had been seen in Philadelphia, and there was the possibility that a priest also betrayed him. Pinkerton's idea was not, however, to pull him out of the danger zone but was for him to be arrested so that, with suspicion diverted, he could continue his operations.

When 'Black Jack' Kehoe called a meeting to denounce McParland, this precipitated the end of his work. It was arranged that this meeting should be at Ferguson's Hall in Shenandoah, where McParland would be given an opportunity to defend himself against the accusations. However, he saw it as a manoeuvre to keep him in the area and under observation. McAndrew, who had travelled back to the meeting to defend his protégé, suggested that they burn the books of the organisation, and this they did.

The next morning, 1 March, two men called at his lodgings saying they had arrived from Scranton. McParland realised that they were his appointed killers – the Scranton train was not yet scheduled. He drove with them in a sleigh to see Kehoe who, the story goes, was sitting down with his friends for a liquid breakfast to celebrate McParland's death. There he learned that it was a Father O'Connor who had put it about that he was a spy, and he demanded to go and see him and hear this from his own lips. The priest had gone to Pittston, however, and McParland now insisted on sending a telegram calling for an explanation. He went to the station, where he ostensibly began to complete a telegram while waiting for a train.

Other Pinkerton men were on the alert and Robert Linden had seen McParland at the station, suspected what he might be doing, and got on board the Scranton train to give help if he could. He could not, for McParland managed by himself. As

9 *Ibid.* pp. 218 *et seq.*

the train was drawing out, McParland said that he must go and see the priest in person and, making his escape, leaped into a carriage.

Another less dramatic version is that McParland went with McAndrew in a sleigh to confront Kehoe before the meeting, and after quarrelling with him turned his back on him and left in the sleigh before catching the train for Frackville, on which he met Linden in the smoking compartment.

> I knew there'd be no bullet in my back. Kehoe was a man even if he was a bad one. He really believed he was a kind of Robin Hood. Now I'm not tryin' to excuse what he did but maybe things'd been different, he could have been a leader of a decent group of miners fightin' for their rights instead of headin' a pack of killers.[10]

Whichever is the correct account, or if there is another somewhere between, amazingly – despite this extraordinary behaviour – the Mollies were not completely convinced of his deception. Kehoe stood his ground.

On 4 May 1876 the trial began of four Mollies – James Carroll, James Roarity, James Boyle and Hugh McGehan – charged with the murder of Yost. The next day John Kehoe, together with three Schuykill bodymasters and five other Mollies, was arrested. The organisation was broken.

McParland first gave evidence in the trial for the murder of Yost. It was, wrote William Linn, a trial observer, a complete shock when he walked down the aisle of the court.

> This was a complete surprise, not only to the Mollies, but to the public which had not hitherto known of his existence. This feeling of surprise deepened into one of wonder and amazement when . . . with perfect coolness

10 Arthur H. Lewis, *A Lament for the Molly Maguires*, p. 240.

and deliberation he told in detail the story of his career among the Mollies.

When he told of being suspected as a detective and related his interviews with his intended assassins, his escapes, etc., judges, jury, counsel, and audience listened with breathless attention; and so completely spellbound were all these by his recital of things the existence of which had not been thought possible, that at anytime the falling of a pin might be heard in the densely crowded room. Much of this narrative which was not relevant was not objected to by counsel for the defendants because of the intense interest they evidently felt.[11]

His evidence continued in a series of trials which led to the conviction of some sixty men including the leader John 'Black Jack' Kehoe. McParland's version of his participation was that he was a bystander who, although he knew of the proposed murders, could not warn the victims or his agency in case he himself was killed. Without success the defence lawyers put it that McParland was an *agent provocateur*. Looking back, Terence Powderley wrote:

. . . that plague spot on American civilisation, the Pinkerton detective, had entered the council chambers of the workingmen of Schuykill County, and, under the guise of friendship, urged the men on to deeds of desperation and blood.[12]

Eleven of the Maguires were hanged and a further fifty-nine were convicted of various offences. One of them, Alec

11 Quoted in *ibid*. p. 240.
12 Terence Powderley, 'The Homestead Strike: A Knight of Labor's View' in *North American Review* 155 (September 1892), pp. 370–75.

Campbell, who owned a bar and was said to have been a bodymaster and to have supplied the gun which killed Jones, continually protested his innocence. On 21 June 1877, as he was taken from his cell in Maunch Chunk jail to the scaffold,

> . . . as if to impress the sheriff with the truth of his protest Campbell bent over, ground his right hand in the dust on the cell floor, and dragging his ball and chain after him took a long stride towards the wall. Then stretching himself to the full height, he smote the wall with his large hand. 'There is the proof of my words,' he said, 'that mark of mine will never be wiped out. There it will remain forever to shame the county that is hanging an innocent man.'
>
> They hanged Campbell that morning, but the imprint of his hand stood out from the wall like truth itself. In vain did the sheriff try to remove it. Succeeding sheriffs also failed. Campbell apparently was right.[13]

The imprint remained until the 1930s, by which time it had become a major tourist attraction. The cell was then replastered.

McParland subsequently travelled west to Colorado where he became head of the Denver branch of the Pinkerton agency. His work in infiltrating the Mollies was acclaimed throughout America and formed the basis of the first Sherlock Holmes' novel, *The Valley of Fear*. Over the years, however, his role has been substantially re-assessed. This began in 1906 with the trial in Boise, Ohio, of Harry Orchard, 'Big' Bill Haywood, George Pettibone and Charles Moyer, the last three of whom were leading members of the Western Federation of Miners.

13 George Korson in *Minstrels of the Mine Patch: Songs and Stories of the Anthracite Industry*.

Haywood went on to become a leading light in the Industrial Workers of the World.[14]

On 30 December 1905 Frank Steunenberg, a former governor of Idaho, had been killed by a bomb attached to his front gate. McParland found two informers, Steve Adams and Harry Orchard, whose confessions led to the arrest of Haywood, Pettibone and Moyer. Adams later withdrew his confession, insisting that his statement was false and had been Pinkerton-inspired.

Orchard, whose real name was Albert F. Horsley, maintained that he had received the bombing instructions from Haywood. Leaving aside the Steunenberg case, Orchard was a self-confessed killer. He had carried out a number of bombings for the Western Federation of Miners, including one in which fourteen non-union members died in an explosion in June 1904, and had probably been involved in other attempts on the Governor's life.

The great lawyer Clarence Darrow, appearing for the defence, created great inroads into Orchard's written confession in which corrections were probably in McParland's handwriting. There were good reasons for Orchard's killing of Steunenberg; in 1899 the then Governor had driven him out of Coeur d'Alene in Idaho, so depriving him of a one-sixteenth share of a mine which would have made him a millionaire. As for the implication of Haywood and the others, it is thought that this was either part and parcel of a power struggle amongst the leadership of the Western Federation

---

14 Known as the Wobblies, this early form of militant American trade union flourished in the first two decades of the twentieth century. The height of its fame came in 1915 with the execution by a firing squad in Utah of one of their leaders, Joe Hill, for murder. The IWW was able to mount international, if ultimately unsuccessful, support including a demonstration of 30,000 workers in Australia for clemency. Hill's last words were said to be, 'Don't mourn, organise.' After his death the influence of the IWW faded quickly and effectively disintegrated with the arrest of their leaders including 'Big' Bill Hayward for sedition in 1920 in the so-called Palmer raids. Haywood was released pending his appeal on bail of $30,000, but fled to the Soviet Union, where he died in the Hotel Lux, Moscow, on 18 May 1928. The Wobblies still maintain a small presence in San Francisco and Denver.

or, more likely, was inspired by the mine-owners. The three Wobblies were acquitted, with Orchard's death sentence being commuted to life imprisonment. Later he petitioned William A. Pinkerton, then head of the agency, to help him obtain parole. Rather contrary to the agency's usual practice of helping their informers whether a conviction had been obtained or not, Pinkerton refused, writing in a memorandum:

I know that McParland always thought Orchard should have been released for testifying, but I still regard Orchard as a cold-blooded murderer who killed many innocent persons and who testified only to save his own skin.

In fact, Orchard was never released, dying in prison on 13 April 1954 at the age of eighty-six. By accounts he was treated as something over and above the ordinary prisoner. Early in his imprisonment he had a room fitted with electricity, and Charles Steunenberg recalled:

Private parties gave him the money with which to buy machinery; the state permitted him to use convict labour for his own private enterprise in which he manufactured shoes for prominent people in Idaho and rolled up a cash reserve of $10,000.

By 1943 Orchard was keeping a chicken farm, although he would tell visitors that he 'just can't bring himself to kill a chicken'. He was described as still fat and sleek, oily-eyed and unctuous. He complained if anyone wished to clear up the 1905 record, and told Irving Stone: 'The trouble with you writers is that you never come here to write about me. You always want to use me to write about somebody else!'[15]

15 Irving Stone, *Clarence Darrow for the Defense*, p. 229.

The incident gets scant mention in Rowan's adulatory account of the Pinkerton agency, which suggests that Haywood and company were imprisoned. Indeed they were, although not quite in the way suggested by Rowan. Pinkerton agents had captured the men in Denver and put them on a special train to Boise, Idaho, where they were kept on death row until their trial. Nor is there any substantial reassessment in the rather more scholarly *The Eye that Never Sleeps*, in which Frank Morn drily comments: 'Third degree methods on Orchard soon produced enough evidence for McParlan [sic] to arrest the three labour leaders and spirit them away to Idaho.'[16]

One Pinkerton man, the stenographer Morris Friedman, was so disenchanted with the affair that he left the agency and wrote his own memoirs, *The Pinkerton Labor Spy*, in which he saw the Pinkerton management as a public menace masquerading as a public necessity and something not far from the Russian Secret Police.

His memoirs did not please the heads of the Pinkerton agency, and operatives who subsequently tried their hands at unauthorised and therefore unadulatory reminiscences found themselves in considerable difficulties. When Charles Siringo wrote *Pinkerton's Cowboy Detective*, he was forced to change the title to *The Cowboy Detective*; Pinkerton becomes Dickenson and Tom Horn, the range-rider and another operative, appears as Tom Corn. There was worse to come. In 1914 Siringo wrote *Two Evil Isms* and sent the manuscript to the agency for approval. Unsurprisingly, since one of the evil isms was Pinkertonism, the Pinkerton management disapproved of the whole concept, took Siringo to court and the printing plates were confiscated.

If the score between McParland and the mineworkers apparently stood at one-all, it was changed when, in January 1979, Kehoe was officially pardoned by the State of Pennsylvania.

16 Frank Morn, *The Eye that Never Sleeps*, p. 158.

As for McParland, the remainder of his life was not a happy one. Shortly after the Haywood fiasco he retired; he married twice and died in the Mercy Hospital, Denver, in 1918. In the last years of his life he had lost a leg and an eye, possibly through drink and diabetes. He had had high walls built around his Denver home and inside the walls had attack dogs always on the loose. Apparently he was in constant fear of being assassinated by descendants of the Molly Maguires:

> In addition, he had bars put on all the lower windows and has a hand gun on every table in the house. He also carried a gun constantly and got up frequently during the night to patrol the house.[17]

Whatever is the truth about the part McParland played in the year and a half when he was actively involved with the Maguires, his feat as an undercover operator – using his landlady's bag of dolly-blue to make ink and sending weekly messages back to Chicago – is one of the great feats of undercover detection and infiltration.

While he may have been the greatest of the early non-military infiltrators, McParland was neither the first nor by any means the last deep-cover man used by the Pinkertons. It was suggested that he was an *agent provocateur*, and it was certainly the case with other deep-cover men that they carried on their own trade side by side with the detective duties.

In 1888 Charles Siringo worked in the Denver office under the aegis of the former safe-blower Doc Williams, and the men cordially disliked each other. His preference was for outdoor investigation rather than office work; he became an undercover man in a Wyoming cowboy gang, and it was his testimony which later had them convicted. In 1889

17 Catherine McParland Schick, quoted by Patrick Campbell in *A Molly Maguire Story*, p. 187.

Eams, a senior man in the Denver office, was caught in a scam charging clients for work not done and pocketing the proceeds. The agency then brought in the gunfighter Tom Horn as an operative.

In 1892 Siringo went deep under cover and, under the name of C. Leon Allison, infiltrated the mining unions in the northern Idaho minefields, becoming a friend of George Pettibone and yet – as McParland had done a decade earlier – all the time sending reports on the union plots. His double role was discovered and he escaped to the hills, returning to town only to give evidence.

One of the mine-owners, John Hammond, recalls Siringo's reappearance.

[He and Siringo] walked together down the middle of the road, each of us carrying two pistols in our coat pockets. There was a running fire of comment from miners on the sidewalk as they expressed their hatred for Siringo in no uncertain language. As he walked, Siringo kept his hands in his pockets. The outline of his guns could clearly be seen as he swayed ominously from side to side.[18]

Eighteen union leaders including Pettibone were jailed.

Siringo had long been a master undercover man. In his younger days he had chased Billy the Kid, losing him when he was cleaned out of his money in a card game, and also had travelled through Indian territory to claim a suspect. In New Mexico he contracted smallpox, which left his face badly pitted. He had posed as a wanted man to persuade Elfie Landusky, a Hole-in-the-Waller, to tell him where Harvey Logan was hiding. After he retired, apart from the indictment of the Pinkertons he wrote a number of fairly

18 John Hays Hammond, *The Autobiography of John Hays Hammond*, Volume 1, p. 195.

successful cowboy thrillers, but died in what were described as poor circumstances in Los Angeles in 1928.[19]

Tom Horn was another of the undercover agents, but this time one whose personal interests were not at odds with those of the agency. He had been an Indian fighter and army scout before he arrived in Denver in 1890 with what were described as impeccable references. For the next few years he was the Pinkerton's Rocky Mountain operative, making a number of arrests of train robbers and cattle-rustlers, killing a number as well. He took time to commit a robbery for himself in Nevada, and was protected by the agency. Siringo wrote:

. . . on one of his trips to Denver, William A. Pinkerton [one of the sons] told me that Tom Horn was guilty of the crime but that his people could not afford to let him go to the penitentiary while in their employ.[20]

Despite the protection, let alone the salary the agency offered, Horn felt tied down and resigned in 1894, becoming a freelance detective and hired gun of the Wyoming Cattlemen's Association. He is described as a tidy, patient and skilful murderer. He would wait hours in driving rain, chewing bacon fat, to ensure he had the one necessary clear shot at his target. After each killing he would leave a stone under the head of his victim so there was no doubt as to the killer. However, in 1901 he made

19 Located in Wyoming, Hole-in-the-Wall was one of the best-known Western safe hideouts. A Hole-in-the-Waller was synonymous with being a member of the Wild Bunch. Harvey Logan, better known as Kid Curry, a notorious member of the Wild Bunch, was widely regarded as one of the more vicious killers of the West. In 1904 he broke out of Knoxville jail after strangling one of the guards and, according to the Pinkertons, formed a new gang in Colorado. He is said to have travelled 1,400 miles in a twelve-day period before being cornered in Glenwood Springs, where he shot himself. He was identified by Pinkerton agents, although the identification was hotly disputed by other agencies including the Union Pacific. His photograph was sent back to Knoxville, where the recognition was confirmed. The alternate and more romantic theory is that he did not go to Colorado but rejoined Butch Cassidy and Harry Longbaugh in Columbia. C. Sifakis, *The Encyclopedia of American Crime* (1982), p. 394.
20 C. Siringo, *Two Evil Isms*, p. 46.

what proved to be a fatal error when he killed fourteen-year-old Willie Nickell, the son of a sheep-farmer, mistaking him in poor light for his father.

For two years, partly because of Horn's powerful protectors, the murder remained unsolved. His eventual undoing was another semi-undercover man, Joe Lefors, a deputy US marshal who became Horn's confidant and, when the latter was well in drink, obtained from him a bragging confession which he took the precaution of being noted by a hidden shorthand-writer and another witness.

Despite his pleas for help from his former employers and a donation of $5,000 to his defence fund from an unknown admirer, Horn was convicted of murder in 1903. He had tried to impugn the confession, suggesting that what he said was just a tall tale and that the stenographer had added pieces of his own. Whilst awaiting execution he escaped from prison but was quickly recaptured and was hanged on 20 November 1903. In recent years efforts have been made – as has often been the case with outlaws – to rehabilitate Horn. It is said that the confession should have been ruled inadmissible and that, indeed, he was not the youth's killer.[21]

Another of the early infiltrating Pinkerton men, A.W. Gratias, managed to infiltrate the Western Federation of Miners so successfully that he became chairman of the union relief committee in a year and president of his local union a year later. He even attended the annual convention, faithfully returning reports on the union activities to the Denver office. It is hardly surprising that the Pinkerton agency was regarded with both fear and loathing amongst the mineworkers of the West. Their talents did, however, provide an example for any self-respecting infiltrator of the twentieth century.

One of the great success stories of twentieth-century police infiltration was that of Mike Malone, who managed to snuggle

21 Dean Krakel, *The Saga of Tom Horn*.

up close to the great Chicago gangster Al Capone and lived
to tell the tale. In 1930 Capone was under investigation by
the Internal Revenue Service in an operation led by Frank
J. Wilson, and was also being attacked on his flanks with no
greater success by the 'Untouchable', Eliot Ness.

Malone is described as being 'black Irish' and coming from
Jersey City; 5 foot 8 tall, barrel-chested, weighing 200 pounds,
with jet-black hair and a brilliant friendly smile, he could easily
pass as Italian, Jewish or Greek. He and his wife had separated
after the death of their young daughter in a road accident,
and after that he seems to have had little interest in anything
but work.

A long and elaborate cover story was invented detailing his
crime history from Brooklyn. He took a room in the Lexington
Hotel next to one of Capone's bodyguards. Malone, using
the name De Angelo, hung about the hotel lobby until he
was approached and asked his business. He was, he said, a
promotor. Did anyone wish to buy gold bricks?[22]

Malone claimed to have been a member of the feared Five
Points Gang and, it appears, just as the punter who is offered the
chance of taking the gold brick to the jeweller for examination
never does so, his story was never checked out. He obtained
a job in one of Capone's casinos, graduated to head croupier,
drank and played with Capone's men and all the time made

22 The gold brick confidence trick has long been a part of American swindles and
survives even today. Indeed 'to gold brick' has passed into slang as meaning to
malinger. The basis of the trick is that the mug punter buys what he thinks are
gold brick ingots and ends up with worthless brass or lead. The trick almost
certainly started in the Californian Gold Rush and there is some evidence that
Wyatt Earp and Dave Mather were involved in the swindle in Mobeetie, Texas,
in 1878. The con was probably brought to New York in 1889 by the talented
Reed Waddell; his bricks were marked in the manner of a regulation brick from
the US Assayer's Office and the mug was always given the chance – or believed
he had the chance – to take the brick to a jeweller of his choice. Thirteen years
later Waddell was still working the trick with a partner Tom O'Brien. Eventually
in 1895 the two fell out and Waddell was killed by O'Brien. A similar scam
is the Green Goods swindle, another well-known confidence trick in which the
mug punter sees banknotes being 'produced' by a machine. He is then given
the choice of purchasing either a large quantity of banknotes at a substantial
discount on the face price or the machine itself. Although very popular in the
late nineteenth century, it is still occasionally practised today.

reports back to Wilson, including a detailed one on Capone's hit-man Frank 'The Enforcer' Nitti. Shortly after this Malone was invited to attend a banquet at which Capone would be present. At a previous such occasion Capone had beaten one of the guests with a baseball bat; now Malone feared that his cover might be blown and he was to be the next. In the event he thought he was being poisoned when he was served spiced steak which burned his mouth; he called for water and was mocked for not drinking champagne until he explained that he had an ulcer. The rest of the dinner passed without incident and Malone was given a friendly pat on the shoulder by the great man.

Shortly after this, Malone was joined by another agent under the pseudonym of Graziano and they learned of the imminent attack on Wilson who was staying at the Sheridan Plaza under an assumed name. Wilson and his superior feared that Malone had indeed been identified and that his life was in danger. Malone insisted it was not, and that both he and Graziano wished to stay under cover. It was fortunate that they did so, because Malone was able to confirm to Wilson that there was indeed a plot against him and that he and his wife must leave the hotel immediately. Later, when Capone had been indicted and was on bail for the revenue frauds and other offences for which he would eventually receive seventeen years, Malone sent another message that Wilson was again under immediate threat.

Malone met Capone one more time. On Saturday 24 October 1931, when Capone was sent to Leavenworth penitentiary on the night he was sentenced, he met Malone in the lift and recognised him – or at least this is the legend. 'The only thing that fooled me was your looks,' he is reported to have said. 'You look like a Wop. You took your chances, and I took mine.'[23]

23 E. L. Irey and W. Slocum, *The Tax Dodgers: The Inside Story of the T-Men's War with America's Political and Underworld Hoodlums*, p. 65. They had some snappy titles in those days.

But what of Eliot Ness, the man who according to criminal mythology was the one who really brought down Al Capone? Sadly for Wilson, who never had a television series of films made about him, and sadly for Ness, who didn't bring down Capone, he played a much lesser part than has been accorded to him over the years. Was he an infiltrator or even a major figure in the destruction of the crime czar?

Not to any great extent, according to Laurence Bergreen in *Capone*, his biography of the gangster. He considers that Ness was very much a second-division player compared with Wilson in bringing about Capone's downfall. He was a member of the 300-strong staff of the Prohibition Bureau in Chicago and certainly from time to time posed either as a corrupt Prohibition agent or a bootlegger, drinking in a Chicago Heights saloon known as Cozy Corners. It seems he was at one time paid $250 a week by racketeers – something he faithfully turned over to his superiors – but it was, to use a pun, strictly small beer. It was not necessarily without danger, however. Shortly after Ness, along with Italian-speaking agent Burt Napoli who was posing as his chauffeur, paid a business call on Joe Martino, then head of the Unione Siciliano, Napoli was murdered. A suspect was arrested, but the man hanged himself in his cell before he could be effectively questioned. Ness's cover was blown and his undercover work came to a halt.[24]

The Capone era abounds with stories of cross and double-cross. One of the more interesting is that of the double life played out by newspaperman Alfred 'Jake' Lingle, a police reporter for the *Chicago Tribune* who was murdered on

24 The career of Eliot Ness, full of promise and now fictionalised probably beyond recognition, never quite achieved the height to which he aspired; throughout much of his life he was overly attractive to women, with the consequent difficulties that brings, and a drink problem to match. After the Capone trial he became the chief investigator of Prohibition violations in Kentucky and Tennessee, and in 1935 the Public Safety Director in Cleveland. He is credited with ridding the town of the Mayfield Road Mob which at that time controlled prostitution and bootlegging. Unfortunately his heavy drinking involved him in a hit-and-run accident on 5 March 1942. He escaped prosecution, but resigned on 30 April 1942. After the war his career slid further into the depths until he died of a heart attack on 16 May 1957 at the age of fifty-four. Laurence Bergreen, *Capone*, pp. 346–9.

9 June 1930. Known as a courageous reporter who had waged a fearless war against the Underworld, Lingle had left the *Tribune* offices saying that he was going to try to get a story about the Moran gang. He was seen a short time later at the corner of Randolph and Clark, and then heading down Randolph to catch a train to the race-track. His movements are well documented; he stopped to buy a racing paper and then headed for the tunnel to the station. A well-dressed young man walked behind him and shot the reporter through the head; he died still clutching cigar and racing paper.

There was an immediate outcry. Lingle was named as a 'first line soldier' in the fight against crime, and rewards of over $50,000 were posted by his paper and local groups. But things were not quite the way they seemed. It transpired that through his police connections he had the ability to award beer-selling and gambling rights, also that he was into demanding money from brothel-keepers and at the time of his death had been wearing a diamond-studded belt given him by Al Capone. His stock slumped and the *Tribune* was reduced to writing articles denouncing other newspaper reporters, notably Julius Rosenheim of the rival *Chicago Daily News* who had been shot to death a few months previously. He, too, had been blackmailing brothel-keepers.

A year later a penniless small-time gangster, Leo V. Brothers, was charged with and later convicted of shooting Lingle. He was expensively defended with a battery of five counsel led by Louis Piquett, who later defended Dillinger, and received fourteen years. 'I can do that standing on my head,' he is said to have announced after the verdict. Over the years there have been persistent suggestions that he was not the killer at all but had been paid to take the rap. He was released after eight years and died in 1951 without disclosing who had paid him either for the contract or for going to prison, whichever was the case. Brothers had been unearthed by a private detective, John Hagan, who had infiltrated the Moran gang and later Egan's Rats in St Louis to do so.[25]

A rather more honourable part in undercover work was played by Jerry Thompson in July 1979 when he was sent by his editor, John Seigethaler, to work on Nashville's *The Tennessean* to infiltrate the Ku Klux Klan. After a decade of dormancy it became clear that at the end of the 1970s the Klan was staging a resurgence in rural communities near Nashville, and Thompson was sent undercover for a few months. This followed the traditional pattern of undercover work, with Thompson leaving his home and setting up a new life in another town.

As with many undercover operations which are intended to last only for a few months, it extended itself in this case to nearly a year and a half. He and his family paid a high price for the investigation, which ended with Thompson returning to his home more as a guest than a family member, an armed guard, and a lawsuit – claiming $1 million – which he successfully defended. In an afterword to his book his wrote:

> It has been almost a decade now since that story broke, and we are still trying to resolve some of the issues which were raised during that turbulent period of our lives.
>
> From a journalist's standpoint, there is the issue of where my commitment to my job – to a story – begins and where it ends. From the standpoint of being a husband and a father, there is the question of when my responsibilities to my family outweigh my responsibilities to search out and expose the truth.[26]

25 Little is known of Jack Hagan, but Egan's Rats were founded in about 1900 by Jack 'Jellyroll' Egan, principally as strike-breakers. By the 1920s, with unions more firmly established, the members turned to safe-breaking and, once Prohibition was announced, entered the game with enthusiasm. It is suggested that one member, Fred Burke, took part in the St Valentine's Day Massacre in 1929. The gang did not survive the end of the era. Their leader, Dinty Colbeck, was shot and the gang split up in the late 1930s.
26 Jerry Thompson, *My Life in the Klan*, p. 321.

The extended length of successful deep-cover investigations is a problem for all investigators. In more recent times there has been a welter of officers who have gone long-term undercover and who have lived to tell the tale. Reading between the lines, particularly of Joe Pistone's autobiography, *Donnie Brasco*, the name he used in his five-year undercover stint with the New York Mafia, there are long-term deep-cover agents working in most cities in the United States.

His is, perhaps, the most interesting of all the stories, if only for the length of time he spent during a period when techniques for the protection of the agent had not been refined in any way and he was at daily, if not hourly, risk of discovery by the highly volatile crowd with whom he mixed. He had originally been part of a relatively minor FBI operation in Tampa in 1975, working on a ring of car and lorry thieves. How the FBI came to be involved is yet another example of how an informant is born. A teenage boy had been arrested on an unrelated charge and his father volunteered, in return for a non-custodial sentence for his son, to blow the whistle on the team who were operating all over the south-eastern United States, stealing bulldozers, Lincolns, Cadillacs and occasionally aeroplanes. In February 1976 the entire ring, consisting of thirty people, was arrested. From there Pistone became part of the Truck and Hijack Squad in New York and it was only a short, but large, step to take to become Donnie Brasco, jewel thief, looking to hang out with the Mafia.

It took him several months of frequenting a local bar, offering to sell stolen jewellery to the barman, before he was gradually accepted into the milieu. He moved on to a knock-out shop dealing in stolen clothing, and from there was taken up by rival mobsters. In the end he was more or less selected by Benjamin 'Lefty Guns' Ruggiero, connected to the Bonanno family, and groomed by him if not for stardom then at least as high as an outsider could rise in the Mafia. After he left and testified against leading lights in the organisation, a contract of $500,000 was put on his head. The people to whom he was closest in the organisation were also under threat. Tony Mirra, who had at one time wanted to use him on a more permanent basis, was murdered in New York in 1982 six months before Brasco began to testify. Then there was Sonny Black, to whom Brasco admits to having had:

> some uncomfortable feelings . . . I felt a kind of kinship with him. But I didn't feel any guilt of betrayal, because I'd always maintained in my own mind and heart the separation of our worlds. In a sense we were both just doing our jobs.[27]

Black was found, handless, in a hospital body-bag in the Mariner's Harbor section of Staten Island, some five months into the trials of other *mafiosi*.[28]

27 J. D. Pistone, *Donnie Brasco*, p. 365.
28 There have been many other accounts of the lives of former undercover agents. They include Derek Agnew's *Undercover Agent – Narcotics*, and Michael Detroit's *Chain of Evidence* which tells the story of a woman police officer who infiltrated bikers in Southern California. This is particularly interesting because it tells the story not only from her point of view but from that of her handler.

9

Infiltrators – England

There is little doubt that infiltrators have been used in Britain in political and religious intrigues since the Tudors. The use of the infiltrator in the criminal Underworld for non-political purposes is more recent. So far as the former is concerned, the playwright Christopher Marlowe may well have begun his career as a spy by himself being the victim of an informer. His atheism had been reported to the authorities and he may well have taken up the offer to work as a Government spy in order to avoid punishment.

Shortly before the establishment of the New Police, there was another outstanding example of the use of the spy and a cover-up of his operations by the authorities. The history books may show that the Cato Street Conspiracy of 1820 was instigated by Arthur Thistlewood who had fallen under the spell of Tom Paine, the great Republican, and, whilst he lived in France, of Robespierre. A closer examination will also indicate the crucial role played by a government spy to bring the conspiracy to fruition and its disastrous conclusion. Thistlewood had risen in the Army to the rank of lieutenant, and married a lady of some wealth; she died, and possibly he soon gambled away her fortune. Other accounts are that he lost his money by an injudicious loan to a friend. His great desire in life, it seems, was to assassinate the members of the Cabinet

and then seize power. The attack was timed for Wednesday,
23 February 1820, when Lord Harrowby was entertaining the
Cabinet in Grosvenor Square. The idea was that one of the
members of the conspiracy should go to the house to deliver
a parcel and then, when the door opened, the others were to
rush the premises and kill the members of the Cabinet. The
plan was for Lord Castlereagh – then Prime Minister – and
Lord Sidmouth to have their heads cut off. However, the plot
had been infiltrated by a government spy, George Edwards,
who ran a shop near Eton School in which he sold models of
the headmaster which the boys could then use as targets. He
was also employed by Sir Robert Birnie and the Bow Street
magistrates.

Sir Robert Birnie himself led the disabling raid on the conspirators. One Runner, Smithers, was stabbed by Thistlewood
and the conspirators – excepting Edwards, who managed to
disappear – were arrested. At their trial they endeavoured to
make him give evidence and sent depositions indicating his
guilt to Viscount Sidmouth, who refused to issue a warrant.
Edwards escaped, it is said with Government assistance, and
fled first to the Channel Islands and then to the Cape.

There was never likely to be much chance of an acquittal
on the charges laid of high treason, but such as there was
disappeared with Edwards. The defending lawyers argued that
the jury should draw the conclusion from Edwards' absence
that the plot had no foundation in reality, and that if it could
be properly investigated the affair would be shown to be that
of a spy and informer. It was said that the idea of attacking the
Cabinet at dinner was that of Edwards. In his speech before
receiving the death sentence, Thistlewood roundly denounced
the absent Edwards, who he said had

  a plan for blowing up the House of Commons. This was not
  my view: I wished to punish the guilty only, and therefore
  I declined it. He next proposed that we should attack the
  Ministers at the fete given by the Spanish Ambassador.

> This I resolutely opposed . . . there were ladies invited to the entertainment – and I, who am shortly to ascend to the scaffold, shuddered with horror at the idea of that, a sample of which had previously been given by the Agents of Government at Manchester . . .[1]

If Thistlewood was right, and there is much to support his view, here was an *agent provocateur de luxe*.

Three years earlier Samuel Bamford, the eighteenth-century North Country radical, had devised a method to thwart the spy system. He and his fellow prisoners had coached themselves to give a single agreed version of events. Then

> if government brought them to trial, it would have to unmask its spies and informers, instead of making them fall by their mutual contradictions, mistrusts and jealousies which as it seemed to me, the government would prefer doing.[2]

Unfortunately, as is so often the case, one of the defendants, Robert Adams, to save himself from the scaffold broke ranks and gave evidence for the Crown. On 28 April the plotters were found guilty of the conspiracy and of the murder of Smithers, and on 1 May they were hanged by James Botting. Much to the disgust of the crowd, who had been kept behind barricades well away from the scaffold to prevent any rescue attempt, they were then decapitated.

When within the decade the New Police marched forth it was never the intention of their founder, Sir Robert Peel, that there should be such a thing as a police spy in his force. The very idea of such a continental device was abhorrent. Nevertheless,

1 Quoted by E. P. Thompson, *The Making of the English Working Class*, p. 772.
2 Samuel Bamford, *Passages in the Life of a Radical*, p. 93. Thistlewood clearly had a death wish. He had previously been acquitted of high treason following the Spa Fields riot in South London in December 1816.

spies there were from a very early stage. Within a few years there was a disaster when the police clashed on open ground in an area between Holborn and Clerkenwell known as Coldbath Fields. One police officer, PC Culley, was killed and an inquest jury later returned a verdict of justifiable homicide. An inquiry followed swiftly.

At the same time as the inquiry into the Coldbath Fields disaster, another inquiry was set up. This stemmed from the behaviour of a former schoolmaster, Sergeant William Stewart Popay, of P division and latterly of the Walworth and Camberwell 'class' of the National Political Union. The Government was highly suspicious of the Union and Lord Melbourne instructed the commissioners to keep him informed of its movements. In turn Popay had been instructed by his superintendent M'Lean to attend the meetings and, as it was found, had interpreted this to mean he should infiltrate the organisation. From 1831 to 1833, masquerading as a coalman put out of work by the Coal Act, Popay did just that.

His radical speeches soon ensured that he was elected to office in the Union. In late April or early May 1833 his cover was blown when he was recognised by a Union member, John Fursey, at his station desk at Park House police station.[3] For the time being he managed to explain away his presence, and indeed he marched with the members to Coldbath Fields, but later – in the course of the defence of another rioter, George Fursey – Popay's behaviour came under scrutiny.

Fanned by the oratory of William Cobbett, author of *Rural Rides*, the House of Commons responded to a petition organised by John Fursey and others including a Frederick Young:

3 The early police forces seem to have had only a rudimentary idea of undercover work. As has been demonstrated throughout police history, others did not learn from the salutary lesson of Sergeant Popay. In 1840 a PC Barnett of the Birmingham City police infiltrated the Chartists in the city. Unfortunately his superiors required him to work in uniform when he was not busy infiltrating, and it was not long before he was seen in a theatre. His explanation that he was working in a private capacity for the theatre manager (an early example of police moonlighting if it was true) was not accepted. (B. Porter, *Plots and Paranoia*, p. 74.)

That he used to urge the members of the Union to use stronger language than they did in their resolutions and other papers, which he sometimes altered with his own pen, in order to introduce such stronger language; that in his conversation with one of your Petitioners particularly, he railed against the Government, damned the Ministers for villains, and said he would expel them from the earth; that he told one of your Petitioners that he should like to establish a shooting-gallery, and wanted some of them to learn the use of the broad-sword, and did give one lesson of the broad-sword to one of your petitioners.

It was the end for Popay who protested, as well he might, that his plain clothes were for his own protection. It was found that:

. . . he complained to several members of the misery to which he and his family had been reduced; he paid frequent private visits to their leaders and never failed to address them as friends; arm in arm with another member he marched to a meeting to celebrate the French Revolution. More serious still he took part in discussions, supporting resolutions, sometimes even proposing that their wording should be strengthened, and encouraged the establishment of an arms depot offering to give members of the Union sword practice.[4]

His conduct was described as 'highly reprehensible' and he was dismissed the force with ignominy. His superiors, who in turn argued that they had employed Popay at the request of the Home Office but only to watch the meetings of the Union, were criticised for not keeping him under closer control. Whilst the Select Committee accepted the need for a plain clothes force, it deprecated 'any approach to the Employment of Spies, in the ordinary acceptance of the term, as a practice most abhorrent

4 Report from Select Committee on Metropolitan Police (675) 1833 Parl. Papers (1833), vol. 13, pp. 401, 409.

to the feelings of the People and most alien to the spirit of the Constitution'.[5]

Looking back, there is little doubt that poor Popay was the sacrificial goat, but were there others like him who remained unmasked? Yes, said Young and others, who maintained they had seen men 'whom they knew to be policemen, disguised in clothing of various descriptions, sometimes in the garb of gentlemen, sometimes in that of tradesmen or artisans, sometimes in sailors' jackets'.[6]

No, replied the police. Popay was a rogue, an original bad and sinful apple, not the tip of an iceberg. Of course, it is now unbelievable that for two years Popay led this double life without the knowledge of any of his superiors. Did no single one of them ever ask how he came by his detailed information?

After the Popay affair, however, the Commissioners were keen to avoid a repetition and in 1839 a Metropolitan Standing Police Order prohibited officers from attending private meetings of any sort. Nor were officers encouraged to adopt a subterfuge to obtain evidence. Indeed, policing in plain clothes was considered unsporting and, with the exception of the small detective branch set up in 1842, all policing was done in uniform. It was something regarded as abhorrent to right-thinking British people generally.

Over the years, however, a number of instances have come to light. On the 'tip of the iceberg' principle it may be that, as with the Special Branch, there was a far greater number of cases when a police officer had donned a disguise than the authorities would care to admit. After all, Rowan, the Police Commissioner, had been an Army officer serving under Wellington in the Peninsular campaign, where he would have became thoroughly versed in infiltration.

In 1845 a constable who had pretended to be a cobbler in order to arrest a counterfeiter was severely reprimanded; as was another who, six years later, hid behind a tree in Hyde Park to

5 *Ibid*. pp. 409–10.
6 *Ibid*. p. 411.

observe an 'indecent offence'. When these scandals broke, the Home Office was at pains to play the matters down.[7]

On the other hand, the detective force led by Field was happy to discuss its success and exploits in disguise with the novelist and social commentator Charles Dickens, who, until he fell out with the police over the actress Ellen Ternan, was their great champion. Dickens was told of an exploit concerning the arrest of silk thieves involving one of the young officers, Henry Smith, who disguised himself as a butcher's boy:

> Never, surely, was a faculty of observation better brought to bear upon a purpose, than that which picked out this officer for the part. Nothing in all creation could have suited him better. Even while he spoke, he became a greasy, sleepy, shy, good-natured chuckle-headed, unsuspicious and confiding young butcher. His very hair seemed to have had suet in it, as he made it smooth upon his head, and his fresh complexion, to be lubricated by large quantities of animal food.

This facility was not altogether unsurprising. Dickens omitted to write that Smith (whom he cleverly disguised as Mith) had been a butcher before he joined the police.[8]

One of the earliest of police officers to put pen to paper, Chief Inspector Andrew Lansdowne, was at pains to correct the view of the newspaper-fed public that a policeman spent his days in donning and shedding disguises with the celerity of a quick-change artist: 'Now all this is fudge. During the

---

7 B. Porter, *The Refugee Question in Mid-Victorian Politics*, pp. 114–15. There was quite clearly a great deal more undercover work going on than the police cared to admit. Officers could be put into civvies for particular operations. See also G. Thurston, *The Clerkenwell Riot*, for an account of the demonstration in Coldbath Fields and the death of PC Robert Culley.
8 Charles Dickens, 'The Detective Police' in *Miscellaneous Papers*, pp. 60 *et seq*. The incident to which Smith referred may have been the arrest of a Richard Elliott and Richard Vincent for breaking and entering and stealing 460 yards of silk and 461 yards of white linen. They appeared at the Central Criminal Court, where Vincent was acquitted and Elliott sentenced to transportation for fifteen years (*The Times*, 12 March 1845).

Whitechapel business a zealous stripling certainly did put on women's attire one night, but he was not commended for his detective instinct in so doing.'

Lansdowne did admit to two other occasions on which a disguise had been worn. Apparently one officer had enterprisingly dressed himself in a baize cloth to resemble a statue in order to catch a thief at the Great Exhibition of 1862. The second time was when an inspector he refers to as 'G' dressed as a clergyman so as to catch a shopkeeper selling indecent prints. Lansdowne was not pleased: 'It was scarcely a credit to the cloth that a clergyman's attire was considered the best disguise, but it was.'[9]

Other officers were more prepared to admit to the use of disguise in run-of-the-mill criminal cases. Detective Inspector J. G. Littlechild maintained that a clergyman's outfit was a favourite with detectives, since it was both easy to put on and it disarmed suspicion. In his time Littlechild had disguised himself as a surveyor and a sanitary inspector as well as a cab-man. Acting was clearly in his line. To win a private bet he had dressed as a minstrel and had been thrown out of a public house.

In the fight against one of the lesser-known aspects of English criminal behaviour – arson, animal maiming and poaching in East Anglia in the nineteenth century – a Superintendent English was hired from the Metropolitan Police in 1844 for the West Suffolk area. Writing on the period, John Archer describes him as: '[to] be considered as the outstanding policeman of the period. He was the forerunner of the plain-clothes policeman, for he dressed and worked as a labourer in order to gain working people's confidence.' English was responsible for the trials of five principals and received an award of £100 and a watch for his effort.[10]

---

9 Joan Lock identifies the clergyman-officer as G. H. Greenham. In his memoirs, the Chief Inspector mentions the instance as the only occasion on which he wore a disguise. Joan Lock, *Scotland Yard Casebook*; G. H. Greenham, *Scotland Yard Experiences from the Diary of G.H. Greenham*.
10 J. E. Archer, *By a Flash and a Scare*, p. 156; *Bury and Norwich Press*, 11 September 1844 and 30 April 1845.

Much of the dislike of disguise can be traced to the attitude of the Commissioner of the time, Sir Charles Warren, who on taking the post relinquished the Governorship of the Red Sea Littoral.[11] He took over from Colonel Sir Edmond Henderson following rioting in Trafalgar Square in February 1886.

Warren lasted two and a half years, during which time there were more troubles on the streets and he quarrelled bitterly with the Home Secretary over the duties and powers of the Commissioner. He also came under severe criticism for the failure of his officers to solve the so-called Jack the Ripper Whitechapel murders, attributed over the years to a wide variety of suspects from the Duke of Clarence downwards. Indeed, one of the more farcical aspects of the Ripper case was the hiring of two bloodhounds from a Mr Brough in Scarborough at the amazing cost of £100. The dogs managed to lose themselves.

There is little doubt that the CID was having a really bad time in the latter part of the 1880s. According to the *Pall Mall Gazette*, whose gadfly-like editor W. T. Stead stung the authorities whenever possible, it had collapsed by October 1888. The reasons given were numerous. First, there was a rule that all officers had to be over 5 foot 10 in height. The *Gazette* also complained that all CID men had to serve two years in the uniform branch, so giving the criminals a chance to get a good look at them and, worse, by the time they did become detectives they could only walk with the characteristic Scotland Yard 'gait' and so were even more readily recognisable. More serious were the limitations on payments to informers and the rule that an officer could not leave London on a case without the permission of the Chief Commissioner. 'Under these circumstances it is not surprising

11 For an account of his early career, see W. Melville Lee, *A History of the Police in England*.

that our detectives do not detect,' chortled the *Gazette* happily.[12]

By November 1887 James Monroe, the Assistant Commissioner head of the CID, was complaining that his department was overworked and under-manned: 'The result has been that Mr Williamson has broken down, and that I am in a fair way to break down also.' Frederick Williamson, the then head of the Detective Branch, was granted three months' sick leave in February 1888. Nor was the CID getting much support from Warren. He believed it was a 'drop in the ocean' compared with the uniform branch, as he wrote in *Murray's Magazine*, adding insult to injury when he concluded that the original function of the police had been prevention and that detective work was not suited to the 'genius of the English race'.[13]

As Bernard Porter says, Warren thought that:

... policing should be open, visible and by the book, rather like cricket, where everything was governed by the rules of fair play. Plain-clothes policing was like taking off the bails at the bowler's end without a warning whilst the batsman was backing up. It was also a constant temptation to corruption as history showed very well. This sort of attitude from a superior was clearly difficult for a dedicated detective like Monroe to live with. Detectives knew that life was not like cricket, and especially among the criminal fraternity. Corruption was the risk you had to run to be effective, and not half so dangerous as the stultifying effects of red tape. This was really the hoary old dilemma of the British

12 *Pall Mall Gazette*, 8 October 1888, p. 3. William Thomas Stead was one of the great crusading English editors campaigning amongst other things against child prostitution. In 1883 he procured a child, handed it to social workers and then wrote an article. Prosecuted, he was imprisoned for three months, but his campaign led to the passing of the Criminal Law Amendment Act 1885. Later he embraced peace and spiritualism, writing a book, *If Christ Came to Chicago*. He died in 1912, a passenger when the *Titanic* sank.
13 Watkin W. Williams, *The Life of General Sir Charles Warren*, pp. 587–90.

police since its earliest days: how to reconcile purity
with results.[14]

The first woman undercover worker employed on more
than a casual basis was almost certainly a Mrs Garner
(or Gardiner):

> In 1916 at the request of the Admiralty, we trained
> and supplied a selected policewoman for anti-espionage
> work, and to help tackle the problem of the drug traffic,
> which was then growing to very dangerous proportions
> amongst soldiers back on leave from the Front . . . Our
> unit disguised herself as a prostitute, got to know all her
> supposed colleagues, moved in circles where she was
> in constant danger from the drug-runner, and obtained
> information of a most important kind, both in connection
> with drug-running and spying.[15]

> . . . who, a florist before the war, developed a positive
> genius for detective work. She was lent to Commander
> Paget, who was engaged in special intelligence work
> for the navy and some very important evidence on
> cocaine was obtained through her, leading to further
> legislation. She was the only woman on the staff of
> the Metropolitan Observer Service for the detection
> and location of enemy aircraft, the only woman who
> understood all the complicated machinery used for the
> purpose.[16]

In February 1920 Mrs Garner was awarded an MBE for her
work with the Metropolitan Observer Service.

Women had been used on a more casual basis before Mrs
Garner, however. In what amounted to an almost classic

14 Bernard Porter, *Origins of the Vigilant State*, p. 84.
15 Mary Allen, *Lady in Blue*, p. 38.
16 Mary Allen, *Pioneer Policewoman*, p. 132.

example of the *agent provocateur*, one undercover woman
was possibly the wife of a police officer (reports vary) who
was used to ask the advice of a chemist, Thomas Titley,
about her pregnancy. He had long been suspected of being an
abortionist, but there was no evidence to go before the Grand
Jury (the rough equivalent of examining magistrates). In 1880
an inspector wrote to Titley explaining that he had seduced a
young woman who was now pregnant and wished to procure
an abortion. Titley was asked to supply the necessary drugs. At
first he seems to have been reluctant to do anything without,
at least, seeing one if not both of the parties. A police sergeant
and a 'female researcher' called at his house in the assumed
characters of the seducer and the mother of the unfortunate
girl. Medicines were supplied and so the evidence was now
in place. The Grand Jury was invited to consider the position
in December 1880 and the Recorder of London set everything
out before them. The first problem they had to overcome was
that it was admitted that the story told to Titley had been
baseless from beginning to end. There was, as the Recorder
pointed out, no young man, no mother and no young woman.
In law the transaction was complete the moment the sale was
effected, but the Recorder had some strong things to say about
the conduct of the police.

> What they did is to be justified only on the assumption
> that all means are fair which lead to the detection of
> crime. But even this is not a sufficient excuse for
> the means employed in the case before us. Thomas
> Titley was suspected, but no more than suspected, of
> having given his help in genuine cases before. What
> if the suspicion is unfounded? What if the temptation
> held out by the police had induced Thomas Titley to
> take his first criminal step? The law knows nothing of
> suspicions. It presumes innocence until guilt has been
> produced. Is it the duty of the police to do all they
> can to lead innocent men into crime and then to turn

around upon them and denounce them for the arranged offence?

There had to be a true bill against Titley, but the Recorder also invited the jury to return one against the police and their witnesses for fraud and conspiracy, and this they did.

The Times was convinced the police had behaved badly. It was in good, thundering form:

Whether the phantom charge against Thomas Titley can be sustained or not is a matter which concerns himself. The charge against the police is of much more general consequence. We must undoubtedly assume that the police and their associates believed that they were doing right. It is even said that they acted under direction which would go far to absolving them from personal liability. But whatever may be the issue of their trial, the result it cannot fail to have will be a clear laying down of the rules by which they are to be guided for the future. Within what limits is it allowable for the police to tempt men to the commission of crime? There are certainly some cases in which the thing in question may be done. The police-constable who is served with drink at forbidden hours or in an unlicensed place does not thereby expose himself to the charge of conspiracy. To send letters by the post containing marked coin is a common practice enough where a letter-carrier is suspected of dishonesty, and, possibly to lead him into an offence of which he may never have been guilty before. But to convey letters with money in them is, it may be urged, one of the regular duties of a letter-carrier. He is subjected to no unfair trial by being set to do what he had undertaken to do and what he may be called on to do any day.

. . . In Thomas Titley's case the whole crime from one end to the other is the mere concoction of the police. He is found engaged in his lawful occupation as a chemist, and he is urged to an unlawful course outside his regular business. There is more here than the detection of crime. The initiative is with the police and not with the offender, each subsequent step is the result of a distinct suggestion on the part of the police. What should we think of a police-constable who instigated a man to open a booth for the unlawful sale of liquor, who then bought liquor from him, and who finally dragged him into court for his breach of the Excise laws? What if a letter-carrier were told of a valuable packet about to come into his charge, and were urged to steal the contents and divide the spoil with his informant? If such courses as these are held to be justifiable, they will cover Thomas Titley's case, as it appears in the charge of the Recorder, but they will hardly more than cover it. If the police have really done what the Recorder's charge implies, and what the finding of the Grand Jury endorses against them, the proceeding is described none too strongly as very greatly to be reprobated in itself and for the abuses to which it obviously lends itself.[17]

Then as now.

It did Titley little good. Two days later the police officers were discharged and Titley was sentenced to eighteen months' hard labour. A series of memorials raised on his behalf were sent to the Home Secretary. One was from his wife, the second was signed by 286 neighbours and the third by 3,800 people from London and the provinces. They did the chemist no good either. Writing to Titley's solicitors, the Home Secretary said that he had examined the allegations by Taylor and Morgan, whose complaints had led to police intervention in the first place, and found there was no ground for interference in the man's sentence.[18]

The so-called golden age of a crime-free Britain of the

17 *The Times*, 14 December 1880.
18 *The Times*, 14 March 1881.

1930s may have been something of a myth, but there is no doubt that the Second World War irrevocably changed the face of British crime. Before the outbreak of hostilities there is little doubt that the ordinary public eschewed crime. They probably saw their involvement as little more than fending for their families, but now new doors were opened for old and new criminals alike. Now, with bomb-damaged shops and buildings open to looting, all kinds of goods came on the black market and into receivers' hands. There was a steady trade in stolen ration books. Under cover of the blackout the smash-and-grab raid proliferated and Billy Hill, for one, found that small post offices were a profitable target for safe-breaking expeditions. By the end of the war it was estimated that there were 20,000 deserters in London alone.

It was in this climate that on 31 December 1945, shortly after the end of the war, one of the more curious and relatively short-lived of Scotland Yard's innovations, the Special Duty Squad, was created. Under the aegis of Sir Ronald Howe, then the Assistant Commissioner (Crime), and Percy Worth, then head of Scotland Yard's CID, four young officers – John Capstick and Henry 'Nobby' Clark, both of whom were then detective inspectors, and Detective Sergeants John Gosling and Matthew Brinn – were given the task to 'carry the war into the enemy's camp'. Each of the men had specialist knowledge of the criminals of a part of London, and their brief was specific. They were to use their extensive knowledge of London's Underworld and live amongst the criminal fraternity. Later they were joined by Detective Sergeant George Burton.

> Neither you nor your men will give evidence in court. As far as the Underworld is concerned, you will have no more material existence than ghosts. How you manage it is your affair but we want results – fast!

From those remarks of Worth the squad took its name. Its official title may have been Special Duty Squad, but it was known to everyone as the Ghost Squad. There were good reasons for its introduction.

Against the depleted ranks of the police was ranged a new type of criminal, cunning, ruthless and well informed. Many had served in the armed forces – some with distinction – and many more were deserters. They were younger, fitter, harder, more resourceful and more energetic than the pre-war criminals.

All Britain was the province of these new criminals. Time, money and distance were no object if the pickings were good. They swooped almost every night. Lorryloads of tea, sugar, butter, clothes, cigarettes and whisky disappeared from the streets or were stolen from warehouses. Jewellery and cash vanished from private houses into the pockets of thieves who worked like phantoms. Fur and rings, clothing and petrol coupons, carpets, lipsticks, typewriters, razor blades, shoes – anything with a ready cash value was loot for the army of the underworld. The figures of stolen property rose to astronomical proportions.[19]

There had been at least one forerunner of the Ghost Squad, recalls Capstick.[20] 'Squibs' Dance, along with his brother Alf, was a member of the Flying Squad:

A rough diamond, he always wore a cap and scarf, like a labouring man, and rolled his own cigarettes from a virulent brand of shag. He never took a cigarette out of his mouth once he had lit it. When the stub was an eighth of an inch long he spat it out, and he didn't care much where it landed. It was never a good idea to stand within a couple of yards of Squibs for that reason.

He more or less lived with thieves in the public-houses,

19 J. Gosling, *The Ghost Squad*, p. 20.
20 J. Capstick, *Given in Evidence*, p. 91 and pp. 53–4.

and was usually accepted by them as a particularly cunning member of their own fraternity. He worked different areas in rotation, and was never tumbled. Drifting into a tavern in South London, cigarette dangling from his lower lip, he would be greeted: 'Blimey! Where have you been?' To which he would mumble, 'Well, I only came out of stir last week.' Then he would work in the far west of London and when asked, 'Been having a lay down for six months?' replied shortly, 'Nah, four.' If somebody ventured to inquire which prison he had been in, and what he had done, Squibs would glare and mutter that he didn't talk. No wonder the underworld looked upon him as a real fly thief.

Another of his favourite disguises was that of a seaman, a common and useful one for police officers generally: 'We paid a visit to a dockland slop shop and emerged as three of the roughest, most drunken seamen who ever lurched ashore from the K. G. Five dock.'[21]

John Gosling describes the early days of the Ghost Squad which lived in an office – something which was, he says, the nearest approach to a cell he had seen outside prison.

Our office was spartan: four walls, two tables, a telephone, and a door with a key in the lock; that was all.

Only one policeman, apart from the members of the Squad, had access to that room during our tenancy. He was Archie, a bald-headed policeman who was the essence of discretion. He was a wonderful character. He brought us cups of tea and sandwiches and sometimes meals. We called him 'the Butler'. He was also invaluable as a 'base camp' man. We were nearly always out and Archie took the phone messages which arrived while we were on the job.

21 Robert Colquhoun, *Life Begins at Midnight*, p. 59.

The members had a *carte blanche* with which to work. They would meet between ten and ten-thirty in the morning, depending on when they had gone to bed the night before, and at six o'clock they would telephone John Capstick to tell him how their day had been spent. At first he sent a weekly report to the Home Secretary, but with the Squad functioning more than satisfactorily this requirement was dropped after three months. For transport the Squad shared an old and dirty Austin 16 which Gosling recalls he once managed to coax to a dramatic fifty-five miles an hour. Perhaps he was a poor driver – Capstick recalls the car as 'super-tuned'.

The Squad had a spectacular success in February 1947, when information was received that a team from North London would raid the Midland Bank in Kentish Town. This was to be one of the earliest examples of kidnapping a manager, stealing his keys and then raiding the vault. The Ghost Squad could find out when but not where the manager was to be snatched. The information was passed to the then head of the Flying Squad, Bob Lee. It shows what dangers lie in undercover work even when precautions are taken.

Lee decided to substitute an officer for the bank manager, and a DS William Davies took the part. Wearing spectacles and a bowler hat, he left the office and travelled towards the manager's home on the Northern line to Woodside Park; he was followed at a discreet distance by two other detectives. As he walked along a footpath by the then semi-rural station, he was attacked and coshed and the officers saw him being bundled into a van. Once the gang had the keys he was thrown out into the snow, still bound and blindfolded. Half the team began an unsuccessful search for Davies; fortunately for him, he was seen by a motorist who drove him to a doctor. The other half kept watch on the bank and when within an hour a man arrived and let himself in, the Ghost Squad swooped. Neil Darbyshire puts it delicately: 'The terrified robber, a window cleaner by day, was in no position to demur and immediately told the furious detectives all they wanted to know.'

At the Old Bailey the team received between three and five years. Davies was awarded the King's Police Medal.[22]

A similar exercise took place the following year when a team of robbers were thwarted in their desire to steal some £250,000 from the BOAC warehouse at London airport. An informer tipped off the police, and fourteen detectives substituted themselves for the guards, mechanics and other staff in the warehouse. The arrangement had been for the guards to be given drugged tea, but the warehouseman who had been approached had contacted the police. When the robbers arrived they found the guards apparently asleep. Fighting broke out and at the end eight robbers were captured. Some reports say it was the whole team, but Underworld legend has it that at least one escaped by hiding under a lorry.[23]

By the late 1940s there were serious doubts about the wisdom of operating the Ghost Squad. The money paid to informers was considerable, and the law of diminishing returns was beginning to apply. Even more seriously, there were fears that accusations could be made that the police were acting as *agents provocateurs*. The original officers had become too well known to the criminals, and officers from the Flying Squad were drafted in and out. Now some officers were thought to be getting too close to their criminal counterparts for their and the force's good; there were also suggestions that reward money was being shared by some officers and their informers.

One of the casualties of the Ghost Squad was Detective Sergeant Robert Robertson who, whilst seconded to the Squad,

---

22 Neil Darbyshire and Brian Hilliard, *The Flying Squad*, pp. 83–4. Since the 1970s, kidnapping and hostage-taking has become a much more common form of crime. Examples include the 1976 Dunstable bank robbery, when a manager's family was held hostage, and the £1 million Security Express robbery in Millwall when a security guard and his family were taken hostage. The aim is to force the key-holder to co-operate and usually the hostages are released relatively unharmed. One of the most highly publicised in recent years was the kidnapping of Elizabeth Kerr, whose husband managed Barclays Bank in Sale, Greater Manchester. It followed an attempt the previous week when Tony Bosson-Williams, the kidnapper, had gone to the wrong house. He received a total of fourteen years at Chester Crown Court on 14 January 1994.
23 Shifty Burke, *Peterman*.

met Morris Page. He was a hanger-on to the notorious Messina brothers – Maltese pimps who had had a grip on vice in Soho over nearly a twenty-year period – and their brother-in-law, Tony Micalleff. Robertson's downfall came as late as 1955 when he was involved in the case of Joseph Grech, charged with housebreaking. The solicitor in the case was Ben Canter, one of the lawyers who had acted for the brothers. Grech seemingly had an unshakable defence. Part of the evidence against him was that the key to the burgled premises had been found on him, but he maintained that it fitted his own front door and therefore was of no significance. However, the jury found that it was and, from his cell where he was serving three years, Grech subsequently unloaded a series of legal bombs.

He had, he said, given Page around £150 to hand to a Detective Sergeant Robert Robertson, the officer in charge of the initial case, who made the key to the burgled premises available so that a locksmith could make a lock to be fitted to Grech's front door. There was to have been a further £150 given to Robertson on an acquittal. He also alleged that Robertson had coached Ben Canter about the questions to be put at the trial.

When Robertson, Page and Canter appeared at the Old Bailey charged with conspiracy to pervert the course of justice, Grech unloaded even more bombs. His conviction, he said, had been brought about by perjured evidence of other officers acting on the instructions of an Inspector Charles Jacobs attached to West End Central.[24] Jacobs, he said, had asked him for £2,000 so that none of his flats or brothels would be raided. After negotiations, the terms had been set at £500 down and £30 a week. Canter, said Grech, had been the bagman, taking £100 to give to Jacobs. According to Grech, Canter came back saying, 'He wants £500.'

24 In February 1956 Jacobs was dismissed the force, having been found guilty by a disciplinary board of assisting a prostitute to obtain premises, of failing to disclose in court a man's previous convictions, and of failing to account for property taken from an arrested man. His application to the High Court for an order quashing the verdict, on the grounds that by reason of his mental health at the time he was unfit to prepare his defence, was rejected.

When he came to give evidence Canter was in difficulties over his relationship with Micalleff, who had been accepted as a surety in the original case by Robertson:

—Can you imagine any honest policeman agreeing to take Micalleff as a surety for this man Grech?
—That is a difficult question to answer.
—I think it is a simple question. Try to answer it . . .
—It depends on the circumstances.

Canter received two years' imprisonment, as did Robertson who for many years continued to protest his innocence, consulting various firms of London solicitors to try to have his conviction overturned. The intermediary, Morris Page, went to prison for fifteen months.

In September 1949 the Ghost Squad was closed down by Sir Harold Scott. During the three years and nine months of its existence, members arrested 789 criminals, solved 1,506 cases and recovered property worth more than a quarter of a million pounds. Despite this undoubted success the autonomy given to the officers, for the best of motives, can be seen as the beginning of the period when the Flying Squad began to operate 'a firm within a firm' which would lead to the great police corruption trials of the 1960s and 1970s.

The Squad may have ceased officially to exist in 1949 but according to the former Commissioner, Sir Harold Scott, in 1954 'a little group of officers continues to act in this way'.[25] This was the Criminal Intelligence Branch, serving the whole of the CID and not merely the Flying Squad.

Although ten years later officers were still being used to infiltrate gangs and carry out jobs with them, it was by no means common practice. According to Leonard 'Nipper' Read, former National Co-ordinator of the Regional Crime Squads:

25 Sir Harold Scott, *Scotland Yard*, p. 168.

Before the Regional Crime Squads, there wasn't the money available and anyway there were considerable dangers for the officers. Without careful handling there is also the danger that the officer seeing money vastly in excess of his salary and pension may be turned.

This has certainly been the case in America.

Whilst there are now numerous accounts of in-depth undercover infiltration by police officers in America, there are few documented examples of English work. Nevertheless, over the years they have taken place.

One recent American example is of a northern Californian officer who went 'deep cover' riding for eighteen months with a group of Hell's Angels. The operation was a great success resulting, as it did, in a very large number of arrests of high-level dealers who until then had been regarded as almost untouchable. The officer was highly praised but the cost to him was a high one. He became personally involved in drugs and fighting and slid into alcoholism; his family life disintegrated and after resigning from the force he took part in a number of bank robberies and received a term of imprisonment.[26] In another case a Chicago police officer who posed as a pimp and infiltrated a prostitution ring became so enamoured with the life that he took it up himself after the investigation.[27] In a third case another officer, a member of an elite drug enforcement unit in Boston, became an addict.[28]

What makes a good undercover officer? Joe Pistone, one of the most successful of all time undercover agents, is clear:

You have to have a strong personality. Strong means

26 Laurence Linderman, 'Underground Angel' in *Playboy*, July 1981, quoted by Gary Marx in 'Who really gets stung? Some issues raised by the New Police undercover work' in *Crime & Delinquency*, April 1982, pp. 165–93, as are the next two examples.
27 *Chicago Daily News*, 24 September 1975.
28 *Boston Globe*, 26 October 1979.

disciplined, controlled, confident. It doesn't mean loud and abrasive or conspicuous. It means your personality can withstand the extraordinary challenges and temptations that routinely go with the work. It means you have an ego strong enough to sustain you from within, when nobody but you knows what you're really doing and thinking.

You have to be street-smart, even cocky sometimes. Every good undercover agent I have known grew up on the street, like I did, and was a good street agent before becoming an undercover agent. On the street you learn what's what and who's who. You learn how to read situations and handle yourself. You can't fake the ability. It shows.[29]

In Britain senior officers look to what Detective Chief Superintendent Roy Ramm calls natural attributes:

By natural attributes I mean their size, shape, colour, gender. Nobody too physically outstanding is selected, and we expect them to have some special skills that we think might be useful in their undercover role, such as speaking a foreign language. We then take them on a training course for two weeks, which gives them a lot of basic about the law, making sure they know how to avoid overstepping the mark.

We are keen to make sure that the officers keep their feet on the ground, that they don't think they are part of Miami Vice, that they don't start to live their undercover role.[30]

Back in 1966, Bobbie James,[31] an officer from a North Country force, was deputed – almost at a moment's notice and certainly

29 J. D. Pistone, *Donnie Brasco*, pp. 98–9.
30 R. Fleming with H. Miller, *Scotland Yard*, pp. 112–13, 115.
31 A pseudonym.

untrained – to infiltrate and report on a London gang of robbers. He had joined the police in Wales before coming to the North where he became a beat officer and then transferred to the CID after some six months. He was seconded to the Regional Crime Squad in April 1965 when 'in those days they were still selling themselves to local forces'.

I came to know a Hungarian who was obviously a true villain with an English wife who was working as a prostitute. He'd been very active in London on smash and grab raids. He was giving me information and I got to know him over a period of time when he was trying to establish himself as a decent member of the community, apart from the prostitution that is. Of course people like that can't. Money is the root of all evil. With a good class villain no matter what money he gets he gets rid of it easily so the villain's wife went on the game in Hull. Some of his pals kept coming up to see him. His name was now Joe and he knew I was a police officer. Initially he tried to soft-soap me and passed me information. He was working as a handyman ferrying other prostitutes.

Then one of his friends, Tibor,[32] another Hungarian successful smash and grab artist, came up to see him. Joe went back down to London with him and rang me and asked if he could see me. I met him at the station and he took me for a drink and five or six of the gang came in. I was passed off as a mate. I was never called by my name – just Taff. Stayed overnight and saw him again the following day. It took a period of time for me to be accepted and gradually I let it be known that I was an escapee from Walton and was willing to assist in anything they did. I had no written guarantee from my superiors. It was never even mentioned. The prime object was to put them away as best you could.

32 The names of all those who were not convicted in the subsequent case are pseudonyms.

The first job was a clothing shop in the Seven Sisters Road in North London. It was led by a Brian Scrivens. He was an absolute charmer, a man who could mix in any circles. He was also totally paranoid. He was speechless before a job – he did nothing but think about it. He'd been on the run for two years after escaping from a six-year sentence for armed robbery and was paying a detective in Fulham weekly rent for his freedom. He would go to the toilet with him to bung him. He used to say, 'Here's another fucking payday for him.'

Another member of the team was another Brian [Johnson] also on the run after two out of four years. A third, Legos Trestyen, had got out of Hungary at the time of the uprising and it was said amongst them that he was wanted for murder back there, but I've no idea if it was true.

The Seven Sisters job was just because someone wanted clothes. We wore the suits for months afterwards but the basic jobs were smash and grab raids on furriers all over the South of England as far as Bournemouth. We would steal a Jaguar and then leave it in a car park for four or five days. There would be four of us on a job. There would be the driver, the one who went for the window, and two on either side would be on the pavement ready to fend off any spirited citizen who wanted to intervene. I would usually be one of those. The m.o. was to circle the place and do it any time of the day when we thought that it would be less busy. Early hours of the morning or mid-afternoon on half-day closing were really best. The men had no fear. If anyone was in our way they'd have no hesitation in carting them on the bonnet.

We'd steam up to the premises, pick-handle through the window and pull the grille out, hit the glass below. There could be thousands in the window. For example the Hull jewellers, Carmichaels, had £220,000 on a pad in the window and that was in the 1960s.

The funniest episode was in Russell's Antiques in Richmond Hill in Bournemouth. We did it in the early hours of one summer morning. We'd broken the window grille and taken £20,000 in jewellery in that time. Then the Borough Force came up the arcade in a vehicle. I was off like a shot. I ended up in the toilet in the centre of Bournemouth. I was actually standing on the ledge of the door when the dog came sniffing around, and if there's one thing of which I'm frightened it's dogs. I stayed in that lavatory for about two hours before I went to catch a train back to London. I was frightened they'd do a second search. I was regarded as quite a hero for getting away. I got back before Tibor and was surreptiously blaming him, 'How can there have been so many bastards', and so on. Very often the people who got caught seemed to get the blame for the failure.

Of course, they were basically bloody evil people. We were living in Bayswater and Joe took his wife and used her as a prostitute there. In turn he befriended a girl from an approved school and got her on the game. Some of the time I lived with yet another Hungarian. I can't remember his name. He had two girls living in a place off Fulham Green with Scrivens and his girlfriend.

The team loved bragging together saying what they'd done and talking in derogatory fashion about Old Bill, how they'd been caught on the job but hadn't had their collars felt because the stuff they'd stolen had been stuck in the back off the police car and away. The gang was on the fringe of the Richardsons and things went in their direction. The firm got 25% of the proceeds if they were lucky. There was a shareout for those who were on the raid and we blew it all in a few days. If you were out of cash it was a treating situation. If you weren't on the job you got a backhander. It meant the man who was treated was now a 'friend' or a 'pal', someone who wouldn't squeal. It proved an affinity. If he was bunged then he was as near a trusted friend as he could become. Whoever was around when the job came up was invited. What we did depended on how much money we had, if a job was coming off or if we were planning one. Work came to us rather than our going out looking. Someone had heard . . . someone had suggested . . . it was easy to do . . . a lot of money . . . jewellery somewhere. We would look at local newspapers to see who was appearing in court and for what. Were the local police up to dealing with us?

There were about thirty who came and went in the gang. There was no team leader. Scrivens wasn't trusted anymore than anyone else. I had to show I wasn't trusting the others without actually saying it. I had to get with Joe without actually seeming to do so.

If we were between jobs things were relaxed. We would get up very late and go to the pub to drink, go for a meal in a café and then back boozing. It was rare we ever ate at the flat. Sometimes the men would stay with a girl for a week or so and then discard her. A number of them had girls on the game, so it was a question of collecting money from them in an evening and possibly going to a nightclub. I was amazed how much the girls earned. They handed it all over. They were far too terrified to hold any back. Once we gatecrashed a party – Scrivens could easily talk his way in somewhere like that. It was quite a society party with everyone swapping partners so no one knew who was with who. Coats and wraps all over the place. Suddenly Scrivens says, 'We're off.' The back seat of the car was laden with coats, jewellery, a couple of pieces of silver. There was never an opportunity missed. He'd obviously done it over a long period of time. He liked to take the piss out of the Establishment and to have a pay day at the same time. It satisfied his ego.

Part of the time I lived with a man known as the Chinaman in N11. He kept a collection of firearms in his place. Then I moved and I lived with Scrivens in the upstairs flat in Fulham Green. I drove the car for him on one occasion. We also did an electrical shop, car radios were packed in oblong boxes. They were piled high along the wall. This was security money for a good Christmas. The women who lived with Scrivens were terrified. They'd take a thumping and next minute be in bed together. The flat was piled high with clothing. We'd wear a different suit every night. A lot of the gear never got taken out of its boxes.

One thing I'll never forget was watching a young girl procured for prostitution in Hull. This lass, she'd dyed jet-black hair. She was married to a fisherman but separated. The fishing fraternity was then very localised. She was very pretty but common as muck. Joe's wife, Tricia, befriended her. A Hungarian came up and took her out, gave her cash which she spent, thinking it was a present. She got a good hiding when she couldn't repay, and he took her to London and put her on the game. There was nothing I could do to stop it.

James's life with Scrivens and his friends wasn't the only problem:

During this time I was liaising with a DI on the Flying Squad. There was an attitude of disbelief that a lad from the sticks was telling them what was happening. We'd heard there was a hell of a lot of bent coppers in London. It was just as well I didn't know too much about them. They could have pressured the people I was living with, and what they'd have got by whispering in their ears who I was. I'd have been a body in the Thames.

I'd spoken to him two or three times before I met him which was about a week after the first job – the clothing shop in the Seven Sisters Road. We'd done it basically because someone wanted some clothing. I passed the information back but no one was ever pulled. I went to the Yard and my contact and his sidekick took me out for a few pints. I had to have some wheels and he took me to a car hire shop and I got a grey Morris 1000 which to my knowledge I've never paid for. We never got a bill for it up here. My story to the boys was that it was a ringer.

With Scrivens and his friends, once there was plenty of money about no one was attached to you. On the other hand, if there was a job you were always chaperoned. It was strange the way they manoeuvred without saying anything directly; two were never left alone together. 'I'll go with X.' 'I'll go with Y.' There was no internal trust. Once it started to be planned, then there was just no way you could get away.

My difficulty was in trusting the Flying Squad.

There were two fraudsmen called Tony and Harry on the edge of the gang. They would take a luxury flat, pay the initial rent and get an extra three months' living. The next thing was they'd hire a chauffeur-driven Bentley, get some stolen credit cards and cheque books, pull up outside stores, always on a Friday afternoon, and have a ball filling the boot. I'd hardly seen credit cards used up to this time.

I went with them this one Friday and we literally filled the boot. They couldn't be served quick enough. We went back with stuff to the flat and there must have been £10,000-£15,000 worth of gear. That particular night we went boozing. It was the time of the purple heart scene. The gang weren't addicts; they used to drink a fair bit and were pushers rather than addicts. Then around 2 a.m. they started on the hearts. Early next morning I got in touch with the D.I., went to Bow Street Magistrates' Court and we got a warrant at 10 a.m. before the court started.

There was a café at the gates of Scotland Yard and I sat there reading a paper whilst a D.I. and his mate went off to turn the flat over. I knew the boys were out to the world. At 12 they came back. I had arranged to meet them at a pub on the corner. They said there was nothing, just a few cheque-book stubs. I was absolutely flabbergasted. The gear was positively there. Even with the answer, 'just a few cheque books', they should have had their collar felt for that.

By the Autumn things were getting difficult. My job was to get information back and not to be involved in a prosecution. There were always people being caught on or after the robberies and there were always people getting away, but I began to think that I was getting away too much and someone would notice. In London my work had put seventeen people away in six months:

The end came in Hull in the December. Joe came back up, and I'd been away from the team for a couple of weeks when Tibor came North. When he saw Carmichaels' window he had eyes like organ stops. When we were all back in London Tibor was telling the group about Carmichaels. There was no problem he said about security. There really wasn't any. The difficulty would be getting out of the city. He'd got a local paper to read the crime and to see what the police were used to. Had they facilities to deal with robbery? The truth was they hadn't. There was another recce, this time with Johnson and Tibor, and it was decided we would come up and do it.

I told them I knew the area because once I had been released from Hull prison and had to make my way home. I said I'd go and find a flat. I could then telephone and tell them where I was, which was going to be in the east of the City. By this time I was pretty well trusted and I was the first of the team to arrive. Johnson, Scrivens, Trestyen all came up in a stolen Austin Cambridge. Some of us were going to get out of the City by train and so one had a ticket to Sheffield, one to Birmingham and so on. Tibor was to be at the station.

Meanwhile Joe had gone back down to London and I got a telephone call from Dover to say he was in the nick for some petty crime. He'd been locked up after he'd come across on a ferry. He wanted to see an officer straight away as he'd found out that there was a pile of cannabis coming into Dover. Thomas Smith, a DS from Yorkshire, and I waited up that day and were told that yet another Hungarian, Peter, would be met by two coloured fellows and we stayed in Dover that night.

I was told the man was a big dealer, Alexander, who had a shop in the Finchley Road and a flat in Golders Green. We went to the Drugs Squad C1 and there a DC and a detective sergeant were assigned to us. We got warrants for both the shop and the flat. On the Wednesday there was a half-day closing and the shop was shut. I went with the detective sergeant to the flat. Who should be there but Tony and Harry.

Not a word of recognition. But as we were searching, a Jag pulled up and Peter shouted something in Hungarian down to an elderly gentleman and a lady. Off they went. Then a couple of minutes later up came another Jag with two coloured lads. Peter yelled, 'Fuck off, Old Bill,' and they were away. We should have moved him from the window.

We took him across to the jeweller's shop and there was nothing. It was just a front, watches, inexpensive stuff. At the back it was virtually empty but there were cement bags and in those bags were polythene bags of cannabis as well as stolen cheque books and passports.

Peter asked to speak to the DS. He came back and said, 'He's just offered me an open cheque.' Walt asked, 'What are you going to do?'

'Bail him under the Magistrates Courts Act.'

Walt said, 'Christ, you can't do that.'

But we were on their midden. We came back disgusted. We kept ringing up and were told the substance had to be tested but the other stuff was obviously stolen. I've no idea whether it ever reached the security lockers. After about six weeks we got in touch with the DS. He'd refused to charge Alexander. 'Why?' 'Insufficient evidence.'

I had to put up with that the whole time. A little later Peter was locked up in Hertfordshire over a load of stolen art treasures from some stately home and started to sing. One day I was in the Crime Squad and the telephone went and who was it but the DC from London. He asked if I had been questioned and indeed I got a call from a DI at Scotland Yard. The DC wanted to know what I'd said and I told him I'd spoken to John Bliss who was then the National Co-ordinator of the Regional Crime Squad when he'd visited our area. So had Thomas Smith. Neither of us heard any more.

The prime object was to put them away as best you could, but the object of some officers in the Met at that time seemed to be to keep them out as long as they were paying. There was no question of my acting as an *agent provocateur*. That kind of person lived by committing crime.

In the meantime I'd told the powers that be and I had my left arm put in plaster to protect me against the police dogs when they arrived. When the team asked what had happened I told them I'd had a long wait at Doncaster to get the connection and so I'd done a job. I told them I'd fallen off a wall whilst doing a screwing. When the police came round I was on my bike and away. They thought this was great. It was the beginning of December. In the flat in Williamson Street there was a provision for open fires. I got a couple of bags of pre-packed coal. I told the men I'd nicked the coal from a shop up the road. Nicking coal, in a strange sort of way, was as good as a high-class burglary. What I was doing was copying the bravado they often showed.

We stayed in the flat six days. Every day we would case the place and we were also looking for a Jaguar as a getaway car. We went miles for the thing – as far as Harrogate. Then came the news that the higher-ups thought it would be too dangerous to try and capture us as we did the robbery. On 6 December 1966 the flat was raided and we were all locked up. When we were nicked a nice fire was glowing.

One of the first things was a de-briefing and I told them about the slaughter in Fulham Green. We kept ringing but for hours and hours there was no reply. Eventually we got through, gave the message and then more hours later the reply came back. There was nothing there. My cover went when I wasn't seen in the dock. It was only then that I learned two of them really were prison escapees.

Within the next year a man who had been serving a sentence for armed robbery was released six months after I had finished. He was a bouncer at the 51 Club and said, 'How's your arm, Taff?' What had happened was Stocken was an escapee and he had spoken with the man who had put two and two together. I said, 'What are you on about?' and he just shrugged. I never had any repercussions. I saw Joe about three years later. He was back with his wife in Hull and now she had two children.

We put away about seventeen people in six months or so on my information, which wasn't bad. As for fear, I don't think I knew fear then. I was young and the adrenelin was flowing.[33]

33 On 12 December 1966 David Johnson, Brian Scrivens and Legos Trestyen appeared before Mr D. N. O'Sullivan, the Hull stipendiary magistrate, and pleaded guilty to receiving a car knowing it had been stolen. The police case was that they had been keeping watch on the car and had seen combinations of the men pass it nine times. Johnson had escaped twice after thirty months of a four-year sentence for possessing forged notes and an automatic pistol. The first escape had been in 1964 and in December 1965 he had escaped from Wormwood Scrubs. Scrivens had received four years in 1962 for office breaking and possession of housebreaking instruments and explosives. Thirteen days later he had received a further six years for armed robbery. He had escaped in 1964. Trestyen had five previous convictions and had been recommended for deportation. All were committed to Leeds Quarter Sessions for sentence. The magistrate told DI Williams, 'I commend you in particular and the Crime Squad generally for your action in causing the apprehension of these three men. I regard this as an important case and it is obvious that a great deal of thought, care, intelligence and powers of observation went into this operation.'

In rather more structured circumstances a Metropolitan officer, Frank, was able to infiltrate the team who planned to rob the KLM warehouse at London airport. On 9 October 1992 Peter White and Carl Harrison were jailed for twenty and sixteen years respectively. White – who, using false references, had obtained a job in the KLM warehouse – and Harrison had planned to kidnap and torture Ann Blake and her daughter, so forcing Ian Blake, a KLM cargo supervisor, into opening the Heathrow strong-room which was said to contain up to £40 million in banknotes and diamonds. It was a thoroughly professional job, with Blake being watched and timed in his movements.

White contacted a former cellmate whom he wanted to fly his share of the proceeds from an airfield at Elstree to Switzerland for him. Unfortunately for him the cellmate had turned informer and a police *Operation Daedalus* was put into effect with Frank being introduced to White as a professional robber. He and Harrison were taken to prearranged venues such as Heston Service Station and the Hounslow East tube station, where up to 40 hours of incriminating tapes were recorded. Later a second officer was introduced as a driver.

On 8 December 1991, armed with handcuffs, wire ties, an imitation revolver and a CS gas canister, Harrison – wearing a balaclava and with Frank in tow – went to Blake's home in Staines, Middlesex, to find more than fifty officers waiting for him. White was arrested later in the day. The surveillance operation had lasted five months.

Detective Chief Inspector Toby Child said of Frank:

He put his life on the line in order to get us the result that we wanted. It is unusual for criminals in this type of offence to plead guilty. The operation was so successful that up until the arrest and even subsequent to the arrest, neither Harrison nor White suspected anything.[34]

34 *Today*, 10 October 1992.

Commenting on his role as an undercover officer, Frank said that the first fifteen minutes were the worst: 'I learn the background of the other person and I live that during the course of the operation.'

Undercover work is now recognised as extremely dangerous and stressful, and officers are now given an 'uncle' to whom they can speak freely without management barriers and paperwork. Although a number of officers have been injured, fortunately in this country none has been killed.[35]

One of the other problems an undercover officer faces is having to stand by and watch the beating of another person rather than break that cover. In 1990 an undercover officer watched a fight in a Newcastle nightclub following which the late Newcastle hardman, Viv Graham, received three years for wounding Stuart Watson, the doorman at Hobo. At the end of the trial the doorman said he was sorry for what had happened, and went on to accuse the Regional Crime Squad of using him as bait to get Graham and the others. There had been an undercover officer posing as a customer when the incident had taken place, who had been under orders not to intervene. Unsurprisingly he came under heavy fire from the defence lawyers and was asked whether, when he realised one of the men had a spiked weapon, he should have stepped in. 'No,' replied the officer. 'I had been briefed and instructed not to.'[36]

One of the most successful long-term operations was *Operation Julie*, the code name – after one of the women officers, a twenty-eight-year-old Detective Sergeant – given to a drug surveillance operation in the late 1970s which ended in trials at the Bristol Crown Court in March 1978 and led to the jailing of Richard Kemp, a brilliant chemist studying nuclear magnetic resonance for his doctorate, who had started the operations with Dr Christine Bott, daughter of an Army officer and sister of a

35 R. Fleming and H. Miller, *Scotland Yard*, pp. 117–18.
36 Graham was shot dead on New Year's Eve 1993. No one has been charged with his murder.

Scotland Yard officer. They met at Liverpool University and, according to her, he 'turned her on to cannabis and LSD'. Early in his career he produced LSD for both an American operation in Paris and a mobile suitcase operation which moved peripatetically around Europe.

Originally there was one laboratory – the Cambridge Connection – run by Kemp, Bott, an American author (a disciple of Timothy Leary, the drug propagandist) and Henry Barclay Todd. It operated from 1970 to 1973 and then, when Kemp and Todd fell out, one laboratory became two. Kemp and Bott moved to Wales, where amongst other things she bred goats and he turned out LSD tablets. The second, larger laboratory was at 23 Seymour Road, Hampton Wick, run by Todd with the assistance of Andy Munro and Brian Cuthbertson, the chemist and general assistant in charge of distribution respectively. Export was undertaken through Amsterdam by Richard Burden, who ran a restaurant in Chelsea.

Operation Julie became a worldwide operation, with the American DEA running a simultaneous operation known as Syntac 10. It was discovered that Bott, alleged to be the group's banker, had a deposit box containing £45,000 in Switzerland, and it was thought there was a supply route to West Germany where another of the defendants had a deposit box. There was also a supposition that supplies had percolated through the Iron Curtain. In February 1978, the Soviet delegate at a narcotics conference in Geneva had proposed a resolution condemning LSD, and none of the other delegates could understand why he had done so.

In 1975 a raid had accidentally been thwarted when quite innocently the wife of a local police officer let slip to bricklayer Alston 'Smiles' Hughes – so-called because of his piano-key teeth and an engaging grin – that her husband was going to visit him. When the detectives, including Martyn Pritchard, went back to Aberystwyth police station, the officers began gossiping and the name of Kemp was mentioned. His name had been on record when earlier that year a man arrested by the Mounties in Montreal had bargained his way to freedom by giving information about drug manufacturers and dealers both in America and in Britain. Kemp had recently been involved in a fatal accident when his Land Rover knocked down a vicar's wife; the vehicle was still in the police garage and it was decided to check it out. Amongst a pile of slates some torn scraps of paper, one with the words 'hydrazine hydrate', an ingredient in LSD, were found. In February 1976 *Operation Julie* was launched, and from then on Kemp and Bott were under surveillance. A detective sergeant and a woman officer rented a cottage near the Kemp home for a two-week fishing holiday. Dick Lee, the acting Chief Inspector, posed as a London businessman recovering from a heart operation and was joined by another officer. Although they spent their time in the pubs, they made no progress with the locals and Lee said: 'I suddenly realised that they thought we were two homosexuals and that was why nobody would accept us.' A young policewoman was hastily summoned as a live-in secretary, and relations with the community improved dramatically.

Meanwhile Pritchard, who had lived five years as an undercover cop on the streets and had been 'arrested' for buying cannabis, returned to London and later to Devizes where again Hughes' name turned up. Now a connection was made, wrongly linking Hughes with Kemp and Bott instead of with Todd.

Two officers, Eric Wright and Steve Bentley, spent eight months, part of the time camping in a van, living amongst the hippies in the village of Llandewi Brefi, targeting Hughes who had been pushing drugs since the 'swinging sixties' in the Kings Road. They met him in the New Inn, Llandewi, public house and became friends, losing £90 to him in a card-game. At first Hughes was suspicious of them and accused them of being officers. Wright grabbed him by the throat and threatened to beat him up. Bentley increased their cover by rowing with the local constable about drinking after hours.

After four months they moved out of the van and began sending messages on a radio transmitter from the loft of their cottage. This stopped abruptly when Hughes told them that when he could not sleep at night he liked to listen to ham radio wavelengths. As the months went by Wright drank and took drugs with Hughes, baby-sat his children and, he says, developed such a friendship that he came close to tipping him off that a raid was pending.

Meanwhile Todd was targeted by a surveillance team of eighteen officers camping out in a three-bedroom house in Hendon. A tail was put on him and when he led the officers to Seymour Road the house was put under constant observation. Even now the police were divided as to whether there was more than one laboratory. Dick Lee was convinced the manufacturing was done only in Wales and said categorically, 'No way is there a lab at Seymour Road.' Later, on his retirement, he would be presented with a plaque:

NO WAY

ITALASR

On 25 March 1977, 800 police made swoops in Wales and Seymour Road. In Wales they found nothing, and it was not until shortly before Christmas that Kemp revealed his hiding-place beneath the quarry-tiled floor of the lounge at his home. The laboratory equipment had been hidden down a well.

Shortly before Christmas 1977 another raid produced a haul of 13 million tablets of LSD worth, it was said, £100 million. In a titillating sidebar to the raid, it was made known that on a previous raid a hippy had been found having sexual intercourse with his girlfriend on the floor of an old caravan: 'The couple were on a "trip" and the man had hammered a six-inch nail through his nose "for a new kick".'[37]

37 *Daily Telegraph*, 24 December 1977.

Kemp received thirteen years, as did his rival Todd, and Cuthbertson eleven, Bott nine and Hughes eight. To the annoyance of many of the officers involved in the surveillance, most of the defendants were paroled after serving half their sentences. Kemp and Bott returned to live together after their release.

An interesting side-note appears in the *Sunday Mirror* for 12 March 1978. Chief crime reporter Norman Lucas writes: 'Many top detectives believe that politicians are closing their eyes to Britain's drug problem.'

One officer claims that

Successive governments have condoned the fiddling of Home Office drug statistics. It could be that only the death of sons or daughters of prominent politicians through drug addiction will start a crusade against those who deal in the dirtiest crime racket in the country.

As is so often the case after a successful operation, jealousy and in-fighting – which had more or less been held at bay during the previous months – now burst out. The hope and belief of Dick Lee was that *Operation Julie* would lead to the formation of a National Drugs Squad, but his hopes were misplaced and instead he soon found himself back in uniform. He resigned, wrote a book on the operation and bought a tobacconist's in the North of England. Six others resigned almost immediately over various criticisms of the way they were treated when they went back to their forces, and there were calls for a Home Office inquiry. Twenty-two members of the squad remained in the force.

What I will say is that the morale in the squad during the operation could not have been higher. Members of the squad lived in filthy, wet accommodation, ate and slept when they could, worked tremendously long hours

and were away from their families a hell of a long time.
I just hope someone remembers all this.[38]

In his account of *Operation Julie*, Lee remembers that:

> . . . within months he and five of his men, Johnny
> McWalters, Martyn Pritchard, Paul Purnell, Alan Buxton
> and Eric Wright resigned from the police. They found the
> work they had done and the experience gained was not
> considered by the Chief Constables to be of any value.[39]

After the Thames Ditton raid three officers ingested drugs
through the skin and wound up in hospital fearful that they
would be sent to the psychiatric unit, something which would
appear on their records:

> We were laughing and smiling about anything . . . When
> we got to hospital we asked for beds well away from
> windows in case it might give us that feeling which has
> affected others that they could fly. It was that scaring.[40]

In his book *Busted!* Pritchard recounts that he was obliged to
visit his mother after dark so as not to shame her in front of the
neighbours. Some time later he resigned and became a publican
in the Midlands. Later, the eponymous Julie left the force to
marry a fireman. Wright was one of the officers who left the
force soon after the operation was completed.

Short-term undercover officers in *Operation Swordfish* were
successful when they posed as the licensee, head barman and
a barmaid for six weeks in 1989. The Cauliflower pub in
Upminster Road, South Rainham, had been going through
managers at the rate of five within eighteen months before
the police went behind the bar to flush out a protection team.

38 *Sunday Telegraph*, 26 February 1978.
39 Dick Lee and Colin Pratt, *Operation Julie*, p. 348.
40 *Daily Express*, 9 March 1978.

In July 1990 the leaders, Donald Hoey and Leonard Sherwood, received six years apiece for counts of blackmail.

The dangers for an undercover officer are obvious, as policewoman Elaine Manson[41] discovered about the same time.

In what the police described as the first serious outbreak of protection racketeering – apparently they had already forgotton *Operation Swordfish* – Frank Salmon, a market trader from Dagenham, was gaoled at the Old Bailey for seven and a half years. He had been convicted of blackmail, affray and an attack during which ammonia was squirted in a victim's face. Robert Mitchell, said to be Salmon's right-hand man, was sentenced to three years for blackmail, affray and possession of a firearm, whilst Gary Pollard received four and a half years and Donald Meason twenty-one months.

Salmon had reigned over a part of the East End and Essex for a little over a year, trying to obtain protection money from twenty-three wine bars, clubs and saunas. He had shot up one bar and pressed a gun under the nose of a barman. In 1989 disc jockey Russell Holt, who played the East End pubs, had forty-two stitches in his head and hand following an assault by four masked men. His ankle was broken by a pool cue and he too went to the police, telling detectives he had been asked to pay Salmon £1,500 as a share of his earnings.

The police used Elaine Manson as the person to trap Salmon. Acting as the friend and business associate of Holt's wife, Denise Seaga, who ran a dress-shop, she met Salmon on five occasions, paying out a total of £800. It was thought that Salmon, known as a womaniser, would be less suspicious than if a male officer had acted as a decoy. On one meeting she was patted down by him for wires when he came to suspect that she was a police officer. His antennae were sound. Another time he accused her of being a policewoman and she told the court, 'He started at me and flicked his fingers . . . He shook his arm and a knife slid down inside his left palm.' On a third

41 A pseudonym.

occasion when she was with him she noticed a bulge in the leg of his trousers and remarked that it looked like the outline of a knife. 'Brains of Britain . . .' he replied. 'In this business you get wankers who don't play ball.'

On 22 May 1989 Manson handed over £600 in marked notes and asked Salmon why he referred to the cash as a present. 'I am not going to shout out it is protection money, am I?' he replied. Shortly afterwards he was arrested.

Operation Motion, hailed as the way ahead in British policing and launched in October 1994 by West London Drugs Squad, involved three women police officers going under cover and posing as prostitutes in a brothel in Queensway.

> We were trying to create the image of tarty street girls. We didn't wash, we left our hair dirty and matted and we deliberately chewed our nails.
>
> We had an AIDS poster, packets of Durex lying around and bottles of water which addicts use to smoke.
>
> If you are playing the part of a prostitute you have to prepare for the worst.
>
> Some would grope you but you just had to grit your teeth.
>
> We had to be very careful not to ask for cocaine directly because that would have been entrapment and they could have got out of it in court.

The thirty-five dealers who were filmed on video pleaded guilty and received sentences of between four and six years.[42]

Undercover work and informers go hand in hand. Here is an old-time criminal recounting his involvement; if it is accurate, it nearly amounts to another instance of the work of an *agent provocateur*.

In 1985 I was sitting indoors when Harry Brand,[43] the kid

42 *Sun*, 11 August 1994.
43 A pseudonym.

who lived next door, came round. He was really the local
bully and he'd offered me bits of crooked gear from time
to time. Usually I declined because it wasn't the stuff I
dealt in. If there was any gear I wanted for myself I did
a deal with him. Sometimes he wanted a bit of advice
and sometimes he told me a few lies but I'd taken them
in my stride. Now he wanted to know if I could get him
any counterfeit £50 notes. I said I wasn't interested in
anything like that. There were too many of the notes
about at that time and people were being nicked. A few
days later he came back again saying he had a friend in
Nottingham who wanted to lay out ten to twenty thousand
pounds for £50 notes. This should have stopped me right
away because he offered £10 a note when the going rate
was £4.

I eventually agreed to go and meet this fellow on the
Saturday morning, 22 June 1985. I was with him and
another man Jackie 'Tinker' Taylor and I arranged the
meet under the flyover at Brent Cross. There were three
men in the car. One was a young man in his late twenties
who said he was Tony Offord. The second was a very
coarse and very nervous Irishman, Paddy Flynn, who
was dripping gold and who said he was the purchaser,
and their driver. I took them for a drink well away to
a pub on Highgate Hill, The Woodman. We had a few
drinks and I wouldn't talk business and from there I split
them up. I suggested we leave Harry Brand, Offord and
the driver there but Paddy insisted his driver stays with
him. I decided I'd take them to a pub over Hackney and
I'd got bad vibes about this meeting. On the way Paddy
asks us if we'll pull into the forecourt of the Archway pub.
I said, 'This is a bit peculiar. You come all the way from
Nottingham yet you want to go to the Archway.' He made
a remark that there wasn't a Paddy in the land that didn't
know the Archway. From there we went to The Swan in
Kingsland Road. We had a drink and he pulled me aside

and said would I sell him some fifties. I asked him how it was to be done and he said he'd bring £20,000 next week but it would have to be the Saturday. He asked if I'd give him a sample and I gave him a straight note. He wanted to keep it but I wouldn't let him.

Jackie and I decided to give it a miss. He didn't feel right about it either; he reckoned the driver was a copper. Paddy and the driver then went back to The Woodman and got Harry Brand to phone us to ask if we'd do business and we said no.

When I got home that night Harry came round and spent two hours trying to persuade me that he'd known Offord for many years and that I should do the business because it meant a good drink from both sides.

I told him we were under the impression it was a set-up and to keep away from it. Every day for the next two weeks he came in begging and pleading for me to do the business. Eventually he asked if I would speak to the Irishman on the phone and come to some arrangements as he'd upped his purchase to £40,000.

From what he said I got the impression the money was for the IRA and I had a talk with Jack who said, 'I can't see the kid next door setting you up, neither can I see his mate Offord setting him up.' So out of greed we decided to do the business.

So, at short notice, we managed to scrape together £110K at face value. It cost £2 a piece. Then we sat down and worked out routes in case it was a ready-eye.

The stuff was taken to Highgate Hill and early on 6 July my nephew put it in black rubbish bags outside a private garage by some shops. There was no danger of anyone picking it up by accident. We'd already given it the once-over and there were no collections that day. I'd spoken to Offord and to the Irishman once on the phone. Now I think he was speaking from a police house.

When I knocked for Harry that morning he said he

couldn't come as his brother had just rung him up and told him he wanted him to drive a lorry. I said to Jackie we'd better swallow it. He didn't think the boy would put it on us and anyway Offord was to be there.

I decided we would go to the meet and I sent my nephew down to a place about two miles from The Woodman and told him once I was satisfied to bring the stuff to me. The Irishman, Detective Constable Valentine O'Rourke, and the same driver, Detective Inspector Roger Hazell, were at The Woodman. Offord wasn't. O'Rourke asked if I had the stuff. He had the cash and we could go round the corner and count it. I wasn't having it. I still had bad vibes and I was afraid of being shot.

So we went to Marler's Wine Bar at the bottom of Highgate Hill. We sat outside giving my eyes a chance. The wine bar was my choice to put them out of position if anything was wrong. I asked to see the cash and Paddy said he wanted to see the notes first. I went to have a world with Jack in the toilet to do a detour round the block and bring back about £10K. I didn't want them to see my nephew.

Roger went and sat in his Volvo. Paddy sat drinking with me as though Scotch was going out of fashion. Jack and I were drinking lemonade. Paddy agreed that he go and pick the cash up. He came back three-quarters of an hour later with a flying bag over his shoulder and I shouted out to Mike to go and get the stuff as everything appeared to be all right.

Next moment Mike brought the stuff up, handed it to Jackie Taylor and the next thing I can remember is being hit over the head with something. There was a Scotsman shouting, 'Where's my piece' and men were jumping on me. I screamed to people sitting outside the wine bar, 'These bastards have fitted me up.' Everyone was herded into the pub and I was taken to Holloway Road police station. When it came to it I was charged with £50K.

Now I know Brand was a police informer. He never gave evidence but his name did come out. While I was in the Scrubs waiting trial Harry came up to see me and said he hoped I didn't think he'd had anything to do with it.

When I got bail though I got him, put a knife to his throat, laid him on the floor and said that if I found he had done it I'd kill him. This bully of the neighbourhood was crying out, 'Please, Mick.'

I wanted to be sure and I went to have a meet with a Chief Inspector I knew and said I'd give £5,000 for the names of the people who'd fitted me up. The message came back two weeks later that there were to be no names but all I had to do was look outside my own front door so I never paid over the money.

Brand used to ring me up crying down the phone, but I had to be very careful with him because I was under twenty-four-hour observation and eventually he was sent to Canada.

I got three years and he came back eighteen months into my sentence. When I came out his family put the house up for sale and then one day the 'For Sale' notice was taken down and I found they'd sneaked out of the back door in the middle of the night. They must have taken all the furniture out that way. That's the last I ever saw of the family. The whole thing cost me £4K and three years.

Even later I learned Brand had stuck up a number of other guys.[44]

44 Some of the police statements in the case appear as the Appendix, and provide a somewhat different account of the incident.

10

The Attitude of the Courts

What then has been the attitude of the courts to the informer, the cell snitch, the undercover agent and the entrapper? Certainly as far as the entrapper is concerned, in Britain and the United States they have followed two differing lines. In one case entrapment was literally that, when a Gary Dawes climbed into a car thoughtfully left by the police for the purpose of luring such people as Mr Dawes who might want to steal from it or take it for a ride around the block. When he shut the door the car locked, and there he was when the police arrived a few minutes later to arrest him. Charged with the offence of aggravated vehicle taking and convicted, he appealed and the Divisional Court said that, on the facts, the process had been a perfectly lawful one. Their Lordships did, however, foresee problems if the officers did not arrive within a short time after the suspect was trapped, and suggested that a recorded message could automatically inform the suspect why he had been arrested.

Entrapment together with the use of informers, both here and in the United States, has always provided problems for the police in terms of just how far the courts in either jurisdiction will admit evidence obtained by such methods. America has always been much stricter in excluding such evidence. There entrapment is in effect a defence, provided it is a relatively innocent person and not an unwary professional criminal who is trapped. The stage was set in the *Sherman v United States* case.

Professional criminals can, at times, be judges. John M. Murphy was an associate county court circuit judge in Illinois from 1972 until 1983, when he was charged with accepting bribes to fix the outcome of hundreds of cases from drink driving to felony, theft and battery. He was assigned to the traffic courts for the first eleven years of his tenure, during which time Judge Richard LeFevour was the supervising judge of the traffic court and the man who had the authority to decide which judge would hear which case. His cousin James LeFevour, of the Chicago police, was assigned to the traffic court throughout almost all that period and organised the movement of cases to Murphy, who would dismiss them or give a supervisory sentence. Money would then pass from the successful lawyer to James for onward transmission to Richard LeFevour. The going rate seems to have been about $100 a case, with 10 per cent in addition for the police officer running the traffic court list.

The state prosecutors expected to win as much as 90 per cent of their traffic cases against public defenders but none against a group of lawyers known as 'miracle workers'. In one drink-driving case the prosecutor asked a woman defendant, 'And don't you think it is fair to say that you were under the influence of intoxicating liquor?' The woman, who had failed the roadside tests and admitted drinking, replied, 'Yes, I guess that is a fair thing to say.' Judge Murphy called a recess, suggesting that the defence attorney have a word with his client. As he left the bench he was heard to call out, 'You won't believe this. The State's Attorney just got the defendant to admit she was drunk.' When the court sat again the defence lawyer asked his client if she was drunk and this time she said she was not. The defence lawyer made no closing argument. Murphy said, 'I still have a reasonable doubt. Not guilty.'

An *Operation Greylord* was set in place in which agents

of the FBI lied on oath about made-up cases. Murphy had an
ingenious defence to the allegation that by his bad behaviour
he was depriving the people in his jurisdiction of his honest
services. It was impossible, he argued, for there to be 'honest
services' because these cases involving the FBI were themselves frauds on the court.

The United States Courts of Appeal disposed of this
quite simply: 'In the pursuit of crime the Government is
not confined to behavior suitable to the drawing rooom.'
The FBI and the prosecutors had, the court found, behaved
honourably in establishing and running *Operation Greylord*.
They had notified the presiding Judge of the Circuit Court's
Criminal Division, the State's Attorney of Cook County and
the Attorney General of Illinois. The *Greylord* cases did not
interfere with the smooth operation of the local courts. In
this respect they were less offensive than 'sting' operations in
which the existence of a well-paid fence may induce people to
steal goods. Here no stranger was at risk. *Operation Greylord*
only harmed the corrupt.[1]

Evidence obtained by the use of entrapment has gone down
two sharply divergent paths in America and in these courts.
In the United States, where entrapment has been shown the
courts have, in the past, rigorously excluded that evidence
where the behaviour has actively encouraged the commission
of a crime.

One of the old American cases, *Grimm v United States*,[2]
points up some of the difficulties and actually sets out the
distinction the courts have often made in these cases and
the thin line they have often walked to uphold or quash a
conviction. Mr Grimm was convicted of mailing information
to a Herman Huntress as to the terms of sale of what were
engagingly described as 'obscene, lewd or lascivious pictures'.
I doubt they would cause a blush on the face of the proverbial

1 *United States of America v John M. Murphy*; 768 Federal Reporter, 2d
Series, p. 1518.
2 156 US 604.

maiden aunt nowadays. Unfortunately for Mr Grimm, however, Herman Huntress was the pseudonym, or perhaps *nom de chasse*, for Mr McAfee, a post office inspector and an agent for the grandly named Western Society for the Suppression of Vice. The US Supreme Court held that McAfee was merely seeking to discover the nature of Grimm's business, as opposed to endeavouring to induce the commission of a crime.

In another example, *Sorrells v United States*,[3] a conviction for selling a half-gallon jar of whisky was overturned. The prohibition agent had posed as a tourist and – something which seems to have aggravated matters, it appears – had either served or pretended to have served with the defendant in the same regiment in the First World War.

In *Sherman v United States*[4] the Supreme Court took a similar view. Here the court roundly condemned the behaviour of a government agent, Kalchinian, who whilst awaiting sentence for drug offences made friends with another man who was trying to wean himself off a drug habit. He was eventually persuaded by Kalchinian's repeated appeals to supply him with drugs. Worse, he went back on to drugs himself. The Court said:

> The case at bar illustrates an evil which the defense of entrapment is designed to overcome. The . . . Government plays on the weakness of an innocent party and beguiles him into committing crimes which he otherwise would not have attempted. Law enforcement does not require methods such as this.

Over the years, as crime and criminal have become more sophisticated, we can see the American horror of entrapment weakening. There are two essential issues in an entrapment defence, says Professor Alan Dershowitz:

3 287 US 435.
4 356 US 369.

The first is whether a government agent *induced* the defendant into committing the crime. If he did, then a second issue arises: the defendant cannot be convicted unless – and this is a big unless – the government can prove that the defendant was *ready and willing* to commit the crime and was just waiting for an opportunity. If the government can prove that the defendant was thus 'predisposed' to commit the crime, then it can convict him even if its agents 'induced' him into committing it on that occasion.[5]

Now in *United States v Williams*,[6] convictions for mail fraud have been upheld even though Federal undercover agents embossed blank credit cards supplied to them by the defendant at their invitation. The courts seem to have had no trouble with undercover agents who run a pawnshop as part of a 'sting' operation or who buy stolen cars. There are, however, American jurists who take the view that an undercover agent may buy but not sell drugs.

The current American position can perhaps be summed up by the case of *United States v Murphy*.[7] Here a conviction for an escape from a Federal prison was upheld notwithstanding a due process claim based on the alleged conduct of prison officials who were said to have encouraged and possibly assisted the escape. The court took the view that even if the allegations were true they failed to establish a due process defence because the government had not engineered the crime from start to finish and its involvement in the crime had not risen to the level of 'creative activity'.

The entrapment defence known to American lawyers as the 'defense of last resort' works only rarely if there is anyone approaching a professional criminal in the dock. They regard it as a defence which can be used only if there is no other chance

5 A. Dershowitz, *The Best Defense*, pp. 236–7.
6 1986, CA9 Cal.
7 1985, CA7 Ill.

of acquittal. The thinking behind it goes that prosecutors can use inducements on the basis that any jury will take the view that organised crime leaders will be predisposed to committing any crime and are just awaiting the opportunity to do so. Entrapment is, therefore, in no way unfair.

Over the years there have been various attempts – mostly unsuccessful – in the English courts to limit the damage to a defence by the use of a police spy or *agent provocateur* as opposed to a co-conspirator or co-accused.

In *Dowling*,[8] a jury was advised to treat with caution the evidence of a man who had entered into a conspiracy in order to betray it. Both the judge, Mr Justice Erle, and another judge, Mr Justice Maule, in *Mullins*,[9] another case that year, were sure that an infiltrator was not an accomplice about whose evidence the jury had to be given a specific warning.[10]

The next step was to try to have the evidence excluded on the grounds that it had been unfairly obtained, so putting it on a par with an improperly obtained confession. In a Courts-Martial case, *Murphy*,[11] the defendant had been convicted of giving information regarding security at a barracks to men whom he believed were Irish terrorists but who were, in fact, undercover agents. Lord Parker, C.J. had said in an earlier case, *Callis v Gunn*:[12]

> That discretion [i.e. the 'overriding discretion' to exclude admissible but unfair evidence], as I understand it, would certainly be exercised by excluding the evidence if there was any suggestion of it having been obtained oppressively by false representations, by a trick, by threats, by bribes, by anything of that sort.

8 (1848) 3 Cox C.C. 509.
9 (1848) 3 Cox C.C. 531.
10 J. D. McLean, *Informers and Agents Provocateurs* [1969] Crim. LR 527.
11 [1965] N.I. 138.
12 [1964] 1 Q.B. 495.

It was now argued that the behaviour of the officers pretending to be members of a terrorist organisation was a trick. The Courts-Martial Appeal Court would have none of that. Oppression would not be satisfied by mere deception by the police which was 'as old as the constable in plain clothes'.

The next tack to be tried was that, as a mark of its disapproval of the conduct of the police, the court should refuse to convict. This is a line which, if raised sufficiently delicately, may appeal to a jury but received no change from the Divisional Court. In *Sneddon v Stevenson*[13] the defendant had spoken to a plain-clothes officer and was subsequently convicted of soliciting for the purposes of prostitution. The argument, which had no success at all, was that the police officer was acting as *agent provocateur* and the court should quash the conviction to show its disapproval. The court said that the police officer had 'merely placed his car so that she [the defendant] could solicit *if she so desired*'. The case would seem to be a relatively early example of what might be described as passive entrapment, as opposed to active entrapment as is exercised in vice cases in America. There a game of cat-and-mouse is played when the undercover officer endeavours to get the girl to make a fatal proposition before she discovers his real identity. As the cases of Titley, Birtles and Macro showed, even active entrapment has only counted towards sentence, and in the first of those cases not even then.

Four years after Birtles in December 1973 the question of law, reality and Northern Ireland all meshed neatly into one case to the eventual benefit of no one. Jeremiah Mealey and Philip Michael Sheridan appealed against their conviction at St Albans Crown Court of conspiracy to rob. The allegation was that they had conspired with a number of other people who lived in Luton to rob a bank and send the proceeds back to Ireland for the benefit of the Republican interests there. They were probably talked into the enterprise by an Irishman,

13 [1967] 2 All E.R. 1277.

Lennon, who at the very least was an informer and probably an
agent provocateur. With some skill he put together the robbery,
but at the last minute pleaded he had a sick child and could not
leave the house. On the way to the robbery – surprise, surprise!
– Mealey and Sheridan, along with two others, were arrested.
They received ten years' imprisonment for their pains.

So far so good, or bad, depending upon one's attitude. The
next stage was that Lennon went to see the National Council for
Civil Liberties and began to make a statement to the secretary,
Larry Grant, part of which made criticisms of the police for
forcing him to become an informer. Unfortunately, although
he said sufficient for Mr Grant to make a reconstruction from
his notes, Lennon did not live long enough to sign a complete
statement. He was shot dead in Surrey.

The Court of Appeal was not sure that Lennon was an *agent
provocateur*, but that he was an informer they had no doubt.
Nor did the Lord Chief Justice mind that he was so.

> . . . It must be accepted today, indeed if the opposite
> was ever considered, that this is a perfectly lawful police
> weapon in appropriate cases and common sense indicates
> that if a police officer or anybody else infiltrates a secret
> society, he has to show a certain amount of enthusiasm
> for what the society is doing if he is to maintain his cover
> for more than five minutes.
> . . . it is, in our judgment, quite clearly established that
> the so-called defence of entrapment, which finds some
> place in the law of the United States of America, finds
> no place in our law here.[14]

The appeals were dismissed.

The discretion of the courts to exclude what could be seen to
be unfairly obtained evidence was largely clarified by *Sang*.[15]
In this case involving forged US notes, the defence was that

14 *R. v Mealey and Sheridan*, 60 Cr. App R p. 62.
15 [1979] 2 All E.R. 1222.

his conduct was the result of behaviour by a police *agent provocateur*. The House of Lords unanimously rejected the decisions which had favoured the discretion of a judge to exclude evidence gained as a result of entrapment.

The question of improperly obtained evidence was to a certain extent codified in the Police and Criminal Evidence Act 1984 *s.* 78 (1). It provides that in any criminal proceedings where the court is asked to allow evidence on which the prosecution proposes to rely to be given, if it appears to the court that, having regard to all the circumstances, including the circumstances in which the evidence was obtained, the admission of the evidence would have such an adverse effect on the fairness of the proceedings, the court ought not to admit it.

It was not long before appeals were being lodged after convictions where the trial judge had refused to exclude evidence. First, however, there is a 1986 Home Office circular to be considered: '. . . No member of a police force, and no public informant should counsel, incite or procure the commission of an offence.'[16]

In *Harwood*[17] the defendant and two others were convicted of conspiracy to evade the prohibition on the exportation of counterfeit currency. It was suggested that X, the person to whom the currency was to be delivered, was either an *agent provocateur* or an informer. The trial judge held that he was not but, even had he been, *s.* 78 was not designed to exclude entrapment evidence. The Court of Appeal observed, *obiter*, that since PACE was an Act dealing with evidential matters it could not be used as another route to abrogate a rule of law that entrapment was no defence.

In *Gill and Ranuana*[18] the defendants were convicted of conspiracy to murder. They alleged that X, through whom they had met undercover police officers, was an *agent provocateur*,

16 Home Office Circular No.35/1986, *Informants who take part in crime.*
17 [1989] Crim.LR 285.
18 [1989] Crim.LR 358.

something the trial judge rejected. The Court of Appeal expressed doubts about the observations in *Harwood*, reverting to *Sang* by saying: 'we have no doubt that the speeches in *Sang* and the import of those speeches are matters to be taken into account by a judge when applying the provisions of *s.* 78.'

It was clear the Court of Appeal was going to have to reconcile these decisions and in effect lay down some guidelines, and it had the opportunity to do so in some domestic undercover operations.

A recent phenomenon – or if not recent, one which has newly surfaced – is that of the disgruntled spouse or lover, usually the former since there is often insurance money involved, who, tired of his or her partner, seeks out a hit-man or woman to remove the incumbrance. Since it is said that the price for disposing of an unwanted lover is around £1,500 it is not surprising that the trend is growing. In a twist to the tale, the hit-man turns out to be an undercover police officer and the enterprise ends in tears and prison. It appears that some officers specialised in these productions, travelling outside their area to assist in the undercover operation. One regional crime squad detective was found to have posed as a contract killer on three occasions.

Barrie Irving, Director of the Police Foundation, said on the Channel Four television programme *Dispatches* which highlighted this line of business:

> The undercover policeman acts the part well, but perhaps too well. The target genuinely believes that the hit-man is a professional killer prepared to murder for a relatively small sum of money.
>
> That generates a high level of fear. The 'hit-man' may then put pressure on the target saying things like, 'Make your mind up – have you got me all the way here for nothing? You're wasting my time.'[19]

19 Quoted in *Police Review*, 15 October 1993.

It was not long before the matter was resolved. In two cases which came before the Court of Appeal in the autumn of 1993, *Smurthwaite* and *Gill*,[20] the court considered in what circumstances evidence obtained by undercover officers should be excluded. Both cases concerned defendants who had been convicted of soliciting to murder. The prosecution case had been that each defendant had tried to arrange the murder of his or her spouse but, in fact, the 'contract killer' turned out to be an undercover policeman. Should the court allow the evidence obtained in what was undoubtedly a trap?

The Lord Chief Justice, Lord Taylor, after emphasising that *s.* 78 of the Police and Criminal Evidence Act 1984 had not afforded a defence of entrapment, set out the considerations the judge should take into account in exercising his discretion in excluding evidence as unfairly obtained. Questions in a not exhaustive list included: Was the officer acting as an *agent provocateur* in the sense that he was enticing the defendant to commit an offence he would not otherwise have committed? What was the nature of the entrapment? Does the evidence consist of admissions to a completed offence or does it consist of the actual commission of the offence? How active or passive was the officer's role in obtaining the evidence? Is there an unassailable record of what had occurred or is it strongly corroborated?

This, it was thought, might have settled the undercover contract killer policeman situation once and for all, but it did not.

In the case of Harbel Mann, who received a six-year sentence at Oxford Crown Court in 1992, he said his marriage had been breaking up and his wife was seeing someone else. A police informer approached him at a club and offered to find a hit-man, who turned out to be an undercover policeman. In the case of Paul Dixon, who received five years at Plymouth Crown Court, also in 1992, the court was told he was having a nervous breakdown and gambling heavily. He was approached in a casino by a man who offered to deal with his wife for him.

The would-be contractor might wish to withdraw but, as in the case of Alan Bainbridge who received seven years in 1989 at Chelmsford Crown Court, they found themselves unable to do so, saying that after meeting the undercover officer he or she was too terrified to do anything but go ahead with the plan. Concerted appeals were launched and the Court of Appeal heard an application for leave to appeal in the cases of Mann and Dixon.[21] The idea was to show that the third person, the one who had contracted the police, was an informer and because he had not given evidence in the trial it was unfair. An informant might have purposes of his own (indeed they all do), and by the time the undercover officer had been introduced, the husband or wife had been incited to commit a crime that would never have been contemplated but for the informer.

Bainbridge's solicitor, John Bacon, had told Duncan Campbell in the *Guardian*:

> This is a nebulous point of law . . . with the undercover police masquerading as hit-men. If you place someone in submissive circumstances their free will will be overborne and they provide evidence against themselves.

The Court, with the Lord Chief Justice presiding, would have none of this.

> One of the main reasons for using undercover police officers in such cases was to avoid having to rely on informants of bad character, who might be regarded by the jury as unreliable witnesses.
>
> In many cases, moreover, there were other good reasons of public policy for not calling informants. They, or

21 Their appeals were dismissed.

their families, might be put at risk of reprisal and their value as informants in ongoing or future cases might be destroyed.[22]

The attitude of the officers involved in these contract killer cases is typified by 'John' in *Scotland Yard*:

What I will never do is talk them into it. But I don't talk them out of it either, because I worry that if I talk them out of it, a week later they'll go and ask someone else.[23]

In *Christou*[24] the Court of Appeal had already decided that discussions between suspects and undercover officers, not overtly acting as police officers, were not within the ambit of the codes under the 1984 Act. Then in *Smurthwaite* the Lord Chief Justice added a proviso that officers should not use their undercover pose so as to circumvent the code. In *Bryce*[25] the court had held that the undercover officer had done just that and acted outside the code. The judge, in deciding whether to admit the evidence, must then consider whether he has abused his role to ask questions which ought properly be asked by a police officer and in accordance with the codes.

Given the law as set out by the Lord Chief Justice, it is easy to see how Mr Justice Waterhouse came to exclude the evidence in the case of Keith Hall. On the other hand, if the defendant is an experienced criminal this may count against him even if there is a deliberate breach. In *Allardice*[26] the defendant had been refused access to a solicitor and then made a confession. In his evidence at the trial, he said that he was well aware of his right to remain silent, and so his confession was given in evidence.

22 *Guardian*, 18 July 1994. *Dixon* (Paul): *Mann* (Harbel); *The Times*, 31 December 1994.
23 R. Fleming and H. Miller, *Scotland Yard*, p. 122.
24 [1992] 4 All E.R. 559.
25 [1992] 4 All E.R. 567.
26 [1988] Crim. LR 608.

Then in 1994 came two cases which set post-crime under-cover work on its head.

Patricia Hall, the mother of two young boys who disappeared from her home in Pudsey, Yorkshire, in January 1992, has not been traced. On 10 March 1994 her husband Keith was acquitted of her murder at Leeds Crown Court. The prosecution case was that Hall, who ran a mobile grocery, had confessed to an undercover policewoman 'Liz' that he had strangled his wife and then incinerated the body. The policewoman had been planted on Hall after he replied to a 'lonely hearts' advertisement in his local paper. All their meetings and telephone calls had been tape-recorded, and when Liz was discussing marriage and expressed a worry that Patricia Hall might return, Hall was alleged to have said, 'I was sleeping downstairs, then I woke up. I strangled her. It wasn't as simple as that, there were voices in my head telling me to do it. I'm sorry. Does that change anything. Do you still want me?'

At the trial the judge, Mr Justice Waterhouse, refused to allow the jury to hear the tape, saying that the questioning by the policewoman had driven a coach and horses through the Police and Criminal Evidence Act 1984 which was designed to protect suspects in interviews. After the verdict he did, however, allow the publication of the contents of the tape. Hall had maintained that his wife, who had had psychiatric treatment, had simply walked out on him after the marriage had deteriorated. He appealed to her to return so that their relationship could be renewed. She does not, so far, appear to have done so.

Perhaps the most gross example of an attempted entrapment to garner a confession came in the case of Rachel Nickell who was savagely killed, stabbed to death on Wimbledon Common in July 1992. There was the usual police sweep of suspects and men living in the area who had convictions for indecent assault or indecent exposure. Amongst them was Colin Stagg, then twenty-nine, who had, it appeared, a compulsive hatred of blonde women whom he told friends were wicked people with loose morals. Many of the women to whom he had exposed himself were blondes. He lived in a poorly furnished council flat in Roehampton near Wimbledon Common, and had a collection of fairly soft-core porn girlie magazines. He was a survival fanatic, and a committed pagan who said he wanted to be thought of as a white witch. What he also craved was a long-term relationship.

He fitted the profile drawn up by Paul Britton, a clinical psychologist, who had been called in to assist the police. Other aspects of the psychological profile concluded that the killer would have a fantasy of using a knife to physically and sexually assault a young submissive adult woman, and sexual excitement from anal and vaginal assault coupled with the victim's fear and submissiveness. Stagg at some time wrote letters to a woman who had placed a 'lonely hearts' advertisement; she told the police that they were 'totally disgusting'. Britton was now invited to mastermind a honeypot trap, using a young policewoman to insinuate herself into Stagg's emotions and so, it was hoped, obtain a confession. A policewoman who was identified as Lizzie James began a correspondence and purported friendship with Stagg.

Guided by Britton, she wrote to him of her fantasies which were described in court by William Clegg QC as 'just about the most hard-core pornography one could imagine'. It was suggested by Mr Clegg that the police and Mr Britton operated a carrot and donkey routine in which Lizzie would 'punish' Stagg by not replying immediately to a letter which was considered not to have gone far enough, and to reward him with a quick response if the letters he sent were suitably deviant. Letters which would probably have been 'rewarded' included those he wrote saying he had never had a sex life, and those containing fantasies such as having sex in the garden and one of having sex in a car.

His rewards included a letter which read, in part:

You write really well, if I close my eyes I can feel you

sitting astride me and pressing me into the grass. I believe this is only the tip of the iceberg. I'm sure your fantasies know no bounds.

In a reply to a letter in which he thought he might have gone too far, she wrote:

My fantasies know no bounds, sometimes my imagination runs riot, sometimes this worries me. I hope I'm not sounding unnatural; but sometimes normal things are just not enough and my demands are much greater, not just straight sex, there is so much to explore. God, don't think I'm a weirdo.

Her later letters contained hints of her past experiences of ritual sexual abuse, her desire to be dominated and, later, of sado-masochism. It was now thought that she must speak to Stagg on the telephone. He was not as forthcoming as was hoped and she offered to take him on holiday. By May 1993 she brought the subject round to murder, and he talked of using a knife in his sexual fantasies. They met for lunch in Hyde Park and he then handed over a letter which contained what were seen to be the common key ingredients – a local common, sunny weather, trees and a knife used to trace marks on the victim. To help things along, Lizzie claimed she had taken part in a satanic murder of a baby and a young woman. 'In certain ways I wish you had [killed Rachel] because it would make things easier for me,' she told him.

Four days later he told her a completely invented story of how he had strangled a young woman in the New Forest and had buried her. At their third and last meeting, Lizzie threatened to break up the burgeoning relationship.

'There can't be anything between us, Colin,' she said, and added in reference to the Rachel murder 'if only it had been you'. According to her evidence Stagg continued to deny the murder but admitted being close to the scene. He started to show signs of sexual arousal and spoke of another fantasy in which on Wimbledon Common he would creep up on Lizzie with a knife. 'If only you had done the Wimbledon Common murder it would be great,' she enticed.

By now, however, Stagg was clearly suspicious and contacted the *Daily Star*. He told Lizzie that he could have admitted to the murder, but that to do so would have been a lie. The operation was wound down, the letters dried up and within weeks Stagg was arrested and charged.

The prosecution's argument was that the psychological profile showed a man who had a sexual fantasy of inflicting anal injuries and who lived near Wimbledon Common in similar circumstances to Stagg. There was a negligible chance of two men with those fantasies being in the same place at the same time.

On 14 September 1994 Mr Justice Ognall refused to allow the evidence of Lizzie James to be given in evidence:

> Any legitimate steps taken by the police and the prosecuting authorities to bring the perpetrators to justice are to be applauded, but the emphasis must be on legitimate. A careful appraisal of the material demonstrates a skilful and sustained enterprise to manipulate the accused, sometimes subtly, sometimes blatantly.

He went on to say that the transcript of the interviews showed an attempt had been made to seduce the accused into exposing his innermost fantasies.

Almost immediately there was a bitter argument between the police and Crown Prosecution Service over where the blame lay for the exclusion of the evidence. On the face of it the rift was healed when Sir Paul Condon, Commissioner of Police for the Metropolis, and Mrs Barbara Mills, Director of Public Prosecutions, metaphorically held hands on television and said the criticism had been misplaced.

Curiously enough, two days after the Hall decision a case

at the Swansea Crown Court showed that the informer-*agent provocateur* is alive and well, albeit having in this instance fled to Greece, and that however gross an entrapment there may be to commit a crime there is still no defence. A police informer, Graham Titley, run by a Midlands Regional Crime Squad officer, managed to persuade a gang to forge £18 million American Express travellers' cheques. He is said to have netted around £100,000 from Amex by way of rewards.[27]

In August 1990, Titley was arrested by the West Midlands police in possession of £10,000 of counterfeit currency. He came under the wing of Detective Constable Alan Ledbrook and began to talk. At his trial in February 1991, Detective Superintendent R. Beards, then second in command of the West Midlands Regional Crime Squad, sent a letter to the judge saying that Titley could help to smash 'major criminals throughout the United Kingdom and Europe . . . who are engaged in the large scale distribution of drugs and counterfeit currency'. It was also thought that he could expose paramilitary organisations in Northern Ireland who were using drugs sales to finance their activities. Titley, who had a string of relatively minor convictions going back to 1970, was sentenced to eighteen months' imprisonment of which he served seven. As befitted a good officer, Ledbrook kept in touch with Titley during his sentence. By the end of the year and now relocated in Staffordshire, Titley was used in a target operation.

The target was sixty-one-year-old David Docker, who said that until he met Titley he was conducting a successful business in factoring and buying and selling end-of-range goods. An undercover operation was set up. First there was an attempt to persuade him to buy a container of drugs from Holland; the undercover police buyers said they would buy it from him. An attempt by Docker to persuade the police to pay up front failed. He made no attempt to contact the 'sellers'.

This operation was not a success and in March 1992 the

27 David Rose and John Merry, 'Scandal of police "fit-ups"' in *Observer*, 25 September 1994.

director of casework at the CPS headquarters, C.W.P. Newall, authorised the police to obtain and try to supply Docker with fake travellers' cheques. Immunity would be given to Titley and an undercover officer known as Mickey for offences they might commit along the way to their target. On 16 May 1992, Docker and some friends were lured to a hotel on the M1 where there were £4 million fake Amex cheques in the boot of a car. Seven men including Docker were arrested. Titley received £37,000 for his efforts.

Nor was the trial a success. Defence lawyers spent a considerable amount of time and effort in trying to get disclosure of documents from the prosecution, including the amount paid to Titley as a reward. In turn he disappeared. When it came to it, Ledbrook did not attend the trial either: he had, said the police, suffered a nervous breakdown. Judge Richard Gibbs dismissed the charges in July 1993, saying that the case was an abuse of process. He was particularly unhappy that the prosecution had not complied with his order for disclosure of documents. He kept an open mind, he said, on why Ledbrook had failed to appear.

What might have been disclosed if the documents had been produced was the sum of £50,000 also paid by Amex to Titley in May 1993 for the Swansea case. By now Titley had been resettled in South Wales and was in contact with a printer, Bernard Wilson, trying to persuade him to print forged Equity cards, MOT certificates and cheques. Wilson, facing bankruptcy with the failure of his business, agreed to print the cards but not the other items. Titley brought pressure on Wilson to go ahead with the whole deal. Wilson claims that threats were made to ensure his full co-operation and, with £5,000 supplied to the police by Amex and handed on to Titley, the necessary equipment was bought. The South Wales police were tipped off and when Wilson and seven others were arrested the raids discovered a world record of $26.6 million forged cheques. Judge Hugh Williams, criticising the conduct of Titley and Ledbrook, said that the eight men arrested were victims of 'scandalous, corrupt incitement' which led them to being 'fitted up to commit crimes which none would have ever dreamed of committing otherwise'.

At least one serving police officer from the Midlands Regional Crime Squad knew or believed that the informer was acting as an *agent provocateur*. Not only that, but he was doing so when he was being handled by a serving police officer from the Midlands. Despite his comments, the judge refused to allow the men to change their pleas to 'not guilty', saying that he was not considering imposing a custodial sentence.[28]

In late October 1994 a third trial involving Titley collapsed when no evidence was offered at Leeds Crown Court against two men, neither of whom had convictions and who had been accused of trying to sell fake travellers' cheques, a situation into which they had been lured by Titley. The Police Complaints Authority began an investigation into all three cases.

Then came a drug importation conspiracy in the Court of Appeal in which, if ever there was a case of entrapment, this was surely it. The facts were simply that a man named Honi, a Pakistani informer used by the United States Drug Enforcement Agency, brought 20 kilos of heroin into this country at the request of Shahzad, a Pakistani dealer, and with the knowledge of at least one customs officer. Honi was then installed in a hotel room and for several weeks tried to persuade Shahzad to come to England. His friend, Latif, arrived the next day, and when both men went to see Honi they were given six bags of Horlicks made up to look like heroin. Both men were promptly arrested. On appeal they claimed first that it was an abuse of process to lure them here, and secondly that Honi's evidence should have been excluded under *s*.78 Police and Criminal Evidence Act 1984.

The Court of Appeal was particularly impressed by the fact that for once a major operator had been arrested. All too

28 *The Times*, 17 September 1994.

often it is the small mule who is caught; sometimes with the connivance of the bigger operator who sacrifices a pawn to enable a smarter move to be made. If on occasions the bigger fish were lured here and then hooked, there was no abuse in that.

There still remained the overall question of whether Honi's evidence would have such an adverse effect on the fairness of the proceedings that it should be excluded. Their Lordships had little sympathy with the argument that s.78 of the Police and Criminal Evidence Act 1984, which was designed to protect the innocent, should be invoked on behalf of an importer of £3.2 million worth of drugs into the country. They thought Parliament might be surprised to hear that the protection of the section extended to such a man. Nor were they impressed with the argument that the evidence should be excluded on the grounds that he was encouraged by an agent of the British Government.

They did not accept that the admission of Honi's evidence had such an adverse effect that it should not have been admitted, and they reiterated that it was for the trial judge to decide; they could not begin to say he was wrong. The appeals were dismissed.

It would seem that once again the court has hardened its heart against the professional criminal and, given there was no bad faith, in future it will take a great deal of persuasion before evidence in such a case would be excluded. Nevertheless the exclusion of evidence under s.78 is a matter for the discretion of the trial judge, and for the present officers should not rely on judges always taking such a robust view. However, overall the heartening part of the appeal from the viewpoint of the police is that it appears the Court of Appeal was, at least obliquely, strengthening the resolve of judges against excluding such evidence. It might seem, however, that the court had rather gone against the principles of *Smurthwaite*.

However, not all cases in which the defence has tried to have evidence excluded under s.78 have gone against the police. In

Bailey[29] a little psycho-drama was acted out for the benefit of
the defendant. The inquiry had reached a stage where there
could be no further questioning because charges had been
brought; now the officers and the custody officer played
out a little charade to fool the defendant. The investigating
officers pretended they did not want the defendants put in a
cell together, but the custody officer said he was going to
do so. The cell was bugged and the defendants then made
damaging admissions in their conversations with each other.
The Court of Appeal upheld the inclusion of the evidence.

What is to be made of these varied cases? It seems clear that
professional criminals may find themselves treated less favourably than the ordinary defendant. There are great dangers in the
use of entrapment evidence, and from the point of view of the
police it is difficult for them to know when evidence obtained
by such means will be admissible. Perhaps it is time for the
Court of Appeal to lay down more detailed guidelines.

If sometimes it is difficult to distinguish between the
decisions of the Court of Appeal, if one compares *Bailey*
and *Mason*, then a line can be drawn. Whilst almost always
bad faith will cause the evidence to be excluded, the courts will
not intervene when defendants have hanged themselves of their
own accord and where by a trick the police have encouraged
them to do so. In *Mason*[30] the investigating officer told the
defendant (and his solicitor) that his fingerprints had been
found near the scene of the crime. This was quite untrue and
the subsequent confession was then excluded. Lord Lane did
however say that 'if the police had acted in bad faith, the
Court would have had little difficulty in ruling any confession
inadmissible'.

In *Williams and O'Hare v DPP*,[31] the defendants were
summoned for interfering with a motor vehicle with intent
to commit a theft contrary to *s.9* (1) of the Criminal Attempts

29 [1993] 3 All E.R. 513.
30 [1987] 3 All E.R. 481.
31 [1993] Crim. L.R. 775.

Act 1981. They based their defence on the entrapment by police officers who in a high crime-rate area, at least so far as vehicle theft was concerned, had left an unattended and open Ford Transit van with what appeared a valuable load of cigarettes apparently there for the taking.

Initially the magistrates found that there had been no communication with the defendants. The justices found the police had not been *agents provocateurs* and that the defendants had been caught through their own dishonesty. The Divisional Court heard the case by way of case stated and concluded that the justices were right to admit the evidence. It was unimpressed by the argument of 'irresistible temptation'.

In the earlier case of *Christou and Wright*[32] it was said that not every trick that produced evidence against an accused would result in unfairness. In this case undercover officers had set up a jeweller's shop in an attempt to recover stolen property and collect evidence against thieves and handlers who took the property to the shop for sale. The appellants had argued that the evidence of fingerprints (they had to sign receipts), conversation which had helped the police trace the owners and general banter should have been excluded either under *Sang* or *s.* 78 of PACE. Further, the claim was that a three-month sting operation such as had been carried on was contrary to public policy. The Court of Appeal would have nothing of it.

In *DPP v Marshall*[33] plain-clothes officers had bought a can of lager and a bottle of wine from a shop licensed only to deal in bulk purchases. The Divisional Court regarded that as a wholly legitimate exercise by the police. It is difficult to see how there could have been any very different ruling. The purchase of drink by police officers in undercover operations in bars and nightclubs has been standard practice for decades.

A slightly different line of cases is where, after the offence has been committed, the police then use a trick to obtain a

32 [1992] 3 W.L.R. 228.
33 [1988] 3 All E.R. 683.

confession. In *Payne*[34] a driver charged with drunken driving was induced to see a doctor to see if he was ill, on the understanding that the doctor would not examine him as to his fitness to drive. The doctor subsequently gave evidence, based on that examination, on his fitness.

When in *Mason*[35] a suspect was induced to confess because of the lies of a police officer, in the presence of the defendant's solicitor, to the effect that the man's fingerprints had been found on a piece of glass, the Court of Appeal, in overturning the conviction, had some harsh words to say on the subject. Curiously these seemed to relate to the deception practised in part on the solicitor rather than the suspect. In *Christou and Wright*, the Court of Appeal was able to differentiate the situation in *Mason*, saying the present case was not a trick within a trick but part of the whole. The fingerprints could have been obtained from dusting the shop counter, and this itself appears to have gone to the overall fairness of the trick.

In *Edwards*[36] undercover police officers offered to buy drugs to provide evidence of an existing conspiracy. The Court of Appeal found, as it was really bound to, that this necessarily involved deceit but in Edwards' case it did not have such an effect on the fairness of the proceedings that it should be excluded. Possibly the *Mason* and *Payne* line of thinking by the court can be justified on the basis that those suspects were in custody when the deception was practised on them, whereas *Edwards* and *Christou and Wright* were out and about.

All this may seem to leave the police with no clear path to tread. Obviously bad faith will count very much against the admission of a confession, but even without this aspect every case is going to be dealt with on its own merits. Senior police officers will have to be involved at an early stage to determine just what is permissible in the way of undercover evidence. Unless great care is taken in difficult cases, then the courts

34 [1963] 1 WLR 637.
35 (1988) 86 Cr. App. R.349.
36 [1991] Crim. L.R. 45.

may not hesitate to exercise their discretion in favour of the accused with what may then seem to the police and public to be bizarre results.

What good judges do like to know are the circumstances of the case, and they get quite het-up when they are kept in the dark. In 1968 Macro was charged with robbing a sub-post office with a man unknown. Quite wrong. The man was definitely known; he was an informer who with the police had warned the impending victim of the proposed raid. The police staked out the premises and the victim went through the charade of allowing himself to be tied up. The court was not pleased when it discovered the true circumstances.

One of the more curious aspects of criminal court procedure has been the use of the cell fink or snitch – the murderer, child rapist or general lowlife – who shares a cell or takes exercise with the defendant against whom there is often not a great deal of evidence, and apparently is able to obtain his confidence to such an extent that he can wheedle a complete confession out of him. The snitch then appears in a shining white shirt at the trial and, having given his evidence, walks off with a much lighter sentence for his own crime.

In fiction, there is now no American thriller in which the defending lawyer does not warn his client against the dangers of self-incrimination in this way. In real life the annals of British and indeed any other nation's criminal cases are littered with notable examples, including success stories for the Crown in, for example, the case of James Hanratty, temporary success in the Luton Post Office murders, and failure in those of John Bindon and the killing of Arthur Thompson junior, the son of Glasgow's King of the Underworld who was shot whilst on home leave from prison as he made his way back to the family fortress after an evening in the local Indian restaurant. Two men were shot to death prior to young Thompson's funeral and in 1992, after a trial lasting fifty-four days, Paul Ferris, suspected of being one of Thompson jnr's murderers, was acquitted.

Much of the evidence against Ferris was from a fellow-prisoner and supergrass Dennis Woodman, a Geordie, who told the jury Ferris had confessed to him in prison. Woodman and his then common-law wife and her brother had been involved in the nasty kidnapping of a farmer in Dumfriesshire in an effort to get him to withdraw money from his bank accounts. How had Ferris made the confession? Shouting through the bars of his cell to Woodman, conveniently in the next cell, whom he had never seen. How had Woodman been placed in the next cell? Well, apparently when in another prison he had been found with escaping tools in his cell, something which he (Woodman) said had been planted by the authorities, and as a result he had been transferred. Woodman, cross-examined by Donald Findlay, told of the tragic death of his children in a road accident, something for which everyone had sympathy for several days until it was revealed that the children were alive and well and living in England and, indeed, Woodman had sent them a Christmas card from prison after their 'death'. Most of his evidence about the case could be traced, almost word for word, to pages from the Scottish editions of the *Sun* newspaper. As the trial went on the normally pro-active Findlay quietly demolished Woodman, who became more and more wild in his allegations, including a suggestion that Ferris's solicitor had endeavoured to bribe him. It was evidence which badly backfired on the prosecution for Woodman was not believed, something which by the end of his two weeks in the witness box surprised few experienced observers.

Sometimes the cell snitch does not have to give evidence. The Flying Squad detective who recruited the man he referred to as the 'Ice-Cream' soon put him to work. He had been informing on receivers at the weekend market in Petticoat Lane in the East End of London with such alacrity that police officers were beginning to rebel against Sunday-morning work.

But it was on a murder in Hackney that the 'Ice-Cream' really proved his worth. It was a sad job, even as murders go. A gang of hooligans about fifteen strong had set out from Islington intent on wreaking revenge on a rival mob in Hackney with whom they had had some previous altercation. They boarded a bus in Essex Road and on arrival at the end of Mare Street they had spotted their intended prey. Mob-handed they left the bus and with knives, hatchets and an assortment of other implements they attacked the luckless Hackney team who seem to have been caught completely unawares. In the fighting an eighteen-year-old boy – from Hackney – was stabbed in the chest with a stiletto-type weapon and drowned in his own blood in the Mare Street gutter.

It was a shocking and quite mindless murder, but happily there was no shortage of witnesses. There were a number of the Hackney mob who knew the names of the Islington gang, and there was the bus conductor as well as some passers-by. There were, however, two problems: no one was giving even the slightest indication as to which one of them had done the actual killing, and certainly no one was admitting the stabbing himself.

Over a period of days we took ten or twelve Islington youths into custody and they were all held in Hackney police station.

Drastic situations need drastic measures and it was agreed we would introduce the Ice cream. The double-cell passages each contained about six cells, and they were full to overflowing even without our hooligans and the nightly stream of drunks and so on who were waiting to go to Old Street court. With the story he had been charged with robbery we planted the Ice cream in one of the cells with one of the suspects. He was an older man and far more experienced and street-wise than any of his cell-mates. Within a relatively short time he had a couple crying on his shoulder. We moved him to other cells with the Islington prisoners – in fact we had him dodging about from cell to cell for a couple of days. By the time he was 'due to go to court' he was able to tell us exactly who had done what in the fight. All the youths he had spoken to had come up with the same name and story about the killer, who we then interrogated at length and who confessed. The Ice cream pulled the whole job down for us.

Occasionally the cell-mate was a police officer, or at least a Pinkerton agent, in disguise. In 1888 David Henderson had been elected Chief of Police in New Orleans, running on a reform ticket at a time of considerable industrial dispute and gang wars with the Provenzano gang then seeking to control the longshoremen. Two years later, on 15 October 1890, he was assassinated and the New Orleans police appeared powerless to do anything until they had 'heard from Pinkerton'.

Frank Dimaio was sent to Louisiana, his reputation being that '[there was no] man in the Agency who is his equal in regard to work among Italians'. Placed in the cell of Emmanuel Politz, he was able to cozy up to him and obtain a confession implicating the Mafia. Despite Dimaio's efforts, amidst allegations of jury tampering, the men were found not guilty. It did them no good, for on 14 March 1891 under the leadership of New Orleans lawyer W.S. Parkerson the jail was stormed and the suspects either lynched or shot.

Dimaio later went on the hunt for Cassidy and Longbaugh before becoming the head of the Pinkerton operation in Pittsburgh.

At one time the judges tended to encourage juries to believe these sinners who repented, giving as they did so the most facile explanations for their assistance in an endeavour to cover the fact that they wanted out as soon as possible. In Bindon's case, the cell-mate was a William Murphy.

Bindon, armed with a machete, had come to the aid of his friend, Roy Dennis, who was being attacked by Johnny Darke, one of a well-known London family, at the Ranelagh Yacht Club in Putney on 21 November 1978. This was not the version of the prosecution, who maintained that Darke's death was a contract killing by Bindon for a fee of £10,000 said to have been put up by a John Twomey. The evidence that it was a contract killing came from the familiar source of a cell-mate to whom Bindon was said to have confessed. The £10,000 was the story of prisoner William Murphy, also on trial for murder. Asked why he grassed Bindon, he piously replied, 'I don't think it's right people should go around killing other people and getting paid for it.' Murphy was convicted.

One of the cases in which it did go right for the police and which involved cell-informer evidence was that of Dudley and Maynard, the so-called Legal and General gang in the Epping Forest murder of Micky Cornwall and Billy Moseley. In two connected gangland killings there still seems to be no general consensus of opinion as to why the victims were executed, nor for that matter is there complete certainty amongst the cognoscenti that the right men were put away. The Legal and General murders was the last major case investigated by Commander Bert Wickstead and concerned the deaths of two top-of-the-second-division robbers – the gaunt, gangling Billy Moseley and his close friend, Micky Cornwall,* the first of whom disappeared in the autumn of 1974 and the second in the spring of the following year.

The Legal and General gang[37] was headed by Reginald Dudley – a hardman who had served a six-year sentence for slashing his first wife – together with a most unlikely villain, Bobby 'Fat Bob' Maynard, a roly-poly amiable man with little in the way of previous convictions, who had a terrible speech impediment caused (it was said) by being severely hit over the head in a fight in a club in Tottenham Court Road. He spoke extremely slowly, with long gaps between words, and was seemingly unaware of this problem because if interrupted

* A pseudonym.
37 The sobriquet 'Legal and General gang' came about when Dudley and Maynard appeared in a Kentish Town public house wearing identical overcoats which resembled a popular television commercial for the Legal and General insurance group.

by the recipient of his telephone call with a 'Hello, Bobby,' he would reply, 'How-do-you-know-it's-me?'

By the middle 1970s Dudley had become a professional receiver and possibly – accounts differ – a police informer. He had, on his own account, been approached by a top London officer to perform that small service. As for receiving, 'He didn't mess about with anything except high quality stuff,' dealing with the Underworld and the police alike. According to one police officer who knew him:

He was well respected in the fraternity. I always thought he could go as far as the Krays and the Richardsons. He had a team and he had the ability and the sense of purpose to do to North London what the Krays did to East London.

There was also a story that Dudley was working with the notorious officer, Alec Eist, shaking down robbers and relieving them of their stolen goods.

On his release from prison in September 1974, Moseley was horrified to find that his old school-friend Maynard had teamed up with the man.

On 26 September 1974 Moseley set off for a meeting at 6.30 p.m. with Ronnie Fright at the Victoria Sporting Club in Stoke Newington. He had been having an affair with Frankie, Ronnie's wife, while Fright was serving a seven-year sentence for armed robbery, and the meeting was to clear the air between them. Moseley was never again seen alive. Parts of his body started to surface a week later in the Thames near Rainham. Although the head and hands were missing, it was possible to make a positive identification of the body since Moseley had suffered from a rare skin disease. The autopsy also showed that he had been tortured; his toenails had been pulled out and he had been burned.

Moseley's other great friend, Micky Cornwall, was released from prison a fortnight after the bits started floating along the river. He was tied in to Dudley through a short liaison he had been having with Dudley's daughter Kathy. Kathy had once been married to a John Dann, known as 'Donuts' – possibly because he had worked in a bakery, but also because it was said that he cut holes in people who offended him. That marriage had broken down and she had taken up with a Ray Baron. When he in turn went to prison, she took up with Cornwall. In theory this was just as heinous a crime as Moseley's affair with Frankie Fright, but neither Baron nor the paterfamilias Dudley seems to have objected.

Cornwall, along with any number of criminals before and after him, was looking for a 'big one'. He now had a new girlfriend, Gloria Hogg, and was looking for sufficient money to buy a place in the country. Again like many other criminals, he lacked discretion and confided his plans to John Moriarty, hardly the best person because Moriarty later turned supergrass after being shot in the leg for the second time. Cornwell left Gloria for the 'big one' on Sunday 3 August. He had been renting a room from another police informer, Colin Saggs, and left shortly before two men came looking for him. Sharon Saggs, his daughter, would identify them at the trial as Dudley and Maynard. Moriarty saw him at a bus-stop in Highgate on 23 August, and that seems to have been the last sighting of him before his body was found in a newly-dug grave at Hatfield, Hertfordshire. He had been shot in the head.

Wickstead's last swoop was on 2 January 1976. Seven people out of eighteen taken were charged; they had been interviewed over a period of four days[38] and included Dudley and his daughter Kathy, Maynard, and Ronnie Fright. During the period in custody they had made admissions which amounted to evidence against them. Dudley was alleged to have said of Cornwall, 'I told him if he had sex with her,

38 The effective implementation of the Police and Criminal Evidence Act 1984 was nearly ten years away. At the time suspects in serious cases could be interviewed almost endlessly. Then such protection as was available to suspects was the informal Judges' Rules, which did not include the right to the presence of a solicitor during interview.

I would kill him.' Maynard allegedly admitted going to the Saggs' house looking for Cornwall. 'It was business,' he said. As for the question put to him that he had told Fright to be late for the rendezvous at the Victoria Sporting Club, he is said to have replied, 'I'm not answering that, otherwise I'm finished.' Apparently, Wickstead had had a tape-recorder fitted into his desk at the police station but had never switched it on. Why not, asked the defence?

'I am a police officer who believes in police methods and tape recorders are not used in police interviews,' replied the Commander.

The prosecution's case as to motive was convoluted. The killings had occurred because (1) Moseley had had an affair with Frankie Fright; (2) he had fallen out with Dudley ten years earlier; (3) Moseley had been suggesting Dudley was a grass; (4) he, Moseley, was sitting on the proceeds of a large jewellery robbery; (5) out of sheer sadism; (6) Cornwall had set out to avenge Moseley's death; (7) he had discovered Dudley and Maynard were the killers and so (8) had had more than a brief liaison with Kathy in order to find out the truth. It was said that Moseley had been shot with a single bullet. The case against Ronnie Fright was that he was deliberately late for his meet with Moseley outside the Victoria Sporting Club and so had lured him to his death.

Much of the rest of the evidence was the rag-bag of serving prisoners who, having seen the light, were able to give evidence against their former cell-mates. One of them was thirty-year-old Tony Wild, who asked the judge if he could sit down as he had a fissure on his anus.[39] He had, he said, been homosexually raped as a young man and, apart from contracting syphilis, he had this permanent reminder of the experience. He had served his apprenticeship in crime as shoplifter, car thief and office breaker; from where it was a

39 I am most grateful for the help I have received from Duncan Campbell and for his permission to quote extensively from the chapter 'The Grass' in *That was Business, This is Personal*.

short step to armed robbery and a series of attacks on Securicor vehicles. The money disappeared into the funds of the Golden Nugget casino in Piccadilly, major London hotels and on a series of presents to himself including a £1,200 fur coat.

In February 1976 he was caught after an attack on a Securicor vehicle which had temporarily netted £7,274. Wild had fired at pursuing Securicor men and escaped in his Volvo, but he crashed and was found hiding in a field. He was fortunate not to be charged with attempted murder and became a grass, receiving the semi-statutory five years for his troubles compared with eighteen for fellow-robber Tony Cook. Wild, it seems, did not want the luxuries accorded notables such as O'Mahoney. He was quite happy in his cell, keeping a diary of his conversations with other inmates such as Oliver Kenny, a publican and old friend of Dudley, and sending selected extracts to the police. Initially they were not impressed with his information and Wild wrote:

Although I have passed on information that I believe would be useful to your inquiries, I have received from your office not even an acknowledgement of the receipt of my letters let alone a routine questioning as to the validity of their content. Perhaps you feel that I am trying to work a ticket or something.

Now he offered them Reggie Dudley, writing to Wickstead:

I hope you will appreciate that I have been very forthright in this letter and that in itself will indicate to you that I have other more serious matters to impart to you.

When he was finally allowed to make a statement:

It's almost a relief to be in the police cell and get it off

my plate. I am caught and am going to spend a long time
in prison. When I come out I want only to spend the rest
of my life quietly with those I love.[40]

Wild told the police that Dudley had boasted about killing
Micky Cornwall, saying, 'He went up in the fucking air, didn't
he, boys?' He added his threepenceworth against Maynard
who, he said, had commented, 'I didn't know guys would
squeal like a pig.' But perhaps the most damaging remarks
he quoted related to Olly Kenny and the Horse and Groom
pub in Brighton. Dudley, he said, had brought a head into the
pub one night and the publican had nearly died of fright when
he saw it.

In the witness box Wild, carrying a copy of the criminal
legal textbook, *Archbold*, was at least the equal, if not the
master, of the legal talent ranged against him. When asked
if he was eating in the witness box he replied, 'I am eating
wine gums. Like all the jury, all the defendants and half the
police in court. Can I carry on?'

The burden of the cross-examination by luminaries such as
Michael West, for Dudley, was that as a disgusting homosexual, real men such as Dudley would not have anything to do
with a man like Wild and therefore would not have given him
the time of day, let alone what amounted to a confession. Wild
would have none of it.

I have been to bed with literally hundreds of women and
I could call five hundred into this court to testify to that
fact. I have also had dozens of jobs of a masculine nature.
I cannot bear men touching me. My crimes, I know, have
got progressively more serious, ending up with armed

40 This is a common enough and probably, at the time, genuine thought. I recall
defending one man on a bank robbery. 'If I get chucked I'm going to give it
all up,' he told me shortly before the trial. 'I'm going to go away and live in
a little town which has a supermarket. That's all I need. Well, make that two
supermarkets.'

robbery. I would interpret that as an attempt – or at least a subconscious attempt – to regain my manhood.

Apart from the confessions and the liaisons between the various dead and accused there was not, as the judge, Mr Justice Swanwick, told the jury 'evidence on which the Crown could ask you to convict'. The police had stated on oath that they were accurate and the defence had said they were fabricated. Whom were the jury to believe?

In the end Ronnie Fright was acquitted, as was another defendant, whilst a third had been acquitted at the direction of the judge. Bobby Maynard was found guilty on a majority decision on the third day of the jury's retirement. He and Dudley were sentenced to life imprisonment; Kathy received a suspended sentence along with an old-time villain, Charlie Clarke. Olly Kenny died before his trial. Six weeks later Moseley's head, wrapped in a plastic bag, was found in a public lavatory in Barnsbury, North London. Perhaps significantly the copy of the *Evening News* wrapped around it was dated 16 June 1977, when the jury had been in retirement.

Some facts emerged from the inquest. Professor James Cameron, who had undertaken the initial autopsy, told the coroner that the head was in 'extremely' good condition. Traces of car paint indicated it had been in a garage for some of the three years since Moseley had choked on his own blood; that removed one of the pillars on which the Crown had based its case. It had also been in a deep-freeze, for it was on the thaw when it was discovered.

In 1980 Wild retracted his evidence. He told the *Guardian* crime reporter Duncan Campbell in a pub in Hove that he had made up the evidence about the head, saying that the police had given him a scenario which he had followed. Campbell reported the interview in *Time Out* and was later interviewed by the Serious Crimes Squad. Wild was soon rearrested for another armed robbery.

On 23 April 1982 Anthony Wild was sentenced to ten

years' imprisonment for a series of five raids in Cheltenham and Croydon between April and October 1981, as well as a bank in Uxbridge. During the raids he had fired several shots, maintaining that he only did so to frighten people. Mr Justice McCowan said he did not regard Wild as a vicious or ruthless man and accepted his story that whilst firing the shots Wild had no intention of harming anyone.

His capture had come about in a none too dissimilar way from his previous escapade. On 9 December 1981 the police received information that he was travelling in a taxi on the A27; a road-block was set up and Wild tried to shoot himself before he dived out into an icy pond. Wild's lover, Margaret Payne, was given two years' probation. Their relationship had begun in April 1981 and they were living together in Somerset in what Charles Whitby QC, prosecuting, said was 'affluent domesticity' and employing a woman as a private tutor for the children.

In October 1981 Wild escaped capture in Somerset, and later Mrs Payne took him clothing and drove him to a hotel. She was arrested two days later and when Wild realised the police were holding her he threatened to go on a rampage. As a matter of expediency they released her, believing that she would lead them to Wild. They met on the Sussex Downs but Wild, who was having something of a charmed existence, escaped again and he was not recaptured for another five weeks.

Wild must have had powerful influences working for him, since he was paroled after serving a little over three years.

After the appeals were rejected, the families of both Dudley and Maynard launched a campaign to prove their innocence. This did not take the extreme course adopted by the friends of George Davis, but tee-shirts were sold and there was a march through Camden Town to Hyde Park Corner. Bobby Maynard junior stood as a candidate in the European Parliament elections in June 1984. Inevitably, however, the campaign

suffered with Davis' conviction for the Bank of Cyprus raid.[41]
Dudley appeared on television in the 1984 BBC programme
Lifers. Nor was the North London Underworld convinced of
their guilt; whilst it was accepted that Dudley was capable of
great violence, few could believe that Maynard had the same
capacity. Over the years various names have been put up as
the potential killers, but no real inquiry has been undertaken
by the authorities.

In 1991 Liberty, formerly the National Council for Civil
Liberties, adopted the Maynard–Dudley case as one for special
consideration in a campaign against wrongful convictions.
With the passing of the Police and Criminal Evidence Act

41 The George Davis case was something of a cause célèbre. In 1974 a robbery
took place at the London Electricity Board in Ley Street, Ilford, in which a PC
Groves – who was in the vicinity quite by chance – ran to tackle the robbers
and was shot in the leg for his pains. Whilst he was on the ground, another of
the team stood over him threatening to shoot him again.
A name in the frame was George Davis. He was first seen by the police
twenty days after the robbery, when he was arrested and gave an alibi that he
had been driving a mini-cab. The books of the firm were gone through and one
of his passengers was interviewed. Eight days later the same thing happened, but
this time the log-books were taken away by the police.
Davis was identified by three officers. Three months after the robbery a second
set of identification parades was held at Brixton prison. Davis was picked out
by two other police officers, but another 34 people failed to pick him out and
three made wrong identifications – two after he had changed his purple shirt
with another man on the parade.
The jury did not accept his alibi and Davis was convicted in March 1975.
He was sentenced to a total of twenty years' imprisonment, reduced on appeal
to seventeen. So began an enormous campaign on Davis' behalf. There were
allegations that he had been fitted up and on his conviction his supporters
mounted protest marches, demonstrations, and the chalking and papering of
most of East London with the slogan 'George Davis is innocent – OK'. In
one incident the cricket pitch at Headingley was dug up during a Test Match.
The 'George Davis is innocent – OK' campaign was successful. He was
released in a blaze of publicity on Tuesday 11 May 1976 by the Home
Secretary, after the publication of the Devlin report on the dangers of convicting
on identification evidence alone. It appears that an additional alibi witness had
also come forward.
Unfortunately the rejoicing was short-lived. He seriously blotted his copybook
as folk hero when, on 23 September 1977, he was captured *in flagrante* during a
raid on the Bank of Cyprus in the Seven Sisters Road, Holloway. Davis' sentence
in the Bank of Cyprus case was reduced to one of eleven years on appeal. But
that was not his last brush with the law. On 21 January 1987 he received
another sentence, this time of eighteen months (with nine of them suspended),
following a raid on the London-to-Brighton mail train in March 1986. Police
guarding postbags on the train tried to force their way into the mail van, but
found Davis blocking the door. He pleaded guilty to attempted theft.

1984 it is doubtful if there would have been convictions in the Legal and General case. It is difficult to know just what, if any, effect the evidence of Wild had on the jury.[42]

Of course what England can do America can, at least in the courts, do a thousand times as well. On 25 April 1989 James Richardson, convicted of murdering his seven children, had his life sentence quashed. He had been convicted in 1967 exclusively on the evidence of three cell informers. On the other hand, the prosecution had declined to take action when another person apparently confessed to the crime.

Richardson's troubles began on 25 October 1967 at his home in, for him, the unhappily named Arcadia, Fla. He and his wife went fruit-picking and left the children in the care of Betsy Reese, a neighbour who fed them beans and rice for their lunch. Six died that afternoon, the seventh survived for twenty-four hours. Richardson's behaviour at the hospital where he went with his wife counted against him. Apparently he remained unmoved; she collapsed. There was also evidence that he had taken out modest insurance for the children of $500 each, as well as policies totalling $3,000 for himself and his wife. The local Sheriff Frank Cline, who was up for re-election, was convinced of Richardson's guilt. The Arcadia Police Chief Richard Barnard fixed his attention on Mrs Reese, who denied that she had either cooked the dinner for the children or even been to the Richardson house. Barnard knew she was lying about this part at least, for he had seen her there. He also discovered that her past was less than desirable: she had served four years in 1956 for shooting her second husband, and her first husband had died after eating her beef stew.

The Richardsons' house was searched for poison and none found, but the next day the police were called to find Reese and a local alcoholic fighting over a bag of parathion. Both said it had come from a shed in Richardson's yard.

The evidence which did for Richardson came from jailhouse

42 For a more detailed account of the case see B. Woffinden, *Miscarriages of Justice*.

informers. James Dean Cunningham was the first to come forward to say that Richardson had confessed to him. In return for his truthful testimony, he would have some time knocked off his sentence. However, he had problems with the facts. When first asked who poisoned the food he replied, 'the mother-in-law' and then when it was apparent that this was an incorrect answer, 'No – the babysitter. The lady who takes care of his kids.' The third time he got it right.

The second informer, gambler James 'Spot' Weaver, said that Richardson had confessed to him that he had poisoned the children while his wife was spending the night with Reese. The motive was jealousy over their uncorroborated lesbian affair. At the trial he said Richardson had never offered a motive. He was not pressed by the prosecution, and the defence were not shown his prior inconsistent statements. The third sneak was shot dead before the trial, but his evidence was read to the jury.

In 1988 Weaver, the only survivor of the trio of informers and then aged sixty-seven, recanted. He told the authorities that he had been beaten until he agreed to make a statement against Richardson. Cunningham had been shot to death in 1969. Meanwhile Betsy Reese, who appears to have been sliding into insanity, had allegedly confessed on numerous occasions to poisoning the children. Moreover, the confessions had been made to nurses well before she became incompetent.

At his re-hearing twenty-one years after he was convicted, it was ruled that Richardson had not received a fair trial because the prosecution had withheld evidence and knowingly used false testimony. There were no plans to re-try him.[43]

At the same time a furore arose in California when inmate Leslie White, who had amassed thirty arrests since the age of nine, decided to tell all and explain how he could garner sufficient evidence to make it seem as though he had been the recipient of a confession from the accused. In the past

43 Mark Curriden, 'No Honor among Thieves' in the *American Bar Association Journal*, June 1989.

he had used these confessions and his willingness to give evidence about them to bargain himself a lighter sentence. Now he changed sides, claiming that defence and prosecution lawyers and even judges knew he was lying. He appeared on CBS' *Sixty Minutes*, saying:

> I've had judges sit up on the bench and look at me like, you know, you lying piece of you-know-what. But what can they do. They can do nothing. If I say one thing, it's believed unless they can prove differently. The defense can't do anything. The defense lawyer will say, 'You're lying, aren't you?' I say, 'No, sir.'
>
> They have no other avenue to disprove my veracity other than the fact they're just trying to verbally attack me on the witness stand.

He went on to recount how he could get information from the telephone in the county jail. Having called the deputy district attorney and identified himself as a detective with the LAPD homicide unit, he then asked for and was given information which could only be known to the actual perpetrator and the police. Because of his disclosure the Los Angeles District Attorney's Office began a review into two hundred cases, including sixteen where the convicted person was on death row.

Eventually, just as they had in England, juries began to express their disapproval of the use of the informer and undercover sting. One of the most significant cases was that of John DeLorean whose trial began on 5 March 1984 in Los Angeles. The one-time millionaire car manufacturer was on a charge of plotting to import $24 million worth of cocaine into the United States. It had been done, said the prosecution, to try to raise money to save his ailing Belfast sports car factory. Time and again the television viewers in the United States had seen him reach into a suitcase of cocaine, lift a package and say, 'It's better than gold. Gold weighs more, for God's sake.'

His defence was that an FBI sting had been up and running to try to force DeLorean into buying the cocaine, something he had made every effort to avoid. A principal government witness was convicted cocaine smuggler James Hoffman who, DeLorean claimed, had threatened him and the life of his six-year-old daughter when he tried to back out of the deal. When it came to it Hoffman, who was cross-examined for twelve days, was never asked about the threats. Indeed the tapes showed the utmost friendliness between the men.

Commenting on the way the case was going, Michael Gillard wrote in the *Observer* (July 1 1984):

> The defence has been helped by a steady stream of prosecution own goals. Missing tapes, erased tapes, destroyed notes, back-dated documents, breached guidelines, contradictory testimony. These have been prised out of Government witnesses and have eaten into the prosecution case, if only around the edges. Only by testifying himself is DeLorean likely to be able to erase the impression on the tapes.

He was only partly right. DeLorean did not give evidence. However, on 16 August 1984 DeLorean was acquitted by the unanimous verdict of the jury who had deliberated for twenty-eight and three-quarter hours. DeLorean, who was by now a born-again Christian, called out 'Praise the Lord'.

Howard Weitzman, the chief defence lawyer, said:

> The jurors are 12 citizens who have sent a message to the nation and the world that the type of conduct that was involved in the investigation, arrest, prosecution and ultimate vindication of John DeLorean will not be tolerated again.

Eight jurors spoke at a press conference after the hearing. They did not wish to be identified as they said they feared themselves being entrapped by government agents.

The veteran lawyer Melvin Belli is reported to have said:

It was one of the great jury verdicts of all time. They stood up and said they were not going to cotton on to cops acting like a bunch of bums.

Harvard Professor Allan Dershowitz, one of the leading American trial lawyers of today,[44] said:

His guilt or innocence played no role in this. All the attention was focused on the Government and he was presented as a victim.[45]

44 Amongst his more famous clients have been Claus von Bulow and O. J. Simpson.
45 *Daily Express*, 18 August 1984.

11

The Police – Undercover Work and Informants

In the manual of best practice provided in 1994 by the Association of Chief Police Officers and designed to overcome problems with informers, officers are enjoined not to use terms such as 'grass', 'snout' and 'snitch'. Nor should officers, however much they despise their informants, allow this to filter through into their dealings with them. As can be seen from the following examples, it will be hard to eradicate these words or thoughts from an officer's (or indeed anyone else's) vocabulary.

I'll tell you right now – it's a tricky game, being an informer. I'll tell you something else: in my seventeen years as a policeman up to 1945 I'd used scores of snouts, but out of them all I could name only ten who were absolutely top class: the men on whose unsupported word I could go in with my head down. It isn't really surprising when you know the circumstances. The snout is a game fellow. He's at one and the same time a crook, engaged in illicit operations, and a detective. He cops it both ways.[1]

1 John Gosling, *The Ghost Squad*, p. 39.

A rather younger officer recalls:

As an aide I was soon to learn the constant dangers that were always to be found with informants. My buck [colleague] and I had 'developed' an active villain – again the name is gone but I recall he lived in the Winchmore Hill area – and everything was going very smoothly. We were getting a job a month on average, receivers, the odd stolen car – all very much run-of-the-mill but very nice for all that. Then, after an association of about six months, trouble loomed. The informant had put us on to a young thief in Southgate who rejoiced in the soubriquet of 'Dig-'em-up Dave': the nick-name derived from the fact that for some years he had worked as a gravedigger and was able to effect no small amount of spare cash by the appalling practice of grave-robbing. It seemed that when Dave was required to dig into an existing family grave prior to the interment of a recently deceased husband or wife, he would return to the cemetery at night prior to the funeral, force open the coffin of the first occupant of the grave and rob the corpse of such rings and other effects as he could find.

In any event, as a result of information from our man we managed to catch 'Dig-'em-up Dave' with a stolen car. Unbeknown to us, Dave's father (Dave was adopted) was a lawyer of some esteem and, it turned out, not altogether unconnected in the 'right' circles. Scarcely before we knew what had happened, allegations of all sorts of malpractice on our part were flying about and a Chief Superintendent and Sergeant from C1 were deputed to investigate. It was suggested that the stolen car had been 'planted' on Dave by the informant and that the whole thing was a conspiracy between ourselves and the informant to implicate the wholly innocent Dave! As I recall, our houses were searched and we were interviewed at great length about the whole thing. Nothing came of it, though, and as both my buck and I continued as aides and were not reverted to uniform duty, I imagine that the powers that be had taken the lawyer's allegations with a pinch of salt.

The sensible use of a snout is essential in promoting career prospects. Even if an officer does not have one himself, from time to time an informer can be borrowed from another officer. A Flying Squad officer recalls his early days:

Towards the end of my aiding career I was to have my first experience of the 'professional snout'. I was due to go on a selection board for secondment to the permanent CID and in those days it was essential for such an interview to be able to present a comprehensive record of arrests. The one thing, it was reckoned, which would always impress was an 'off-duty job' and it was with this in mind that I was taken to King's Cross by an old and very experienced Detective Sergeant Brian Kelly to meet 'Spotty' Larwood.[2]

'Spotty', apparently, could invariably be found in an all-night snack bar in the Euston Road named 'Jon-Jaks' and sure enough this is where we found him. He was a small man, painfully thin and ultra-scruffy. In later years, when watching the TV programme *Callan*, I felt convinced that admirable actor Russell Hunter had known 'Spotty' Larwood well and upon him had based his portrayal of Callan's informant 'Lonely'.

'Spotty,' said Brian Kelly, with an air of authority, 'this is Mr R. He's going on a board in a couple of weeks and he needs a nice little job.'

'Hooo,' said 'Spotty' with a sharp sucking noise and in the manner adopted by car salesman when viewing one's prized Escort which is being presented for part-exchange.

2 A pseudonym.

'I don't know about that, Mr Kelly.' He produced a filthy diary or note-book and the conversation which followed took this form, and I give my word there is no exaggeration: *Spotty*: 'No, can't do nuffink for at least a munf, Mr Kelly (loud and very fluid sniff); 's'always the same, in't it, this time of the year – bloody aides boards[3] everywhere and they all want 'elpin', don't they?' Another quick look at the book followed by frenzied hacking at awful teeth with the pencil, and then: 'See, I got me own aides at Clerkenwell to look after, Mr Kelly, ain't I? Then I got to put one in for a skipper from the Cally (Caledonian Road) who's going on the DI's board, I got a DC at Narrowbone Lane (Marylebone Lane) in the shit and 'e needs a bit of 'elp (pause for disgusting throat clearance and relocation of nasal mucous), an' on top of all that, I got the 'Eavy Mob (Flying Squad) an' if I don't look after them Gawd knows what'll 'appen.' *Kelly*: 'And Gawd knows what'll happen if you don't help Mr R, you scruffy little bastard.'

What followed was pure theatre: for a quarter of an hour Brian Kelly alternated between threatening and pleading and Spotty, well, the man was a star! He moaned about the pressures of his profession and at the low rates being paid by the Informants Fund. He ridiculed the sentences being handed down by the stipendiaries at Clerkenwell Court and Messrs Seaton and Elam over at the London Sessions. Between sinus-clearing exercises and the insertion of various instruments into what I imagined must have been a whole cavern of dental cavities, he protested time, weather conditions, risk and likely reward. He (rightly) accused Kelly and I as being 'orf yer own manor' and suggested that before long there would be officers 'from bleedin' Brighton comin' up 'ere after me',

3 If an Aide to CID wished to be confirmed in the job he had to go before a promotion board, at the same time producing evidence (in the form of arrests) of his ability. The Aide to CID has been discontinued.

but eventually he came round. Ten minutes he'd give me, he said grudgingly: 'Free o'clock Saturday afternoon – outside the pictures in Clerkenwell Road.'

And so there I was, as directed; I recall it was freezing cold and raining and a wind-swept corner in the Clerkenwell Road is not the best place to be when one is off-duty. After about a quarter of an hour I saw Spotty walking towards me from the direction of the station on the other side of the road. Beside him, and clutching an enormous canvas sack, was a younger but equally scruffy man. As they came adjacent with me Spotty looked across and nodding towards his companion dodged up an alley and disappeared. I ran across the road and producing my warrant card stopped his friend, who was still striding confidently along seemingly oblivious of Spotty's sudden absence.

The sack contained about 60 towels and various other linen articles, all marked as coming from one of the large hotels round the Russell Square area. Spotty's chum was charged with alternatively stealing them or receiving them and he pleaded guilty the next morning, as they say 'like a good 'un', and got three months without a word of complaint.

As I gave the brief facts to the magistrate, I spied Spotty in the public gallery watching the results of his handiwork. I never knew whether his chum was some sort of volunteer. I never knew how Spotty got paid and I never saw him again.

Some years later, though, I heard that he was involved in something of a scandal: it seemed that throughout his professional career he had kept some sort of diary (and probably accounts) relative to his activities, and suddenly he decided to put this to good use. The story – although it may be apocryphal – was to this effect: late one winter's night Spotty was taking coffee at the all-night coffee stall at The Cross [King's Cross] when he encountered a down-and-out vagrant of even more straitened circumstances than himself. On learning that this poor man had neither lodgings nor the wherewithal to acquire them, Spotty immediately offered the spare bed in his room. He then treated the unsuspecting dosser to several cups of coffee and a bacon sandwich or two and then suggested they make their way to Spotty's drum. On the way, Spotty suddenly remembered a meeting that he had with a friend, and suggested that his new-found friend might like to continue on to the house and let himself in. For this purpose Spotty handed him an enormous bunch of keys and selecting one of these as being the key to the door of his lodgings, suggested that his friend may like to keep hold of it to save trying the lot in the lock. At the time he also happened to be carrying a large holdall which he handed over with instructions that his room was 'first on the left inside the front door' and that as he did not wish to take the bag with him on his 'meet' it should just be put on the bed.

He then disappeared into the night leaving the unsuspecting vagrant to make his way to some address off Argyll Square or that area. When he arrived, the key which Spotty had selected did not fit the lock of the front door and as he was trying key after key off the bunch in the lock he was collared by the local Q car crew – a plain-clothes mobile patrolling unit. The keys turned out to be a bunch of twirls (skeleton keys) and the holdall contained an assortment of housebreaking implements including, it was said, a rope ladder!

In those days possessing housebreaking implements by night was a matter for the Quarter Sessions (Crown Court) and it was there that things started to go wrong. It developed that the defendant was the errant son of very wealthy people from the North and, incensed by what had befallen their offspring, they instructed solicitors to brief the late Victor Durand QC to defend him. Private enquiry agents were told to find Spotty Larwood but before he was located – and being well aware of what was going on – he turned up at New Scotland Yard one night complete with diary *et al* and put a lifetime of wickedness on paper. The defendant was quite rightly acquitted and in the months that followed countless CID officers from all over London were seen and interviewed.

As I say, this story may be apocryphal, but I recall speaking to several of the officers who were mentioned in his statement and from what they said I think it is true in substance.

More seriously, one of the problems with informants has been the danger that, to improve their standing with the officer running them, to get a licence, albeit a limited one, to steal or to deal in drugs or reward money, they will turn themselves into *agents provocateurs*. A very early example of this may have occurred in the running by the Special Branch of an informer, Auguste Coulon.

In 1892 a number of Fenians were arrested in connection with a bomb factory in Walsall. Almost certainly they had been acting under the aegis of Auguste Coulon. Indeed one of the conspirators Frederick Charles – who had the highest reputation in the area, 'would never,' – according to Patrick McIntyre, who on the eve of his promotion to inspector was suddenly demoted to constable – 'have gone of his own accord into any diabolical plot'. It may be that McIntyre, who made his denunciation of his superiors in *Reynolds Weekly*, had a grudge to argue, but Coulon was regarded as the property of a senior officer. Papers show that an order for the arrest of Coulon was countermanded by the Chief of Walsall police, Taylor.

Until the 1970s an informant to a Flying Squad officer could effectively remain anonymous. All the officer had to do was to put in a report to the information fund saying that an informant wished to be known as John Smith and had been instrumental (a favourite police word) in the arrest of Tom Brown, as a result of which a considerable amount of property had been recovered. The senior officer who authorised the ensuing payment did not have to know Smith's real name. It was a system which led to innumerable instances of abuse, one of which was the sharing of the reward money between the informer and the police officer.

It is also possible that the officers who run them, both for reasons financial and for advancement in the force, will turn their informers into *agents provocateurs*. Almost certainly in the bad days of Scotland Yard in the 1960s and 1970s, there were examples of officers who would arrange with an informer to set up a robbery and then after the arrest of his colleagues claim the reward from the bank which was never in real danger of an attack.

One of the more disturbing uses of the reward system came in 1968 in the case of David Cooper,[4] Michael McMahon and Patrick Murphy who were convicted of the murder of sub-postmaster Reginald Stevens who on 10 September 1969 was shot dead, probably accidentally, in his car in a Luton car-park. Four robbers had intended to persuade him to hand over the keys to the post office. The driver of one of the cars involved was thought to be in his forties or early fifties, with greying hair. A reward of £5,000 was offered by the Post-Master General.

A Vauxhall car, wiped clean of fingerprints and belonging to an Alfred Matthews, was identified as being in the area at the time of the murder. He had a number of convictions for violence and dishonesty, was known as a good getaway driver and had previously robbed a post office. The car had been transferred to a non-existent person at a non-existent address on the day before the murder. When the police went round, Matthews was said by his wife to be away. Eventually, his brother Albert Elliott told the police he was with him. Matthews was arrested, and by way of explanation

4 David Cooper was known also as John Disher. He died in 1993.

said that the man to whom he had sold his car must have been involved. He was never placed on an identification parade. He was, however, according to Detective Chief Superintendent Kenneth Drury, 'leaned on a bit' to turn Queen's Evidence against Cooper, McMahon and Murphy. This he did. Although charged with the others, no evidence was offered against him and he appeared as the major prosecution witness.

His story at the Crown Court was the traditional one of the informer – one which, in these less disingenuous times, might not have had the same degree of acceptance. He said that he had been asked to collect some parcels in his Vauxhall from the railway station at Luton, for which service he was to receive £10. By the time he realised that he was the dupe of the robbers, he was well on his way up the M1. Once in Luton the others went on ahead of him; he was asked to keep look-out on a shop which he suddenly realised was a post office. The three others, one of whom was covered in blood, collected him in a van. He wanted to drive away on his own but the man, wiping off the blood, got into the Vauxhall. After a mile or so he managed to persuade the man with him to get out.

Some of the other evidence against the men was provided by Thomas Weyers and Derek Jackson to whom McMahon, on remand in Leicester prison, supposedly confessed his guilt. He, Cooper and Murphy were convicted.

The reward money was duly paid with Alfred Matthews receiving £2,000, and his brother Albert Elliott, Thomas Weyers and Derek Jackson each receiving £500. There were suggestions that Drury had received up to half Matthews' share of the reward; his bank statement showed that when the £2,000 was deposited there was a withdrawal of £700.

Matthews was quite unable to accept that he had received a reward. He regarded the money as compensation for loss of work and inconvenience resulting from his decision to turn Queen's Evidence and the resulting police protection.

The struggles of Murphy, McMahon and Cooper to obtain their freedom, denied repeatedly by the Court of Appeal, occupied the next eleven years. On 13 November 1973, with a new alibi witness whom the court believed, Murphy was freed, the court having decided that the identification of Murphy by Matthews was too weak to be allowed to stand. Cooper and McMahon were not so fortunate. With the court protecting Matthews over the next decade, it was not until the Home Secretary, William Whitelaw, asked the Queen to remit the sentences that they were released on 18 July 1980.

In the meantime the officer in the case, Detective Chief Superintendent Kenneth Drury, had been promoted to Commander and then relegated to the status of prisoner. His downfall is an interesting insight into what happens when thieves, or grasses, fall out with their employing officers.

On 27 February 1972 the *Sunday People* announced that Commander Drury and his wife had recently returned from Cyprus, where they had been guests of porn dealers James and Rusty Humphreys.

For a time Drury tried to bluff his way out. Yes, he had been to Cyprus. No, he had not been a guest, he had paid his share. No, it had not been a holiday; in reality he was looking for the escaped train robber Ronnie Biggs. At the time, and for what it was worth, Humphreys supported him. But it wasn't worth much. On 6 March Drury was suspended from duty and served with disciplinary papers; he resigned on 1 May. Then foolishly he turned on his former friend. He sold his story to the *News of the World* for £10,000 and as part of his confessions amazingly he publicly named Humphreys as a grass. It is not surprising that Humphreys took umbrage and gave his alternative version, saying that far from being a grass or getting money from Drury it had all been the other way around. The money, the wine, the good life had all flowed from the Humphreys' cornucopia.[5]

On 7 July 1977 Drury was convicted of corruption for his part in the activities of some members of the Porn Squad.

5 Just to complete the somewhat tortuous story, in 1994 Humphreys returned to prison following his conviction at the Inner London Crown Court for dealing in pornography.

He received eight years' imprisonment, reduced on appeal to five. With the gift of hindsight it is possible to speculate that Matthews had been an informant for Drury all along, not simply on this one instance at Luton, and as such was protected by him. Even if that were not the case, the higher echelons of the police took a dim view of the shenanigans of Drury and Matthews. Commenting on the situation, Assistant Commissioner Gilbert Kelland later wrote:

> An immediate policy decision was made that no reward money would ever be recommended or paid by us to anyone who had turned Queen's Evidence.
>
> In 1980 I wrote a confidential letter to all the major banks, insurance companies and loss assessors pointing out the dangers of offering rewards so large that they might in themselves generate crime.[6]

It may be the case that subsequent to that no payments were made or recommended to those who turned Queen's Evidence, but certainly massive sums were paid out to actively involved criminals. In fact the rule was broken in spirit more than it was observed in practice.

However well-intentioned their plans, the police did not always achieve the desired ends when using informers. In St Paul, Minnesota, the Police Chief introduced the eponymous O'Connor system, the aim of which was to stem the flow of, and control, major crime within the system. The scheme was to allow hoodlums to use St Paul as a safe city to which they could go for rest, recreation and freedom from arrest provided they 'committed no depredations against the citizens of St Paul'. Gambling and prostitution were allowed to flourish on the basis that prostitutes and gamblers were the eyes and the ears of a police department.

The scheme appears to have worked well enough for a time

6 Gilbert Kelland, *Crime in London*, pp. 217–18.

in St Paul. Unfortunately, however, the effects were long-term.
First, the local police force became lazy; it was now too easy
for them to make arrests. More widely, criminals transferred
their operations to other nearby towns and cities whose crime
rates soared. The original *status quo* was restored.[7]

In more recent times members of the police have been used
to infiltrate their own. In all instances this has been in an effort
to eradicate corruption. In some cases the officers may have
been reluctant but have been uncoerced; in others, it has been
the price of their own freedom. As is almost invariably the
case, the bulk of examples come from America. In 1970 the
mayor of New York, John Lindsay, empanelled the Knapp
Commission and over the next two years dozens of police
officers were implicated in taking bribes and participating
in gambling, prostitution and drug operations. Much of the
evidence came from honest officers such as Sergeant David
Durk and Detective Frank Serpico, who had infiltrated the
operations of these corrupt officers. Sometimes officers were,
like common criminals, given the option of turning informer
or being prosecuted. One such was Officer William Phillips,
accused of taking bribes and fixing court cases. Supplied with
a tape recorder, he was used by the Knapp Commission to
show that officers were obtaining up to $4 million a year in
bribes. His evidence did not appeal to the Police Commissioner
Patrick V. Murphy, who denounced the operation in general
and Phillips in particular as a rogue cop caught in the act
and 'squirming to get off the hook'. The Commission was
disbanded with inconclusive results, but at the beginning at
least it did have a dramatic effect. Two days after it first sat,
113 plain-clothes officers were transferred.

Another officer who gave evidence at the time of the Knapp
Commission was the thirty-one-year-old Bob Leuci. He was

7 M. L. Harney and J. C. Cross, *The Informer in Law Enforcement*. In criminal
circles St Paul was known as Home because of these facilities. It was not the
only city which operated such a scheme. For a time at least Toledo, Ohio, had
similar rules but was never given the accolade of a nickname.

called before the Commission in mid-February 1971 and left in an ante-room waiting to be interviewed by Nicholas Scoppetta. Leuci, one of the Princes of the City, so-called because the Special Investigating Unit for which he worked had a citywide jurisdiction, was not a happy man. Although he was unaware of it, the Crime Commission had nothing on him; he was not, however, clean and it did not take Scoppetta too long to suspect that Leuci was hiding something. According to Leuci's biography,[8] Scoppetta asked him to dinner and the two men struck an almost immediate rapport. Leuci admitted three occasions on which he had taken part in a scam – he had taken money from a drug-dealer on the premise that he and his colleagues could influence a prosecution which was in any event going to be dropped – but said he was otherwise clean. What he really wanted to do was not to inform on his colleagues but to go after the lawyers for both prosecution and defence who, depending upon which side of the fence they sat, were either taking bribes to drop cases or paying them to police officers. Leuci began to talk to Scoppetta, with everything being recorded. Unfortunately for posterity, the arrangement was that after the lawyer had finished with them the tapes should be returned to Leuci. He burned them.

At one time it was suggested by a superior of Scoppetta that there should be a scam practised on the criminals. Not only would Leuci find corruption, but it would be manufactured in the sense that active criminals would be told they were being prosecuted for tax evasion. Opportunities would then be created for active criminals to bribe Leuci – who was connected to the Mafia through family ties – to get their IRS files. They would then be arrested for attempting to bribe an officer. Leuci refused to play along, saying that this was a total frame.

Instead it was decided that an attack should be made on the Baxter Street gang, a group of lawyers and bail bondsmen who were suspected of fixing cases and who worked near the

8 R. Daley, *Prince of the City*, p. 13.

criminal courts on Center Street. Leuci went undercover, and
the story of his investigation of lawyer Edmund Rosner and
bondsman Nick DeStefano is an almost classic account of what
can go wrong with undercover work and the subsequent court
case. Both men were having considerable legal difficulties
over an indictment alleging they had suborned perjury in
a case involving Pedro Hernandez. Unfortunately for the
Government, Hernandez had disappeared in July 1971 and
without him there would be no case. It was thought that
he might have been murdered. It seems that if they could
not prevent the collapse of the Hernandez case, with the
help of Leuci they could still put together another against
Rosner. On 30 September 1971, Leuci, wearing a wire, had
lunch with DeStefano and Nick Lamattina, a New York City
police detective, in a Chinese restaurant. Leuci offered to find
out whatever Rosner and DeStefano wished to know about the
case. DeStefano seems to have relayed this most useful piece
of information to Rosner, who said he did not wish to get
involved. The next day DeStefano said that the lawyer was
convinced he could win the case without help.

This did not actually suit DeStefano or Lamattina who
wanted the information. The next step was to try to get Rosner
to pay for the information for them even if he did not use it
himself. DeStefano now told Rosner that Hernandez had been
killed and that the government was putting a case together in
which they would claim that Rosner was the contractor. Surely
he now wanted information? It is easy to see how Rosner was in
a bind. He had not arranged the killing. Was he being framed?
Was Hernandez really dead? Could he explain his position to
a judge? He agreed to see Leuci with DeStefano.

On the day of the meeting Leuci did not wear a wire. It was
probably fortunate for him because this was the time when he
was rubbed down by DeStefano and Lamattina. Immediately
there were evidential problems. He maintained that Rosner had
given DeStefano $400 to give to Leuci to give to his contact.
Rosner's version was that he had resolutely refused to pay over

any money. At the next meeting, however, Leuci was wired up but the results were inconclusive. The meeting had been in an Italian restaurant where the other customers, unaware of the importance of clarity on the tape, had inconsiderately laughed and talked, so ruining it. Thoughtlessly the management had had music playing as well.

It was arranged by Leuci's handlers that another meeting should take place, but this did not go too well either. It became apparent to DeStefano and Lamattina that Leuci was an undercover agent. Fearing for his life and after a series of misunderstood signals to his back-ups, he had them arrested. Within a few hours they had themselves become undercover agents. In terms Rosner didn't have a prayer.

What was more serious, however, was that Leuci's crimes were not limited to the three shake-downs of the drug-dealers. They amounted to a whole career of misbehaviour including destroying evidence and, when he finally confessed, enough crimes to fill an eighty-plus-page booklet. It did not do Rosner any good, however. At his trial Leuci stuck to the three crimes he had committed and the jurors tended to believe the good-looking police officer. Eventually Rosner served eight months of a three years' sentence. Leuci was never prosecuted and went on to become a successful crime novelist. One of the reasons for not prosecuting him was because it was thought that such an action would deter future informers.[9]

Despite the criticisms of the use of corrupt police to infiltrate and inform on other corrupt officers, this has become widespread in America. One major instance came in May 1986 when Henry Winter and his partner Tony Magno, from the notorious Precinct 77 in Brooklyn, were offered the choice of being indicted or turning informer/undercover officers on their own people. They had both been dealing in drugs and ripping off drug-dealers. The choice was clear: freedom or nine years.

9 For the record, Hernandez turned up alive and well in Mexico City.

—I want to go home tonight, Henry. Do you want to go home tonight?

—Yeah, I want to go home too.

—Then I guess we have no choice, Henry. I guess we'll cooperate.

And co-operate they did, to such great effect that at the end of their compulsory tour of duty one other officer had agreed to testify against his colleagues and one had committed suicide.[10]

There is, however, one entertaining instance from the fighting corruption days of the Met. It occurred in the Albion public house in Ludgate Circus, near the Old Bailey and used as a drinking hole for police and criminals alike (the Prince of Wales in Lant Street and the Premier Club in Soho were others) and as a place where business such as the arrangement of bail and negotiation of a reduction in charges could safely be undertaken.

Early one evening in March 1980 a scuffle broke out between two well-dressed men in the bar there, one of whom was trying to remove a tape-recorder from the other younger man. The story goes that the publican's wife leaned over the bar and said, 'Right. If you two don't stop now, I'll call the police. I'll call the police.'

The fighting stopped and the younger man hissed back at her, 'We are the police.' In fact they were Detective Superintendent John Keane and the younger Detective Inspector Bernard Gent. The fight had been in an endeavour to switch off a tape-recorder which had recorded an 'arrangement' that for £10,000 Gent, who had gone equipped with the device, would do his best to assist in the release of a man charged with robbery. At the Old Bailey, following a majority decision of the jury, Keane received a sentence of three years' imprisonment.

There has been little in the way of academic research into

10 M. McAlary, *Buddy Boys*, pp. 26–7.

the use of the informer in England and Wales, but recently studies have been undertaken at various universities, including the University of Hull, where Dr Clive Norris and Colin Dunnighan have carried out a survey of two forces, involving a sample of over 200 officers, both uniform and detective. Their findings, which seem to be matched by a second survey into another force, to a certain extent run counter to anecdotal evidence from officers who, it must be said, have been in the main from the Met, many dealing with serious organised crime.

Norris and Dunnighan issued a questionnaire to officers who were beginning their shifts. Generally these were completed in the canteen before starting work, although a number returned them at a later stage. They also had access to the records and people, based on the official payments made to informers. They then interviewed every detective (but not every officer) and a dozen informers. The first of their findings was that most officers said that the most important thing in the life of an informer was money. It was a response which Dr Norris doubted as being wholly accurate.

Money is a way of negotiating trust. It is a way of cementing a relationship. Informers ask for money as a sign that what they are saying is valuable, but things cut across money particularly when you think that with a registered informer the average payment is £115.

Now, informers fall into two categories – registered and unregistered – with the difference being that as a rule (but not a completely inflexible one) only registered informers are paid. Since the cases of Macro and Birtles, this has become – in theory at least – standard police practice throughout the country. Indeed, the Association of Chief Police Officers has spent some time trying to arrange the adoption of a national policy, including providing an informer manual which includes 'best practice' for dealing with informers. In its unadopted form it has had a strong influence, but it has never been officially launched.

What Dr Norris and Colin Dunnighan found was that Home Office guidelines were regularly and routinely broken: 'For example – they ban the setting-up of jobs without authorisation from a senior officer. In practice, however, such authorisation was rarely sought.'

The statistics of the sample make for interesting reading.

Of registered informers, 80 per cent are male with half in their twenties, a third in their thirties and a fifth over 40. Two-thirds are unemployed. Half are either married or in a settled relationship. Only one in eight has no previous convictions; one-third have between one and five, and half have six or more.

A strong difference was found between registered and unregistered informers. The latter were more likely to be older, female, married, employed, and with significantly fewer convictions.

They also found that recruitment of registered informers almost invariably took place in the police station at the instigation of the police, with only one in ten of the informers beginning negotiations themselves. Half of the initial discussions occurred while the potential informer was under arrest, a third after an arrest but when they were no longer in custody, and one in ten came from those who were involved in an investigation into a crime but were not formal suspects. Sixty per cent of the negotiations began in a police station, with a further 25 per cent starting at either the recruit's home or place of work. Only one in seven conversations with people who became registered informers began in a club or pub. There was no single instance of a solicitor or his clerk acting as an initiator. As for unregistered informers, one-third volunteered themselves.

Once an informer is registered, it seems that officers spend a good deal of time keeping them sweet in what sometimes develops into a long-lasting relationship – although many

informers give only one bit of information and are not heard
of again. The longest-serving informer in the survey had been
providing information for over twenty-two years. Nearly half
of the officers had given their principal informer their home
telephone number. The reason behind this is twofold. First, to
maintain a successful informer twenty-four-hour-a-day access
is little short of essential. Second are the childish names under
which informers operate. It is hardly surprising that when
'Bugs Bunny' rings up Detective Sergeant White at the police
station he has a hard time getting through or even leaving a
message.

The research found that officers are extremely reluctant to
ask for advice from their controlling officers, usually a Detective Chief Inspector and sometimes a Detective Inspector. Over
half the officers running registered informers said that they had
never asked for advice at all. Even then they would not, they
said, ask the controller. Two-thirds would approach another
constable or sergeant whom they would consider to be more
sympathetic. Officers, in theory, should make applications
to their controlling officer for authorisation of participating
informers. It would seem that if the DCI is 'into' informers,
the officer is likely to be given a free hand, and if the controller
is not in favour of the informer scheme he will be subverted
by the detective.

How does one handle an informer? Only slightly over a
third of the officers said that they had received training, and
half of those who had thought it to be of little use. Other
training came from informal talks with other officers or was
self-acquired. This presents a worrying feature, because it is
clear that a number of younger officers are working without
either training, instruction or support and consequently are
likely to get themselves into problematical situations – for
example, deals with their informers which they cannot possibly
carry through. The use of the informer presents a dilemma. In
theory, plea, charge and bail bargaining are frowned upon but,
given there is no law requiring the police to charge anybody,

there is no breach of the law if they do not. The use of the reduced charge and the grant of bail is essential to a successful relationship with an informer. Norris and Dunnighan found that was why so many officers said that money was the most essential part of a relationship with an informer. 'It doesn't raise moral questions.'

Much more worrying appears to be the disclosure, or rather non-disclosure, of the use of participating informers. In theory a decision to use a participating informer must be taken at either Head of CID or Assistant Chief Constable level. In fact the requests are granted rarely, particularly because, says Dr Norris, they are rarely made. And, when they are, his research suggests that they are not disclosed to the Crown Prosecution Service.

Whether they are granted will depend much on the person to whom they are made. A regional co-ordinator of the Regional Crime Squad is much more likely to sanction requests, since he will receive them on a regular basis. At force level, the authoriser is likely to be much more wary and will be bypassed.

From a detective's point of view informers are a continuous risk, one of the problems being the uncertainty of the information provided. There is the risk that the informer will provide the wrong information; he may provide the wrong time, date or place, or the job will simply not go down. This leads to a waste of time if, for example, the police have provided a stake-out, and it also leads to a loss of face for the detective running the informer. There is also the risk that the informer has watered down his actual role, and hence the problems that will arise when it is discovered he is in it up to his eyeballs rather than his ankles. Thirdly, there is the risk of physical harm being done to the informer.

On the other hand, 94 per cent of detectives were quite or very confident of the usefulness of the information supplied by their principal informer. Six out of ten thought that over three-quarters of the information he provided was useful. A substantial majority of the detectives (as opposed to the uniformed police who took part in the survey) believed that three-quarters of people turned in by their principal registered informer were actively involved in crime. Provided the informer was himself actively involved in the criminal sub-culture, they believed that some three-quarters of his information was useful. The less deeply involved, the less useful the information.

Anecdotal evidence that officers have paid informers out of their own pockets is substantiated. The last time an informer had been paid, slightly under half of the officers had paid from their own pockets sums up to £50, with half paying between £10 and £20. The highest sum ever paid from an officer's own pocket was £200, with only a handful paying more than £50.

Officers were found to be both protective and demanding of their informers. In one instance a detective had allowed his informer to escape, and to divert suspicion had taken him to hospital to have his arm put in plaster. In another, where good information was being received, an officer had protected a man whom he knew to be an escapee from prison. On the other hand, officers kept their informers in line by retaining papers which could lead to a prosecution and by threatening to blow their cover.

Only one in three had managed to recoup the money officially. There were, however, found to be a number of ways in which a sort of slush fund could be developed. For example, if an officer was over six miles from his station he could claim a luncheon allowance of £3.15, and supervisors encouraged officers to take advantage of this so that a fund of around £60 could be put together.

12

A Threatened Species?

Where does it all lead? Or is it just a circle with temporary breaks as the courts for a while turn against the testimony of the informer and undercover agent? Should a species seen to be endangered be protected? Apart from anything else a grass is cheap at the price. For example, the No.4 (Midlands) Regional Crime Squad had a £47,000 budget for the year 1993–94. On the other hand, in America there is a considerable reaction to the enormous sums being paid out to informants.

Critics of the supergrass system and of undercover police work argue that there are very considerable dangers not merely for officers but for the judicial system. One of the pre-eminent figures in American criminal law, Professor Alan Dershowitz, is clear:

> Informers are very important. They give you leads and tips. They tell you where the guns are buried. That's all fine. It's when the informant's word, his credibility, is used in court – that's the problem.[1]

Stephen Trott, a judge on the US 9th Circuit Court of Appeals

1 Quoted in Mark Curriden, 'No Honor among Thieves' in the *American Bar Association Journal*, June 1989.

and former assistant attorney general for the Criminal Division, was quoted in the same article: 'I tell prosecutors, "Don't use these kinds of witnesses unless you absolutely have to."' He accepts, however, that the criminal justice system would collapse without the use of informants. The system tolerates informants – often the only witnesses – as essential:

> The FBI will tell you that if you don't have informants, you're out of luck when it comes to investigating heavy-duty crime. Out of luck! So you've got to balance this thing. It's not a question of not using them, it's a question of when and where.

Now in 1995, Professor Al Alschuler, of the University of Chicago, has firmed his opinion on the use of the supergrass:

> The informant system is a dark corner of law enforcement all but immune from judicial supervision. As the war on drugs escalates, so does the extent of the intrusion on privacy, the use of brutal methods to 'turn' snitches, and the unreliability of the informant-provided information upon which the police act.[2]

Unsurprisingly, there have also been problems with informants and supergrasses. Jack Slipper, who in principle likes the scheme, also recognises the dangers:

> I found the average informant was a man who had been dealt with by an officer who'd treated him fairly and not bullied him and the man had been fortunate enough to have got a light sentence. Then if the officer was any good he'd meet him soon after the case, if he hadn't gone away, or when he came out, buy him a drink and say, 'Look, it's up to you but if . . .'

2 Letter to the author.

Looking back, I think it is one of the most dangerous ways of retaining your credibility because no matter how clean, how straight you want to keep it the officers who run with professional informers find themselves bound in a web into which the layman would read corruption. But it could well have been nothing of the kind. I've known good officers, who've done excellent work and who've finished up their career with a cloud over their heads because of informers.

Over the years efforts have been made to provide a code for officers. In 1992 the Association of Chief Police Officers put together a document which was due to be put to the crime committee for ratification, but none was forthcoming. Some police forces used it as a blueprint, but for some reason it was never official policy. In September 1994 a document was prepared and accepted which sets out the rules to be followed by police using informers. To what extent it can or will be followed is another matter, and Clive Norris of Hull University has doubts:

In many respects the new guidelines merely codify the existing rules and regulations. Our research suggests that many of these rules were routinely broken. Unless there is a profound change in the manner in which detective/informer dealings are supervised, it is unlikely that they will have much impact on the day-to-day use of informers. In short, so-called 'noble cause' corruption will remain.

In the guide officers are urged to keep their distance from the informants. Whether it is actually possible to do this and maintain the necessary bond is another matter. Officers may be reminded that the informer belongs not to them but to the police, but the practice is a different matter entirely.

Here is a police officer who joined in the 1970s, speaking of

his younger days when the grass was loyal to the officer, and
fine concepts of belonging to the police as a body did not
occur to him:

> In the 1970s the cultivation of informers was an active
> part of the CID. What are you doing? Are you getting
> to know them? These were questions asked by senior
> officers of young men in the CID. How you did it was
> left up to you. If it resulted in turning a blind eye and
> operating an unofficial licensing system, then that was
> not necessarily frowned upon. A set of double standards
> existed. The people you were sending to prison, as long as
> you treated them in a way they felt was their due, had no
> resentment. If you dealt with their family by their lights
> they'd be willing to become informers on their release.
>
> I knew officers who looked after wives, making sure
> they didn't behave too widely; who looked after post
> office and building society books, bringing money each
> week for the wife.
>
> The relationship between the police and villainy was
> wholly different from today. We were encouraged to be
> much closer.
>
> Informers were a wholly personal thing. You didn't
> allow anyone else to know who your informant was. If
> you went to your DI or DCI and said, 'My informant tells
> me . . .,' if you were accepted as a working DC, then
> your superior officer would never dream of asking the
> informant's name, or if he did he wouldn't expect you
> to name him.
>
> Informants expected to be paid out of the rewards,
> but in many cases the reward money paid out bore no
> resemblance to the amount the informant received. If they
> got a good drink they were lucky.
>
> I was on late turn at the CID at Peckham one night. I
> was the only one in the office when the phone rang about
> 9.30 p.m. A voice said he wanted to speak to such and

such an officer. I said he wasn't here and I'd leave a message for him. No, it was urgent. Would I meet the caller, who said he had information. I went and met him in a pub. He'd just come out of a three-year sentence. He'd been the driver in a robbery fifteen years earlier and had been grassed by a supergrass. He said whilst he was in prison he'd been visited by officers from Countryman who wanted him to tell them about Officer X. 'Tell us and you can walk out within the next few weeks.' He named the officer and I said I knew him well. 'If you know him, tell him I've nothing against him and I didn't tell on him. I did my full time but tell him they're looking into him.'

A new problem for the police and the courts has been the protection of their informers and ordinary witnesses from identification in court. In the past the witness appeared and then either took his chance or disappeared into a witness protection programme.

The Metropolitan Police have had a witness protection system for the last twenty years; it is one which has grown out of the use of the supergrass in the trials of the seventies. The police work on informality, and to make formal rules often presents problems. 'We wanted to make sure that people coming into the supergrass system survived giving evidence,' says Commander Roy Ramm, who ran the scheme.

The Metropolitan Police Criminal Justice Protection Unit (CJPU) has three categories into which witnesses in the context of organised criminal groups will fall. The witness is defined as being frequently a co-conspirator or associate mixing with members of the particular criminal group. They vary slightly from the ACPO definitions.

Resident Informant – An active participant in a succession of serious crimes who, after arrest, elects to identify, give evidence against and provide intelligence about fellow criminals involved in those or other offences.

Protected Informant – A person informing on associates participating in crime whose identity and activity is exposed.

Protected Witness – A person who can provide essential evidence, generally about the most serious offences, and a substantial threat exists to their well-being.

The scheme has dealt with several hundred witnesses over the years with, in 1994, about thirty cases outstanding. The figures provided by the Association of Chief Police Officers, Police Superintendents' Association and the Police Federation, in answer to a written question by the House of Commons Home Affairs Committee on Organised Crime, are:

In the period	No. of cases dealt with by the Witness Protection Unit	Breakdown by status
1977–82	48	96% Resident Informants 2%Protected Witness
1983–87	24	25% Resident Informants 50% Protected Witness 25% Protected Informants
1988–93	61	31% Resident Informants 58% Protected Witness 8% Protected Informants 3% Other

In cases where protection had been sought between 1 February and 20 June 1994, there had been fifty-seven applications for protection of which forty-one were witnesses seeking protection and forty dependants, making a total of eighty-one. Eight people were seeking resident informant status, forty-four protected witness status and five protected informant status.[3]

Curiously, Ramm believes that as more importance is placed on scientific evidence, so witness intimidation will increase:

> The more we are able to provide incontrovertible proof through DNA, fingerprints and forensic evidence in general, the more the witness provides the only vulnerable area in the prosecution.[4]

Nowadays, with (it appears) a much more active programme by professional criminals to discourage evidence being given against them, more steps have been taken to repair the situation. Quite apart from cases involving children, in what the authorities deem to be appropriate circumstances screens have gone up between the witness and the dock and the public gallery. There are now instances where pseudonyms and voice distorters are being used.

Nor is it clear what, if any, signal of guilt this sends out to the jury. The judge can say until he is blue in the face that the erection of such a screen should not be held against any of the defendants, but whether the jury puts two and two together and makes four or an even greater number, who can tell?

Given the self-interest of informers and the fact that they and ordinary witnesses have had very close links with the police for months, defence lawyers fear that there is likely to be a bond between them and the witnesses will be unlikely to say a word against their helpers. If the witness appears under a pseudonym, behind screens and with a voice distorter, it

3 House of Commons, Home Affairs Committee, *Organised Crime*, 1994, HMSO.
4 Michael Clarke, 'Witnesses in Fear' in *Police Review*, 6 May 1994.

is difficult to see how the defendant can mount any sort of cross-examination, let alone an effective one. It may be, for example, that he has had an abortive affair with the witness who holds a grudge against him. It may be the woman's husband. He may have sacked the witness, or fought him in a pub on a previous occasion. Who can tell?

The Court of Appeal was convinced that the defendant should have the right to know his accused even if he did not see him. In the case of Vincent Agar, heard at Teesside Crown Court, the judge had refused to allow the defence to put questions to police officers which might lead to the identification of the informer. Agar received eighteen months for possessing amphetamines with intent to supply. In February 1989 the Court of Appeal said that although there was a well-established rule of public policy inhibiting the disclosure of the identity of informants, there was an even stronger public interest in allowing a defendant to put forward a tenable defence in the best light.[5] The appeal was allowed.

One detective in a large metropolitan force is probably speaking for a great number of his colleagues when he says that:

> . . . it is a right of the defendant in British law to be faced by their accusers and this really flies in the face of that: but when you look at undercover officers or the security forces, they're allowed to do it, and this is just an extension of that.[6]

It is small wonder that the defence, where the money is available – and that of course is only in serious crime cases – have resorted to employing private detectives to try to identify the witnesses.

5 (1989) 90 Cr. App. R. 318.
6 Michael Clarke, *op. cit.*

Part of the problem has come about because of the reluctance of the prosecution over the years to disclose to the defence what material it has which it is not using. There have, unfortunately, been a number of highly publicised cases at appeal level which have shown that the prosecution has, before trial, had in its possession evidence which would either tend to show the innocence of the defendant or actually exculpate him completely.[7] In theory, for many years the prosecution has had a duty to pass over unused material but has not been doing so. Now the defending lawyers have adopted a more aggressive stance, and to a great extent they have been supported by the courts.

In 1993 David Shattock, Chief Constable of Avon and Somerset, spoke up against the practice of disclosure, saying that since the previous September at least ten cases had been withdrawn because the disclosure rulings would have put witnesses or informants at risk:

> Certain solicitors and barristers are exploiting the rules of disclosure, knowing we will withdraw the prosecution rather than face the fear of reprisals when information becomes known to their clients.
>
> One never wants to stop information being passed on to solicitors and barristers who have a duty to look after the best interests of their clients. After what has happened in the past, we don't want to be the sole keepers of information.
>
> But there are occasions where we think that the information that they are asking for is not necessary.

Examples given by the Avon constabulary – not one would

7 A particularly sad example is that of Stefan Kisko, convicted of the rape and murder of Lesley Molseed. The prosecution, which relied heavily on a confession, had evidence to show that physically he could not have been her attacker. Kisko was released from a mental hospital after many years and died before he could be awarded compensation for his ordeal. Later, after Kisko's release, another man was arrested but was never charged.

immediately think of as being the centre for major organised crime – included the kidnapping of two men who were taken to a flat, tied up and handcuffed. Their money was stolen from them and their kidnappers threatened to pour boiling water over them. The offenders were caught in the act, but the witnesses failed to appear at court, telling the police they were in fear of their lives. A second case involved a man who was hacked with a meat cleaver, and others were attacked with baseball bats. Several days later one of the victims was threatened by men who stole and burned his car; he later withdrew the complaint. The third of Avon's instances involved a man who was beaten unconscious and when he awoke found himself naked in a bath; he then had boiling water poured over him. The case was dropped after witnesses were too scared to help the police.

On average it appears that the police (really the Crown Prosecution Service) are dropping a case a week to protect informants. Assuming it is a multi-handed defence case, this means that over the last two years 200–300 serious criminals are on the streets who would, and should, have been in prison. This is the opinion of Detective Chief Superintendent Brian Ridley of the Metropolitan Police.

The police also complain that the disclosure rulings are physically restrictive and financially ruinous. Lawyers defending Robert Black, the paedophile convicted of killing three girls in April 1994, asked for and received twenty-three tons of documents obtained in the ten-year investigation. In the Asil Nadir – Polly Peck fraud case, over one million documents were produced.

The police have also complained about the tactics used by defence lawyers when they have obtained the information. In one rape case in the South of England, it is claimed that the police had routinely interviewed a man who had had a rape conviction many years earlier. The defence obtained this information under the rules of disclosure and called the man as a defence witness. He was asked whether he had ever been convicted and whether he had been questioned over the present incident. Their defendant was acquitted.

In the case of an allegation of a robbery at a supermarket in the Midlands, details were obtained of all other supermarket robberies in the area – on which there was no evidence against the defendant – and for which he was able to supply alibis. He was acquitted.

This, say the police, is unfair play, maintaining that in the first case the jury had the impression that the witness was the guilty man, and in the second that they had never made any allegations against the accused in relation to the other robberies.[8]

It may be that there can be restrictions on the amount of documents to be produced, but that still does not solve the problem of protecting the identity of witnesses.

As for the use of the informer, now big business for drug-enforcement agencies, there are allegations that there is little control exercised by the agencies that use and pay them, and that many informants continue their illegal activity while being paid by the agencies. Further it is claimed, particularly in America, that deals are concealed from the defence.

There is clear evidence that informants have lied on oath, so sending innocent people to jail, and that the informers frequently entrap people to build cases for the agents for whom they work and with whom they bond.

In Great Britain there is a suggestion that informers should be put on a weekly wage, and this is almost the practice at present in the case of a principal registered informer. It certainly appears to have been the case in Northern Ireland. As always, America is ahead of the game. Back in 1991 FBI agent Bensch, who at the time supervised over 250 confidential informants, acknowledged that:

Many informants working on a long-term case will get

8 *Independent on Sunday*, 18 December 1994.

a weekly allowance of $1,000 and a large reward at the end, as much as $100,000 . . . actually, some of the bigger informants are a downright bargain.[9]

'We will pay an informant anything from £50 to £100 at the bottom to several thousand pounds of public money for the recovery of large quantities of drugs,' says Detective Chief Superintendent Roy Ramm, thereby showing that Scotland Yard is in a different league from the forces researched by Dr Norris. He adds:

And I wouldn't want to put a ceiling on it, because, so far as we're concerned, there is no ceiling. We don't say we pay up to a maximum, it depends on the work.[10]

Apart from paying from their own resources, informants are funded by Scotland Yard which sends out begging letters to banks, building societies, and insurance companies asking for a contribution for informers. 'Informing has become, if not an honorable trade, a mass occupation,' says Dershowitz. 'They manufacture crime to sell their product. They lie to give their employers – the authorities – what the informant thinks they want to hear.'

Says Professor Al Alschuler:

With money and leniency, there are tremendous pressures on informants just to make things up. Any honest law enforcement officer will tell you informants put spins on their stories all the time. You cannot trust these people. What is more disturbing is that the government is giving informers a licence to conduct their criminal conduct. The government is basically subsidizing the drug trade.

9 _American Bar Association Journal_, June 1991.
10 R. Fleming with H. Miller, _Scotland Yard_, pp. 126–7.

There is plenty of anecdotal evidence that this is being mirrored here, with drug shipments being allowed through to wait for 'the big one'. If concrete evidence is needed, then a case which was eventually heard at Newcastle Crown Court gives ground for considerable concern.

At the beginning of 1994 there was a major disaster in the case of Joseph Kassar, a Manchester businessman convicted of a plot to smuggle £67 million of cocaine imported amongst lead ingots from Venezuela. The shipment had gone through and had been distributed through sources in Liverpool, but the planners tried a second time. On this occasion Customs and Excise found nearly £150 million, in street terms, of 95 per cent pure cocaine at a warehouse in Stoke-on-Trent. They removed the drugs from the crates of thirty-two lead ingots which, this time, had come in through Felixstowe and were on their way to Liverpool. Customs tried to prove that the £67 million had gone through Kassar's hands, but in the end they were able to show that only £300,000 had passed that way.

That was bad enough, but the full story of the investigation and its repercussions was yet to come out. When it did, it showed a complete lack of co-operation between the Customs and the police. The success story which turned to ashes had begun on 26 June 1992 when the Customs were waiting as Brian Charrington landed in his private aircraft at Teesside airport. Six months previously Customs officers had drilled into the lead ingots stored in the Stoke warehouse, and they believed Charrington was the organiser of the shipment.

It appears that members of the drug wing of the No. 2 (North East) Regional Crime Squad had been working with Customs to prepare a case against him. Unfortunately, what appears not to have been mentioned is that quite apart from him being Target One, Charrington was just about the *Numero Uno* police informant. The moment he was arrested, the police went to his rescue. If need be, they would give evidence in his defence.

In fact this is not uncommon practice. For example in January 1989 Detective Superintendent Tony Lundy was allowed to give evidence *in camera* on behalf of his protégé, supergrass Roy Garner, and towards the end of 1994 a major furore broke out when it was discovered that Commander John Allinson, former head of operations at Scotland Yard, had privately intervened at the trial of a man linked to a contract killing. Allinson later resigned.

During the search for the killer of Donald Urquhart, shot in a professional hit, a suspect's home in Sussex was raided. There detectives found a huge cache of arms and ammunition. Allinson gave evidence in the judge's private room, saying that the man had helped to solve a major robbery ten years previously. It was a move which did not please either London or Sussex detectives. In the end the weapons were confiscated and the man fined.

The Customs officers in the Charrington case complained that, far from producing major drug-related arrests, Charrington had only implicated small-time if professional criminals. Gilbert Gray QC, the barrister for Charrington, asked for and was granted a meeting with Sir Nicholas Lyell, the Attorney General. Five weeks later, on 28 January 1993, all charges against Charrington were withdrawn by the Crown Prosecution Service; he and ten others were due to be committed for trial to the Crown Court. In their turn the police complained that the bust of Charrington had pre-empted a major strike against a Colombian cartel.

In January 1994 the only person to be convicted for his part in the whole affair was Kassar, described by the trial judge, Mr Justice May, as 'not one of the principal organisers, but very much a middleman'. It is interesting to speculate on the sentences which would have been passed on the leaders. His solicitor complained that the case had been surrounded by secrecy and that the press had been deliberately gagged to prevent the truth being known. John Merry, who runs a news agency in Darlington, claims that a prominent politician telephoned him urging him not to publicise the case. At the time of Kassar's trial, Charrington was believed to be in Hong

Kong. According to the *Observer*, one of the police officers involved in thwarting the Customs inquiry left the force in January 1993 and that September drove to Spain with his wife, a serving police constable, in an £87,000 BMW registered to Charrington.[11]

It is only when a situation or an informer begins to unravel that the damage he or she has caused can begin to be seen, and by then it is often too late to do anything about it except to begin a damage limitation exercise.

One such American informer was the former nude dancer, Darlene McKinney, who became so addicted to cocaine that the only person she could find to employ her was not a topless-bar-owner but the Georgia law authorities. She laid the first information because a supplier refused her credit, and from then an officer in the drug squad in Rome, Georgia, took her up with some enthusiasm. She was told there was more money in addition to her first reward if she continued to help bust drug-dealers and she co-operated enthusiastically. Later she turned on the agent who ran her when the head of the town's narcotics unit was himself charged with trafficking.

During spring 1988 her activities, which included luring men into using or selling drugs after sex with her, led to eighteen arrests. McKinney also maintained that her supervisor not only had sex with her but let her walk off with part of the drugs. She also received 10 per cent of cash or assets seized.

> The reason I was doing all these things [offering sex if friends would buy her cocaine specifically from the undercover agent] was because I would do anything for drugs.

She went on to testify that after each arrest agents would spread the bags of cocaine they seized on the table.

11 The *Observer* was about the only newspaper to carry what would appear to be a major story. See David Rose and John Merry, 'Drugs bust victory turned to dust' in the *Observer*, 16 January 1994.

I'd just get a little out and he'd kind of turn his back. He never actually handed me the bags and said, 'Here, take some cocaine out of it,' but he knew what I was doing. He'd have to be pretty dumb not to.[12]

Apart from those who suffered at Darlene McKinney's hands, all this may seem mildly amusing and remote from the real world. After all, where exactly is Rome, Georgia? Of course, the denizens of that town may ask, who is John Banks? The sort of question a judge asks on a slack afternoon, or late morning, with an eye on a place on page one of the tabloids: 'Who are the Beatles?' He might also have asked, 'What on earth were the authorities doing using him?'

The Beatles may have written and performed 'Lucy in the Sky with Diamonds', said to be a homage to LSD, but John Banks was another proposition altogether. In April 1993 the thief, mercenary, blackmailer and would-be contract killer, as journalist David Rose described him, was in hiding, protected by police and Customs squads who, Rose said, had paid him as an agent for many years. The wheels had finally come off.

In the first week of April a jury at Southwark Crown Court had unanimously found an alleged heroin dealer, Raymond Okudzeto, not guilty. Okudzeto was, he claimed, the victim of a classic reverse sting. He thought he was acting with and on behalf of the authorities, but he was not. The jury found that he had been entrapped by Banks acting as an *agent provocateur*, and threw out the case.

Banks' career is both lengthy and noteworthy, and it is

12 *American Bar Association Journal*, June 1991. Another story in the same article tells of how a sixty-year-old electronics expert was prevailed upon to make a briefcase bomb. He was told that the explosive was necessary to destroy a Mafia shipment of drugs. He wanted to back out but he was then told the Mob would harm his family. In a third story, marijuana dealer Woody Moore seems to have gone completely off the rails. First he testified that leading Georgians, including a judge and his law partner, had helped him launder drugs. The partner was indicted but along with all other defendants was acquitted. During this period Moore continued importing drugs. He then turned on the authorities, alleging they had known all the time he was still importing.

interesting that anyone should have used him as a trustworthy informer for any period of time at all. A self-styled major, he served in the British Army from which he was dishonourably discharged in 1969 for theft. The commission was, he said, awarded him by the government of South Vietnam shortly before its collapse.

His career as a mercenary began some six years after his compulsory retirement from the British Army. Operating from an office above a laundrette in Sandhurst, he endeavoured to recruit mercenaries for the African cause in what was then Rhodesia with an advertisement in the *Daily Telegraph*. The initial group of dogs of war did not last long; some were discharged for getting drunk in a London hotel, and within six months Banks was back recruiting once more – now for the anti-Marxists in Angola.

This time some of the dogs did not return to home kennels. Of the 180 who went, fourteen were murdered by a Greek fighting on their side. Two were executed by the victorious MPLA, and others were killed in action.

Banks' first appearance as a government witness was in the spring of 1977, when he appeared at the Old Bailey in a case where three men were said to have negotiated a deal to buy what now seems to be a modest £25,000 of arms. They received long sentences. At the trial Rock Tansey, appearing for the defence, alleged that Banks had incited the men into dealing in arms, probably against their will and certainly against their better judgement. Gerald Smiley, Joseph Higgins and James Davidson were found guilty on 10–2 majorities of being involved in soliciting Banks and two other men to supply 1,000 American-made M1 carbines. Smiley called to the judge, 'You gave Banks a chance to perjure himself and these fools [the jury] believed him.'

Three years later Banks was back in the Old Bailey, this time in the dock accused of blackmail and uttering threats to kill. So far as the blackmail went, he claimed he had information about a Cuban plot to assassinate the Nicaraguan president, Antonio

Somozo. Banks had sent two men to collect $250,000 from the Nicaraguan embassy in London. His defence was interesting, including not only claims that he was a past agent for the British Secret Service but also details of plots to kill 'Carlos the Jackal' and of assassinations in Yemen. He received two years' imprisonment.

Six months later in April 1981, he was in Coldingley open prison and absconded, staying out for eight months. On his return, he lost twenty-eight days' remission and suffered fourteen days' loss of privileges, a punishment which hardened prison discipline observers would describe as little more than a slap on the wrist.

Throughout the remainder of the 1980s Banks seems to have flourished. He became a security consultant, a military adviser and a wheeler-dealer. He had a substantial property in Lincolnshire. Nevertheless, he found time to become involved in situations which led to his appearances as a prosecution witness or a behind-the-scenes manipulator in cases where others gave evidence. In 1991 he was giving evidence in the contract killing of a former-loved-one case; the woman was acquitted. That same year, allegations of dishonest handling and theft against a man said to be a member of the Ulster Defence Association were dropped at Isleworth Crown Court. They related to some £20 million worth of paintings, part of the theft of the Alfred Beit Collection stolen in Ireland. He had posed as a potential buyer at the Penta Hotel at Heathrow.

Next year, he did not give evidence when Martin Poole and James Collis were prosecuted at Winchester Crown Court for trying to buy 75 kilos of cannabis from the Customs in the form of officer Michael Stephenson in an undercover scam. Their defence was that Banks had bullied them into purchasing the cannabis, telling them that it was compensation for the failure of a deal he had made with one of their associates.

The defence, although severely hampered, managed to provide at least marginal evidence that Banks existed and was involved. They found his computer telephone records, but Stephenson gave evidence that he did not know the whereabouts of Banks. Later, it would appear that he was in regular contact with Banks, who was 'an informant whose identity we were trying to protect'. This would seem to be not the only time that Banks was being protected.

The Okudzeto trial related to £40,000 of heroin found at the defendant's flat shortly after he had offered a sample to an undercover Customs officer, who went to the flat, posing as a buyer for £15,000 of heroin. Okudzeto had been approached in Kenya by a man called Evans Anyona, and had immediately told Banks, his former business associate, in the belief that he would pass the information on to the authorities. Instead, Banks persauded him to take an active part in the sting.

The Customs sheltered Banks for eight months, refusing to admit that he had played any part in the sting; it was only at a pre-trial review that his existence was admitted. When he did give evidence, Banks denied he had ever spoken to Anyona. Later during the trial a logged record was produced showing that Michael Stephenson, the undercover officer in charge of the case, had spoken with Banks about putting in a buyer, and that Banks had been in touch with Anyona in Kenya.

Banks gave evidence and under cross-examination denied setting people up. He also denied he owed Okudzeto money and claimed he had been paid £750 by customs officials. His only motivation, he said, was his hatred of drugs. Asked about his involvement in Africa, he cannot have charmed the jury when he replied, 'I didn't mind which side [I was working for] as long as it was paid for.' He was asked how much he charged for a contract assassination and replied, 'There is no fixed price. I'm sorry, we're not Tesco's.'

Summing up, Judge Eugene Cotran said:

The log reveals the discrepancy between Banks and Stephenson. The credibility of one or both of them is suspect. There was some misdemeanour by the Customs team . . . There were certain disturbing features. You

must ask yourself why were these things done. You may
say the rot starts from the top downwards or you may
question the credibility of this case.

The jury failed to agree, and now Okudzeto, who had been in
custody for eleven months, was released on bail. The re-trial
took place the following April. At the second trial Banks did
not give evidence and Okudzeto was acquitted.

In July 1994 Banks resurfaced in South Africa organising
bodyguards for Winnie Mandela. He was now, it appears,
her main security adviser, and had been in the country since
October 1993 when he came to the notice of the police over a
Mercedes Benz hired car. He was held in prison until payment
of £21,000 was made anonymously.

As for the use of undercover police, there is an argument
that this itself leads to the licensing of criminals to commit
crime. Jean-Paul Brodeur argues that whilst all guidelines on
handling informers proclaim that the law is not to be broken in
the course of their assignment with the police, the application
of the guidelines is progressively suspended as handlers get
more deeply involved with their informers in risky operations.
He cites the case of a Royal Canadian Mounted Police officer
who appealed against his conviction for drug trafficking on
the grounds that he accepted only a part of the benefits that his
informer was making in selling drugs. The informer apparently
had found it unfair that his handler should not get his slice of
the cake.[13] He also sees the subversion of the law as inevitably
following, and the informer as a shield for misconduct:

I was struck by how often police officers whose behaviour
was under review tried to justify the the fact that they were
at the wrong place (e.g. a strip joint), at a wrong time
(being on duty) and doing the wrong thing (getting drunk)
by alleging that they were 'meeting with an informer'.

13 J.P. Brodeur, 'Undercover policing in Canada: Wanting what is wrong' in *Crime,
Law and Social Change* 18.

A senior Scotland Yard officer believes that undercover officers have to be committed.

> Totally. And they have to keep remembering where they come from. They have a need to be conscious of what their parent organisation is trying to achieve.

There is also the danger, more prevalent in America than here, that the undercover officer will become a casualty. Gary Marx cites a number of cases when undercover black officers have been killed in mistake for offenders.

The benefits are, however, attractive. Police morale can be strengthened by the knowledge that officers are actively taking steps to prevent and detect crime. The results of an undercover operation can serve as a warning to the semi-professional as opposed to career criminal. For the latter, undercover work may not break up an organisation but its presence, perceived or real, may serve to disorganise their businesses.

On a lighter side, surveillance and undercover investigators are used by insurance companies investigating fraudulent claims. Willy McNicholas was injured carrying mats at the Moss Side Leisure Centre in 1987. He was still claiming to be suffering from the effects of his injuries when he went to Fuertaventura where he carried the luggage for his family, swam and carried his son's buggy. Posing as a tourist, the investigator filmed him in these operations. McNicholas was later invited to see edited highlights of the film of his holiday. Within half an hour he abandoned his claim, though he thought the behaviour of the council was unsporting: 'It's normal business practice to check out compensation claims but to video my wife and kids as well as me is a bit much. No privacy laws were broken because we were filmed in public places, not in our room or anything like that.'[14]

Many would like to see the range of undercover work extended. A senior Scotland Yard officer believes that the

14 *Observer*, 25 September 1994.

road down which the police should think of travelling is that of the undercover officer, and says:

> Courts seem to be much more comfortable with undercover officers than with informers. Society is better off with undercover officers, but the historical context says that society is uncomfortable with secretive let alone secret police.

More positively, he notes that there is an increasing number of appearances of undercover officers because of the difficulties with informers.

> We can protect undercover officers better. For decades we have been seeking to limit the role of the informant, looking to get an undercover officer in or to get corroboration.

Rowan Bosworth-Davies, formerly a police officer and now with a major City firm of solicitors, comments:

> I'm a fan of undercover policing. The future of investigating real City crime is the use of undercover policing with target surveillance and target hardening. If you accept City crime is organised crime then why not investigate it as such? If the authorities want to combat City fraud effectively then the way they go about it at present is farcical.

In America, where perhaps the technique of the use of the informer has been most highly developed, it would seem that in 1993 the Justice Department spent some $97 million on informers of one kind or another annually. It has raised the hackles of many, including one lawyer who commented:

> Many of these individuals, because of their special relationships with law enforcement or prosecutors, are

able to continue committing crimes and doing drugs. I consider this to be an absolute disgrace. As a lawyer I understand that the government may need informants at times, but this level of cash payments (let alone other benefits conferred on informants) is outrageous.

As with all forms of policing, there is a price to be paid. There is little doubt that, if asked to vote on the subject, the vast majority of the public would shut their collective minds to the dangers of the informant, the informer, the entrapper and the cell fink. They would think only of the resulting convictions and say, 'Yes, siree, that is indeed what we want.'

Appendix

STATEMENT OF WITNESS

(M.C. Act, 1980, S101; C.J. Act, 1967, s.9; M.C. Rules, 1981, r. 70)

Statement of ....

Age of Witness (if over 21 enter 'over 21') ....

Occupation of Witness ....

Address and Telephone Number ....

....

....

This statement, consisting of   pages each signed by me, is true to the best of my knowledgevidence, I shall be liable to prosecution if I have wilfully stated in it anything which I know to be false or do not believe to be true.

Dated the   day of   , 19   .

Signed ....

Signature witnessed by ....

On Saturday 22nd June 1985 with a man called Roger I and a man known as Tom MORRIS went to the roundabout on the North Circular Road at the junction of the M1 motorway where we met a man known as Tony, I now know this man to be Michael BAILEY, and another man named Garry, I now know this man to be Harry Brand. I had £10,000 in cash in my constructive possession with the authority of my Detective Inspector. BAILEY and BRAND arrived in a Ford Granada colour blue index no: CEV 185R. I was introduced to them and we then followed to the Woodman Public House, in Highgate, N.6 where we entered the car park at the rear. BAILEY and I discussed the fact that he said that he had a quantity of forged £50 notes for sale. He said that he had £50,000 worth and wanted £10,000 sterling for them. I agreed to this and I said I would show him my money (i.e. £10,000) BAILEY also said, that he had one sample on him but it was down his trousers and he would show it to me at a later stage. Then Roger, BAILEY and I went in Roger's car to the Archway Public House, Archway Road, N.19 where I showed BAILEY my £10,000. He said that there was no need as he trusted me fully. He also said that everything was sweet and that he would take us to a public house in the East End where we could exchange the £50,000 worth of forged £50 notes for my £10,000 cash. Meanwhile we had left Harry and MORRIS drinking in the Woodman Public House. With BAILEY Roger and I went to the Swan Public House, Kingsland Road, Dalston, E.8. where I met a number of men and was introduced by BAILEY to a man named Frank. I now know this man to be Jack TAYLOR. TAYLOR stated that they had £50,000 worth of forged £50 notes in a car nearby and he wanted to do the swap i.e. £10,000 sterling for the forged £50,000 rather quickly. I said to TAYLOR, 'As they had seen my money, I wanted to see theirs before the transaction was completed.' TAYLOR was reluctant to show his forged £50 notes at this stage. TAYLOR said that he wanted my £10,000 first before he passed me his forged £50,000 currency. I would not agree to this and insisted that I had to see their money first. TAYLOR said that as we all trusted each other there were no problems and that he had definitely got the forged money in a car nearby. I said that if that is so, show it to me. TAYLOR was still reluctant to do this. BAILEY who was present all the time during this conversation then said that he [had] a forged £50 note in his possession and that I could have a look at it in the toilet if I wished. He gave me a £50 note and I went into the Gents toilet with BAILEY, and carefully examined this particular £50 note. The note appeared to me to be a genuine £50 note. BAILEY and I returned to the bar, again to the company of TAYLOR. BAILEY said to TAYLOR, that he had shown me a forged sample and TAYLOR asked me what I thought of the quality of the forged £50 note. I said to BAILEY and TAYLOR that if the rest of their merchandise was as good as that one then they would be just about perfect. I said to TAYLOR, 'Would you show me the £50's.' TAYLOR said, 'There are too many people about, I can't show it to you in the car.' I said to TAYLOR and BAILEY, 'In that case, I'm going to return to Nottingham.' Roger and I returned to the Woodman Public House where we met BRAND and MORRIS. I said to BRAND that TAYLOR and BAILEY would not show their £50's and that I was going to return to Nottingham. BRAND used the telephone and he told me that TAYLOR would contact me in due course at Nottingham.

On Tuesday 2nd July 1985 I went to Nottingham where at 7.30 pm BAILEY telephoned me from London to say that the deal was on and that business could definitely be done this time. He also said he could double up. I asked him to explain this and he said that he had £100,000 in forged £50 notes and wanted me to produce £20,000 for this amount. I said that this was okay. He then said he would ring me the following evening and confirm when and where we should meet in London. BAILEY did in actual fact telephone again the following evening, 3rd July 1985, but stated that he would definitely confirm a meeting in London for Saturday morning, but before he was able to do this he would ring again at 7.30pm on the following Friday night. I stated I may be unable to take his telephone due to business I had to do in Manchester. As a result of further information received on Saturday 6th July 1985, Roger and I met BAILEY and TAYLOR in the Woodman Public House, TAYLOR stated that they had the forged £50 notes nearby and they had £100,000 worth. BAILEY said that it is all good stuff and that it was as good as the sample he had shown me previously. We had a few drinks and then TAYLOR suggested we leave the Woodman Public House and follow him. TAYLOR left alone in his Vauxhall motor car and BAILEY came with Roger and I in Roger's car. We followed TAYLOR down the Archway Road and eventually stopped outside Marlers Wine Bar, Archway Road, N.6. where TAYLOR, BAILEY and I had a drink at the table outside the Wine Bar. Roger stayed in his car. BAILEY then introduced me to a young man who had in his possession a plastic shopping bag with some shopping in it. BAILEY then took the bag from the young man and showed me a large quantity of forged £50 Bank of England notes, which were at the bottom of the bag underneath the shopping. I checked them, they looked good and all the numbers appeared to be the same. Due to the length of time I spent checking them, BAILEY said, 'You're not going to count them all one by one.' I said, 'No, I trust you.' Whilst checking the forged money it did not appear to me that there was £100,000 notes present, and it was in my opinion their idea to 'have me over'. (By pretending there was £100,000 but in actual fact there was approximately £50,000) I then arranged to go and get my money: (i.e. £20,000). I returned a short time later to Marlers Wine Bar and again spoke to TAYLOR and

BAILEY. I was carrying a flight bag and said I had the £20,000 in there. TAYLOR and BAILEY then signalled to the young man who was in the vicinity. The young man approached and then BAILEY handed me the plastic bag. I looked inside and checked to see that the forged money was still there. It was. I then gave a pre-arranged signal to my colleagues and I ran away up Highgate Hill.

Bibliography

Agnew, D., *Undercover Agent – Narcotics* (1959), London, Souvenir Press.

Albanese, J., *Organised Crime in America* (1989), Cincinnati, Anderson Publishing Co.

Allen, M., *Pioneer Policewoman* (1925), London, Chatto & Windus.

————*Lady in Blue* (1936), London, Stanley Paul.

Archer, J.E., *By a Flash and a Scare* (1990), Oxford, Clarendon Press.

Ayling J., with Barnao, T. and Lipson, N., *Nothing But the Truth* (1993), Chippendale, Pan Macmillan.

Babington, A., *A House in Bow Street* (1969), London, Macdonald.

Bamford, S., *Passages in the Life of a Radical* (1984), Oxford, Oxford University Press.

Bean, J.P., *Over the Wall* (1994), London, Headline.

Bergreen, L., *Capone* (1994), London, Macmillan.

Bland, J., *Crime, Strange but True* (1991), London, Futura.

Bleakley, H., *The Hangmen of England* (1929), London, Chapman & Hall.

Block, A., *East Side – West Side* (1980), Cardiff, University College Cardiff Press.

Bogen, J.I., *The Anthracite Railroads* (1927), New York, Roland Press.

Bonanno, J., *A Man of Honor* (1983), New York, Simon & Schuster.

Borrell, C. and Cashinella, B., *Crime in Britain Today* (1975), London, Routledge & Kegan Paul.

Boyd, A., *The Informers* (1984), Dublin, The Mercier Press Ltd.

Brown, M. (ed), *Australian Crime* (1993), Sydney, Lansdowne.

Burke, S., *Peterman* (1966), London, Arthur Barker.

Campbell, D., *That was Business, This is Personal* (1990), London, Secker & Warburg.

————*The Underworld* (1994), London, BBC Books.

Campbell, P., *A Molly Maguire Story* (1992), New Jersey, Templecrome.

Capstick, J., *Given in Evidence* (1960), London, John Long.

Coleman, J.W., *The Molly Maguire Riots* (1936), Richmond, Va., Garrett & Massie.

Colquhoun, P., *A Treatise on the Functions and Duties of a Constable etc.* (1803), London.

Colquhoun, R., *Life Begins at Midnight* (1962), London, John Long.

Cox, J., *A Faithful Narrative of the Most Wicked and Inhuman Transactions of that Bloody-Minded Gang of Thief-Takers alias Thief Makers,* in *Villainy Detected, Being a Collection of the Most Sensational True Crimes and the Most Notorious Real Criminals that Blotted the Name of Britain in the Years 1660–1800* (1947), New York, D. Appleton-Century.

Cyriax, O., *Crime* (1993), London, André Deutsch.

Daley, R., *Prince of the City* (1978), New York, Houghton Mifflin.

Darbyshire, N. and Hilliard, B., *The Flying Squad* (1993), London, Headline.

Demaris, O., *The Last Mafioso: The Treacherous World of Jimmy Fratianno* (1981), New York, Times Books.

Dershowitz, A.M., *The Best Defense* (1983), New York, Vintage Books.

Detroit, M., *Chain of Evidence* (1994), London, Headline.

Donaghue, A., and Short, M., *The Krays' Lieutenant* (1995), London, Smith Gryphon.

Dunne, D., *Fatal Charms* (1988), New York, Bantam.

Dvornik, F., *Origins of Intelligence Services* (1974), New Brunswick, N.J.

Enright, S. and Morton J., *Taking Liberties* (1990), London, Weidenfeld & Nicolson.

Fitzpatrick, W.J., *Secret Service Under Pitt* (1892), London, Longman.

Fleming, R. with Miller, H., *Scotland Yard* (1994), London, Michael Joseph.

Follain, J., *Dishonoured Society* (1995), London, Little, Brown.

Fordham, P., *Inside the Underworld* (1972), London, George Allen & Unwin.

Fox, S., *Blood and Power* (1990), London, Penguin.

Frankos, D., *Contract Killer* (1993), London, Warner.

Fraser, F., *Mad Frank* (1994), London, Little, Brown.

Friedman, M., *The Pinkerton Labor Spy* (1907), New York, Wilshire Book Co.

Fry, C. with Kray, C., *Doing the Business* (1993), London, Smith Gryphon.

Gardner, P., *The Drug Smugglers* (1989), London, Robert Hale.

Giradin, G.R. and Helmer, W.J., *Dillinger: The Untold Story* (1994), Bloomingdale, University of Indiana Press.

Goddard, D., *The Insider* (1992), New York, Arrow Books.

Gosling, J., *The Ghost Squad* (1959), London, W.H. Allen.

Graeff, R., *Talking Blues* (1989), London, Collins Harvill.

Greenham, G.H., *Scotland Yard Experiences from the Diary of G H Greenham* (1904), London, George Routledge.

Greere, S., 'The Rise and Fall of the Northern Ireland Supergrass System' in *Criminal Law Review*, October 1987.
———*Supergrasses* (1995), Oxford, Clarendon Press.

Grover, D.H., *Debators and Dynamiters: The Story of the Haywood Trial* (1964), Corvallis, Oregon State University Press.

Hammer, R., *Playboy's Illustrated History of Organised Crime* (1975), Chicago, Playboy Press.

Halper, A. (ed), *The Chicago Crime Book* (1968), London, Souvenir Press.

Hammond, J.H., *The Autobiography of John Hays Hammond* (1935) (2 volumes), New York, Farrar and Rinehart.

Harney, M.L. and Cross, J.C., *The Informer in Law Enforcement* (1960), Springfield, Ill, Charles C. Thomas Publishers.

Hay, D. et al, *Albion's Fatal Tree* (1977), London, Peregrine Books.

Horn, T., *Life of Tom Horn: Government Scout and Interpreter, written by Himself* (1964), Norman, University of Oklahoma Press.

Irey, E.L. and Slocum, W., *The Tax Dodgers: The Inside Story of the T-Men's War with America's Political and Underworld Hoodlums* (1948), New York, Greenberg.

Irwin, W.R., *The Making of Jonathan Wild: A Study of the Literary Method of Henry Fielding* (1966), Hamden, Conn., Archon Books.

Jennings, A., Lashmar, P. and Simson, V., *Scotland Yard's Cocaine Connection* (1990), London, Jonathan Cape.

Kelland, G., *Crime in London* (1981), London, Bodley Head.

Knightley, P., *Second Oldest Profession* (1986), London, André Deutsch.

Korson, G., *Minstrels of the Mine Patch* (1938), Philadelphia.

Kray, R., *Villains We Have Known* (1993), Leeds, N.K. Publications.

Lacey, R., *Little Man* (1991), London, Constable.

Lansdowne, A. A., *Life's Reminiscences of Scotland Yard* (1890), London, Leadenhall Press.

le Caron, H., *Twenty-five years in the Secret Service: The Recollections of a Spy* (1892), London.

Lee, R. and Pratt, C., *Operation Julie* (1978), London, W.H. Allen.

Lee, W.M., *A History of the Police in England* (1901), London, Methuen.

Lewis, A.H., *Lament for the Molly Maguires* (1964), New York, Harcourt, Brace & World Inc.

Littlechild, J.G., *Reminiscences of Chief Inspector Littlechild* (1894), London, Leadenhall Press.

Lock, J., *Scotland Yard Casebook* (1993), London, Robert Hale.

Maas, P., *The Valachi Papers* (1970), St Albans, Panther.

Marx, G. T., *Under Cover: Police Surveillance in America* (1988), Los Angeles, University of California Press.

Maxwell, W.H., *History of the Irish Rebellion of 1778* (1845–1903), London.

McAlary, M., *Buddy Boys* (1988), New York, G. P. Putnam's Sons.

Mills, L., *Crimewatch* (1994), London, Penguin.

Morn, F., *The Eye that Never Sleeps* (1982), Bloomington, Indiana University Press.

Morton, J., *Gangland* (1992), London, Little, Brown.

——*Bent Coppers* (1993), London, Little, Brown.

——*Gangland* 2 (1994), London, Little, Brown.

Murphy, R., *Smash and Grab* (1991), London, Faber & Faber.

Nash, J.R., *World Encyclopedia of Organised Crime* (1993), London, Headline.

Nash, J.R. and Offen, R., *Dillinger: Dead or Alive?* (1970) Chicago, Henry Regnery.

Nelli, H.S., *The Business of Crime: Italians and Syndicate Crime* (1981), Chicago, University of Chicago Press.

Niederhoffer, A., *Behind the Shield* (1969), New York, Anchor.

Noble, T., *Neddy* (1993), Balmain, Kerr Publishing Pty Ltd.

Norman, F., *Bang to Rights* (1958), London, Secker & Warburg.

O'Brien, J. and Kurins, A., *Boss of Bosses*, (1991), London, Simon & Schuster.

O'Mahoney, M., *King Squealer* (1978), London, W.H. Allen.

Petrow, S., *Policing Morals* (1994), Oxford, Clarendon Press.

Pistone, J.D. with Woodley, R., *Donnie Brasco* (1988), London, Sidgwick & Jackson.

Porter, B., *The Refugee Question in Mid-Victorian Politics* (1979), Cambridge, Cambridge University Press.

———*The Origins of the Vigilant State* (1987), London, Weidenfeld & Nicolson.

———*Plots and Paranoia* (1989), London, Unwin Hyman.

Poulter, J., *The Discoveries of John Poulter, alias Baxter* (1778), Worcester, Michael Russell.

Powis, D., *The Signs of Crime* (1977), Maidenhead, McGraw-Hill.

Pringle, P., *The Thief Takers* (1958), London, Museum Press.

Pritchard, M. and Laxton, E., *Busted!* (1978), London, Mirror Books.

Radzinowicz, L., *A History of the English Criminal Law, volume ii* (1956), London, Stevens.

Read, L. and Morton, J., *Nipper* (1991), London, Macdonald.

Renner, T.C. and Kirby, C., *Mafia Enforcer* (1988), London, Corgi.

Rozenberg, J., *The Case for the Crown* (1987), Wellingborough, Equation.

Rowan, R. W., *The Pinkertons* (1931), London, Hurst & Blackett.

Scott, H., *Scotland Yard* (1954), London, André Deutsch.

———(ed), *Crime and Criminals* (1961), London, Bookplan.

Short, M., *Crime Inc.* (1991), London, Mandarin.

———*Lundy* (1991), London, Grafton.

Sifakis, C., *An Encyclopedia of American Crime* (1982), New York, Facts on File.

Siringo, C.A., *Two Evil Isms: Pinkertonism and Anarchism* (1915), Chicago, Charles A. Siringo.

Slipper, J., *Slipper of the Yard* (1981), London, Sidgwick & Jackson.

Smith, D.C., *The Mafia Mystique* (1975), New York, Basic Books.

Spiering, F., *The Man Who Got Capone* (1976), Indianapolis, Bobbs-Merrill.

Starr, C.G., *Civilisation and the Caesars* (1954), Ithaca, NY.

Stone, I., *Clarence Darrow for the Defense* (1941), New York, Doubleday.

Summers, A., *Official and Confidential: The Secret Life of J. Edgar Hoover* (1993), London, Gollancz.

Sunday Times Insight Team, *Ulster* (1972), Harmondsworth, Penguin.

Taylor, I., *In the Underworld* (1983), London, Guild Publishing.

Teresa, V. with Renner, T.C., *My Life in the Mafia* (1973), London, Hart-Davis, MacGibbon.

Thompson, E.P., *The Making of the English Working Class* (1963), London, Victor Gollancz.

Thompson, J., *My Life in the Klan* (1988), Nashville, Tenn., Rutledge Hill Press.

Thurston, G., *The Clerkenwell Riot* (1967), London, George Allen & Unwin.

Tremlett, G., *Little Legs* (1989), London, Unwin Hyman.

Unger, S.J., *FBI* (1976), Boston, Little, Brown.

Whittington-Egan, R. and M., *The Bedside Book of Murder* (1988), Newton Abott, David & Charles.

Wilkinson, L., *Behind the Face of Crime* (1957), London, Frederick Muller.

Williams, W. W., *The Life of General Sir Charles Warren* (1941), Oxford, Oxford University Press.

Wilson, F.S. and Day, B., *Special Agent: A Quarter Century with the Treasury Department and the Secret Service* (1965), New York, Holt, Rinehart and Winston.

Woffinden, B., *Miscarriages of Justice* (1987), London, Hodder & Stoughton.

Index

BENT COPPERS

Contents

Acknowledgements

My thanks go to Brian Hilliard, whose help has been unfailing, and in strictly alphabetical order, to Dock Bateson, Julian Bean, Keith Bottomley, Harry Clement, Clive Coleman, Walter Easey, Michael Fitz-James, John Frost, Dominique Harvie, Frances Hegarty, Tony Judge, Jennifer Kavanagh, Joan Lock, Brian McConnell, Mike McConville, Bernard Porter, Jim Ratcliffe, Nipper and Pat Read, Julian Rice, C.H. Rolph, Mike Seabrook, Martin Short, Edda Tasiemka, Frank Williamson, Richard Whittington-Egan, Ann Wilson, Alice Wood, and the many other people who have allowed me to quote from their material, as well as those who have helped and advised me but who have asked that I do not name them.

'Those who cannot remember the past are condemned to repeat it.'

George Santayana, *Life of Reason* (1905–6)

Introduction

There is an old story of a school class set to write essays on the police. One boy finished his within seconds. On inspection it consisted of one sentence: 'All coppers are bastards.' It was decided this viewpoint should be changed – the story is obviously old, for such re-education would not be deemed appropriate today – so it was arranged for the lad to visit the local station, after which he would write another essay. The visit passed off well but the revised essay took no longer to write. It read: 'All coppers are cunning bastards.'

As the years pass and large sections of the public, for good or bad reasons, become disaffected with the police, many would subscribe to that generalization or, to use a sociological term, stereotypicalization, which means just about the same thing but sounds more impressive. To some extent it is the fault of the police that this view pervades much of the community, where one aspect which particularly troubles people is police corruption.

I once acquired a bibliography of police corruption published in the United States. It ran to 190 pages. There is no similar bibliography in this country. Could this mean there is no corruption here or simply that no one has got round to writing about it? I am afraid it is the latter. Although there have been fine books on, for example, Challenor and on the Porn and Drug Squad trials, there has been nothing dealing with the subject in the round. A number of books on general as opposed to specific police corruption have been threatened and even appeared in publishers' lists in Britain, but none has so far materialized.

One notable failure to make it out of the starting gates

was the horse ridden by former armed robber and prison escaper John McVicar. He had written *The Rotten Orchard* in conjunction with Laurie Cork, once the youngest officer on the Flying Squad, who had been acquitted at the Central Criminal Court of allegations of his involvement in a major drug smuggling exercise. At the time, Cork, like many retired police officers, had what used to be called a road house in Devon. The arrangement was that McVicar would tape-record his memoirs, switching off the machine at moments when the revelations of misconduct in the force became too personal. He did just that but, unable to resist 'the real thing', he left running a second recorder attached to his ankle. This did not augur well for the partnership and Cork obtained an injunction in the Chancery Division against McVicar and the *Daily Express*, which wished to serialize extracts. The injunction was partly lifted and some, but by no means necessarily the most interesting, revelations duly appeared, although the book did not.

Nor have the police in their memoirs been that forthcoming. 'Perhaps the pension has always exerted an exemplary bridle on the tongue,' wrote the criminologist Richard Whittington-Egan. Certainly permission for the publication of memoirs was and, in theory, still is required before Knacker of the Yard can tell all, or at least a little. However, the pension cannot have been the bridle for crime writers, who, with the notable exception of Arthur Tietjen,[1] have eschewed the gory details of the bad behaviour of the police. In some ways this is not surprising. The journalists of, say, the 1950s and 1960s, the golden era of policing in general and Scotland Yard in particular, were in the pockets of the great detectives such as Hannam, Fabian and Spooner. Fabian would deliberately delay press conferences until late in the evening to show who was the master but there was always a tidbit for the first edition. Percy Hoskins, the great *Daily Express* crime reporter, would travel to conferences abroad with senior officers from Scotland Yard and was kept by Beaverbrook in a flat in Park Lane to which the top brass had access. Hoskins was never going to blow a whistle. There certainly was one to blow and he should have done so. 'He must have known enough to blow the Houses of Parliament into the Thames,' said one former Chief Constable. For Hoskins was

---

[1] A. Tietjen, *Soho*.

writing at the time when Detective Sergeant Harold 'Tanky' Challenor was the scourge of Soho.

For over a century barely a chapter about corruption could be garnered from the hundreds of memoirs and books written about Scotland Yard and, in much smaller numbers, the other forces. 'Almost no social science research exists on the subject of deviant behaviour in the police force,' wrote van Laere and Geerts. 'This is not only because this is a sensitive issue. Many police believe that deviant behaviour occurs so rarely in their forces that it presents no real problem – that it is merely a case of a few rotten apples.'[2]

Rather as in those carefree pre-AIDS days when social diseases were swept under the carpet and into the asylum, the attitude seems to be, well, it did happen once but that was a long time ago and, anyway, the bloke resigned. Provincial forces in particular believe themselves to be clean, blaming all the dirt, or as much as possible, on the Met. Their argument is that they are a small tight-knit community who would know and root out evil-doers, assuming there were any; an attitude that others would say could well lead the other way and produce a more closely knit community which would protect its members.

One Chief Inspector in a Home Counties force considered that 'corruption is at a much higher level in London than in provincial forces. The culture is more inclined to tolerate corruption in the Met.' And as for the Met: 'We are not worried about corruption on the old scale. Not at all . . . The top men have gone now, and the others keep their heads down,' was the comment of one Superintendent. While an Assistant Chief Constable in a large northern force who was formerly with the Met, said, 'I do find it disappointing that people are still prepared to take money despite all the restrictions. But the situation is one thousand per cent better now, it really is.'[3]

Of course, some did not wear blinkers. A former Met Inspector with sixteen years' service recounted:

> I was just leaving the job when my Superintendent came up and said, 'You're going. Not a bad time to leave this job. The

[2] E.M.P. van Laere and R.W.M. Geerts, 'Deviant Police Behaviour', *Policing*, vol 1, no 3, p. 5.
[3] R. Graef, *Talking Blues*, chapter 10.

only thing you can say is that corruption is on the way out.' I said, 'You must be joking.' And he said, 'Oh, I think we can pat ourselves on the back here. I think I can happily say that Mark finally put an end to that.' And I said, 'You are just not looking round you guv'nor. You should spend a little more time away from your desk. It's nothing to do with me, but don't think it's all gone.'

The trouble is the guys who were DCs and DSs stopped taking money in '73, '75, when Mark actually started hitting them for corruption. But if they start again they are DIs and DCIs and more by now. It doesn't bode well.[4]

But even when officers proposed to try to throw some light on the subject they were dissuaded. The former head of the CID, Gilbert Kelland, recalls an early experience:

During the course [at residential staff college] we were required to write a thesis on a subject of our choice and, influenced by some American literature particularly the 1951 Senator Kefauver's Committee findings, and my own experiences, I chose as a subject 'Police and Public Corruption'. After discussions with my syndicate director, a superintendent, I was persuaded that as there was insufficient written material on which to base my research I should instead write a paper on crowds and police responsibilities. It seemed that even at the Police Staff College the subject of corruption was not open for discussion.[5]

Of course, 'It is always in a villain's interest to put about that he is able to bung coppers.'[6]

When I did a little research into the subject in 1985, as far as the Met was concerned any corruption happened in another division from the one in which the questioned officer was serving. Indeed, there was some support for this. Although in 1981 necessary anti-corruption measures cost £5,800,000 in the Met alone, it was believed that it had the lowest rate of corruption in any major police force in the world.

[4] Ibid.
[5] G. Kelland, *Crime in London*, p. 23.
[6] P. Laurie, *Scotland Yard*, p. 249.

Over the years less than ten per cent of complaints against the police have been substantiated; for example in 1982 the figure was only nine per cent. It is estimated that one third of initial complaints are withdrawn and a further one third of the remainder are not proceeded with, although they should be. If in 1982 thirty per cent of these latter complaints should have been substantiated, then a massive 8,000-plus complaints would have been justifiable that year.[7]

The other division theory was, and still is, one which the police are naturally keen to promote. And if the promotion is done resourcefully it can spill over on to writers who are allowed to watch the police at work and play, and who in turn may be used to clothe the myth in a shroud of respectability. The police have long been adroit at a process of disinformation. Here is Peter Laurie writing shortly before the great scandals of the late 1960s and 1970s: 'The very fact that bribery is hardly discussed is, I think, quite strong evidence that it is almost as rare amongst the Metropolitan Police as its senior officers claim.'[8]

Nor were the police themselves always forthcoming about things which went wrong. Following the 1986 conviction of officers for assaulting youths in London's Holloway Road, John Cleal resigned as editor of the Met's fortnightly paper *The Job*. He had been required to print an article defending Scotland Yard's approach to the case, which was presented to him as written by a serving officer. Technically the article may have been correct but it had in fact been written by Scotland Yard's public relations branch, of whom only two of a strength of seventy were serving officers. Cleal had wished to publish the article acknowledging that it had come from the public relations department but had been overruled.[9]

Of course, the vast majority of officers are honest, hard working, brave and committed to their forces. (Corrupt officers too may be brave and hard working, and, in their own way, committed to their forces.) It is also in the interests of criminals and the disaffected to play up the amount of corruption prevalent at any one time. Nevertheless, much goes on to which decent, honest, committed officers turn blind eyes on a daily basis. Where does that leave them?

[7] K. Russell, *Complaints against the Police which are Withdrawn*.
[8] P. Laurie, *Scotland Yard*, p. 246.
[9] *Observer*, 30 March 1986.

Without going too much into the realms of criminology and
sociology, there have been two sorts of histories of the police.
First, there is the orthodox version by such writers as T. A.
Critchley and Douglas Browne, who championed the police
and exculpated them at every turn. Critchley, for example,
writing as late as 1967, cannot bring himself to mention Sergeant
George Goddard who amassed a fortune in protection money
in the 1920s. For Critchley, Goddard was a non-person who
has conveniently been erased from police history. Then, as the
pendulum swung, came the revisionists of the 1960s, some of
whom saw fault, default and preferably perjury lying in the
gutter of every investigation.

Just where the truth lay in some of the earlier inquiries of
the 1900s is extremely difficult to divine. Either the police
were telling the whole truth and it was right that they were
absolved from any wrongdoing or, less palatable but, in the
light of current events, more plausible, the authorities covered
up for them wherever possible.

I have tried throughout the text to give examples from other
people's research, both English and American, in addition to
material garnered from my own experiences. The result is, I
hope, cumulative rather than repetitive. It is almost always
possible to find completely opposite theories and views from
officers and researchers. One example is the different attitudes
to the benefits of the large and small force, mentioned earlier.
A former Chief Inspector in a northern provincial force states:
'Up here there wasn't any opportunity for corruption. It was
a smaller force. We all knew each other. There was greater
supervision. We would know if anyone was corrupt.' This is
diametrically opposed to the theory that the smaller and more
cohesive the group, such as the West Midlands Serious Crime
Squad, the more it will stick together and, if need be, take the
necessary steps to thwart authority.

I hope this book does not read like so many of those theses
turned into sociological tracts which bored me stiff when I was
reading for my degree. If it does, I have failed on that count, as
well as failing to make some sort of comprehensive assessment
of the extent of corruption in policing in England over the last
160 years, the reasons it flourishes and, more importantly, what
may be done in the future to control and mitigate its influences.
I do not think anyone seriously believes it can be eradicated.

Certainly not the former Commissioner, Sir David McNee: 'Corruption in a police force is like sin in society at large. You will never wholly eradicate it for it is embedded in the greed and selfishness of human nature.'[10]

I have tried to set parameters of deviance by excluding behaviour which, whilst at the very least aberrant and often criminal, did not derive from the police officer's special position. So, for example, the cases of officers accused of making fraudulent multiple share applications for stock exchange flotations fall outside the scope set here, although, in passing, it must be questioned whether officers who behave in this way are sufficiently scrupulous in observing proper conduct in their professional lives to remain in the force. Set against that, I know a barrister still in practice in the criminal courts whose court manners and knowledge of the law are impeccable and masterful respectively, though in his private life he has behaved no better, and on occasions considerably worse, than his clients. Private misdemeanours may not necessarily affect a public life. But it is a matter to be considered.

Nor have I said anything about officers who have killed people in their private as opposed to their public lives. So, in this instance, there is nothing of the case of the Glasgow Constable, James Robertson, who was executed in December 1950 for the murder of his unwanted mistress.

One of the problems of research into the police applies equally to other forms of research, perhaps even more so. The police are a tightly knit community. They are adroit in avoiding the importunities of a researcher over the short, if not long, term. It is therefore difficult to know which of the handouts which present them in a particularly good light are true. I spent one afternoon discussing policing generally with a number of police constables with up to five years' service. Part of the time a Chief Inspector was present, part of the time not. No, there was no corruption, no brutality, no sexism, except for one officer who was possibly about to face a discipline charge over harassment of a female PC, certainly no racism.

We discussed that most minor aspect of corruption, the free cup of tea in a café. At first the constables thought yes, it would be acceptable to go into a café in uniform provided you paid for

10 D. McNee, *McNee's Law*, p. 205.

the tea. Then they bent a little and agreed that if, for example, they bought a sandwich they could have a free cup of tea with it. But under no circumstances was there to be anything such as a free plate of bacon and eggs. This led inexorably to the downhill spiral of such things as twenty-five per cent off pizzas, and the use of the warrant card known as the International Disco Card, which gets a police officer into nightclubs for free and goodness knows what else. And as for special constables, that wrongly derided branch of the force, there was no question but that they loved them, salt of the earth, etc. etc. Perhaps my problem was that I spoke with them as a group.

Afterwards their Inspector told me they had been economical with the truth.

'There's a café in town owned by an old DS where they spend their mornings getting free food. He doesn't mind. It only costs him a few eggs and it's company for him when he's not busy. In fact if I want them to do something I ring him up and ask him to get them over to such and such a place. As for specials – they can't stand them.' Perhaps the DI also recalled that a few years earlier he and I had gone to a nightclub in the town, to find a queue trailing round the block. We went to its head, produced his 'International Disco Card', said of me 'Visiting DI from London', and in we went.

On the other hand Professor Mike McConville of the University of Warwick, who has spent many years researching various aspects of legal and police behaviour, believes that by and large the police are genuine in their responses. 'Provided you can strike up a relationship they'll very quickly give you the trade secrets. I don't want to be a victim of self-delusion in that I think they'll tell everything but in a way there's no one else knowledgeable about policing to whom they can talk. At home their families don't want to know.'

In this survey I have concentrated mainly on the Metropolitan Police. This is for a number of reasons: first, because they were the 'new police'; second, because they are the biggest single force in the United Kingdom; and third, because their history is the most documented. I have added contributions from various other forces, amongst them Liverpool, Manchester, Leeds, West Midlands, Cardiff, Brighton and Southend, which I hope give a fair spectrum of policing throughout England, Wales and Scotland. It should not, however, be thought that police deviance here is essentially any different from that in other countries in the Western world. The stories and comments about the Met or Greater Manchester could be applied equally to Miami, Dallas, Paris, or for that matter Sydney and Hong Hong. Indeed the problems here may seem to fade into insignificance compared with those of officers in Miami or other American cities. After all, whilst over the years several of our Chief Constables have gone down the tube, so to speak, none can emulate Mr Billy Hart, the well-respected Chief of Police of Detroit, who is presently serving eighteen years on corruption charges. Nor, whatever our officers have got up to, have they yet achieved the scale of notoriety of the Miami Police in 1986:

> The beleaguered Miami Police Department with more than a dozen officers facing charges ranging from drug dealing to murder, is the focus of an inquiry by the Federal Bureau of Investigation into drug-related corruption. Twenty-five other police officers, some of them of high rank, have been subpoenaed as witnesses or as targets of the investigation.
>   . . . while the temptation is greater in Miami than in most American cities because of the great volume of cocaine smuggled into south Florida from Latin America, the epidemic of police corruption is not seen as a purely local problem. Experts expect increased corruption to unfold in other cities with the rise in consumption of crack, a cheap and powerful cocaine derivative.[11]

The *New York Times*'s last comment was certainly right as far as its own city was concerned. In September of the same year twelve New York City Police officers from the 77th precinct in Brooklyn were suspended after being charged with some 250 counts, including sale and possession of crack and other drugs, burglary, thefts, attempted gun selling, trespass and bribery. A thirteenth officer, said to be one of the ringleaders, committed suicide several months later.

In case it should be thought that this could not happen here, at some time or another in the past decade officers in the Met and other city forces have been charged and convicted of each and every one of the offences the Brooklyn officers faced. The

11 *New York Times*, 2 August 1986.

rise in the scale of drug dealing has already provided evidence that some officers are prepared to deal with the importers or their middlemen. Indeed in some respects the sad story of the Drug Squad shows that, when they put their minds to it, British officers can do just as well as their American brothers.

And if there is any thought that since the purges of the 1970s and 1980s there is no longer a potential problem, then one need only to read *Scotland Yard's Cocaine Connection*[12] and to look at the allegations made throughout 1992 surrounding certain officers at the Stoke Newington police station in North London, who are said to be behaving in exactly the same way as their Brooklyn and Bronx counterparts, to be stripped of complacency.

'There can be few more daunting tasks imaginable than embarking on a project of research into the incidence of wrongdoing amongst police officers. Where does one begin?' wrote barrister David Wolchover, introducing his admittedly informal survey of the attitudes of barristers to police evidence at the Inner London Crown Court. From a poll of fifty-five of his colleagues who both prosecuted and defended, just under seventy-five per cent agreed that the police lied in three out of ten trials.[13]

Where should I start? I have adopted at least the first part of the advice of Lewis Carroll's King of Hearts in *Alice in Wonderland*. 'Begin at the beginning,' the King said gravely, 'and go on until you come to the end: then stop.' If I were to follow the second part of the advice, it might be that, to mix quotations, I would follow Macbeth's line to the crack of doom. Instead, for all practical purposes, I have come to a stop at the end of December 1992.

[12] A. Jennings et al.
[13] *New Law Journal*, 1986, p. 181.

Part 1

1

Before the New Police

It is tempting to think that the Metropolitan Police sprang, like Rabelais's Pantagruel, fully formed and calling for bread and wine, on the day of their birth in 1829. It would be the first of many wrong assumptions people have had about the police since that day. Whilst Robert Peel's 'blue lobsters' were a fairly radical concept, there had been many an effort to establish some form of law to police the London streets. For one reason or another – lack of funding, indiscipline, petty rivalry and dishonesty are just four – the efforts had failed; but efforts there certainly had been.

Rudimentary attempts at policing, not only in London but the rest of England, had been made before the Norman Conquest. Nearly a century after that invasion the 1164 Assize at Clarendon commanded sheriffs to assist each other in the pursuit of 'reputed felons'. Thirty-one years later in 1195 Richard I appointed certain knights to 'swear to the King' all men over fifteen to keep the peace. Over the years the knights became known as Conservators of the Peace. In 1285 the Statute of Westminster laid out the duty of all citizens to police their own areas; two constables in every 100 people were appointed to inspect arms on a half-yearly basis.

In the reign of Edward III these Conservators, whose office had been an executive one, had their functions enlarged so that by the end of the century they had become Justices of the Peace, forerunners of today's lay magistracy. Meanwhile parish constables were established. The men served a year at a time, as did the magistrates, and their duties were to arrest malefactors

3

and vagrants. They took an oath not dissimilar from that of the present day police constable. The hierarchy was therefore sheriff, justice, constable.

All in all, in rural areas it was a system which worked reasonably well. The justice was usually a well-known local figure, who had to have an estate worth twenty pounds a year and who understood how the community ticked. Apart from times of large-scale rebellions such as the Peasants' Revolt he could cope adequately. It was not the same in urban areas. Here, corruption was rife.

As early as 1601 justices had become known as basket-justices following an attack by a Member of Parliament who said that many of them carried a basket for the reception of gifts from those who came before them. The justices also regularly skirted the income qualification and used their offices to make money. The contemporary writer Lambarde comments that they 'were men of small substance whose povertie made them both covetous and contemptible'. In 1693 another writer, Bohun, described a justice as 'a living creature that for half a dozen chickens would dispense with a whole dozen of penal statutes'. One would have hoped that a statute would at least have been worth two chickens rather than the reverse.

In turn their subordinates, the constables, hired substitutes to appear for them – as, it must be said, over the years, did farmers called for war service; and in the twentieth century, jurors, if the interruption of their businesses would prove to be costly, have done the same. One step lower down the scale, night-watchmen in their turn hired assistants whose sole ability was to sniff out those who could pay money to avoid arrest and prosecution.

London was a particular problem. There was the City of London and the City and Borough of Westminster. In addition there was the mass of buildings running from Charing Cross to where they met the City in Fleet Street; there was Holborn, Smithfield, Clerkenwell, as well as places south of the Thames. Maintenance of such law and order as existed was claimed by church authorities, county justices for Middlesex and Surrey, plus public and semi-public bodies which supplied private watches. It was not until the reign of Elizabeth I that a real attempt was made to police London. Then, under an Act of Parliament, the City and Borough of Westminster was divided into twelve wards each having an unpaid burgess and an assistant, along parallel lines with the aldermen of the City of London. Even so, whilst the City of London was regulated, the City and Borough of Westminster was not. The burgesses fought with the justices over what could be a lucrative business. Pity the poor constables. In 1572 an Act was passed which provided stricter punishment for beggars as well as providing a compulsory poor-rate. In addition a constable could be fined six shillings and eight pence, a tidy sum, if he failed to arrest a beggar. In practice he left this to a deputy whom he paid.

In the next century Cromwell's administration saw the country divided into twelve divisions, including one for Westminster and Middlesex and another for the City, each with a commanding major-general. A by-product of this system of essentially military rule was that it did away with the powers of many of the petty authorities whose conflicting interests ensured that nothing was done. But the system produced a network of spies and oppression, a legacy Peel would have to try to overcome when he introduced his Police Bill nearly 200 years later.

The restoration of the monarchy produced sweeping changes in Westminster. Apart from improved sanitation, street lighting and paving, a force of paid bellmen, known as 'Charleys' after the monarch, was introduced. There were also additional powers given to magistrates, including the power to swear in extra men at times of crisis.

Efforts to prevent crime seem to have been established on a fairly ad hoc basis. All were no doubt well intentioned. Many were swiftly abused. One gambit introduced at the end of the seventeenth century to combat the rise of the highwayman, the coiner and other felons was the reward for apprehending such criminals of a judge's certificate which exempted the recipient or his nominee from holding any office, in practice a constable, in the parish where the crime had been committed. Known as blood-money or a Tyburn ticket, the certificates soon became currency, usually fetching between £10 and £50 but on occasions up to £200 or even £300. The proceeds of sale would be divided between prosecutor and the constable. A result was that criminals were given licence to commit small misdemeanours in the expectation they would graduate to the felony for which arrest would bring the reward.

By the beginning of the nineteenth century the standard of

petty justice in the Metropolis had virtually hit rock bottom. Now a Justice of the Peace had become a Trading Justice. Nominally unpaid, he could expect to clear £1,000 from his 'office' – both a position and literally a room. In the country the magistrate was traditionally the local squire, who settled disputes, punished offenders and generally kept the poor in their place. He usually had sufficient means not to need or be tempted to be corrupt on the small scale available.[1] In Gloucestershire, for example, at one time the magistrates refused all fees to which they were entitled. This philanthropy led to vexatious litigation and the magistrates were obliged once more to charge fees, which they then gave to charity.

The situation was not the same in the towns and cities. One view is that the Trading Justice was by no means necessarily corrupt in the sense of being totally dishonest but he had too much work. The conditions in which they lived were often dangerous – there are accounts of magistrates who caught gaol-fever – and if they made a mistake in their office, they, like the constable, could be prosecuted. Others see the incentive for their office as the fees available to them rather than the gain from accepting bribes or giving perverse decisions.[2]

'Men of profligate lives, needy, mean, ignorant and rapacious who often acted from the most scandalous principles of selfish avarice,' wrote Tobias Smollett of justices in his *History of England* in 1760. And his contemporary Edmund Burke told the House of Commons, 'The justices of Middlesex are generally the scum of the earth: carpenters, brick-makers, and shoe-makers, some of whom are notoriously men of infamous character that they are unworthy of any employ whatsoever, and others so ignorant that they can scarcely write their own names.'

Yet, if for nothing else, they were needed to maintain the social status quo. 'The metropolitan magistrates, although despised by their superiors as needy mercenary tools, and

---

[1] The squirearchy may not have been corrupt about money but they were certainly not even-handed. Sidney and Beatrice Webb cite the case of a farmer who was coursing hares on his own land with the permission of his own landlord when he was summoned by Lord Buckingham, the owner of the adjoining land. The luckless man asked for time to arrange legal representation and was refused. He was tried and convicted by the Duke in his own parlour and on the evidence of the Duke's servant. S. and B. Webb, *English Local Government: The Parish and the County*

[2] For an account of the magistracy of the time, see S. and B. Webb, op.cit.

hated by their inferiors as instruments of oppression, are yet absolutely necessary to keep the common people within bounds.'[3]

Their greatest source of revenue was in the granting of bail, something which continued well into the nineteenth century. Townshend, a Bow Street Runner, told a Parliamentary Committee, 'The plan used to be to issue warrants and take up all the poor devils in the street and then there was the bailing them, 2/4d., which the magistrate had; and taking up a hundred girls, that would make, at 2/4d., £11.13s.4d. They sent none to gaol, for bailing them was so much better.'[4]

It was under the licence of the Trading Justice that the celebrated criminal 'thief-taker' Jonathan Wild operated so successfully. Wild, who carried a silver-mounted staff as an emblem of his self-styled rank, was a broker for stolen goods. Provided no questions were asked and there were adequate rewards, the goods were returned to the warehouses from which he had often arranged their theft. Indeed he seems to have provided a role model for some policemen to the present day.[5]

It was a Colonel Thomas de Veil, who had fought in

[3] Patrick Pringle, *The Thief Takers*, p. 53, quoting a writer in *Gentleman's Magazine*.

[4] Anthony Babington, *A House in Bow Street*, p. 36.

[5] Wild's career was an interesting one. Born in Wolverhampton in 1683, he was apprenticed to a buckle-maker. In 1708 he was imprisoned for debt and was discharged four years later, when he set up house in Drury Lane with his mistress Mary Milliner, a prostitute whom he had met in prison. Initially he was what was called a twang, the pickpocket who would take the wallets of Milliner's clients. (In those days intercourse with prostitutes was almost invariably undertaken vertically.) He began his criminal apprenticeship proper with a Charles Hitchin, a City marshal who taught him the trade of receiver, which Wild was to perfect. For twelve years he was able to maintain such a successful double life that by 1724 he petitioned to be made a freeman of the City. His end came when he was indicted for receiving ten guineas as a reward for helping a Mrs Steham to recover stolen lace, the theft of which he had arranged. Convicted, he was hanged on 24 May 1725. He had tried to commit suicide the night before and, still drowsy, was pelted by the mob on the way to Tyburn. He was survived by both Mary Milliner and Charles Hitchin. Ms Milliner, whose ear had been sliced off by Wild in a temper, had been paid a pension by him to the date of his death. Hitchin remained a City under-marshal for a further three years, when he was tried for sodomy. He was acquitted of the capital offence but convicted of a kindred misdemeanour. He was sentenced to a term in the pillory, as well as six months' imprisonment, and fined £20. For a full account of Wild's life, see *The Thief Takers* by Patrick Pringle. The character MacHeath in John Gay's *The Beggar's Opera* was based on Wild.

Portugal and Spain under the Earl of Galway, who established something approaching a comprehensive system of justice in the Metropolis. Working as a half-pay captain operating appropriately enough from Scotland Yard, he had set himself up as an adviser to fellow officers in the presentation of petitions for preferment. He studied law and expanded his activities. In 1729 he held a commission as Justice of the Peace for Westminster and Middlesex and ten years later he established an office in Bow Street. By now he was also the *de facto* chief magistrate, a title officially bestowed on Sir John Gonson, then chairman of the Westminster bench.[6]

According to some accounts it was two years after de Veil's death in 1746 that his position was occupied by Henry Fielding, later famous as a novelist, who as the senior stipendiary magistrate at Bow Street established the Bow Street Runners.[7] It was their misfortune that they were also referred to as thief-takers, a label which, with its tones of Wild, they hated. Sadly, many of them were little better than their well-known if not illustrious predecessor but, given the history of the behaviour of their elders and supposed betters, it is not surprising that they continued to practise some of Wild's less respectable activities. What is surprising is that more did not do so.

The earliest reference to the Runners is in 1785. Little is known of their origins, partly because their methods were kept secret and also because of the general aversion to thief-takers. A decade later their strength was put at six or perhaps eight. At first thief-taking was a spare-time activity but under Henry Fielding's brother, Blind John Fielding, who

[6] De Veil, although he did not establish a detective force, was himself something of an amateur detective and by skilled cross-examination of witnesses often discovered the truth. A man of some courage, he read the Riot Act to mobs on at least two occasions. A great womanizer, he was married four times, had twenty-five legitimate children and a 'like number of concubines'. Said *Gentleman's Magazine* in its obituary: 'he served himself by means of his office with a variety of women.' He seems to have held examination of female witnesses in a special closet. P. Pringle, *The Thief Takers*, p. 78.
[7] These accounts suggest that a Justice Poulson lived at Bow Street for two years. Others say that the date of de Veil's death is wrongly recorded. Possibly both are wrong and in the intervening period the house was occupied by yet another justice, Thomas Burdus. See A. Babington, *A House in Bow Street*, p. 61.

succeeded him in office, they received a weekly salary of 11s.6d., later increased to 25s. together with 14s. a week allowance. Nevertheless, they still relied on private work for their real income. From about 1790 Townshend and another Runner, John Sayer, would report to the Bank of England for ten days in every quarter, acting as security men when dividends were being paid. Another was regularly seconded to the Post Office and others were hired by theatre owners both to prevent crowd disturbances and deter pickpockets.[8] From the beginning of the nineteenth century a Runner was employed in the lobby of the House of Commons whilst Parliament was sitting.

Following an attack on George III by the mad Margaret Nicholson in 1786, Runners were used for the protection of the monarchy, for which an annual fee of 200 guineas each was paid. There was also a foot patrol, sixty-eight strong and divided into thirteen companies, set up by Sir Sampson Wright in 1790. The men were armed with cutlasses and the captains of the five- or six-men teams carried a carbine and a pair of pistols. Their task was to prevent robberies. Fifteen years later the horse patrol, established by Sir John Fielding, was revived. There had been an upsurge in the number of highwaymen and this fifty-four-strong paramilitary force, togged out in double-breasted blue coats with yellow buttons, blue trousers, black leather hats and white gloves, carried cutlasses and handcuffs. They received twenty-eight shillings a week together with an allowance for their horses.

They operated on a military system to such a degree that one highwayman when captured was found to be in possession of a complete and accurate route- and time-schedule of the patrols. Either the reconnaissance of the criminal classes was operating at a high level of efficiency or there was a certain amount of corruption going on amongst the patrol members.

---

[8] One of the Runners, Donaldson, would call out to the patrons leaving and entering the theatre, 'Take care of your pockets.' Another, Bond, provides an early example of an allegation of 'police' brutality. A man from Soho Square complained that during one performance of a piece in the Drury Lane theatre he had been sitting in the pit 'applauding and booing' when Bond had seized him by the collar and ripped his shirt. A. Babington, *A House in Bow Street*, p. 189.

There is one thing that appears to me most extraordinary, when I remember in very likely a week there would be from ten to fifteen highway robberies. We have not seen a man committed for highway robbery lately; I speak of persons on horseback; formerly there were two, three and four, highwaymen, some on Hounslow Heath, some on Wimbledon Common, some on Finchley Common, some on the Romford Road . . . People travel now safely by means of the Horse Patrol that Sir Richard Ford planned. Where are the highway robberies now?[9]

The Runners, who had no uniform but who carried a small baton with a gilt crown, were in effect the small private army of the senior magistrate at Bow Street, and their prime function was the pursuit of criminals. To this effect they could be dispatched to magistrates in any part of England who sought their help. On private missions a fee of a guinea a day was payable, plus 14 shillings a week travelling expenses. If the mission was successful a substantial bonus could be expected. Townshend, the best known of the Runners, was said to have an estate of £20,000 on his death, and Sayer £10,000 more.[10] Much of this money must have derived from acting as intermediaries between thieves and insurance companies, and complaints were made that agreements were reached in which rewards would be paid for the return of property coupled with an undertaking not to prosecute.

In 1828 Sir Richard Birnie, then Chief Magistrate at Bow

---

[9] Townshend in his evidence to the Parliamentary Select Committee 1828, quoted in A. Babington, *A House in Bow Street*, p. 194.

[10] Townshend is described by Captain Gronow (*The Reminiscences and Recollections of Captain Gronow*, pp. 202–3) as 'a little fat man with a flaxen wig . . . To the most daring courage he added great dexterity and cunning.' Invited to write his memoirs by the Duke of Clarence, he appears to have been an early example of the police officer who attracted groupies. 'Oh sir,' he told his patron, 'you've got me into the devil of a scrape! I had begun to write my amours, as you desired, when Mrs Townshend caught me in the act of writing them, and swore she'd be revenged; for you know, your Royal Highness, I was obliged to divulge many secrets about women, for which she'll never forgive me.' He had been a costermonger before joining the Runners and had acquired much of his knowledge of the underworld by attending trials at the Old Bailey. He had, it seems, a reputation for honesty, one not shared by Sayer.

Street, told the House of Commons Committee that he did not believe that such practices ever occurred, a comment which set the tone for many years of official blindness or cupidity. The Committee did not believe him. In their view 'compromises had repeatedly taken place by the intervention of police officers . . . It has been distinctly asserted to your committee by officers that they have had the sanction of higher persons of their establishment for engaging in such negotiations.'[11]

Other magistrates' offices had their own forces and indeed some Runners managed to have themselves attached to more than one office, thereby drawing double pay. But the days of the Bow Street Runners were numbered, even before they had achieved their greatest successes.

In the 1760s John Wilkes, a former MP for Aylesbury, and his followers had clearly demonstrated the inability of the magistracy to control the streets.

In 1763 Wilkes, said to be the ugliest man in Middlesex but one who could charm any woman from under an umbrella, had published a paper *The North Briton* which was found to contain a libel on the King. He was arrested, deprived of his membership of parliament and outlawed. He was promptly re-elected for the Middlesex constituency. *The North Briton* was ordered to be burned by the public hangman, Thomas Turlis, in front of the Royal Exchange on 5 December. When Turlis stepped forward, the crowd pelted Sheriff Thomas Harley, who was in charge of the ceremony, as well as the hangman. Turlis pushed the sheets in the flames, from which they were rescued by a workman, and the crowd then stormed

---

[11] The report cited three cases in which banks which had been robbed of a considerable sum paid £1,000 for the recovery of the money or bonds. In those cases there had been an undertaking not to prosecute. See A. Babington, *A House in Bow Street*, p. 192. One of the cases was the Paisley Bank Robbery, to the investigation of which Sayer had been seconded. The banks were then by no means as keen on prosecution; rather their sights were turned towards the return of the money stolen. On this occasion Sayer arrested two high-class thieves, James Mackoull and Huffey White. Mackoull offered to return all the money he had in return for an undertaking not to prosecute. This was accepted but the bank found that only a fraction of the stolen money found its way back into their coffers. There was considerable suspicion that much had stuck with Sayer. Mackoull tried to work the same trick on two further occasions. On the first he was successful. On the second he was prosecuted, found guilty and sentenced to death. His wife obtained a reprieve but he went mad and died in prison. Sir R. Howe, *The Story of Scotland Yard*, p.20.

the officials who, along with Turlis, fled for safety into the Mansion House.[12]

When in March 1768 Wilkes, still an outlaw, returned from his exile in Paris, there were further disturbances and it became apparent that the magistrates were almost powerless to deal with serious crowd trouble. Sir John Fielding, who three years earlier had been blamed for not suppressing crowd demonstrations over the importation of French silks, again initially declined to call out the troops to disperse the crowds which had gathered to celebrate Wilkes' further reelection to Parliament. He believed that their presence 'would provoke what it is intended to prevent'. Wilkes agreed to appear before the Court of King's Bench on 20 April. A week later he was back in court, when bail was refused. Put into a coach to take him to the King's Bench prison, he was rescued by the mob and then, with John Fielding and the other magistrates chasing after his coach, he surrendered himself to the gaol. Fielding was threatened with dismissal if a similar incident took place.

On 10 May the Guards fired on the mob which had gathered outside the prison to cheer Wilkes and, it was feared, to try to free him. A young farmer named Allen was first bayoneted and then shot. When brought before a coroner, the soldier who fired the shot was acquitted. Later he received £30 from the government and was highly commended for his part in what came to be known as the St George's Fields Massacre. In 1770 a Parliamentary Committee was set up to inquire into recent robberies in the City and in Westminster.

More serious than the Wilkes' disturbances, on 6 June 1780 the new Newgate prison was destroyed in the anti-Catholic Gordon Riots following the passing of the Catholics Disability Bill. For a week London was in the hands of a looting and

---

[12] *Gentleman's Magazine*, 1763, p. 614. Turlis, along with William Marwood, who a century later invented the long drop, has always been regarded as one of the greatest hangmen. This is despite the fact that in January 1763 he was caught stealing coals from a neighbour's cellar, itself a capital offence. Turlis pleaded in mitigation that the hanging trade had been poor in recent months. The sheriffs of London, saddened that their official had reached such depths of depravity, obtained him a pardon and he was appointed Finisher of the Law for the County of Surrey to help supplement his income. One of his particular claims to fame is that he hanged Laurence, Earl Ferrers, who had shot and killed his steward. H. Bleackley, *The Hangmen of England*, pp. 94–103.

rioting mob, led by the unstable and fanatical Lord George Gordon. Sir John Fielding, now a dying man, was in Brompton and the chief police office was sacked and looted, as was the Old Bailey and the Sessions House next door, plus the Fleet and King's Bench prisons. The magistrates in general were absent and although troops were on the streets, they merely patrolled and made no attempt to intervene. The rioting ended when rumours began to circulate that the Bank of England would be attacked. Guards marched to Threadneedle Street and the mob was met with gunfire. Scores were killed and this effectively ended the riots.[13]

Five years later in 1785 the government introduced the London and Westminster Police Bill, which recommended a District of the Metropolis, including the City, with nine administrative divisions each presided over by a stipendiary magistrate, who would use the fines he collected to pay the expenses of the office. Each division was to have twenty-five fit and able men, properly equipped and armed, to act as full-time salaried constables. They would have greater powers than parish peace-officers, with powers to arrest any person in possession of articles which they had 'probable grounds to suspect'. They would have special power of control over pawnbrokers and publicans. They would be able to enter licensed premises at any hour of the day or night without a warrant.

The Bill was not a success. It met with criticism on all fronts. For a start the City was incensed at its inclusion. The Middlesex justices, who regarded it as a slur on them and who also resented the creation of a stipendiary magistracy, condemned it as 'inexpedient and totally unnecessary'. The press was hostile and there was general resentment at the idea of creating what was seen as an independent armed police force. The Bill was withdrawn and the government promised to produce a new, amended

[13] Continuing the sad stories of public hangmen of the time, Ned Dennis, who succeeded Turlis, was caught up with the mob when it attacked a shop in New Turnstile, Holborn, owned by a Catholic, Edmund Boggis. At the least he tore down pieces of wainscoting and burned them. He appeared at the Old Bailey charged with riot and despite a sympathetic summing up by the trial judge, James Adair the Recorder of London, he was convicted on 3 July and sentenced to death. Following petitions he was reprieved and given a free pardon, which enabled him to continue his good work by hanging his fellow rioters.

and, of course, improved version. It never saw light of day.[14]

The next major problem for the administration was the spate of killings in Ratcliffe Highway, Shadwell, in December 1811. There were allegations in the newspapers of the increase in crimes of violence, the corruption of the Runners and the inefficiency of the magistrates who controlled them. It is characteristic of the whole history of the police that whilst there could be major explosions taking place up and down the country, a relatively minor domestic incident would ultimately lead to a major shake-up of the authorities. In this instance the background was the Napoleonic Wars, with the Peninsula campaign going none too well; further troubles with the United States; and the Luddite Riots, which had spread to Yorkshire and Lancashire, while in the Midlands there were serious disturbances caused by rising unemployment. Nevertheless, it was the Ratcliffe Highway murders which were to provide another substantial plank from which would-be reformers of the police could launch their campaign.

The murders were those of the Marr family on 7 December and Mr and Mrs Williamson, a publican and his wife, together with their servant, on 19 December. The motive was robbery and the victims had been brutally attacked with a maul and ripping hook. On 20 December a carpenter, John Williams, was arrested. The evidence against him was clear. Three days before his arrest he had borrowed sixpence; now he was found in possession of new clothes. The women who had washed his old shirts had found them to be stained with blood and a knife in his possession could have caused the throat-wounds to the victims. He was strenuously interrogated and held overnight in the Coldbath Fields House of Correction, where the next morning he was found to have hanged himself. He had gone to some trouble because the beam was so low he had had to sit to do so. The Shadwell justices were authorized to have him dressed in his finery – a brown greatcoat lined with silk, a blue undercoat with yellow buttons, blue and white waistcoat,

[14] Curiously, Ireland led the way in these matters. What Dublin did today London did half a century later. In 1786 the Irish Parliament in Dublin passed a Bill which was very largely based on the London and Westminster Police Bill. As a result magistrates, who no longer had to control peace-officers, took a great deal more interest in their judicial functions. A. Babington, *A House in Bow Street*, p.169.

striped blue pantaloons, brown worsted stockings and shoes –
strapped to a board, together with the ripping hook and maul,
and paraded through Shadwell followed by magistrates, police
officers and the Bow Street patrol. The procession stopped
outside the Marrs' house and finally the body was thrown into
the ground at New Gravel Lane and, as a suicide, had a stake
driven through it.

But the investigating officers did not come out of the case
with any great credit. The Shadwell justices' office consisted of
three magistrates and they had applied to Bow Street for help,
which was readily supplied.[15] At one time no less than seventeen
police magistrates, a score of Runners from the various offices
and what was described as a 'strong corps' of the Bow Street
patrol helped in the inquiry, which lasted a little over two weeks.
There were now renewed calls for a complete reorganization of
the nightly watch as well as the formation of an enlarged and
'unpolitical' police force. One of the wilder suggestions was
that 'the most distinguished pugilists of good character' (itself
almost an oxymoron), such as Tom Cribb, should be recruited
as parochial watchmen.[16]

The next year, however, some progress was made. There
had been Luddite rioting in the Midlands and a more domestic
scandal when George Skene, chief clerk in the Queen Square
office and nominally the first officer in the police, was convicted
of forgery, then a capital offence. Another Select Committee
was established, this time to inquire into the state of the nightly
watch. Its report, published on 17 April 1812, was a radical one
and the findings were in keeping with the Bill of 1785. Police
magistrates and those at Bow Street, itself intended to be a central bureau for the police, were to be given superintending powers over all constables, beadles and watchmen. The police were
to have increased powers of arrest and would be paid, for particularly good work, irrespective of a conviction by magistrates.

[15] 'We never stop a moment in the case of a serious offence to the public; if a
person at the farthest end of the neighbouring counties gave notice of a murder or
any atrocious offence being committed, I should send, one, two or three officers
immediately to the spot for information, and send others in all directions to search
out the offenders, and no party would ever be applied to for the expense' – the then
chief magistrate, Sir Nathaniel Conant, giving evidence in 1816 before the Select
Committee.
[16] For a full account of the Ratcliffe Highway murders, see D.G. Browne, *The Rise
of Scotland Yard*, chapter 6.

The report came to nothing. On 11 May in the lobby of the House, where for some reason there were no Bow Street Runners at the time, Prime Minister Spencer Perceval was shot dead by John Bellingham. With his death went the proposed police reforms.[17] The new Tory administration produced a watered-down version of the Bill but this met with stern opposition. It was abandoned and there, politically, the matter rested until 1823. In the meantime, however, there were a number of events which would inexorably lead to the establishment of a Metropolitan police force.

In 1815 the introduction of the Corn Bill led to riots which, if not quite on the scale of the Gordon Riots, were of considerable concern. The same year a Select Committee was appointed to consider the 'state of mendicity in the Metropolis'. In its way, says Douglas Browne, it was to be 'regarded as a sort of curtain-raiser to the most elaborate investigation into the state of London's police that Parliament had yet undertaken'.[18]

There can be no doubt that the magistracy, and with it the police in the Metropolis, was at one of its lowest ebbs. There was a substantial increase in the number of burglaries and shop-breakings. Indeed the Worship Street and other Runners were not operating nightly patrols. There was a call for yet another inquiry into the reform of the police. Hiley Addington, an Under-Secretary, told the House of Commons that the police magistrates believed the Metropolis had never been in a more tranquil state, but the Committee was set

---

[17] Bellingham held no personal grudge against Perceval, who appears to have been a dull and somewhat mediocre Prime Minister in his short tenure. Bellingham was a bankrupt Liverpool broker from a family with a history of insanity. His complaint appears to have been that the British government had not assisted him sufficiently when he had been imprisoned in Archangel over a fraudulent insurance claim in 1808. In his murder trial Bellingham was given little help in his defence. Applications for adjournments to prepare his case properly were refused and the jury retired for only fourteen minutes before rejecting his insanity defence. He was hanged six days after the shooting. The hangman, this time William Brunskill, came in for a good deal of abuse from the crowd and it is said that Bellingham's hanging ended his career. He took to dreaming of the man saying 'He's made a Mr Perceval out of me.' His dreams may, however, have been incipient *delirium tremens* for he drank to help him through this and other executions. Brunskill was retired on a pension of 15 shillings a week. Perceval's widow received £2,000 a year to go with a lump sum of £50,000. Spencer Perceval's last words are said to have been, 'Give me one of Bellamy's veal pies.'

[18] D. G. Browne, *The Rise of Scotland Yard*, p. 66.

up and received evidence from, amongst others, the London magistrates, their clerks, Runners and the Recorder of London. Now it was discovered that a George Vaughan, a member of the foot patrol at Bow Street, had been emulating Jonathan Wild, planning a series of robberies and then arresting his colleagues, two of whom were ex-City of London officers, who carried them out. Vaughan was arrested when he was denounced by two thirteen-year-old boys recruited by him to burgle a Mrs Macdonald, a wealthy widow. They were caught in the act and under questioning named the foot patroller. It was subsequently discovered that he had taken part in one robbery himself and, on conviction, he was duly transported.

When the Committee finally reported in 1818 there was nothing much new; they declared that they 'would deprecate a severe system of police as inconsistent with the liberties of the people'. Here raising its head once again was the fear of the continental system, Fouché and the police spy.[19] Clearly there was considerable internal mistrust of the police. For example, it was only at the very end of the investigation into the Cato Street conspiracy of February 1820 that the Runners were brought into action.[20]

[19] Joseph Fouché (1759–1820) was the Minister of Police under Napoleon. He was first appointed under the *Directoire* and shared in the *coup d'état* of 18 *Brumaire* which brought the Emperor to power. He organized a powerful system of espionage which he developed over the years. He was a man capable of playing many parts. After Waterloo he transferred his allegiance to Louis XVIII. He died in retirement in Trieste.

[20] The Cato Street conspiracy was instigated by an Arthur Thistlewood who had fallen under the spell of Tom Paine, the great Republican, and, whilst he lived in France, of Robespierre. Thistlewood had risen in the army to the rank of lieutenant and had married a lady of some wealth. She died and he soon gambled away her fortune. His great desire in life was to assassinate the members of the Cabinet and then seize power. The attack was timed for Wednesday, 23 February 1820, when Lord Harrowby was entertaining the Cabinet in Grosvenor Square. The idea was that one of the members of the conspiracy should go to the house to deliver a parcel and then, when the door opened, the others were to rush the premises and kill the members of the Cabinet. Lord Castlereagh, the then Prime Minister who later cut his throat with a rusty razor, and Lord Sidmouth, were to have their heads cut off. A man named Edwards, used as a police spy, joined the plotters and the Bow Street magistrate, Sir Richard Birnie, led the disabling raid on the conspirators. One Runner, Smithers, was stabbed by Thistlewood and on 17 April the plotters were found guilty of high treason and the murder of Smithers. They were hanged by James Botting. Much to the disgust of the crowd they were then decapitated. In 1826 Botting was released from a debtor's prison, where he had been for two years, when the City Corporation granted him a freedom at the rate of 5s a week.

In 1822 Sir Robert Peel became Home Secretary and within two months set up yet another Select Committee to examine the police. Little came of this one either, except that a head constable – in effect a police inspector – was appointed for each office and there was to be a daily patrol, dressed in the red and blue uniforms of the horse patrol, who were to 'distribute themselves judiciously' from 9 am to 7 pm when they would be relieved by the night parties. The thinking behind the uniform was that since most of the members were ex-soldiers the uniform would help them 'to be proud of their establishment'. But slowly and surely Peel brought about change. For example, the horse patrol was found a new headquarters in Cannon Row and the foot patrol's status in the hierarchy was upgraded, with the rank and file encouraged to apply for promotion as police inspectors. Peel also had a rather more grandiose scheme to rebuild the Bow Street office but this project foundered.

In 1826 Peel turned his attention to his long-held plan for the wholesale reform of the policing system in London. He had already had a successful trial run for what was to become the Met. In Ireland the Peace Preservation Force had been established by an 1814 Act of Parliament. As Fenian activities grew, in 1822 a further Act established the armed Irish Constabulary which had four training schools.[21] Here was Peel's blueprint. At first there was to be no New Police; instead the Metropolis in a ten-mile radius of St Pauls was to be 'one great city, divided into six divisions'. The City's square mile was, however, to be left alone. Peel, like most people, felt unable to tackle the powerful organizations which held political control there.

That nothing progressed until 1828 was due to the religious difficulties which bedevilled politics at the time. Peel had felt obliged to resign on the Roman Catholic question and it was not until the Duke of Wellington became Prime Minister in early 1828 that he returned. The Iron Duke was enthusiastic about a New Police. After the refusal by the third regiment of Guards to march to Portsmouth he had commented, 'In my opinion the government ought, without the loss of a moment's time, to adopt measures to form either a police in London or a military corps which should be of a different description from the regular military force, or both.'

---

[21] The separate Dublin Metropolitan Police Force was founded in 1836.

18

With Peel back in the Cabinet yet another Select Committee was established and at last there was a positive report, with a proposal to create an office of police under the Home Secretary which would have control over all police establishments in the Metropolis – except the City. Peel's mind was made up within weeks. There must be a 'new' police. Out must go the Runners and the watchmen, the beadles and so on. There must be a genuine Metropolitan Police.

Curiously there was now little opposition to Peel's proposals. After the first reading, the Bill was submitted to a tribunal of Peel's nominees for revision. His initial suggestion that control should be under three magistrates was converted into two commissioners. Royal assent was received on 19 July 1829. And so, under the control of the new commissioners, the middle-aged Colonel Charles Rowan CB, and a thirty-two-year-old Irish barrister, Richard Mayne, the New Police was born.

For some years the Runners continued their existence alongside the new force. Part of the troubles which had to be faced by the New Police was the antagonism of the senior magistrate at Bow Street, who regarded them, and their commissioners, as a usurpation of his authority, although, on occasions, there was a transfer of personnel between the two forces. The Bow Street Runners horse patrol was removed from the control of the senior magistrate in 1838 and a year later, on 24 August, the Runners were disbanded by an Act of Parliament.

2

The First Seventy Years

On Tuesday, 29 September 1829, the six companies of the Metropolitan Police Force paraded in Old Palace Yard, Westminster, and marched in single file on the outer edge of the pavement – a tradition that has continued to the present – from their barracks to the new station houses. They were kitted in all their glory: blue swallow-tail coats, broad leather belts fastened with brass buckles, half-Wellington boots and specially strengthened top hats on which the officers could stand, the better to view the surrounding countryside. The smart, unflashy and uncomfortable uniform – at one time Sir Robert Peel had suggested the more military scarlet and gold rather than blue – had been studiously designed to avoid any suggestion that this was a European-type army by another name. Each man had his divisional number and letter sewn on to his collar.[1]

The first police Commissioners, Rowan and Mayne, had also compiled a book of General Instructions for the police. 'It should be understood, at the outset, that the principal object to be attained is the prevention of crime.' The instructions went on to caution recruits against drunkenness and accepting money from the public without the permission of the Commissioners.

The force had been chosen carefully. Honest and unobjectionable – each man had had to present a signed recommendation as to his character – under thirty-five, able to read and

[1] There were seventeen divisions, arranged as letters of the alphabet, a system which has survived to the present although the boundaries of the divisions have changed. For example A division is no longer responsible for patrolling Westminster. The divisions ranged from Kensington to Whitechapel and from Hampstead to Southwark.

write, and not less than five feet seven inches tall, they had been selected from the ranks of the army (402) and the navy (101); from butchers (135), bakers (109) and candlestick makers (well not quite), and included shoemakers (198), labourers (1,154), clerks (152), servants (205), plumbers and painters (46), with their pay deliberately pitched at a level insufficient to attract the military officer classes.[2] Constables were paid 21 shillings a week less two shillings towards the cost of a uniform allowance. Pay for superintendents was £200 per annum, with inspectors earning half that amount, and these ranks were almost exclusively filled by former warrant officers and NCOs of the Guards and the Cavalry. Applications from commissioned officers had been rejected irrespective of merit, although during the 1830s a handful of commissioned men would be recruited.

Peel wrote to his friend Croker that he was determined to refuse employment to 'gentlemen – commissioned officers, for instance – as superintendents and as inspectors, because I am certain they would be above their work . . . A Sergeant of the Guards at £200 is a better man for my purpose than a captain of high military reputation, if he would serve for nothing, or if I could give him a thousand a year. For somewhat similar reasons, a three shillings a day man is better than a five shillings a day man.' He feared the officer class 'would refuse to associate with other persons holding the same offices who were not of equal rank' and that such behaviour would 'therefore degrade the latter in the eyes of the men'.[3]

Then, as now, promotion was to be from the bottom. In theory, if not in practice, a ranker could become the Commissioner. Over the years it was indeed the policy of many a Chief Constable to promote on seniority and not on merit, on the basis that the men knew where they stood and it caused less dissent amongst them. So from the first it is possible to see a potentially fatal flaw in the refusal to establish an officer class in the police force.

Despite the screening process, some of the men who presented such a fine sight that September day either could not read or, if they could, did not comprehend the General

---

[2] Those who made up the rank of constable included 51 tailors, 141 carpenters, 75 bricklayers, 55 blacksmiths, 20 turners, 141 shopmen, 141 superior mechanics, 51 weavers and 8 stonemasons.

[3] Sir Robert Peel to John Wilson Croker, 10 October 1829.

Instructions. Five were dismissed for drunkenness after the first patrol. There were other problems: 'In the lower ranks of the force there was a tendency to think that promotion would depend on the number of convictions secured. Drunkards and prostitutes were obvious prey, and so many of the latter were brought to the Hatton Garden office that one of the magistrates there, Allen Laing, was reported to have directed the police to "drive all such women into the City".'[4]

Peel's 'blue lobsters' were from the beginning objects of public hostility and derision. Within two years, there were 1,250 resignations from a force strength of 4,000. Worse, 1,989 had been dismissed, mainly for drunkenness. By 1839 over 6,000 had resigned and a further 5,200 had been dismissed; of the original 3,314 men who had paraded nine years earlier, only 850 remained in the service.

The first attacks and scandals had not been long in coming. Over the two or three years since the creation of the force there had been considerable political unrest, due in part to the work of the Ultra-Radicals, known as the Ultras. An assassination plot against William IV was discovered and a visit to a banquet cancelled. Pamphlets, hostile to the police, were circulated:

LIBERTY OR DEATH! BRITONS!! AND HONEST MEN!!! The time has at last arrived. All London meets on Tuesday. We assure you from ocular demonstration that 6,000 cutlasses have been removed from the Tower for the use of Peel's bloody gang. Remember the cursed speech from the throne!! These damned police are now to be armed. Englishmen, will you put up with this?

---

[4] D. G. Browne, *The Rise of Scotland Yard*, p. 90. Such a tendency persisted well into the twentieth century. The former policeman turned journalist C. H. Rolph, writing of his poor arrest record – six in four years – which was threatening his promotion to sergeant, tells of the sergeant who advised him to look around and 'get some summonses'. Rather shamefacedly Rolph stopped a window-cleaner for not fastening himself with a strap to something heavy inside the room; the man was fined five shillings, which Rolph paid. He adds, 'But the kindly sergeant's idea was that I should embark on a sort of prosecuting blitz . . . Myself, I should have thought any promotion board would look with suspicion upon a record of this kind acquired with such sudden timeliness. But there was a fairly general belief in it.' (*The Police and the Public*, p. 182.) It was certainly the belief of the aides to the CID in the 1960s, who relied on a good arrest record to avoid being returned to uniform.

Good rabble-rousing stuff. And roused the rabble was. Skirmishes between police and the mob were common, with the latter retreating – just as the magistrate had hoped – to the safety of the City of London boundaries. On 9 November 1830 a crowd had gathered at Temple Bar, the dividing line between the City of London and the City of Westminster. At the time the Public Records Office in Chancery Lane was under construction and the mob collected stones and wood from the building works. Rowan's men, stationed down the Strand near Charing Cross, were able to march down through them and the rioters fled into the safety of the City.

As a result of information received, the police were able to thwart a meeting of the Ultras in November 1831 and the police routed a mob in Finsbury Square in April 1832. The first fatal clash came just over a year later, on 13 May 1833, at Coldbath Fields near the prison in Clerkenwell. The handbills printed to promote the meeting were deliberately inflammatory. There were calls to abolish the House of Lords and the monarchy. Police spies had kept the Commissioners informed of the newly formed National Union of the Working Classes, whose meetings were taking place regularly throughout the country with attendances and memberships at a respectable eighty-plus. Following information from a police spy in K division that 'If the meeting takes place the members of the Union will go armed,' the Home Secretary banned the demonstration. The Prime Minister, Lord Melbourne, no great friend of the police, instructed Rowan and Mayne that their men were to stand by, initially concealed but to break up the meeting if anyone attempted to address it, in which case the leaders were to be arrested.

During the morning of 13 May the crowd and the police began to gather at the Fields. At first the atmosphere appeared good-humoured; men sat around playing jackstones and the police, who had been given some beer, seem to have been calm and constrained, if not in good humour, in the midday sun. By two o'clock it was estimated that up to 1,000 were present but there was no sign of the Union members, who, apparently, were still in a local public house deciding who should chair the meeting. Meanwhile Richard Egan Lee, who later admitted to being the printer of some of the pamphlets, proposed another named Mee as chairman.

At 2.45 the Union members marched up Calthorpe Street

carrying banners as well as the tricolour and the American flag. Mee began to address the meeting. He clearly did not wish there to be trouble, warning the crowd of the 'hirelings of the Government who are paid to induce you to commit a breach of the peace. We are grateful to the Whigs for advertising our meeting for us but as the government has threatened you so that in your excitement you may act offensively and so be led to the slaughter be peaceful and orderly.'

He urged the crowd to furl the flags and when there was a roar of disapproval, called on them to take the spikes from the end of the flagpoles they were carrying.[5] Almost immediately he saw the police begin their march down Calthorpe Street. Mee jumped from the railings and ran off towards Bagnigge Wells Road. A respectably dressed man called on the crowd, then beginning to waver, to stand firm but without Mee their mood turned violent and they prepared to confront the police head on.

The fighting lasted ten minutes, during which time three police officers were stabbed, one of them, Robert Culley, fatally. Later George Fursey was charged with the attempted murder of a PC Redwood and a Sergeant Brooks.[6] No one was ever charged with the murder of Culley.

There was, however, an inquest, conducted on 15 May at the Calthorpe Arms with a jury of seventeen and a coroner, Thomas Stirling, who was then aged eighty-eight. It was remarkable for the hostility shown by the jurors to the police and their evidence. By the third day Stirling had completely lost control of the jury, who had effectively abandoned their inquiry into Culley's death and were holding an investigation into the conduct of the police that afternoon. When Stirling told them they were inquiring into

[5] These were called Maceroni pikes after the eponymous colonel who had devised them for the use of crowds attacked by cavalry. This all-purpose weapon was about six feet in length and hinged in the middle. When extended, a metal sleeve slid over the hinge to increase stability. There was a nine-inch detachable blade which could be used as a dagger, while the butt end could be used as a bludgeon. Maceroni's textbook on the subject was entitled *Defensive Instructions to the People*.

[6] George Fursey was tried at the Central Criminal Court. His defence was provocation and he alleged that Redwood and his colleagues were drunk. The judge began his summing up at five minutes to eleven in the evening. The jury complained that they did not wish to hear more and had already made up their minds but they eventually retired at ten past one in the morning and returned a not guilty verdict an hour and ten minutes later. A dinner was given in Fursey's honour at the Sawyers Arms in Camberwell. The police were given instructions to stay clear.

Culley's death and that the police conduct would be investigated by another tribunal later, the foreman replied:

'I beg your pardon, sir. The summons which we received, and a copy of which I now hold in my hand, enjoins us "to inquire, on His Majesty's behalf, touching the death of the deceased" and also contains this important intimation – "and further, to do and execute such other matters and things as shall be then and there given you in charge".'

'But it is not necessary for you to inquire as to the conduct of the police after the man was killed.'

'But if the witnesses that you object to are examined, circumstances may come out which we are anxious to investigate. As tradesmen we are not anxious to waste our time, and we entered on this inquiry purely with a spirit of justice.'

And later in the dialogue the foreman had this to say: 'Persons who have been beaten are fearful of coming forward, we are convinced that unless their evidence is heard the course of justice will be impeded.'

Towards the end of the hearing Mary Hamilton, a servant at the Magpie and Stump, Fetter Lane, gave evidence:

I came through the posts in Calthorpe Street and, on going up the right hand side, between three and four o'clock, I met the policeman who is now dead. While I was talking to him I perceived a man rush towards him from the mob with something in his hand, with which he made a thrust at the policeman, but I could not distinguish what it was. The man said, 'I shall do for the bugger.' I said, 'For God's sake let me get out', and I hastened away as fast as I could. I saw the deceased after he was dead and knew him to be the same who spoke to me. The instrument which the man who had rushed towards me had was like an instrument used to sharpen knives on. I was knocked down and my clothes were torn. I did not see the policeman strike the man first, nor had he said anything to provoke him.[7]

[7] For a detailed account of the inquest and its aftermath, see Gavin Thurston, *The Clerkenwell Riot.*

Her evidence did not appeal to the jurors at all. She had been interrupted when she said the instrument was 'like a butcher's steel and was as long as my finger'.

> 'Then it may have been a piece of wire for ought you know?'
> 'The witness has said nothing about wire. Good God, gentlemen, witnesses are not to be treated in this way.'

The jurors began arguing with the coroner when he reminded them of her testimony:

> 'We do not believe her – no, not one of us!'
> 'And why not?'
> (Juror): 'Because she was contradicted by other witnesses. She said she was two minutes talking to the policeman and it was proved that that was impossible by all the other witnesses. She was tutored.'
> (Another juror): 'She was tutored by the police, she acknowledged having been with them since that day. Why ask us to give a verdict against our consciences?'

Later, as the argument raged, the jurors declared her evidence not worthy of credit. 'I have seen her drinking gin on the leads of this house with a crowd of policemen, with whom she admits she has been since the day of the meeting.' Despite the efforts of the coroner, the jury was adamant in returning its verdict of justifiable homicide on the grounds

> that no Riot Act was read, nor any proclamation advising the people to disperse; that the Government did not take the proper precautions to prevent the meeting from assembling; and that the conduct of the police was ferocious, brutal and unprovoked by the people; and we moreover, express our anxious hope that the Government will in future take better precautions to prevent the recurrence of such disgraceful transactions in the Metropolis.

The verdict was greeted with public acclaim. The jurors were given beer and escorted to their homes in triumph. The police were jeered. Later there was more fêting of the jury with a dinner, a riverboat trip and dancing; a banner bore the legend, 'In Honour of the Independent & Heroic 17 Jurymen who in defiance of Tyrannic Dictation returned an Honest Verdict', and a series of medals were struck in their names.

The verdict was unsupportable. There was, for example, no necessity to read the Riot Act, the procedure under which a magistrate called upon an unruly crowd to disperse. All that that would have accomplished was to turn the meeting into a capital offence for those who lingered more than another hour.

On 30 May 1833 the Solicitor General petitioned the Court of King's Bench to quash the verdict and it did so without hesitation, saying the only possible verdict on the evidence was wilful murder by persons unknown.[8] But the jury and its backers were nothing if not tenacious. On 7 June they petitioned parliament on the grounds that 'they heard with great pain and alarm that their conscientious verdict had been quashed in the King's Bench and that a slur had thereby been cast on their character as jurymen acting under the solemn obligations of an oath and that they prayed the House to take the subject into consideration and pursue such means as might seem requisite to free the petitioners from blame and secure to future jurymen the privileges conferred on them by law.' Parliament reacted favourably. A Select Committee of the House of Commons was established to inquire into the affray at Coldbath Fields.

On 17 May Culley was buried in the graveyard of St Anne's, Soho. His pregnant widow was granted a gratuity of £200 by the government and newspapers opened a subscription for her which raised another £50. At his funeral the two hundred or

---

[8] The verdict on the death of PC Culley was in marked contrast to that on the death of the second police constable to die on duty. John Long had been a night-watchman and was regarded as having an excellent character and experience. On 18 August 1830, whilst patrolling what is now Gray's Inn Road, he was stabbed to death by a well-known burglar, John Sapwell, whom he was about to question. Sapwell's defence was that he had heard the cry 'stop thief' and had joined in the pursuit. A subscription list was opened for Long's family and for a time both the public and press were very sympathetic towards the police. Whilst awaiting his execution on 20 September 1830, Sapwell continued to protest his innocence. His body was later dissected. Long is usually considered to be the first police officer to have died on duty. In fact the first was a PC Grantham who on 29 June 1830 died whilst breaking up a fight in Somers Town. He was knocked to the ground and kicked on the temple. His death has gone almost unremarked.

so of his colleagues who attended were jeered and booed once again by a crowd of around three hundred.

At the same time as the inquiry into the Coldbath Fields disaster, another inquiry was set up. It all stemmed from the behaviour of a former schoolmaster, Sergeant William Steward Popay, of both P division and latterly the Walworth and Camberwell 'class' of the National Political Union. Lord Melbourne had instructed the Commissioners to keep him informed of the Union's movements and, in turn, Popay had been instructed by his Superintendent to attend its meetings. Popay had interpreted this to mean he should infiltrate the organization, and from 1831 to 1833, masquerading as a coalman put out of work by the Coal Act, he did just that.

His radical speeches soon ensured he was elected to office in the Union. In late April or early May 1833 his cover was blown when he was recognized by a Union member, John Fursey, at his station desk at Park House police station.[9] He managed to explain away his presence, and indeed marched with the members to Coldbath Fields, but his behaviour later came under scrutiny.

Fanned by the oratory of that old radical campaigner William Cobbett, the House of Commons responded to a petition got up by John Fursey and others, including a Frederick Young, in which they said that Popay

> used to urge the members of the Union to use stronger language than they did in their resolutions and other papers, which he sometimes altered with his own pen, in order to introduce such stronger language; that in his conversation with one of your Petitioners particularly, he railed against the Government, damned the Ministers for villains, and said he would expel them from the earth; that he told one of your Petitioners that he should like to establish a shooting-gallery, and wanted some of them to learn the use of the broad-sword,

[9] The early police forces seem to have had only a rudimentary idea of undercover work and others did not learn from the salutary lesson of Sergeant Popay. In 1840 a PC Barnett of Birmingham City police infiltrated the Chartists in the city. His superiors required him to work in uniform when he was not busy infiltrating and it was not long before he was seen in a theatre. His explanation that he was working in a private capacity for the theatre manager (an early example of moonlighting if it was true) was not accepted. (B. Porter, *Plots and Paranoia*, p. 74.)

and did give one lesson of the broad-sword to one of your Petitioners.

It was the end for Popay, who protested, as well he might, that his plain clothes were for his own protection. The parliamentary inquiry found that, besides complaining of the misery to which he and his family had been reduced, Popay had marched arm in arm with another member to a meeting to celebrate the French Revolution. 'More serious still he took part in discussions, supporting resolutions, sometimes even proposing that their wording should be strengthened, and encouraged the establishment of an arms depot offering to give members of the Union sword practice.'[10]

His conduct was described as 'highly reprehensible' and he was dismissed the force with ignominy. His superiors, who argued that they had employed Popay at the request of the Home Office, though only to watch the meetings of the Union, were criticized for not keeping him under closer control. Whilst the Select Committee accepted the need for a plain clothes force, it deprecated 'any approach to the Employment of Spies, in the ordinary acceptance of the term, as a practice most abhorrent to the feelings of the People and most alien to the spirit of the Constitution'.[11]

Looking back, there is little doubt that poor Popay was the sacrificial goat, the sop to Cerberus. But were there others like him who remained unmasked? Yes, said Young and others, who maintained they had seen men 'whom they knew to be policemen, disguised in clothing of various descriptions, sometimes in the garb of gentlemen, sometimes in that of tradesmen or artisans, sometimes in sailors' jackets'.[12] 'No, replied the police. Popay was a rogue, an original bad and sinful apple, not the tip of an iceberg.

It is of course unbelievable now that for two years Popay led his double life without the knowledge of any of his superiors. Did no single one of them ever ask how he came by his detailed information? And so at an early stage in the development of the

---

10 Report from Select Committee on Metropolitan Police (675), Parliamentary Papers (1833), vol 13, pp. 401, 409.
11 Ibid., pp. 409–10.
12 Ibid., p. 411.

police, the public, possibly with some justification, anticipated Hilaire Belloc by answering 'Little Liar'. Relations, which had tended to improve after the funeral of Culley and some articles in *The Times* supportive of the police, were once more soured. It might have been some consolation for Popay to know that he would be regarded by some as the true 'founder of the detective system'.[13]

After the Popay affair, the Commissioners were keen to avoid a repetition and in 1839 a Metropolitan Standing Police Order prohibited officers from attending private meetings of any sort. Nor were officers encouraged to adopt a subterfuge to obtain evidence. It was something regarded as abhorrent to right-thinking British people generally. In 1845 a constable who had pretended to be a cobbler to arrest a counterfeiter was severely reprimanded, as was another who six years later hid behind a tree in Hyde Park to observe an 'indecent offence'. When these scandals broke the Home Office was at pains to play the matters down.[14]

Much of the police troubles of the period stemmed from internecine warfare and if the police were not permitted to spy on the public, they were encouraged to spy on each other by the guerrilla war being undertaken by the Chief Magistrate at Bow Street, Frederick Roe, against the Commissioners. On 19 June 1834 an allegation of rape was made by a prostitute, Ruth Morris, against an Inspector Wovenden. The offence was alleged to have occurred in a police cell after she had been arrested for being drunk and disorderly. She made her complaint the following morning to a Superintendent Lazenby, who saw it as patently untrue and refused to accept it. He did however report the matter to the Commissioners. Lazenby was told to get the woman to tell her story to the magistrate when she appeared. But, as is often the case in these matters, there was an administrative blunder. Her case had been heard by the time the message was relayed and she was long gone back into the streets.

---

[13] C. Reith, *British Police and the Democratic Ideal*.

[14] B. Porter, *The Refugee Question in Mid-Victorian Politics*, pp. 114–15. There was clearly much more undercover work going on than the police cared to admit. Officers could be put into civvies for particular operations, for example, in the 1840s an Inspector Anderson, regarded as one of the finest police officers in the Met, was sent to East Anglia to act undercover in the poaching wars which raged throughout the counties.

Commissioner Mayne decided that a charge should be brought so that Wovenden's name could be properly cleared. In theory that was the end of the matter. In practice it was not.

A month later a Sergeant clerk working undercover in Lazenby's office for Roe gave the details of the case to his master. In turn he reported to Lord Duncannon, brother-in-law of Melbourne the Prime Minister, who called for another inquiry. A further charge was brought and Wovenden appeared before the Grand Jury.[15] They refused to prefer a Bill of Indictment and he was discharged.

This should have been the end of the matter but again it was not. In September the Commissioners had submitted a report to Duncannon, clearing both Lazenby and Wovenden of any misconduct and maintaining that they were the victims of Roe's malicious conduct. It did no one any good. On 31 October the Home Secretary ordered the Commissioners to dismiss the men. Ascoli maintains that the correspondence shows that Roe's aim was to force the resignation of the Commissioners.[16] In this Roe did not succeed. Rowan and Mayne believed that they should act for the greater public good and so Lazenby and Wovenden, both veterans of Wellington's Peninsula campaign, were sacrificed. Despite efforts on their behalf and a petition by Lazenby to the Duke himself,[17] they were never reinstated.

Certainly, however, the New Police had some admirers:

> The integrity and trustworthiness of the New Police considered as a body, are above all praise. It is surprising in how few instances charges of corruption have been preferred, far less proved, against any of their number. One scarcely ever hears of such a charge. There seems to be a spirit of rivalry as to who shall be the most honest – if the expression be a

[15] The Grand Jury acted as a filter to weed out unmeritorious cases before the defendant was arraigned in front of the petty jury, who would decide his guilt or innocence. With the rise of the magistracy in the nineteenth century, who took over the duties of the Grand Jury, the latter lost its power. It was finally abolished in 1934. A long, spoon-like lance with which the Grand Jury handed down its last Bill of Indictment hung in St Alban's Crown Court for many years. The Grand Jury is still used in a number of states in America, including New York and Maryland, although there too it is falling into disuse.

[16] D. Ascoli, *The Queen's Peace*, p. 108.

[17] 12 December 1834, HO 61/13.

proper one – as well as to who shall be the most active and enterprising among the body.[18]

By the end of the 1830s Nicholas Pearce, an Inspector nominally attached to A division in North London, had been given the special duty of keeping observation on known London criminals. On 1 February 1840 there was a serious jewel theft in Welbeck Street and in the Police Orders for the next day instructions were issued for 'an active man in each division' to trace the property. Two years later Pearce was given a Sergeant Thornton from E division as his assistant and so, *pace* Popay, the first fledgling detective force was founded in the Yard. The concept initially foundered however.

Pearce himself, a former member of the Bow Street foot patrol which, together with the more famous Bow Street Runners, was amalgamated with the Metropolitan Police in 1839, may have done well. Others were not so capable, or perhaps so interested, in the work. There was a marked lack of cooperation between the divisions and the police, who had always been the targets of sniper fire from the popular press, now came into the sights of the much heavier guns of *The Times*, which could usually be relied on for support. Their perceived bad behaviour on this occasion was their failure to apprehend a middle-aged Irishman, Daniel Good, who, on 6 April 1842, had escaped from custody and had locked the investigating policemen in a barn. Why, asked *The Times*, had the police force of 3,800 men, 'maintained at heavy cost', been unable to lay their hands on a man who had 'already crossed their path' many times? The *Weekly Dispatch* complained that the police behaviour had been 'marked with a looseness and want of decision which proves that unless a decided change is made in the present system, it is idle to expect that it can be an efficient detective force'.

The complaints lay in the failure of a Superintendent Thomas Bicknell to circulate details of the wanted man. From about 1838 there appears to have been what was called a 'route-paper' system in operation. Brief details of a crime, together with a description of any suspect, were circulated to divisions by horseback riders. Each station marked on the back of

[18] J. Grant, *Sketches in London*, p. 392.

the route-paper the time at which it was received and the Commissioners then examined it to see what information on it should be given in their daily report. On receipt of the route-paper the Inspector or Sergeant in charge of the station was expected to circulate details to the men on the beat as soon as possible. Bicknell simply did not include the information on his route-paper that Good was known to be living with a woman in South Street off Manchester Square. Good was not arrested until nearly a fortnight later, when he was seen in Tonbridge, Kent, by a one-time officer from V division. There had already been difficulty in concentrating the minds of station officers on the need to follow up information in route-papers and indeed on 5 March 1842 Rowan and Mayne had sent out a tersely worded order about it. Now, as a result of the failure of senior officers to pay attention to the importance of the Good route-paper, five were suspended.[19]

Almost immediately after the fiasco over Daniel Good, on 5 May there came the shooting of Constable Timothy Daly by a Thomas Good, described as a bricklayer but in reality a member of an Islington street gang. A baker who went to the help of Daly was also shot dead. A PC Moss who had been keeping Good under observation was wounded. Now there was a swing in the pendulum of public affection and questions were asked in the press as to why single, unarmed and uniformed officers should be exposed to such dangers. Rowan and Mayne acted promptly. On 14 June they presented a memorandum requesting the appointment of two Inspectors and eight Sergeants to a new detective branch, with rates of pay which would mean promotion for those selected. Six days later, bolstered no doubt by a second attempt on the life of

---

[19] Good had originally been chased by the police for the theft of a pair of trousers from a tailor in Wandsworth High Street. He was in service to a Mr Shiell, who lived at Roehampton some two miles away. Good was followed into the stables area and under the bales of hay the mutilated torso of a woman was discovered. It was then that Good made his escape, locking the stable door behind him. The dead woman was a Jane Jones with whom Good had at one time lived and by whom he may have had a child. His hanging was watched by the largest crowd since the execution of Henry Fauntleroy, the banker, who was hanged for forgery on 24 November 1824; he had swindled the Bank of England of £250,000. Despite, or because of, this Fauntleroy was popular with the crowds who expected and hoped for a reprieve. After his execution there were rumours he had escaped alive and was living on the continent, where he may still be, along with Elvis and Jack Kennedy.

Queen Victoria, the Home Secretary gave permission for the establishment of the experimental detective force.[20]

The New Police in London were only a small part of Peel's reforms. He had already planned a general police measure for the English counties, as opposed to the towns in 1828. On the whole the towns were reasonably well policed already, and it has been suggested that the reason the New Police spread into urban areas was because the Met had driven the criminals out of London. But more to the point are the riots relating to the Reform Bill which erupted in 1831 in Bristol, Nottingham, Derby, Exeter, Coventry and Preston. Emergency legislation followed emergency legislation. The Special Constables Act of 1831 enabled local justices to conscript special constables if a riot was threatened. This was followed by the Lighting and Watching Act 1833, whilst the Royal Commission on Municipal Corporations was appointed in July of that year. This, in turn, gave way to the Municipal Corporations Act 1835 and policing in the provinces was up and running.

The Act originally applied to the 178 boroughs in England and Wales which had already been granted charters of self-government. Watch committees were to be formed which, within three weeks of formation, would appoint a 'sufficient number of fit men' as constables. The watch committee would have the power of firing as well as hiring. In practice many boroughs simply appointed the night-watchmen and day constables who were already *in situ*. There was no need, it was thought, to have new brooms sweeping the streets clean. Others, notably Bristol, followed the London example. Many other industrial towns, including Birmingham, Manchester and Bradford, which did not have a charter of incorporation by 1835, were not obliged to have a police force until incorporation.

As a result standards of policing and its control varied

[20] At the time there were a considerable number of threats to the life of Queen Victoria. On 30 May 1841 a John Francis fired at the royal carriage when she was driving in Constitution Hill. He was sentenced to death but reprieved on 3 July, the same day that a hunchback, Bean, pointed a pistol at the Queen when she was driving to the Chapel Royal in St James'. The weapon – loaded with gunpowder and pipe tobacco – failed to go off. In all, by May 1842 thirty-seven people had swum into the view of the police for offences relating to the Queen, many of them minor offences such as throwing letters into her carriage or trespassing in Buckingham Palace. (D. G. Browne, *The Rise of Scotland Yard*, p. 120.)

considerably, depending to a great extent on how much money was made available for a force. There was, for example, no bar on tipping, something which at least in theory was frowned upon in the Met. Part-time officers were common and in 1830 Swansea appointed a former Bow Street Runner to organize things for them. He and his team lasted three years before they were dismissed and three regular full-time Constables were appointed, to be followed two years later by an Inspector, who proved to be illiterate. To be fair, things improved there considerably over the next decade. By 1844 the Inspector (not the same one) was required to report in person every Friday morning to the whole council, sitting as the watch committee. Other boroughs displayed great reticence in spending their hard-collected money on policing. In 1838 only about half the boroughs had police forces and in 1845 thirty-plus boroughs had ignored the Act. Eleven years later there were still thirteen defaulters.

Meanwhile back in London the detective branch of the force was having troubles. Rowan and Mayne were, with justification, by no means sure of its reception and the formation went unannounced. It was another month before the press got wind of the force, which was promptly labelled 'Defectives' in the popular press. It suffered at the hands of the public, who believed that here indeed were the continent's police spies in their own backyards. By 11 November 1846 it was clear that the detective branch needed the application of a choke-chain. Rowan wrote, 'I have reiterated to the Superintendents that there shall be no particular men in the Divisions called Plain Clothes Men, and that no man shall disguise himself without particular orders from the Superintendent, and that this should not be done even by them without some very strong case of necessity being made out.'

The detective force suffered too from the reaction of the uniformed branch, partly because of the higher rates of pay the men earned and partly because they were regarded as Commissioners' men. In turn the detectives seem to have displayed an arrogance towards the uniform branch which has persisted until the present day. On 24 March 1845 an order was sent reminding the detectives that they must cooperate with their colleagues and at all times show respect to senior officers.

In 1846, in an effort to improve relations, Rowan began a system under which two Constables from each division were trained in detective work and then sent to the force. Despite an increasing workload the division was not strengthened until 1864. By this time public hostility had to a large extent died down. In part this was due to Charles Dickens, who printed a eulogy in *Household Words* after he had invited the force to the editorial offices for tea.[21]

Even at that period there was an opportunity for considerable personal reward over and above the detective's salary. Pearce, for example, had benefited considerably from the £400 on offer following the successful investigation into the murder of Lord William Russell in May 1840,[22] and detectives were positively encouraged to take private commissions with the consent of the Commissioners. Indeed Wilkie Collins' early detective novel *The Moonstone* (1868) might well have been called *The Moonlighter* for, in that book, Lady Verinder hires Sergeant Cuff away from the Yard for his investigations.[23] It was, however, Charles Dickens, champion of the police, who called that particular concept into question. He believed, probably correctly, that a 'swell' or gentleman, but perhaps one with underworld connections, had hired a policeman from the Yard to make inquiries into the private lives of two young actresses who lived at 31 Berners Street, Soho, then, as now, a raffish area of London. The 'actresses' were Maria Ternan and her sister Ellen with whom Dickens was conducting an affair which he maintained was strictly platonic. He wrote to his sub-editor Willis asking him to make a protest to the police.[24]

Reward money could also lead to difficult questions in cross-examination, as Pearce discovered in the Courvoisier trial:

[21] See A. Trodd, *The Policeman and the Lady: Significant Encounters in Mid-Victorian Fiction*, *Victorian Studies*, vol 27, no 4 (1984), p. 439.

[22] The elderly Lord William Russell was found dead on a bloodstained bed at his home in Norfolk Street, Park Lane. At first it was thought he had committed suicide but this was discounted when it was found that silverware was missing. His French valet, Courvoisier, was later charged and indeed confessed to his counsel Charles Phillips. Despite a spirited defence Courvoisier was found guilty and later made a further gallows confession in which he admitted stripping naked before killing Russell to avoid any traces of blood on his clothes.

[23] It would, however, have been an anachronism, for the word moonlighting did not come into use until between the World Wars.

[24] The letter of 25 October 1858 is in the Huntington Library. *See also* A. Nisbet, *Dickens and Ellen Ternan* and P. Ackroyd, *Dickens*.

'Do you expect to get any of this reward if the prisoner is found guilty?'

'Yes.'

'Have you formed any notion of what your share of the reward will be if the prisoner should be convicted?'

'No.'

'If this prisoner is acquitted, you will of course get no reward?'

'None.'

Pearce left the detective force following a row over pay and became a Superintendent in the East End. He was replaced as its head by an Inspector Shackell. It was not the end of his career as a detective, however. In 1846 he was involved in the investigation into the death of PC 313K George Clark, who had disappeared whilst on the night-shift at Dagenham, Essex. It was to become an investigation from which few of the officers involved would emerge with much credit.[25] Indeed the affair encapsulates just about every kind of misconduct and deviance which one could lay at the police door and, as with all the best of so many later examples, there was never a really satisfactory result.

In 1846 Dagenham was not the urban sprawl of today. It was no more than a village, a number of whose inhabitants smuggled goods from Thames' boats over the marshes. The arrival of the police had not been welcomed. Constables had been assaulted and it was believed, both in and out of the force, that a number were quite prepared to turn a blind eye to the locals' efforts to gain more than a marginal living from the scrubby smallholdings. As a result there was a high turnover of men. Those who had been threatened by the locals departed alongside those who were thought to have been bribed. The latter were not dismissed but merely transferred to less testing areas. Nor when arrests were made could the police rely on the local magistracy, who were handing out light sentences, possibly as a retaliation for the loss of their authority but also because they were almost certainly being bribed.

Because of the danger of the area, Constable Clark was allowed to carry a cutlass as well as a truncheon. He took over

[25] For a full account of the investigations, see J. Lock, *Dreadful Deeds and Awful Murders*, pp. 90–107.

a beat on the edges of the area, replacing a PC Abia Butfoy who had been seriously threatened and so transferred. When Clark failed to report on the morning of 30 June a mounted patrol was sent out to look for him. Meanwhile his fellow officers said they had not seen him since they had left for their beats at 9 pm. A Sergeant William Parsons reported leaving Clark at the Four Wants crossroad and seeing him again at 1 am, but Clark had failed to meet a PC Kempton shortly after that; nor had he kept his next official appointment with Parsons at 3 am.

The search for Clark continued throughout the day and recommenced at dawn on the Thursday. By Friday night Clark's body had still not been found and Kempton and Butfoy, recalled to the area, were dragging one of the ponds of a local farmer, Ralph Page, when it was suggested that there was yet another pond which might usefully be looked at. On the way Kempton found a damaged police truncheon and also immediately one of the young boys sent with the officers as guides found a bloodstained cutlass in the hedge and nearby the already decomposing body of Clark. He was on his back, his legs crossed and his right hand clutching a handful of corn. His face was bruised and there was a large cut along the top of his skull, and also cuts to his back and neck. His money, watch and rattle were still in his pockets, which effectively ruled out robbery as a motive.

The magistrates required the police to use every vigilance in their power and this included calling out Inspector Shackell. Various theories for the killing were on offer. One was that it was a mistaken identity case, with the unfortunate Clark mistaken for Butfoy, or possibly for his Sergeant, Parsons. Both of these men had fallen foul of the local Walker brothers, Amos and Moses: Butfoy had asked Moses to empty the contents of a bag he was carrying and Parsons had questioned Amos over possession of some stolen hemlock. Parsons had been active in his prosecution of Amos, pressing on with the case even though the complainant had failed to appear. Walker had, in accord with local custom, been given a small fine. There was also a theory that Clark had been killed because of his refusal to turn a blind eye to the smuggling prevalent on the marshes and in which other officers acquiesced.

The Times was in full cry. The reason, it thundered, that no progress had been made was because there had been no reward money on offer. Meanwhile the inquest reopened with a statement from the Walker brothers that they were innocent and, more importantly, evidence from Ralph Page's wife Elizabeth that after the discovery of Clark's body she had invited three of the officers to supper during which Kempton had said that Parsons had not been on duty, for most of the night of Clark's disappearance. He had, apparently, reported sick and Kempton had finished his duty for him. Kempton and another officer, Jonas Stevens, who had fainted at the sight of Clark's body, both denied this. Parsons denied any absence from duty and in this he was backed by the constables under his command.

The coroner ranged far and wide in questions during the inquest, from asking why Clark's box, in which he kept his possessions at the police station, had been broken open, to whether Clark was disliked by his colleagues. Was he lending them money? Had there been arguments over religion? A PC Isaac gave evidence that Clark had broken open his own box but Isaac put his disappearance much earlier in the night, saying that Clark had not kept a rendezvous at Miller's Farm at 11 pm. The coroner then adjourned with the news that 'certain information' had come into his possession which might lead to the exhumation of Clark's body. The 'certain information' was a letter from Bristol and as a result officers, metaphorically, leaped on their horses and galloped off in all directions.

When the inquest reopened there was evidence that Clark's wounds were made by his own cutlass. The body had been exhumed to see if he had been shot. This proved not to be the case but suspicion was now transferred to Parsons. Mrs Page stuck to her story that Kempton had told her Parsons was not on duty. She was contradicted by a witness who in turn was contradicted by a juryman, who said that the witness had told him Kempton regularly did Parsons' duty. Parsons interrupted to say he believed that he was being set up as the murderer, which he denied he was and said he could produce witnesses who would deny the statements made by Mrs Page. To further confuse matters, Julia Parsons, the Sergeant's sister, told the jury that she had seen Parsons and Clark together about 9 pm that evening; her brother was on a horse, with Clark walking beside him. She went on to say he had been home around midnight to write up his report and had left again at 1 am, not returning for a further eight hours.

Parsons produced evidence that he had been served a pint of porter by the landlord at the Cross Keys public house around midnight and that a carter had seen him on horseback between three and four in the morning. The coroner accepted that Parsons had been on duty all night; the problem was whether Kempton had said he had taken the Sergeant's duty and if so why. The inquest was further adjourned.

On 12 August 1846 Dennis Flinn, John Hennessy and Eileen Rankin were brought before magistrates at Ilford on suspicion of murdering Clark. The evidence depended on a rambling confession by Eileen Rankin to an Irish labourer to the effect that Hennessy and Flinn had been involved in a fight with a policeman who was found dead the next morning. The case was remanded a week, during which time it was established that both men had a perfectly good alibi.

On 18 August *The Times* reported that several Dagenham policemen had been arrested on a charge of murder. In fact five policemen – Kempton, Hickton, Farnes, Butfoy and Parsons – had merely been suspended. The inquest was reopened.

Butfoy went first, admitting he had told lies. He had not seen the Sergeant that night. He had not even been on duty. Parsons and he had been to a police court earlier in the day and he, Butfoy, had got so drunk that he was excused duty. He had no explanation for the death of Clark, he told the jury, 'only it looks strange that the Sergeant does not acount for his time from half past nine o'clock until eleven and that Clark was not seen by a man who was invariably in the habit of seeing him at eleven o'clock at the Four Wants'.

Kempton went next, admitting to taking over Parsons' duty at midnight. He had expected to meet Clark but the officer had not appeared. Farnes now retracted his statement that he had seen Parsons previously and that he had changed his story at Kempton's request. Parsons' response was a simple denial. 'They have sworn falsely.' When it was pointed out that they now all contradicted him, he replied, 'I can't help that.'

There was further damaging evidence from a labourer who said he had seen PC Clark on duty at 10.30 pm and had agreed to wake him up between three and four. A porter,

Henry Clements, then said that he had seen Parsons in the public bar murmuring, 'Poor fellow, I wish I had not done it now.' Clements had asked, 'Done what?' Parsons did not reply.

But suspicions soon shifted from Parsons. It was discovered that the hymn-singing, tract-bearing Clark had two girlfriends, the second of them a married, though separated woman, Susan Perry. Her husband, said to be very jealous, had been seen in a Dagenham public house the night of the murder. An officer was instructed to become friendly with the husband and try to worm out any confidences from him. He failed to do so.

On the last day of the inquest yet another witness was called. This time a PC George Dunning gave evidence that he had heard Parsons quarrelling with his sister Julia. Parsons had begun to cry and later had threatened to throw her down the stairs if she did not hold her tongue. Julia Parsons admitted the quarrel but maintained it was to do with family matters.

When it came to it, the coroner told the jury that in his opinion both Butfoy and Parsons were lying and the jury must make up their minds whether there was sufficient evidence to bring in a verdict of wilful murder against anyone. The motive must have been one of revenge in view of the dreadful injuries. The jury returned a verdict of murder by persons unknown.

The police and Inspector Pearce came in for some further criticism. There was an allegation that the police had planted a bloodstained handkerchief in the field deliberately to complicate the investigation. Since this allegation came from the Reverend Lewis, the coroner's brother, it was not something to be taken lightly.

The charges of perjury against officers Farnes, Butfoy and another named Stevens were dropped. They had not been on oath when first examined so whilst they may have lied they could not have committed perjury. They were dismissed the force and now, wearing their bright new hats, appeared as the main prosecution witnesses against Parsons, Hickton and Kempton for conspiracy to pervert and against Kempton and Hickton for perjury.

A bail hearing was arranged for the end of March 1847

but only Kempton appeared. Hickton and Parsons had fled. Kempton, unable to find a £400 surety, remained in custody, with the trial fixed for 14 July. On 30 June Hickton was brought into Arbour Square police station in the East End by an old friend, Sergeant Harvey, having been handed over by his father. Hickton had persuaded his father to tell Harvey his whereabouts so that the reward for finding him could be claimed jointly. Despite considerable doubts of the validity of the scheme, £25 was awarded, to be shared between Harvey and Hickton *père*. As Joan Lock points out, the sum was 'riches – when one considers that a policeman's pay was only £1 a week'.[26]

At the trial Kempton and Hickton were found guilty and each received a sentence of seven years' transportation. In the end neither served the sentence. Hickton had his commuted and, on a petition by Kempton's father, Kempton too was released. He had, after all, had 'only one report for neglect of duty'. Parsons was acquitted at the Old Bailey in 1848 on the direction of Lord Justice Denman, who ruled that the Sergeant had not been conspiring to defeat justice but only to cover up his own dereliction of duty.[27] Looking back on the Clark case, it has all the classic ingredients of subsequent police trials: perjury, conspiracy, allegations of planted evidence, extra-marital sex, absconding bail, rewards paid to the wrong people and finally a splendidly ambiguous decision by the trial judge.

In 1855 came the case of the officer who paved the way of organized corruption. Charles King, a plain clothes officer in C division, was indicted for larceny and receiving. 'The chief occupation of this cumulative offender for many years has been to train young thieves to the occupation of picking pockets, he himself conducting them to the places where their profession might be most advantageously exercised, pointing out the victims, and covering his pupils in the performance of

---

[26] J. Lock, *Dreadful Deeds and Awful Murders*, p. 105.

[27] In 1858 Mrs Page came forward to tell the story that the murderers were her husband Ralph, conveniently dead, and three other men, one of whom had already hanged himself and another gone to Australia. The third, George Blewett, was acquitted when a Grand Jury refused to return a true bill. Later that year the police received a letter from Australia to the effect that Clark had been killed when he came upon some tobacco smugglers. A final version of his death was that he was killed because of an affair with Parsons' wife.

their tasks. He was sentenced to transportation for fourteen years.'[28] One of his companions in crime, a PC Jesse 'Juicy Lips' Jeapes, survived prosecution but was dismissed the force after fifteen years' service.

Nor was the general reputation of the uniform police too high. The phrase 'if you want to know the time ask a policeman' taught to children in the twentieth century had a more cynical origin. It was a reflection on the ability of the police to separate drunks from their watches and part of the oral history of distrust of the police. Not that, in the mid-Victorian years, sobriety on the part of the police themselves counted for much: in 1863 no fewer than three Sergeants and 212 Constables were discharged for drunkenness on duty.

Whilst the Clark case may perhaps be dismissed as something of a localized difficulty for the Metropolitan Police, other cases on a far greater scale followed. The first was incompetence of the highest order, the second corruption of the highest order. Neither endeared the force to the public.

At a quarter to four in the afternoon of 13 December 1867 the Fenian Michael Barrett blew up part of Clerkenwell prison, with the loss of thirty-seven lives. In one of the simplest acts of terrorism, he had placed what appeared to be a barrel of beer, but which in fact contained gunpowder, against the walls of the prison. The police had been informed of the likely attempt. Indeed the day before, a Constable had actually seen an unsuccessful attempt to blow down the wall – the fuse was damp and the gunpowder failed to explode – and he had apparently taken so little notice that he allowed the conspirators to return and remove the package. Three people were captured and later Barrett was caught in Glasgow. On 26 May 1868, two days after he was executed in what was the last public hanging in England, the Treasury put a Bill through parliament alloting a sum 'not exceeding £300 a year' as an allowance for house rent to each of the three Assistant Commissioners.

The *Daily Telegraph* for one was appalled:

Surely there must be some member of the House who will

[28] Annual Register for 13 April 1855. See also A. Lieck, *Bow Street World* and C. Emsley, *The English Police*.

stop this questionable proposal and insist on a thorough inquiry. The other day a sergeant of constabulary, who against the orders of his superior officer had subscribed for a forbidden newspaper, was summarily dismissed; but for permitting Clerkenwell to be blown up, three of the men primarily responsible are rewarded with an extra £300 per annum. At this rate, if the Houses of Parliament are blown up, the officers will deserve two or three thousand a year.

The facts of the Clerkenwell case are extremely simple . . . the London event was distinctly foretold to the authorities in Scotland-yard, and they took what they considered precautions. They were warned that an explosion was planned, and they posted their constables around the gaol. The policemen saw the barrel placed near the wall but, according to the official excuse, it was suggestive of nothing save beer. One may see in a pantomime a simplicity of that kind affected by the Clown; but in real life surely nothing so grossly idiotic ever occurred before. Another excuse given is, that the police expected an explosion from below; they were prepared for a mine, but not a lateral attack . . . It is plain to anybody that five or six men patrolling outside the prison could have watched the whole exterior wall, and that, unless they shut their eyes, they must have observed the death-bearing barrel, and might have conjectured its consequences. Of two things one: either Sir Richard Mayne and the Assistant Commissioners gave the sentinel police no information of what was expected, and, if so, grossly neglected their duty; or they selected the most marvellously stupid men in the force.[29]

And so on for another several hundred well-thought-out words.

In the same year, with fears of returning ticket-of-leave men as a growing menace to London society, a departmental committee was set up to investigate policing. Its findings included a suggestion for an increase in the detective force. And it was the pure and simple greed of those detectives

[29] *Daily Telegraph*, 28 May 1868.

which was to set Scotland Yard back on its heels when in 1877 came the first of the great police corruption scandals – the Turf Fraud, in which five senior officers from the detective division were arrested and appeared at the Old Bailey. In turn this led to the foundation of the Criminal Investigation Department (CID). However, in accepting bribes, suppressing evidence and giving advance notice of raids, the behaviour of the officers involved was to provide a blueprint for behaviour by corrupt policemen in that CID and other detective forces for the next 115 years.[30]

The background to the 1877 Trial of the Detectives is that of two high-class fraudsmen, William Kurr and Harry Benson, who operated a series of racing scams. Benson, educated in France, had previously run a series of swindles, including one in 1872 in which he had posed in London as the Count de Montague, Mayor of Chateaudun, supposedly raising money for refugees from the Franco-Prussian War. He extracted £1,000 from the Lord Mayor but was arrested almost immediately. Fearful of a prison sentence, he set fire to the bedding in his cell and had to be carried into court on the back of a warder to receive his twelve-month sentence. On his release he teamed up with William Kurr, the son of a wealthy Scottish baker. From at least the previous year Detective Sergeant, later promoted Inspector, John Meiklejohn had been taking bribes from Kurr, whom he had met by chance in a bar and whom he tipped off about the progress of police inquiries in connection with racing frauds. A Chief Inspector George Clarke, a freemason, then approaching sixty, was roped in, possibly after a hint of blackmail by Kurr. Clarke at the time was using a man who had absconded bail as an informant and Benson let it be known that a letter sent by Clarke was in their possession. One of Scotland Yard's most able detectives, the multilingual Nathaniel Druscovich, was also recruited. He had backed a bill for his brother in the sum of £60, a quarter of a year's salary, and could not pay. Kurr kindly lent him the money and he too was hooked. The fourth officer involved, William Palmer, was recruited through Meiklejohn.

The monies they received were considerable. For informing

[30] The principal account of the case is in George Dilnot's *The Trial of the Detectives* but there are many shorter versions in a number of books, including Joan Lock's *Dreadful Deeds and Awful Murders*, pp. 185–6.

Bent Coppers

Kurr that a fraud charge could be 'settled', Meiklejohn received
£100. Later Druscovich declined £1,000 for not travelling to
Scotland to continue inquiries but on another occasion took
£100 and a piece of jewellery for his wife. He was also given
a cigar-box containing £200 in gold as a *douceur* for delaying
inquiries. Clarke received £150 in gold. For assisting in the
changing of certain banknotes, Meiklejohn asked £2,000 from
Benson.

The most audacious of the racing swindles was perpetrated
on the Countess de Goncourt in Paris. She was persuaded to
place bets on horses through a commission agent in London
and to be sent her winnings by cheques drawn on a non-existent
bank. In a matter of weeks she had been swindled out of
£10,000. Outside solicitors pressed Superintendent Frederick
Williamson into pushing along the inquiries and, despite the
efforts of Meiklejohn and Druscovich to delay matters, Kurr
and Benson were arrested. Kurr received ten and Benson
fifteen years of penal servitude. Setting a precedent, they
now cooperated with the authorities, in return, they hoped,
for an early release. On their evidence Meiklejohn, Palmer,
Druscovich, Clarke and a solicitor, Edward Froggatt, were
charged. Clarke was acquitted. The others received two years'
apiece.

Sentencing the men, Baron Pollock stated, 'The spirit and
rule of the law in England have been, and I trust always will
be, to make a wide distinction between offences committed
under either sudden impulse or under the pressure of want
or poverty, and offences committed by persons placed in a
position of trust.'

But the officers were the tip of the iceberg. The best that can
be said for Williamson was that he was extraordinarily slow to
realize what was going on. Others take a less charitable view.
'It seems inconceivable that Williamson was unaware of the
conduct of so many of his officers, but a hundred years later,
in not dissimilar circumstances, it was a question which was
again to be asked of Scotland Yard.'[31] As for others in the
department, Dilnot comments, 'Any person studying this case
cannot fail to come to the suspicion that many other detectives
both inside and outside Scotland Yard were in the pay of Kurr

[31] D. Ascoli, *The Queen's Peace*, p. 145.

and Benson. It is doubtful if the full ramifications of this great plot were ever brought to light.'[32]

There had already been complaints about the conduct of the detective branch when in 1872 Druscovich and Meiklejohn had allowed Warren, Bidwell and Macdonnell, part of a team of American swindlers dealing in forged securities, time to escape across the Atlantic to the temporary safety of the United States. Nor was general discipline any too good at the Yard at the time. One of the crucial pieces of evidence against Druscovich to corroborate that of Kurr and Benson came from Detective Sergeant William Reivers. Under cross-examination he admitted that he was one of two detectives in line for promotion if Meiklejohn and Druscovich were dismissed from the force. Later in the trial it was established that during his fifteen-year service he had had eight disciplinary offences recorded against him, including disobedience, incivility, drunkenness and assault. In October 1876 he had been given the opportunity to resign over a complaint by a private inquiry agent. He had declined the offer and had 'been reduced'.

The whole affair, wrote Douglas Browne, wearing blinkers at the time, was 'a net of corruption happily unique in the history of the Metropolitan Police'.[33]

Even as the trial was going on a departmental commission had been set up by Colonel Henderson, a former regular officer of the Royal Engineers who had been appointed Commissioner on

[32] G. Dilnot, *The Trial of the Detectives*, pp. 54–6.

Druscovich was a broken man and died shortly after his release from prison. Palmer became a prosperous publican, as did Clarke, who retired on a pension after his acquittal. Meiklejohn became a private inquiry agent and lost a libel action over his involvement in the Turf case. Froggatt, the solicitor, received a further sentence after tricking Lord Eustace into marrying a lady of doubtful history; he became one of the trustees and later embezzler of the £10,000 marriage settlement. He died in the Lambeth workhouse. William Kurr and Harry Benson continued to operate a series of swindles, mainly in the United States. Benson eventually committed suicide in the Tombs prison, New York. He was about to be extradited to Mexico for selling fake tickets for a tour of Madame Patti, the soprano.

Williamson, who had joined the force in 1852, retired in 1889 and died the same year. He had been given leave of absence following fainting fits in 1888, said to have been brought on because of his involvement with anti-Fenian activities. He was fifty-nine. In 1888 he is said to have commented to Sir Robert Anderson, then just appointed Assistant Commissioner,' You're coming to a very funny place. You'll be blamed if you do your duty, and you'll be blamed if you don't.' (D. G. Browne, *The Rise of Scotland Yard*, p. 201).

[33] D. G. Browne, op. cit., p. 184.

Mayne's death on Boxing Day, 1868. Its terms were to inquire into the 'state, discipline and organization of the Detective Force of the Metropolitan Police'. In this he was aided by a young barrister, Howard Vincent, who presented a paper on the centralized detective operations in Paris,

The commission reported on 25 January, recommending that a completely reorganized detective branch be formed, separate from the uniform police. It should have an Assistant Commissioner who should be a lawyer, with magisterial experience, and who should have charge of the whole force in the absence of the Commissioner. As for the detective branch, it was recommended that the men should 'in their respective ranks take precedence over the uniform or preventive branch of the service'. They were also to receive higher pay.

Just under two months later Vincent was appointed as Director of Criminal Investigations, ranking as Assistant Commissioner only so far as pay was concerned. As to power, he had *carte blanche* in his own department, with direct access to the Home Secretary, and was instructed 'not to pay too much attention to what was said of him, either by the Commissioner, or by anyone else at Scotland Yard'.[34]

There was also a shuffling of the personnel. The new CID would have a Chief Superintendent at Central Office, with three Chief Inspectors, three first-class and seventeen second-class Inspectors under him. In divisions there were to be a further 15 Inspectors, 159 Sergeants, 60 divisional patrols and 20 special patrols. And who survived the purge to become the Chief Super? None other than the innocent or thick, depending on how you view him, Frederick Williamson. Clearly no lesson had been learned from the earlier débâcle. However, Vincent took no chances with other officers. All but twenty of them were on three months' probation.

If Williamson's was a foolish appointment, the structuring of the CID in relation to the uniform men also left a great deal to be desired and set the scene for a further 120 years of internecine warfare. 'The special pay and status of the CID aroused the understandable jealousy of uniform men at the "sharp end" of policing, while divisional Superintendents reacted so strongly to the presence on their ground of police

[34] D. Ascoli, *The Queen's Peace*, p. 148.

officers over whom they had no authority that it was at once
laid down that all reports from detectives in divisions must be
submitted through Superintendents and that the former must
cooperate closely with the latter. None the less, a dangerous
precedent had been set.'[35]

Williamson had a different view, but of course he had
first-hand experience of the matter. He believed the CID failed
to attract the best and brightest of recruits: 'the uncertainty and
irregularity of the duties, which are also no doubt in many cases
very distasteful and repugnant to the better class of men in the
service, as their duties constantly bring them into contact with
the worst classes, frequently cause unnecessary drinking, and
compel them at times to resort to trickey [sic] practices which
they dislike.'[36]

Vincent also experimented with the concept of gentlemen
officers, totally rejected by Peel. He appreciated that CID
work required more intelligence than was possessed by the run
of the street Constable and advertised for 'gentlemen of good
education and social standing'. They were to be drawn from
the military and were particularly sought after if they spoke a
foreign language – as had Druscovich and look where that led
him. The scheme was doomed to failure, partly because it was
found there was no substitute for basic training as a policeman
but also because of discontent amongst the rank and file CID
officers in an early display of the subversion of their seniors'
wishes.

Vincent also agreed with Williamson's view of the recruitment problem:

I do not think that there is any possible system of exercising
continuous and effective disciplinary supervision over upwards
of 250 detective officers, operating over a wide area, who
must necessarily by the nature of their duties, be allowed
wide individual freedom.

I am also of the opinion that it is impossible for the
majority of men to be in contact for any length of time
with all the worst features of human nature, in its most
repulsive aspects, without incurring enormous danger of

[35] Ibid, p. 149.
[36] Memorandum by A. F. Williamson, 22 October 1880 (MEPO 2/134)

moral contagion. Proofs of this are not, unfortunately, wanting.[37]

It was during Vincent's short tenure, before he left for the more comfortable benches of the House of Commons, that the police were involved in yet another case in which they were seen as acting as *agents provocateurs*. A chemist, Titley, was believed to be an abortionist and, in what must be one of the earliest examples of the use of a woman by the police, a policeman's wife was recruited to ask his advice on the pretence of being pregnant. He was convicted but once more questions about the propriety of the behaviour of the officers involved were raised and an indictment, subsequently quashed, was brought against them.[38]

Nor was the lot of the Commissioners a very happy one. Rowan and Mayne had struggled for many years against the magistracy – resentful of the loss of their powers – the press and bureaucracy. Mayne was broken by the Fenian bombing of Clerkenwell and his successor, Henderson, resigned following the rioting in Trafalgar Square in 1886. On Monday, 8 February of that year the London United Workmen's Committee held a meeting complaining about rising unemployment. The police response to potential trouble from a rival organization, the Social Democratic Front, was puny. In charge was an old District Superintendent, Robert Walker. At the age of seventy-four perhaps he should not even have been expected to take charge and, dressed in civilian clothes, he was swamped by the crowd. Adding insult to injury he also had his pocket picked. The meeting went off well enough but then the crowd broke ranks and surged down Pall Mall. The police reserve of some 560 men was wrongly directed to the Mall and the mob marched uninterruptedly to Oxford Street where they were broken up by the enterprising Inspector Cuthbert from Marylebone police

[37] Memorandum by Howard Vincent, October 1880, ibid.

[38] However, if they could get away with it, they did. A Superintendent English was actively engaged in undercover work in the investigation of rural incendiaries in East Anglia in 1844. He is described as an outstanding policeman of the period by John Archer in *By a flash and a scare: incendiarism, animal maiming and poaching in East Anglia 1815–1870*. It is likely that a great deal of undercover work took place from the earliest days of the force, only to be denounced when the agents were flushed out.

station, who managed the trick with a sergeant and fifteen men due to go on night duty.

The same day a committee was appointed, and chaired, by the Home Secretary, Hugh Childers, to look into both the trouble and 'the conduct of the Police Authorities in relation thereto'. It reported a fortnight later, recommending that the administration and organization of the Metropolitan Police Force be thoroughly investigated; 'and we hope that this investigation will take place without delay'. Henderson resigned the next day. He was replaced by [General] Sir Charles Warren, who on taking the post relinquished the governorship of the Red Sea Littoral.[39]

Warren lasted two and a half years, during which time there were more troubles on the streets and he quarrelled bitterly with the Home Secretary over the duties and powers of the Commissioner. The street troubles had arisen over organized squatting in Trafalgar Square where charitable citizens 'moved by this spectacle of squalor, provided bread-vans and soup kitchens and soon the Square became an unoffical welfare centre'.[40] But soon it was not merely the poor and homeless who were in the Square. It became used for political meetings and Warren issued an order, promptly ignored, banning them. On 8 November 1889 he issued another notice banning assemblies in the Square. The confrontation came five days later, on Sunday, 13 November, when 2,000 police, helped for the first time by the mounted police and with both the Life and Foot Guards standing by, kept a mob out of the Square.

On a more localized level Warren was under severe criticism for the failure of his officers to solve the so-called Jack the Ripper Whitechapel murders, attributed over the years to a wide variety of suspects from the Duke of Clarence downwards. One of the more farcical aspects of the Ripper case was the hiring of two bloodhounds from a Mr Brough in Scarborough at the amazing cost of £100. More seriously the Home Secretary wanted the East End brothels closed. Warren replied pragmatically that the eviction of the owners of the brothels was no remedy. The women would simply be driven on to the streets whilst 'in driving the brothel-keepers away from

---

[39] W. M. Lee, *A History of the Police in England*.
[40] D. Ascoli, *The Queen's Peace*, p. 159.

certain neighbourhoods much would be done to demoralize London generally. It is impossible to stop the supply where the demand exists.' It seems that at the time there were about 1,200 prostitutes in W division where the murders were taking place and at least sixty-three known brothels.[41]

In 1887 the behaviour of the police managed to bring about the defeat of the government by five votes, following a PC Endacott mistaking a Stockton-on-Tees virgin, Miss Emily Cass, for a prostitute and arresting her for soliciting on Jubilee night. Witnesses were called as to her character – under the law of the time she was not allowed to give evidence herself – and the charge was dismissed by the Marlborough Street magistrate, Mr Newton. Unfortunately he then chose to say to her, 'Don't walk alone in Regent Street at ten o'clock.' All hell broke about his shoulders, with the press in full cry and derisive songs sung in the music hall. An inquiry was announced and Warren saw Miss Cass and her lawyer at Scotland Yard. Miss Cass made a favourable impression with the Lord Chancellor and in the end Endacott was made the scapegoat. He was suspended and charged with perjury. Mr Justice Stephen directed the jury to acquit the Constable and he was returned to duty.[42]

There is little doubt that the CID was having a very bad time in the late 1880s. According to the *Pall Mall Gazette*, whose gadfly-like editor, W. T. Stead, stung the authorities whenever possible, it had collapsed by October 1888. The reasons given were numerous, beginning with the rule that all officers had to be over five foot ten inches in height. The *Gazette* also complained that all CID men had to serve two years in the uniform branch, so giving the criminals a chance to get a good look at them, and, worse, by the time they became detectives they could only walk with the characteristic Scotland Yard 'gait', making them even more readily recognizable. More serious were the limitations on payments to informers and the rule that an officer could not leave London on a case without the

[41] D. G. Browne, *The Rise of Scotland Yard*, p. 207.
[42] History repeats itself. In 1928 the police treatment of a Miss Irene Savidge in not dissimilar circumstances led to a Royal Commission. In the 1980s a magistrate at Highbury Corner in London made a comment to the effect that women walking at 1 am in a road near Finsbury Park, a noted area of prostitution, were likely to be thought to be on the game. Since the street contained a nurses' hostel he too was attacked for his comment.

permission of the Chief Commissioner – the separate powers granted to Vincent had long since been merged. 'Under these circumstances it is not surprising that our detectives do not detect,' chortled the *Gazette*.[43]

By November 1887 James Monroc, the Assistant Commissioner head of the CID, was complaining his department was overworked and undermanned. 'The result has been that Mr Williamson has broken down, and that I am in a fair way to break down also.' Williamson was granted three months' sick leave in February 1888. Nor was the CID getting much support from Warren. He believed it was a 'drop in the ocean' compared with the uniform branch, as he wrote in *Murray's Magazine*, adding insult to injury when he concluded that the original function of the police had been prevention and that detective work was not suited to the 'genius of the English race'.[44]

As Bernard Porter says, Warren thought that

policing should be open, visible and by the book, rather like cricket, where everything was governed by the rules of fair play. Plain-clothes policing was like taking off the bails at the bowler's end without a warning whilst the batsman was backing up. It was also a constant temptation to corruption as history showed very well. This sort of attitude from a superior was clearly difficult for a dedicated detective like Monroe to live with. Detectives knew that life was not like cricket, and especially among the criminal fraternity. Corruption was the risk you had to run to be effective, and not half so dangerous as the stultifying effects of red tape. This was really the hoary old dilemma of the British police since its earliest days: how to reconcile purity with results.[45]

But officers of the uniform section could still wreak havoc

[43] *Pall Mall Gazette*, 8 October 1888, p. 3. William Thomas Stead was one of the great crusading English editors, campaigning amongst other things against child prostitution. In 1883 he procured a child, handed it to social workers and then wrote an article. Prosecuted, he was imprisoned for three months but his campaign led to the passing of the Criminal Law Amendment Act 1885. Later he embraced peace and spiritualism, writing a book *If Christ Came to Chicago*. He died in 1912, a passenger when the *Titanic* sank.
[44] W. W. Williams, *The Life of General Sir Charles Warren*, pp. 587–90.
[45] B. Porter, *Origins of the Vigilant State*, p. 84.

and outside the Metropolis the century closed with a splendid scandal in Manchester which showed that a corrupt officer could, if he put his mind to it, flourish almost without hindrance. William Bannister had been a Constable in 1871, a Sergeant in 1875, an Inspector in 1880 and a Superintendent in 1882. In the 1890s he was in charge of D district in which there were an abnormally high number of brothels [and disorderly houses]. In particular in Shepley Street houses were kept by a woman named 'Mother' Wilson and a man named Taylor. Bannister not only drew up Sarah 'Mother' Wilson's will but also was a beneficiary. After her death the houses were carried on for immoral purposes, and there was evidence from constables that Bannister carried on the management of them.

In 1893 Bannister had been brought before a watch committee on two charges of misconduct and at one time in the debate it seemed as though he might be dismissed. Some members of the committee then protested this would mean the loss of his pension and a reprimand was substituted. All the constables involved with the 1897 inquiry before Mr Recorder Dugdale gave the reason why they were afraid to move against him as that they were afraid of being 'swamped by their colleagues'. Others said that D division was no worse than other divisions. He was also seen by a Constable Wilkinson in company with a Mrs Julia Davis, separated from her husband in the Falstaff Public House in Hulme behaving in a way which 'if true would have degraded him'. Bannister's explanation that he was in the pub for the purposes of making another will and that there had been a robbery committed was accepted. Wilkinson resigned. Bannister had also brought an action against the Rev John Kelty for defamation. Kelty had said that Bannister had gone in a cab drunk with two prostitutes to Raby Street police station. The words had been held to be privileged but Mr Justice Kennedy had whitewashed Bannister telling him he left the court without a stain on his character.

On 7th December 1896 Bannister resigned before the Watch Committee. His last act had been to help his old friend William Taylor escape a charge of brothel-keeping. According to Dugdale's report issued on July 9 1897 Bannister had been promoted over four other inspectors and against the recommendation of the Chief Constable.

3

1901–1939

The new century did not start well for the Metropolitan Police Force. There was now a Liberal government with a substantial majority and the Liberals and their allies could be relied upon to pose rather more questions into police behaviour than their Conservative counterparts. Almost immediately there were two opportunities.

The first was the appalling case of Adolf Beck, which led to the establishment of the Court of Appeal. The police may not have come out of this case as badly as the lawyers and the judiciary but nevertheless their investigations left a great deal to be desired. The Beck case also showed how the establishment's ranks close in an inquiry into a case that has gone horribly wrong. In this instance, however, the eminent barrister Horace, later Mr Justice, Avory was heavily criticized, at least by the media and the public, for his conduct.

In 1877 a John Smith was convicted at the Old Bailey of frauds on women of the *demi-monde* whom he deprived of their money and jewellery. He would pose as a member of the aristocracy, Lord Willoughby, with a home in St John's Wood and then offer the woman a position as his mistress. She would be purchased a new outfit on a forged cheque and he would decamp with her jewels and whatever money he could borrow from her. Smith was sentenced to five years' penal servitude and remained in prison until 1881.

In 1894 the swindles began again, carried out by a Lord Wilton or Lord Winton de Willoughby still living in St John's Wood. Unfortunately for Adolf Beck, a Norwegian seaman, a woman he met quite by chance, Ottilie Meissonier, on 16 December 1895 in Victoria Street identified him as Lord Wilton. Beck called a policeman to whom he denied his guilt but he was arrested and charged. A rudimentary identification parade was held and several other women identified Beck. After the committal proceedings a man, not a policeman, communicated with Scotland Yard to say that Beck was the swindler John Smith. He was then identified by PC Spurrell and another officer who had arrested Smith fifteen years previously. Handwriting evidence was given by the expert, Gurrin, who said the handwriting and exhibits 'must have been written by the same person'. Beck's solicitor made two applications to the Commissioner of the police to inspect John Smith's record. Both applications were turned down and Beck, prosecuted by Horace Avory, went on trial at the Old Bailey.

Charles Gill, defending Beck, asked for leave to cross-examine Gurrin to the effect that the 1877 exhibits had been written by Beck. If Gurrin confirmed this, there was an immediate defence available: there was clear evidence that Beck had been in South America in 1877. Avory objected on the grounds that this was a collateral issue and should not be inquired into until the jury had reached its verdict. His objection was upheld and Beck received a sentence of seven years' penal servitude.

In prison he was treated as the ex-convict Smith. Dutton, his solicitor, appealed to the Home Office to be allowed to prove that Beck had been in Peru when Smith was convicted. His applications were turned down and Beck had been in prison for two years before it was discovered that he could not be Smith. Smith was a Jew and circumcised. Beck, a Gentile, was not. The prison governor consulted the trial judge, the Common Sergeant, Forrest Fulton, but it was decided that whilst Beck, since he could not be Smith, should now be treated as a first offender, nothing had happened which invalidated his conviction. His further petitions were turned down and he was released on licence in 1901.

Curiously, during Beck's time in prison the swindles ceased, only to begin again in 1903. The next year Beck was once more arrested, committed for trial and convicted. Again the swindles stopped but whilst Beck was in custody a William Thomas was arrested trying to pawn the rings of two actress sisters, Violet and Beulah Turner, who had been swindled. Mr Justice Grantham postponed sentence on Beck to allow further inquiries to be made. Thomas was found to be Smith, alias Lord Wilton; Gurrin withdrew his evidence and Beck was released to general acclaim on 19 July 1904.

Public opinion now ran high in favour of the Norwegian and the £2,000 offered to Beck as an act of grace was roundly condemned. An internal Home Office inquiry was pooh-poohed in the *Daily Mail* by Sir George Lewis, the eminent solicitor now acting for Beck. There must be one held by a judge. And indeed there was. The Home Secretary appointed the Master of the Rolls to head the inquiry. Curiously the tribunal did not recommend a Court of Appeal. The fault in the present case was considered to be that of the judge. In future the right to compel the court to 'state a case' to the higher court would be sufficient. As for Mr Avory, he was in a high old temper.

> . . . my attention has been called to certain passages in the *Daily Mail* in which I am accused of having been a party to a conspiracy to secure the conviction of a prisoner by suppressing facts which would have ensured his triumphal acquittal . . . I do desire to call your attention to the fact that at a later date, Sir George Lewis, the solicitor to the *Daily Mail*, is reported in an interview to have stated that the conduct of the prosecution was open to the gravest suspicion, and that my conduct was apparently designed in order to deprive Adolf Beck of his defence to this charge. Seeing that Sir George Lewis is a man who ought to know something of the criminal law and who ought to know something of me . . . it is only for that reason that I have even mentioned allegations . . .

No, Mr Avory didn't remember the details of the case. When Sir George Lewis asked 'whether, after the evidence that was given of Mr Beck being in Peru during the whole of the years that Smith was in prison – whether after hearing that evidence Mr Avory was satisfied that Mr Beck was not John Smith,' Avory replied: 'To ask me what I thought at a particular moment in 1896 about one case of several that I did during 1896 is an impossible question to answer.'

That was the end of the matter. The committee found

'nothing whatever to complain of in the conduct of the trial by the prosecution. Mr Avory, as counsel for the Crown, in the view of the case which he held, was perfectly justified in taking the objection, as well as in every step he took in the conduct of the prosecution. He has given his reasons in evidence, and it would be quite superfluous to refer to them here.'[1] Quite.

The second case to highlight police behaviour started over what was essentially a minor incident, although there must have been deep resentment smouldering in the background. On 1 May 1905 Eva D'Angeley was arrested in Regent Street for 'riotous and indecent behaviour' or, in plain language, prostitution. The charge was dismissed after a Mr D'Angeley told the magistrate that he was married to the lady and that she was merely waiting for him, something she had done on a regular basis. Better still, Sub-Divisional Inspector MacKay told the court he believed the D'Angeleys to be a respectable couple. The experienced Marlborough Street magistrate, Denman, dismissed the charges and another desert storm blew up with allegations of harassment, bribery and corruption. A Royal Commission was set up to inquire into methods and discipline in the force.

Although the D'Angeley case is the one cited as the grounds of the Royal Commission – and one which exonerates the police of any wrongdoing – it was not the only case to cause concern. One of the other cases which led to the Commission was that of a PC Rolls who, it was alleged, had planted a hammer on a cabinet-maker sleeping on a bench at London Fields and had then arrested him. The case was dismissed at the North London Police Court by the eccentric magistrate Edward Snow Fordham. Rolls was later prosecuted at the Central Criminal Court and received five years' penal servitude. Another officer was allowed to resign.

This led to the formation of the Public Vigilance Society, and such success as the public had in establishing any misconduct by the police was largely due to it and to Earl Russell, who appeared for the Society and who later wrote modestly:

I was instructed by a curious body called the Police and Public

[1] Official report of the Committee of Enquiry (CD 2315), November 1904.

Vigilance Society run by a fanatic called Timewell. He was prepared always to believe anything he was told against the police and to resent with some indignation the demand for proof which a lawyer always makes. However, we selected about twelve of the likeliest cases, and in spite of the extreme poverty on our side and the whole force of the Treasury and the police against us on the other we succeeded in getting home seven of them, largely on my cross-examination of the police.[2]

One of the cases which they 'succeeded in getting home' was that of PC Ashford, who is described by the old East End villain Arthur Harding as having a nice wife 'but always after the women. He wasn't intelligent enough to catch a thief, but he was good at perjury and he could do a man an injury by strength.'[3] In August 1906 Ashford came across a young man named Gamble out walking with a prostitute, Ethel Griffiths. It appears he wanted the girl for himself and told Gamble to clear off. Mrs Griffiths told Ashford she did not want him and the officer then knocked Gamble down and kicked him. A police sergeant, Sheedy, came up and told Gamble to get up and fight like a man. Then when he saw how badly the man was injured he told Ashford to go away as he had done enough. Gamble was in hospital for four months and was operated on four times. He later spent nearly a month in a convalescent home. One member of the Commission compared his injuries to those which would have been sustained by falling on a railing.

The Public Vigilance Society was aided and abetted in this case by Arthur Harding. He discovered two witnesses and arranged for the Commission's investigator to take statements from them. Later another witness was found. The Commission found that PC Ashford was guilty of the misconduct alleged, that is kicking Gamble, but that he did not intend to do him the serious injury which resulted. In Sergeant Sheedy's case it was found that he had not stopped the assault and that he had failed to make a report to his superiors. The investigation of the incident by an Inspector Hewison had aborted when he found no trace of Gamble's name at the London Hospital –

[2] *My Life and Adventures*, pp. 304–5.
[3] R. Samuel, *East End Underworld*, p. 191.

he had been wrongly listed under the name Pearce – and the Commission found that Hewison had done 'all that could be reasonably expected'.

The aftermath was the prosecution of Ashford. Proceedings were begun immediately after the Royal Commission published its findings and at the Old Bailey in September 1908 the jury was instructed to disregard the evidence of Ethel Griffiths because she was a prostitute. The defence also claimed that there had been no proper identification of Ashford as the kicking officer. After a two-hour retirement by the jury, he was found guilty and sentenced to nine months' hard labour. Leave to appeal was refused.

Within days of the appointment of the Commission its members had been inundated with letters and postcards alleging police corruption, perjury and bribery, often in language 'foul and intemperate'. From these, nineteen cases, including that of Mme D'Angeley, were closely scrutinized by the Commissioners who sat on sixty-four occasions over a period of eleven months. The rag-bag of witnesses who came before them included Arthur Harding, a.k.a. Tresidern, who would later lead an armed siege of Old Street Police Court.

Unsurprisingly the Commission, increasingly bored with the East End witnesses, exonerated the police and declared that, far from harassing street offenders, they were kind and conciliating to them. (One wonders whether a similar Commission sitting today would reach the same conclusions.) True, in some nine cases there had been reprehensible conduct but by and large the Commission found that 'The Metropolitan Police is entitled to the confidence of all classes of the community.'

The Times for one was enchanted. 'We have no hesitation in saying that the Metropolitan Police as a whole discharge their duties with honesty, discretion and efficiency.' It was unfortunate that the same year a constable was convicted of perjury.

What the Commission did reveal was an unofficial earner for the force. They were expected to act as wakers-up, for which they received call-money from the sleepers. Police Orders put a stop to this little touch: 'Though the police should, when they can, render this or any other service in their power to the inhabitants, this particular service is one which can very rarely be rendered, and when rendered should be gratuitous;

the police cannot undertake to be at a given place at a fixed hour every day.'[4]

As to the D'Angeleys, MacKay had conducted further inquiries and now came to the conclusion he had been mistaken in his assessment of the pair. One is tempted to wonder how he was deceived in the first place. Did not he or his colleagues know the French girls who worked his area? Could he not tell D'Angeley was a pimp? Why did he not ask for a short adjournment to make proper inquiries? Meanwhile, both the D'Angeleys had retreated to Paris and sensibly stayed there despite the entreaties of the police, who offered to pay the lady's fare back so she could give evidence to the Commission. Their return to France had been hasty: when they caught the packet they had not had time to pay for their lodgings and had left behind a few empty trunks.

The Royal Commission was hardly out of the way when internal strife broke out. The level of police pay has long ceased to be a valid reason for corruption but this has not always been so. The early years of the century saw a long and bitter battle over pay and the right to found a union, the so-called 'right to confer'. There was nothing new in this. There had been short-lived strikes in the Met in 1872 and 1890.[5] The demands were similar – the right to confer, higher wages, a pension as of right and a weekly rest-day. There had been some excitement in the 1890 strike when the Life Guards were called in to deal with disorder outside Bow Street court. Lessons were there for the learning for any potential strikers: after the 1872 strike a hundred men were dismissed but later allowed to return to the service on reduced pay; after the 1890 strike none of the thirty-nine men dismissed was reinstated. Now, however, at the beginning of the First World War, the police had a champion in the newly founded *Police Review* and a martyr in ex-Detective Inspector Syme.

As a young Inspector in the Metropolitan Police, John Syme had shown great promise, but in 1909 he fell out with his superiors, accusing them of oppression and injustice.

[4] Police Orders, 30 July 1907.
[5] The police obtained their pensions charter in 1890 and their weekly rest-day in 1900.

Syme, as an inquiry many years later showed, had right on his side, but he lacked discretion. He inspired an agitation in the Press and in Parliament against the senior officers of the force. Disciplinary action was taken against him, and he was dismissed. An uncompromising bigot, he embarked on a vendetta against the Commissioner, Sir Edward Henry, a patriarchal ex-Indian civil servant who administered the force on pro-consular lines. He published libellous pamphlets about Henry and associated himself with Kempster, the founder of the *Police Review*; then in 1913 he started a clandestine union, the Metropolitan Police Union, afterwards styled the National Union of Police and Prison Officers.[6]

What Syme had done was dare to challenge his superiors. As with so many disputes in the police it began over a triviality and escalated. In 1909 two young officers in Pimlico found two men banging on a door demanding to be let in. They were told by the officers to go away, refused and were arrested. They were taken to the police station to be charged under the Metropolitan Police Act with banging on doors without a reasonable excuse. Syme, who was the duty Inspector, discovered that one of them lived at the house. This would have provided the defence of reasonable excuse and he refused the charge.

To have an entry in the refused charge was one of the cardinal sins in the Met in the early years of the century and it was decided the officers should be put on report. Syme went on their behalf to the Superintendent and in turn was reported as being too familiar with the Constables. He then made an allegation that his superior officers were hated for their tyranny. The superiors were cleared and for making a false accusation against a senior officer Syme was reduced to the rank of station Sergeant. Syme said he would appeal to his MP and for this was summoned before a board at Scotland Yard and sacked. He now began a twenty-year campaign to clear his name.

His actions brought down the full weight of the hierarchy and he was prosecuted on a number of occasions for criminal libel. As a result Syme spent much time in Pentonville Prison,

[6] T. A. Critchley, *A History of Police in England and Wales*, p. 184.

often on hunger strike. In 1924 Rayner Goddard, the future Lord Chief Justice, headed a board of inquiry which found that the matter had been clumsily handled but that Syme had no justifiable grievance. Syme, nevertheless, had powerful supporters, including a number of Labour MPs and the *Police Review* which had championed him at some cost; the editor had had to settle a libel claim over allegations in the magazine.

In 1931 the Home Secretary announced that Syme's claims would be dealt with in an adequate manner. He was granted a pension of £72 per annum back-dated to 1909, which meant he received £1,200. 'There has never been any question of Mr Syme's sincerity. It is acknowledged that while he was a police officer he discharged his duties conscientiously, and no stigma of any kind attaches in this settlement to him,' said the Home Secretary, J. R. Clynes. This was well received: 'Thus Mr Syme has triumphed after a strenuous struggle of twenty-two years' duration! Surely an astonishing object-lesson in what may be achieved by perseverance . . . It is mooted Mr Symes may stand for Parliament as a Labour candidate.'[7] This was unlikely, for by then Syme's 'mind was unhinged, and he ended his days, a pitiful creature, throwing bricks through the windows of the Home Office. He died in 1955. Long before this, however, the Police Union had rid itself of so embarrassing a member.'[8]

But Syme had begun to pave the way. Police pay had failed to keep pace with the cost of living, which had doubled during the First World War. Now the police were paid unfavourably in comparison with munitions workers. Despite the risk of retribution in the form of instant dismissal, more and more police, many in the provinces, joined the Union. Critchley writes: '[the police] were an easy prey for the malcontents with mutinous talk. By 1918 many policemen and their families had sunk so low in poverty that they were actually under-nourished and the temptations held out by bribes of food and money must at times have been irresistible.'[9]

By 1918 matters reached a head. The Home Office called a conference to discuss police pay and at the same time there

[7] H. L. Adam, *Behind the Scenes at Scotland Yard*, p. 38.
[8] For a full account of Syme and the Police Union's struggle, see A. Judge, *The Night the Police Went on Strike*.
[9] T. A. Critchley, *A History of Police in England and Wales*, p. 184.

was a move by several of the larger authorities to co-ordinate their rates. Meanwhile the still outlawed Police Union was believing in the power of collective bargaining. Over the years there had been some parliamentary support for the right to confer, notably, if sporadically, from Ramsay MacDonald and Philip Snowden; now the Union had support from the Socialist members. It did not have the support of the Commissioner, Sir Edward Henry, who could not understand why the police should wish to have a union, nor what it could do if there was one.

In August there was a further deterioration in relations between the rank and file police and their elders and betters. A promised pay and pension review did not materialize and on 25 August an officer was dismissed for union activities. Two days later the Police Union made three demands to the Home Secretary: a substantial increase in pay, reinstatement of the dismissed policeman and complete recognition of the Police Union. If the demands were not met by midnight on Wednesday, 28 August, strike action would be threatened. They were not; and on Friday, 30 August, 6,000 from a strength of around 19,000 of the Metropolitan Police went on strike, marching down Whitehall headed by a lone piper. The government tried divide and rule tactics. General Smuts, in the absence of the Home Secretary who had declined to return from his holiday in Somerset, offered to meet two men from each division but not the representatives of the union. In turn the union threatened to bring out the City Police, and did so. Effectively London was defenceless.

The government now invited Charles Duncan, both a Member of Parliament and chairman of the Police Union plus general secretary of the Workers' Union to which the Police Union was affiliated, to negotiate with the strikers on the basis they would have a substantial increase in pay but no recognition of the union. Clearly there had to be some concessions, for both the public and the press were on the side of the police. And whilst concessions there were, the outcome of the meeting the next day, at 10 Downing Street, remains confused. It was certainly agreed that there would be a substantial pay increase and that the dismissed officer would be reinstated; the third, difficult point was that there would be a representative board at Scotland Yard and – this was the problem – possibly the recognition of the union at the end of the war. The government was terrified that if they conceded the right to a union to the police, then the army would want one also. The Bolshevik uprising in Russia had occurred only a few months previously and the thought of reds under beds, particularly army ones, whilst not a slogan for another forty years, was already a fear.

Unfortunately there was no agreed record of what had actually been decided at the meeting and dispute and further bitterness broke out. The Union claimed it had been promised recognition after the war and the Home Secretary denied it. Sir Edward Henry, the Commissioner, resigned that night and was replaced by General Sir Nevil Macready, who had dealt with the miners' strike at Tonypandy in 1910. The General fell out with the police representatives on the board almost immediately. He thought them subversive and in return they considered him autocratic.

After the war, the union requested formal recognition and was refused. By the spring of 1919 marches were taking place in London denouncing Macready as a militarist and calling for his resignation. Special branch members were now required to report on their colleagues' activities. Infiltration was a tactic the good General had already employed with some success in the Glamorgan miners' strike nine years' earlier. The government was simultaneously endeavouring to head off action by legislation. The Desborough Committee appointed on 1 March 1919 had recommended much higher pay which would be standardized for all forces, and machinery for police and police authorities to make representations to the Home Office. At the end of May the Home Secretary announced that a Constable's starting wage would be raised by £2 to £3.10s a week. Legislation was introduced to prevent officers belonging to a trades union but provided for the establishment of the Police Federation, at the same time creating a Police Council as a consultative body. Striking officers would be summarily dismissed. The legislation went swiftly through parliament and was due to complete its passage on 1 August.

The Police Union, fighting for its survival, called a second strike for 31 July. It was not a spectacular success, although a total of 2,364 men responded. There were 1,056 strikers in the Met, 954 in Liverpool and varying numbers from five other forces, ranging from 119 in Birmingham and four less than that in Birkenhead down to one in Wallasey. There was rioting in Liverpool and the troops were called in. The other unions did not keep their promises of support and the strike effectively collapsed within twenty-four hours. All the men were dismissed and for the next thirty years unsuccessfully applied for reinstatement. The Police Union had outlived its function. It died the night of the strike. In many respects it resembled the early American trade union, the International Workers of the World. It too had its successes and its martyrs but ultimately it was replaced by more acceptable negotiators.

Whilst there had been considerable public support for the Met and the rest of the police in their efforts to obtain a decent wage, the tide in public opinion about the force was again just beginning to turn. Throughout the 1920s there were some highly publicized cases involving an eminent archaeologist, a major in the Indian army, an ex-Crown official, an ex-police official of senior rank and finally an ex-MP with considerable political clout. All fell foul of the police. One police historian disposes of the situation quite neatly: 'the worst that can be said of most of the [police] officers concerned was that their actions were sometimes injudicious. Three constables were convicted of giving false evidence; but the majority of the cases which were to provoke an uproar between 1922 and 1928 fell in that very difficult and controversial class involving women who either are of doubtful reputation, or act in a highly indiscreet manner.'[10] Naughty women.

Following the investigation of the last of these indiscreet women, another Royal Commission loomed and as with the 1906 one it involved the treatment of the woman, or rather women, for in part it related to the use of women police officers generally. There had been no place in the New Police for women. Admittedly one had been used to trap an abortioner but this was strictly on a part-time, one-off basis and anyway the subterfuge had been frowned upon. However, during the First World War women were allowed, in limited circumstances, to act as Special Constables. Their main tasks were to keep a look-out for suspicious persons and a light on the beach.[11]

The first official policewoman was Mrs Edith Grant from

[10] D. G. Browne, *The Rise of Scotland Yard*, p. 326.
[11] *The Vote*, 28 August 1914.

Grantham. She appears to have been a motherly body, much of whose duties consisted of keeping Hyde Park free from misbehaviour; the wildlife was not to be frightened. 'When [she] found couples wrapped around each other in the grass of Hyde Park, she would point out the dangers (which were then, of course, considerable) with motherly frankness and appeal to the men to be chivalrous towards the girls. Her manner was such, Miss Peto claims, as to make this perfectly acceptable and they would respond with thanks and desist.'[12]

Towards the end of the First World War it was announced:

A force of women police is to be created for London, officially recognised, under the control of the Commissioner of Metropolitan Police, and subject to the same discipline as the men. This is another 'break through' by women of that long line of positions that were assumed only to be fitting for men.

Women are likely to be firm and efficient constables. Our urban life will be cleaner by the presence of the woman constable.

In the woman constable's dealing with the venal minor male offender against the law she is likely to be less lenient than the policeman and be less inclined to 'look the other way'. Man is apt to be merciful with man – and woman. Woman is not to be cajoled. When a woman has a sense of duty, she is inflexible. There is some amusement in the prospect that those who hear the chimes o'midnight will have to be wary of women police. These would be ill days for Sir John Falstaff.[13]

'And there is little doubt that the mercy and flexibility of the male constable was in direct proportion to the bribe he could extract.'[14] Women officers were thus to be employed mainly in cleaning up the streets and the parks.[15]

[12] J. Lock, *The British Police Woman*, p. 47, quoting Dorothy Peto's *Memoirs*, pp. 16–17.
[13] *Daily Mail*, 3 October 1918.
[14] *The British Police Woman*, p. 89.
[15] Clear up the parks they did. In April 1928, the month of the Savidge incident, sixty-four persons were charged in thirty-three separate cases. In a reply to a question in the House of Commons the Home Secretary said that in only one of the cases was there anything other than police evidence. *Police Review and Parade Gossip*, 22 June 1928.

Meanwhile there were difficulties with police and prostitutes, whom the former considered fair game for convictions or extortion:

In 1924 a sergeant made an entirely unjustifiable arrest of a lady for street corruption and was himself convicted of assaulting her. An unpleasant feature of the case was that the police solicitor endeavoured to put in a report from the Commissioner saying that he had inquired into the charge and exonerated the sergeant.

This irregularity was, of course, repulsed by the magistrate but the sergeant was kept on duty after his caution. He appealed unsuccessfully. A comic feature then came into the matter. A constable got frightfully angry with the sergeant about something and they had a set-to with truncheons in a public street. The local costermongers put up a fund for the defence of the constable who was, against the weight of the evidence, acquitted by the jury, so bad an impression did the sergeant make.[16]

In 1927 there was a report which recommended that prostitutes should no longer face immediate imprisonment and that riotous behaviour, which had previously consisted of touching an arm and saying 'hello dearie', be replaced with the requirement that annoyance actually be proved.

For a time the police sulked, but now they deal with proper cases in a reasonable way. Under these provisions annoyance has to be proved. It is a little disconcerting to a purist in evidence like myself to hear a magistrate inquire of the policeman 'Was he annoyed?', the very issue for the court. I flummoxed a policeman once by asking 'How did he show his annoyance?' But as an old inspector once observed to me, 'Once a policeman knows what is wanted it's all right sir.' Quite soon officers thus interrogated answered 'By the expression of his face', a reply difficult to counter.[17]

That same year a Major Graham Murray was convicted by Mead, the magistrate sitting at Marlborough Street, of being

[16] A. Lieck, *Bow Street World*, pp. 228 ff.
[17] Ibid., p. 220.

drunk and disorderly. The Major appealed and the case against him was stopped at the Inner London Sessions. Later Murray was awarded £500 compensation by a sub-committee of the Street Offences Committee. He did rather better than a lady charged at Bow Street with being a common prostitute. She was able to bring medical evidence which caused the magistrate to stop the case, but it was not until the Home Secretary faced some sharp questioning as to why the good Major should have £500 and a working-class girl should receive no compensation for being charged with being a prostitute, that compensation was paid to her.

In September 1928 two officers, Clayton and Stevens, brought a false charge against a girl, Helen Adele, who 'refused to be complacent' with them. They were later charged and convicted of conspiracy to pervert the course of justice. Then in the same year came the final straw when the Savidge case blew up in the face of the Commissioner. With hindsight it would seem that the original complaint against the officers was probably unjustified. What was wrong was the handling of the subsequent inquiry. As so often, the attitude was 'when in danger or in doubt shout and scream and run about'.

At about 9.45 pm on 23 April 1928, fifty-eight-year-old Sir Leo Chiozzo Money, ex-Liberal MP who had resigned the whip and failed to win a Labour seat, writer on financial affairs and a married man with a daughter, was found sitting under a tree in Hyde Park with Irene Savidge, a twenty-two-year-old from New Southgate; her occupation, appropriately enough for the case, was that of a valve-tester. According to two plain-clothes officers, their behaviour was thought to be likely to offend public decency. 'I am not the usual riff-raff, I am a man of substance. For God's sake let me go,' said Sir Leo when they approached him. If the mention of being a man of substance was an appeal to the pockets as opposed to pocket books of the officers, it fell on deaf ears. He struggled violently all the way to the police station, where he was allowed to telephone his friend, the Home Secretary.

His defence was simple – a complete denial – and the magistrate Henry Cancellor, sitting at Marlborough Street, decided he had heard enough after the evidence of Sir Leo. Cancellor had heard that a man had run after Sir Leo and the police trying to return his umbrella. The police agreed this, and accepted they had not thought to ask the man his name and address. Cancellor dismissed the charge against Money and Miss Savidge and awarded £10 costs against the police. He also criticized them first for not obtaining corroborative evidence, which would seem to have been available from the man with the umbrella and, secondly, for not referring the case to Scotland Yard so the matter could, if necessary, have been dealt with by summons. 'If that had been done,' said Cancellor, 'I think that the case would never have been brought and a great deal of pain would have been spared the defendants.'

The police were outraged. The Divisional Superintendent alleged bias by the magistrate; in fairness to him, magistrates throughout the ages have tended to side with their social equals or superiors. He suggested that there should be a retrial, which showed he knew nothing of the law of *autrefois acquit*,[18] and complained that the magistrate had not heard the evidence of Irene Savidge, which showed he did not understand the right of a court to stop the case when it felt that at any stage there was sufficient doubt to acquit the defendant. The police solicitors seem to have agreed with the beliefs but, pointing out the law, said nothing could be done.[19]

Sir Leo, however, was not one to rest and a question was asked by a Labour member in the House of Commons. What did the Home Secretary propose to do about a case where two persons of good character and position were charged and costs were then awarded against the police? Answer: Sir William Joynson-Hicks proposed to consider – with the appropriate authorities – whether the police were guilty of a breach of their duties or even perjury.

Sir William decided that the case must be investigated by Chief Inspector Collins, a man with thirty-two years' service and, better still, ninety-three judges' commendations to his credit. Unfortunately Collins had not studied the papers in the case of Miss Cass half a century earlier to see the traps into which officers could fall when investigating this sort of allegation. His instructions were to make his inquiries in the following order: first, he was to examine the records relating to the officers; next, he was to interview the officers; and third,

---

[18] By which, in general, once a person has been acquitted on the facts, he or she cannot be retried.
[19] For a fuller account, see J. Lock, *The British Police Woman*, p. 157.

he was to see Miss Savidge. After that he had to see a Miss Egan, who had introduced Miss Savidge to Sir Leo, and then finally Sir Leo himself.

What Collins totally failed to appreciate was the delicacy of the case and the prevailing attitude to womanhood, particularly to a woman who was, as Miss Savidge proved to be, *virgo intacta*. The first two parts of his mission were successfully accomplished, but unfortunately he failed to arrange suitable facilities for interviewing Miss Savidge at her local New Southgate police station. He then sent a car to bring her to Scotland Yard, if she would agree to come. (One can imagine the choice she had in the matter.) In any event she was to be accompanied by the woman Inspector, Lilian Wyles. Collins collected Lilian Wyles from Marylebone, where she had been giving evidence in another indecent exposure case, and according to her memoirs, Collins complained angrily about the requirement that a woman should accompany him.[20] Miss Savidge was collected from her place of work and was refused permission to go home to change. Inspector Wyles was dismissed once they had reached Scotland Yard.

In his turn Sir Leo refused to cooperate. He would not go to the Yard and when Collins went to the mountain he refused to allow 'roving questions as to his past history and his relationship with Miss Savidge'. Collins reported back to the DPP, Archibald Bodkin, who wrote a stiff letter saying that if Money did not toe the line, other steps would have to be taken. When it came to it, the only other steps taken were by Sir Leo. On his behalf a question was asked as to how Miss Savidge could have been taken to Scotland Yard and cross-questioned there about an already closed case without recourse to legal advice or even that of friends.[21]

The following day it was the turn of Inspector Wyles to be scooped up. She was taken to the House of Commons, where she was questioned by a Home Office official. As she says, she was tempted to tell all to obtain revenge for the years of insults from male officers but in the end she said nothing which would harm Collins, who was by now on the rack. After the questioning she was placed in a glassed-in chamber

[20] L. Wyles, *A Woman at Scotland Yard*.
[21] Ibid.

behind the Speaker's chair, where she was mistaken for Irene Savidge. Collins was at first seemingly broken but recovered his composure and demanded Inspector Wyles write a statement at his dictation, something she refused. She said she would write exactly what she had told the Home Secretary 'and of you, nothing but good, which you did not deserve'.

The Home Secretary promised the fullest inquiry and one was held in public at the law courts, with Sir John Eldon Bankes, a former Lord Justice of Appeal, as chairman and two MPs, a Conservative J. J. Withers and a Labour member Hastings Bernard Lees-Smith, comprising the tribunal.

According to Miss Savidge, who was represented by Sir Patrick Hastings KC, with Henry Curtis Bennett KC for Money and Norman Birkett KC for the police, Collins had alternately cajoled and bullied her with remarks such as 'Now you are really a good girl, and you never have had a man, have you? But there are several things one can do without really sinning: do not be afraid to tell us, as we are looking after you.' She complained that he distorted and altered what she had said to suit his statement. He would also take hold of her arm and say things such as 'My dear Irene, are you sure of this?' He would then put his arm around her and hold her hands in a reconstruction of how she and Sir Leo had been sitting. There was certainly an unfortunate incident when the note-taker, a Sergeant Clarke, found there was only one sugar spoon when tea was brought into the room during the four-and-a-half-hour interrogation. According to Miss Savidge Clarke said, 'Now Irene will spoon with me.' His version was, 'Now Irene will use this spoon with me.'

The outcome was that Miss Savidge stood up well during her five and a half hours in the witness box and an intense cross-examination by Birkett, although she admitted that by going to restaurants and the cinematograph house with Money, she was deceiving a young man with whom she was also walking out. In relation to a statement that Sir Leo's hand was on her knee, she said that 'the Inspector suggested it' and she had let it go as she was 'fed up' by that time and felt 'awful' and would have signed 'anything to get away'.

Collins was possibly less convincing. Sir Patrick Hastings got to him early in the cross-examination:

'On May 15 a motor-car, which I think is known in the Force as the fast car – the most important police car – arrived where Miss Savidge works with two policemen and a policewoman in it and another policeman awaiting it?

'Yes.'

'It arrived without the slightest indication to her parents or any of her friends that they were coming?'

'Yes.'

'Was it intended to take that girl to Scotland Yard if possible?'

'Very well, sir, yes.'

Collins denied that he had ever said words to the effect, 'You are a good girl, you have never had a man', agreeing that 'it would have been a most disgusting thing for anyone to say, let alone a police officer'.

A month later the tribunal announced its split decision. Perhaps predictably the chairman and the Conservative member found in favour of the police, completely exonerating them. The demonstration about how Sir Leo sat with the girl did not happen and the remark about being a 'good girl' was not uttered.

We are unable therefore to accept Miss Savidge's statement on the material matters as to which there was a conflict of evidence between her and Chief Inspector Collins and we acquit him of any improper conduct during the taking of Miss Savidge's statement. We are satisfied that the interrogation followed the lines indicated to him by the Director of Public Prosecutions and was not unduly extended.

The Labour member Lees-Smith had something else to say:

The test is the credibility of Miss Savidge on the one side and the two police officers on the other. My conclusion is that Miss Savidge is the more credible witness. The impression that she made in the witness box was that of a frank, simple and somewhat child-like witness, whose evidence remained unshaken under cross-examination. The police officers did not give the impression that they were equally frank in their evidence, but denied both the probable and improbable with equal force. The mechanical precision with which the chief police witnesses corroborated every detail of each other's statements cast suspicion upon their evidence.[22]

Despite the exoneration of the police by the majority of the tribunal the affair lingered on. The best thing that came out of it were important recommendations for how witnesses and defendants who might appear in subsequent criminal proceedings should be interrogated. The person should be clearly informed beforehand of the nature of the statement and the possible consequences involved in making it; the statement should normally be taken at the person's home and not at his or her place of employment and, in the case of a statement to be taken from a woman by the police which 'involves matters intimately affecting her morals, a woman should be present unless the woman being interrogated expressed a desire to the contrary.'

The Labour opposition was not satisfied and the debate raged until on 11 August the government, under heavy fire, announced the usual sovereign remedy for their ills, a Royal Commission. This one was

to consider the general powers and duties of police in England and Wales in the investigation of crimes and offences, including the functions of the Director of Public Prosecutions and the police respectively; to inquire into the practice followed in interrogating or taking statements from persons interviewed in the course of the investigation of crime; and to report whether, in their opinion, such powers and duties are properly exercised and discharged, with due regard to the rights and liberties of the subject, the interests of justice, and the observance of the Judges' Rules both in the letter and the spirit; and to make any recommendations necessary in respect of such powers and duties and their proper exercise.

When it came to it the Director of Public Prosecutions, Sir

22 Montgomery Hyde, *Norman Birkett*, pp. 229–44, contains a full account of the hearing before the tribunal. The then enormous legal expenses of Miss Savidge, amounting to some £1,449. 7s.8d, were paid for by the Metropolitan Police.

Archibald Bodkin, resigned. In a lecture given in 1979 Sir
Thomas Hetherington explained Bodkin's situation:

> It may well have seemed, from the way he was instructing
> the police to carry out their investigation, that his aim was to
> show that Sir Leo and Miss Savidge had after all committed
> the offence of which they had been acquitted, rather than to
> discover whether there was evidence that the police officers
> had committed perjury. However, there is no doubt that
> the criticism which Bodkin had to undergo at the time –
> and subsequently – had a very severe impact on him. The
> challenge to his integrity, unjustified as it may well have been,
> was a shock to him . . . There is no direct evidence that the
> Savidge incident led to Bodkin's resignation. Nevertheless,
> not long afterwards he suddenly summoned all members of
> his staff to his office one morning and announced that he
> was departing that afternoon.[23]

General Horwood, the Assistant Commissioner of Police for
the Metropolis, also resigned.

And the other players? According to Wyles, Collins had been
in such a state before the hearing at the tribunal, his moods
swinging between elation and depression, that she was directed
by the Chief Constable to keep him calm at all costs. She had
refused him anything from the 'small stock of cheering liquid
of which I constituted myself bartender'. In retrospect Wyles
clearly lied at the tribunal to protect Collins and used the case
to show that she was really one of the boys who could be relied
on to back them up when outsiders sought to throw dirt at the
force. Joan Lock, herself a policewoman and ignoring the fairly
humble background of Irene Savidge, believes she was right to
do so: 'who could blame her or them when truth and justice had
been held in such contempt by their betters?' Later, in her book,
Wyles recanted and agreed with what Irene Savidge had said.

Collins never made it to Superintendent, the next rank
up. There were, however, consolations. He was asked to
investigate a murder 'in the country', where the local police

---

[23] Upjohn Memorial Lecture 1979, quoted in Joshua Rozenberg, *The Case for the Crown*, pp. 24–5.

were itching for him to interrogate the suspected woman. He does seem to have profited by his earlier mistake. He refused to see her until a policewoman was present. He also received substantial damages for libel relating to the case.

On the other hand Sir Leo Chiozza Money pushed his luck that bit too far. In September 1933 he appeared at Epsom Magistrates' Court on two summonses arising out of an incident in a train on the Southern Railway. According to a report in the *Daily Telegraph* it was alleged he forced his attentions on a Miss Ivy Ruxton, a thirty-year-old shop assistant, and that he had embraced her against her will. By this time Sir Leo's friends in high circles had had enough and he was fined 40 shillings. This time no parliamentary tribunal was called.

Now, with hindsight, it is possible to reconstruct the Savidge affair in a number of ways. Given the circumstances of the arrest it is certainly possible that the arresting officers believed what they saw and that deliberate perjury can be eliminated. On the other hand this had the makings of a cheap arrest. Two officers saw an elderly man and a young woman under a tree late in the evening. Easy pickings. What is absolutely clear is that the behaviour of Collins when he investigated the arrest has all the hallmarks of a police cover-up. He was determined to exculpate his officers and, at some cost to himself, he did so. There was no need to arrest Miss Savidge as he did. There was no need to dismiss Inspector Wyles from the room. The interrogation today of a young woman for four and a half hours without a solicitor by two male officers would cause the greatest suspicion, let alone the exclusion of statements under the Codes of Practice set out in the Police and Criminal Evidence Act 1984. We now know Inspector Wyles lied, possibly for the good of the force, probably for her own benefit. Bent for self, bent for the job. It was part of an ever repeating tapestry.

As if that was not sufficient, another major public scandal came at the end of the year when a uniform Sergeant, George Goddard, stationed at Vine Street and detailed to clean up vice in the West End, did so with such success that when he was investigated he was found, on pay of £6. 15s. 0d. a week, to have a £2,000 house. He also had £500 in a Selfridges deposit box and £12,000 in an account in Pall Mall. He had been a police officer for exactly twenty-eight years.

On 23 September 1928, the Commissioner for Police received a letter:

Dear Sir,
I am desirous of bringing a matter of great public importance to your direct notice in order that you may cause immediate necessary action to be taken. It concerns the activities of Sergeant Goddard at Marylebone Station, who not only accepts bribes for services made and offered, but has financial interests in some of London's most notorious nightclubs. Goddard resides in his own freehold residence in Streatham, and he also owns a beautiful Chrysler motor-car. His brother-in-law is also in business provided by money supplied by Goddard. No notice was taken of my last letter to the authorities, and before approaching the political candidate for this constituency I am prompted to write this letter to you. I suggest that you call on officers under your personal control to inquire into this communication.

From where had the money come? Sir Percival Clarke, for the Crown, said it had come from the person in the dock with him, Kate Meyrick, the undoubted queen of the nightclubs. Known throughout the upper echelons of English society as Ma, she ruled principally at the Forty-Three Club in Gerrard Street,[25] although in her time she opened dozens of clubs including Dalton's (in Leicester Square), Brett's, the Silver Slipper and, after her release from Holloway, the Bunch of Keys. She was by no means a conventional Irish beauty; sad-eyed, drab and dowdy, according to some reports, she would sit behind her desk in the narrow entrance hall collecting the £1 entrance fee. She was an astute businesswoman, even though she had not taken up her career until her forties. From the profits she

[25] She was immortalized as Ma Maybrick in the novel *Brideshead Revisited* by Evelyn Waugh. Part of her fortune came from her friendship with the Belgian financier Alfred Lowenstein, who was a patron of her clubs and who advised her on her investments. Lowenstein died in the most peculiar circumstances. Whilst flying across the Channel in his private plane he fell out. The pilot put down on the nearest French beach and launched an immediate search but the body was never found. Various theories were advanced and in her memoirs Mrs Meyrick hints at suicide. Murder was eliminated and the most popular theory is that he mistook the exit door for the lavatory. Curiously, the aircraft from which he had fallen crashed in South Africa in 1931, killing the pilot Commander Glen Kidston.

educated her eight children well. One son went to Harrow, the daughters to Roedean. Time and again her clubs were raided, mainly for selling drinks after hours and running unlicensed premises.

Kate Meyrick had first gone to prison in 1924 and continued to do so sporadically throughout much of the next decade, but her most celebrated appearance in court was in 1929 with Goddard. During a six months' sentence in 1928 when she was visited in Holloway prison by an Inspector, she declined to answer questions. On her release she fled to Paris, heard of the warrant for her arrest and with some style telegraphed the Chief Commissioner and the Chief Magistrate, Sir Charles Biron, to announce her return on the Boulogne-Folkestone packet.[26]

Goddard certainly could not have come by his money honestly and it was said he had acquired his considerable fortune by gifts from Mrs Meyrick in return for tip-offs over raids. Initially he said he had obtained his house and motor-car through thrift. This he then denied throughout the trial, maintaining he was no more than a successful gambler – £7,000 had come from winnings on the turf – and an investor in Silbermans, a music publishing business, which had netted him another £5,000. Ever the astute businessman, he had invested money in a scheme to sell rock – edible rather than audible – at the Wembley Exhibition of 1924 and then had dabbled on the foreign exchange market. These ventures had produced £4,000 and £2,000 each. He had, he said, reported irregularities in the running of the Meyrick clubs.

He was done for by the evidence that a secret observation had been kept on him by senior officers, so that he had not been able to tip off the nightclub queen. Nor had he been totally discreet. He would give a young Constable, John Wilkins, who later gave evidence against him, £1 or 30 shillings, telling him he was going to Regent's Park to meet Mrs Meyrick. Fourteen £100 notes in the Pall Mall safe deposit box were traced to a restaurant keeper in Soho and thirteen £10 notes to Mrs Meyrick, with a further nine attributable to her manager Luigi Ribuffi. Goddard was also alleged to have been taking sweeteners from Mrs Gadda, who 'kept a certain house in Greek Street, Soho'. He was

[26] K. Meyrick, *Secrets of the 43*, p. 186.

sentenced to eighteen months' hard labour and ordered to pay £2,000. Mrs Meyrick received fifteen months' hard labour.

On his release Goddard was back in court, this time as plaintiff. After his conviction the Commissioner of Police had, somewhat prematurely, confiscated all his money, claiming it to be the property of the Crown. In fact Goddard had been convicted of taking only some £900 in bribes and an order was made that a substantial part of the money be returned to him. He retired to the country and lived off his investments.

After her sentence Kate Meyrick returned to the West End, opening fresh clubs until in 1932, following yet another spell in Holloway, she promised to stop. She died the next year at the age of fifty-six. Dance bands throughout the West End observed a two minutes' silence in her memory.[27]

That tribute may be the attractive part of the story. What was unattractive was the fact that as early as 1922 a young officer, Josling, who had arrested a bookmaker, had been warned by Goddard to 'leave the betting boys alone'. In return Goddard would 'see him all right'. The young officer reported the matter to his seniors, who charged him with making false statements about Goddard and dismissed him from the force. Once again the questions which went unanswered are first, how did Goddard manage to deceive his superiors for so long, and secondly, is it possible there were no other officers involved with him?

It was a question asked, and partially answered, almost immediately after the trial:

> But the one thing that mystifies one most of all is how an officer in Goddard's humble position – that of a mere sergeant – was able to carry on such an extensive system of 'graft' without being unmasked or in any serious degree interfered with. That is the real mystery of the Goddard case. However, there are certain thin portions of the veil of obscurity through which one may get unpleasant glimpses of the truth.[28]

But neither the author nor anyone else ever cared to lift

[27] A. Tietjen, *Soho*, p. 138.
[28] H. L. Adam, *CID*, p. 30.

that veil. 'Of course,' says writer Anthony Judge, 'at that time police discipline was rigid. It is laughable that he could be thought to control corruption on that scale. He must have been protected.'[29] It is interesting to note that in 1922 the police had managed to obtain an apology from the *Daily Graphic*, which had alleged that certain gambling houses in London 'can afford to bribe the police to a certain extent'.

Suggestions that Goddard was a blackmailer were refuted. According to H. L. Adam,

> What he was really guilty of was the offence of receiving bribes, which is quite a different thing. The people who run night clubs make enormous profits and they can well afford if it suits their purpose, to 'buy' anybody's silence by means of liberal payment. Let me illustrate this with a little incident that actually happened. While the Goddard case was pending, Scotland Yard had occasion to send an officer to one of these clubs for the purpose of obtaining certain information. Directly the officer presented himself at the club the proprietress went straight to a cash-box, took out a roll of notes, representing quite a large sum of money, and passed them across to the officer. The latter observed, as he pushed them back again, 'No, thank you, I'm not here for that sort of thing!' The woman, however, would not accept this intimation, and actually thrust them in the officer's pocket. When the latter got outside he pushed the notes back through the letter-box.[30]

But why did he not arrest her for attempted bribery?

The second Royal Commission of the century again more or less found in total favour of the police. 'The acceptance of tips for services rendered or indulgencies allowed by the police is liable to create in the public mind an impression of venality, which is readily expanded from small to large things until it is held to cover the whole sphere of police duty.' However, police corruption 'where it exists seems to be mainly associated with the enforcement of laws which are out of harmony with public opinion, or in enforcing which the police are compelled by lack

[29] Interview with author. The happier side of the story is that Josling became a teacher and ended his career a much loved headmaster.
[30] H. L. Adam, *CID*, p. 28.

of adequate powers to have recourse to unsatisfactory methods of detection.'

As Douglas Browne commented, 'Among 60,000 men there were bound to be occasional cases of misconduct. The majority had never been better behaved, and the public was well protected against the actions of the rare exceptions. As a whole the police were competent and highly efficient. It had all been said before.'[31]

Shortly afterwards Lord Byng, former commander of the Third Army in France and Governor General of Canada, became the twelfth Commissioner. There were cries (unjustified and foolish, says Browne) that he had been appointed so the force could be disciplined. But he immediately retired several senior officers, and he did tighten discipline. He also took steps to muzzle press criticism, seen as unfounded and unwarranted in the Savidge and other cases, and approached Lord Riddell, then chairman of the Newspaper Proprietors' Association, to such effect that for two or three years the doings of the Metropolitan Police almost ceased to be news.[32]

Whether, in retrospect, that actually helped is another matter, for the Met was not regarded as trustworthy by other forces, let alone the public. Frank Williamson, a former Chief Inspector HMI, recalled:

In 1927 I was walking through the police station yard at Northampton with my hand in my father's, he being the Chief Constable of Northampton. The Exchange cinema had been broken into the night before and they had some information about two men who'd stayed at the Queen's Hotel and they were cockneys. Before my very ears, I would have been ten, my father said to his Detective Inspector, 'These two

---

[31] D. G. Browne, *The Rise of Scotland Yard*, p. 338. The majority did not include PCs Arthur Cheshire and Joseph Lucas, who each received a sentence of six months' hard labour for receiving a corrupt gift of silver coins from an Edwin Bottom at Goodwood Races. 'Let this be a lesson to others,' said Mr Justice Horridge, 'and let us hope it will do something to purify the Police Force.' It is clear that Lucas and Cheshire were not alone in their dealings. Bottom had a piece of paper on which the following tariff was written: 'Sergeant 5s, Bizzy 5s, Free Flatty, Extra Flatty 2s, Sergeant Extra 2s.6d. and Private Flatty 2s.6d.' A bizzy was racecourse slang for a detective, a flatty a uniformed constable and a private flatty meant a detective constable. *Police Review and Parade Gossip*, 18 March 1927.
[32] D. G. Browne, *CID*, p. 343.

men are in London, go and interview them and don't tell the Metropolitan Police you're coming.' That was the first indication I ever had. It was years before I ever thought of being a policeman.

Certainly one officer thought the arrival of Byng was of benefit to the force:

In recent years the underpaid police were thought less likely to be tempted to corruption if their pay was increased. I am not so sure. In our case it was a question of example. We knew that many, though not all, of our superiors were taking bribes. It went higher than that. After the Commissioner's sudden retirement we learnt that, among other things, free cases of whisky were delivered regularly to his house; and that the dentist with the police contract, a bad-tempered snob, was exposed charging full dentures for the teeth to be pulled. We were comparatively well paid in those days, and had we been given higher wages I don't suppose we should have decided bookmakers' half-crowns were no longer necessary, any more than rich men decide not to go to endless trouble and ingenuity to dodge the taxes they can well afford to pay. When our superior officers were known to be honest, the majority of us followed suit.[33]

Byng, who retired through ill health, was replaced in 1931 by Hugh Trenchard, a Commissioner described by Ascoli, who could never be said to have been a hostile historian, as 'constantly alive to the extent of CID corruption and his correspondence during 1934 is a curious commentary on his intellectual cowardice. The man who could talk to Kings seemed frightened of corrupt constables.' Nor was he really able to handle the CID. Trenchard, while deluding himself that he had stopped the rot, constantly shirked the issue. Detectives played the game according to their own rules, confident that neither their superiors nor the courts would accept the word of known or convicted criminals.

In 1934 Trenchard wrote to Ramsay Macdonald that 'the state of jealous rivalry . . . which has so long existed between the CID

33 H. Daley, *This Small Cloud*, p. 109.

and the uniform branch is gradually being put to an end, and the two branches integrated into one harmonious whole'. He was deceiving himself, says Ascoli, who adds, 'indeed many of his reforms went far towards widening a rift which had existed for sixty years'.[34] One of those reforms was the ill fated endeavour for the last time to establish an officer class.

Trenchard took over the role of Commissioner on 2 November 1931. His life had been devoted to the Royal Air Force and the position was not wholly a pleasing one. It was put to him that the police were going through a difficult period and needed firm leadership. Additionally the Royal Commission had made numerous recommendations. Trenchard was not moved by the appeal and it appears to have been only at the intercession of King George V that he was persuaded. According to Ascoli his arrival was not that 'of a new broom but of a seismic disturbance. He questioned, probed, hectored, and bullied. A constabulary wag described him as the only man he had met who would never take yes for an answer. Yet with his sharp brain and eye for detail went a curious inability to communicate clearly, with the result that he was often incoherent in conversation and unintelligible when dictating.'[35]

A note in his papers identifies the areas which particularly concerned him:

> I found that the state of discipline in the force was not good. There was a great deal of discontent with the conditions of service.
>
> The Police Federation was holding 480 meetings a year and this had been going on for 12 years. The Police Act of 1919 only sanctioned 12 meetings a year of one day only.
>
> Many police constables were still patrolling the beats which were laid down by Sir Robert Peel a hundred years before.
>
> The Statistical Branch, if it could be called such, did not show where crime was most prevalent and was completely out of date.
>
> There was no map-room.
>
> There was no scientific laboratory.
>
> There was no welfare officer.

---

[34] D. Ascoli, *The Queen's Peace*, p. 240.
[35] Ibid., p. 228.

The facilities for sport and recreation were completely inadequate.

The police section houses . . . were appalling, the married quarters even worse.

There was a very large proportion of constables compared with officers.

There was too much corruption.

There was too much tipping.[36]

The Royal Commission of 1929 had specifically frowned on 'tipping', as had the earlier one of 1906. Now Trenchard decided to try to eliminate it once and for all and the Metropolitan Police Act 1933 proscribed the practice. It was a long-held custom, going back to Victorian days when it may have been officially recognized – there is some conflicting evidence – to hire policemen, but being employed in uniform outside duty hours led to all kinds of abuse. Much of the duty was performed at the new greyhound racing tracks, which were then, in London, firmly under the control of the Sabini brothers from Saffron Hill, who ran horseracing, greyhound tracks and nightclubs. They had controlled the racetracks by force for well over a decade, fending off their arch rivals, the Brummagem Boys. Ex-Inspector Tom Divall, who had had a long and unhealthy relationship with both the Sabinis and the Brummagen Boys during their power struggle, had little good to say about greyhound racing:

> My advice to working men and women is to cut it out. Have nothing to do with any of it; from what I have seen at the meetings . . . it is just about as straight as a butcher's hook . . . Some of the good bookmakers are disgusted with greyhound racing. One told me he was getting a hundred pounds a week out of it, but he would like to see it smashed up. Another rattling good fellow told me that he was doing well at it but nevertheless it was a dirty game and it was terrible for the working man, especially to those who could not control themselves.[37]

---

[36] Ascoli points out that Trenchard cannot have been correct in relation to Peel's beats. These were devised by Charles Rowan but the London geography had changed over the century so that none of the original beats remained.

[37] T. Divall, *Scallywags and Scoundrels*, p. 225.

And here were London's finest making, according to Trenchard, about £1,000 a week collectively from policing the tracks in their spare time. Small wonder there were opportunities for further graft and corruption.[38]

Accordingly, the Act provided that 'the legitimate requirements of all the employers concerned will be met by the supply of such police as are necessary, on payment to the Police Fund at the approved rates'. Such was the new law; and who shall say how many half-crowns continued to pass from hand to hand? asks Ascoli wryly.[39] Indeed, if Trenchard thought he had stamped on this sort of thing he was sadly mistaken. Until the end of Covent Garden market in the centre of London there was a thriving trade in unofficial policing. A Chief Superintendent in 1992 recalled those days:

I don't think the police thought of it as corruption with a capital C. In the Covent Garden market you had cart-minders, and lorries could park if you said they could. Then when the market finished it became a derestricted area but between 8.30 and 9.00 for the moment car parkers had to pay and the cart-minders took money from private motorists and paid the sergeants a percentage.

When I was on duty I was given £5 by a lorry driver and I said, 'What's that for?' and he said, 'I've given it to the wrong person.' Later the sergeant said, 'I think you've got something for me, son.'

The same applied to filming in the street. In theory forms should be made out and fees should be paid by cheque to the Finance Branch but money was paid in a packet to F department. The best example was getting the traffic stopped on Sunday morning in the Aldwych for a film and over £1,000 was paid in cash.

The comment by Ascoli that Trenchard was frightened of corrupt Constables seems a little unfair. In his shake-up of men and institutions he uncovered substantial evidence of graft in high places. 'With regard to the attitude of the police,' he wrote to the Home Secretary on 21 September 1933, 'the older men

---

[38] A. Boyle, *Trenchard*, p. 664.
[39] D. Ascoli, *The Queen's Peace*, p. 235.

are still – as I said they would be – very sulky. Two of the three superintendents who were told to go in six months' time have sent in their resignations to go in a month. So have one or two chief inspectors.' He added, 'It will be a good thing when they have gone, but it will be better still if I can only get in some chief inspectors who are gentlemen to keep an eye on what is happening. I have found out a good deal more since I saw you, and it is really important that I should have some more people I can trust in the districts.'

Certain CID officers had been found taking bribes. A Superintendent had been dismissed and had appealed. Then came a case which worried Trenchard considerably. It also says something about the accessibility of the Commissioner to the public in those days and the fairly amateur way in which matters were handled over what seems to be a confusion between a criminal prosecution and a civil suit. Trenchard wrote in a letter to Sir John Gilmour, the Home Secretary:

> You may be interested to know of another piece of roguery. Norman Kendal, in charge of the CID, says it's one of the worst cases he has known. The other night, at home, I was called up on the phone by a man called Watson who said he had been a notorious crook and that he was – to use his own language – being 'bled white' by certain senior officers of the CID. In fact he was being blackmailed. My wife, who pretended to be the secretary, talked to him on the phone and we eventually fixed up a meeting between this man and Sir Francis Griffith, my new man here.
>
> With the information received, Kendal arranged a trap to be set for the senior officers whose names had now been given by Watson, and a few hours later we arrested a first-class detective-sergeant and a second-class detective-sergeant in company with this man who, after they'd had drinks together, handed over to the two detectives some money we had already marked and given to Watson. Watson vowed he had been paying money out like this for some six weeks.
>
> It is really rather a horrible case because Watson is really, I fancy, living on money which is coming from unfortunate unemployed persons with very little means. The detectives must have known this . . . I am now told by the Director of Public Prosecutions, and all my legal people that we cannot

put the detectives in the dock. We can only dismiss them, as legally there is no offence we can convict them of in a civil court . . . Though Kendal hopes there are no more like it, I feel there are more than we think. We just have not enough people to unearth them.[40]

From the information garnered from his tours of police stations Trenchard was depressed by the number of elderly time-serving Constables simply awaiting their pensions, as well as coming to the firm belief that corruption was endemic.

It seems clear that corruption was on a grand scale at the time and, if one accepts the belief that the police were riddled with masonry, brother officer protected brother officer. Reginald Morrish, a Met officer from 1911 to 1937, worked in the CID for sixteen of those years. Before he died, having served as senior instructor at Hendon Police College, he burned all his papers. His son Ivor wrote:

During the whole of my early life at home, including a period in which we lived at a very busy police station in South London, my father's chief topics of conversation were the police, religion, bribery and corruption (which he saw as rife at all levels in the police force) and freemasonry. The one thing which seemed to worry him most of all was the connection which he felt existed between freemasonry and corruption, and between freemasonry and self-advancement in the force. In his view there was no doubt about these connections . . .

The most common expressions used by my father in relation to work were 'he is on the take', 'he is taking backhanders', 'he is receiving the drop', until I personally (quite wrongly?) came to equate being 'on the square' with being amenable to bribes, corruption and perjury, so often did he use these phrases in juxtaposition.[41]

In August 1933 Leopold Harris, a notorious fire-raiser, was sentenced to fourteen years' imprisonment after pleading guilty to eighteen counts of arson, conspiracy to commit

[40] A. Boyle, *Trenchard*, p. 640.
[41] M. Short, *Inside the Brotherhood*, p. 271.

arson, conspiracy to defraud and obtaining money by false pretences. His brother David had received a term of five years following his conviction on two counts of arson. Six months later both Leopold and David Harris were interviewed at length in Maidstone Prison by Superintendent George Yardell over allegations that senior police officers, mainly from the East End, had suppressed evidence in return for bribes, participated in mock burglaries for insurance purposes and dropped charges in exchange for cash. Harris told the investigating officer how money had been handed over at a billiard hall in the East End and at a police sports ground. He named two Chief Constables, six Superintendents and three Chief Inspectors. No prosecutions were ever brought.

Trenchard's biographer writes:

> Few senior officers at headquarters realised the depths of his horror at the corrupt practices of individual members of the CID and uniformed branch. His gift for nosing out the facts and keeping them to himself, or when disciplinary action had to be taken, confiding in only one or two close collaborators like Drummond or Kendal, proved an unmixed asset. Offenders were usually apprehended without warning. Yet his biographer has heard men who now hold some of the biggest police posts question whether Trenchard did not exaggerate the amount of corruption prevalent in the Metropolitan Force at a time when they themselves were novices. Allowing for his own lofty personal standards, and for his life-long belief that 'nothing is worse than the corruption of the best', these latter-day critics err in disallowing Trenchard credit for being able to judge how far the rot had gone; many did not commit the unforgivable crime of being caught; and those who did represented only a fraction of the culprits.
>
> 'You can't measure corruption as exactly as you can measure crime,' he told his biographer. 'But you can smell it, and you can prevent occasions for it. I had time enough to deal only with the flagrant cases and to hope that the uncaught people would profit by the example I made of those to mend their ways.'[42]

[42] A. Boyle, *Trenchard*, pp. 641–2.

It was in part to counter this that Trenchard devised the direct entry system of the middle classes into the upper echelons of the force – junior Station Inspectors – through the Police College at Hendon, something which Peel had eschewed and the force as a whole deeply resented and ridiculed. In November 1933 the rules for admission were published to an accompaniment of derisive cheers. Candidates were required to present themselves with a dinner jacket suit, four dress shirts and patent leather shoes. There were over 105 applications for the twelve places available to those from outside the police force. Cadets had fifteen months of intensive training, which included six months on the beat. Of the next year twenty-nine candidates entering the college, twenty came from the police themselves. Had Trenchard's scheme been left in operation the Metropolitan Police would have become a self-supporting profession producing its own leaders by the mid-1950s. It was not permitted to be so. Trenchard's structure was dismantled and the college closed in 1939 with the outbreak of war. By then the competitive examination for entry had been abolished. It had been recommended that direct entry candidates should serve one year on the beat before entering the college and that the upper age of Hendon men drawn from the force should be raised by four years to thirty.

4

1945–1964

During and for some years after the war, so far as the public was concerned, the police were epitomized by George Dixon, the officer who, in the guise of Jack Warner, was gunned down by that young tearaway, Dirk Bogarde, near the Metropolitan Music Hall, Edgware Road, in the film *The Blue Lamp*. If ever there was a golden age of policing, this was it. There was no point in criminals suggesting that the police had fabricated evidence, that their confessions were not what they had seemed; the magistrates, or the jury guided by the trial judge, would not believe them. The police were 'our police' and whatever they said and did was beyond both reproach and question.

But at the time when the Metropolitan Police should have been self-supporting if Trenchard's scheme had been allowed to flourish, there were considerable ripples under the calm surface both in the capital and in the provincial forces. The middle to late 1950s saw the beginning of a series of crises for the police throughout the country. For a start, if the authorities had had their eyes open and been able to do their multiplication tables, they might have cared to consider the case of a Chief Inspector who died in the mid-1950s leaving a six-figure sum amassed on pay of £8 a week. Around the same time, in 1955, came one of the first, albeit small corruption cases. It involved a police officer, a burglar and a solicitor, and would have far-reaching repercussions.

Ben Canter was one of the solicitors who had acted for the notorious Messina brothers, who controlled vice in Soho up to the 1950s. He was now acting for Joseph Grech,

90

another Maltese, who was sent to prison for three years for a housebreaking offence. Grech had seemingly had an unshakable defence. Part of the evidence against him had been that the key to the burgled premises had been found on him, but Grech maintained that it fitted his own front door and therefore was of no significance. The jury found it was. From his cell, Grech unloaded a series of legal bombs. He had, he said, given a Morris Page around £150 to hand to a Detective Sergeant Robert Robertson, the officer in charge of the initial case, who made the key to the burgled premises available so that a locksmith could make a lock to be fitted to Grech's front door. There was to have been a further £150 paid to Robertson on an acquittal. Grech also alleged that Robertson had coached Ben Canter about the questions to be put at the trial.

When Robertson, Page and Canter appeared at the Old Bailey charged with conspiracy to pervert the course of justice, Grech unloaded some more bombs. His conviction, he said, had been brought about by perjured evidence of other officers acting on the instructions of an Inspector Charles Jacobs, attached to West End Central. Jacobs, he said, had asked him for £2,000 so that none of his flats or brothels would be raided. After negotiations the terms had been set at £500 down and £30 a week. Cantor, said Grech, had been the bagman, taking the £100 to give to Jacobs. According to Grech, Cantor came back saying, 'He wants £500.'

When he came to give evidence Cantor was in difficulties over his relationship with Tony Micalleff, a brother-in-law of the Messinas, who had been accepted as a surety in the original case by Robertson:

> 'Can you imagine any honest policeman agreeing to take Micalleff as a surety for this man Grech?'
> 'That is a difficult question to answer.'
> 'I think it is a simple question. Try to answer it . . .'
> 'It depends on the circumstances.'

Cantor received two years' imprisonment, as did Robertson; the intermediary, Morris Page, fifteen months. Robertson had apparently met Page whilst working in the Ghost Squad. This was a squad of young officers either new to the force or from a different district whose duty was to mix with the underworld posing as genuine members and to report back what they had learned. Although the Ghost Squad was officially disbanded by 1957, there is no doubt something very similar has continued to operate on perhaps a more informal basis, with officers either working undercover on specific cases or occasionally being sent to infiltrate a specific gang.

On 17 November 1955 the *Daily Mail* revealed that Detective Superintendent Bert Hannam had lodged a report with the Commissioner, Sir John Nott-Bower, revealing 'a vast amount of bribery and corruption among certain uniformed officers attached to West End Station'. According to Hannam's report, the corruption involved 'club proprietors, prostitutes, gaming-house owners, brothel-keepers and men living on immoral earnings'. It appeared that Hannam had interviewed no fewer than forty men serving prison sentences arising out of West End vice. 'The extent of corruption can be gauged by the fact that it was found that some uniformed patrolmen in the vice-ridden streets of Soho were receiving up to £60 a week in bribes.'

Hannam found, so the article said, that 'evidence was "cooked" by police officers to benefit accused people. Details of previous convictions were suppressed in many cases so that men standing on charges were fined nominal sums instead of going to prison.' Under a heading 'Tipped Off?' readers were treated to the following:

Gaming houses, where faro and chemin de fer were being played quite openly, were tipped off at a fee when a raid was to take place. Proprietors were warned to get 'mugs' in on a certain day, so that the regular customers could escape arrest. Brothel-keepers were told that certain evidence could be adjusted for a price. Huge sums of money changed hands. The 'adjustment' was for an officer to say in evidence that upon the raid taking place he found a number of fully clothed women on the premises, whereas, in fact, they were nude. That gave the premises an air of respectability – and halved the fine.

The hundreds of prostitutes who infest the West End streets are included in the bribery racket.

One officer is pointed out by them to be the richest policeman in the Force.

Most of these unfortunate girls appear on a special 'roster' due for appearance at a magistrates' court on a certain day for the usual £2 fine for soliciting. If the day does not happen to suit the woman, a 'fee' is paid for postponement.

Nott-Bower acted swiftly. Summoning effectively the whole of C division at West End Central station, he climbed on to two tables and gave his men a pep-talk:

I wish to tell you how much I deplore the imputations which have recently been made in the press which reflect on the reputation of the whole force and, in particular, all of C division.

In one of today's papers reference has been made to certain statements regarding the officers of C division in a report submitted to me by Detective-Superintendent Herbert Hannam.

I want it to be known that there is no truth whatever in this, and that none of the subjects referred to in that report have been so much as mentioned in any report submitted to me by the Superintendent.

There was something of what would now be called a damage limitation exercise approach from the authorities. In a statement to the press, Nott-Bower stated: 'The Metropolitan Police are a fine and conscientious body of men and women whose good relations with the public whom they serve may be impaired by irresponsible charges made against them.' He went on to deny that 450 men, practically the whole of C division, might be transferred from central London. 'In fact no transfers are under consideration.'

There were, however, 'certain matters under rigorous investigation which might lead to disciplinary action and criminal proceedings', said Sir Hugh Lucas-Tooth, Under-Secretary, Home Office. 'It is deplorable that such things should be said at a time when owing to a serious shortgage of manpower all officers were working overtime to fulfil their duties.' There was no truth in suggestions that 'many officers' had come under suspicion. Certain confidential papers had, it was true, gone missing but no ' "top secret" or even "secret" papers have been missed from Scotland Yard. Those that were found in a house have no security importance whatever.'

The next day Sir Lawrence Dunne, then Chief Magistrate, appeared at Bow Street and spoke out against 'reckless and irresponsible allegations': 'The aim could not be other than to sap the confidence of the public in law enforcement, both outside and, perhaps of even greater significance, inside this court.' He went on to exculpate C division, adding that the newspaper article so far as it purported to reproduce Hannam's report was 'utterly misleading and most mischievous'. He had not, he said, read the report. And in the House of Commons Sir Hugh Lucas-Tooth commented that the 'general accusations made in certain quarters against the police are unwarranted and unsubstantiated'.

In fact, there is every reason to believe that, with the exception of one or two sentences, the article was substantially accurate.[1] The newspapers were not satisfied. Cassandra in the *Daily Mirror*[2] and the then *Manchester Guardian* both rose in defence of the *Mail*. 'The Police Commissioner, the magistrates and the Home Office should reserve some of their congratulations for the day when Central London is cleansed of blackguards, thieves, and pimps who publicly flaunt their power and their riches,' wrote Cassandra.

In December 1955 it was revealed that the wardrobe locker of a Detective Sergeant who had been assisting Detective Superintendent Stephen Glander (who was either helping Hannam or working independently on an inquiry investigating 'allegations of professional misconduct among policemen') had been forced. Papers had been disturbed but nothing had been taken. An inquiry which involved a number of officers submitting their fingerprints for comparison seems to have come to nothing.

In January 1956 a Detective Sergeant employed in the central records office of Scotland Yard was charged with stealing a file and communicating it to the man to whom it referred.

The next month Inspector Reuben Jacobs was dismissed the force. A disciplinary board had found him guilty of assisting a prostitute to obtain premises, failing to account for a prisoner's property and failing to disclose in court a man's previous

---

[1] S. Chibnell, *Law and Order News*, p. 163.

[2] Cassandra, the Greek goddess who had the gift of prophecy coupled with the curse that no one would believe her, was the name taken by the *Mirror*'s journalist in his famous columns. He was sued, successfully, by Liberace over an article which implied Liberace was homosexual.

conviction. Jacobs took it hard and applied to the Divisional Court to quash the conviction on the grounds that by reason of his mental health at the time he was unfit to prepare his defence, to cross-examine witnesses and to give evidence on his own behalf and call his witnesses. The application was rejected.

'Jacobs was a very nice pleasant man,' recalls solicitor Jeffrey Gordon. 'It completely disillusioned me about the police. I had admired him so much.' Gordon had been articled to the firm which undertook prosecutions of brothels on behalf of what was then Westminster City Council. 'My principal would have been consulted on what was required for the prosecution, for example, was there more than one girl working from the flat or house? When the likely raid was leaked the whole of our office fell under suspicion. Jacobs was tipping the girls off.'

But the rank and file were not happy and expressed their displeasure over the next few months. In a display of strength to show just how much control the lower ranks have, they held a go-slow over their duties and the *Daily Sketch* duly reported on 15 March 1956:

> Sir John Nott-Bower will hold a formal inquiry into a go-slow at some West End police stations. Officers are annoyed at disciplinary action taken against an inspector, station sergeant and constable. The inspector was reprimanded, the sergeant reduced in rank and the police constable asked to resign after twenty years' service. Since the discontent began six days ago the number of prostitutes appearing before magistrates has dropped. The number of motorists reported for parking offences has also been reduced.[3]

The tribulations of the police continued in Brighton with the

---

[3] The police were quite capable of subversive behaviour. Two years later in an unofficial go-slow over tea-break discipline, only one prostitute appeared at Bow Street instead of the usual thirty. The problem had been at B division Gerard Road, 'when an inspector told last night's late men going on duty that there was too much slackness and there would be disciplinary action against any man caught going to the canteen for tea during duty hours. Indignant policemen spread the word to colleagues on nearby C beats. Result, a quiet night for the tarts.' *Star*, 24 September 1958.

'Who is cop strike ringleader?' asked the *Daily Sketch* the next day. Feeling spread to other divisions, notably N and E covering Caledonian Road and Kings Cross and G covering City Road. Motorists also benefited from a temporary truce. This continued for a few days before petering out.

arrest of the Chief Constable and several of his merry men. The case echoed the efforts of Meiklejohn and Druscovich and the blackmailing of Waters in the 1930s. Indeed the *modus operandi* of corrupt officers changes little; wrinkles are just added from time to time.

On 25 October 1957 – the day Albert Anastasia, the New York gangster king, was shot to death in a barber's shop in the Park Sheraton, the body of Christian Dior was flown back to France and pop singer David Whitfield was reported as having flu – Chief Constable Charles Field William Ridge along with Detective Inspector John Hammersley, the second in command of the Brighton CID, and Anthony John Lyons, proprietor of Sherry's Bar, were charged that they, 'between January 1 1948 and October 18 1957 at Brighton did conspire together and with persons unknown corruptly to solicit and obtain rewards for the said Trevor Ernest Heath, John Richard Hammersley and Charles Field William Ridge for showing or promising favours contrary to their duty as police officers and thereby obstructing and defeating the course of public justice'.

At that stage bail was refused. Heath, a Detective Sergeant, had been arrested the previous week. Joining them later was Samuel Bellson, owner of the Burlesque Club, who had given evidence in one of the Jack Spot trials and was well known in the more *louche* areas of town.[4] Officially Bellson was a commission agent, which translated meant bookmaker. In fact he ran a chain of gambling clubs from which he was said to have made a fortune. His method was to sort the 'toffs' from 'the boys' and give them separate clubs. Running illegal gambling clubs was his idea of going straight.

Ridge had worked his way up through the force, which he had joined in 1925. He became a Detective Constable in 1928, rose to Detective Sergeant in 1935 and after the war was promoted Detective Chief Inspector, in 1949, and Deputy Chief Constable

[4] The 1955–56 Spot trials related literally to a running fight between Albert Dimes, a close friend of Billy Hill and the Sabinis, and Jack Spot (Comer) over control of London's underworld. Both men were acquitted of causing an affray but later Spot was charged with and acquitted of slashing Scarface Russo. In the meantime Spot's wife had been convicted, along with two others, of procuring a clergyman to give false evidence in the first trial. Finally a number of London's villains were sentenced to terms of up to seven years for slashing Spot. He retired from the London scene, leaving the door open for Dimes and Hill.

in 1955. He had been gassed during the First World War and as a result spoke with what was described as a gruffness in his voice at emotional times, when his calmness disappeared. Over-fond of quotations, which he used to offer at his morning police conferences, he remarked to the *Daily Telegraph* reporter at the committal proceedings: 'My strength is as the strength of ten, because my heart is pure.'[5]

In the April before his arrest he had had grandiose plans for himself and the police, telling the local Chamber of Commerce that a grey horse had been purchased from the Met and that it would be ridden along the seafront by a police officer in jackboots and a white helmet. 'Brighton today is a law-abiding town. It is my experience that these [clubs] are breeding places of vice and crime, and recently they have received fairly frequent visits from the police. It is my intention that these visits will go on with increasing momentum because I am determined to stamp them out.'

Hammersley, who had been a major in the war, had joined the force in 1937. Heath had joined in 1941 and had been a sub-lieutenant in the navy, in command of a landing craft on D Day.

Scotland Yard officers had had suspicions about the Brighton Police Force for some years. Rather as with complaints from forces about the Met, inquiries in Brighton would frequently fail: sometimes information was not forthcoming or suspects had vanished before they could be questioned. There was no hard evidence on which to act until a man called Alan Bennett, also known as Ferguson and Brown, went to Scotland Yard to ask about the existence of a warrant for his arrest. Bennett, who had accumulated fourteen convictions by the time of the trial, had had a variety of occupations, working as a chef, running a café on the Isle of Wight and operating in the scrap metal market. He is pictured either as a flamboyant character who now ran the Astor Club in Brighton, with a Rolls-Royce and offices in London and on the Continent, or, as solicitor John Bosley described him, 'a shady picturesque bit of a dandy running a rotten little one-room club with a bar in the corner'.

---

5 *Daily Telegraph*, 28 February 1958 the quotation is from Tennyson's *Sir Galahad*.

Bennett told the police and later the court that he was seen by Heath, who told him he was wanted in connection with the burglary of a jeweller's shop in Bournemouth. He gave Heath £10 and went into the station to see Hammersley. Bennett denied any part in the robbery but as he left dropped two screwed up £50 notes on the floor by the Inspector. Heath later called Bennett to tell him there was a warrant out for him in relation to a robbery in Folkestone on 30 May 1957; he had been picked out by a photograph and he was 'in plenty of trouble'. He was told to meet Heath in the Bodega Bar in Ship Street that night. Instead Bennett went to Scotland Yard.

The inquiry was run by Detective Superintendents Forbes-Leith and Radford. A Trenchard man, Forbes-Leith was one of the graduates of Hendon and was known as 'the Governor in the bowler'. Radford was appointed to be the guard of Bennett. Also on the team was Peter Vibart.[6] Vibart gave evidence that he had met Bellson in Brighton and had told him it was believed he had been paying money to certain officers over a long period in connection with the Burlesque Club. Bellson had replied:

> I could tell you a lot. I will help you all I can. One of the worst cases I know about is a woman doing fifteen months . . . Her name is Brabiner. The one who can tell you all about it is Betty Lawrence. There is someone else you ought to see. That is old Harry Leach who lives in Stamford Avenue. They did his son over his jewellery. Ridge sent me along to do some business for him. I went to Leach but he would not pay enough and later Ridge went himself. I have been in this town a long time. If I can help you I will.

But, when it came to it, he did not help either the police or himself enough. Later he refused to make a statement, denied his conversation with Vibart and appeared in the dock with the others instead of as a star witness on the other side of the court. So did Lyons, to whom Radford put it that it was he who had introduced Ridge to Alan Bennett to fix up protection if the club sold drinks after hours. Lyons denied it.

---

[6] Vibart was later to be involved in numerous cases including the Great Train Robbery. He was a close friend of Tommy Butler, who headed part of the inquiry, and, in line with the soubriquets given to Scotland Yard officers at the time, they were known as the Terrible Twins.

There was other evidence from a PC Frank Knight, who told of a conversation when Heath came into his office and asked if he was interested in earning £10 a week. Knight asked him what he meant and Heath replied, 'Mr Hammersley has asked me to see you. Sammy will pay you a tenner a week just to keep him informed when his club is going to be done.' Knight had told him he was not interested and Heath replied, 'It will be all right. Your job won't fall flat.' Knight again told him he was not interested and this time Heath said, 'All right, it is up to you. I was to get a fiver out of it for fixing it up, but that won't break me. I have my other fiddles, you know that.'

The Leach affair came about when John Leach lent a customer money as a security for stolen goods. Heath and Hammersley, investigating the theft, had, he said, asked for money, telling him that if he had to go to court he would have to get a solicitor and barrister and that might cost £300 to £400. Leach had asked, 'What can I do?' Hammersley was alleged to have replied, 'Well for £250 the evidence can be taken down and slung in the sea.' Leach had refused, been charged and convicted but on appeal he was awarded costs against the police.

As for the notorious Astor Club, which opened at Easter 1955 and was known as the Bucket of Blood because of the claret spilled during the fights there, Bennett's evidence was that Lyons had told him it was possible to serve drinks all night without being bothered by anyone. He had left Lyons to make arrangements and he later took Ridge to the club, when it was decided to pay the officer £20 a week. He told the court he had given Ridge £20 on five occasions and then Heath had arrived at the club to say that 'from now on, I will be calling for the presents from the club'. Bennett had asked him if Ridge had sent him and Heath said, 'Yes, I will be calling in the future.' Which he did.

But there were others less well able to look after themselves. A Sheila Swaby had asked Heath if she could see him about her husband, then on remand in Lewes Prison. He had said it would be difficult but he would do his best for her and asked how she was fixed for £50. She told him she would have to speak to her husband. She did not raise the money and Swaby received five years for housebreaking. Later Heath told her, 'You see now what has happened. You did not look after me, so I did not look after you.'

The day after William Page, a local bookmaker, gave evidence at the committal proceedings, fire swept through his club in Castle Street. Another who gave evidence was Alice Brabiner, a charwoman, whom Bellson had told the police about. She told the court that she had paid bribes so that her son would not know the trouble she was in. The 'trouble' was performing abortions. 'Heath said he could not get me out of trouble but he would do what he could to help me if I paid him. Even if I won the pools it would not get me out of the trouble I was in, he said.'

Altogether she gave him £68, of which £25 was paid on the first occasion. She cried when she told the court, 'He said I could get fourteen years. On one occasion he threatened to bring me corrective training papers to sign. I did not know what he meant. I paid him £15, went back into the sitting-room and fainted.'[7]

Less sinister but equally rewarding, according to another witness, was the conduct of one of the officers. 'He would order two or three pounds of groceries – the best of course – and offers 10 shillings change . . . says he's coming down on such a date for his Christmas turkey and presents. So I has it all ready for him – a tenner with the turkey.' Coincidentally but almost simultaneously a man serving a sentence in Maidstone Prison gave information to the Kent police that he had been paying protection money to the Brighton police.

At the Old Bailey on 27 February 1958 Ridge was found not guilty, along with Lyons. Heath, Hammersley and a commission agent who had joined the indictment were found guilty. The jury, which had to give a unanimous verdict, had been out for four hours and twenty minutes, hardly a blink of an eye by today's standards, when they returned to say they were disagreed about the cases of Bellson and Ridge. Minutes later they returned again, this time to convict Bellson, and an hour

---

[7] Corrective training was introduced by the Criminal Justice Act 1948 and allowed a court to impose a longer period of imprisonment than would be normal in the case of an offender aged between twenty-one and thirty whose record was such that it appeared he was becoming a recidivist. There is no way this could have applied to Alice Brabiner, who was far too old. Corrective training was abolished by the Criminal Justice Act 1967.

and a quarter later they found Ridge not guilty. After he had discharged the Chief Constable, the judge, Mr Justice Donovan, commented that the Brighton force needed a leader 'who will be a new influence and will set a different example from that which has lately obtained'. The trial had cost Brighton ratepayers £15,000.[8]

Despite his acquittal Ridge came under further heavy fire from the judge when next day he sentenced Heath and Hammersley to five years' imprisonment apiece:

Neither of you had the professional or moral leadership which both of you were entitled to expect and should have had from the Chief Constable of Brighton, now acquitted. For if he can contrive as he did, to go to a suspected briber of police in private and alone, it is small wonder that you, Heath, followed that example, and if he could admit, as he did, to his private room a much convicted and hectoring bookmaker and there discuss with him almost as a colleague the policy of the police in certain matters it is small wonder that you, Hammersley, saw little or no wrong in going off on holiday with a local man with a serious record.

Jokes were instantaneous. On the night of his acquittal a group of London CID officers were dining *en famille* when one handed a banknote to a waiter. 'I can't accept this,' he said, holding it to the light. 'It has a ridge in it.'

The Watch Committee met almost immediately to dismiss Ridge as being negligent in the discharge of his duty and unfit for the same. With his dismissal he lost his pension of £20 a week. On 14 March 1963, just over five years after his acquittal, Ridge succeeded in the House of Lords in overturning the decision of the committee because they had not informed him what charges he was to face before them, nor was he invited to attend the disciplinary proceedings. As a result he retrieved his pension, of which half was paid by the Home Office.

After the Brighton case the Home Office began to insist that

[8] Ridge was defended by Mr Geoffrey Lawrence QC, fresh from his triumphant defence of Dr Bodkin Adams, accused of murdering several of his female patients in Eastbourne. Victor Durand defended Bellson and Edward Clarke defended Heath.

Chief Constables had experience in outside forces. It was not a conspicuous success. The new Chief Constable of Brighton had instructions to clean up the force but as Sir David Napley has remarked, 'all these improvements are short-lived. For a period after either a case or a Royal Commission the matter is stirred up and the situation marginally improves, but these sort of things are soon forgotten and they soon revert to previous habits.'[9] This was certainly true in Brighton, for in 1971 nine young Constables were arrested and charged with theft from motor vehicles.

It was not long after the fall of the Brighton officers in 1955 that another Chief Constable was in trouble. This time it was the one from Southend, described wittily as a 'dipsomaniac and megalomaniac – in that order', who had paid for his daughter's wedding with the police funds. Frank Williamson, the investigating officer, recalls: 'He had had his hands in the till and the Home Office was petrified at having to pay half his pension if he was acquitted. They were perpetually on the line to the Old Bailey asking "Is there any news?" But with Mars-Jones prosecuting and George Waller on the bench, if we couldn't get a conviction with that we might as well have given up.' In the event, after a thirteen-hour retirement until 1 am – there were no overnight stays in hotels in those days – the jury returned verdicts of guilty. Apparently one juror had been holding out against a not guilty verdict on one count.

The next hiccough which followed the arrest of the Brighton detectives arose from a small incident. Again it was one which was mishandled until it blew up to the proportions of a national scandal. The first question was whether, on 7 December 1957, Thurso policemen Robert Gunn and PC Harper hit John Waters, a boy who was being cheeky, and then, more seriously, whether an approach was made to the boy's father to drop the case in return for a payment.

What thirty years later seems a trivial affair had begun when the two officers had entered the Bay Café in Thurso on a routine visit. In it were six boys, including John Waters, then aged fifteen. One of the youths remarked, 'Here's our friends,' perhaps adding 'Two smart guys'. Harper then told the boy, 'If there's any more cheek I'll mark you for life', a comment the

---

[9] Letter to the author.

tribunal found to be highly improper but in no way sinister, nor one which was taken seriously. Waters, so the tribunal found, made a grunting noise at the officers. He was asked his name, would not give it and swore at the officers. He was then taken outside, where he gave his name and was told not to be cheeky. He then returned to his friends and the officers moved off down the High Street.

Later, so the report said, Waters found his jacket was torn, and 'saw in this the opportunity to turn the tables against the constables'. He ran after them and, according to the finding of the tribunal, said, 'You bastards tore my jacket.' The tribunal also found that Harper told the boy that if he had done so he was sorry and to go away. Instead Waters 'came on and made an obscene and offensive reply'. It was then the officers decided things had gone far enough. Each took an arm and led him into an alleyway between two shops.

> We are prepared to believe that, after entering the alley, Constable Gunn told Waters he was going to book him and asked for particulars.
> We are prepared to believe that the boy was still unsubdued and that he gave truculent and obscene replies.
> But we cannot accept Constable Gunn's account of the way the boy sustained his injuries.

According to Gunn, after using the words 'Gestapo bastards', Waters made a dash for the exit and on the way came into contact with his outstretched wrist. The tribunal found that the 'nature of the boy's injury is consistent with a blow and in the circumstances as we know them it is, to say the least, highly improbable that it could have been caused by the boy colliding with a fist or an arm'.[10] The tribunal was also able to say that when the boy was taken into the alleyway there was not 'common purpose to inflict chastisement upon him' and it accordingly exonerated Constable Harper from any complicity in striking the blow.

But it was not quite as easy as that. Waters' father alleged that after he had made a complaint he had been approached with an offer of money to drop the matter.

[10] Tribunal report, April 1959.

We consider the probabilities are that Constable Harper did offer to pay money for the dropping of the complaint. Our view of the incident is that it was wrong for Constable Harper to have attempted to get the complaint withdrawn for a money payment. It is fair to point out that Constable Harper was not attempting in any way to tamper with the evidence. If he had confined himself to making an appeal we might have had no comment to make, but it was certainly wrong for him to have attempted to buy Mr Waters off.

There had been no disciplinary action taken against the police because the Procurator Fiscal had marked the papers 'No proceedings'. Constable Harper had destroyed his notebook the following year, citing limited space in his locker. Surplus papers had been burned to make room. The tribunal found the action taken by the Caithness police authorities after the incident to be 'all that it should have been'. And there was nothing but praise for Inspector Carter, who had done 'an excellent bit of work'.

Given the violence meted out to and by the police of later years this case seems to have been a storm in a tea shop but it shows how seriously police indiscipline was regarded in those days. Two hundred MPs had lobbied the government to set up an inquiry: The *Daily Mirror* wrote:

The actions of the police must ALWAYS AND AT ONCE be subject to impartial examination – whenever and wherever these actions appear open to suspicion of injustice. **Nothing less can be fair to the police**. OR TO THE PUBLIC.[11]

Small though the Thurso case may have seemed at the time it was another rung on the ladder which led to the Royal Commission of 1960.

If constables misbehaved, so did their elders and betters. Quite apart from Mr Ridge and the now imprisoned Chief Constable of Southend, the Chief Constable of Worcestershire was also embroiled in a dispute, mainly because he too had been dishonest. He too received a short prison sentence. Why

[11] *Daily Mirror*, 20 March 1959.

did such senior officers, who were, after all, the closest things to gentlemen the police has ever known, put their hands in the till? Frank Williamson, who was also a Chief Constable, taking over Carlisle from a predecessor who never paid full value to any tradesman, believes that it was because of the increased financial burden placed on a Chief Constable. Suddenly a whole new standard of living was required of him on pay not substantially different from that of a Chief Superintendent.

In fact this had long been the case. In 1894 the former Chief Constable of Bradford, Philip Woodman, who had been appointed Chief Constable of Surrey, stood in the dock of his old court and pleaded guilty to specimen charges of embezzlement. The total money involved came to around £200. He had spent the money supporting his father, a veteran of the Crimean war, an unfortunate brother and a wife who was delicate.

> The stipendiary: What was his salary?
> The town clerk: £2 per week, £104 per year.
> The stipendiary: Was that all?
> The town clerk: Yes sir. The great object of police officers is not the salary, but the fact it is a competency for a man. This is a pension but that is now gone forever.

Woodman received a sentence of five months' imprisonment with hard labour.[12]

Now in the 1950s, up in Lancashire, the Chief Constable of Blackpool, Stanley Parr, was displaying a lack of judgment and authority that would have repercussions spreading down south to the City of London Police Force twenty years later. Incidental to this, on 18 November 1959 Home Secretary R. A. Butler said it was his impression that the time had come for an independent inquiry to examine such questions as the recruitment, training, discipline and organization of the police, the relation of central and local government authorities to the police and the relations between the police and the public.

The announcement was the culmination of another seemingly stupid little quarrel. However it was one which – as with the 1929 inquiry – featured a prominent figure. Brian Rix, whose

---

[12] *Police Review and Parade Gossip*, 14 December 1894.

trouser-losing comedies at the Whitehall Theatre had followed the tradition of the Aldwych farces of the 1930s and were just as much loved by audiences, had been involved in an altercation with a traffic policeman. It was a tragi-comedy which was to play and play. Earlier in 1959 Rix had been stopped by PC Eastmond for speeding on Putney Heath. Following behind the police car was a civil servant named Garrett who became involved in the dispute over the actor's speed. 'There followed allegations of assault on both sides.'[13] In fact Garrett alleged he had been pushed over a hedge before he was taken to the police station, where the Inspector refused to accept the charge of assaulting a police officer in the execution of his duty. Garrett later brought an action for assault and battery, which was settled on a no admission of liability basis in the sum of £300.

An Opposition motion in the Commons censured the Home Secretary for his failure adequately to explain the payment of £300 in the case of Garrett v Eastmond in which the alleged misconduct of a Metropolitan Police officer was involved. Mr Butler replied:

There is a feeling that if the published version of the events of December 17 was true the police officer had been allowed to get away with grave misconduct without public exposure in the court and without any disciplinary punishment. There was also the feeling that it was the corollary of public cooperation with the police that a policeman who misbehaved and abused his power in relation to the public should be severely punished.[14]

Although the incident which had finally sparked the Royal Commission, the fifth in police history, came from the Met, the inquiry became involved almost exclusively with provincial affairs. The terms included 'the constitution and functions of local police authorities; the status and accountability of all members of police forces; relations between the police and the public' and "the broad principles" which should determine the level of police pay'.

In November 1960 the Commission, under the chairmanship

[13] D. Ascoli, *The Queen's Peace*, p. 275.
[14] *The Times*, 19 November 1959.

of Sir Henry Willink QC, reported: 'We do not think that anyone acquainted with the facts can be satisfied with the state of law and order in Great Britain in 1960. Society has, in our opinion, a duty not to leave untried any measure which may lead not only to the detection, but above all to the prevention of crime.' Later the report concluded: 'The evidence we have heard and the information we have obtained in the course of our visits convince us that police pay is at present inadequate either to inspire in the police and the community a sense of fair treatment, or to attract to the service as a whole and retain in it, enough recruits of the right standard.'[15]

The remainder of the report was delivered in May 1962 and offered some clear thoughts on the role of the Chief Constable, and the appointment of a Chief Inspector of Constabulary who would act as adviser on provincial matters to the Home Secretary as well as supervising a research and planning unit. According to the report, relations between the police and public were good except in isolated instances, and there was no need (three members dissenting) to establish an independent system of investigating complaints against the police.[16] The Police Complaints Board was still fourteen years away. In the meantime, however, the Police Act 1964 established that when a complaint was made against a policeman the chief officer of his force was to set up an investigation 'and for that purpose may, and shall if directed by the Secretary of State, request the chief officer of police for any other police area to provide an officer of the police for that area to carry out the investigation'.

This did not, however, include the Met, which held firm against outside interference in its disciplinary processes. With a force of over 21,000, the Met believed or at least maintained that it was quite capable of appointing an officer from within its ranks who did not know the alleged culprit and who could be relied on to conduct an unbiased inquiry. So agreed the Royal Commission. In fact, this was a wholly misplaced belief. Since 1879 the investigation of a complaint of serious misconduct could only be carried out by the CID. A complaint against a member of the CID, which, with the exception of Goddard,

---

[15] HMSO 1960, Cmnd 1222.
[16] HMSO 1962, Cmnd 1728.

was where most systematic corruption could occur, would thus be investigated by a CID officer. This was very far from a pool of 21,000 men – rather it was one of 3,000. Because an allegation might only be investigated by an officer of senior rank the pool was reduced to a depth whereby it was almost impossible that the investigating officer did not know at least something of the man under investigation. It was not until the reforms of Sir Robert Mark in 1972 that the Met changed its position. By then, however, the damage had been done.

But if things were thought to be going well at that time – except in isolated instances – some people were deceiving themselves and, had the public known about it and senior officers had not swept it under the carpet, the Royal Commission might have had to spend more time on a rather more serious incident than the Garrett-Eastmond farce. Unfortunately it took five years to surface and when it did, it was the first publicly aired hearing of what would be twenty years of allegations of incidents of lies, brutality, planting, and the fabrication and suppression of evidence which would eventually lead to the introduction of the Police and Criminal Evidence Act 1984. The golden age of policing was at an end.

At 12.30 am on 6 August 1959 three youths, Patrick Albert Tisdall, Thomas Alfred Kingston and Sidney Hill-Burton, were charged with possessing offensive weapons without lawful authority or excuse.[17] They had been in the Manor House public house just by Finsbury Park playing Russian billiards from about 8.30 that evening. One had a conviction for theft for which he had been fined £10, another for breaking a window and the third for letting off a firework. Not by any means were they major local criminals. As they left the pub at closing time Tisdall and Kingston were stopped by a PC Tonge. Hill-Burton was spoken to by two other young officers, Walden and Taylor. All agreed to go to the police station.

Tonge, Walden and Taylor were what were known as aides to CID. The aide scheme, which was heavily criticized, enabled uniform officers who showed aptitude and interest to be transferred to the plain clothes branch as an aide to CID on a temporary basis. Initially an aide would be placed with

---

[17] A full account of the case appears in Sir D. Napley, *Not Without Prejudice*, chapter 13.

either a young CID officer or, more likely, a more experienced aide. If he made good he could remain in the CID. And making good meant making arrests – 'a factor which is regarded as one of significance throughout the CID for all officers and not only aides, despite the denials of many senior officers that this is so. It is a canker in police administration which should long since have been eliminated, since it lies at the root of many wrongful arrests and charges but is something to which the Force tenaciously and misguidedly clings.'[18]

Walden was certainly making good. He had been an aide for fifteen months and had notched up more arrests than any other. In the last year he had been responsible for twelve of the twenty-one arrests for possessing offensive weapons. He had four commendations in his short career; Taylor had two.

At first Tisdall, Kingston and Hill-Burton believed they were being questioned over an assault. Hill-Burton asked how he would get home and was told 'That's your worry.' Tisdall and Kingston went in another car. At this time none of them was searched. They were charged at half past midnight, released from the police station at 5 am and told to be at Tottenham Magistrates' Court at 10 am that day.

They went immediately to see David Napley, the well-known London solicitor who later became president of the Law Society. Napley's managing clerk, once he had arranged an adjournment for a week, set about taking their statements.

This was a case in which, on the face of it, the three accused had been caught, in the police vernacular, bang to rights with the weapons on them. In those circumstances defendants could only take one of two courses: admit their crimes or allege that the weapons had been planted. Too many chose the latter . . . Experience is an enormous asset for judges and magistrates but there is an exception to every rule, and long experience, if not carefully watched, can result in injustice. The bench tends to become case-hardened – so often does the shoplifter say she intended to pay but forgot, the person charged with handling stolen goods says he bought them from a chap called Joe in a pub and thought they were straight and those charged with possessing offensive weapons say they

[18] Sir D. Napley, *Not Without Prejudice*, p. 145.

were planted – that scant respect is given to the explanation which every now and again turns out to be true.[19]

The youths ran the defence that the weapons had been planted. When they were searched at the police station in the presence of a Detective Sergeant Bolongaro, Walden put his hand into Kingston's pocket and withdrew a barber's razor. Kingston protested it was not his. Walden suggested it might have been planted in the pub. No, replied Kingston, he, Walden, had planted it. Kingston, according to his statement, received a blow for his pains and when he continued to deny the razor was his, he was threatened with a truncheon.

More or less the same thing happened to Tisdal, except that when he denied that Walden had found the razor he was not struck. Hill-Burton was told to take off his jacket by PC Tonge, who found a cosh inside, an event witnessed by a PC Rust. Hill-Burton vehemently denied the cosh was his and Walden picked it up, struck the desk and asked, 'How would you like a belt over the head with this?'

Sorrell, Napley's managing clerk, asked his principal if he would take the case himself as he believed in the youths' statements. Napley vigorously cross-examined them himself. He found them to be of limited education and he believed them. His inquiries showed that the officers from Y division were out of their area. The Manor House pub was on N division ground. Normally, suspects would have been taken to a station in the area of their arrest. Hornsey police station was outside it.

On 13 August, despite a spirited defence by Napley, the youths were convicted and fined £10 each. Napley comments, 'If they were guilty they should have had a far more severe penalty for possessing such dangerous and unpleasant weapons in a public place for an unlawful purpose.' It was a typical case of the fudged reasoning of magistrates of the time: by convicting in dubious cases the magistrates not only fail in their duty to give the accused the benefit of the doubt and acquit the defendant but by imposing a nominal fine they compound the offence by also failing to impose the proper sentence.

A conviction in the magistrates' court carries with it an automatic right of appeal, against either the conviction itself

[19] Ibid. p. 146.

110

or the sentence or both. Cases were re-heard in those days by the Quarter Sessions Appeals Committee (now by the Crown Court) with a qualified chairman and lay magistrates from a different petty sessional division from the one which heard the original case. There is no right to a jury trial for the appeal. One danger of the appeal system is that even if the appeal is only against conviction, the Crown Court has the right to deal with the sentencing aspect and, if it thinks fit, increase it. This is one of the reasons why many convictions in magistrates' courts are not appealed.

Despite the advice both of Napley and James Burge, whom he instructed, that they would be unlikely to win the appeal and that their sentences would be up for reconsideration, the youths were adamant they would appeal. They raised the money and appealed to Middlesex Quarter Sessions Appeals Committee. The police now called Inspector Ward, Sergeant Cottam, DS Bolongaro, DC Rust and DC Anderson, in addition to PCs Walden, Taylor and Tonge. The result was a foregone conclusion.

Ewan Montagu, the presiding judge who ruled Middlesex Quarter Sessions with a rod of iron,[20] dismissed the appeal and, ante-dating the Court of Appeal in the Birmingham Six case, commented, 'If there was any possibility that the charges [ie the young men's allegations] were true, one would obviously have to take action, and also, in a case of this kind, allow the appeal . . . We are absolutely satisfied that there is not a vestige of truth in their [the accuseds'] account of what occurred.' Each boy received a sentence of twenty-eight days' imprisonment.

Not unnaturally Napley was extremely upset and on 25 November 1959 wrote to the Home Secretary, R. A. Butler, calling for a public inquiry. Six months later he received a reply to the effect that a full inquiry had been conducted and there were no grounds for interfering with the conviction. It was not until February 1964, by which time the Police Bill was under consideration, that Eric Fletcher, a solicitor Member

[20] Montagu was one of the last of the old-fashioned bullying chairmen of Quarter Sessions. Outside court, a man of great charm and wit, inside, whenever a mother entered the witness box to give evidence in mitigation, he would write GBAH to stand for good boy at home as she took the oath. It rarely did the child much good. It was he who devised the wartime plot to deceive the Germans over the Normandy landings. The story was made into a film, *The Man Who Never Was*.

of Parliament, raised the question in the House, this time linking it with the case of Harold Challenor and one of two Irish constituents who had, he believed, been the subjects of a beating that had been covered up.

A month later, in March 1964, the then Home Secretary Henry Brooke ordered an inquiry into the youths' case. It was headed by William Mars-Jones QC, later to become a High Court judge, and sat for forty-six days. Unfortunately Brooke undertook that if the officers involved agreed to give evidence before the tribunal they would be free from disciplinary proceedings.

As the evidence was heard a new picture began to emerge. On receipt of Napley's complaint the Home Office had merely asked the police to conduct their own inquiry. The papers were sent to a Chief Superintendent Fieldsend, who delegated the inquiry to Detective Superintendent Radford from Kings Cross, 'a congenial but not over-intelligent policeman', says Napley. In his initial report Radford had made a scathing attack on Napley and his clerk, suggesting they would make a complaint against the police at the drop of a hat. As Mars-Jones commented, 'It was not the work of a detective but that of an advocate urging the cause of his trusted subordinates.'

It also became clear that Fieldsend was pursuing his own line of inquiry and statements were taken from witnesses who would have confirmed the youths' story as to the timing of the incident. 'I have come to the conclusion,' said Mars-Jones, 'that Detective Superintendent Radford never did place these additional statements and documents in the bundles he made up for the Home Office. His final report has been so prepared as to omit all references to matters raised in these additional statements.'

Fieldsend had been unhappy all along, even though he drafted his report to exculpate the police. He nevertheless suggested the aides be returned to uniform duties, a recommendation overruled. As Mars-Jones commented, 'In the whole of my service I have never known so many irregularities being committed by so few officers in so short a time.' The first inquiry had been abruptly halted by Assistant Commissioner Jackson, an action which made Mars-Jones 'reluctantly come to the conclusions that in this instance the Assistant Commissioner did not give the matter the consideration which it deserved . . .

He allowed his judgment to be swayed by his dislike of Chief Supt Fieldsend and his branch. He was also a victim of the pressure being exerted to have a report submitted to the Home Office as soon as possible.'

W.L. Mars-Jones QC found that Sir Richard Jackson, Assistant Commissioner and by this time head of Securicor, 'acted hastily and without proper consideration' and that a Detective Chief Superintendent Hatherill and Detective Superintendent Radford were partial to the officers involved in the inquiry. He found the five police officers had lied and that the evidence tended to support the allegations of three young men convicted five years ago that razors and a rubber cosh had been 'planted' on them. All the significant points of conflict between the police and the youths were resolved in the latter's favour, but when it came to it he added, 'The evidence disclosed in this inquiry is not sufficient for me to be able to find, five years after the incident, that the allegations [of planting the weapons] are established beyond all reasonable doubt.'[21]

As Napley comments: 'Thus an otherwise exemplary piece of work by Mars-Jones was somewhat marred by a degree of timidity at the end . . . one might have hoped for a marginally more courageous and robust finding as to the planting of the weapons.' The youths were pardoned and given compensation 'in an amount, which in my view was far from generous'.[22]

Had Mr Mars-Jones had the benefit of hearing from an officer serving on Y division immediately after the incident on how evidence was obtained, he would no doubt have been even more horrified.

The guy's stopped for sus. He's taken to the police station. The officer has to justify the charge. He has to convince the officer there is sufficient evidence to support the charge. He's got to produce the evidence. It's at that point he might be searched and suddenly a bunch of keys goes down on the chargeroom desk to his amazement. 'I found this in his

[21] *The Times*, 4 December 1964.
[22] The quotations are from Sir D. Napley, *Not Without Prejudice*, and the Mars-Jones Report. Counsel for the inquiry was Geoffrey Lane who as Lord Lane, Lord Chief Justice, presided over the Birmingham Six appeal. In his book *Occupied with Crime* written in 1967, Sir Richard Jackson makes no reference to the incident.

right hand jacket pocket.' The guy's protesting like mad, quite rightly. This is the sort of thing which would occur.

The station officer might suspect the pattern. Here is John Smith again coming in with another suspected person who is squealing but he's there as a functionary. He can't say I'm not going to charge this guy because you're fetching too many of these people in.

But by the time the inquiry was concluded things were beginning to tumble around the heads of the Met. The Challenor case was in full flow.

The very odd Detective Sergeant Harold Challenor – 'he was mad before he joined the Met' – feared by villains everywhere, was a singular influence in Soho at the time. Born in 1922, he had had an elementary education and had worked as a male nurse, a lorry driver and a motor mechanic before joining the army at the age of twenty. He had a distinguished war record, winning the Military Medal and attaining the rank of company quartermaster sergeant. He had spent several years in the Flying Squad when, in 1962, he was sent to West End Central police station (Savile Row) as a second-class sergeant. In the 1960s, when he was already showing signs of deafness and irrational behaviour and the time between arrest and trial by jury at the Old Bailey or the Inner London Sessions was only a matter of a few weeks, he soon made a great impact both on the community and the courts.

Soho sounded like Chicago when Challenor described it. The courts were obviously impressed, although magistrates, judges and members of juries all knew that perfectly respectable people – like magistrates, judges and members of juries – could spend a pleasant evening in Soho without indulging in crime or coming to any harm. London's West End has the best theatres, restaurants, cinemas, clubs and pubs in the country, and they are frequented by regular customers and provincial visitors who never once catch a glimpse of a drug-orgy or a gun-fight. Yet the detective-sergeant was not only believed when he brought his conspiracy and offensive weapon charges; he was increasingly admired for his skill and courage in tackling the bandits.[23]

23 M. Grigg, *The Challenor Case*, p. 16.

His finest hour came in September 1962 with his smashing of the 'protection racket' being run by Riccardo Pedrini, Joseph Oliva, John Ford, Alan Cheeseman and James Fraser. That, at least, was the evidence of Wilfred Gardiner, a man with a conviction for living off immoral earnings, who ran the two strip-tease clubs, the Phoenix and the Geisha. Gardiner gave evidence of threats, damage to his car, demands to be 'looked after' and 'If you try nicking us I shall shoot you. You're a dead man anyway. You won't live the rest of the year.' He also spoke of another occasion when he saw Oliva cutting the hood of his car. 'That's how we're going to cut your face,' he was told.

On 21 September Riccardo Pedrini and Alan Cheeseman were arrested outside the Phoenix Club by two of Challener's aides. They were taken to Savile Row and told to put their belongings on a table. Cheeseman was slapped and, so he said at the trial, Pedrini was taken into a cell and beaten. Both he and Cheeseman had weapons planted on them. John Ford, who had been involved in a long-standing quarrel with Gardiner, lived in the next block of flats to Pedrini. There is no doubt there had been trouble on a fairly regular basis between them. He was arrested on 22 September and charged with demanding money with menaces. On 24 September Joseph Oliva was arrested driving along Berwick Street. Challenor and two younger officers dragged him from his car. He was found to have a bottle of turpentine with a piece of torn-up towel in the neck and a knife in his pocket. At the trial Challenor said he had information that Oliva intended to attack the Phoenix Club; Oliva was said to have remarked, 'If I don't burn him someone else will.' James Fraser was arrested on 26 September when he was pointed out to police officers by Gardiner. He was found to have a knife. It seems that the only connection between him and the others was that he had once been in a van with Oliva when there had been a near accident with Gardiner in his open car. On that occasion both had called the police.

On 6 December, charged with conspiracy to demand money with menaces, demanding money with menaces and possessing offensive weapons, the five men appeared at the Old Bailey. After a retirement of two and a half hours Fraser was acquitted of conspiracy, and the others found guilty. Their convictions were quashed by the Court of Appeal in 1964, by which time Challenor was in disgrace.

His war on Soho characters had been perfectly successful whilst he stuck to the *louche* element who had a few convictions in their background, or even their associates with no convictions but on whom the tar would stick. They were not likely to be believed by a jury when they flatly contradicted the evidence of a Detective Sergeant, who in addition to being a rising star in the Met was a well-decorated war hero from the Tank Corps. Indeed, in the summer of 1963, £1,000 was on offer in Soho for anyone without a criminal record who would set himself up as a Challenor victim and then turn the tables on him. When it came to it, however, there was no need to spend the money. Challenor managed to bring about his own downfall. The first step was an incident which could almost be overlooked. The second could not.

The first concerned Harold Padmore, a Barbadian and former well-known cricketer, whose mistress, Patricia Hawkins, was arrested for obtaining money by false pretences at the clip joint where she worked. On 6 July Challenor went with two other officers to arrest the thirty-eight-year-old Mrs Hawkins, who supervised the club's hostesses, one of whom, when accused of being a prostitute, described what was going on in the club. 'I have to earn a few pounds sometimes. We kid the punters they can have a bit of the other, and then send them down Wardour Street where friend Padmore speaks to them about his girl. They don't come back.'

Challenor had now found someone, a young man from Switzerland, who would complain. Mrs Hawkins was arrested and Padmore went to the West End Central police station to arrange her bail. According to Padmore he was shown into a room with six or seven plain-clothes officers together with Challenor. 'What does a black ponce like you want in a white police station?' demanded Challenor and, when Padmore told him, replied, 'We'll have some fun with this coon.' The evidence at the inquiry was that Challenor made Padmore turn out his pockets and then hit him repeatedly, saying, 'Take that black bastard out of my sight. I wish I was in South Africa. I'd have a nigger for breakfast every morning.' He then began to sing 'Bongo, bongo bongo, I don't want to leave the Congo', a popular tune of the time. The watching officers, whilst enjoying themselves, appeared to be afraid of Challenor.

Padmore was then arrested and charged with obtaining money by false pretences and, when he asked to see a solicitor, was again punched. The following day his solicitor applied for a summons for assault against Challenor but the magistrate refused to grant it. The case against him, Mrs Hawkins and Jeanne Browne, the girl who worked in the clip joint, was dismissed after the first jury disagreed. In the event the medical evidence did not bear out Padmore's allegations of serious injury. Nevertheless he agreed a settlement of £750 for assault and false imprisonment.

The James inquiry, which took place in 1964, went into the Padmore case in some detail, finding in favour of Challenor wherever possible. Padmore's evidence being uncorroborated, it was not accepted by Arthur James, nor was that of the solicitor's clerk who supported it in some instances. Mr James did, however, find that Padmore had been struck by Challenor and that, with one exception, the officers who gave evidence to the inquiry had played down what they must have realized was improper conduct.

Unfortunately for himself and the police, Challenor next lighted upon political demonstrators rather than underworld figures, in what was to prove his undoing. On 11 July 1963 a demonstration took place around Claridge's hotel to protest against a state visit by Queen Frederika of Greece.[24] One of the men arrested was a Donald Rooum who, fortunately, happened to be a member of the National Council for Civil Liberties. He was arrested carrying a banner by four plain-clothes policemen, one of whom was described by Rooum as 'a big, stocky, flat-nosed man with a dark suit, boots and a very short back and sides'. 'You're fucking nicked, my old beauty,' said the policeman.

At West End Central, Rooum was pushed upstairs to a detention room by Challenor, who repeatedly hit him on the ear. 'Boo the Queen would you?' he asked. 'No, not at all,' replied Rooum and was rewarded with another blow. 'There you are, my old darling,' said Challenor, 'have that with me. And just to make sure we haven't forgotten it . . . there you are, my old beauty. Carrying an offensive weapon. You can get two

[24] The origins of the protest, now almost forgotten, had arisen following the death of a Greek political activist, Lambrakis. A banner carried by Donald Rooum read 'Lambrakis RIP'.

years for that.' And with that, said Rooum, Challenor produced from his own pocket a piece of brick wrapped in paper. That evening six other men and a juvenile were arrested. Each was given a piece of brick by Challenor or his subordinates. Each refused to sign for their property, denying the bricks had been in their possession.

In the event Rooum was doubly fortunate. He had been refused bail by the police and he was represented by Stanley Clinton Davis, a well-known criminal lawyer. Rooum's case was adjourned for trial until 19 July. The basis of his defence was that he could not have been carrying a brick because there was no brickdust found in his pocket. An independent expert was found who confirmed this. Here was Rooum's good fortune. As he had been refused bail he had had no chance to change his clothes before handing them over to Clinton Davis after the initial remand hearing. At the hearing Rooum was defended by Michael Sherrard, who would later defend Hanratty. A forensic scientist gave evidence that there could have been no brick because not only was there no dust but a broken brick, the size of the one produced, would inevitably have scratched the lining. Edward Robey, son of the comedian Sir George, was the magistrate sitting at Marlborough Street when the case was heard. After he had handled the brick and found how easily it crumbled he expressed his doubts and acquitted Rooum, refusing an application for his costs to cover his expenses.

Another of the defendants, John Apostolou, was not so fortunate. With the same solicitor, barrister, forensic scientist and the same story, Robey, incredibly, found him guilty and fined him £10. Two juveniles, Ronald Ede and Gregory Hill, were due to appear at Chelsea Juvenile Court. The case was first adjourned because Challenor was ill and then, on 9 October, the prosecution offered no evidence. Apostolou appealed against his conviction and on 22 October the prosecution indicated they would not seek to support the conviction. Later Rooum was awarded £500 and Apostolou £400. There had been a number of convictions of other defendants, who had been fined £5 and in one case given a conditional discharge.

Challenor found himself at the Old Bailey on 4 June 1964 on a charge of corruption. Defended by Manny Fryde, of Sampson & Co, solicitors for the Krays, he was committed to a mental hospital having been found unfit to plead. Three other officers were found guilty, receiving sentences of four and three years. At the end of the trial Mr Justice Lawton called for John du Rose, known as 'Four Day Johnny' because of the speed with which he solved his cases:

> Chief Superintendent du Rose, I would be very grateful if you would bring to the attention of the Commissioner my grave disturbance at the fact that Detective Sergeant Challenor was on duty at all on 11th July 1963. On the evidence which I heard from the doctors when he was arraigned, it seems likely that he had been mentally unbalanced for some time, and the evidence which I heard from Superintendent Burdett in the case has worried me a great deal. It seems to me the matter ought to be looked into further.

At the inquiry which followed, Arthur James QC, later to preside over the Great Train Robbery, reported into the circumstances in which it was possible for Challenor to have continued on duty at a time when he appeared to have been affected by the onset of mental illness. As with so many official investigations into alleged police misconduct, the report was a whitewash. Mr James found that Challenor was allowed to continue because of the extreme difficulty in diagnosing paranoid schizophrenia and it was no fault of his fellow officers that they had failed to notice his unsocial behaviour. Presumably it was unremarkable that an officer should jump on the table and sing or that he should walk home to Kent every night after his duty ended. If there was a clash of evidence between witnesses to the inquiry and police officers, then the evidence of the latter was invariably preferred, mainly because there was no independent evidence. Allegations that Challenor had taken bribes were dismissed almost out of hand, Mr James saying, 'Such allegations form part of the armoury of the criminal and are directed at any target which it wished to destroy.'

In the Pedrini case, a former police officer who had become a barrister, William Hemming, along with Margaret Laville, a solicitor's clerk through whom he obtained much of his work, gave evidence. Not only was Hemming a member of the Bar, he was a long-time member of the *louche* Soho drinking club, the Premier, as was Miss Laville.[25] Evidence that Cheeseman had met Challenor in the club in her presence could not be accurate, she said, and Mr James unhesitatingly accepted it. Hemming gave evidence that he had held Challenor in high regard as an officer. The allegation that Challenor had received a £50 bribe was dismissed.

Later Challenor found work as a solicitor's clerk taking instructions in criminal cases. He was certainly not able to accept the acquittal of Rooum with good grace. In his own memoirs he wrote:

. . . soon afterwards Rooum heard me repeating details of his arrest and stating that I had found the brick in his pocket.

Whether Mr Rooum had prepared himself for such an eventuality I do not know, but he certainly had his wits about him for his mind went back to a book he had read entitled, *Science in the Detection of Crime*, by a former Scotland Yard officer, and he realised that if he could prevent the brick being placed in his pocket he could prove his innocence because there would be no trace of dust in his pocket and no fingerprints on the brick. This would make nonsense of my evidence.

To achieve this, however, it was essential for him to remain in custody over night in order to prove that he was wearing the same clothing when he was examined by an independent forensic expert. For that reason he did not seek bail, but refused to sign for his property which included the brick.[26]

Whatever the truth behind the Challenor illness there is no doubt he presented a formidable figure to the Soho villains, and was certainly feared by them. He knew the gang leaders and believed that 'fighting crime in Soho was like trying to swim against a tide of sewage; you made two strokes forward

---

[25] The Premier Club was a dingy little place in Little Compton Street. It was inhabited by an amazing cross-section of people, including villains, bookmakers and police, who came together on neutral ground. 'I never saw money changing hands there,' says one Flying Squad officer, 'but it must have done.' The clientele also included a surgeon who was described as 'the greatest drinker I ever saw', surely an accolade coming from a group which prided itself on alcohol intake.

[26] H. Challenor with A. Draper, *Tanky Challenor*.

and were swept back three. For every villain you put behind bars there were always two more to take their place.'[27]

Was it possible, asked *The Times*, for a Detective Sergeant to remain on duty for five months after the onset of an acute form of paranoid schizophrenia, and to the accompaniment of a crescendo of serious allegations as to his conduct, without someone or something being seriously at fault? Was it possible for the Detective Sergeant's intermittent outbursts which on the most lenient interpretation amounted to grossly culpable excess of zeal, to go unchecked for that period, unless there existed at his station the atmosphere in which the lower ranks of a disciplined force know that there are certain things which are contrary to regulations and which are wrong, and that they also know that they are allowed to do those things provided they are not found out, and no one is going to try very hard to find out?

The answer, of course, is yes, it was. Harold 'Tanky' Challenor was merely a scapegoat. As 'Nipper' Read commented:

Suddenly everyone realized he was crazy. He was known for his erratic behaviour and, in fact, senior officers encouraged him. He was called a personality. The senior officers only realized his outrageous behaviour when it was too late. They forgave the things he did. Harry and his kids had a very good arrest rate. If the Queen of Greece hadn't been on a visit I don't suppose he'd even have been caught out.

Perhaps the final word on the Challenor affair should go to Paul O'Higgins, a fellow of Christ's College, Cambridge, who wrote:

When certain newspapers published news of the Report under such headlines as 'Challenor: Police Cleared', they gave a misleading impression, because the Report, while exculpating the police with respect to their failure to detect Challenor's incipient insanity, did no more than that, and did not deal directly with the questions which have given rise to public concern, namely whether there was a lack

[27] Ibid., p. 154.

of proper control over the activities of police officers in the London West End Central police station and in the Metropolitan Police generally, and whether there was any foundation for the belief that violence and other forms of illegality were prevalent on the part of a number of police officers.[28]

But now it was not only the Met who were having troubles. Despite great efforts by the Sheffield police to sweep things under the carpet, the Rhino-whip case refused to stay down with the underlay and the force was embroiled in an inquiry.

From 1946 until 1963 there had been an impressive detection rate of indictable crime in Sheffield. It had never fallen below forty-nine per cent and in the heady year of 1955 it had reached nearly sixty-six per cent; in 1962 it was some eighteen per cent above the national average. But in the early months of 1963 there was a significant drop. So on 9 March 1963 a special Crime Squad of seven officers was established under the overall control of Detective Chief Superintendent George Carnill, who had joined the force in the days when strong-arm tactics by the police, under the supervision of successive Chief Constables, had cleared up the Garvin-Mooney gambling and protection gangs of the 1920s.

The squad was relieved of the boredom of covering day-to-day crime and instead was set to concentrate on serious crime, mainly break-ins. There were two shifts in which two young Constables, Derek Millicheap and Derek Streets, described as 'likely youngsters', worked together. There were, however, no immediate results and on 14 March all members were called to a meeting where devotion to duty and the need for commitment and long hours were stressed. In fact at the time no days off were being allowed the special squad. In the previous two years, the regular squad of fifty had worked 16,000 hours between them and in that time Streets had headed the list, working in excess of 380 hours' overtime. There is little doubt that Streets and Millicheap believed they were part of an elite squad who thought they could use tough methods to deal with tough criminals and take risks to achieve speedy results. Indeed at the meeting Detective Chief Inspector Wells pointed out

[28] *Criminal Law Review* 1965 p.663.

they would be dealing with hardened criminals who might be expected to plead not guilty.

Equally certainly he related (possibly with humorous touches) an incident when a member of the 1957 squad was accused in court of using a 'lie detector'. By this he certainly meant an instrument used to extract a confession by violence, and we do not accept those witnesses still in the service who say they thought the reference was to a scientific instrument or tape recorder . . . Upon the whole we have come reluctantly to the conclusion that the admitted reference to a 'lie detector', which had otherwise little point, did contain a veiled hint to those who wished to take it that force might have to be resorted to, coupled, as we find it was, with reference to 'taking chances'.[29]

Shortly after the meeting, the squad, which had been on duty since 8 am 'with little food and no success', received some information and members went to the White Horse public house in Malinda Street. There they arrested three well-known local faces, two of them brothers, and took them to the CID headquarters in Water Lane.

Apart from a screwdriver and a pair of gloves (which we are satisfied were found on a search of the van at CID headquarters and not dropped by Kenneth Hartley at the time of his arrest as DI Rowley said) there was no evidence to justify this precipitate action and at an informal meeting at the Wheatsheaf public house . . . DI Rowley expressed the view that confessions must be obtained or Detective Chief Superintendent Carnill (using his nickname Chang) would be furious.[30]

The men were interrogated in the upstairs conference room and blinds were drawn to shut out the view from overlooking flats. The aim of the interrogations, which included beating with a truncheon and an instrument known as a rhino-tail, about eight

---

[29] *Sheffield Police Appeal Inquiry*, 1963 (HMSO), Cmd 2176.
[30] There is a full and excellent account of the case in J. P. Bean's *Crime in Sheffield*, chapter 12.

inches long and made of a gut-like material with a plaited loop at one end, was to get confessions to break-ins at the Crookes Valley Park Café and the Forum Cinema.

The two brothers were charged; the third man was released. Next morning the brothers appeared in court and were remanded in custody. But one stripped to the waist and showed the marks on his body to the magistrates. The men were given the opportunity for photographs and a medical inspection. After the hearing Chief Constable Eric Staines asked Carnill to make a full and immediate inquiry to find out what had happened. However, for a week no statements were taken from the detectives involved and no other member of the Crime Squad made a statement at all. As for notebooks, these were compiled a week after the allegation. Of the rhino-whip there was no trace. One of the detectives involved had, very sensibly, burned it, along with the offending truncheon. Charges of burglary against the brothers were dropped.

And charges against the detectives? The Chief Constable wished the matter to be dealt with internally and on 27 March Arthur Hewitt, the solicitor for the brothers, was granted summonses against Millicheap and Streets under s18 (triable only on indictment) and s20 (triable in either the magistrates' court or before a jury) of Offences Against the Person Act 1861. The Chief Constable, when shown the photographs of the injuries, was totally unwilling to accept that any member of his force could have been responsible for them. Indeed one of the first suggestions made by the police to explain away the bruising was that the brothers were sado-masochists and the injuries were self-inflicted. When Millicheap and Streets were served with the summonses neither made a reply. Later, in the canteen, according to a Detective Chief Inspector, Millicheap indicated he would plead guilty to the lesser charge, s20, saying 'Well, it was a vicious assault'. Streets said, 'We must have been mad.'

On 2 May Streets and Millicheap pleaded guilty to the s20 summonses, in return for which the s18 charges were dropped. Hewitt, prosecuting privately, told the magistrates the allegations against the police officers. In turn their counsel put forward what was the policemen's new, improved and just as mendacious version of events. The sado-masochist story had flown out of the window by now. No, there had been no systematic beating; the men had been drunk and abusive and had started fighting amongst themselves. In breaking it up the officers had done that bit too much. Mr Peter Baker for the defence said, 'They were so truculent, foul-mouthed, obscene and quarrelsome among themselves they had to be restrained by these two officers. They did not stop at restraining them but laid into them and gave them what some may think these men possibly deserved. But they went too far.'[31]

The magistrates clearly accepted the defence version of the matter. 'When police are assaulted courts regard the offence as more than usually serious and the converse must also apply,' said chairman Bryan Pye-Smith. 'In instances, and how few they are, where the police are guilty of violence and assault on members of the public, the offence must be taken with extreme seriousness.'

Streets was fined £75 for his assault on Albert Hartley, his brother Kenneth and on Patrick Clifford Bowman. Derek Edward Millicheap pleaded guilty to similar offences against Bowman and Albert Hartley, and was fined £50. Each was ordered to pay £49.6s.8d. costs. There had been a whip-round to pay for their defence. Now an officer started a collection to pay their fines; £73.10s.0d. was paid by one anonymous donor. An effort to persuade other officers to contribute failed.

There is not much doubt that Streets and Millicheap believed the matter would end there. Indeed they had, they thought, been promised that it would, apart perhaps from a small disciplinary ticking-off. It did not. They were dismissed the force by the Chief Constable, whose decision was confirmed by the Watch Committee. They appealed the decision and then the whole shabby truth began to emerge before the tribunal, chaired by Graham Swanwick, and heard under the Police (Appeals) Rules, 1943. There was, the tribunal found, a concerted effort amongst the squad to explain away the injuries.

The first thought of Streets and Millicheap was to pin their hopes on a previous fight between the brothers and another man. That was discovered to have been some time earlier and no injuries had resulted. As the tribunal report said, 'Five days were spent in anxious deliberation by the squad, concocting versions that might meet or mitigate the allegations.

[31] *News of the World*, 5 May 1963.

The evidence of Mr Streets that Detective Inspector Rowley was the main author of the concocted versions and what their successive nature was, is confirmed beyond doubt.'[32]

Disregarding the suggestion that the injuries had been self-inflicted for sexual gratification, the versions put forward were: first, a fight on arrest; second, when it was thought that four officers might be charged, that there had been a fight in the lavatory with the brothers fighting the third man; and third, the fight had been broken up by Streets and Millicheap with DC Rowlands coming to help and in turn being joined by DI Rowley. When it was learned that only Streets and Millicheap would be charged, they were left as the only ones involved in the fight. 'This was embodied in two typewritten, but unsigned, statements by the appellants, bearing the date 15 March, but in fact not drafted in their final form until the 20th or 21st.'

Why did the two 'likely youngsters' agree to take all the blame? For a start, they were the ones who administered the beating, though admittedly with the connivance of other officers. Secondly, they were afraid that if they implicated other officers, they would 'gang up' against them. Thirdly, they thought that if they told the true story implicating senior officers, they would not be believed by the justices and that an apparent effort to shift blame and seeming disloyalty would count against them. Finally they told the tribunal that they had received advice to plead guilty and hints from DCS Carnill, DI Rowley and another officer that they would not lose their jobs.

The tribunal roundly criticized the senior officers. DI Rowley had handed in his resignation shortly after the incident, a resignation that the tribunal thought should not have been permitted. It thought that the Chief Constable lived in an ivory tower and was barely able to accept that men under his command could be guilty of truly infamous conduct. It considered that he had leaned far too heavily on Chief Superintendent Carnill, left too much to him and was over-influenced by him: 'When the appellants were convicted (and indeed before) we consider that he shut his eyes to the evidence of the photographs supporting the prosecution version as given in court, and was

[32] *Sheffield Police Appeal Inquiry*, 1963 (HMSO), Cmd 2176. This and the following quotations are from the Swanwick report.

content to accept the version of the fight in the lavatory without further inquiring into its probable falsity.'

Carnill was criticized over his investigations.

He was content that no statement should be forthcoming from the squad for at least five days, although they had hardly anything else to do: although known to be strict on notebooks, he neither examined nor caused to be examined a single one: he never insisted on a statement from any of the squad except the appellants, and he accepted unsigned typewritten statements from them: he neither made nor instructed an immediate search for weapons such as it was alleged on March 15 were used.

The appeals by Streets and Millicheap were dismissed.

On 6 November the Watch Committee announced the suspension of the Chief Constable and Carnill. Two weeks later Carnill and DCI Wells announced their retirements. They were followed by the Chief Constable, who resigned his £4,000 a year post on 20 November. He died in Bournemouth in 1979. The editor of the *Sheffield Telegraph*, who had done much to keep the issue in front of the public, was named journalist of the year.

5

From the 1960s onwards

Police problems in Yorkshire had turned from Sheffield in the early 1960s to Leeds by the end of the decade. The troubles had started as early as 1953 when two officers were dismissed for taking money from bookmakers. Over the years there had been considerable laxness, until between 1969 and 1971 eleven members of the Leeds constabulary were charged with a variety of offences, ranging from theft to indecent assault on children. One of the charges included a conspiracy to pervert the course of justice following the death of an elderly widow on a pedestrian crossing on Christmas Eve and involving Superintendent Derek Holmes, who had been the driver.

Known as the 'Big Red' affair, after the nickname of the Superintendent, it came to light when the two Constables involved went, after the inquest, to the coroner to tell him what they really knew. They had felt unable to confide in their superior officers and alleged a cover-up, including an allegation that beer had been smelled on the breath of the teetotal widow, Minni Wein. The case resulted in prison sentences of nine months for Brian Nicholson and Inspector Geoffrey Ellerker. Three other officers, including the head of the traffic police, were cleared. It was, said the trial judge Mr Justice Mocatta, tragic that through a misguided sense of loyalty the officers should have committed misconduct. Mr Justice Mocatta did not know the full story.

With Ellerker in prison, investigations began again into the case of David Oluwale, a lame, mentally disturbed Nigerian vagrant who had been found drowned in the River Aire.

Described as violent and dirty, he had been tormented by Ellerker and Sergeant Kenneth Kitching, who were later cleared of his manslaughter but found guilty of a series of assaults. Their trial revealed a nine-month campaign of harassment and bullying of Oluwale. Other officers gave evidence that both the Inspector and the Sergeant had assaulted the man in front of them and they had stood by and done nothing. During the investigation almost all the 1,100 members of the force were interviewed in secret. Ellerker and Kitching received prison sentences of three years and twenty-seven months respectively but it was clear that camaraderie was stronger than the lesson learned by colleagues in Sheffield.

Indeed the Leeds force at the time paraded a thoroughly unattractive collection of incidents which virtually covered the spectrum of corruption a force could reasonably manage. Back in 1963 a Constable had been jailed for four years for conspiracy to pervert the course of justice. Two years later a Sergeant and a Constable were fined for the same offence and were reinstated by the Chief Constable. In 1969 a Sergeant, acting as a coroner's officer, was given a two-year suspended sentence for forgery and for stealing money found on bodies awaiting inquest. Later that year a Constable was fined for stealing from a supermarket. The next year, in April, a Constable was jailed for nine months for burglary and in July a Constable was fined for stealing from a woman's handbag at the police station. In 1970 three police officers were found guilty of theft. The ringleader, a Sergeant, was given three years' imprisonment and a Constable twenty-seven months. The same month a Constable received nine months' for indecent assault on two boys and a girl, whilst in September 1971 a Panda car Constable had been fined £50 after admitting a charge of attempted bribery arising out of a friend's speeding offence in another police area. Suggestions that a public inquiry should be held into the force were rejected.

Meanwhile, back in London, it was not until the great *Times*' exposure in 1969 that the public realized that there were still serious questions to be raised about the behaviour of the Metropolitan Police. On Saturday, 29 November that year an article was published alleging corruption by Detective Sergeants John Symonds and Gordon Harris and Detective Inspector Bernard Robson. It also gave rise to the phrase 'a firm within a firm'. Symonds, Robson and Harris had, said the article, been systematically blackmailing Michael Smith (real name Michael Perry), a small-time Peckham thief, whilst offering him both help if he should find himself in difficulties and advice as to where he should hide his ill-gotten gains for safe-keeping (putting them into a little sweet shop with a bird running it). 'Then if a wheel comes off so what? You've got a home and a – business.'

> Disturbing evidence of bribery and corruption among certain London detectives was handed by *The Times* to Scotland Yard last night. We have, we believe, proved that at least three detectives are taking large sums of money in exchange for dropping charges, for being lenient with evidence offered in court, and for allowing a criminal to work unhindered.
>
> Our investigations into the activities of these three men convince us that their cases are not isolated. We cannot prove that other officers are guilty but we do believe that there is enough suspicion to justify a full inquiry.
>
> The possible scope of corruption is disclosed by the admission of a detective sergeant who has taken £150. The total haul of this detective, Sgt John Symonds of Camberwell, and two others, Detective Inspector Bernard Robson of Scotland Yard's C9 division, and Detective Sergeant Gordon Harris, a regional crime squad officer on detachment from Brighton to Scotland Yard, was more than £400 in the past from one man alone.[1]

The squad had been investigating a series of burglaries by a gang using skeleton keys and Michael Perry had been a suspect. During a raid on his flat in Nunhead Lane, Peckham, the detectives had found twelve bottles of stolen whisky and equipment of a type used by safebreakers. Robson threatened to 'find some gelignite' to complete the kit. The next day Perry paid Harris £25 for not telling the court about a previous conviction for receiving and shortly after that, when Robson saw Perry in a car, he thrust a packet into the man's hand pretending it contained a stick of gelignite.

Perry took the advice of a friend, South-East London crime

---

[1] *The Times*, 29 November 1969.

boss Joey Pyle, and went to *The Times*.[2] Senior reporters Garry Lloyd and Julian Mounter wired up Perry, whilst his conversations were monitored by an independent sound-recording engineer. In all, thirteen tapes were produced in evidence and included such comments as: 'Don't forget, always to let me know straight away because I know people everywhere' and 'If you are nicked anywhere in London . . . I can get someone on the blower to someone in my firm who will know someone somewhere who can get something done.'[3] During October and November 1969 Perry paid £250 to the officers, £200 so that the planted gelignite could be forgotten and £50 in respect of information of an impending police raid. The press investigation continued with, on one occasion, the observant Robson noticing the reporters and asking Perry who they were.

The tapes and statements were handed to Detective Inspector Brett, the night duty officer at the Yard, at 10 pm on Friday evening, the 28th. It was arranged that two Chief Superintendents, Roy Yorke and Fred Lambert, should go through the material with a view to briefing Assistant Commissioner (Crime) Peter Brodie the next morning. By then, however, the named, and unnamed, men were well aware of the allegations made against them. Symonds had already contacted one potential witness against him before summoning Victor Lissack, the portly and able London solicitor, to his home in Kent, to instruct him to issue a writ for libel and to make a statement denying the allegations. Robson, meanwhile, was discussing his position with a colleague in the Regional Crime Squad.[4]

In *The Fall of Scotland Yard* the authors adroitly point out what would have happened had the allegations been made

[2] Pyle had a long and successful career as a major figure in the London underworld. Apart from a sentence of eighteen months' imprisonment for his part in a fight in the Pen Club in Stepney in 1961, when Selwyn Cooney was shot dead, he avoided prison sentences until November 1992, when he received fourteen years for being involved in the distribution of heroin.

[3] Garry Lloyd and Julian Mounter in *The Times*, 29 November 1969.

[4] Lambert did at least make efforts to unravel what was a very tangled web of corruption. Unfortunately at the time he was, perhaps, not a suitable person to have been on the inquiry. He was under great strain and having matrimonial difficulties. He was eventually removed from the inquiry in May 1970 by Moody's superior, Wally Virgo when he disagreed with DAC Dick Chitty. In turn Virgo was convicted with Moody in the Porn trial (see below).

against someone outside the police: 'The normal conduct of a criminal inquiry – searching the suspects' homes, desks, lockers – seems to have been totally neglected.'[5] As they say, little effort was made to take the investigatory action which might have led to the officers being able to clear their names. Instead many days were spent trying to intimidate and discredit *The Times* reporters and their tapes. In this they were unsuccessful. Despite being questioned for eight hours a day over a three-week period, Lloyd and Mounter were unshaken. The tapes were sent for a series of examinations. The fee of one expert at this stage was £1,500. He later appeared as a defence witness for Harris and Robson.

In the face of this sort of evidence, what was the Met to do? The answer, say some, was far from the exhaustive investigation called for by the allegations; it was, rather, a cover-up. And there is a good deal of support for this theory. For a start, much of the investigation was left in the hands of the notably corrupt Chief Detective Superintendent Bill Moody, who was at the time taking the kind of sums from Soho pornographers that would make Symonds and Co seem strictly third division.[6] Nor was much interest taken in the man described by Lloyd and Mounter as a 'senior police officer . . . said to have operated for years a sophisticated system using two scrap-metal dealers as middlemen. The alleged activities of this officer are well known to South London's petty thieves.' He remained on duty.

Then, in a blaze of publicity, Frank Williamson, aged fifty-two and Her Majesty's Inspector of Constabulary for Crime, was appointed as adviser to oversee the inquiry. However, Williamson, former Chief Constable of Cumbria with a reputation as an honest and painstaking detective, was seen by the Met as an intruder who, it was feared, would ensure that a damning report was produced. He had been the officer in the successful prosecution of William McConnach, the Chief Constable of Southend, which had resulted in a conviction on thirty-two of thirty-five counts of dishonesty and a sentence of two years' imprisonment. The McConnach investigation was looked on as a model investigation, as opposed to the Brighton case in which the inquiry had been conducted by Met

[5] B. Cox et al, *The Fall of Scotland Yard*, p. 42.

[6] He later received a sentence of twelve years' imprisonment (see chapter 7).

officers and which had resulted in the acquittal of Ridge and the ensuing litigation over his wrongful dismissal. Williamson's views on police corruption were well known and he had stated at many detective training schools that until the words 'except police officers' were written into certain statutes, they must be dealt with in just the same way as any other offender.

He recalls his appointment by James Callaghan, Home Secretary at the time:

The article was published on that Saturday morning in December 1969 and I heard nothing that weekend at all. I had no remit in the Metropolitan Police. I heard nothing in the office during the week until on the following Thursday I was going to Dishforth in North Yorkshire to lecture to a senior detective officers' course. When I arrived I was told, 'You're to speak on the phone to Mr Callaghan's private secretary and you're to return to London immediately.' So I turned round and my driver and I made it by the skin of our teeth. I saw Callaghan alone and he asked had I read the exposé in *The Times*. 'What do you think ought to be done?' I said, 'Well, it's too late now but you should have had an independent inquiry.'

Callaghan said, 'What do you mean, it's too late?' I said, 'Well, if they were going to do any damage they'll have done it. Papers and records will have been destroyed and gelignite wrappers will have been thrown away and the whole thing will be blown wide open.' The first thing that happened on the night this was offered to the Yard by *The Times* everybody named on the tapes was warned by C1 what was coming.

Callaghan said, 'You've just got yourself a job.' I said that although I had no police powers, no remit in the Metropolitan Police, I was prepared to do anything he wanted but 'I want to make it clear I'm five days behind the ball and that's too much start to give these people. If you want me to do something I'll do it but it'll need you to tell the Commissioner and you'll have a battle.'

I went in on the following Monday. At about 11.30 the staff officer brought the *Evening Standard* in and put it on my desk. It said words like 'Outsider appointed to Head Police Inquiry', 'Frank Williamson invited by the Commissioner'. I wasn't or, if I was, he had been forced to invite me – to advise on the nature, scope and extent of the inquiries into the allegations made by *The Times*.

It was the start of the troubles which were to lead to Williamson's early retirement.

By the time I got there, du Rose had got Moody into the inquiry on the pretext he was going to deal with the Warwickshire officers involved in Perry's tape. Moody was clearly sent in to that inquiry to sabotage it. Du Rose was active in the obstruction of *The Times* inquiry right from the word go. He was responsible for getting Moody into it and there was only one reason for that.

Du Rose and I fell out on the very first day I was there. He came into the office and said, 'I don't know what you're doing here', and I said, 'I'll tell you what I'm doing here. I'm here to make a contribution to this inquiry' and I said, 'Let me just tell you something while you're here with the door shut. If it comes to a competition as to who can be the most diabolical between you and I, I'll win that bloody contest, John, hands down.' It wasn't very long before he put his ticket in and went to National Car Parks. I can't prove why, but I know why. Because he got the wind up. He realized the game was partially up.

From that moment on Brodie, who was Assistant Chief Commissioner, and Waldron, who was the Commissioner, never spoke to me. They shut the door completely on me, with the effect that from the day it was announced Brodie was virulent, poisonous, said things about me which if I'd been of that frame of mind I'd taken him to the cleaners.

Leonard 'Nipper' Read, who also fell foul of the mandarins on the fifth floor, confirms Williamson's problems:

At the time of the inquiry I was a Chief Superintendent at Scotland Yard and Frank, a good friend of mine, would confide in me both the difficulties he was experiencing and the attitude of some of the top brass of the CID. It can be summed up quite neatly. One day he asked to see me and I said, 'I'll meet you at the Yard.' 'Good God,' he said, 'we can't do that, Nipper.' And when asked why ever not, he said, 'I'm *persona non grata* at the Yard.' I was dumbfounded. Here was a man who had been a provincial Chief Constable and who was now an Inspector of Constabulary whose presence in the Yard was being questioned.

We had to meet in a pub and there he expressed his concern at the quality and ability of officers seconded to his inquiry from the Yard, giving as an example Detective Chief Superintendent Bill Moody.[7]

Robert Mark, who became the Commissioner, believes *The Times* affair was mishandled by the Home Office and wrote:

The Secretary of State should have immediately exercised his power under Section 49 of the Police Act 1964, and insisted that the matter be investigated by a suitably senior chief constable assisted by a specially selected team of provincial and Metropolitan officers. The Home Office, however, decided to follow a different course. The inquiry was left in the hands of the Metropolitan Police, with Frank Williamson, HM Inspector of Constabulary (Crime), being assigned to the task of advising and overseeing the operation. Inspectors of Constabulary are not police officers and have no police powers. They are not able to give orders to police officers at any level. Their duties are inspectorial and advisory and their authority depends entirely upon the willingness of the Home Secretary to support them on a particular issue, if necessary, in extreme cases, by threat of withholding the Exchequer grant of half the cost of the force. It can hardly have come as a surprise to Frank Williamson that in the circumstances of this kind he was not likely to see the inquiry conducted in the way in which he would have wished. He did, however, fight tenaciously and was able to insist on the inclusion of provincial detective officers in the investigating team. It is largely to his credit that it ended, but not before March 1972, with the conviction of two detectives and their subsequent imprisonment. A third fled the country and has not been seen since.[8]

[7] L. Read and J. Morton, *Nipper*, pp. 44–45.
[8] R. Mark, *In the Office of Constable*, p. 108.

Williamson says that if he had had 'another dozen good men I'd have beaten them. If I'd had someone I could say to, just go out and do that job properly for me and take a proper statement, if I'd had twenty senior officers from the provinces, I'd have beaten them.' He thinks that if he had had a properly defined position on the inquiry, he would have been able to do something about the thirty-odd officers mentioned in *The Times* inquiry against whom no action was taken. 'If I'd had Jim Callaghan on my own I think we would have made a dramatic difference to *The Times* inquiry but not with Brodie and Waldron because Brodie and Waldron were feeding Philip Allan, then the head of the Permanent Civil Service in the Home Office, with what were nothing more than lies which had been fed up to them from the Deputy Assistant Commander level in the CID.'

Mark apparently also kept his head down. 'If I wanted to speak to Bob Mark, who was the Deputy Commissioner, I had to meet him at the Scilly Isles pub outside Esher on his way home. He wouldn't be identified as having anything to do with me while the inquiry was going on.'

The Yard was seemingly quite keen to nobble witnesses, smearing both them and Williamson, who says:

Just before I finished in 1971 I did a final inspection of Essex police. You had to interview anyone who requested to see you. I had a request from a DI called Larby. I saw him at Brentwood on my own and he said he had been carrying a weight on his mind for a long time. I said 'What is it?' and he said, 'I was in C9 when *The Times*' allegations were published. I came into the office in the morning about a quarter past nine and in the office was Detective Inspector Robson and he said, "We're in the shit because the piece about the gelignite is true."' The committal proceedings had already taken place and there had been a number of officers from the Met who had said the gelignite incident had never happened. Here we had a man from Essex saying categorically Robson had admitted having gelignite which he had put in Perry's hand.

I said, 'You know this is going to the Old Bailey?' and he said 'Yes' and I said, 'You know what's going to happen to you when you get in the witness box in the Old Bailey?' and he said, 'I shall have a bloody rough time.' I said, 'I should accelerate that a little bit, it'll be worse than that,' so he said, 'Well, so be it.'

I said, 'You've walked about with this information in your head for two years. Who did you tell?' And he said, 'I told my Chief Constable John Nightingale on the afternoon it happened. I went specially to Chelmsford headquarters and asked to see the Chief on a matter of urgency.' I queried whether that was true and he said it was.

Nightingale was out in an anteroom and I said, 'John, I want a senior detective officer to take a statement off this man and I want it as a complete issue from beginning to end.' He said, 'Why do you want one off my detective officer?' I said, 'There's a very serious situation which now I want you to talk about.' A Detective Chief Superintendent took the statement and it confirmed he had told his Chief Constable, so I said to Nightingale, 'What did you do about this, an allegation of fearful corruption and collusion between police officers?' He said, 'The Met's nothing to do with me. I did nothing about it.' I said, 'You're a police officer, you've got a responsibility.'

I rang Skelhorn and told him I wanted to see him immediately because I had some dynamite in my hands. I saw him at Buckingham Gate and he told me to go the next morning and take a statement from Nightingale and he would deal with him as far as he was able. Nothing happened to Nightingale except he got knighted some six years later.

That was only part of the story. Within a matter of days two Flying Squad men went down to Brentwood, sorted him out in his office and said, 'Withdraw that statement or else.' The or else was that the *People* newspaper the following Sunday published an article that a DI in Essex had been keeping company with the wife of a thief who was in prison.[9] He was identified by the fact that he liked to have intercourse with his socks on.

When we submitted the officer's statement I thought the roof was going to come off the Yard. They called me all

[9] *People*, 23 April 1972. The story revealed that the officer had been having an affair with the wife of a man then serving a seven-year sentence for receiving.

the bastards they could lay their tongues to, Brodie in the officer's mess accusing me of being dishonest during my service in Manchester. There was a campaign of vilification such as I have never known, and I wasn't brought up in the cupboard. They sent two Flying Squad officers to Manchester to see Bobby McDermott, the King of the Barrow Boys, who had a cellar in New Barn Street. These two officers went to see McDermott and tried to get him to say something about me being dishonest but he wouldn't.

He did not appear at the trial. Robson now accepted the gelignite incident, saying he was not trying to obtain money but evidence from Perry, but his acceptance did neither him nor the officer any good. After disciplinary proceedings he was dismissed from the Essex Police.

Why did Brodie behave so badly towards Williamson? Can he possibly have been dishonest himself? There had, at the time and subsequently, been persistent rumours in the underworld that it was possible to reach as high as Assistant Commissioner level. Writing while he was still alive, the authors of *The Fall of Scotland Yard* speak highly of him: 'As Chief Constable, first of Stirling and Clackmannan and then of Warwickshire, Brodie had pursued corruption when it became apparent with a zeal which some had thought excessive. He had also had the task, as an Inspector of Constabulary himself from 1964 to 1968, of overseeing Williamson's involvement in the Southend inquiry, on which he had given Williamson strong backing.'[10]

Williamson was in as good a position to form a view as anyone:

I would love to be able to tell you Brodie was bent because it would be a retribution. I cannot. It would be totally irresponsible for me to say I knew he was in any way bent but I can tell you this: he was completely and utterly stupid and he accepted the advice of the senior officers like Du Rose and Millen. Anything they said became gospel and they were twisting him right, left and centre. They were putting the umbrella up over the dishonest troops in the CID in London. They had nothing to worry about because Peter Brodie would

[10] B. Cox et al, *The Fall of Scotland Yard*, pp. 34–5.

say to me, 'You've got it wrong, my chaps wouldn't do this to me.'

One night on the 5th floor, Brodie came along the passage. I said to him, 'Just the man I want to see', and I put a proposition to him about Moody being dishonest because of him driving motor cars which had originated from Humphries, and he said, 'I'm not interested in the motor cars that Moody drives.' I said, 'You ought to bloody well be,' and we had a right shouting match.[11]

The consensus of opinion amongst senior officers of the time is that Brodie, whom they point out was 'a Trenchard man', was a fool rather than a knave. This is Nipper Read:

Although I had always liked Brodie, my assessment of him as being ill advised was borne out later at the corruption trials when he gave evidence on behalf of convicted officers. His misguided loyalty to the wrong people made him the implacable foe of Sir Robert Mark, who destroyed him with the observation that the CID were 'the most routinely corrupt organization in London' and who removed the command of the CID from Brodie and placed it in the hands of the Divisional Commanders. Perhaps it is to Brodie's credit that he still tried to defend his 'chaps', saying they were a straight bunch of guys, but with *The Times* enquiry and the Porn Squad investigation, his position was becoming intolerable. From that point on he almost relinquished his command to the mandarins, who relished the situation.

Brodie was one of the 'old school' of officers who tried to freeze Mark out but it was he who was offered the position of Commissioner on the death of Joseph Simpson. Mark turned it down, suggesting the caretaker appointment of Waldron, hoping that by Waldron's retirement he, Mark, would have learned sufficient about the Met to know how to deal with it when he took over. When Mark was appointed Deputy Commissioner Brodie knew his chance had gone.

I didn't see Brodie again until 1972 when I went to the Home Office where I had been called for interview for the post of National Co-Ordinator of the Regional Crime

[11] L. Read and J. Morton, *Nipper*, chapter 12.

Squads. Brodie was one of the members of the panel. He greeted me warmly when we met outside, shook my hand, said how nice it was to see me again and wished me all the best. 'I'm sorry to tell you the competition against you is very strong,' he said. 'I don't think you're going to get it this time. I've got three Commanders in for it and one is first favourite for the job. Never mind . . . Good luck anyway.' The first favourite was Commander Ken Drury who in July 1977 was sentenced to eight years' imprisonment after he had been found guilty of corruption.

Nor did Williamson have any help from Commissioner Sir John Waldron. On the death of Commissioner Joe Simpson, a Trenchard man, Callaghan had appointed a stop-gap in Waldron, then aged fifty-eight. It was made clear at the time that the next Commissioner would be Robert Mark, then an Assistant Commissioner who had been Chief Constable of Leicestershire and whose arrival at the Yard was deeply resented by senior officers in the Met. Mark had been approached by Callaghan and been told that Waldron was to have a two-year appointment. In the event, with a change of government and Waldron's reluctance to hand in his spurs, it was to last four years, with Mark as Deputy Chief Commissioner. Williamson says that Waldron 'enjoyed being Commissioner so much that he stayed. The only reason was, he didn't understand the nature of the problem he was sitting on. I once said to Jack Waldron in a fit of temper, I regret to say, when I was getting blank walls and obtuse contributions, "Jack, the playing fields of Winchester are not the place to find the facts of life." But the relationship between he and I at that stage was well beyond repair.

After a two-month trial on 3 March 1972 Robson, who had been the former head of a crime-busting operation codenamed Coathanger, received seven years, whilst his second in command, Harris, was sentenced to six years' imprisment. They stood to attention in the Old Bailey dock as Mr Justice Sebag Shaw pontificated in the manner all judges adopt when sentencing police officers: 'What you did was wicked and reprehensible. You destroyed respect for the law where it required to be preserved. You weakened its authority where it was your duty to support and assert it.'

The senior police officer was James Silvester, a Detective Inspector at Peckham. At disciplinary proceedings in May 1971 for failing to make notes of an arrest and making a false statement in relation to an alibi, he was demoted to the rank of Police Sergeant (second class CID). Appeals against the demotion failed and Silvester later resigned from the force.

As Robert Mark noted, the third detective – Symonds – had fled the country before his trial but he returned and was sent to prison for twenty-four months when he surrendered seven years later. On his release he had an extraordinary tale to tell, including allegations that a senior officer attempted to solicit £500,000 from a rich suspect. Other allegations, aimed mainly at the staff of the Director of Public Prosecutions, were that a barrister with close links to the DPP's office was bisexual, a gambler and had been corrupted; that senior DPP officials leaked police documents to suspects who could then frustrate police inquiries; that a law officer had been lured into corruption by his love of pornography and that sensitive information had been passed to a solicitor and a private detective. He also claimed that officers whom he believed to be corrupt whilst he was at Scotland Yard had been promoted as high as Commander and that masonic links were used for protective purposes.[12] Three months later Symonds, who had defended himself, went on to say that he had been a spy for the KGB. Although it was privately conceded that there may have been a good deal in what he said regarding corruption at the top, after so many years had elapsed it was not possible to obtain corroboration. In any event Symonds would have been an easily destroyed witness.[13]

Whilst Deputy Commissioner, Robert Mark had endeavoured to take steps to deal with the CID, whom he saw as dangerously out of control. In his book he quotes an example of the disastrous state of relations between the CID and provincial forces. There had been a break-in on a trading estate in the Thames Valley region, when soap-pads valued at the not inconsiderable amount of around £5,000 had been stolen. There was information that a London team had been involved and as Mark wrote:

[12] *Daily Express*, 22 September 1984.
[13] *Daily Express*, 22 January 1985.

Two Metropolitan detectives had arrested two men, both of whom had bad records . . . they charged the men and notified the provincial force who undertook to send two officers to court on the following day. When they arrived they found the charges against the two men had been withdrawn, the store-keeper to whom they were trying to sell the stolen goods having pleaded guilty to a charge of dishonest handling, a previous conviction for dishonesty not having been revealed to the court. Needless to say the two provincials were speechless with rage. Withdrawal from the court of a charge of an indictable offence requires the consent of the Director of Public Prosecutions and he had not been consulted. The provincial chief constable complained to the commissioner and an inquiry was mounted by CID, the deputy commissioner, of course, having no status in the matter because the allegation was of crime.

The resultant report was a classic of its kind. The Metropolitan Police solicitor to whom I sent it described the report as so partisan as to be virtually worthless. No gloss favourable to the two Metropolitan officers had been omitted, however fatuous. He described the investigation as a travesty and said that the investigating officer had shown himself to be unfit to conduct any future investigation into allegations against police officers. He emphasized that if ever the report was disclosed to a court it would bring our system of investigation into contempt and went on in much the same vein. It is important to understand that he was not assuming corruption on the part of the two officers and that there might have been a satisfactory explanation for what they did. In the event neither they, nor anyone else, proffered one and the investigation was such as to pre-empt the possibility of criminal or even disciplinary proceedings. C department were asked to answer many pointed questions but replied immediately and simply with an assurance that there was no question of corruption.[14]

The outcome was that the investigating officer was promoted to Chief Superintendent and one of the investigating detectives was also promoted a few days later.

[14] R. Mark, *In the Office of Constable*, p. 114.

Williamson believes that even though on this occasion he was crying in the wind, this was the case which established Mark as a serious force with which to be reckoned. Mark became Commissioner on 17 April 1972, not long after the *People* had run the story that the Commander of the Flying Squad had been on holiday with James Humphreys, the Soho pornographer. Mark, as acting Commissioner designate, was able to force Brodie into suspending the officer. Mark wryly comments: 'Nine days later the Assistant Commissioner (Crime) went to hospital for observation, having obviously suffered a long period of excessive strain. He never returned to duty, though we were all relieved to hear that there was nothing fundamentally wrong with him.'

Williamson did not receive the praise and thanks he deserved. Over the years he spoke out against corruption in the police and as a result earned the displeasure of many, including Sir David 'The Hammer' McNee, who, in somewhat of a surprise appointment, became Commissioner in 1976 on Sir Robert Mark's retirement. Williamson took the trouble to meet him for luncheon and had given him papers regarding his thoughts on *The Times* inquiry and his recommendations for changes in the CID of the Met. For this he was rewarded in McNee's autobiography: 'They were helpful recommendations. If Frank Williamson had cared to check when I had been Commissioner for a few years he would have found that each had been acted upon. Some had already been implemented before I became Commissioner.'

Sir Robert Mark in his autobiography said of Williamson 'an honourable man unable to accept any longer the frustration and difficulties of the ideals of the police service in which he believed', to which McNee commented in his book, 'Fair enough, but not so fair to keep bobbing in and out of retirement to attack those who were trying to succeed where he failed.'[15] Anthony Judge says of Williamson that the experience ruined his life: 'Here was a man who had lived for the police and he had to live with the realisation that a key section was suffering from endemic corruption and no one would do anything about it.'

But before Mark's retirement and McNee's appointment the Drugs Squad had come under scrutiny. For some time there

[15] D. McNee, *McNee's Law*, p. 202.

had been reports that drugs taken from arrested criminals did not appear on the charge sheets and were being recycled by the Drugs Squad. Two years earlier, in 1976, the civil rights group, Release, had published a report which was highly critical of the police and which included allegations of planting. Release had also received some allegations of bribery too late for inclusion in the report. Efforts by Release to cooperate with Scotland Yard over the substantiation of the allegations broke down when Release became convinced that Scotland Yard was not taking the matter sufficiently seriously.

In November 1972 the high-flying Scotland Yard officer DCI Victor Kelaher and four other members of the squad were charged with conspiracy to pervert the course of justice and, with the exception of Kelaher, with perjury. This time HM Customs and Excise officers, who at times seem to have waged as long a war with Scotland Yard as they have with drug importers, complained about the relationship between the Drugs Squad and a major importer of cannabis. An inquiry by Lancashire detectives was led by Assistant Chief Constable Harold Prescott. It failed to provide sufficient evidence for a prosecution but a Met officer, Commander George Clarkson, led a second investigation into breaches of disciplinary regulations. There was evidence, for example, that in July 1970 Drugs Squad officers took part in a drug deal in London. A Ken Lee had tried to sell a gram of LSD, then worth around £450. Instead of arresting Lee, one of Kelaher's team had arranged for the drug to be sold to an agent of the Bureau of Narcotics and Dangerous Drugs (BNDD). In turn the agent had persuaded Lee to provide the names of his American contacts, who were duly arrested. So here was the sale and purchase of LSD in London with no arrest to show for it. Indeed it was all done under the supervision of a Scotland Yard officer. It was this sort of breach of regulations which led to the criminal charges.[16]

Kelaher, as *de facto* head of the Drugs Squad, had persuaded the gullible Brodie that his men should establish a presence at Heathrow, something which infuriated Customs and Excise who felt their best cases were being pinched by the Yard. It

[16] See B. Cox et al, *The Fall of Scotland Yard*, for a detailed account of the affair.

must have provided them with considerable satisfaction when in December 1970 Kelaher was found in a Holland Park flat with a prostitute, a Mrs Roberts, whose former husband was a Ghanaian diplomat whom Kelaher had arrested for a drugs importation in 1967. The officers confiscated some jewellery as well as a watch which Kelaher said he had given her.

Shortly before that incident, in the autumn of 1970, two Arabs came to London to try to sell two kilos of heroin and during their stay became friendly with a Bahamanian pimp and hustler, Basil Sands. Sands, who had known Kelaher through the club circuit in 1967, told the Chief Inspector about the heroin and over the next two months Kelaher and two of his aides met the Arabs in various London hotels to try to arrange buyers. Nothing came of the negotiations and the Arabs returned to Beirut. Meanwhile Sands had arranged to send out a British girl as a courier for further drug shipments. Unfortunately the Arabs acted independently and sent Sands a shipment of cannabis in a parcel of oriental goods. These arrived in the middle of a postal strike and Sands' telephone call to British European Airways to inquire if they had arrived was tapped by Customs and Excise. The Customs officers allowed the consignment, without the drugs, to be delivered. Sands had arranged with Kelaher that they should go to the Melba House Hotel in Earls Court, owned by Ghassan Idriss, a friend of Mr and Mrs Roberts. On 5 March the Customs officers surrounded the Melba House and arrested Sands and his friends, including Kelaher when he returned later in the evening. Kelaher was questioned by Customs officers for five hours, said nothing and was released.

What followed appears to have been a power struggle between the Home Office, the Customs and the Yard, with DAC Dick Chitty firmly against the idea of prosecuting Kelaher. It would, he said, lead to a further deterioration in the none too satisfactory relations with Customs. At least some people inside the Home Office, which had now accumulated considerable material, wished to have an independent investigation into the Drugs Squad. Again this was something not welcomed or permitted by the Yard. Kelaher was transferred to administrative duties at Tintagel House.

At his trial Sands took the line that he was an informant of Kelaher, who together with three of his Drugs Squad detectives, Pilcher, Prichard and Lilley, gave evidence for the defence. Of

Kelaher, John Marriage for Customs said, 'The more those of us concerned in this matter thought about [Kelaher's] statement, the less we came to the conclusion that Mr Kelaher could be believed.' The judge Alan Trapnell in his summing up had this to say: 'A forthright attack has been made on the character of Chief Inspector Kelaher, but the jury must not let their opinion of the Inspector sway their verdict even if in private they believe he was in the middle of the smuggling ring. If he is to be judged, let him be judged properly by another tribunal on some other occasion.' Sands received seven years for conspiracy to import cannabis.

When the prosecution of Kelaher and other members of his squad finally came, they were not helped in their case by the evidence of Commander Wally Virgo, whose testimony in fact favoured the defence. In the end, three of the junior officers were convicted of perjury. Prichard received four years; the others eighteen months each. Melford Stevenson, the judge, spoke of the more junior officers as 'the victims of dishonest superiors'. As for Prichard, he received another of those judicial homilies:

> You poisoned the wells of criminal justice and set about it deliberately. What is equally bad is that you have betrayed your comrades in the Metropolitan Police Force, which enjoys the respect of the civilized world – what remains of it – and not the least grave aspect of what you have done is to provide material for the crooks, cranks and do-gooders who unite to attack the police whenever opportunity occurs.[17]

Kelaher, in one of the smart cover-ups favoured by the Yard, was allowed to resign and given a medical discharge. In the shades of Challenor, he had spent a year attending St Thomas' Hospital for treatment for a nervous complaint. It did not work as well as might have been hoped. 'I am allowed by the Commissioner to say that had he not done so serious allegations would have been made against him in disciplinary proceedings,' said Alex Lyon, Minister of State for the Home Office.[18] Kelaher, recovered from his nervous

[17] A very full and dispassionate account of the disgrace of the Drugs Squad appears in B. Cox et al, *The Fall of Scotland Yard*, chapter 2; *Adam's Tale* by Gordon Honeycombe is the story of one of the officers who was acquitted.
[18] *Hansard*, 14 May 1974, p. 1262.

complaint, later wrote a book which, following representations by Scotland Yard, was never published in England.

But perhaps the biggest scandal of all was narrowly averted when the principal complainant, Albert, commonly called Charles, Taylor, conveniently died of a heart attack whilst on the way back to prison from the Old Bailey trial in which he was a defendant. In the inquiry it was quite apparent that there were still high-ranking officers who had escaped Sir Robert Mark's purge.

In the autumn of 1976 Taylor was under investigation in connection with a dollar premium fraud.[19] He was a well-known figure in the underworld and it had been at his hotel, the Leigham Court, in Streatham that an attack had been made on Peter Garfath, the lover of Rusty Humphreys, wife of the pornographer Jimmy Humphreys. Whilst on the run in Holland Humphreys had complained that a DCI John Bland of the Serious Crime Squad had framed him for the attack. Bland was a frequenter of Taylor's hotel. The information on Taylor was that he was being 'minded' by corrupt officers and that he was running the fraud.

Gilbert Kelland, then head of the CID, arranged for Bert Wickstead to lead an investigation. Wickstead selected his own staff but reported that he was being asked by a Deputy Assistant Commissioner from C department to explain their use.

Taylor was arrested and charged with a conspiracy to counterfeit gold half-sovereigns as well as with the dollar premium fraud. Lodged well out of the way in Bedford Prison, he now began to make lengthy statements about his involvement with very senior officers and Barry Pain, Chief Constable of Kent, was called in to conduct an inquiry under s49 of the Police Act 1964. Bland was suspended.

During the inquiry Wickstead received a call from the wife of a man with whom he had dealt as a junior officer in the PEN club shooting in the East End in 1959. The man, then in custody, told Wickstead that he had received an offer to set Wickstead up and was being supplied with dates and places where Wickstead was

[19] A dollar premium fraud operated when the Exchange Control Act was in force. It was only possible to buy a foreign investment by using currency from other British residents. This produced a shortage of investment currency and created a premium of up to half the value of the pound. In essence the fraud involved selling a foreign security on which it was claimed the premium had been paid when it had not.

alleged to have taken money. Wickstead sought the assistance of the new Commissioner, David McNee, but with the death of Taylor the inquiry was closed down. The Director of Public Prosecutions decided there was not sufficient evidence to bring charges. Bland resigned before disciplinary proceedings could be taken. The DAC in question also resigned at short notice on the grounds of ill health, as did a Commander. Wickstead was not pleased.

Meanwhile, things had not been going well in the City of London Police. Following allegations by a supergrass in August 1978, Operation Countryman was set up, originally to inquire into the City of London Police but later extended to cover the Met as well.

The inquiry began when the Commander of the Flying Squad, Don Neesham, reported what he saw as a corrupt association between professional criminals and officers in the City of London Police. This was reported to that force who, in turn, asked the Met to conduct an inquiry. As the inquiry progressed it became apparent that the Met itself might be implicated and it was decided that an outside force be involved in the inquiry. Leonard Burt, then an Assistant Chief Constable of the Dorset constabulary, was appointed with the agreement of his Chief Constable, Arthur Hambleton. Operation Countryman was established.

The problem of the City police stemmed not from misbehaviour by the lower ranks but lax behaviour at top level, where the Acting Commissioner was James Page, a former Superintendent in the Met who had been transferred in 1967. An active freemason, he was standing in for Sir Arthur Young who had been seconded to the Royal Ulster Constabulary. Page, who had served under the now disgraced Chief Constable of Blackpool, Stanley Parr, was warned of two freemasons in the City police who were known to be corrupt.[20] It was a warning he later ignored.

[20] There is a full account of Page's behaviour, his 'drinking with the lads' who were encouraged to call him 'Jim' and the need to take him home in a patrol car, in Stephen Knight's *The Brotherhood*, p. 87. Serious drinking and its accompanying problems were not confined to senior officers in the City force. The Police Federation complained after one Commander who had decided to pay an impromptu visit to the night duty squad at Holborn fell down, and shortly afterwards a Chief Constable of Hampshire fell whilst alighting from an official car at Hendon Police College following a luncheon and was unable to rise. He resigned.

In November 1971, when Sir Arthur Young retired, Page surprisingly beat John Alderson, later to become Chief Constable of Devon and Cornwall, in a two-horse race for the post of Commissioner. Page was

'mad about his masonry,' said one uniformed superintendent. Others of all ranks, some freemasons among them, have confirmed this. When the already highly masonic City force learned of the new Commissioner's passionate commitment to the brotherhood, many more officers joined the lodges. Page had a simple faith in masonry's power for good: officers who were masons were good officers because masonry was good.[21]

It was an interesting syllogism and one which the two officers ultimately proved wrong. Indeed Page compounded matters by refusing to discharge an unsuitable probationary Constable because he too was a mason.

In May 1976 £175,000 was stolen in an armed raid at the offices of the *Daily Express*. Sixteen months later another armed raid took place at Williams & Glyn's Bank in Birchin Lane off Lombard Street. This time £520,000 in wages was stolen. Six men in balaclava helmets and armed with shotguns ambushed a Securicor van. One of the guards was shot in the legs. After the Williams & Glyn's raid a number of well-known faces – Francis Fraser Jnr, James Fraser, George Copley, Harry Wright, Tony White and Allen Roberts – were arrested and freed on bail.[22] Then in the following year all charges were dropped.

[21] S. Knight, *The Brotherhood*, p. 92.
[22] Francis Fraser Jnr was not the well-known Frankie Fraser but a relation. Several of these men were career criminals. Copley, for example, scuppered a prosecution for robbery in 1981 by taping an interview with a Sergeant Pook who visited him in Reading Gaol. Pook confirmed an offer that if Copley would admit his part in the Williams & Glyn's robbery and also give evidence of corruption against certain London detectives, he would receive only a five-year sentence for the present charge. The tape was produced at the trial and Stephen Wooller for the Director of Public Prosecutions admitted it was 'hopelessly compromised'. In 1981 Roberts was shot by his partner John Hilton in a raid on a jewellers, which also resulted in the death of the jeweller. Harry Wright disappeared shortly after his release, since when there have been persistent rumours of his death in an execution (see J. Morton, *Gangland*, pp. 291–4).

In May 1977 a raid took place literally in the *Daily Mirror* building, where the security van had been locked in. Disguised as printers the gang escaped with £197,000. The driver of the security van was shot in the heart and died on the way to hospital. Two weeks after the *Mirror* robbery Tony White, just cleared of the Williams & Glyn's bank robbery, and Billy Tobin were arrested. At the subsequent trial of Chief Inspector Phillip Cuthbert for accepting bribes, an Alfie Sheppard said he acted as the middleman in bail and other negotiations. White was granted bail and later had all charges against him dropped. Tobin put up £3,000 for bail and Cuthbert provided Tobin's solicitor with a question and answer form. Bail was still refused but Tobin was later acquitted. He was sentenced to sixteen years' imprisonment in 1981 when he was caught *in flagrante* robbing a security van in Dulwich.

Knight advances an interesting argument about the crimes, concluding they would never have occurred if Page had not become a mason. If he had not been, he would never have had the masonic help necessary to beat Alderson and become the Commissioner in 1971. If he had not been a mason he would have listened to advice and not promoted the masonic officers of whom he had been warned. If they had not been promoted they could not have influenced the promotion of others who cooperated in setting up the raids at Williams & Glyn's and the *Mirror*.

The officers conducting Countryman were derisively referred to by the Met as the Sweedey, and they made little progress. In the end the eight Met officers who were finally charged were all acquitted. Later three of them were dismissed following disciplinary proceedings, one resigned and four resumed duty. The inquiry ended with allegations by the investigating officer Arthur Hambledon that he had been treated in a way which many villains have alleged to the courts over the years. He said that he had signed a statement as a result of inducements. And like the statements of many others with a good deal of right on their side, his explanation was not accepted.

However, the trial of two of the officers charged in the Countryman inquiry cast some interesting light on the City Police – and indeed the Met to whom the inquiry had spread. On a tape played at the Old Bailey, DCI Philip Cuthbert, then on trial for selling bail to criminals, named a senior officer as 'the greatest unhung villain' in London and a greedy bastard. He said that the man had taken money from two robberies, survived an official inquiry into his activities and had told Cuthbert he would take money as long as it was sensible.

Cuthbert alleged that the head of Scotland Yard's Robbery Squad and all his men had taken money in return for helping three of the men who had been arrested. In a conversation between Cuthbert and an Inspector John Simmonds, when Simmonds carried a concealed tape-recorder and microphone, Cuthbert said, 'Don't pretend, I used to bung X and Y and it used to go up the fucking top of the tree, used to go up to the AC.'

Cuthbert was explaining that the senior officer was trying to make him the patsy for the Countryman Operation and referred to the robbery at the *Daily Express* in 1976: 'He did the *Daily Express* job, governor, and I know what he copped on the *Daily Express* job. I know, only it doesn't matter. I mean you're new on the firm. It doesn't matter, but I know what he did. I know who got it for him and I know what he give them back.' Questioned, he said two more junior officers handled the distribution. One Sergeant got £300 out of £20,000 and 'he got the hump with it, thought it was a liberty'.

It's happened in the Met. It's happened in the City. It's happened in all the counties. It has happened for years and years. The job is different now. I don't do things like that.

I'm not saying somebody doesn't get a bit of bail. That will always happen. You will never stop it, but we don't let robbers go for money. I've never let robbers go for money in my life. I never would. And if anybody has it's not down to me.

He also said that the senior officer received money from the robbery at Williams and Glyn's bank because he was in a position of power up there on the Regional Crime Squad and covered things, 'same as all the blokes on the robbery squad had a drink out of it, going right up to the top of the tree, Z and the rest of them'. Cuthbert maintained that the amount of money which had changed hands after the Williams & Glyn's raid had been between £60,000 and £90,000.[23]

The senior officer made a statement saying the allegations were totally unfounded:

Between 1976 and 1978 I was seconded to the Home Office and played no part whatsoever into the investigation into the Williams & Glyn's robbery. I did commence the investigation into the *Daily Express* robbery but moved to the Home Office many months before any arrests were made and I never had any contact at all with those arrested.

I have never accepted a bribe nor been involved in any way with any criminal activities. No evidence was given at the trial to suggest otherwise – contrary to what might have been supposed by readers of some media coverage.

It is also suggested during the tape that I may have tipped off one of the accused, Mr Cuthbert, of Operation Countryman's interest in him. Again this is totally unfounded and there is no truth whatsoever in the allegation. On the day that Mr Cuthbert alleged that I had tipped him off I was not even aware of the investigation by an outside force other than the Metropolitan Police.

Reference was made on the tape to an inquiry some years before and the inference was made by Mr Cuthbert that the complaints against myself and other officers were true although 'not proved'. In fact the complainants have since admitted that the complaints were false and in an attempt to 'frame' the investigating officers.

Mr Cuthbert has since withdrawn his allegation also.

The senior officer was, however, obliged to apologize for inaccurate evidence he had given in the case. When his turn came to give evidence Cuthbert claimed he was drunk when he made the allegations taped by Simmonds.

On 20 July 1982 DI Philip Cuthbert, at the end of the six weeks' trial, was sentenced to thirty-six months' and ex-DS John Goldbourn to twenty-four months' imprisonment. The jury's verdicts were 'inevitable and sensible', said the trial judge.

[23] *Guardian*, 23 August 1982.

You tried to pull the wool over the eyes of sensible jurors – you failed.

Justice in England has been for countless years the admiration of the whole world and corruption by police officers strikes at its very roots.

I have watched jurors understandably refusing to convict on the uncorroborated word of decent police officers and I do not blame them with their knowledge of how men like you behave.

The jury had heard how criminals arrested after major robberies were allowed bail and, it was alleged but denied by Cuthbert, that outers – watered down evidence – were also on offer.

Thousands of pounds had been handed over to Cuthbert by an intermediary, Alfred Sheppard, in a restaurant opposite Bishopsgate police station. After his conviction there were suggestions that Cuthbert might turn out to be the first police supergrass but nothing came of them.

In another prosecution Inspector James Jolly was acquitted of trying to frame major robber, Billy Tobin. Later he was dismissed the force along with two others for tampering with records of suspects' interviews.

If Countryman had no great success with the investigation into the City Police, it had an even more conspicuous lack of success when in 1978 it tangled with the Flying Squad and its subsidiary, the Robbery Squad. Much of the problem stemmed from Countryman's use of the supergrass, ironically a technique much favoured by the Robbery Squad.

On 23 November 1978 the then head of the Flying Squad, Commander Don Neesham, initialled a complaint about Countryman's dealings with supergrasses in general and, in particular, a protest from a DCI in the Robbery Squad about an approach by Countryman to a Kenneth Warne, one of the DI's witnesses. The report complained that Countryman was dangling soft options before criminals. A month later another DCI on the Robbery Squad obtained a statement from a criminal named Shackleton claiming that one of the Robbery Squad's officers in whom Countryman was interested was being framed.

Four months later, on 3 April 1979, Neesham resigned, complaining that three of his men, all Detective Sergeants, had been disciplined and fined £250 for failing to notify a provincial force they were searching premises in the area. He believed they had been demoted as a result of complaints which were nothing to do with Countryman. Sir David McNee, then the Commissioner, recalls it slightly differently:

> After the meeting [with Leonard Burt in December 1979], Pat Kavanagh [McNee's deputy] told me Hambledon had alleged that Don Neesham had been unhelpful to the Countryman team. No firm evidence was produced to support the allegation – only the thought that Neesham was being over-protective of the men under his command. In order once again to avoid any accusation of obstruction to the Countryman inquiry, it was decided to move Neesham to other duties. When told of this, however, he exercised his right to retire on pension.[24]

Later that year, on 13 November, there were further disagreements between the Countryman team and the DPP. A DPP official, Kenneth Dowling, forbade a Countryman Superintendent to interview a defendant at Brixton. Nevertheless the Superintendent visited the prison and a letter was written signed by Sir Thomas Hetherington, then the Director of Public Prosecutions: 'I find this cavalier treatment of Treasury Counsel and my department quite unacceptable.'

On 7 December Hambledon had his fatal meeting with Pat Kavanagh and Hetherington. The DPP said that if Hambledon continued to complain about being obstructed he would have to resign. Hambledon eventually agreed to sign a statement that there had been no obstruction. When it was produced against him he maintained he had signed it only in a desperate effort to save Operation Countryman as an independent inquiry.[25] If this was the case he suffered no worse a fate than the defendant who puts his name to a confession 'to get bail'.

Nor was there much success for the three-year inquiry during the 1980s under the control of Detective Chief Superintendent Stagg. Although the Director of Public Prosecutions was quite content to allow common criminals to be convicted on the evidence of supergrass Billy Young, he was not happy with

[24] D. McNee, *McNee's Law*, p. 194.
[25] *Observer*, 8 August 1982.

the prospect of putting serving police officers at such risk.[26] One officer was suspended and, in May 1983, served with internal disciplinary charges. Would he possibly become the first police supergrass? No, was the emphatic answer. Only traffic policemen bite their colleagues. The officer knew nothing. He was allowed to resign and a reference was given to him by the Yard enabling him to become a member of the Institute of Professional Investigators.[27]

Not all police corruption at the time was on such a grand scale as this but one incident throws some light on just how high a criminal could go for help. In 1980 a fight took place in the Albion public house in Ludgate Circus, one of the known meeting places for criminals and police where deals could be arranged. The men were respectable and well dressed; one was Detective Superintendent John Keane and the other Detective Inspector Bernard Gent. The fight was started by Keane in an effort to snatch a tape-recorder from Gent's pocket. He considered that Gent was being unsporting in taping the conversation, which recorded an agreement that in return for a £10,000 bribe Gent would do his best to secure the release of a man suspected of a substantial robbery. It appears that Keane had simply telephoned Gent as the officer in the case asking 'if anything could be done'. Keane received a three-year sentence. He would have been a junior officer at the time of Mark's purge in the early 1970s.

The last to go in the great Scotland Yard trials of the 1970s was the Porn Squad. Theirs was the greatest fall of all. For the first time in living memory not only did officers of the rank of Commander stand in the dock of the Old Bailey. They were convicted.

In 1969, shortly before Christmas, pornographer James Humphreys and his wife Rusty were guests with senior CID officers, including Commander Wally Virgo, at the Criterion Restaurant in Piccadilly. Humphreys took the opportunity to

---

[26] Billy Young had an interesting track record. In 1980 he had supplied another supergrass, Micky Gervaise, with a policeman's uniform, obtained from a Sergeant in the Met, which facilitated the flagging down of a lorry containing £3.4 million of silver bullion. Later Young was himself grassed on by a fairly minor robber, Freddie Sinfield, over the robbery of a security van some years earlier. Billy Young's career is well documented in M. Short, *Lundy*.

[27] A. Jennings et al, *Scotland Yard's Cocaine Connection*, p. 104.

complain that DCS Moody, then in charge of CI Obscene
Publications Squad, would not give him a 'licence' to use his
properties in Soho as dirty bookshops. Another pornographer,
Bernard Silver, who together with Tony Mifsud ruled vice in
the West End for two decades, was also present. It was he
who arranged a meeting with Moody in a Mayfair restaurant at
which negotiations were opened. Could a bookshop be opened
in Rupert Street? Nothing was finalized. Silver and Moody
would meet the next day when the porn king would make a
formal offer.

When terms were agreed they were staggering: £14,000 was
to be paid for the licence; Silver would become a partner, so
satisfying Moody who did not want to see outsiders creeping
in; and a further £2,000 a month would be paid to prevent
raids and closure. It was never a particularly happy association,
in part because Humphreys took the opportunity of Silver's
absence abroad to begin an affair with his mistress, Dominique
Ferguson, a move which soon became Soho gossip and went
straight back to Silver. Reprisals were threatened, including a
suggestion that Humphreys be fitted up for a crime. In turn,
he contacted Commander Drury, whom he had met at a party
he had given to celebrate the promotion of a Flying Squad
colleague, and the threats came to nothing. The fee for this
service, said Humphreys later, was £1,050. From the moment
Humphreys met Drury he seems to have had the Commander
in his pocket, wining and dining him and taking him to boxing
tournaments at the World Sporting Club.

The first cracks in the empire began to appear in 1971 when
the *Sunday People* named a variety of operators as the pornographers of Soho, including Silver, Mifsud and Humphreys
along with two others, Jeff Mason and John Mason. The
Sunday People also made allegations that there were corrupt
dealings with detectives. A Detective Chief Superintendent was
appointed to investigate the allegations but, with one exception,
all denied they had paid over any money to the police. The
exception was Humphreys, who refused to be interviewed,
ostensibly on the advice of his solicitor but in practice on the
advice of a friend in the police.

The first exposé by the *Sunday People* had come to nothing.
But in 1972 the paper produced a second round. On 27
February it announced that Commander Drury and his wife

had recently returned from Cyprus, where they had been guests of Humphreys. The gaff was blown in a curious way. When something went wrong in London one person at whom the police looked was Joey Pyle, the old-time friend of the Nash family from Islington and drinking companion of Humphreys. When the police were looking for Freddie Sewell, killer of Blackpool Superintendent Gerald Richardson, they turned over Pyle's home. Nothing was found to link him with Sewell but he was charged with possessing a firearm and ammunition, a charge he strenuously denied and of which he was acquitted at the Old Bailey. He then had the hump with the Met in general and told a reporter of Humphreys' holidays in Cyprus with police officers.[28]

For a time Drury tried to bluff his way out. Yes, he had been to Cyprus. No, he had not been a guest, he had paid his share. No, it had not been a holiday; in reality he was looking for the escaped train robber Ronnie Biggs. At the time and for what it was worth, Humphreys supported him. It wasn't worth much. On 6 March Drury was suspended from duty and served with disciplinary papers. He resigned on 1 May. Then foolishly he turned on his former friend. He sold his story to the *News of the World* for £10,000 and as part of his confessions he named Humphreys as a grass, something guaranteed to destroy his reputation amongst the criminal fraternity, if not to get him a good beating to go with it. It is not surprising that Humphreys took umbrage and gave his alternative version, saying that far from being a grass or getting money from Drury it had been all the other way round. The money, the wine, the good life, had all flowed from the Humphreys cornucopia.

But now the foundations of the porn empire were cracking and Humphreys was investigated over the slashing of Peter 'Pookey' Garfath in the lavatory of the Dauphine Club in Marylebone as punishment for daring to have an affair with his wife Rusty. Three days before the attack she had been

[28] In the summing up of the trial of Pyle for possessing the gun and ammunition, the judge told the jury that to acquit Pyle would mean that the police officers had committed perjury. At Lewes Crown Court on 30 June 1975 one of the officers on the search, Harold Hannigan, who had been on the same Regional Crime Squad as George Fenwick, was found guilty of trying to bribe a Sussex detective. He was given a conditional discharge by Melford Stevenson, who called him 'a very, very, conceited fool', and advised him to see a psychiatrist (B. Cox et al, *The Fall of Scotland Yard*, p. 191).

released from Holloway where she had served a four months' sentence for possessing a firearm. Garfath named Humphreys as one of six assailants and a warrant was issued for his arrest. Humphreys, who was in Holland at the time, launched a counter-attack. He was not involved in the assault on Garfath, rather it was a frame-up, organized by a Detective Inspector Bland in concert with some criminals from Streatham led by Alfred Taylor as a reprisal over the resignation of Drury. Meanwhile Rusty Humphreys was arrested and charged with conspiracy to pervert the course of justice and conspiracy to cause grievous bodily harm to Garfath.[29] She went to A10 to complain about senior detectives, backing up her claims with details from her diaries which had been taken from her on her arrest three months earlier.

Gilbert Kelland, later to become an Assistant Commissioner, was appointed to lead the investigation. At first he found Rusty Humphreys' statement difficult to accept. If the diaries were all that important, why had nothing been done for the past three months? Why had they never been sent to the Deputy Commissioner during that time? 'The explanation I was given for this oversight was the pressure of work on the senior officers of the squad dealing with her case, but I have always found this difficult to accept.'[30]

Kelland and his team began their inquiries in earnest and in mid-October they visited Humphreys in prison in Amsterdam where he was awaiting extradition. At first he was prepared to talk but the next day he refused to see them and he maintained this stance until after his conviction on 25 April 1974, when he was sentenced to eight years for the assault on Garfath. Even when, in May, he did consent to make statements and later give evidence, he proved to be a temperamental witness. Looking for a witness who in police terms would remain staunch, Kelland turned to Soho pornographer John Mason.

On 27 February 1976 Drury, Virgo and Moody were arrested along with nine other officers. The pool included two ex-Commanders, an ex-Detective Chief Superintendent, an ex-Detective Chief Inspector and a host of smaller fry. It was, in any language, a major scandal.

[29] She was later acquitted of both these charges.
[30] G. Kelland, *Crime in London*, p. 127.

In April 1976 at Knightsbridge Crown Court Mason was fined a total of £25,000 for possessing obscene publications and now began to make detailed statements to Kelland. His revelations were remarkable. One ex-Detective Superintendent had attended Mason's offices once a week to advise on articles for the magazine and generally to subedit the contributions. He had been paid £10 a week until, on his death in 1972, the job had been taken over by DCI George Fenwick. At the other end of the scale Mason recalled how his routine monthly contribution to the Porn Squad, which had been £60 in 1953, had risen to £1,000 by 1971. His relationship with the squad had been such that he was lent a squad tie to attend the basement at Holborn police station, from where, at a price of between £500 and £1,000, he could buy material confiscated from other shops and dealers.

At the first of the three Porn Squad trials Humphreys, like Achilles many years earlier, was sulking in his tent, and refused to take part. Even so Fenwick received ten years' imprisonment and four other former officers received between four and eight years'. In the second trial, which began the next March, Virgo and Moody, together with four junior officers, faced an indictment with twenty-seven counts alleging bribery and corruption totalling £87,485. This time when faced with the story that his 'bottle' had gone and that Mason was by far the more important witness, Humphreys emerged. Now all sorts of skeletons were dug from the cupboard, including that of the dismissal of Lambert from *The Times* inquiry. After he had been removed by Virgo, Lambert had dealt with Humphreys' correspondence. He was little more than a functionary but was still able to see how the Obscene Publications Squad was behaving and in his opinion it was not behaving adequately. He sent back numerous reports to the squad's officers for correction but, although they should have been returned to him, they never were. He was chastised by Virgo, who said he was upsetting the morale of CI, the Obscene Publications Squad, and told he was going to be posted to Interpol. In September 1970 he went on permanent sick leave and retired at the end of March 1971.

At Virgo's trial it was suggested on his behalf that Lambert was a drunk who took time off work and who had been dismissed from *The Times* inquiry because of his incompetence and because he knew one of the officers involved. Brodie gave evidence that this was not the reason. The correct version was that Frank Williamson had expressed dissatisfaction with him. No, said Williamson, now long retired and who came to give evidence for the prosecution, this was not the case; nor was Lambert incompetent. It was even put to Williamson that he had specifically asked Virgo to have Moody on his team.

All six defendants were convicted, receiving between four and twelve years' imprisonment. Later the conviction of ex-Commander Virgo was quashed by the Court of Appeal.

The third trial involved Drury and two others, and again Humphreys had to be coaxed into the witness box. Now he was an essential witness. Arrangements were made for him to see a journalist from the *Sunday People*, who had assured him that a full inquiry was taking place into his own conviction for the assault on Garfath. Humphreys' evidence at the third trial led to the acquittal of one officer, DI Legge, who had admitted he had gone to stay in Humphreys' apartment in Ibiza. Humphreys gave evidence that he was one of the very few officers he knew who had never wanted or accepted a penny from him. The case was stopped against Legge, who later resigned from the force. On 7 July 1977 Drury received eight years' imprisonment; the other officer half that sentence.

Humphreys was released at the end of August of that year by exercise of the royal prerogative of mercy. In 1982 he was circulated as wanted over the manufacture of amphetamine drugs in Eire.

Meanwhile there had been further problems with the Drugs Squad. When No 5 Regional Crime Squad made an arrest in Romford in 1977 they found drugs which came from a haul of 1,200 lb seized in February of the previous year. The haul had been recorded as having been destroyed. The market trader, John Goss, who had been arrested, told the police that he was being pressured into selling the drug by officers. His story was accepted and at the Chelmsford Crown Court he was given an absolute discharge. In June 1977 a Detective Sergeant and a Constable were suspended whilst inquiries were made into the possible involvement of more senior members of the Drugs Squad. Investigations showed that the drugs sent for burning had been removed from the bags before destruction and some other substance substituted. The independent observer required to witness the destruction had merely examined the labels and not the contents. Clear plastic bags should have been used instead of black sacks.

Later a Detective Chief Inspector, two Detective Inspectors and a Detective Constable faced disciplinary boards. All except one Inspector, who was reduced to the rank of Constable, were required to resign. Earlier a Detective Sergeant had been convicted at the Old Bailey and sent to prison.

Just how far did Scotland Yard's upper echelons of the 1960s and 1970s know what went on? Not very much if it could be helped, it seems. Frank Williamson says:

> Ernie Millen would absolutely guarantee that no bad news would get to the Assistant Commissioner. He saw it as his job to protect the ACC from the unpleasant facts of life. Now whether there was any side benefit arising out of things I don't know because if you start getting in the position where you're fixing things it soon becomes valuable to someone else other than you.

But it was a case involving no major villains or major corruption which would lead to great changes in the organization of the police forces throughout England and Wales and promote the twin pieces of legislation, the Police and Criminal Evidence Act 1984 and the Prosecution of Offences Act 1985, which, in theory and to a certain extent in practice, changed the investigation and prosecution of criminal cases, in the latter case effectively emasculating the police, certainly the Met. The incident was the killing of the transvestite prostitute, Maxwell Confait, and the subsequent conviction of three youths for his murder.

6

Confait, PACE and after

On 22 April 1972 a fire broke out in a house in Doggett Road, Catford, South-east London and in a room on the first floor firemen discovered the body of Maxwell Confait, a transvestite prostitute. Two days later a police officer saw two boys running away from a fire which had been started in a shed in a nearby park. The information was passed to other officers and three boys, Colin Lattimore, Ronnie Leighton and Ahmet Salih, were arrested. All confessed to the murder of Confait and the subsequent arson. At the time Lattimore was eighteen but was said to have a mental age of eight. He had been diagnosed educationally subnormal and, later, psychiatrists were to say he was highly suggestible, 'so that the slightest indication of the expected answer will produce it'. Leighton was fifteen and although considerably brighter than his friend Colin he was described as 'borderline subnormal' and 'really an immature, inadequate, simple dullard'. Salih was described as reasonably intelligent. He was just fourteen.

The crucial question for the prosecution was the time Confait died. Lattimore, who had allegedly admitted strangling Confait, had a watertight alibi for the night of his death. Independent witnesses could trace his movements from 6 pm to 11.40 pm. Another had seen him at home at 11.45 pm and his father could place him in the house at 12.35 am.

The doctors at the committal proceedings put the time of death between 6.30 and 10.00 pm, basing their conclusions on the onset of *rigor mortis*, and once the case was committed the boys were obliged to give details of any alibis they had under the provisions of the Criminal Justice Act 1967.

> [It] was never contemplated when this change went through that it would also favour the prosecution in providing a chance to blur the edges of its evidence when that was found to be in conflict with a disclosed alibi. Colin, Ronnie and Ahmet were caught by this disclosure, which alerted the prosecution to its only chance of a guilty verdict. If the alibi had not been disclosed, the evidence about the time of death would have remained as clear and unequivocal as it was at Woolwich Magistrates Court.[1]

The boys were convicted in November 1972. Lattimore was convicted of manslaughter on the grounds of diminished responsibility, Leighton of murder and Salih of arson. Lattimore was ordered to be detained under the Mental Health Act without limit of time, Leighton during Her Majesty's pleasure and Salih sentenced to four years' detention. Their appeals were dismissed.

Their families did not accept the verdicts and with the assistance of their MP, Christopher Price, they set about obtaining a referral of the case to the Court of Appeal. In June 1975 the Confait case was referred by Roy Jenkins, then Home Secretary, back to the Court of Appeal. Over the years this has been something of a graveyard for the hopes of appellants but on this occasion their convictions were quashed. Jenkins, in his letter referring the case, had written that if Confait's death took place 'some appreciable time before midnight, it appears that the evidence of the boys' whereabouts would assume greater importance and that doubt would be thrown on the accuracy of their statements of admission to the police, the truth of which they denied at the trial'.

When the case came before the Court of Appeal in October 1975 it was established by further medical evidence that Confait's death took place 'some appreciable time before midnight'. Lord Justice Scarman said the effect of this fresh medical evidence was 'to destroy the lynch-pin of the Crown's case and to demonstrate that the version of events contained in the admissions relied upon by the Crown cannot be true'. He

[1] C. Price and J. Caplan, *The Confait Confessions*.

accepted that it was still possible that the boys' confessions to the arson at 27 Doggett Road could be correct but added that their statements could not be 'regarded as sufficiently reliable evidence standing as they do, alone, to justify the convictions for arson which were based solely upon them'.

Recriminations followed swiftly upon the boys' release. How could they have confessed to a killing they never committed and, moreover, how could the Director of Public Prosecutions, Sir Norman Skelhorn, have authorized the prosecution? Sir Henry Fisher, a former High Court judge, was appointed to hold an inquiry. It was held in private and in his report published at the end of 1977 he found that Detective Superintendent Graham Stockwell, one of the interviewing officers, 'gave his evidence[to the inquiry] convincingly and made a favourable impression on me. He has a frank and open manner; he seemed calm, steady, careful and intelligent (as his posting to the Fraud Squad indicates); I judged him to be wholly trustworthy.' Not so Ronnie Leighton, who had had a quick spat with Donald, later Lord Justice, Farquerson who represented the police. Early in his cross-examination by Mr Farquerson, when Leighton was asked why he started fires, he replied, 'I tell you I don't know. If you keep on, mate, I will knock you one.' He then left the room saying, 'I have fucking had enough of this.'

Sir Henry Fisher's findings went as follows: (a) Lattimore's alibi was genuine and that he could have taken no part in the killing; (b) Leighton and Salih could have taken part in the killing; and (c) all three could have set light to 27 Doggett Road. He could not accept that the confessions could have been made without at least one of the boys having been involved in the killing and arson. The most likely scenario was, he thought, that Lattimore's confession to his part in the arson was true and that he had been persuaded to confess to the killing by either Leighton or Salih. He thought Leighton's and Salih's confessions to the arson were true and that their answers to the killing had been falsified to include Lattimore. They had both been involved in the killing.

This was not the case. In January 1980 the then Director of Public Prosecutions, Sir Thomas Hetherington, received 'new information' about the case and Sir Michael Havers, the Attorney General, told the House of Commons eight months later that he was satisfied that Confait had died even earlier:

before midnight on 21 April. 'I am also satisfied that if the evidence now available had been before Sir Henry Fisher he would not have come to the conclusion that any of the three young men was responsible for the death of Confait or the arson at 27 Doggett Road. Counsel has advised, and the Director of Public Prosecutions and I agree, that there is insufficient evidence to prosecute any other person.'

The new information had come through an Inspector Eddie Ellison who investigated the story of a man who claimed he was being blackmailed for a murder he had committed. There were two men each of whom maintained he had seen the other kill Confait but not to have been involved himself. It was not thought there was sufficient evidence to prosecute either.[2]

What Sir Henry did correctly identify, however, was the need for changes in the way suspects were interviewed, as well as the need for 'an analysis and evaluation of a case by a legally qualified person at as early a stage as possible'. He found that there had been breaches of the so-called Judges Rules which governed police interrogation of suspects. He also found that the questioning of Lattimore was unfair and oppressive. The investigating officer, DCS Alan Jones, could see Lattimore was mentally handicapped and he should have waited until someone, a parent or friend, could attend the interview.

As for the lawyers, and in particular the DPP's officer in the case, Dorian Williams, Sir Henry had this to say:

so far from trying to make the time of death more precise . . . Detective Chief Superintendent Jones, Mr Williams – so far as he was aware of the problem – and Mr [Richard] Du Cann [Treasury Counsel who conducted the prosecution case at the trial] made every effort to keep it as vague as possible. The reason for this was that they were concerned to establish a case which rested wholly or mainly on the confessions, which could not be entirely true unless the time of death was outside the brackets given by Dr Bain, the police surgeon, and Dr Cameron, the pathologist.

---

[2] The next year the Home Office offered the youths a total of £65,000 in compensation for their wrongful imprisonment.

He accepted that Williams was an experienced and conscientious officer. 'I believe he did as much as under prevailing practice was expected of him. Sir Norman Skelhorn did not criticize him.' Sir Henry commented, however, 'The scrutiny which Mr Williams provided in this case fell short of the scrutiny which I believe is required and which (in theory at least) the procurator fiscal would carry out under the Scottish system.' He concluded: 'If I am right in thinking that Mr Williams did as much as under the prevailing system was expected of him, then I am driven to the conclusion that the practice was unsatisfactory.' And he pointed out that 'The purpose of such evaluation should be not only to judge the narrow question of whether there is evidence to support the prosecution's case, but to look into the strength and weakness of the prosecution's case in an objective way to determine whether continued prosecution is justifiable.'

In his memoirs Sir Norman Skelhorn had little to say on one of the major blots of his career:

In view . . . of the developments that have now taken place, resulting from fresh evidence having come to life – which was apparently not available either at the time of the prosecution or at the time of Sir Henry's inquiry – I do not think that any useful purpose would be served by now dealing with these matters. Sir Henry's report was of course published appreciably later than my retirement, but in so far as he suggested revision of procedures, both by the department and by the police, I feel sure that they will have received careful consideration.[3]

It was the start of the road which led to the Police and Criminal Evidence Act 1984 (PACE), and the Prosecution of Offences Act 1985 which saw the foundation of the Crown Prosecution Service as well as the end of much of the autonomy of the Metropolitan Police to prosecute their own cases without qualified legal assistance unless they specifically requested it.

---

[3] Joshua Rozenberg, *The Case for the Crown*, pp. 60–64; Sir Norman Skelhorn, *Public Prosecutor*; C. Price and J. Caplan, *The Confait Confessions*; Sir Henry Fisher, *Report of an Inquiry by the Hon Sir Henry Fisher into the circumstances leading to the trial of three persons on charges arising out of the death of Maxwell Confait and the fire at 27 Doggett Road, London SE6.*

By providing very considerable safeguards for suspects in the form questioning may take, the recording of interviews and the provision of legal representation, PACE substantially curtailed the way in which the police throughout the country could conduct their inquiries. The removal of the right of the police to conduct their own cases not only removed opportunities for direct corruption but also lessened their bargaining power to persuade defendants to plead guilty at an early opportunity.

The next step along the road to these reforms came on 23 June 1977 when the government announced its intention to set up a Royal Commission on Criminal Procedure under the chairmanship of the Vice Chancellor of the University of London and professor of oriental history, Sir Cyril Phillips. The Commission was under way by February 1978 and reported in January 1981.[4] Three years later came the Police and Criminal Evidence Act accompanied by a series of Codes of Practice which established the required police behaviour in all aspects of an investigation – stop and search, arrest, interrogation, and general behaviour at the police station.

PACE became law the year after what was known as the Holloway Road incident took place. In August 1983 four youths, Gary Foley, Eric Ranger and his brother Baltimore, and Daniel Jenkins, had been walking home from a fair when the officers from transit van November 33 waded into the youths 'for a laugh'. There is little doubt the officers had been jeered at by other youths who had made off and now the police ordered the boys against a fence and started beating them. One boy, kneed in the face, suffered a broken nose. Another was punched in both the stomach and the face; a third was dealt with similarly and thirteen-year-old Eric Ranger was struck with a truncheon. All the boys were later treated in hospital.

An inquiry was begun and got nowhere. It was not possible

---

[4] The terms of reference were as follows: 'to examine, having regard both to the interests of the community in bringing offenders to justice and to the rights and liberties of persons suspected or accused of crime, and taking into account also the need for the efficient and economical use of resources, whether changes are needed in England and Wales in (i) the powers and duties of the police in respect of the investigation of criminal offences and the rights and duties of suspect and accused persons, including the means by which they are secured; (ii) the process of and responsibility for the prosecution of criminal offences; and (iii) such other features of criminal procedure and evidence as relate to the above'; and to make recommendations.

to identify the officers. Two and a half years later, in February 1986, the Police Complaints Authority (PCA) issued a statement saying that there was insufficient evidence to charge anyone with a criminal offence or to institute disciplinary proceedings. As part of the abortive inquiry the PCA had asked the Met to parade all the officers who might have been involved in the incident and to 'warn' them of their behaviour. Some thirty officers were required to parade before a Deputy Assistant Commissioner and in the words of the PCA statement, they 'were told in no uncertain terms of the anger and disquiet felt about the incident. They were told that, although the officers in only one of the vans were involved, all the officers in that van must have known what happened.'

The Met denied that this was an official reprimand or that it would affect individual officers' careers. The general warning was given because the police investigation had failed to establish which of three personnel carriers on duty in the area at the time was involved in the incident. Relying on descriptions given by the youths, the investigation had narrowed its inquiry to the crew of one particular vehicle. In fact it was later established – after a series of identification parades at which no officer was picked out – that the vehicle in question had nothing to do with the incident and that its personnel could not have known anything about the assaults.

On 7 February 1986 the *Police Review* reported the findings of the PCA and, opening with an editorial 'A Conspiracy of Bastards', began a campaign attacking the guilty officers both for their assaults and for allowing suspicion to fall on fellow officers whom they knew to be blameless. The editorial said that police officers used the term bastard to describe the worst type of criminal. 'They apply it to the cruel, the ruthless, the vicious and the sneaking pervert. There are five bastards serving in the Metropolitan Police.'

A week later the editor, Brian Hilliard, received an anonymous telephone call from a woman. Was there a possibility that someone who had given evidence about the assaults could be given immunity from prosecution? It seemed to Hilliard that when she rang back repeating the question she was reading from a prepared statement. Hilliard went to see Commander Ken Merton, of the Met's Complaints Investigation Bureau.

He promised he would recommend to both the DPP and the CPA that immunity should be granted to any officer who gave evidence and 'who was not directly concerned with the assaults'.

The offer of immunity was announced in the *Police Review* the following week. On the advice of a psychologist who had been consulted, no mention was made of the anonymous caller. He felt that any mention of the caller would cause her to withdraw to avoid any chance of identification. It was believed that the best method of obtaining further co-operation was to provide some means for her to contact publicly an authoritative source who would guarantee the immunity. The same day, 21 February, a press conference was held at Scotland Yard to confirm the offer and to establish a hot line over which potential witnesses could provide evidence about the assaults.

By 8 pm that evening the Yard had received the first of four calls from officers willing to give evidence against the suspects. Within a week four Constables, who were later convicted, had been arrested along with Colin Edwards, their supervising Sergeant on the night. He had tried to take advantage of the immunity offer.

Judge Kenneth Jones, sentencing the officers for their part in the Holloway Road incident',[5] said: 'You behaved like vicious hooligans and lied like common criminals. This was a brutal, appalling and unprovoked attack. By these assaults you have betrayed your own manhood and been false to the high traditions of the police. To save your own skins you all conspired together to lie again. You were even prepared to allow suspicion to fall on your fellow officers.'

Nicholas Wise, Edward Main and Michael Gavin were jailed for four years. Sergeant Colin Edwards, who organized cover-up on behalf of his men, was jailed for three years. Michael Parr, acquitted of assault but convicted of conspiracy to pervert, received eighteen months. The men had held a clandestine meeting in Whittington Park, North London, the day after the attack, in order, the prosecution alleged, to discuss the tactics of the situation. On the same day as the officers were sentenced, PC Victor Weekes was jailed for nine months at the Old Bailey over an unrelated incident.

[5] Brian Hilliard, 'The Holloway Incident', *Police Review*, 17 July 1987.

He had been convicted of repeatedly punching a man cleared of threatening behaviour.

In the Holloway Road incident it was only the offer of immunity from prosecution that tempted three officers to give evidence. Of them, Derek Jamieson resigned the force after an incident in which his wife was stabbed, Kevin Luxford remained in the Met, whilst Philip Boak transferred to Manchester.

Later, officers from November 30, another of the police vans in the area on the evening of the assaults, won libel damages of up to £30,000 in the High Court from the *Evening Standard*, which along with the *Police Review* had campaigned for the continued investigation. This compared favourably with the awards totalling £5,000 to the assaulted boys. On 15 December 1988 police in the other vans won £175,000 from the BBC and Labour politician Gerald Kaufmann over a TV interview which wrongly linked the officers to the van.

DAC Robert Innes said of the incident, 'The public pressure, through the media, actually caused us to look at it again. There was a wave of public feeling that I can't remember before. That caused us to rethink.'

Almost immediately after the Holloway Road incident came the report of a 'new scandal of beaten boys'. This time the allegation related to a vanload of policemen on duty after a Northampton Town vs Peterborough United game in September 1985; they were said to have assaulted supporters. No progress had been made in the investigation by the end of February 1986 and Northamptonshire police asked the PCA to take close supervision of the case in a final attempt to allay fears of a cover-up.

By 1990 it was quite apparent that things were not well in police forces up and down the country. During the years 1989 and 1990 there were no less than thirty-seven investigations being carried out into one force by another. There were three into the West Midlands concerning the Birmingham Six, an investigation into an arson, and the failure to secure the Serious Crime Squad headquarters on the announcement of the squad's dissolution. There were three into the Essex constabulary. One concerned an unsubstantiated allegation of bribery in the Number 5 Regional Crime Squad but, more unpalatably, neither the PCA nor the police forces involved were prepared to release the relevant information about the other investigations. Indeed this was something of a feature of the time. During those years the Thames Valley Police were also investigated; in three cases the investigating forces were Bedfordshire, Surrey and Hertfordshire but it was not disclosed what the complaints were about, and in the fourth case neither the complaint nor the investigating force was disclosed. When the Humberside Police were investigated over a death in custody the investigating force was not disclosed.

The most significant of these investigations, both for its outcome and for the quashing of a number of convictions obtained by the Serious Crime Squad in the force, was that into the West Midlands. During the latter part of 1988 and in 1989 when it was disbanded there was growing concern about the activities of the West Midlands Serious Crime Squad. The whisper against it was that certain officers had consistently flouted the requirements of PACE and its Codes of Practice in their investigation into crime and their interrogation of suspects.

Clare Short, MP for Birmingham Ladywood, raised the case of Paul Dandy in the House of Commons on 25 January 1989:

> In February 1987 a Paul Dandy was arrested and held as a Category A prisoner at Winson Green Prison in Birmingham.[6] During his detention, which lasted ten months, he attempted to commit suicide. In November 1987 all charges against him were dropped because his solicitor had obtained forensic evidence which showed that his confession – the charge against him as based on his confession – had been forged by the police.[7]

Short requested that the Home Secretary set up an inquiry into the squad by HM Inspectorate of Constabulary. In his reply Mr Douglas Hogg, then Under Secretary of State for the Home Office, said, 'The inspectorate is not the proper method of dealing with problems of that nature . . . Home Office ministers have no power to intervene. There is a thorough and

---

[6] A Category A prisoner is a likely escaper and/or one who will be a danger to the public if he, or much more rarely she, does escape.
[7] *Hansard*, 25 January 1989, col. 1155.

Bent Coppers

fair system for dealing with allegations against police officers
and it provides for an independent element in the form of the
Police Complaints Authority.'[8]

In the first part of his answer he was correct. HM Inspectorate
of Constabulary was little more than an observing force, as
Frank Williamson had found to his cost when he investigated
The Times inquiry of 1969. Whether because of the constraints
under which it works the PCA has been able to live up
to Mr Hogg's hopes and expectations is a totally different
matter.

Unfortunately the PCA had continually declined to supervise the investigation of Dandy's case, which was conducted
internally by the West Midlands Police itself. It was when the
case had been concluded and was in the public domain that
the Authority began to take an interest and wrote to Dandy
in Winson Green. He had been released five months earlier.
Once it had reviewed the procedures adopted by the internal
inquiry, the PCA gave its imprimatur to the recommendation
that the appropriate disciplinary action was a reprimand to the
officers involved. The penalty imposed was not for the manner
of obtaining Dandy's 'confession'. Instead it was for having
disposed of the original record of his interview.[9]

Over the weeks and months it became clear that, even before
the case of Paul Dandy, a number of other cases investigated
by the West Midlands Crime Squad had aborted in similar
circumstances. Because of doubts about the conduct of some
of the squad's officers, several other cases failed after the release
of Mr Dandy. The tar caused by the improper behaviour of some
stuck to the many.

On 22 June 1989 Ronald [Ronnie] Bolden, who had been
two years on remand at Winson Green Prison, was acquitted
at Birmingham Crown Court of two bank robberies at city
banks. The jury had heard defence allegations that interview
records as well as forensic evidence had been fabricated. The
trial judge, Richard Curtis QC, described some of the police
evidence as 'unattractive' and 'totally misleading'. From his
remarks in court it seems that prosecuting counsel also accepted
that all was not well with the police evidence.

[8] Ibid., col. 1160.
[9] See *Hansard*, 25 January 1989, col. 1159.

172

This was over eighteen months after the collapse of the Dandy case and by now the press hounds were up and running. The problems surrounding the squad and their cases were increasingly brought to the attention of the public. It was known that five other cases investigated by the squad had collapsed since the end of 1989. Now the PCA agreed to the supervision of four investigations. Immediately after the end of the Bolden case, West Midlands Police spokesman Superintendent Martin Burton announced that the then Chief Constable, Geoffrey Dear, was 'taking a critical look at [the squad's] structure, function and supervision . . . It was recognized some months ago that a root-and-branch review was necessary to allay doubts.'[10]

Following the review five officers were transferred to other duties as the size of the squad was reduced. It was also announced that the rest of the squad would be merged later in the summer with the Stolen Vehicle Squad and the Drugs Squad to form a new Organized Crime Squad. The announcement did not please the *Birmingham Post*: 'Concern about the activities of the West Midlands Police Serious Crimes Squad has abounded for many months. The dispersal of the team should not be used as a means of avoiding the apportionment of any culpability that might exist.'

Six weeks later, on 14 August, Geoffrey Dear asked the PCA to supervise its own investigation into the squad under the terms of s88 of the Police and Criminal Evidence Act 1984. In an investigation under s88 the PCA provides a supervisory element but the groundwork is done by the officers of the investigating force, in this case the West Yorkshire constabulary.[11] The *Birmingham Evening Mail* had this to say:

Mr Dear has now called in another police force to investigate the activities of the squad. While it is in the nature of things

10 *The Times*, 24 June 1989.
11 The terms of reference under PACE s88 are [any matter which] (a) appears to the appropriate authority to indicate that an officer may have committed a criminal offence or an offence against discipline; and (b) is not the subject of a complaint, if it appears to the appropriate authority that it ought to be referred by reason (i) of its gravity; (ii) of exceptional circumstances. Under PACE s98 the PCA can only provide a brief report of its findings. The section prohibits the publication of all but the barest detail.

for policemen to investigate other policemen there must be a certain amount of disquiet over that decision. There are bound to be doubts, allegations of a cover-up or whitewash, no matter what assurances to the contrary are given. The police authority should over-ride the Chief Constable and insist on an independent public inquiry . . . It would be a traumatic, breast-baring period for the force. But it is necessary. Doubts would be removed, public confidence restored, and at the end the force would be healthier, tougher and untainted.[12]

The PCA at first set a time limit of events which took place after 1 January 1986, but this was subsequently amended so that specific complaints in the period from 29 April 1984 to 31 December 1985 would also be included.

In early 1989 Geoffrey Dear asked the PCA whether it believed the squad had been systematically flouting the rules. The PCA replied that it had no such evidence. Later Sir Cecil Clothier, on his retirement from the chairmanship of the PCA, told the *Guardian* that the squad was 'an aberration. I don't know any other place where anything on this scale has happened. Obviously there is a nucleus of officers there willing to misbehave in order to secure convictions which they probably think are justified.'[13]

Parallel with the PCA investigation an independent inquiry funded by the Civil Liberties Trust, and based in the law faculty at the University of Birmingham, began research in October 1989. It had been set up following efforts by Clare Short, the MP who had originally placed the questions in the House of Commons. The West Midlands force partially cooperated with this second inquiry, of which the *Birmingham Post* said:

. . . all the more important that West Midlands Police agrees to co-operate in an independent inquiry . . . It obviously doesn't have to, but the public will be able to read only one thing into a refusal – that there is something to hide . . . The public want[s] . . . an assurance from an impartial

[12] 15 August 1989.
[13] 28 July 1989.

investigation that if there was something wrong there is full atonement and that any fear of a repeat is removed.[14]

The West Midlands Police Serious Crime Squad had begun life in 1952 as the Special Crime Squad in the City of Birmingham Police. Its function was to assist the regular CID unit in investigating serious crime. This was not an uncommon practice; where there was an outbreak of serious crime, often burglaries, a small task force would be set up to break up the pattern. One example, and one which went severely wrong, is that set up in Sheffield (see Chapter 4).

By 1959 the unit had changed its name twice and was known as the Birmingham Crime Squad. Its work was going well, not so much in terms of the quantity of arrests, although that was good, but the quality of them, and that year the City Police's annual report commented delightedly: 'It would be difficult now to envisage the investigation of serious crime in the Midlands without the aid of the Birmingham and Regional Crime Squads.'

Although it is easy to play with police clear-up figures, and indeed almost make them stand on their heads to achieve the desired result from their interpretation, it seems that that 1959 period was one of the high points for the squad. The next year it made 579 arrests and detected 1,060 crimes. By 1976 the totals had fallen to 254 and 660 respectively.

In 1974 the City of Birmingham force was amalgamated into the new, enlarged and improved West Midlands Organization. The squad underwent one final change of name which it retained until its disbandment fifteen years later – the Serious Crime Squad. In 1979 the annual report was pleased to record that the squad – in liaison with the Robbery Squad – had cleared up Ronnie Brown and the Thursday Gang, a collection of criminals who carried out robberies on that day of the week. 'Their concerted efforts are proving successful in maintaining the impetus against this class of dangerous criminal,' the report stated, in what, it seems, was a reference to Operation Cat, which had been the joint effort of three squads.

The 1980 report said of the Operation that it had 'met with considerable success whereby [several persons] have been

[14] 26 June 1989.

arrested and charged with offences of armed robbery and in one instance the murder of a security guard in the course of committing armed robbery'. The author of the independent inquiry's report, Tim Kaye, believes this was a reference to John Patrick Irvine who, along with George Keith Twitchell, was arrested for the murder. Both were convicted and continue to argue their innocence.

That year's report also contained the following passage: 'There is some indication that professional criminals are becoming very much harder to apprehend, are not amenable to interview at any stage and make every effort to avoid conviction.'[15]

From 1982, although there had been two new Detective Sergeants and three Detective Constables added to the squad, there was a decrease in the number of arrests made. In 1984 the annual report found that this was because the Serious Crime Squad had been 'heavily involved in dealing with a protected police informant'. This must have taken up a considerable amount of the squad's time but it came to nothing. Albert McCabe, on whom hopes were pinned, wrote to the solicitors of the suspects he had named saying his allegations were untrue and he had only become an informant because of improper threats and inducements by officers of the squad. McCabe was promptly dropped as a prosecution witness. But, by now, Operation Cat, which had been a conspicuous success, was under fire from local solicitors.

Geoffrey Dear was appointed Chief Constable of the West Midlands in 1985, the year that the Police and Criminal Act 1984 came into force, and the Serious Crime Squad continued its concentration on robberies of cash in transit and at banks and building societies. The annual reports for the next two years included these laudatory passages:

> Since its inception in the early 1950s the Serious Crime Squad has been at the forefront in the detection and apprehension of criminals involved in the commission of very serious crime.

---

[15] There does seem to have been a tendency to think that when rounded up the usual suspects should have put up their hands and admitted all. In 1988 the annual report, explaining away a low arrest and conviction rate, commented rather peevishly, 'Investigations are protracted, and masks, disguises, false number plates and other means of evading capture are frequently used.'

> The squad is a flexible mobile unit comprising teams of experienced detective officers able to give invaluable and immediate support to their divisional colleagues. [1985]

> . . . a comprehensive and timely training programme ensured that the new legislation [PACE] was quickly understood, effectively implemented and did not unduly affect police efficiency. [1986]

Three years later Geoffrey Dear was not so happy with the squad's attitude to PACE, which he described as 'cavalier and sloppy'.[16]

In the period 1974–88 the number of reported robberies and assaults with intent to rob increased by a factor of nearly six, from 437 to 2,557. In 1980 some thirteen per cent of arrests made by the squad were for offences of armed robbery. In 1988 the percentage had dropped to just two. Now the annual report read: 'Recent reorganization has necessitated changes in recruitment to the squad. In the forthcoming year a greater devolvement of staff will take place with district branches being established. These reorganizations will improve the already valued service provided by the Serious Crime Squad to territorial divisions.'

Those officers who joined the Serious Crime Squad after the reorganization of April 1974 came mostly from the Birmingham Crime Squad. Recommendations to join came mainly from serving members. The independent inquiry found that the pool from which the officers was drawn was shallow and that the squad was moulded in its own image. Many of the recruits to the squad would already have served in Number 4 Regional Crime Squad with which many joint operations had been mounted. It has also to be said that in the early years the Regional Crime Squads had been the dumping ground of many of the less able or indeed politically acceptable members of forces. Another complaint is that the squad should have been subject to the two-year transfer of officers in specialist units. Members of the Drug Squad and even the Child Liaison Unit were moved. Why not the Serious Crime Squad? One argument, also applied to the Commercial Branch, is that it takes at least two years for detectives to acquire the necessary understanding of the world in which they operate.

Officers questioned in the independent inquiry thought that most members served only a short period. Vehicle drivers, it is true, did a twelve-month stint, but DS Michael Hornsby served for sixteen years and DC Hugh McLelland for fifteen. Meffen, talking to the independent inquiry, believed that only four officers had served for a protracted time and that one of the officers had been left on the squad for 'personal reasons'.[17] In fact twenty officers served for more than two years and several for over five; a result of this would be that the squad was a thoroughly cohesive unit and one which, like many another, was resistant to change.

One effort to reorganize operational practices came in 1988 when the annual report stated: 'In the forthcoming year a greater devolvement of staff will take place with district branches being established.' A second effort was made by Dear in June 1989. It met with no greater success and in August he told the *Birmingham Post*: 'In June I got the squad together and lectured them on leadership, on standards and quality of work. Afterwards I considered the matter dealt with and water under the bridge, since to my knowledge there were no further cases emerging. I now know that there were people who apparently decided to stick two fingers up at the boss.'[18]

There also appear to have been problems over the number of civilian staff operating with the squad. According to the district auditor there were seventeen civilians but no police officers employed in the press office. According to *Unsafe and Unsatisfactory* there were, in fact, eight police officers who acted as press officers, one ranking as high as Superintendent.

On Friday, 11 August 1989 the offices of the Serious Crime Squad at Bradford Street police station were raided by officers from the West Midlands force's Complaints and Discipline Department on the orders of the Chief Constable. Desks, cupboards, briefcases, files, personal belongings and cars were searched. The Complaints and Discipline Department then left the building without securing it. This failure was to

---

[17] The inquiry believed that this was Hornsby who, for over ten years, had suffered from a form of diabetes which impaired his eyesight; T. Kaye, *Unsafe and Unsatisfactory*, p. 27.
[18] 16 August 1989.

be the subject of much controversy and rancour. One Serious Crime Squad detective described the raid:

> I arrived at Bradford Street at about 8.45 am on Friday, August 11 with two colleagues in a crew car. The rear gates were always kept locked for security reasons but there was a coded padlock. We were joined by a senior officer and we all drove into the yard.
>
> As we did so a number of officers – about four or five – from Complaints and Discipline came out of their places of hiding. As we reached the door they closed it on us. They had obviously been watching out for us from the old controller's office and the door of the old charge room.
>
> We were ushered into the crew room. We were told that we were not allowed to leave our car to telephone anybody. The same happened to the other crews . . .
>
> The Complaints and Discipline people wanted to find DCs Clifford and Woodley and they were located on air.
>
> At Bradford Street they started the search. They took our desks apart, emptied drawers, baskets, briefcases, files. They emptied everything. Any cupboards that did not open, they demanded the keys. Every part of that office was searched. All the crew cars were brought into the yard. They stripped them right down to the carpets, both linings and glove compartments.
>
> If there had been anything there that should not have been there, we would have been done. That is why we were so surprised and angry over later allegations that files could be missing. Because from Friday and that time on, they knew exactly what was in our desks and our offices.[19]

That afternoon Roger Clifford and David Woodley were questioned for several hours, under caution, over the alleged rifling of court files in the case of Michael Bromwell, charged with armed robbery. At 5 pm they were allowed to leave and a senior officer told colleagues there was no evidence against them. Three days later, on the Monday, Geoffrey Dear announced the disbandment of the squad. In the event Clifford and Woodley were to be suspended until January

[19] *Police Review*, 11 August 1991.

1990, when they were reinstated. Other officers were placed on non-operational duty.[20]

The same Monday officers acting for the Police Complaints Authority found that papers relating to Michael Bromwell's conviction were missing from the files at Warwick Crown Court.

In late autumn 1991 the Police Complaints Authority published the findings of its two-year inquiry conducted by West Yorkshire police. It had gone on for over two years against Dear's initial expectation of lasting no longer than twelve months and involving no more than twelve officers. In the end the investigators looked at 694 arrests made by the squad since 1986. There were complaints against the investigators that they had questioned people regarding pre-1986 arrests, thereby exceeding their brief, and had endangered informants by questioning them in front of their friends and workmates.

As for the report, its complaints of mismanagement covered a wide spectrum and related particularly to overtime which, the report claimed, was paid whether worked or not, with some detectives clocking up 200 hours as opposed to the average ninety-six extra hours worked in a twenty-eight-day period. Most of the overtime was run up by detectives 'meeting contacts' in pubs. It was not possible to identify the authorization or justification for individual overtime applications because the original application forms were not recovered by West Yorkshire. The Headquarters City CID Operations had exceeded its overtime by 13,500 hours for 1988–89. Of this excess expenditure, which was paid for by the Major Crime Contingency Fund, itself something regarded as an abuse by the PCA, eighty-eight per cent of the funding was claimed by the squad.

Detectives on the squad spent an average of £600 a year –

---

[20] DCs Woodley and Clifford received £40,000 damages for libel from two newspapers which reported them as removing the papers. At the time of writing a further action is pending against a third newspaper.

In Bromwell's successful appeal his counsel argued that 'Notes had disappeared and had disappeared in circumstances which suggested most powerfully that officers colluded to take them.' The Lord Chief Justice, Lord Taylor, in allowing Bromwell's appeal, said it was very likely that the papers had been stolen, adding, 'Mr Birnbaum [counsel] prays in aid that they [the notes] were stolen. It is not necessary for me to make a finding, but the material before me raises a very real possibility that this may be the case.'

not including payments to registered informants – cultivating contacts. The Detective Chief Inspector and Detective Inspector claimed around £39 a month and the others an average of £51. The PCA reported: 'These individual claims had minimal pocket book justification.'

There was more of the same criticism over the way in which subsistence claims, of around the same monthly amounts, were made. 'Owing to the unacceptable manner in which squad officers completed their pocket books it has proved impossible to determine whether their claims were justified.'

Nor was the PCA happy with the way the informants were paid. At best, senior officers were found to be confused as to their responsibilities to ensure that payments were valid. At worst, they were party to false claims of money drawn but not paid to informants.

Pocket books were generally found to be inadequately kept and poorly maintained. In many cases the place of the start and finish of duty were not recorded and there were spaces left between entries. Some days had no entries at all.

Judge Francis Petrie of the PCA recommended that custody records be retained for six years, there should be more effective supervision of payments to informants, force orders on pocket books should be revised and the overtime system be overhauled.

Former officers of the West Midlands Serious Crime Squad reacted angrily to the report, claiming, in effect, a complete vindication of the squad. DCI Bob Goodchild said, 'I am astonished that, after two and a quarter years and umpteen millions of pounds that has been spent, this is the sum total that they can come up with. All they can complain about is overtime, expenses and a slight criticism of working practices.'[21]

In fact there had already been a report in 1985 which had criticized the squad's working practices. Commander Ron Hay of the Metropolitan Police had criticized the use and supervision of pocket books following his investigation, which had centred on a man kept in custody on a murder charge for eight months. He had apparently confessed and was released after the arrest of another man who was subsequently convicted of the offence. Hay's report was seen by several officers of chief officer rank

[21] *Police Review*, 22 May 1992.

but the mistakes made were repeated in a number of other investigations. The Hay report, apparently, never reached the eyes of Geoffrey Dear.

There was, moreover, a second report, this time made in 1987 by a John Brown, then a Detective Chief Inspector. It had called for urgent changes but, although there is a memorandum mentioning its existence, it appears that the report itself was mislaid. Brown had already complained that the decision to axe the Serious Crime Squad had been precipitate: 'Publicity seems to have been the main factor. If only Geoffrey Dear had waited – just delved deeper and secured all the information he required – none of this need have happened.'

Goodchild, who had spent some time on traffic management, echoed him. When told of the disbandment of the squad, 'My reaction was of total disbelief at the most outrageous piece of disloyalty coming from a police officer.'

In a separate report Dear was criticized by Roger Birch, the Chief Constable of Sussex, for failing to secure the safety of documents relevant to the inquiry. In particular he was blamed for not securing the Bradford Street office, from which most of the squad operated, for three days after it was disbanded. Dear has always maintained that a direction to seal Bradford Street was included with instructions to see another thirty-nine venues. The failure, he says, was a result of a misunderstanding between two Assistant Chief Constables. In any event, according to *Police Review*, Bradford Street was in reality a booking office where no important documents were held.[22]

In the meantime there had been a string of dropped charges, acquittals – many by direction of the trial judges – and quashings of convictions of defendants by the Court of Appeal in cases involving the Serious Crime Squad. The alleged defects in the cases included missing documents, fabricated confessions, planted forensic evidence, duress, missing surveillance equipment and lost exhibits.

In the case of George Twitchell he was paid £20,000 compensation following his acquittal in 1982. Officers in some other cases were demoted to the rank of uniform Constable, or fined under police regulations for making false and untruthful records. In June 1991 four squad officers stood trial at Oxford

---

[22] 'The Mud that Never Stuck', *Police Review*, 22 May 1992.

Crown Court charged with conspiracy to pervert the course of justice in the trial of a Keith Parchment whose conviction for robbery had been quashed in July 1987. It was alleged that the officers had obtained admissions by getting Parchment to sign blank sheets and then claiming that they had taken down his confession at his dictation. One was acquitted by the direction of the judge at the beginning of the trial. The other three did not give evidence and were acquitted.

The West Yorkshire inquiry also reported to the Director of Public Prosecutions on their investigation into eleven officers. The outcome of this was not known for a further six months until Mrs Barbara Mills, the Director of Public Prosecutions, announced she did not intend to proceed against any of the men. Later she took the unprecedented step of justifying her actions in the *Independent*. In a letter she wrote, 'It is my duty to make the right decision, not the expedient one . . . There is an enormous difference between poor supervision and sloppy management practice, and criminality.'

But Dear was by no means finished. On the BBC television programme, *Geoffrey Dear, A Costly Mistake*, which examined his decision to disband the Serious Crime Squad, he said that, whatever Mrs Mills might think, some of the squad members should have been prosecuted. He accepted, however, that a large number of officers affected by his decision would have good reason to feel both distressed and aggrieved. 'I was making deep cuts into good wood . . . It was necessary to be unswerving and ruthless.' He went on to explain that his decision to remove everyone from the squad and to disband it had been based on his experience on how Operation Countryman had been conducted in the Metropolitan Police. Unsurprisingly, his comments were not well received by the officers whose squad he had disbanded.

The decision not to prosecute was, predictably, applauded by the West Midlands branch of the Police Superintendents' Association. 'Many of the complaints were made by dangerous criminals who did not miss this opportunity to attempt to damage the reputation of a professional and very effective team of police officers who served the public of the West Midlands very well for many years,' said a spokesman.

Others viewed the situation differently. Gareth Williams, then Chairman of the Bar, said: 'It troubles me and members of the Bar generally that you have these appalling miscarriages of justice and no-one is brought to book. It cannot be right that people serve imprisonment for fifteen and sixteen years and no criminal sanction is imposed.'

A twelfth victim, Michael Thomas Bromwell, was cleared on 22 June 1992; his first appeal had been rejected in 1988. The crown did not oppose the appeal of Bromwell, who had served four years of a seven-year jail sentence for a reprisal gangland shooting. Notes of his interviews with the squad disappeared from the court file. Lord Justice Taylor commented that the explanation that the officers had sought the notes to answer a Criminal Injuries Compensation Board inquiry was highly unlikely to have been sound and truthful.[23]

The cases continued to be heard by the Court of Appeal in 1993. In the case of Binham, the Crown conceded that it could not support the conviction. Eight statements had disappeared from five different places. The Crown did not believe this was sheer coincidence. One statement had disappeared from the files of the Crown Prosecution Service, although there was no suggestion of impropriety on their behalf.

Jeff Crawford, who had supervised the investigation from the point of view of the Police Complaints Authority, said that he was shocked but not entirely surprised by the decision not to prosecute: 'I think it is tragic the nation will not be given the opportunity to hear what did go on. It would have been better if some officers who the investigators and myself thought should have been charged were charged, so the nation could be reassured the investigation was thorough and there was no attempt to cover up activities of the officers.'[24]

Frank Williamson, former Head of HMI Constabulary, commented: 'I used to be able to deny corruption in the provinces. I can't now. I'm old enough to remember Birmingham Crime Squad in its inception and I'm here to tell you I'm not surprised about West Midlands. The Birmingham City Crime Squad in the old days were a hard, tough, no-care-for-the-rules outfit and that's when it started.'

Mrs Mills also studied eleven reports of possible misappropriation from police funds by officers. In nine cases there was

[23] *Guardian*, 23 June 1992.
[24] *Times*, 20 May 1992.

insufficient evidence to prosecute. In the other two 'the public interest did not require a prosecution'. Those two cases were referred for possible disciplinary action. On 15 January 1992 it was announced that seven West Midlands officers were to face a total of twenty-eight disciplinary charges covering falsehood and prevarication, and altering or destroying documentation records. Ten former officers had escaped charges because they had resigned. A further 102 officers had been or would be 'advised' for not following procedures or codes of practice or irregularities in recording interviews.

Peter Moorhouse, deputy chairman of the PCA responsible for discipline, said that the inquiry had achieved disciplinary results, released twelve people from jail and brought about 'major changes to the operating practices of specialist police squads. That is a pretty substantial return on a long inquiry.'

There were also the 'political' cases which were beginning to surface and resurface after the convicted had spent a decade and a half in prison. In the mid-1970s there were a series of IRA attacks on targets in mainland Britain, including public houses and the Old Bailey. On 5 October 1974 time-bombs were planted in the Horse and Groom and the Seven Stars pubs in Guildford; five people were killed and many more maimed. On 7 November two people died at a pub bombing in Woolwich, South London. In 1975 the 'Guildford Four', Gerard Conlon, Paul Hill, Patrick Armstrong and Carole Richardson, were jailed for life for what was alleged to be their part in these bombings. They were freed by the Court of Appeal in October 1989 following an investigation into the case by the Avon and Somerset Police. The prosecution had been based almost entirely on forensic evidence which established that there were traces of nitro-glycerine on the hands of six of the accused and on the gloves of the seventh. This could only have occurred, said the scientists at the trial, by reason of the deliberate handling of explosives. In July 1990 Sir John May began the hearing of his public inquiry into the circumstances of the conviction and referred the case back to the Court of Appeal, which quashed the convictions.

In 1991 three former officers were charged with conspiracy to pervert the course of justice and in June of that year Mr Ronald Bartle, a stipendiary magistrate sitting at Bow Street, discharged the officers on the grounds of the lapse of time since the alleged offence, the delay in the preparation of their case, media publicity and the failure of certain of the Avon officers to caution them properly.

In January 1992 the Divisional Court ruled that the officers must stand trial. 'The jurisdiction to halt criminal proceedings for delay has to be exercised with great care,' said Lord Justice Neill, 'particularly where the delay is not the fault of the prosecution but arises because the matters giving rise to the criminal proceedings have only come to light after a long period.' Lyn Williams, assistant general secretary of the Police Federation, said the decision to proceed against the officers was 'regrettable and disappointing after the amount of time that has elapsed'.[25]

In 1992 the 'Birmingham Six', jailed for life for their alleged part in an IRA bombing in Birmingham in November 1974 in which twenty-one people died, were released when their convictions were quashed; this was after years of effort by their supporters and finally the appointment in March 1990 of the Devon and Cornwall investigation into the case, which led the Home Secretary, David Waddington, to refer the matter to the Court of Appeal. There the appeal was effectively conceded by the Crown when the police and scientific evidence on which the six were convicted was conceded to be unsafe. The case had been before the court on a number of previous occasions and the prior appeal had elicited the comment from the then Lord Chief Justice, Lord Lane, that the longer the case continued the more convinced he and his colleagues were of the guilt of the Birmingham Six. Lord Denning, the former Master of the Rolls, had previously pronounced on the subject when, in one of the by-products of the case, the six had tried to bring a civil action:

> Just consider the course of events if this action is allowed to proceed to trial. If the six men fail, it will mean that much time and money will have been expended by many people for no good purpose. If the six men win, it will mean that the police were guilty of perjury, that they were guilty of violence and threats, that the confessions were involuntary and were improperly admitted in evidence and that the convictions

[25] *Guardian*, 25 January 1992. The officers were acquitted by a jury in May 1993.

were erroneous. That would mean the Home Secretary would either have to recommend they be pardoned or he would have to remit the case to the Court of Appeal. This is such an appalling vista that every sensible person in the land would say: It cannot be right these actions should go any further.

This case shows what a civilized country we are. Here are six men who have been proved guilty of the most wicked murder of twenty-one innocent people. They have no money. Yet the state has lavished large sums on their defence. They were convicted of murder and sentenced to imprisonment for life. In their evidence they were guilty of gross perjury. Yet the state continued to lavish large sums on them in actions against the police. It is high time it stopped. It is really an attempt to set aside the convictions on a side wind. It is a scandal that it should be allowed to continue.

Quite apart from the alleged misdemeanours of the Serious Crime Squad, the West Midlands Police had trouble nearer to the ground, and once again the case encompassed the problems – drinking on duty, pressure on suspects, lies and cover-ups, an attitude to those they regard as being inferior – which have bedevilled the police throughout their history. On 13 December 1991 Chris Mullin, the Labour MP for Sunderland South who had done so much to bring about the release of the Birmingham Six, raised the matter of a two-year-old case in an adjournment debate in the House of Commons, saying 'The West Midlands Police have been caught fabricating evidence.' He alleged that they did so in the knowledge that 'they can rely on their superiors up to the Chief Constable himself to make sure the truth is covered up. They can rely, too, on the Crown Prosecution Service to connive in the disappearance of inconvenient evidence.'

He was referring to the death of PC Tony Salt, a community policeman in Small Heath, Birmingham, who, on 16 April 1989 with his colleague Mark Berry, had been keeping observation on an illegal Afro-Caribbean drinking club. Salt left his post and then went to the Grapes, a nearby public house, where he drank seven or eight pints, a short and a can of strong lager. After leaving the pub Salt wandered down the alleyway in the direction of the drinking club and twenty minutes later Berry saw him collapse at the mouth of the alley. He was dead on arrival at the hospital.

Three West Indians, Peter Gibbs, Mark Samuels and Tony Francis, were arrested. Gibbs was interviewed and eventually agreed to confess to stealing Salt's wallet and a martial arts instrument known as a cubiton which Salt always carried with him. Samuels maintained he was in Sparkhill police station and ultimately confessed on tape to stealing the wallet and the cubiton. The third member, Tony Francis, the doorman at the club, agreed on tape that he had prevented Salt from entering the club. All were charged with murder.

'No sooner had the men been charged than things began to go wrong,' Mr Mullin said. A taxi driver said he had taken Gibbs and Samuels away before Salt died. Two pathologists said a blow from Francis could not have killed Salt and that he had most likely fallen drunkenly on the bucket of a parked JCB digger. PC Salt's widow then said she had found the cubiton in the family car. Her statement was not disclosed to the defence by the Crown Prosecution Service. It was nearly a year before no evidence was offered against the men.[26]

And if things are going badly, they tend sometimes to get worse rather than better. Two masked raiders stole £150,000 worth of drugs from the West Midlands police station at Perry Barr. They knew it was unmanned at night except for a civilian security guard, who was threatened with an axe. They disabled the alarm system and stole the drugs – 66 kilos of cannabis resin in bags weighing a kilo each and resembling a bag of sugar. Substantial piles of heroin, cocaine and crack were ignored, which led officers to believe that the drugs may have been taken to thwart a trial. Without the exhibits the prosecution would have a hard time in proving their case.[27]

But as one door closed on potential prosecutions of officers, several more opened; one in fact had been open for some time. The Greater Manchester Police had been having a bad time in the late 1980s but even before then there had been the case of Steven Shaw, a twenty-five-year-old student at Manchester University. It was a curious incident, resulting from a visit to the university by Leon Brittan, then the Home Secretary, on

[26] *Guardian*, 14 December 1991.
[27] *Daily Mirror*, 7 July 1992.

1 March 1985. Violence had flared between demonstrating students and the police outside the university and thirty-seven people including officers were injured. Soon afterwards, Shaw, a politics and philosophy student, alleged that his flat had been burgled and that he had been beaten up in a deserted alleyway by the police. When he complained to the police he was subjected to a five-hour interrogation during which he was tortured by a lighted cigarette being thrust into his face and having his hands stamped on. His position was not helped, however, by the fact that initially his fellow students would not cooperate with an independent inquiry by the Avon and Somerset Police, which finally resulted in complaints by thirty-three students of mistreatment and seventy-one allegations of general police misconduct on that night. To obtain any sort of cooperation the police had been forced to hire off-campus accommodation so students could make contact without the knowledge of their colleagues. The identities of the two officers alleged to be involved were not discovered.

The left-wing-controlled local authority's magazine *Police Watch* carried a front page artist's impression of the officers said to be involved, and the council authorized a £3,500 independent investigation into the affair by a former graduate in history and archaeology. By now Shaw, with a warrant for conspiracy to pervert the course of justice out for his arrest, fled abroad. However, by no means everyone was convinced of Shaw's guilt. Anthony McCardell, member of the Greater Manchester Police Authority and former chairman of the City Council Police Monitoring Committee, urged the Home Secretary to grant immunity to any Greater Manchester Police officer 'willing to break the secrecy pact', saying that only if policemen were guaranteed immunity from prosecution would the full facts of the case emerge:

> I am not suggesting these two policemen were ordered to rough up Steven Shaw . . . What I am saying is that as events progressed senior officers gradually became aware of what had taken place and wrongly thought it better to stay silent and hope the affair blew over. But that has not happened because so many people are convinced both . . . and Steven became scapegoats for policemen determined to

protect their own reputation or mask the misdemeanours of colleagues.[28]

Nothing ever came of the request and the affair died a natural death. Eventually the summonses against Shaw were dropped by the Crown Prosecution Service on the basis that there was no reasonable chance of a successful prosecution.

The Shaw affair ran almost parallel with that of John Stalker. Amidst allegations, counter-allegations and a multitude of recriminations, the Deputy Chief Constable of Greater Manchester had been suspended and then reinstated before he finally resigned. His acquaintance and a local Conservative Party chairman, Kevin Taylor, himself a friend of the so-called Quality Street Gang and a property developer, who had built his fortunes on his skill as a professional card player, had been ruined by a prosecution which eventually collapsed.

In May 1984 John Stalker had been appointed to lead an inquiry into the shooting in 1982 of six unarmed men by the Royal Ulster Constabulary, an appointment which, if it was by no means welcomed enthusiastically by the RUC Constable, Sir John Hermon, was certainly not welcomed at all by others. In May 1984 when Stalker lunched with Hermon, he maintains that he was handed a flattened-out cigarette packet tracing Stalker's family tree on his mother's side and showing her Catholic links.

Within the year Stalker had made substantial progress in his inquiry. By February 1985 he was chasing what was known as the 'Hayshed' tape, which, if genuine, he believed would prove that RUC officers had shot an unarmed teenager without warning and in cold blood. Despite requests and assurances he was never to see the tape and fifteen months later he was told that a squad had been set up to investigate a Manchester policeman.

Simultaneously Greater Manchester Police were beginning their investigation into Kevin Taylor over allegations of fraud. The Taylor inquiry was pursued ruthlessly:

Surveillance equipment had been set up to spy on his palatial Bury home. Friends and relations were being quizzed by

28 *The Times*, 14 September 1987.

senior detectives. His phones were being tapped, his mail opened and (on one occasion) his accountant's office burgled. His bankers all over the world were getting requests from Manchester detectives for confidential documents. Taylor asked his lawyers to find out what the police wanted. They would not say. Taylor told the police he was ready and willing to talk to them at any time they wanted. He got a promise from the Chief Constable James Anderton that if the police ever wanted to speak to him they would get in touch with his lawyers. That was not the way it happened. When Taylor's house was raided in May 1986 there was no advance warning. The police took away a few old papers from the 1970s – and the real loot: three photographs of John Stalker.[29]

Inquiries continued into the working of Taylor's bank accounts. Certainly he had borrowed £1 million but the properties were valued at £1.6 million and no customer or client ever suggested that Taylor was involved in fraud. Nor did bank officials. The next step was to approach the Crown Court and ask for access orders to seize Taylor's accounts. In a sworn statement to Judge Preest, DI Arthur Stephenson suggested that Taylor was involved with drugs. Preest granted the orders. The statement was kept in a sealed envelope for over two years.

Now Taylor was charged, along with his accountant, a Co-op bank official and a surveyor, with conspiracy to defraud the bank by overvaluing property. The result was a disaster for Taylor. His companies collapsed, as did the prosecution, but not before Taylor was ruined.

As the trial progressed Stephenson, one of the officers to be reprimanded, was under severe cross-examination by Taylor's counsel, David Hood. Driven ever deeper into damaging admissions over the conduct of the case and, in particular, into the evidence given on the application before Judge Preest, the case was destroyed. At lunchtime on 18 January 1990 Michael Corkery, a London barrister who had unexpectedly been instructed on behalf of the Crown rather than a local person, received instructions from the Director of Public Prosecutions to offer no further evidence.

[29] Paul Foot in *The Spectator*, 9 June 1990.

Stalker by this time had resigned. He had been removed from the Northern Ireland inquiry on 29 May 1986 and had been given extended leave pending the outcome of disciplinary offences. Inquiries into his relationship with Kevin Taylor continued for the next three months until after a 36 to 6 vote by the Police Committee he was reinstated on 23 August of that year. At worst the allegations were reduced to the use of a police car for his own purposes. On his reinstatement he maintained an unhappy relationship with the Chief Constable, James Anderton. It was clear to Stalker that he had no future in the force, particularly when Peter Topping was appointed Chief Superintendent in preference to Stalker's choice, John Thorburn. It was Topping who had been the senior officer in the unhappy prosecution of Kevin Taylor. Stalker retired on 13 March 1987.[30]

Stalker went into journalism which was, perhaps, his first love. There is little doubt he had been treated badly by the force. His legal costs for defending himself before the Police Committee had amounted to something over £21,000. Despite his reinstatement without charges the Police Authority refused to make any contribution to the costs, which were paid for largely by public subscription and a concert organized by a Frankie 'Frou-Frou' Davies. Even this did not please certain police officers, who may not have the facts actually quite right but who give a flavour of their attitude, in the words of one former Chief Constable:

> That's no way for an ACC to carry on whether he's been railroaded or not. Yet there is the victimized ACC up on the boards with him, playing the drums in a pub. There's no dignity left in the business. What sort of an impression he left as the disciplinary controller of the Manchester City Police, God only knows.

But whatever the Stalker–Taylor problems, at last there was a triumph. In May 1989 came a great feather in the force's cap when it rooted out from its ranks the 'bullying and crooked' police officer, Thomas Gerald 'Ged' Corley, a constable with

---

[30] There are three basic accounts of the two cases. J. Stalker, *Stalker*, and K. Taylor with K. Mumby, *The Poisoned Tree*, are in one pan of the scales. P. Topping, *Topping*, is in the other. Each is intensely personal.

wide-ranging contacts in the underworld. The list of complaints compiled against Corley, described as a nineteen-stone thug, and certainly a six foot four, nineteen-stone weightlifter, included conspiracy to rob and supplying a firearm.

Despite his continued protestations of innocence and that he was being fitted-up, Corley was found guilty at Manchester Crown Court of conspiracy to rob – an attack on a security guard at Walkden near Manchester in 1987 – and transferring a firearm. He received a sentence of seventeen years' imprisonment.

But within weeks of Corley's conviction the cream on the top of the milk had soured. An inquiry began into the investigation which led to Corley's conviction.

At the end of August officers were suspended. What, asked *Police Review*, would be the effect on the Corley conviction?

The answer is that in March 1990 it was quashed. Ged Corley, who described his last two years as a nightmare (doubtless rightly considering the treatment meted out to convicted police officers), was acquitted by the Court of Appeal which described his trial as a travesty of justice. He had been released on bail by the Court of Appeal in the autumn of 1989, not something which that Court does regularly or lightly. If the Crown Prosecution Service had known only a quarter of what had emerged since the trial, Corley would never have appeared in court, said Lord Lane, the Lord Chief Justice.

The South Wales Police had troubles too. In February 1992 seven officers were suspended after an investigation of the force's handling of the 1985 murder of Sandra Phillips, a sex shop manageress, and the subsequent conviction of a pair of homeless out of work brothers, Paul and Wayne Darvell. A further eighty officers up to the rank of Superintendent level were issued with formal warnings of complaint. Again the trouble was inconsistencies in the notebooks of officers. The notebooks were dated within a day of the interviews but it appears that the notebooks themselves had not been issued to them for another month. In June the Darvell brothers were released by the Court of Appeal when their case was referred back by the Home Secretary. The Crown did not oppose their appeal. A further twelve other convictions were being reviewed by the Devon and Cornwall Police who had conducted the Darvell investigation.

Whilst this was going on the Court of Appeal freed Stefan Kisko. He had been convicted at Leeds Crown Court of the murder of schoolgirl Lesley Molseed in 1975 after signing a confession to the murder. Now semen tests showed he could not possibly be the killer. It transpired that this vital information had not been passed to the defence. Later in the year Judith Ward, convicted of the bombing incident which killed a number of soldiers on a coach in 1975, was also cleared by the Court of Appeal. Her confession was regarded as unreliable, as was that of McKenzie[31], whose conviction led to the Lord Chief Justice laying down guidelines on how the judge should approach confessions from clearly unstable and unreliable defendants.

In November and December 1991, first Winston Silcott and then Engin Raghip and Mark Braithwaite were cleared by the Court of Appeal, which overturned their convictions for the killing of PC Keith Blakelock during rioting on the Broadwater Farm Estate, Tottenham, in 1985. The Crown, through Mr Roy Amlot QC, conceded the case. 'We say unequivocally we would not have gone on against Raghip or Braithwaite or any of the other defendants having learned of the apparent dishonesty of the officer in charge of the case. I say that because the Crown has to depend on the honesty and integrity of officers in a case, especially where he has close control of the case.'

It was the ESDA (Electrostatic Deposition Analysis) test which proved the undoing of the Crown's case.[32] Mr Amlot agreed that it demonstrated that key passages in the confessions had been added later. The Crown's case had been based on admissions made during interviews. There was no other corroborative evidence.

During the trial itself Mr Justice Hodgson had ruled on the confessions in the case of Y, a juvenile aged fifteen but with a mental age of seven. On his arrest he had been taken to Wood

[31] Shades of Confait. McKenzie, a 38-year-old man with an IQ of between 73 and 76 had been arrested in connection with fires started at addresses after he had been seen in the vicinity acting suspiciously. He confessed to 12 murders, 10 of which confessions the police did not believe. However he was charged with the murder of two elderly ladies. The Court of Appeal quashed his conviction on the basis that the absence of an adult rendered the confessions unreliable. *New Law Journal*, 14 August, 1992.
[32] In lay terms the ESDA test can show whether pages of narrative have been written consecutively or whether additional sheets have been inserted into the original sheaf.

Green police station where he had been held in isolation in a cell for four fours. He had been questioned on six occasions for a total of approximately ten hours. He was denied access to a solicitor, who was turned away when she attended the police station to make inquiries. The boy's mother was not requested to be present during the interviews; instead a school teacher was the 'appropriate adult' required to be present. Medical evidence called on behalf of the boy showed he was completely illiterate and innumerate with severely diminished capacity to recall and remember events. Clearly no heed had been paid to the Confait case.

The trial judge, refusing to admit the confession in evidence, said that 'four hours of isolation, reinforced halfway through, for a boy of fifteen with a mental age of seven who should not have been in a cell at all, is oppression. He went on to list seven further acts, including failure to notify teachers who had been designated as the appropriate adults as to the allegations being investigated, and the holding of the boy without access to the outside world in circumstances that must have been 'disquieting and crushing', as significant in his ruling that the custodial conditions were oppressive. In the Broadwater Farm inquiry, of the 127 people arrested in the investigations who asked for a solicitor, seventy-seven had access delayed or denied. Fifty-four of those arrested, mostly juveniles, were interviewed in the presence of a friend rather than a solicitor.[33]

There was still one running sore relating to the Met. It involved their star thief-taker, Detective Superintendent Tony Lundy, and his involvement with Roy Garner, an informer *de luxe*. Once more it brought into question the desirability of a close link between an officer, however senior, and an informer, however valuable.

One of the problems which has bedevilled all police forces at all times is that the chances of happening upon a theft taking place are remote in the extreme. If the thief does not leave behind any sort of evidence which may be forensically examined then the chances of his being apprehended rest on chance and, more prosaically, the use of an informant. And it is the informant who, whilst producing the solution to crimes, without public and, he hopes, friends', recognition,

[33] Quoted in the Burnham Report. pp. 10–12.

has caused many problems to the police forces to whom he has sold his services. A former Commander of the Flying Squad comments:

Shepherds Bush was an interesting ground – there was the White City Estate, sprawling, a very good ground for training as a CID. There were some very good thieves living on the ground. There was a very good DI there. Keen you should develop informants. 'A detective is only as good as his informants' he would say, and I think that's true today. A lot of people in the CID didn't develop their informants as they should have done. Perhaps they felt unsafe. Informants could certainly be regarded as unsafe but they didn't have to be. It depended on who was the governor. It depends on the officer's own personality – if he is prepared to allow too much it can get out of hand. That's where things have gone wrong in part. Informants mustn't get involved.

They were paid buttons. You had to make it look at least respectable yourself and it's amazing the information that came in. You claimed incidentals. The informants you were running, you had to sub them as a way of insurance. If they went inside you gave their wives a couple of quid now and again.

A Chief Inspector in a provincial force speaking in 1992 said, 'The big problem is knowing what their ulterior motives are. They're paid peanuts and you don't know if they're setting up jobs for you. Now it's strictly supervised. Names in sealed brown envelopes deposited with a superior officer and just what you can and can't do.'

'In the main informants are both feckless and, as their role suggests, devious,' commented a Detective Sergeant in the Flying Squad. 'A grass I had, had £16,000 in reward money in a year – and this was in the late sixties – and he borrowed £200 from me for Christmas.' His view was echoed by a Chief Inspector:

There was one DC who had a very good informant and he took him out of the cells to go and identify the properties he'd screwed. He parked out in a rural area and by arrangement the girl friend turns up for a conjugal visit. So the DC leaves them alone and the informant does a runner. The Detective Superintendent looks in the envelope and says it says you could take him out of the cells but nothing about conjugals. And the DC is back in uniform.

The same Detective Sergeant comments that Alec Eist, a former Flying Squad officer, 'was the best informed policeman in London. He knew all the villains. You don't get information without going some way towards them. He could turn fifty per cent of all his suspects. There is no villain in London who will not give you information if you go about it the right way.'

At times major informants were protected by the officers, to excessive lengths. Not only were their names kept secret but they often had a licence to commit crime, secure in the knowledge that their runner in the force would dig them out of trouble. Often they are major criminals. For example, when the Kray inquiry was nearing its conclusion and there was evidence that Alan Bruce Cooper, who had been dealing in LSD, had hired another man as a contract killer, Read, the investigating officer, had Cooper arrested. Cooper told Read to contact du Rose as he had been that officer's spy and informant for two years, something which du Rose admitted although he tried to play down the contact.

A former Flying Squad Detective Sergeant tells the story:

When I was on the squad I was working with a guy and we got some info both from a man I'd had on my firm for years and also from a country housebreaker. The guy came to me one day through another contact and told me about a man S who lived in East London. The man was flooding London with forged $100 notes. My guy told me he was real cautious and would only deal with people he trusted. Apparently he would send out for the notes whilst the buyer stayed in the shop. Now, if this went right there was a lot of money for my grass and he didn't work for nothing. What we would have to do was put a buyer in, then follow the man sent from the shop to get the notes, and we knew this would be very difficult.

Anyway we arranged a set-up and the surveillance with motorbikes standing by. On the day in question we went down in a taxi and with an intercept van. It was pissing with rain and our two men, my guy and the burglar, goes in. S's man comes out, gets in his van and off he goes with the motorbike after him. Then, apparently, he does a swift right on an amber and the bike's on the floor trying to go after him.

When we got back to the station one of the motorbike blokes came up to me and said could he have a private word. I said of course and he said, 'The guy you're looking at is called SN isn't he?' And I said, 'Well, you're right but why?' 'I think you should know he's X's man. [X was a DCI.] Last week I delivered a wedding present from him to the DCI's daughter.'

I went back and discussed it with my man and the talk was that S was minded by someone very high up. All intercepts went through the minder and so we realized that we could not put one on S. If it was right that S was being minded it would be blown out. I tried again to find someone who S might trust as a buyer but the next man fucked up as well. So we decided to go and see the DCI; tell him we understood he knew S and that we were anxious to locate the premises, and as an inducement for the DCI not to go bent on us we would say that there would be substantial reward money from the FBI and we would see that he got his whack. The DCI said that was fine and he'd do what he could. This was a Tuesday. Later he told us the money was being kept in a second flat where S lived and so we planned the next one for the Thursday.

On the Thursday I'd been to take a statement about something completely different and at 10.30 I had a call to go into the Yard. We were hauled into an office and another DCI there said, 'You've been to Bow Street to get a warrant.' I said we hadn't and he said yes we had. I told him if he didn't believe me to ring Bow Street court. He said we might like to know that a Superintendent was already at S's flat along with *The Times* and it was all wired up waiting for us to go there.

Later I had a statement taken from me by a Deputy Assistant Commissioner and afterwards he gave me the form 163 which set out the complaint against me. It said that S had met two senior Scotland Yard officers who had told him that members of the Flying Squad were going to search his premises for forged bills and if they didn't find any they would plant some and blackmail him for £500. The DCI'd turned us over to protect his man. It was a terrible thing to do to us. For me that was the turning point in the job.

Chief Superintendent Harry Clement recalls:

In the old days, if you'd got a police officer of DAC rank and he got to hear that two operational detectives were involved with the same man, one running the man as an informant and the other chasing him, he would have them both in and he would ask what information the man was giving. Then he would ask the other what evidence he had against the man, and what he was wanted for, and he would come down on the side of the chaser. He would tell the first to get the man to come in and put his hands up. So he would come in with a few charges and he would get the message he'd had it his own way for too long.

An informant could earn anything from £5 upwards. Roy Garner, the snout for Tony Lundy, was reputed to have cleared £300,000 in rewards during his career, which ended in a sixteen-year prison sentence for trafficking in cocaine. In 1992 an informant who assisted Customs officers was paid £30,000. At the other end of the scale, however, in 1991 the Inspectorate of Constabulary disclosed in a report that South Wales detectives were empowered to pay only £5 to their snouts without prior authority. Even senior detectives were obliged to obtain written permission from an officer of the rank of Detective Chief Superintendent.

'What sort of information do you think you can get for a fiver? It does not buy an awful lot,' said a forlorn South Wales detective. The Inspectorate of Constabulary agreed, saying there was little evidence of use of informants in the force. 'This practice does not encourage detectives to seek out, use or handle information. The proper use of informants could save time and manpower,' the report added, recommending that arrangements in South Wales be reviewed.[34]

Just as there has been a divergence of opinion on whether

---

[34] *Daily Telegraph*, 18 January 1992.

having a free cup of tea in a café is the first step towards corruption, so have there been mixed feelings as to whether the police should mix, on a regular basis, with criminals and so, whilst obtaining information, leave themselves open to the risk of the approach.

Former Assistant Commissioner Sir Ronald Howe was one of those who favoured mingling. 'I always insisted that detectives should go to race meetings, dog tracks and clubs of ill-repute. That is where information is found.' In an interview with the *Sunday Times* he went on to suggest that the minimum height restrictions need not apply to detectives His ambition was to see a national detective force which would be completely separate from the uniformed branch.[35]

In the Royal Commission of 1961 it was recalled how in the 1928 Commission police were being actively discouraged from mixing with informers and criminals. Now the rules and regulations relating to informants were more circumscribed than in the past.

But in the 1980s the rise and fall of the arch informant Roy Garner, together with the destruction of Scotland Yard's whizz-kid Superintendent Tony Lundy, protégé of former Commander of the Flying Squad Don Neesham, showed the true dangers of running informants. It came with Garner's increasing involvement in the cocaine trade. Before that, quite apart from his informing abilities, he had been involved in 1982 in a VAT fraud which worked by importing exempt coins, such as Krugerrands under £50,000, and then selling them on with the VAT added. This in itself was perfectly legal. The only problem was that the VAT had to be repaid within three months. It was not. Given that flights were being made on an almost daily basis, the profits were enormous.

In November 1984 Garner went to prison for the maximum term of two years' consecutive on two counts and was fined, as well as being made the subject of a criminal bankruptcy order. The Court of Appeal later reduced the sentence by a year and quashed the fine. The Court expressed the hope that the criminal bankruptcy would be pursued by the authorities. It was something of a vain hope. Garner's stud farm belonged to his father; the family home was mortgaged to the hilt; his share

[35] 29 October 1961.

of Elton's, the nightclub behind Tottenham police station, went to repay a loan on the club; and as for the reward money – that had gone too, probably on his string of racehorses.[36]

Garner, put forward as the grass over the case of the Brinks-Mat laundering, was arrested along with a drug dealer, Nicholas Chrastny, and Mickey Hennessey (one of the notorious South London family of criminals), over the importation of fifty-seven kilos of cocaine found in suitcases in Chrastny's flat in Harley Street. Chrastny was given conditional bail. He was to become a supergrass on the usual terms of residence in a police station. Off he was sent to the wilds of Yorkshire where his wife was allowed to give him £500 in cash for his daily needs, and to while away the time he was given modelling plasticine, paint and glue. By the morning of 5 October he had finished sawing through the bars of his cell, making his escape through the doctor's room in the police station and out of the window into a waiting car. He has not been seen or heard of since. As always, there are various stories, the principal ones being that he is either dead or has left the country. One of them must surely be the case.

Lundy appeared at Garner's trial, giving evidence *in camera* along with another officer, DCS Roy Ramm. The trial judge, Keith Machin, had allowed an application by Michael Corkery QC to hear this part of the case without the scrutiny of either public or press. Later the *Observer* published an account of the *in camera* part of the trial:

> Lawyers representing HM Customs accused a senior Scotland Yard detective of corruption in a secret session during an Old Bailey drugs trial . . . Lundy was cross-examined *in camera* about two leaks to the cocaine smugglers which occurred after he allegedly gained knowledge of the case. His answers were inconsistent with subsequent statements by Florida police.
>
> Mr Derek Spencer, cross-examining him for Customs, said the nature of the corrupt relationship was that Garner gave Lundy information to further his career and Lundy gave Garner police information. He told Lundy: 'You found out Garner was being inquired into and you told him.' Lundy denied the allegations.[37]

---

[36] See A. Jennings et al, *Scotland Yard's Cocaine Connection*, p. 112.
[37] 23 April 1989.

On his conviction Garner received a twenty-two-year sentence. Lundy was investigated uphill and down dale and in the end only a disciplinary matter over the receipt of some fencing for his home was brought against him. He decided not to contest the allegation, maintaining it would cost him over £20,000 to do so. He was allowed to retire on the grounds of ill health and sold his two-part story, 'Bent or Brilliant?' to the *News of the World*. There are no prizes on offer for correctly guessing his answer. He is now living in Spain, protected by the Spanish police from villains released from longish terms of imprisonment who are less than enthusiastic about him, and untroubled by repeated rumours that, from his cell and with the prospect of parole looming large, his former protégé, Garner, is busy telling his version of all to fascinated police officers. Efforts by a number of television companies and journalists to persuade him to sue them for libel have so far been unavailing.

Meanwhile back in London all has not been well in either Tottenham or Stoke Newington, whose court, North London, in the High Street had once been described by its resident magistrate, Evelyn Russell, as the last outpost of the British Empire. In 1992 allegations were being made that a substantial number of officers in the local police station were actively involved in the drug trade. Shades of the Goss case in 1976 but on a considerably wider scale. There were also allegations of planting, bribery and protection of both dealers and drinking clubs. There was also a complaint that one officer was independently running a protection and machine racket in Turkish cafés in the area, at the same time swindling the Customs and Excise of a sum in excess of £1 million.

Operation Jackpot launched by Scotland Yard in April 1991 was designed to root out these officers. Its remit was, in the words of Assistant Commissioner Peter Winship, 'to investigate allegations of drug dealing, theft and conspiracy to pervert the course of justice'. A report in the *Guardian* revealed that twenty-five police officers from Stoke Newington were named in a report on corruption sent to the Director of Public Prosecutions; three of them were alleged to have profited from drug dealing. A number of other officers are alleged to have fabricated evidence, planted drugs and committed perjury. One officer, said by his colleagues to have had personal problems and to be suffering from the disturbing condition of tinnitus, a persistent ringing in the ears, committed suicide at Barkingside custody unit on 29 January 1992. He was said to have been named by several dealers as being involved in the dealings, something angrily denied by his colleagues.[38]

In July 1992 Pearl Cameron was sentenced to five years' imprisonment at Snaresbrook Crown Court. She had pleaded guilty to supplying crack to up to 100 people daily, from which she was said to have made some £70,000. Part of the profit had, she alleged, been paid at the rate of between £1,000 and £2,000 a week to a police officer, her co-conspirator and back-up man. She believed that the officer was responsible for the raid on her house when she refused to continue dealing. Sentencing her, Judge Grigson said he did so on the basis that her dealing had stemmed from a corrupt officer, although this did not mean he accepted the allegations.[39]

Other cases involving officers from the station had been halted, including the case against Dennis Bramble alleged to have been found in possession of heroin. This was stopped by the CPS who indicated that one of their witnesses had lied on oath in a previous case in which the trial judge had invited the CPS to consider taking proceedings against the officer. None was formulated.

It may be several years before it is established whether the Stoke Newington allegations are isolated incidents or are symptomatic of another major outbreak of corruption which can rank with some of the larger-scale efforts, including bribe taking and drug dealing, by American officers such as those of Precinct 77 in Brooklyn in the middle to late 1980s.[40]

[38] *Guardian*, 21 November 1992.
[39] *Guardian*, 11 July 1992. The judge was in something of a legal bind. Where this sort of mitigation is put forward the judge is either obliged for the purposes of sentencing, to accept it or, to hold a mini-trial to determine its truth. With the potential legal consequences of holding such a trial if he found in favour of Mrs Cameron this is the last thing which would have been desirable.
[40] M. McAlary's *Buddy Boys* is an account of major racketeering by officers in that precinct over a period of years. Arrests were made following the use of already corrupt officers to inform on and wire-tap their colleagues.

Part II

7

Bent for Self

Perhaps one of the reasons why corruption in the police exists is that no one has ever been able satisfactorily to define it, and without an accurate definition it is next to impossible to assess its extent. It is difficult enough for criminologists to agree on a definition of crime. In his *Criminology in Focus* Keith Bottomley devotes the first thirty-eight pages to a discussion of the definition, and he is by no means alone in the quest. 'For as long as there have been police, there has been police corruption. For as long as there have been social theorists there have been theories of police corruption,' wrote James Richardson.[1]

In practice it would seem easy enough. Like the story of the blind men and the elephant, they can't describe it but they can recognize it. But corruption is not that easy to recognize. Just what does one make of the attitude of the former Met Detective Chief Superintendent who had this to say in 1993: 'I don't say he was corrupt but he took a few bob or so. There were people who were doing things and people who were corrupt. There's a difference.' As D. H. Lawrence said, what is pornography to one man is the laughter of genius to another.[2] So one policeman, police force or police department may regard an activity as either corrupt or providing a service to the public.

Take the free cup of coffee as an example. Just where does this fit into the following definition of corruption devised after a questionnaire was sent to 500 police departments?

[1] J. F. Richardson, *The New York Police: Colonial Times to 1901*.
[2] D. H. Lawrence, *Pornography and Obscenity* (1929), London (Faber & Faber).

Police corruption consists of acts which involve the misuse of police authority for the police employee's personal gain: activity of the police employee which compromises, or has the potential to compromise, his ability to enforce the law or provide other services impartially; the protection of illicit activities from police enforcement, whether or not the police employee's involvement is promoting the business of one person whilst discouraging that of another person.[3]

Most police departments took the view that a free cup of coffee was perfectly acceptable but a few took totally the opposite view:

Restaurant owners offering free cups of coffee or meals, newspaper vendors offering free newspapers, storekeepers offering free cigarettes or magazines, cannot be considered in the same way as individuals displaying a sense of hospitality in a private home. Usually any 'free' offer is made by store-owners with the expectation that special consideration will be returned by the police officer for the 'free' cup of coffee. In a few instances, an owner may make an offer without any expectations of a return favour by the officer. However, the appearance of an owner's expectations is perceived by the public, and when appearances to the general public are improper, the involved behaviour is prohibited.[4]

'Asked by the prosecutor, Pamela Haynes, how long he had been a corrupt cop, a definition which she defined as including accepting gratuities like free cigarettes and coffee, Magno had replied, "My whole career".'[5] 'No police force in a large city is really that different from any other, and nor are the allegations of deviant behaviour made against them.'[6]

As to the extent of deviance, in 1962 C. H. Rolph wrote of police malpractice that, whilst a combing of the daily newspapers would reveal the sad fact that many police get convicted of some form of dishonesty, a daily combing would not reveal it. Today this would not be the case. Now, hardly a

[3] National Advisory Commission 1975, p. 473.
[4] Richard Ward and Robert McCormack, 'An anti-corruption manual for administrators in law enforcement' in *Managing Police Corruption*, p. 99.
[5] Mike McAlary, *Buddy Boys*, p. 303.
[6] L. Sherman, *Police Corruption*.

EFFICIENCY OF FEMALE POLICE IN WHAT IS VULGARLY CALLED A "JOLLY ROW."

1852: a fanciful view of the then-ludicrous notion of women police.
(Illustrated London News)

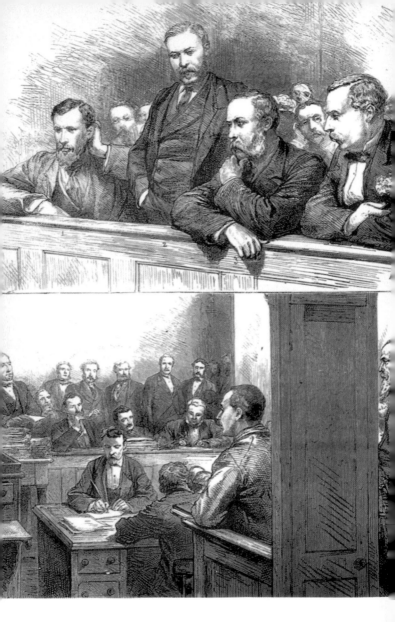

The fall of Scotland Yard, 1877. *(Illustrated London News)*

One of the early causes of middle-class discontent with the police.
(*Illustrated London News*)

above: Inspector Wiles, who covered up for Chief Inspector Collins in the Savidge case. *(Illustrated London News)*

ACQUITTED : Sir Leo Chiozza Money, the noted economist, who was arrested in Hyde Park with Miss Savidge, but whose trial was stopped and who was discharged by the magistrate, Mr. Cancellor

SIR LEO MONEY'S FRIEND : Miss Irene Savidge, the manner of whose interrogation at Scotland Yard is the cause of the present inquiry into English police methods

'The Governor of Brighton': Samuel Bellson, who was charged with Heath, Hammersley and Ridge. *(Associated Press Photo)*

George Goddard, who while a sergeant at Vine Street on pay of £6 15s a week had £12,000 in an account in Pall Mall. He received 18 months. *(S & G Press Agency Ltd)*

above: Detective Inspector John Richard Hammersley (above right). *(Topham)*

Chief Constable Charles Ridge. He was acquitted, and later took his dismissal by Brighton Council to the House of Lords. *(Topham)*

right: Detective Sergeant Trevor Heath: each received five years' imprisonment. *(Topham)*

Detective Superintendent Harry Challenor, the 'scourge of Soho', who was found unfit to stand trial at the Old Bailey *(Topham)*

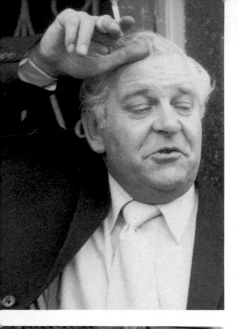

Commander Kenneth Drury relaxes with a cigarette outside his home on the day of his resignation. He was later convicted at the Old Bailey. *(Popperfoto)*

Rusty Humphreys (left) attending the Old Bailey with her legal adviser. The evidence of her husband Jimmy led to the conviction of Porn Squad officers. *(Topham)*

day passes without the report of a prosecution of a policeman or woman in the national let alone local newspapers.

The organization JUSTICE applied specifically British considerations when it compiled a list of what it deemed was deviant behaviour.[7] (The terms are more understandable, if less graphic, than the American collection which follows later.) Divided into two categories, the first, corruption which influences the course of justice, contained: (a) requesting or accepting bribes for not opposing bail or for not bringing charges; (b) making arrangements with known criminals to protect them for personal gain. In the second category, criminal dishonesty, came: (c) theft from premises under police surveillance; (d) appropriation of parts of the proceeds of theft; (e) appropriation of, or carelessness with, prisoners' property. To these might usefully be added: (f) the suppression of evidence on behalf of the defendant; and the all-embracing (g) obtaining any pecuniary or other benefit by reason of the use of uniform or office of policeman. All these are methods by which an officer may enrich himself in one way or another; what may be called bent for self. So the list does not include the fabrication of evidence to obtain a conviction, which forms a totally separate, but connected, part of the overall subject – bent for the job.

One American sociologist[8] has suggested that the ladder of police corruption in ascending rungs goes 'mooching' – eating on the arm, i.e. receiving free coffee, meals etc; 'chiselling', – gaining free admission and obtaining price discounts; 'favouritism' – granting immunity from traffic prosecutions and prejudice (where minority groups receive less than impartial treatment because of their lack of influence); 'shopping' – taking small items from unlocked stores during the rounds, extortion, a system whereby advertisements taken in police magazines can wipe out small traffic offences; 'bribery' – payments of cash or 'gifts' for past or future help to avoid prosecution (gifts are of higher value than in mooching and services must be performed to mutual understanding); 'shakedown' – appropriating large and expensive items when investigating a break-in; 'perjury' – providing an alibi for other officers apprehended in unlawful

[7] B. Whitaker, *The Police in Society*, pp. 255–7.
[8] E. R. Stoddard, 'The Informal Code of Police Deviancy: a group approach to Blue Coat Crime'. *Journal of Criminal Law, Criminology and Police Science* (1968), 59(2), 291–313.

activity; 'premeditated theft' – providing an alibi for planned burglary as opposed to shakedown. These would seem to be the opportunities available mostly to the patrol or uniform branch. Can these be applied to a specifically British police force?

Perhaps at the very bottom of the list there should appear 'mumping', an eighteenth-century word meaning skulking or loitering, which spawned the American police officers' mumpholes where an officer could coop, or sleep, for a few hours and have a cigarette or, indeed, some other pleasure without being found by his Sergeant. An early example comes from the Liverpool Watch Committee's minutes of 1843: 'Found drunk in privy with prostitute. Dismissed'. And more prosaically if less succinctly from a police constable in 1992:

> First time I did it was at Christmas. We'd been sent down to help direct pedestrians in the Christmas shopping and we just went to the pictures in the afternoon.
>
> On my night posting I used to take a space blanket, put the wireless up on full and go to sleep in the park. It all came to an end when I was found out having a sun bed during my refreshment break. It turned out the woman who was hiring out the bed was keeping a log of all the police who were in and out of her house. There was dozens of us. It would have been all right if I'd just been having tea with her.
>
> The inspector said, 'I can't believe it. You took all your clothes off.' I said, 'I didn't want to get white lines.' I thought he was going to hit me. I was taken off home beat and put back on relief.

In theory mumping was quite a harmless pastime and one which could bring benefits by way of information to the officer concerned. It could constitute good, old-fashioned policing:

> Several of the perks . . . probably contributed to the policeman's acceptance within the community which he patrolled. The receipt of food and drink especially could demonstrate a constable's friendliness and willingness to comply with the norms and standards of the local community. It was also useful to the policeman, not only because of the respite which the receipt of certain perks provided from the monotony of

the beat but also because it gave him the opportunity to talk with people in a relaxed manner, to learn about, and to get information from them.[9]

Ex-Detective Chief Superintendent Jack Slipper says, 'I'd like to see a return to the old days on the beat. In the old days you could go into a block of flats and have a cup of tea with the boilerman. You got to know everybody.' Such mooching, the first on the American list, could also lead completely the other way from Slipper's concept of good policing. An American officer described his attitude to a man who regularly gave him free meals: 'If I had run across Sam doing anything short of murder, I think I would have treaded very lightly.'[10]

The American researcher Banton, who had prepared a survey of officers in Carolina and Georgia, believed that in his limited experience mooching was initially restricted to Patrolman rank. He also believed that the British officer was above such things: 'In Britain the idea of mooching by policemen is regarded as intolerable . . . In Britain a constable who was given a free meal would probably feel under an obligation to the giver because such an action is exceptional.'[11] What know they of England who only America know? 'You don't need to pay for your meals. When your money has been turned down five or six times you don't offer any more.' And there are plenty of other stories:

. . . she used to give the local policeman breakfast every morning before the place opened. He never paid nor offered. Implicit in the understanding was the understanding that he would look out for burglars, turn a blind eye to any licensing infringements such as drinking after hours and if called on to do so would side with the owner in any trouble with an unruly customer.[12]

---

[9] C. Emsley, *The English Police*, p. 224, citing 'Society and the Policeman's Role', p. 37.
[10] E. R. Stoddard, 'The Informal Code of Police Deviancy: A Group Approach to Blue Coat Crime', *Journal of Criminal Law, Criminology and Police Science* (1968), 59:2.
[11] M. Banton, *The Policeman in the Community*, p. 223.
[12] J. Morton, 'Police Corruption', *Policing*, 1986, vol. 2, No 1.

There were pints of beer left outside a pub, tea in the back room of a sweet shop. Complimentary tickets for the cinema or theatre and, for the rural customer, eggs, vegetables and game.[13] For police in a mining community there was coal sent around. In Central London at the time of the motor show there was the opportunity of helping men park their cars and minding them whilst they were absent. Harry Daley believed it was possible to make as much as £30 in a week from such a posting.

Although this sort of thing is probably best done at the lower levels of policing, there is no reason why it cannot be done at any level. A former Chief Constable of Penrith after the Second World War is said never to have paid full price for anything in the town.

Unsurprisingly some critics see this as the thin end of the wedge. Simon Holdaway, describing mump-holes, wrote: 'Yet all of these places implicitly require a reciprocal exchange: nurses, caretakers, publicans and shopkeepers occasionally require prompt assistance with disorderly customers or patients. Further, some shops, usually take-aways, are known to be 'GTP' [good to police]. Again, this relationship is not without implicit reciprocal obligations.'[14]

The next step up the ladder is chiselling, something of which Joseph Wambaugh's character Bumper in *The Blue Knight* made a speciality. Bumper is a fictional character but the consensus of opinion is that, in his early novels at least, Wambaugh was giving an accurate portrait of contemporary urban policemen: *Lines and Shadows* is his first-hand account of the behaviour of the San Diego police and their border patrol. Chiselling probably does not even occur to most officers as deviance, any more than an average office worker regards using the telephone for private purposes or stocking up with disposable ball-point pens as theft.

Chiselling can be described euphemistically as going too far. Emsley described a variety of little scams from the mid-nineteenth century such as that of the enterprising Mr Gittings

[13] C. Emsley, *The English Police*, p. 224 quoting amongst others H. Daley, *This Small Cloud*, p. 107, and J. Wainwright, *Wainwright's Beat*, p. 17
[14] S. Holdaway, *Inside the British Police Force*, p. 43.

of the Ipswich Borough force who in August 1868 was reprimanded for taking two people to see a prisoner in the cells
and receiving payment for the same; or there were the cases
of members of the Thames division who were disciplined for
collecting money from wharfingers, and officers from a number
of forces who went round their beats asking for Christmas
boxes. Others took advantage of the free pint of beer by asking
for more or, worse, the money to buy more. In July 1890
Jonathan Haigh of the Hull City Police was required to resign
after twenty years' service: a local publican had complained he
had not paid for his beer for six weeks. And in the 1940s two
officers in Whitley Bay more or less persecuted a local landlord
by going to the back door of his pub in the early hours and
making him open and keep open the bar until 4 am.[15]

The warrant card, too, may be an open sesame for various
perks and discounts: free entry to nightclubs, a percentage off
pizzas, discounts on fitness clubs. Yet behind many of these
perks is the implicit understanding that the officer will be on
the side of the provider if there is any localized difficulty. 'You
don't want to be looking over your shoulder the whole time.
I'd rather pay,' said one Police Constable. But that officer was
one of the group who had been maintaining, contrary to the
evidence of their group leader, that a free slice of bacon in a
café would never pass their lips.

Favouritism, such as providing immunity from traffic prosecution, comes next. This can work at street level, of which
a particularly good example is the attitude of the police to
the three-card tricksters who work pavements and race-tracks.
This could work both ways: 'If we wanted an arrest they'd say,
look we'll give you a body. You went to court with him and got
overtime,' said a Detective Chief Superintendent in 1992. On
the other hand:

In due course every PC who served in the West End got
to know all the gamers and they got to know you, which
is how the look-outs were so effective. And it was known
for hard-up PCs to bestow an outsize wink on the look-out
from time to time, before he had had time to raise an alarm.
This signalled to the look-out that he need not raise it today,

[15] C. Emsley, *The English Police*, p. 226.

He would then smile beatifically at the PC and whistle in a different note. The PC would then drift past the team, who would carry on happily rooking some innocent soul and smile pleasantly at the PCs, even sometimes inviting them politely if they would care for a little game. As they passed one of the stooges would detach himself unobtrusively from the crowd and brush against one of the PCs in passing him. No one could possibly see it, so well was it done, but a couple of grubby ten pound notes would have passed from one hand to the other. It took perhaps five seconds and no one faltered in his pace for a second. The two PCs would make for the nearest pub and split the money between them and that was that.[16]

In the words of a Detective Sergeant speaking of the 1960s:

It's really all a question of degree. Did you ever go to Cranbourne Street–Lisle Street where the Church of our Lady of Paris is? There used to be escape artists there. The crowd would gather and the barker would tie the bloke up, chains all round, push him on the floor and he'd start writhing. Then he'd go round with a hat. He never escaped from the bloody bag. A copper would come and move the crowd on. He'd get 5s. They used to queue up at West End Central to do that beat.

Sometimes the police officer would decline a bribe but this was often out of prudence. A Police Constable speaking of the 1980s said, 'I was the gaoler and was offered £1,000 when the vice squad brought in a publican. He had already offered them £1,000 each to let him go but you just daren't do it. You never know when the Gay Police monitoring group have set a trap.'

Many criminals carry what is known as dropsy, known in America as fall money.(In the States dropsy has the more sinister meaning of an offensive weapon or of drugs which could be dropped near the suspect, thereby giving reasonable cause to justify a search.) As Leonard 'Nipper' Read explains:

Situations will always arise where an officer – either uniform or plain clothes – is faced with a situation where he is alone

---

[16] M. Seabrook, *Coppers*, p. 124.

with a criminal who has committed some offence, be it petty or serious. If the criminal is of a mind he can then make an offer to the policeman, which may or may not be accepted, but if it is the officer has then become inextricably corrupted. He knows it, as does the criminal, who may well use such knowledge at some time in the future to further his own, or his associates', interests.

To illustrate this I quote from the case of Raymond Jones, a famous and successful cat burglar of the fifties and sixties. I dealt with him at Marylebone Lane for an offence of burglary and when he was searched a pad of notes amounting to £150 or £200 was found in his pocket. When I questioned him about this he said, 'Well, that's my getting out money.' He then explained that on a number of occasions he had been arrested by a pair of aides to CID or uniformed officers from a car. Before being taken away he pointed out that as no one else was involved there was no need for the case to go any further and then made his offer of the cash.

He told me, 'And Nipper, you'd be surprised how many times that got me out of trouble.'

It worked for ordinary folk as well, albeit on a much reduced financial scale. In Chicago in the early 1960s it was common practice for citizens to keep a $5 bill clipped to their driver's licence. When stopped for a traffic violation the driver would hand the licence to the police officer, who would remove the $5 and wave the driver on. Such practices spread, becoming more expensive with time. By 1970 the going rate in New York was $10.[17] Amongst the criminal fraternity the signal expressions used to a police officer whom it is hoped will give some help are 'May I have a word with you?' or 'May I have a word in your ear?'

Laurie Taylor recounts a typical example of how a deal is worked from start to finish, described to him by Geoff, a long-time successful con man. Geoff had been arrested in relation to a wedge of phoney travellers' cheques and asked the young officer in charge of the cells to see the governor of the nick, an officer he knew to be 'dead crooked'. The officer

[17] R. L. Smith, *The Tarnished Badge*, p. 176 and 'How corruption is built in the system', by David Burnham, *New York*, 21 September 1970.

came down to the cells and asked, 'What are you doing here?' "Listen Mike, you've got to get me out." I mean it's really funny. There's this young wally thinking Mike's setting me up to make a statement, and there he is doing his best to get me out of it.' There were however complications:

> In a situation like this, the cost of the deal depends upon how much evidence has to be buried or lost, and unfortunately for Geoff the search of his house had turned up a parcel of £8,000 worth of travellers' cheques and the paraphernalia needed to change them up. This also meant that other people, such as those on the search party, were in the know, and would have to be paid. But they were wise enough to this sort of trading, and a small team happily came down to take Littlewood's [an arresting officer] place, and work out the fine points of the deal. Geoff started the bargaining.

'Right. Now I wanna walk out of it *completely*. But there is no way they're going to have that. So I say to them, "You can have a thousand pounds; and I'll duck me nut [plead guilty] to a little tiny one." So they say, "That's all right." And I'm ducking me nut to four hundred dollars' worth in the magistrates' court next morning.'

As this is such well-established practice among professional criminals and certain policemen the next step is obvious. If the police are going to be given their money – and this is hardly the sort of set-up which encourages trust in credit arrangements – then Geoff has to be got out of the cell on bail.

'So I'm bailed that evening. Straightaway bailed, and later I meet 'em and they get their grand. Met 'em in a pub and gave 'em the thousand pound. Sweet.'

Unfortunately for Geoff he had a number of previous convictions and as such there was still the possibility of a prison sentence. It was not enough that '"We'll say you've been right helpful, and we're looking for the person that gave you the TCs. You've given us his [fictitious] name and been very helpful and we expect to make another arrest soon . . ." and all that bollocks.'

But Geoff required more insurance and paid over a further £1,000 for the police to leave out one of the previous convictions. It was 'buried'. Even so he received a six months' sentence suspended for two years. 'A bit close,' said Geoff.[18]

That is a classic example of obtaining money first for bail, then to reduce the charge, to falsify the evidence given to the court and finally to conceal a previous conviction. In this instance clearly a number of officers were involved in the payment.

The officer may, of course, use his own initiative. A traffic officer, X, used to approach solitary drivers and in one case approached a motorist named Simpson, alleging he had been speeding.

X: Do you realize you can lose your licence?
Simpson: Yes.
X: How much is it worth?
Simpson: A lot.
X: Can you give me any reason why I should not report you?
S: No.
X: I'm sticking my neck out for you and getting nothing in return.

X waited a few seconds and when no response was forthcoming said, 'Get out of here.'

Simpson reported the matter after discussing it with his girlfriend. Those involved in 15 out of 116 stops by the officer in the previous six months were seen and said they had been asked for money. On 21 January 1975 he was jailed for fifteen months. It was said that 325 cases were being investigated.[19]

Of course this officer was neither the first, nor the last. For four years the Chief Constable of Manchester denied that any of his men took bribes in these circumstances until in 1930 he dismissed a Constable for precisely that:

Members of the force enjoy good conditions of service and are in receipt of pay and allowances of a sufficiently high standard to ensure independent and faithful service and the conscientious discharge of duties entrusted to them.

[18] I. Taylor, *Inside the Underworld*, pp. 137–9.
[19] P. Knightley, 'Straightening Bent Coppers', *Sunday Times*, 13 April 1975.

The Watch Committee and the Chief Constable take a very serious view of what is nothing but a corrupt practice, and any member of the force who may in future be found guilty of this offence will not only be dismissed the force but will be taken before the court and prosecuted.[20]

Help may also be sought at a higher level than the officer on the beat. The Cardigan inquiry revealed that one member of the standing joint committee had approached the Chief of Police about a friend's speeding offence and another member admitted he had been asked to use his influence to get a police officer promoted but he had refused. A Chief Inspector in a provincial force said in 1992: 'We had a TV celebrity come up here to do a promotion for us and he got stopped on the way doing around 120. He asked me if I could do anything for him with the Met, on whose patch it was. I rang up, asked if they could help and ten minutes later it came back "written caution".'

One of thirty-seven disciplinary charges against Stanley Parr, one time Chief Constable of Blackpool, alleged that he had intervened improperly to prevent a hotel owner being prosecuted for traffic offences. A tribunal in the wake of the Osmond report heard how the hotel owner's son had collided with another vehicle while driving his father's Jaguar on the day the two families returned from Tenerife. The son had told the police who interviewed him, 'My father is on holiday in Tenerife with Stanley Parr and I'll see Mr Parr when he returns home tonight.' He was not prosecuted.[21]

Parr was one of the less attractive Chief Constables, even of a small town force. He had effectively been blackballed when he had applied to be Chief Constable of Lancashire. Frank Williamson comments:

Without a crystal ball if anyone had said to me Stanley Parr will end as Chief Constable I would have said, 'You're out of your mind.' I knew him as a Constable and he crawled his way to the top of the Lancashire County Police. When Parr was on the short-list for Lancashire the papers came on my

20 Cited in C. Emsley, *The English Police*, p. 226.
21 S. Knight, *The Brotherhood*, pp. 100–101.

desk. There were five categories. A: suitable; B: suitable but
not yet; C: suitable in the future; D: unsuitable; and E: I don't
know enough about him. I marked him down as unsuitable
and I was telephoned by Phillip Allen to say I was upsetting
the balance of inspectorate opinion. I replied, 'You can say
I wasn't here but I won't alter it.' I said that if this man
was appointed the Chief Constable of Lancashire a disaster
would ensue. The rest had marked him as an A because Eric
St Johnstone had said he was suitable.

I remember when he was in Blackpool as Chief Constable
there was an ACPO [Association of Chief Police Officers]
meeting followed by a dinner given by the Blackpool Corporation. Parr left a bit early and as we came out onto the
landing there he was with an Omo box. He offered each of
us a stick of rock with ACPO Blackpool 61 on it. I said,
'I notice it comes from the North Shore Rock Company.'
I'd locked the owner up for receiving sugar. He thought it
was a suitable gesture and some officers thought it suitable
to accept.

Another fairly easy touch for the police are prostitutes, either
for cash or sexual favours. One of the allegations inquired into
by the Royal Commission of 1908 was that prostitutes were
being blackmailed by the police, and Harry Daley recalls that
the infamous George Goddard not only made a steady income
through his business relationship with Mrs Meyrick but also
through his control of prostitutes.

He and a constable, both in plain clothes, had for a long
time been given exclusive control over common prostitutes.
The rot must have developed almost automatically. Each
whore paid a lump sum to Goddard, which entitled her to
be arrested in proper rotation with other girls, never unexpectedly, and enabled her to give full attention to passing
men without the nervous wear and tear of keeping constant
look-out for coppers. The arrangement was so convenient
to the girls that on the appointed day, in places like Lisle
Street they formed small queues waiting to pay their dues
to Goddard. It must have been wonderful.[22]

22 H. Daley, *This Small Cloud*, p. 149.

But cash could change hands in return for a caution rather than a charge. An Inspector on a provincial force, speaking in 1992, says, 'The girls used to be brought into the station by the Vice Squad, their possessions were put on the counter and the money put on one side. After that they got a caution. It happened in Leeds as well.'

Although if one reads American police procedurals the inescapable conclusion is that police officers there spend much of their spare and duty time with prostitutes of one class or another, this was not the finding of the Knapp Commission, which reported that police officers in New York steered clear of prostitutes on the grounds they were unreliable and dangerous.

Chiselling continues at all levels. In the late 1980s the Assistant Chief Constable and a Chief Superintendent of a northern force were said by their men to have had new rockeries dug in their gardens laid with paving stones from the police sports club. Only the groundsman was sacked for doing the work on police time. A Chief Inspector commented, 'When he had his rockery done with stuff from the sports ground, the attitude was "Sod this; we know he's not going to get done. What's the point in making waves?"' Commenting further, he said, 'Our Chief Constable was investigated in the early 1980s and again in the middle eighties. The first time the Chief Constable appointed to do the investigation stayed with him and subsequently gave him a clean bill of health. The second time it was agreed he would resign.'

There is nowhere in the list for gratuities offered by pleased civilians for services rendered, something banned by the Royal Commission of 1906 and the Police Act 1933, but ever present and, from time to time, converted into a thriving little business. The scam run by a traffic Sergeant at Covent Garden is described by Mike Seabrook, author of *Coppers*, who worked at Bow Street, as the largest-scale single racket run by the Met. It was in all but name a protection racket.

It was the most lucrative ever because of its size and the efficiency with which it was run. It was a real scam. It was run by a Ron Toms whose official title was traffic sergeant and duty sergeant at Bow Street. Bow Street covered Covent Garden with its little narrow streets made for horsedrawn vehicles, not the lorries which filled the market. There were three shifts plus a fourth on weekdays which was effectively a second early turn. It started at 5.30 and Toms sat in his office with the duty roster in his hands. Only known and trusted PCs would go on the junctions where hold-ups were likely. Any driver which came and left Covent Garden dropped between 5s and £5 into the hands of the PCs, depending on the size of his vehicle. And this was done at several junctions. Every vehicle and every night. He ran it for twenty-five years. Very senior PCs gave him half. Young ones on semi-probation gave him two-thirds and he would give half to the station officer or reserve depending who was in his pocket.

When he died there was a cartoon pinned on the notice board with a coffin being carried down the winding stairs. There was a hand coming out of the lid holding a £5 note.

Despite the instructions over the last hundred years, officers in the 1960s and 1970s at least were still taking on extracurricular duties. One Detective Chief Superintendent recalls his early days:

'Every week as a young PC I used to go with a member of staff of the Arsenal Football Club to collect the wages from the bank. The Sergeant who gave me the instructions had a season ticket for the stand for which he hadn't paid.' Similar semi-unofficial arrangements continued into the 1970s. A former Inspector with the Met says, 'There were a considerable number of armed robberies at the time and the local CID were encouraged to provide escorts. The two officers who provided the escort were given £5. That was £2 each and £1 to the DI.'

Nor were officers above preying on each other. A Commander, speaking of the 1950s, recalls: 'I and a colleague were coming up as possible aides to CID. The sergeant says, "I'll expect a bottle of scotch on my desk from each of you tomorrow morning." We discussed it and my colleague said he wasn't going to buy one. I did. He ended up looking through letterboxes for the whole of his career.' Drink seems to have been popular currency. A Chief Inspector remembers that 'The big thing was to get on miners' strike duty and you wouldn't get up there unless you gave the duty sergeant a bottle', while in the memory of a Police Constable talking of the 1960s: 'The governor of the department was always surrounded by hopefuls.

The only time I saw the DI angry was when someone nicked his bottle of whisky. Junior officers had to provide him with his bottle of whisky. The people who paid out were the ones who were being made up. Jimmy N. was unwilling to toe the whisky line and so he stayed in uniform.'

'I had to pay ten shillings to the sergeant for my annual leave and when I first went in a police car I paid the driver. That would be around 1969–70,' recalls a Chief Superintendent; and a former Police Constable at Bow Street tells how 'Toms used to charge you if you wanted to shift from night duty to day or the other way about. Later he did mellow a bit.'

It's the same the whole world over, or at least on the other side of the Atlantic. William Brashler, a District Attorney in Chicago, says 'One [rookie policeman] told me that the first thing he learned on the job was to pay a sergeant $2 a month to forget the mandatory hourly call-in from a beat telephone box.'[23]

And once in, it is very difficult to opt out. 'When one CID officer became so nauseated by the corruption that he decided to get out, he was forced to pay a bribe to obtain his transfer.'[24]

Until the 1980s, in the United Kingdom, there was little fear of a prosecution being mounted over racial prejudice, let alone punishment by the courts or disciplinary bodies. This applied also to complaints by the public. In 1991, principally because of evidence requirements, the Police Complaints Authority did not accept one single complaint of racial abuse. More recently, however, there have been claims made under the Race Relations Act, and dismissals and reductions in rank, mostly over allegations of racism towards black and Asian officers.[25]

> [An officer] of the Northamptonshire Police Training Centre at Ryton near Coventry was required to resign following a special inquiry ordered by the Chief Constable, David O'Dowd. He was found guilty of misconduct during a training course following allegations by an Asian recruit.[26]

Andy Atkins was harassed and quit the force at the end

[23] H. A. Beigel, *Beneath the Badge*, p. x.
[24] B. Whitaker, *The Police in Society*, p. 266.
[25] See chapter 10.
[26] *Police Review*, 23 March 1990.

of his fourteen-week training period. The sergeant had said, 'I've met your sort before – all bastards, you're just here for a free ride.' Other classmates signed his class photo with 'Dear Nigger', 'Black Bastard' and 'Blackbird'.[27]

In a separate, well-publicized incident the Nottingham Police were rebuked for not allowing university graduate Surinder Singh to join the CID; he had been called a curry muncher. His action had been financed by the Commission for Racial Equality. It was pointed out in 1990 that 'whilst just over one per cent of Britain's police officers are black, only 1,339 out of 126,868 have achieved promotion'.[28]

Returning to the American list of deviance, extortion seems to have a much harsher meaning here than is evidently the case in the United States. The American sociologist cites as an example a system whereby advertisements taken in police magazines can wipe out small traffic offences. If that is extortion, then here the pressure is perhaps more subtle. Lawyers as well as local shopkeepers are prevailed upon to make contributions to raffles and tickets for police boxing tournaments. The police have a series of Rupert Bear badges which are sold for charitable purposes, and who can reasonably refuse to make a suitable contribution? There was no overt suggestion that the lawyer who did not contribute to the raffle would find his case at the back of the morning list, or that there would be delays in letting him into or more often out of the cell when he visited his client, but there was a distinct feeling it could happen. Until the establishment of the Crown Prosecution Service by the Prosecution of Offences Act 1985 and the establishment of a duty solicitor scheme in police stations and courts throughout the country, police officers both in the station and at court were in a position of very real influence over the distribution of legal aid work. The purchase of a ticket, the gift of a case of Scotch at Christmas, might well have ensured that an arrested person went to the purchasing solicitor's firm:

I was the court reporter at a London court and a serious case

[27] *Sun*, 2 November 1990.
[28] *Today*, 31 October 1990.

came up on a Saturday morning which needed a solicitor. The case was adjourned to get one. I was going to have lunch with a solicitor friend and I knew he was in his flat so I told the gaoler his name. 'Oh, no,' he said. 'Mr X gets all these sort of cases. I've got to ask him first. If he's not about then we'll get on to your friend.'

But, of course, life in Britain is no different from the States:

Desk sergeants informed bondsmen and attorneys whenever a prisoner needed their services. The bondsmen and attorneys gave the deskman a percentage of the fees they collected. At one time the chief of the department issued a listing of approved bondsmen and attorneys who paid the chief a set percentage. The chief, in turn, paid the desk sergeant and sometimes the arresting officers received a monthly stipend.[29]

The practice of solicitors delivering cases of Scotch to court Christmas parties was outlawed by the clerk of at least one London magistrates' court in the 1980s. But the transactions could be on a more commercial and explicit basis. A North London solicitor, speaking of the 1960s, recalled how 'the gaoler at a North London court approached me in the lavatory and said he could send me as much work as I wanted. It would cost £5 for every case in the magistrates and a further £2.10s. if it went to the Quarter Sessions or Assizes. That week I'd had a case of murder which had run two days at the Old Bailey and I had been paid £23. I told him I couldn't afford it.'

A barrister's clerk says:

The briefs used to come down with a star on them. This meant it was a cash case and my member of chambers knew that of the brief fee one third had to go back in cash to the officer who had recommended him through a firm of solicitors. Once I had to take the money but I refused after that, and it was usually done by the solicitor's clerk who very often paid over the money in a drinking club called the Premier in Soho.

[29] William A. Westley, *Violence and the Police*, p. 33.

In 1993 a solicitor's clerk pointed out, 'Of course the police are still in a position to send cases to you. And they're not going to do so if you're hostile.'

One of the quid pro quos would be that the solicitor who had been sent the case would not attempt to make too much of a meal of it and would let the police officers down lightly if there were discrepancies in their evidence. It was the same in the provinces where, before the Crown Prosecution Service was established, local solicitors would be instructed to appear to prosecute on behalf of the police in some cases, whilst defending in others. In the 1970s one young solicitor who had given the police a hard time whilst defending and obtained an acquittal in the morning was called in by the senior partner after lunch, who told him he had received a call from a senior officer reminding him that the firm also relied on the police for their prosecution work.

It was all part of a system of back-scratching and kickbacks which still continues between the police and various professions. Under it garages would be prepared to leave money on the seat of a police car in return for being given the tow-away job and therefore, in all probability, the repair work following a car accident. Beat officers could easily steer a driver who had a bald tyre to a co-operative garage rather than issue a summons. Mike Seabrook, ex-Metropolitan Police officer, says 'There was £25 on the front seat of the front lift truck. Half for the reserve man (the station officer's assistant) who we hoped had a hook-up with the front lift firm.' And an Inspector recalls that 'Before the days of the M 25 if you had a wide load which required a convoy round the North Circular, you had to enter into an auction with the rats [traffic officers] otherwise your lorry stayed where it was.'

Speaking of the 1970s, a London solicitor tells the story:

I was in Hampshire. I'd parked and when I returned to my car I found two officers looking at my tyres. They were well worn even though the car was only a few months old. I believe there was a tracking problem. I showed them the mileage and they said that if I had the tyres changed there and then they wouldn't report me. Did I know a garage? No, I did not. Well then, Henry's is just around the corner. Tell him officers had sent me.

It was only later I realized there was probably an arrangement going on between Henry and the constables. But so
what? I didn't know a garage in the town. They'd helped
me out. Good luck if they made a fiver.

Others would ensure that solicitors who reduced the price
of a conveyance (particularly in the days when it was a Law
Society disciplinary offence to do so) received legal aid cases.
The Law Society rules were circumvented by the kickback being
in cash. No doubt it was swallowed up in the accounting system
somewhere.

Coroners' officers would be able to recommend funeral
directors to bereaved relatives, and who is to say that it did
not ease the latter's load to find things went smoothly because
of the assistance of the officer? Of course this was not merely
an English practice. In New York in the 1960s the kickback
from the undertaker was a modest $10.

The *Liverpool Daily Post* commented back in 1932:

Discretionary power of prosecution could also be used in
deviant ways. The formal rules could be used by the rank
and file for their own personal advantage. A shopkeeper
who refused to sell constables cigarettes at a discount and
complained of the illegal sale of similar goods to the public
from their own trading organization, the Police Guild, could
find himself summonsed by the same officers for employing
children under age (which in turn gave rise to the banning
of the Police Guild by the Watch Committee).[30]

Says a Detective Constable from North London, 'At Christmas
as the junior officer I would be sent round the shops and pubs
collecting tributes. It went for the Christmas party and what
was left at the end was shared amongst those who were still
standing.'

Bribery in relation to suppressed evidence, the granting of
bail, reduced or dismissed charges and warning of impending
raids or prosecutions has been one of the great problems of the
police from the Trial of the Detectives in 1878 until the present.

[30] Quoted in M. Brogden, *On the Mersey Beat*, p. 70.

According to the American scale, the bribery payments of cash or gifts for past or future help must be of higher value than in mooching and the services performed must be to a mutual understanding.

The following tale is by an old-time villain who had been arrested in the mid-1950s after a stabbing incident in which he accidentally cut himself. The victim had refused to identify his assailant but, in theory, there was still the cut to be explained.

I was taken to have a couple of stitches and was then locked up. I had a few quid with me, reasonable money. The DS came in to see me and asked if I wanted anything. I said I'd like a sandwich and I gave him four fivers or something like that, anyway much more than a sandwich cost. He didn't say it won't come to that and he went off and came back with the sandwich but he did bring back the change and I said you can keep it and he did. So I knew I was halfway. Then he said, 'You're lucky that I'm on tonight. The DDI's on holiday, the DI is sick and that's how I'm in charge. I'll have to hold you for a while but I'll let you out.' I was let out and met him down the road. He wanted a couple of hundred quid so I gave him a drink and arranged a meet later.

Until the Crown Prosecution Service was established one of the favourite ways of obtaining money was the bribe for bail. In criminal circles bail has always been especially prized. The dreadful immediacy of being swept up leaves no time to arrange one's affairs – do another job to provide for the wife and children, arrange a minder for the wife lest she strays with another man. Such preparation is not so different from that of the holidaymaker who before a trip cancels the milk and newspapers and disconnects the television – except that the criminal's trip is likely to be much longer. Small wonder that a whole industry grew up whereby opposition to bail minimized following a financial arrangement with the police officer in the case.

'You can ask Sergeant Blank anything you like to help me, sir.'
　'What, anything?'

'Anything you like, sir. He'll play. He's been well sweetened. He won't let you down.'

Ironically enough the corrupted officer is not only rewarded by his 'sweetener', he is often complimented by the court on his fairness to the prisoner.[31]

The police can go soft to ensure a defendant gets bail or can even forget evidence to ensure he is acquitted. Said Laurie Cork, an ex-Flying Squad officer:

You always oppose bail on serious offences like robbery. But you let the situation be ruled by the defending solicitor or counsel by them putting words into your mouth that you have got to agree with: such as you know he won't abscond – which is the be-all-and-end-all of the situation. You sort of do it reluctantly. That is the way it is done.

There is a Flying Squad expression: only the poor get held in custody; the rich get bail.[32]

Arrangements in London in the 1970s and up to the mid-1980s were dealt with by such men as Frankie Alberts[33] and the interestingly named Red-faced Tommy, with the transactions carried out in pubs like The Albion at Ludgate Circus or such clubs as The Premier off the Charing Cross Road. Money would be paid half down with the balance on a successful bail application. The negotiator's fees would be on top, possibly the same as the bribe, paid for by the defendant, or none at all if the favour was for a close friend or relative.

Of course, outsiders as opposed to 'family' would not stand bail without a fee, particularly if they had been required to negotiate with the police in the first place. They were also required to try to eliminate or have watered down certain damaging pieces of evidence. A former armed robber related:

The first time I ever knew about the police being bent was in 1963 in Borehamwood. A mate and I were nicked in a stolen

---

[31] C.G.L. DuCann, *The Police and the Public*, pp. 146–9.
[32] *Daily Express*, 19 October 1984.
[33] Alberts fell off a roof and was killed during a police raid on the premises. It had been persistently rumoured in the underworld that he had in his possession a considerable amount of evidence about corrupt officers. None was ever found.

car with pick-axe handles. The copper comes into the cell and asks if I'm from Kentish Town and I say yes. Then he asks me if I know GB. I think he's on the pump [seeking information] but I still say yeah. That evening I get a visit from a friend who says, 'I've done the business.' And he had. It cost £300 to get six months and it was good value. We pleaded to the car and offensive weapons. It could have been a conspiracy. In them days the police stood by their word. They dropped evidence or you wound up with a very small sentence.[34]

Sometimes only half the money would be paid in advance but often this was unnecessary. 'If a publican or bookmaker could get the business done for £500, then I would expect to pay £1,000. In those days the police were honest. If they agreed something they honoured it.'

There were professional straighteners such as Harry Sheeney who owned greetings card shops and was said to have a lock on a Commander at the Yard. Another was Joe Stafford, the father of Dennis who was one half of the celebrated Stafford and Luvaglio case. Says one former customer.

Old Bill knows you've got a few quid and it's not your time to go – they can save you for a better day. They've got two or three of you so they can afford to leave you out. A friend'll go to Red-face Tommy Plumley, or Frankie Alberts, or Jo Stafford, and they go and straighten it up. You get bail to show good faith. How much? Depending on what you're on and how much they know you've got in your pocket. Can be anything. Likely you never see them. They've got the SP [starting price, i.e. information] and they won't take money unless they know you're not iffy.

Sometimes it went wrong. In the words of a former armed robber, 'I only recall one case when the cozzer went bent and that was when a West End copper agreed to get my mate out of a drink driving for £1,000. It all went wrong but I think that was because my friend was a spade and the copper didn't like spades.'

A Commander recalls the 1960s: 'When I was a DC I went

[34] J. Morton, *Gangland*, p. 277.

to the local scrapyard and there were twelve bags of coal which had obviously come from the coal yard. So I arrested him. When I got back to the station I was told he was the super's man and I should drop the charge. I said I wouldn't, so I was told that I should leave out some of his convictions the next morning. I thought, not bloody likely. The man came up in front of one of the local stipendiary magistrates and he got six months, the maximum. I went back to the station again and now no one would look at me let alone talk to me. I was sitting there and the phone rang. I was told I was being transferred across London. 'When will it appear in police orders?' I asked. 'It won't,' was the reply.' Report at 2 pm.'

Sometimes it appeared to have gone all wrong but it hadn't. Says a London solicitor:

I attended an identification parade at Brixton Prison in the late 1960s for two of my clients charged with bank robberies. The parade took hours with probably about twenty witnesses. Just at the end they were picked out by one person. I telephoned one of the wives to tell them what had happened and she just wailed down the telephone, 'They can't have been; we paid £6,000 for that parade.' Now, of course, for a variety of reasons criminals like to pretend they have the police in their pockets but I think she was telling the truth for two reasons. The first is that the person turned out to be a police constable who later made a statement saying that whilst he believed the two he had identified were the people he had seen, he could not be sure. The second was that I met one of the wives twenty years later and the first thing she said was, 'I haven't seen you since we paid all that money for the ID.'

On other occasions it was never quite clear whether the money had been well spent, as in a case in the 1980s remembered by a London solicitor:

Just before a bail application in a very substantial jewellery robbery the defendant's wife came up to me and said, 'He's sweet as a nut. You can ask him anything you want.' But any question I asked got a wrong answer. Like – 'He's married with two children?' and the reply came, 'I don't think he's married to the woman he's living with. I know the children are by a different father.' It took me half an hour to convince the bench to give the man bail. The client's wife ran up to the police officer afterwards and said, 'Thank you, you were wonderful.' Personally I thought I was the wonderful one. I thought she'd have been better giving her money to me. But then at the trial the officer got up and said the principal witness had gone to Switzerland. There was no point in having an adjournment because he had told him he wouldn't come back.

Negotiations took place in clubs like the Premier, where detectives, barristers, solicitors' clerks and the underworld mixed, or in public houses such as the Prince of Wales in Lant Street in South London where there was a less cosmopolitan clientele and which was run by a member of the Foreman family. Peta Fordham described it:

At one end sit the bloods – a lot of failed boxers etc. who are gang strong-arm men. At the other sit the wives, chastely excluded from the conversation of their lords, and drinking port and lemon. This is where the dishonest police get their wages.

The Prince of Wales is a well-known place to fix surrender bargains, as well as to pay over, so that the Flies have legitimate grounds in being there. X and Y [senior police officers] are said to get their wages there through an informer called Z.[35]

Fordham, a slightly eccentric middle-aged journalist, had her heart in the right place. Her private papers show a draft letter she wrote to the then Home Secretary complaining that X and Y were allowed to flourish without let or hindrance. Nothing seems to have come of her complaint. Perhaps it was never posted.

Some deals went wrong in a completely unexpected way. On 17 January 1973, at the Central Criminal Court, Eric Price was found guilty of taking a £500 bribe over a revolver. The gun had

---

[35] P. Fordham, *Inside the Underworld*. Fly was a Victorian term for a police officer and also for a cadger or beggar. Peta Fordham had something of a sense of humour.

been brought into the country in March 1969 by an American on a gambling junket. He left the gun in a safe-deposit box but hotel staff told the police. Price, then a DC, told the visitor he could be jailed for five years but that the matter could be squared. The police officer then introduced the visitor to Edmund Bridge, a clerk, as his 'guv'nor'. In September 1971 the visitor returned and called at West End Central police station seeking the return of the gun. No trace could be found but several days later an anonymous call to Scotland Yard said the gun had been thrown in the Thames at Chelsea. It was fished out and checked but it had not been used in any British crimes. Price's deal, however, was discovered.

Price had been promoted Sergeant because of his work on the Buggy case.[36] Price's link man with the vanished London gambler Jack Buggy was Edmund Bridge – there is a curious little photograph of the pair of them in Vienna on their way to see a man who had agreed to help with the police inquiries but was not prepared to leave Austria to do so. Quite how Bridge had acquired police status is not clear.

Some police have a pragmatic approach. A retired North London Detective Constable remarks:

Who are the police working for? Why should they be criticized? I've no doubt you could find some members of the public who would not want to criticize the police. They'd say, 'Look at the hours they do. So they copped a oner off the guy for bail the magistrates would have given to him anyway.'

And what do you know, then the guy came in and gave him information because he thought he'd formed a relationship. At long last he'd found somebody he could speak to. This is what was often the case. If you had some sort of financial dealings with the guy he would frequently come up and give information about things of much more serious nature than he was before the court for. He felt he had formed a relationship. 'Ah, there's somebody I can talk to. We have done something together.' But nowadays

---

[36] Jack Buggy was believed to have been shot in a rather seedy card club, the Mount Street Club, in Mayfair and was possibly connected with the minding of part of the proceeds of the Great Train Robbery. There is a full account into the investigation into Buggy's killing in J. Morton, *Gangland*, pp. 269–72.

this sort of thing doesn't go on, we understand. They may have sanitized the police to an extent but look at the crime figures. How well is the general public served by what they have been doing?

At the top end of the scale in Stoddard's list comes the shakedown, an American example of which is given in Bob Leuci's *Prince of the City*, the story of a corrupt New York officer who gave evidence against his former colleagues of the wholesale looting of an electrical shop by police officers. It has been echoed in England.

In early 1980 British Transport police officers received lengthy sentences: Derek Ridgewell seven years, Douglas Ellis six years and Alan Keeling two years. There had been a long series of weekend thefts in the fifteen months between January 1977 and April 1978; parcels containing property valued at £364,000 were plundered from the BR parcels depot at Bricklayers Arms, Bermondsey. Months earlier Ridgewell and Ellis had detained Anthony Jeff (who now received three years) and another man (who now received a twelve-month suspended sentence) for stealing from the depot. On the first occasion Jeff had received a suspended sentence and the second man had been fined at the magistrates' court. Ridgewell and Ellis had then approached the thieves and taken part in the first of a series of raids on the parcels depot. They tricked the depot security man with false explanations of their presence and then loaded up vans. Allan Keeling, another Detective Constable, was involved but became frightened and asked for transfer. Jeff was finally arrested by RCS officers in the act of transferring parcels and found on him was a typewritten list provided by Ridgewell.

On 1 September of the same year, at a time when the *Countryman* inquiry was at its height, officers called to a break-in at Austin Reeds in Fenchurch Street took clothes, suitcases, squash rackets and golf balls and transferred them to their CID car and van. DI Brian Deacon (forty-one) received eighteen months, Sergent Stanley Ilsley (forty-five) twelve months, Detective Leslie Nugent (forty-three) twelve months and Acting Sergeant Frederick Jolley (forty-seven), a dog handler and holder of the British Empire Medal, with twenty-seven years' service, nine months.

Giving evidence against DC David Chapman, PC Cruttenden said that Chapman was stopped when entering the scene by an Inspector who told him not to worry, he would get a coat anyway. When Cruttenden went in, four officers were removing clothing and Chapman pushed two wallets in his anorak: 'Go on take them, they are tasty wallets.' Cruttenden threw them on the floor. Perhaps one of the most troubling aspects of this case were the efforts of a senior officer to discredit Cruttenden.

At some point in his criminal career a dishonest officer crosses the line which promotes him from being a grass-eater to a meat-eater. The former simply accepts the payoffs that happenstances of police work throw his way, whilst the meat-eater aggressively uses his police powers for personal gain. A former Detective Constable recalls his experience over scrap merchants in the 1970s:

When I was at X as an aide it would seem to be a wonderful source to plot outside the depot in Smith Road. The thieves would come along and in due course enter the gates of the merchant with sacks on their backs. Logical, if you look in every sack you'll get some arrests. Another guy and I did this. I think we did it for one afternoon and we were called into the DI's office and told we'd got to cut this out. A scrap merchant had been on that the aides were going to ruin his business. If it got out the police were searching sacks which had been brought in, then he wasn't going to get any gear brought to his yard. We were told to look elsewhere.

Later I was at another station and we had a change of DI. The biggest scrap merchant was jumping up and down because the new DI hadn't been round to see him. All he wanted was to form a relationship of the kind he had with previous DIs. The fact that the new DI wasn't into that sort of thing disturbed him. If he wasn't paying for protection and his business wasn't being protected it could be severely damaged.

In America some authorities regard the grass-eater, and the man who has once turned his head, as their root problem. It becomes progressively more difficult to break the chain:

Their great numbers tend to make corruption respectable. They also tend to encourage the code of silence that brands anyone who exposes corruption a traitor. At the time our investigation began any policeman violating the code did so at his own peril . . . The rookie who comes into the department is faced with the situation when it is easier for him to become corrupt than to remain honest.[37]

It was when the police became meat-eaters on a grand scale that the troubles really started. As always the United States has the best examples. 'In the early 1960s the three principal members of a group of safecrackers in the Denver police were probably the most skilled in the nation at that time.'[38] Since 1960 in America there have been organized police burglary teams in Denver, Chicago, Nassau County, Des Moines, Nashville, Memphis, Birmingham, Cleveland, Bristol (Conn), Burlington (Vermont), Miami and doubtless a dozen other cities. And if that was not bad enough, in 1972 a number of Chicago policemen stood trial for murdering heroin wholesalers who had refused or stopped payoffs.[39] But Britain, quite apart from the great investigations into the Flying, Porn and Drugs Squads, has had her fair share of police villains, even if they sometimes operated on a more modest scale than their American counterparts. On 23 June 1975, for example, four members of a gang of policemen from the same shift at Felling police station, Tyneside, under the leadership of Sergeant Robert Storey, were jailed at Newcastle Crown Court for eighteen months to five years. Two more were given suspended sentences. Over thirty shops and warehouses had been raided over eighteen months, with the policemen investigating their own crimes and stealing a range of goods from meat to furniture.

Members were recruited quite simply. Ian Calderwood (given eighteen months) was investigating a burglary at a radio shop when he was joined by Storey and two others. He was about to contact the shop manager when Storey told him to hold on; then Storey (five years) and Barry Robinson (four years) began to stack electrical goods. Storey told him to take what he wanted as it would be the insurance company and not the shopkeeper who would be the loser. Later Calderwood stole some kitchen units

[37] Knapp Commission, 1972.
[38] R. L. Smith, *The Tarnished Badge*, p. 14–31.
[39] *Time*, 10 July 1972, p. 22.

and sold them to his father, a well-respected and liked member of the community. 'I can only say that my actions were induced by the attitudes of others – long-serving police officers on my shift, particularly Storey,' said Calderwood in a statement.[40]

Criminals on the run or who had escaped from prison could also pay a weekly or monthly sum to officers to keep them off their backs. Frankie Fraser, speaking of the 1940s, recounted:

> A DC nicked me when I was about fifteen and about four years later when I was nineteen I met him in a pub, the Temple Bar, known as the Doctors, in the Walworth Road. It was Christmas and I was on the run from the army. He was as crooked as anything. He had another copper with him and I could see he wasn't after nicking me. I give him a score and he could have licked my boots.

Things do not appear to have changed. This is a Detective Sergeant from a provincial force speaking of the late 1980s:

> Our Crime Squad had good information that a high class crim was living at an address in London. They sent a message to the Met and the answer came back that he wasn't living there. So a DS and a DC went down themselves. They knocked on the door and there he was. And what he had to say was, 'Fuck off, I only paid you lads £200 yesterday.'

Finally, although violence does not normally appear in lists of police corruption – and in the view of some commentators cannot be included since there appears to be no commercial gain – it does seem that the police sometimes use violence for violence sake. Indeed the last thirty years have been a chapter of deaths in police custody which have never been satisfactorily explained.

In 1976 Liddle Towers, a thirty-nine-year-old electrician, died from injuries allegedly received from the police in Gateshead. His doctor, Alan Towney, said, 'I've never seen injuries like them. He has been pulped. He had about forty bruises and seven large abrasions.' When dying Towers had

[40] *Sun*, 24 June 1975.

told his doctor, 'They've killed me Doc . . . They shouldn't do this to a dog.' The police version is that one officer accidentally fell on top of Mr Towers, but eyewitnesses saw three officers kicking him as he lay handcuffed on the ground. The first inquest returned a verdict of 'justifiable homicide' and the second inquest resulted in an equally unsatisfactory verdict of 'misadventure'; but the Home Secretary has unfortunately and astonishingly to date declined to set up an inquiry under section 32 of the Police Act 1964.[41]

On 11 March 1983 Jimmy Davey was arrested in Coventry and held in custody to await the arrival of the London police for questioning over the death of Paddy O'Nione, who had been shot in a street near Tower Bridge. On their arrival Davey, who had already served a six-year sentence for the brutal attack on a Coventry-based policeman, is said to have lunged at one of the officers who promptly put him in a choke-hold. Eleven days later, with Davey still in a coma, the life support machine was switched off.

On 5 May 1988 Patrick Shevlin and Hamish Montgomery were convicted of the murder of Owen Roberts in a police cell at Morecambe. The court heard that he had received a methodical beating after he had been arrested. He had been thrown out of a nightclub and returned to perform his favourite trick of smashing glasses on his head. On appeal, the convictions were quashed and manslaughter convictions substituted.

There can be little doubt that Roberts would have provided a major headache to the good administration of the night duty shift. It is more difficult to appreciate the damage that Henry Foley, sixty-seven, was causing as he lay handcuffed in a cell in Southport after being arrested for drunkenness. On 18 April 1986 Sergeant Alwyn Sawyer received seven years for his manslaughter. The imprint of Sawyer's left boot matched marks on the victim's shirt. Sawyer did not give evidence.

A former Detective Chief Superintendent, speaking of the 1960s, relates:

I arrested this man for being drunk and took him back to the station. In those days the night duty officer slept upstairs.

[41] B. Whitaker, *The Police in Society*, p. 282.

What happened was the drunk was making a noise and the sergeant came down and gave him a few bangs. When I came in to take the man to court there he was marked up. I asked what I was going to do and the sergeant replied, 'Like that when I found him.' That's just what I did say to the magistrates, 'Like that when I found him, sir.' He gave me a curious look and fined the bloke ten shillings. Afterwards the man said he was sorry for causing me trouble. He'd been so drunk he couldn't remember.

In *Policing Police Violence*, based in part on research in Glasgow between 1982 and 1986, two Dutch researchers, Uildriks and van Mastrigt, concluded that there were five categories of police violence. The first is the 'fair fight', a private confrontation with a police officer in which neither side complains. This seems to have some tradition behind it. The first Chief of Police of Milwaukee believed that before you could arrest a man, 'you had to whip his ass in a fair fight'.[42] It was a view held until well into the second half of the century in some districts of London, where a new policeman in certain stations in the East End had to fight the local champion before he could gain respect.[43]

The second category is 'effective policing', or, less euphemistically, the use of force on a known criminal, usually to make an arrest. The third, 'informal punishment', is when officers dispense summary justice and violence, sometimes against juveniles, as punishment. 'Acts of war', the fourth category, is where there is a struggle for power between police and local communities or gangs, as occurs in some inner city neighbourhoods. An example would be the gang-busting behaviour of the police in the 1920s in Sheffield where gang wars raged and where Sir Percy Sillitoe, later head of MI5, suppressed them in a way which is quite alien to today's liberal attitudes. The gangs, led by George Mooney and Sam Garvin, controlled organized betting in the area; the game was called tossing and odds were laid against which of five half-crowns landed heads or tails. According to Sillitoe, each gang had hundreds of members who, quite apart from running the pitching rings, controlled

---

[42] J.F. Richardson, *Urban Police in the United States*, p. 27.
[43] P. Laurie, *Scotland Yard*, p. 240.

the poor quarters such as the Crofts, Norfolk Bridge and the Park, collecting protection from the publicans.

> I called my senior officers together and asked them to select very carefully for me some of the strongest, hardest-hitting men under their commands . . . It was not difficult to pick a dozen of the best of these to form a 'flying squad' specially to deal with the gangster problem. These men were taught ju-jitsu and various other methods of attack and defence, and it was surprising how little teaching they needed. They had just been waiting for the chance to learn![44]

The final category of violence, 'police riots', occurs, the authors suggest, when police have lost control of public order, as at, say, Wapping. According to Uildriks and van Mastrigt, police management often fails to see police violence as a problem or simply denies its existence. The reaction of one Assistant Chief Constable is a blatant example: when confronted with a report that an officer had hit someone on the head with a baton, he pointed out that this could not possibly be the case since 'regulations stipulated that a baton should only be used to hit someone on the shoulder'.

Unsurprisingly the police were not amused by the book. The Strathclyde force in rejecting it said that it was based on anecdotal research conducted many years previously and no longer reflected the force. The Association of Chief Police Officers said that it did not take into account the enormous changes in professionalism and discipline that had taken place in the service.[45]

[44] P. Sillitoe, *Cloak without Dagger*.
[45] *Independent*, 14 October 1991.

8

Bent for the Job

In a high percentage of cases conviction in a criminal trial results at least in part from some form of admission or confession by the defendant. In a study carried out for the Phillips' Royal Commission on Criminal Procedure and based on the Birmingham Crown Court, it was found that between thirty and forty per cent of prosecution cases would have been fatally flawed without a confession.[1]

> The work of any investigator . . . is made much easier if a suspect can be induced to confess. It saves a lot of legwork. And it can be considered as the most conclusive sort of evidence if the person with the greatest vested interest in opposing the prosecution actually supports it.
> Every investigator is under pressure to obtain a conviction, especially after a crime that causes public alarm. This pressure is public and external and takes the form of praise and promotion if the investigator is successful; criticism and opprobrium if not. The pressure on the investigator to obtain a true confession is slighter. For once a confession has been obtained, it is generally taken for granted by all and sundry that it was correct. So basically it boils down to the pressure of the investigator's own conscience, or the fear of being found out if he should concoct a confession or otherwise falsify evidence.[2]

[1] J. Baldwin & M. McConville, *Courts, Prosecution and Conviction.*
[2] Torquil Ericson in *New Law Journal*, 22 June 1990, p. 884.

This is confirmed by a former Assistant Chief Constable:

> We were both DIs investigating a major crime and he gets
> two boys in. They won't say anything, so he writes out the
> statement and I say I won't witness it. He says, 'They've done
> it.' I say, 'That's not the point, you've got to have evidence.
> I'm going home for the weekend and we'll talk on Monday.'
> Next day he rings up and says they've found a third boy with
> all the gear. I say, 'Well then, there's your evidence.'

There are three main kinds of confession, argue psychologists
Gudjonsson and MacKeith.[3] The first is the voluntary confession, for which no pressure of any kind is required. They are not
necessarily true confessions. In many murder cases, particularly
those with any public profile, the police have to cope with a
number of totally spurious ones, so they do not disclose a
piece of information (e.g. the victim has six toes or a toe
missing) in order to eliminate purported confessors by asking
them a question which they are unable to answer correctly. In
the second category come the confessions which Gudjonsson
and MacKeith call coerced compliance. By this they mean that
after a period of stress under investigation, the suspect will say
almost anything to bring an end to the questioning regardless
of the long-term consequences of so doing. The third type
of confession is that when, as a result of the interrogation,
suspects actually come to believe in their own guilt, even
though they are entirely innocent. As Dr Cohen in the *New
Scientist* commented, 'The very certainty of the police evidence
makes the accused doubt the truth of what he or she remembers
. . . [Suspects] become very suggestible.'

Defendants are rarely caught *in flagrante* so other pieces
of evidence which will tie them to the crime are needed:
identification, forensic evidence, being found in possession of
all or some part of the stolen property or a weapon used, or
the evidence of a partner in the crime who is either confessing
his part in the particular offence or a string of offences and is
thereby turning supergrass. If all else fails there is usually a
fellow prisoner who will come forward and say that whilst on
exercise the major criminal now on trial confessed all to him.

[3] 'Retracted Confessions', *Medical Science and the Law*, 1988, vol. 28, p. 187.

The early 1970s introduced a new word – supergrass – into the English language. It also gave a new phrase to criminal slang – 'to do a Bertie', or inform to the police. For a time one of the foolproof ways of obtaining convictions was to use a supergrass, a development of the use of the cellmate, and this continued for over ten years until the use of the supergrass was more or less discredited.

Grassing, however, remains perhaps the principal method by which the police obtain information which will lead either to the prevention of a crime or to the arrest of the villains and recovery of stolen property.[4] As we have seen, any good detective keeps a small, or sometimes large, string of informers who may be active thieves themselves or who may simply hang about on the fringes of the underworld. In the past they were paid out of a police information fund or sometimes out of the pocket of the officer who ran them. It was regarded as a good investment towards promotion. Sometimes in the case of a drug bust the informer was given a part of the bust itself as his reward. Sometimes an informer had a licence to commit crimes, short of violence, in a particular area. Sometimes all three.

The singularly corrupt Flying Squad officer of the 1960s, Alec Eist, is described in admiring terms by a former colleague: 'He was the best informed police officer in London. What he took off one criminal he gave back to another. If he got £200 from a villain for giving him bail, Eist would give £195 to cultivate an informant.[5] Another says of the practice: 'You find three pounds of heroin and put only one on the charge sheet. The villains are pleased; less they're found with means less bird, and you give the other two to the informant. The job won't pay the informant so the only way is you give it back.'

But grassing changed gear on to a wholly different level with the arrest in 1970 of Derek, better known as Bertie, Creighton Smalls. It became the era of the supergrass, the criminal who, to dig himself out of trouble, would inform not just on his colleagues on a particular job but on his associates and their

---

[4] The origin of the term is in doubt. It might come from rhyming slang, grasshopper–copper.
[5] Eist, a florid, handsome, black-haired man, was acquitted in one of the trials of police officers and solicitors in the 1970s. Later he had a dress shop. 'It did no good. He was always having fires and burglaries – it was an embarrassment.' Later still he owned a public house near Newmarket. He died of a heart attack.

efforts going back years and years. In turn he could expect to receive a minimal sentence compared with that handed out to his former friends. He could also expect, through a nominee, a share of the insurance rewards.[6]

In the late 1960s and early 1970s Bertie Smalls led a highly successful team of armed robbers in a series of attacks on banks, mainly in North and North-West London but on occasions as far afield as Bournemouth. Each time the operational method was almost identical. The robbers wore balaclavas, possibly with a nylon stocking underneath, and masks. The raids were in banking hours. A ladder was used to get over, and a sledge-hammer to smash, the security grilles put up in the 1960s, which were not yet made ceiling to counter. A shotgun would be fired into the ceiling to concentrate the minds of staff and any customers there might be in the bank. There would be one or two getaway cars waiting. The haul was usually substantial.

Smalls' name was 'in the frame'. He had been wanted for the Bournemouth Lloyds Bank job in September 1970 and his wife, Diane, had been arrested along with others, including a Donald Barrett who had made a confession naming names. At the trial at Winchester Crown Court, Barrett pleaded guilty. His reward was a sentence of twelve years and a card posted from Spain from the others, who had all been acquitted, reading, 'Wish you were here.'

Smalls had also been identified from a photograph in the Rogues Gallery at Scotland Yard as being involved in the National Westminster raid at Palmers Green in May 1972. The number plate of a Jaguar car which had been used in a trial run had been noted by an off-duty police officer. It was traced back to a garage at Tower Bridge in which Smalls was known to have an interest. That was certainly not sufficient to bring a charge. After a robbery at Barclays Bank on Wembley High Road in August 1972, which had netted over £138,000 in old notes, a special unit was formed by the police under the direction of Jim Marshall. It would eventually become the nucleus of the Robbery Squad.

---

[6] Although Bertie Smalls was undoubtedly the first of the modern supergrasses, in 1706 John Smith, a convicted housebreaker known as Half Hanged Smith because he had survived an attempt to hang him, was pardoned after he had named about 350 pickpockets and housebreakers. He may well have been the original supergrass.

The team began to accumulate snippets of evidence against Smalls. A woman clerk picked out his photograph as being involved at a robbery amassing £296,000 at Ralli Brothers in Hatton Garden in March 1969. Now the Bournemouth robbery was cross-checked, even though Smalls had never been arrested for it. Indeed at one time the Hampshire Police had thought he had done away with the principal witness, Stella Robinson, the Smalls' au pair. Only her presenting herself to the police in London after the acquittal of Diane Smalls and the others had prevented a murder inquiry.

Three days before Christmas 1972 Inspector Victor Wilding went to see Smalls at his home in Selsdon. The police now had sufficient evidence to justify an arrest. The only person there was Stella Robinson, who when pressed, told them Smalls was spending Christmas near Northampton. At 5.30 am the police grouped outside the house and DCI Brewster of the Regional Crime Squad knocked on the door. Smalls in his underpants opened it and the police rushed forward, knocking Brewster over in the rush. Smalls said he had opened the door to let the cat in. It had a trick of scratching to gain admission. Diane Smalls commented, 'You let the rats in, not the cat.'

The arrest was totally unexpected. Members of the gang had paid £5,000 each to a 'bent copper' to get an early warning of any arrest. Bertie had not paid his whack. Whether there was such a police officer able to obtain information is doubtful. It may have been a double scam to lure the robbers into a false sense of security.

Smalls was arrested for the Wembley bank robbery and was taken from Northampton to Wembley where he was questioned. On the journey he had made a tentative suggestion about doing a deal but when formally questioned he had said nothing. He was remanded in custody by Harrow Magistrates' Court for committal papers to be prepared. It was when the papers were served on the defence that Peter Donnelly, the solicitor's managing clerk who had acted for Smalls over the years, noticed a reference in them to 'outers'. Smalls would, so the statement of a police officer read, give names if he had 'outers'.

Donnelly began negotiations with the police to provide Smalls with the 'outer' at the expense of his former colleagues. Donnelly recalls: 'One of the final conditions was that if Smalls' statement wasn't used and he was not to be a witness and immunity given, then what amounted to a total confession would remain on police files and not be used against him at a trial.' He adds, 'But there was such a level of corruption at that time that sooner or later it would have got out and he'd have been dead.' During those three days Smalls stayed at Wembley with an armed guard. On the third day the police had to say yes or no. They said yes, and so Smalls became the first modern supergrass.

In July 1974 at the Central Criminal Court, Smalls' former friends received up to twenty-one years' imprisonment, although some sentences were reduced on appeal. The Court of Appeal was none too pleased with the Director of Public Prosecutions, Sir Norman Skelhorn, and his deal with Smalls. 'Above all else the spectacle of the Director recording in writing, at the behest of a criminal like Smalls, his undertaking to give immunity from further prosecution is one which we find distasteful. Nothing of a similar kind must happen again,' said Lord Justice Lawton.

But Smalls had set the tone for the 1970s. The opprobrium attached to most supergrasses never seems to have stuck to him. In a curious way he seems to have been regarded as an innovator. The next in line to repent, recant and recount all was a man who published his memoirs designating himself as *King Squealer*, Maurice O'Mahoney. He had been suspected for the attack on a Securicor van at Heston in West London. The van had been rammed with a tipper truck but the take had been a disappointing £20,000. He had been the victim of a tip-off that the raid would take place. After his arrest and that of other members of the gang, the whisper went around that O'Mahoney was going to squeal. Two members of the team threatened to gouge out his eyes if he talked. According to Jack Slipper, who had unsuccessfully chased the train robber Ronald Biggs to Brazil and in whose charge Mahoney was, this was the turning point. He asked to see a senior officer. In his turn O'Mahoney's evidence led to some 200 convictions and from then on the floodgates were opened.

After the Court of Appeal's comments on the Smalls' deal, supergrasses could not expect to walk free. What they could expect was a sentence of around five years – the supergrass tariff – instead of one of twenty, during which time they would be kept in police custody whilst they gave their evidence and, allowing for remission and parole, released immediately or very soon after they had completed it. They could expect reasonable accommodation visits from their wives and sometimes the opportunity to go out to the local pubs with the detectives guarding them. There would be reward money and a new identity at the end of their sentence. It is hardly surprising that there was a steady queue of men willing to turn in their former colleagues. Whatever successes Marshall and Slipper had had with Smalls and O'Mahoney, it was nothing to the success which would come to a rising star in the Met, Tony Lundy. In May 1977 Detective Chief Inspector Tony Lundy rejoined the Flying Squad, soon to be reorganized in part as the Robbery Squad with its headquarters at Finchley.

Within six months he had his first major success with David Smith, arrested for an attack in September 1977 on two elderly men who collected their company's wages near The Thatched Barn, a restaurant at Borehamwood in Hertfordshire. The money was snatched but then one of the team, Alf Berkley, tore off the glasses of one of the men and squirted ammonia in his eyes. The man was almost completely blinded.

Smith turned supergrass, confessing to over sixty armed robberies. He was kept at Finchley police station for over fifteen months, at the end of which, as a result of his efforts, sixty-nine people were charged, of whom ninety per cent pleaded guilty. Two of the other robbers in the Thatched Barn team were also allowed to become supergrasses. One of them, George Williams, who had been offered the supergrass deal before Smith had rolled over but had initially held out, also received five years for a total of eighty robberies.

His evidence was necessary because there was a small problem with Smith. He had actually killed a man. Smith had coshed Kurt Hess, an elderly factory owner, during a robbery in Shoreditch. Hess had died three weeks later. The DPP's policy was to require a plea of guilty to a murder – which carried a mandatory life sentence – and so Smith could not be considered a credible witness. However Smith's luck was in. A statement was obtained from a pathologist which showed that Hess's poor health had contributed to his death. A charge of manslaughter was sufficient, so Smith could be reinstated as a prosecution witness[7]. Later the rules were relaxed and supergrasses who had pleaded guilty to murder were allowed to give evidence for the Crown, in one case with fairly disastrous results.

In fact George Williams' hands were none too clean either. In 1967 he and Smith had kidnapped the manager of a North London supermarket, Walter Price, to get the keys from his safe. The sixteen-stone Williams, known as 'Fat George', coshed Price, who died eight weeks later from heart failure. Price had staggered home with a lump on his head described by his widow as 'as big as an egg'. When she heard Williams had received the tariff five years she commented, 'That seems a very light sentence for murder.'[8] Judge Michael Argyle, his hands tied by public policy, commented that he considered Smith and Williams 'two of the most dangerous criminals in British history', adding that whilst he accepted they were telling the truth, 'it was nauseating to hear these hypocrites and that as a matter of policy they have only been sentenced to five years each'.

But Smith did not last long on the outside. Throughout his adult life as an unsuccessful career criminal, he only spent short periods out of prison. On 29 September 1986 he was caught in a raid on a Securicor vehicle in Golders Green along with another former supergrass, Ron Simpson. Smith again turned supergrass but this time he did not live long enough to testify. In a cell which had been hung with balloons for his birthday five days earlier, Smith cut his throat with a razor blade on Monday, 13 October. Simpson was gaoled for twenty-one years. Perhaps, when it came to it, Smith was the better off.

Recruit followed recruit through the Lundy supergrass factory, some thirty of them defended by Roland Pelly, a Bishop Stortford solicitor who had been outside the main stream of criminal defence practice. In fact he had been the DPP's agent in Hertfordshire in the early 1970s when the DPP used to send cases to local firms of solicitors.

One of Lundy's less successful supergrasses was one who,

---

[7] Smith was also reputed to have killed a bookmaker, Harry Barham, found shot in the back of the head in his car in Hackney; £40,000 had been stolen from him. There was no hard evidence against Smith and he was never charged.

[8] For a detailed account of the successes and more importantly the failures of the supergrass system, see A. Jennings et al, *Scotland Yard's Cocaine Connection*.

dressed as a policeman, had threatened his victim in a robbery with castration and had the man's daughter stripped to her underwear asking 'How would you like to see your daughter raped?' He served only twenty-four months in prison, but although he had named fifty-eight criminals it seems he was responsible for the conviction of only five.

On 24 March 1980 a robbery went off which surpassed the Great Train Robbers' caper. It was also one which would have the greatest repercussions on the credibility of Scotland Yard and, in particular, Tony Lundy. The haul was 321 silver ingots of bullion, worth £3.4 million, which were stolen from a lorry on its way from London to Tilbury Docks. A gang of bogus traffic officials together with a man wearing a police uniform flagged down the lorry into a lay-by and held up the crew at gun-point.

The instigator of the enterprise was Michael Gervaise, six foot, a fluent linguist and a skilled burglar alarm engineer, described as a 'balding figure with the mild air of a retail tobacconist'. He was another who would become a supergrass. He had received eighteen months' for his part in the 1975 Bank of America robbery but otherwise had no record worth speaking of. Together with an old friend, Micky Sewell, Gervaise had put together a team which included Lennie Gibson, Rudolpho Aguda and Aguda's nephew, Renalto 'Ron' Aguda. Ron's specialities included the ability to uncouple trailers from their tractor units at speed. Gervaise also had on his team a number of bent police officers who were paid to overlook his activities. One, Terence Donovan, who later served a prison sentence, was employed as a 'security adviser' after his retirement from the force. His job was to advise Gervaise of suitable places to burgle. Another bribed by Gervaise was the notorious Alec Eist.

The lorry was stopped by Gervaise, who flagged it down wearing his policeman's uniform – supplied by a Sergeant in the Met to Billy Young, who had passed it and some others to Lennie Gibson – and directed it into a lay-by for a bogus traffic census. The guards were threatened that their kneecaps would be blown off if they did not co-operate. Gervaise and Co went off with the silver to store it in a 'slaughter', a rented lock-up garage, near Oakwood tube station at the northern end of the Piccadilly line. Gibson and Aguda senior were the only ones to hold keys to it and they had them on them when arrested.

Sewell was on bail at the time for a £200,000 wages snatch and was being used as a snout by the then DCI Bill Peters, a large and flamboyant officer on the Flying Squad. His mission for Peters was to infiltrate another robbery team headed by Ronnie Johnson and his information led to the arrest of that team hours after they had shot a guard in a robbery at a bank in East Finchley. One of the men soon accepted Lundy's offer to turn supergrass and he named Tony Fiori, an Islington thief, who graduated from grass to supergrass with some facility. In turn he named Gervaise.

It was only a matter of time before Gervaise joined the supergrass circuit. And it was only a matter of time before someone claimed the £300,000 reward being put up by the insurers. The claimant would be Roy Garner, part owner of a thoroughly disreputable nightclub, Eltons, which more or less backed on to Tottenham police station, and a man closely associated with Lundy as well as Gibson. He had turned down an approach to do the silver bullion job.

The important thing was the recovery of the silver. Gibson when arrested held out for some time as to its whereabouts until he had spoken with Aguda senior. On the night of 4 June 1980 the police went to the lock-up at Oakwood, kicked in the door and recovered the silver – all but twelve bars worth £120,000. No one has ever been able to establish where they went to, but there again no one has ever seemed to worry too much about it. Nor has anyone ever satisfactorily explained why it was necessary to kick the door down; after all Aguda and Gibson had been arrested with their keys to the slaughter on them.

Gibson and the Agudas received ten years' each on pleas of guilty, which was rather more than the seven they had been half promised. Micky Sewell had long disappeared – tipped off by a police officer – and Gervaise had his five years. 'Dave Granger', a pseudonym for Roy Garner, received the £180,000 reward. Garner also submitted claims through Lundy for payment for information from a Brinks-Mat security van hold-up in Hampstead in December 1979 and a fraudulent insurance claim based on a faked armed robbery, the reward for which was £75,000. After much haggling Garner received £178,000. Over the years he is believed to have accumulated over £500,000 through rewards recommended by Lundy.

The beauty of the supergrass system was that little actual detective work was required. In the 1970s and 1980s London juries were perfectly happy to convict on the evidence of a recanting criminal. Indeed they continued to convict in the provinces throughout the 1980s. But In London the supergrass system was becoming more and more complicated. There now seemed to be competing teams of supergrass: those who gave evidence under Lundy's aegis and those, such as John Moriarty, who gave evidence against Lundy's friend Garner. Moriarty had twice been shot by rivals and had served periods of imprisonment. Now he decided to give evidence and to implicate Roy Garner. In the early 1970s Garner, together with a friend Kenny Ross, had purchased premises in Upper Street, Islington, and then tried to evict the tenants. When this failed the premises were fired. Now Moriarty was prepared to name them in his statement as the organizers of the arson attacks.

Yet another series of supergrasses were being run under the name Operation Carter from Reading by Number 5 Regional Crime Squad. In 1977 a security van at Hemel Hempstead in Hertfordshire had been taken for £34,000 and three years later a North London robber, Freddie Sinfield, was arrested. The name he put in the frame was Billy Young, Gervaise's police uniform supplier. And this time a supergrass was prepared to talk about corrupt police officers.

Those were the heydays of the supergrass:

Supergrass trials have fallen into disrepute and supergrasses aren't used quite as much. But what they did was present to your stock gangland criminal a real threat. Gangs haven't stayed together because of that risk. The risk of being supergrassed got very high about seven or eight years ago. Then jurors started to acquit because supergrasses were being offered immunity or extremely low sentences, money was being offered or facilities in custody, so they died off.[9]

There was also the fact that defence barristers had worked out

[9] Michael Mansfield QC in D. Campbell, *That was Business, This is Personal*.

a sufficiently damaging technique to deal with the supergrass. In the times of Charlie Lowe they had been defeated by the apparent revivalist confession which had been made. There was also still an innocence around. After all, argued defending lawyers amongst themselves, why would the supergrass confess to masturbating with a defendant in a contest to see who could ejaculate over his girlfriend if it wasn't true? By a process of logic, if that was true then surely they did rob the bank together. Quite apart from that, possibly a number of years had elapsed between the robbery and the trial, and the defendants were not the sort of people who kept appointment books. It was almost flawless. Nor did it require that much work.

But as time went on and the supergrasses were shown to have been so much more evil than those against whom they now gave evidence, juries were simply not prepared to convict on their word alone. And very often there was little else.

The three basic methods of obtaining a conviction improperly are the 'verbal' or, as it was known, 'gilding the lily' (inserting words to produce a confession), brutality or trickery to extract a confession, and planting evidence. Until well into the 1970s it was not accepted that any of these occurred except in the rarest, and most exceptional, circumstances. Then attitudes changed, so that it was just about acknowledged that gilding the lily might take place. But it could not be accepted publicly in Great Britain by police, or judges for that matter, that in modern times officers ever resorted to violence to extract a confession, although this practice was accepted as common in the United States.[10]

Torture had been the common way of extracting confessions until the middle of the seventeenth century. A trial could not proceed if the accused refused to plead guilty or not guilty. He could not be tried without his consent and by remaining mute he could delay his trial indefinitely. In a felony case, on conviction the defendant's property was forfeit to the Crown. The twisting of thumbs with whipcord, a procedure which was carried out in court, was found to be a relatively easy way of

[10] One of the world's first pictures of the police shows them administering a beating to a prisoner. It is not quite clear from the drawings found in 2000 BC tombs in Beni Hassan, Egypt, whether the prisoner was a suspect or being punished. He is being beaten with a stick by one policeman whilst his arms and legs are being held by three others. (C. Franklin, *The Third Degree*, p. 11.)

obtaining the required plea. For the more obdurate, stronger measures were required and the punishment *peine forte et dure* was found to be the most effective. A statute of 1275 details the procedure:

> That the prisoner be sent back to the place from whence he came and there put into a mean room where no light can enter, that he be laid upon his back with his body bare, save something to cover his privy parts, that the arms be stretched forth with a cord one of each side of the prison, and in like manner his legs shall be used, that upon his body shall be laid as much iron and stone as he can bear and more, that the first day he shall have three morsels of barley bread and the next day he shall drink thrice of the water in the next channel to the prison door, but no fountain of spring water, and this shall be his punishment until he dies.

In this punishment the prisoner was bound to die but if he could hold out against an admission then at least he saved something for his family. It seems that few actually died from the punishment. Not surprisingly the threat usually proved sufficient, just as the threat rather than the administration of a beating is usually enough to obtain a confession in modern times.[11]

Whilst the last recorded instance of torture, as opposed to the *peine*, in England is in 1640, the rack survived in Scotland for another half century. By the end of the eighteenth century it had become accepted that a confession would be excluded if it could be shown that it was made under the pressure of fear, or in return for some promised benefit such as a pardon or lighter sentence. From the eighteenth century accused persons were given the form of caution which has effectively lasted to the present: 'You are not obliged to say anything unless you wish

[11] One who did suffer the press was a Major Strangeways. In 1658 he was accused of shooting a lawyer named Fussel who wished to marry the Major's middle-aged sister, Marbellah. Strangeways' objection to the marriage was that he had made over all his property to his sister because he had fought with the Royalists and feared Cromwell would sequestrate the estate. Strangeways shot Fussel to frustrate the loss of his property. He refused to plead and was put to the press in the yard at Newgate on 28 February 1658. He lasted only ten minutes and at his request his friends added their weight to the stones. (*The Newgate Calendar*.)

to, but anything you do say will be written down and may be used in evidence against you.'

Later the 'against you' was dropped for fear that the innocent might be deterred from making an exculpatory statement.

One of the problems of the English criminal trial of the nineteenth century was that in theory, until the passing of the Criminal Evidence Act 1898, the sworn evidence of the accused was not admissible. The accused could not give evidence on his own behalf, but evidence of what he or she said to others was admissible. So, for example, in the murder trial of Thomas Wainwright in 1875, statements made by him to the police were admissible and in another case eleven years later the hearsay statement made by Adelaide Bartlett to her doctor was admitted.[12]

The earliest form of written rules to be observed by the police when questioning suspects and obtaining confessions from them was provided by Mr Justice Hawkins in 1882. Not, of course, that the police always followed His Lordship's observations. They were quite prepared to accept the ticking-off which came their way when the breaches were too flagrant. The Hawkins' directives became the basis of the Judges' Rules first set down in 1912 and amended in 1918. These nine-point rules – boiled down they stated that when a police officer had made up his mind to charge a person he should caution him and that a person in custody should not be questioned – to which lip service was paid in court were finally revised in 1964 when it was said that their application 'unduly hampers the detection and punishment of crime'.[13]

In 1984 the Police and Criminal Evidence Act together with its attendant Codes of Practice set out in detail how interviews with suspects were to be conducted. Sections 76 and 78 gave the trial judge, or magistrate, power to exclude evidence which had

---

[12] Wainwright was convicted of the murder of his mistress. A respectable tradesman and zealous churchman, like many a Victorian he led a double life. He buried the corpse in a grave in his workshop and it would probably not have been discovered had he not been seen moving it to a more satisfactory hiding place. Despite overwhelming evidence he persisted in maintaining his innocence. On appearing on the scaffold on 21 December 1875 he was not pleased to find the Sheriff had given permission for 100 people to attend the execution. He was hanged by William Marwood.

Adelaide Bartlett was found not guilty of poisoning her pusillanimous husband with chloroform. After her acquittal it was suggested that in the interests of medical science she disclose how she had managed the trick. She did not.

[13] Home Office Circular No 31/1964, Appendix A.

been obtained unfairly.[14] In theory there should now not have been problems with obtaining proper 'voluntary confessions' which would be admissible in evidence. In practice it has been very different. The Act called for the presence of the custody officer, the independent policeman to supervise matters and protect the suspect against brutality and oppression; and the opportunity for the suspect to communicate with a solicitor and have him present at the station before any questioning could take place. Here surely was enough to ensure that confessions would truly be voluntary and that roughing up suspects would be a thing of the past. Sadly as with most things in this best of all possible worlds, it has not quite worked out like that. Lawyers have spent some of the happiest, and most profitable, days of their lives arguing in the Crown Court and in the Court of Appeal over the admissibility of confessions allegedly made in breach of the Code of Practice.

On 10 December 1992 the Lord Chief Justice presiding over the Court of Appeal quashed the convictions, at Swansea Crown Court in November 1990, of three men, Stephen Miller, Tony Paris and Yusef Abdullahi, for the murder of Cardiff prostitute, Lynette White. She had been found hacked to death on St Valentine's Day 1988 in her 'punter's room', a seedy flat in James Street, Cardiff, where she charged £10 a time. She had been stabbed over fifty times and her throat had been cut through to the spine. She had been due to give evidence at the trial of a woman accused of trying to kill a prostitute. Witnesses saw a dark-haired white man with cut hands and wearing bloodstained clothes outside the flat and the police

[14] s76(2): If, in any proceedings where the prosecution proposes to give in evidence a confession made by an accused person, it is represented to the court that the confession was or may have been obtained (a) by oppression of the person who made it; or (b) in consequence of anything said or done which was likely, in the circumstances existing at the time, to render unreliable any confession which might have been made by him in consequence thereof, the court shall not allow the confession to be given in evidence against him except in so far as the prosecution proves to the court beyond reasonable doubt that the confession (notwithstanding that it may be true) was not obtained as aforesaid.

(8): In this section 'oppression' includes torture, inhuman or degrading treatment and the threat of violence (whether or not amounting to torture).

s78(1): In any proceedings the court may refuse to allow evidence on which the prosecution proposes to rely to be given if it appears to the court that, having regard to all the circumstances, including the circumstances in which the evidence was obtained, the admission of the evidence would have such an adverse effect on the fairness of the proceedings that the court ought not to admit it.

duly issued a photofit. Ten months later, although the white man had not been eliminated from the inquiries, five black men including Stephen Miller, White's boyfriend, were charged.

With the shades of the Confait case hovering over the police station, Miller, who had an IQ of 75, was repeatedly questioned. He denied the offence on no less than 300 occasions during his nineteen-hour questioning which reduced him to tears. Said Lord Justice Taylor: 'If you go on asking somebody questions, and tell him he is going to sit there until he says what you want, there will come a time when most people will crack. Oppression may be of the obvious, crude variety or it may be just by relentlessness.'

The Crown conceded that if the tapes of the interview should not have been admitted at the trial, then they could not seek to uphold the convictions. In giving judgment the Lord Chief Justice spoke harshly about the oppressive conduct of the investigating officers and the supine behaviour of the solicitor who had sat in on the interviews. Apparently at the trial the really offensive tape (No 7) had not been played. Had this happened there was no doubt, thought His Lordship, that the trial judge would have excluded the confession. It was never satisfactorily explained why that tape had not been not played.[15]

---

[15] Nothing, however, compares with the Japanese system of *Daiyo-Kangoku*. Under the Japanese Code of Criminal Procedure a suspect must be brought before a judge within three days of his arrest. The judge may, if he wishes, decide that the suspect be detained pending judgment. He is then sent to a detention centre for up to ten days. This is a pre-indictment detention and can be, and usually is, extended for a further period of ten days. In special cases another period, this time of five days, may be granted. Unfortunately under the code a detention centre may, and routinely does, mean a police cell and during the detention the suspect may be continually interrogated by the police. The cells are ten square metres in size and may be inhabited by a number of other detainees. There are separate, but visible, cells for women who are subject to harassment by other prisoners. The police officer in charge observes and records every movement of the suspect, such as waking, washing, eating, reading, sleeping and excreting. Standing up, walking and talking to other prisoners is prohibited. Rules about the correct sitting position are strictly enforced. Baths are taken once a week and there may be exercise in the police station but the exercise area is, in reality, a smoking room. Communication with visitors is extremely limited and prisoners may not communicate with counsel without permission. Interviews are limited to office hours, although the police may continue to question suspects until midnight. If a suspect does not confess, he or she is treated even worse. Conversely, if a confession is obtained, the suspect is accorded preferential treatment. (Japan Federation of Bar Associations) The conviction rate in Japanese courts where there is no jury system is over ninety-nine per cent.

A week later Anthony Gilbey was awarded £85,000 damages and costs against the police. He had been wrongly arrested on a charge of gross indecency in a public lavatory in Beccles, Suffolk, in June 1989, and been acquitted at Ipswich Crown Court a year later on the direction of the trial judge because of the unreliability of the evidence of the police. After the settlement of his claim – at which counsel for the Chief Constable of Suffolk conceded that Mr Gilbey should not have been detained, charged or committed to trial, and made an unreserved apology – Gilbey said:

> You hear about these things happening but it is grotesque when it happens to you. I was locked up and after they failed to browbeat a confession out of me they then tried to link me to a murder. Some people might just have confessed, but not me. I was prepared to fight them. It was perfectly clear I had not behaved in the way alleged but unless you have a wife to stand by you as my dear wife did, it would be very difficult to go on. They even cross-questioned my wife at home without telling her why. They frightened the life out of her.[16]

But these are instances where the police have merely infringed the rules rather than deliberately cheated. In 1970 journalist Peter Laurie was allowed a more or less free run of Scotland Yard. Here are a number of comments made to him by officers: 'People do get fixed up, but they're always good villains.' 'If you went by the rules the clear-up rate would be down from twenty-five per cent to two per cent.' 'If I thought there was a one per cent chance he hadn't done it, I wouldn't screw him down. But, let's face it, if stories weren't given a nudge along, the crime situation would get out of hand.'[17]

Nor were there any perceived dangers to the practice. The trial judge and magistrate generally would simply refuse to believe it had happened and any hope of a lenient sentence on a conviction flew out of the window. G.L. DuCann, known as the Duke, and father of politician Edward and Treasury

16 *Times*, 16 December 1992.
17 P. Laurie, *Scotland Yard*, p. 232.

Counsel Richard who prosecuted in the Confait case, wrote the following of the 1950s, but little has changed:

> Forced by his calling to be a professional witness, the policeman's familiarity with the witness box breeds contempt of its obligations . . . He very quickly learns that in most of his evidence he cannot tell the truth about anything and will not be allowed to by the judge, or magistrate or counsel.
>
> Moreover police perjury – unlike some other perjuries – carries no risks. Police witnesses are sometimes discredited but rarely prosecuted for perjury in my experience. The profession appears to give immunity from this misfortune.[18]

Today the Police and Criminal Evidence Act 1984 is supposed to have eliminated the opportunity for police to fabricate confessions in the police station. Again it has signally failed to do so. Sooner or later the bright, committed and deviant police officer will get around the problem. One way has been the insertion of additional sheets of paper into the stack on which a statement has been written, adroitly turning it into a confession. But there have long been other means.

From the very beginning of their careers young police officers were taught that there were certain requirements to be observed to obtain a conviction. Prime examples of convictions that could be obtained by false means were the fraudulent arrests of bookmakers' runners and the illegal round up of prostitutes for soliciting, undertaken on a rota basis. In the latter case, the offence under the Metropolitan Police Act 1839 was being a common prostitute soliciting in the street to the annoyance of passers by. But –

> Almost all the arrests were illegal. Men were hardly ever annoyed, police in uniform would be unlikely to see any girl cause annoyance to two, at least, as the law demanded. If the law required the men to give evidence, or merely to give their names and addresses, the arrests would have stopped immediately . . . I made my share of these illegal

[18] C. H. Rolph (ed), *The Police and the Public*, pp. 146–9.

arrests and my conscience was no more troubled than, apparently, were those of Bible-punching Home Secretaries like Joynson-Hicks and John Simon, or that of pious Sir Rollo Graham-Campbell, the Chief Magistrate at Bow Street, all of whom were aware of the injustice and did nothing about it.

The girls were aware they had not broken the law, but didn't seem to mind The smart girls in Burlington Gardens were usually arrested two or three times a week and sometimes jibbed a bit at the third. The rougher girls in the Leicester Square area were hooked in about once a fortnight, and occasionally could say, 'Well, I can't grumble dear – I haven't been in for a month.'[19]

Another example concerned the requirement of a passer-by to be aggrieved if a conviction for insulting behaviour was to be obtained. This led to evidence, readily accepted by magistrates, which bore little resemblance to the truth. To obtain a conviction the officer was always obliged to have seen a woman with a child, or a gentleman of clerical appearance, cross to the other side of the street in horror at the words uttered. Neither the mother, the reverend gentleman nor, if the officer was a humorist or chancer, the two nuns who crossed themselves before speeding away, ever gave evidence. Nor had they given their names to the officer, who was too busy arresting the unruly prisoner to go in search of them.

It was the same with the suspected person laws, applied first to white criminals when they tried car door handles and later to black youths when they tried to pick from the handbags of women watching the Changing of the Guard. There were never descriptions of the cars or their number plates or of the women. Perhaps it could be argued that the women moved on but the cars remained where they were for some time. A London solicitor speaking of the late 1960s said:

It got to the stage where provided your client came up with some sort of story, however improbable, such as still being drunk at 11 am after a night out and touching car door handles for support on the way home, some magistrates would acquit. But woe betide the client who had you challenge the police officer flat out and put it to him he was lying. Down you went.

'Magistrates especially were happy to accept the word of the police officer,' said a Chief Inspector. 'They connived in it, and protected police witnesses in court. It was expediency. The feeling was that if you knew the result it was easier to do it this way. Why make life more difficult for yourself? Those are the thoughts that went through police officers' minds.'

An apologia for the behaviour comes from no less a person than the former Commissioner, Sir David McNee:

Many police officers have, early in their careers, learned to use methods bordering on trickery or stealth in their investigations because they were deprived of proper powers by the legislature. They have risked civil actions frequently when doing so . . . One fears that sometimes so-called pious perjury of this nature from junior officers can lead to even more serious perjury on other matters later in their careers.[20]

The pious perjury referred to is the obverse side of the coin. Pious perjury was practised by judges in the eighteenth and nineteenth centuries to militate against the brutal laws of the time when, for example, the theft of goods worth over five shillings was a capital offence. Juries would simply devalue the item stolen. Prisoners who were able to read a short passage from the Bible were given the so-called benefit of clergy and were absolved from further punishment. In time any prisoner who could memorize the passage received the benefit. When a prisoner was to be branded, very often it was done with a cold iron. It is small wonder that the police forces of the time, seeing the connivance of the players in defeating the law, behaved in a like manner for their particular ends.

And modern forces behaved similarly. In the words of a now retired Police Constable: 'At an early age the officer has already twisted the evidence to suit what Parliament wants and he's

[20] D. McNee, *McNee's Law*, p. 2.

amazed to find he's been believed . . . From the start he's got to twist the evidence and tailor it to what the law wants it to be. And so it goes on.'

The same sentiments are expressed by ex-Flying Squad officer Laurie Cork. 'What happens is you get taken under the wing of a senior detective and are gradually brought into the system, that there are certain people who should be charged with certain offences, even if there is no evidence there.'

Verballing became a way of life in his police career. 'If you don't do it, it takes a lot longer to succeed and at that time you would have got no chance of going on the Flying Squad, which was obviously my goal.' He explains: 'You either nick someone, fix someone up or you earn from them [take money]. That's one of the first rules you learn as a CID officer, to do one or the other. The criminal fraternity don't dislike someone earning a few quid but they do dislike being fitted up.'[21]

The concept of the verbal does not seem to have been fully recognized outside the police and their criminal clients until the 1970s. Even today there is considerable dispute as to how much it existed prior to the Police and Criminal Evidence Act 1984 which in theory, if not in practice, made verballing impossible.

> Verballing was once regarded as something that could be talked about only in hushed tones but, more recently, its existence as a social phenomenon whatever its actual incidence has gained widespread acceptance. Verballing occurs when a statement of admission is attributed to a suspect even though the suspect did not in fact make any such statement. Sometimes this is referred to as fabrication, sometimes as gilding the lily. Occasionally verballing is established to have occurred. More usually it remains as an allegation with more or less suspicion attached to it.[22]

Some judges did however recognize that all was not perfect with the police and the accuracy of their statement-taking. 'Statements have sometimes been put in evidence which have been said to be the prisoner's own unaided work as taken down

[21] Quoted by John McVicar in the *Daily Express*, 19 October 1984.
[22] M. McConville et al, *The Case for the Prosecution*, p.84.

by the police officer and in which the prisoner has recounted in the stately language of the police station (where, for example, people never eat but partake of refreshment and never quarrel but indulge in altercations) the tale of his misdeed.'[23]

Not surprisingly the police themselves were keen to challenge the allegation that the widespread use of the verbal could ever happen. There is little doubt that some did have amazing recall:

> To see Hannam giving evidence was an education. He had an almost photographic memory and, if need be, would demonstrate this by quoting extensively without referring to documents in front of him. He was actually able to recite pages and pages of statements, and he taught me how to do it as well, so that in the future if notes weren't taken by one of my sergeants, I was able to recall great passages. It wasn't a question of being selective: you wrote down what you remembered and Hannam was brillant at this.[24]

What excited Hannam to a high degree was standing in the witness box and pitting his skills against an opposing counsel. Many of his colleagues regarded him as a lawyer *manqué*

A rare opportunity for exhibiting those skills came in 1953 with the famous towpath murder case: two young girls had been murdered and thrown into the Thames near Teddington lock. The accused man, Alfred Whiteway, of whose guilt there was little doubt, strenuously denied the signed confession which the prosecution produced in court. This confession had been the main plank in the case produced for the prosecution by Inspector Hannam, the man in charge of the inquiry. It

[23] Lord Devlin, *The Criminal Prosecution in England*, p. 39. Throughout the century there have been intermittent complaints in legal and police magazines about officers' pedantry. The officer never 'walks or runs', he always 'proceeds'; he never 'asks', he always 'requests', he never finds people 'quarrelling', they are always 'having an altercation' (*Justice of the Peace*, 10 February 1917; also *Solicitors Journal* 1932. p. 767 and *Police Review*, 27 June 1924, p. 348 and 22 February 1952, p. 134). Perhaps the best example is the constable who 'saw a man and woman having intellectual course', meaning 'sexual intercourse' (quoted in both *Solicitors Journal* and *Justice of the Peace*). This pedantry apparently continues. A person is never dead until certified by a doctor; he is 'apparently lifeless'. A corpse does not wear pyjamas but 'night attire'.

[24] L. Read and J. Morton, *Nipper*, p. 40.

was challenged vigorously by the young barrister defending the accused, thirty-seven-year-old Mr Peter Rawlinson, later Lord Rawlinson QC, who also used to do libel reading for the *Daily Express* and was doing so whilst conducting the Whiteway trial.

> Acting on the instructions of his solicitor, Rawlinson put Inspector Hannam through a rigorous two-day cross-examination on the methods he had adopted in drawing up the signed confession. Hannam never forgot those two days. Rawlinson, in a merciless pursuit, opened up gaps of doubt in Hannam's evidence.
>
> Rawlinson left [Edward] Pickering [then editor of the *Daily Express*] in no doubt of his opinion of Hannam's methods in obtaining the signed confession. It was not that Hannam was lying, Rawlinson said. It was the method he had adopted to secure the self-damning confession. A piece here and a piece there. A juggling of context. A clever manipulation. Then the collation. At the best, it was an unsavoury method of conducting a police investigation.[25]

C. H. Rolph recalled the allegations slightly differently, as well as the public reaction to them:

> . . . his trial produced the most direct and explicit attack on the evidence of a police witness that I have ever known. Counsel for the defence said that the Superintendent had invented the whole statement attributed to Whiteway – that it was 'a completely manufactured piece of fiction written by the officer'. The jury rejected this and found Whiteway guilty. I remember that when Mr Hannam's cross-examination was reported in the newspapers, about a dozen complete strangers wrote to me at the *New Statesman* office to express their anger that a police officer should thus be accused, in open court, of what would have amounted to perjury with intent to murder. I can't say that such a thing has never happened; only that in half a lifetime of intimate contact with policemen I never met one who was remotely likely to do it, even though he knew (as he so often *thinks*

[25] P. Hoskins, *Two Were Acquitted*, p. 47.

he does) that he was dealing with a guilty man who was otherwise going to escape conviction.[26]

Another problem for the police officer, the defence and the court was that of the note or pocket book:

> The trial of the Liverpool bookmaker and nine ex-constables of Liverpool, concluded at Liverpool Assizes on Monday, all ten being found guilty of corruption and conspiracy. The allegation was that all the policemen . . . accepted bribes from [a bookmaker] so that he might not be interfered with in carrying on street betting. One of the constables, when dealing with the arrest of a 'dummy', said four officers were working together, and one made up his notebook for the purpose of his evidence. 'We would all make it up the same. That was a matter of form.'

> Mr Justice Swift: 'I have often heard it suggested that policemen do these things but I have never heard a policeman on oath say that he did them.'
> Constable: 'Well they do. It does not say we would say exactly the words in our notebook.'
> 'Are you saying, as an officer of seven years experience, the usual thing is to make items agree, whether it is true or not?'
> 'If I had to go into the witness box, I would make my notebooks up true.'[27]

The difficulty was that if the police admitted they had made up their notebooks sitting together in the canteen and pooling their joint recollections, this left them as sitting ducks for cross-examination. Instead they went through the farce of producing notebooks made up identically down to the last comma and, in the teeth of the evidence, stood their ground denying there had been any collaboration with other officers. And however much they were made to look at best foolish and at worst liars, time and time again they were backed by the magistrates and judges. Eventually the process was legitimated with the decision in the *Bass* case.[28]

---

26 C. H. Rolph, *The Police and the Public*, pp. 181–2.
27 *Sunday News*, 1927, quoted in M. Blogden, *On the Mersey Beat*, p. 121.
28 1953:1 QB 680.

Bent Coppers

But this was basically kids' stuff. The lawyers did not realize what really went on. A Detective Constable, talking about the 1960s, explained:

> As a CID officer you're going to come across a higher level of irregularity. You would be involved in more important cases and then you would come across another practice. It was scriptwriting.
> Certain officers had the ability, the talent, following an arrest of a number of people involving officers with ranks ranging from DC to the highest of the CID on division, to write up a case. At some point that case had to be put on a report and DC A's evidence mustn't clash with the evidence of DS B which mustn't clash with what Chief Inspector C gave. It used to be the case that when questioned one gave one's evidence to say that I made my notes independently. It was said that if all the officers sat round and concurred it was wrong but later the court changed the practice so that officers said they sat round and made sure it was absolutely right. But in point of fact it was essential because the technology didn't exist. All officers could do it but at pretty near every police station there would be some guys who excelled at being scriptwriters.
> One officer who was later to be Chief Inspector of HM Constabulary was a great scriptwriter. There was a robbery in the town. We heard the robbers were going to wear some disguises. We more or less knew what was going to happen but it was a complicated affair. He pulled it all together He was a well-known scriptwriter.
> You would go there and do the physical. The guys would be carted off to the station, pulled out one by one and questioned, so you would have some observation, and some when questioned, and the whole thing had to be coordinated to make a case. What would actually happen, you made no entries in the pocket book but at a later date you would be handed a carbon of a statement and you would put that in your pocket book in a certain way.

Another officer from the same division confirms the ability of that 'great scriptwriter': 'He came as a first class sergeant and it seemed then he was being groomed. He went right up from the ranks. He was a dapper little man, very clever, erudite. It [scriptwriting] was common.' And an ex-Commander adds: 'Scriptwriting – know what you mean. The Chief Inspector of Constabulary? I know who that was.'

Perhaps one of the best examples of misbehaviour with the notebook was that of an officer who in March 1986 was asked by defending counsel to produce his notebook. It was discovered that the notebook to which he had been referring when he gave his evidence was in fact blank.

One of the complaints often made by defendants, and one which led their lawyers to look at the total of their allegations with some disbelief, was that the person who gave evidence of their arrest had never been there. 'Why on earth should the man do that?' asked the incredulous solicitor, fast losing faith in his client. 'What was in it for him?' But it did occur from time to time and it was not frowned upon particularly heavily by the courts. When two officers were charged with perjury in these circumstances it was accepted that they had acted out of misplaced loyalty to the job and had been saving the time of their senior officers by volunteering to undertake the wasteful and boring job of attending court. Imposing absolute discharges, the judge hoped that there would be no disciplinary action taken against them.

Officers who were not prepared to give evidence were looked on with some contempt by their colleagues. Speaking of the notorious Alec Eist, one former Flying Squad colleague maintained, 'He was no scriptwriter. He hadn't the intelligence, nor would he go to court on a job. He had no bottle. The only time he went he had a bad time and like so many you get one bad go and that's it. Instead he'd get a job, stick it up [tell his colleagues] and make sure he wasn't there.'

Some aspects of the law were held in deliberate contempt by all who participated in the play. One such was the arrest of street bookmakers when street betting was in force. Leonard 'Nipper' Read, talking about a successful raid on an illegal betting office in Albany Street near Regent's Park in the early 1950s, said, 'It was a perfect snatch but whilst we were in there the phone went and I recognized the voice of a local Detective Sergeant ringing up to place a bet. "Sorry Sid," I said, "the office is closed today."'[29]

Brian McConnell recalled that in the 1950s 'I was a cub reporter on the local paper and I wanted to see what happened. I was in the pub when a call came through that they wanted six volunteers for the afternoon's register [list of cases] so I sat with the others on the bench at the entrance. The police van was parked near the Magistrates Court, I went in and was fined five shillings and that was that.'

It was not something new, nor was it confined to London. The Chief Constable of Liverpool's report to the Watch Committee, 1927, stated:

> The forms of corruption were of two kinds, receipt of monies a week on consideration of a partial stay of police action ... the other, an arrangement whereby certain arrests were made, followed by pleas of guilty and convictions of men provided with betting slips for the purpose so that complaints of street betting in particular localities might be satisfied, meanwhile there would be immunity from arrest at other places ... The bookmakers carefully selected men to be convicted who had no previous convictions, so that light fines should be inflicted.

From time to time officers did get a rush of conscience, possibly because they had turned to religion, and often with unpleasant consequences to themselves. On 24 August 1974 an officer was suspended on full pay after he admitted he had planted evidence during a disturbance at Twickenham. He had confessed because of his faith in the Pentecostal Church. In May 1988 a policeman of thirteen years' standing and a younger officer admitted making false statements that they had seen a fifteen-year-old youth driving a stolen car and a twenty-two-year-old in the passenger seat. The incident occurred in November 1986 when they were following two youths driving through Walthamstow. They lost the car but later found the youths standing nearby. At the police station they both said they had seen one of the boys in the car. They received nine months' imprisonment, six of which were suspended, and six (with four suspended) respectively. Whilst the youths were awaiting trial the older officer had broken down and told one of his seniors that he was now a Born Again Christian: 'I have now found religion. I cannot go through with taking a religious oath and lying in the face of God.'

So far as the more straightforward interrogation goes, the widely read American police manual by Inban and Reid outlines twenty-six specific techniques to be used in interrogating a suspect. The author comments:

> . . . most of these techniques will inevitably involve some sort of deception because they require an officer to make statements that he knows are untrue or play a role that is inconsistent with his actual feelings. The effectiveness of those techniques is amply documented by the authors as they recount case after case in which a strategic lie or timely false show of sympathy was instrumental in leading a suspect to confess.[30]

Welsh goes on to give a number of examples from American cases, including the recital of the burial service to a deeply religious suspect, telling a suspect the victim was still alive (and therefore could make an identification), and the converse, telling him the victim was dead.

What America could do so could the United Kingdom and there are a wealth of stories of officers, one of whom eventually reached the rank of Commissioner, who donned a white coat to act as the doctor called out for the suspect. The benefits of this were legion. There could be a denial that the suspect had called for a doctor. There would be no record of a doctor attending the station. And the defendant's wild accusations could be seen as now embracing the uniform branch as well as the CID, so that if he was to be believed, the court would have to find that there was a major conspiracy not simply between two or possibly three officers but one which embraced the whole police station.

Other ruses are still more subtle. A Detective Constable tells a tale from the 1960s:

[30] S. Welsh, 'Police Trickery in Inducing Confessions', *University of Pennsylvania Law Review*, vol 127, No 3 January 1979, p. 3.

An Irish young female comes in, said father had been having intercourse with her. In fact alleged incest but wanted to stop it happening to the younger sister. The guy was taken into the nick. Various methods were used because the guys serving the public were concerned about the need to save the girl giving evidence. It would be much easier to have a confession from the father. We had an Irish officer and the suspect was a Catholic and the officer dressed up as a priest and paid a visit to the guy in the cell. As a result of what was said the guy confessed. Now that's a police irregularity but judge the result.

Of course this was not a new technique. According to the ballad *The Croppy Boy*, it had been employed during the Troubles of the 1920s, and not merely in Ireland either. In 1926 a London detective had posed as a lawyer to obtain a confession. It produced comment but no more: 'If a defendant were to masquerade as a priest and extract information through the confessional there would be an outcry.'[31]

When the English courts did find that the police had deliberately deceived the suspect's lawyer (as opposed to the suspect), they excluded the confession. In the case of *Mason*, where the defendant was suspected of arson, during the course of an interview the defendant and his solicitor were told by the police deliberately and untruthfully that the defendant's fingerprints had been found on fragments of a bottle. The defendant then admitted he had handled the glass. On appeal the Court of Appeal excluded the confession, saying that the judge should have considered the deception on the solicitor.[32]

More serious was the 'sus' charge, an example of which led to the Mars-Jones inquiry. The law required two overt acts for the police to stop a person on suspicion and, in the words of a Detective Constable,

they would give the guy two or three car door handles or two or three house doors they would push against, or shop doors. I've no doubt there were some genuine sus person arrests – but I would say the greater proportion weren't, and the kind

[31] *Police Review and Parade Gossip*, 1 October 1926.
[32] (1987) 86 Cr App R 349.

of guys who would be swifted for sus would be the yobs, guys hanging about with nothing specific to do, vagrants, people hitching North, they would find themselves getting the attention of a couple of aides. I don't think often the guys who really deserve it were nicked. I believe when the coloured element increased they were frequently the victims of such police attention.

But such behaviour would be the police officer's earliest introduction to irregular conduct leading to arrest and his first introduction to committing perjury. A Detective Sergeant recalls that 'Just about my first day out I was dropped off by the Inspector on one side of Waterloo Station and told to have an arrest for him by the time he'd driven round to the other side. It was a kind of test.'

As for magistrates, in the words of a Detective Constable:

They sit there and have the same officers before them week after week and they would surely detect a pattern that this officer has a tendency to fall over this kind of criminal situation, but what is their discretion? If the prisoner is there, his name's on the list and the evidence is given by two separate officers and that coincides, they're not caught out. It's been well rehearsed. Can they say if they've heard perfect evidence of a suspected person, can they say, 'No, we believe what the guy says that he was walking down the road when you suddenly pounced on him and he was astounded?' Where should the magistrates' discretion go? It should go surely to the police witnesses? Weight of evidence. Case proved.

A Detective Sergeant, formerly of the Flying Squad, recounts how in the 1970s, 'We found this old dear of a magistrate and we learned she liked a drop of Scotch, so on a Saturday we'd get a name and address out of the phone book and ask if we could come over with a warrant to be signed. We'd sit with her from two till five drinking her Scotch and then say 'Thank you ma'am' and tear up the warrant after we left. But who's she going to believe? The villains or us?'

It was not only the lay magistracy which fell prey to the charms of young enthusiastic officers. An ex-Chief Superintendent remembers in the 1960s that 'The magistrate at Old Street used to lap up the evidence of the aides. He would have them back in his room for a chat.' Indeed some magistrates, even senior stipendiary ones, display an almost blind faith in the police. Ronald Bartle, who has sat for a number of years at Bow Street, wrote in *The Law and the Lawless* that in his years at the Bar and on the bench he had never known a police officer 'to exaggerate in the slightest degree the circumstances of the offence'.

And when there was absolutely no way out for the police then the magistrate would often do nothing except pass it off with a pleasantry. This is a barrister speaking of a case in the 1970s:

> I defended a man charged with a series of armed robberies on betting shops in Charlotte Street. The evidence was two and a half pages of verbal admissions to a Flying Squad officer including words to the effect, 'It was D-Day (June 4), well this was my D-Day. I took the shooters to frighten them, I wasn't going to use them.' At first he declined to give any explanation and said he would produce it to his solicitor at the proper time. When the case came up at Marlborough Street for committal he produced a letter from the governor of Brixton saying that on the day of the robberies he was in custody on burglary charges. I suggested to the stipendiary magistrate he might wish to send the papers to the Director of Public Prosecutions but he replied he did not think it was necessary, adding that defendants often played tricks such as this on hard-working officers.

Another instance was that of Arthur John Saunders, convicted for his part in a substantial robbery in Essex. The evidence against him consisted largely of verbal admissions made to Commander Albert Wickstead. Asked if he was on the robbery, Saunders had replied, 'There's no point in saying no, is there?' He put up an alibi defence but his witness let him down. His appeal was dismissed in December 1971 but later Bertie Smalls, the supergrass, said in one of his statements that Saunders had not been on the raid. This presented the authorities with a dilemma. How could Smalls be put forward as truthful in one instance and not in another? The Court of

Appeal quashed the conviction, pointing out in explanation that Saunders had been drinking when he made the admissions.

But the officer had to make sure of the status of the person he was swifting – arresting falsely. He might get a conviction but it could come back to haunt him. A Detective Constable recalls in the 1970s:

> Guys got swifted for flashing – exposing their person with intent to insult a female. This particular officer X was very concerned to have high arrest figures and I worked with him on the Q car. Once he had arrested a middle-aged guy for flashing at Highgate. He was found guilty, as a result of which he lost quite an important civil service job. It became the guy's practice to follow X around the various court appearances. It was said he was taking notes with the intent of eventually vindicating himself because most of X's arrests were contentious. Similar methods as those used in sus. Therein lies the danger of deviating from your normal sources of looney susses and yobs and vagrants. Looney susses – often they would plead guilty, save everyone trouble.

But did not the station Sergeant do anything about what must have seemed like an unbroken line of suspects all arrested in exactly the same fashion? There appears to have been at the very least tacit approval. 'If I'd seen anything I would have reported it but the officers weren't foolish. Anyway these were compliant prisoners. Whatever had been said or done to them, they were going to plead guilty' – an ex-Inspector speaking of the 1970s.

There were, of course, other ways of obtaining a conviction, i.e. brutality. Again the police and courts have, in general, been reluctant to accept there has been any violence offered to prisoners. One regular claim by defendants is that they have been beaten into a confession. 'I've been present when prisoners have been assaulted in the charge room on a handful of occasions,' says a Chief Inspector. 'The majority were when the prisoner was being quite violent. A couple of occasions were when prisoners were mildly assaulted – no worse than a common assault – through frustration. But I've read the reports. Perhaps my experience is naïve and not typical.' A Detective

Chief Superintendent recounts how he 'had a sergeant who'd smacked a guy who then spilled the beans. From this he was always smacking prisoners. If the first didn't work, then he smacked them again. Eventually he was reported and the Mafia closed around him. They weren't going to see their sergeant go down.'

Occasionally, however, officers will accept something has happened. One Detective Constable, speaking of the 1960s, recalls: 'He was brought into Kings Cross Road for robbery. He's interrogated by the DI in the police cell. I was with half a dozen officers in the corridor, and the guy was really interrogated. We had quite a job cleaning up the blood after the interrogation.' More succinctly, 'We slaughtered him,' was how an ex-Assistant Chief Constable recalled the interrogation of a man suspected of the killing of two young children in the 1960s.

Amongst the allegations against the West Midlands Police was that five men arrested by the Serious Crime Squad had had some form of plastic bag put over their heads until they were about to pass out. The object of the exercise was either to induce an admission to a given crime or to obtain their signature to a previously prepared written confession.

The first allegation of 'plastic bagging' came from a George Twitchell in 1980 when he was arrested and charged with the murder of a Securicor guard. Twitchell submitted to a lie detector test and later was injected with sodium amytal, a so-called truth drug, under the aegis of a Professor Canning, who concluded that he was inclined to believe Twitchell's account of the events. His evidence was ruled inadmissible and on 22 February 1982 Twitchell was sentenced to a period of twenty years' imprisonment on his conviction for manslaughter and robbery.

The same allegations were raised by a Harry Tredaway, who was examined shortly after the alleged incident by a Home Office pathologist who concluded:

> . . . the finding of petechial haemorrhages on the shoulder and on the front of the chest is exactly where I would expect to find them if a plastic bag has been held over his head in the manner he described . . . Furthermore, the finding of abrasions of the mucous membrane inside the right corner

of the mouth is fully consistent with the statement of the complainant that hands were put over his mouth.[33]

All the defendants in cases where there were allegations of 'plastic bagging' were convicted. Tredaway brought a civil action against the West Midlands Police. It was struck out on procedural grounds in August 1990.

Surely plastic bagging is just too far fetched to attract credibility? Says Professor Mike McConville of the University of Warwick:

> I remember looking at cases where people had alleged plastic bagging, all of which seemed to be rather preposterous at the time. This was repeated by a number of defendants who, on their own admissions, were repeat criminals. I was a witness when one was given a truth drug and he came out with allegations of this kind. He went through his questioning – yes, he'd had a gun and so forth and then came out with these stories. There was another man who alleged the officer had been drinking and had threatened him with a gun.
>
> My view was changed. Initially I had believed these were fanciful rumours which I had heard from criminal sources and which didn't even deserve investigation because they seemed to involve extreme allegations which were highly improbable. Now there had been structured interviews with defendants who had never spoken to each other and who had no opportunity to contact each other. They had come out with stories which agreed with each other in important respects. In one case the convicted individual never made an official complaint and didn't regard what had occurred as having any bearing on the outcome of his case. He only saw it as another demonstration of the poor treatment he had received over the years from other police officers. One can only get a feeling and that is that the stories were certainly plausible. At the end of the day you have to make a judgment and mine was that the stories were very likely to be true.

The independent West Midlands inquiry reported that a

---

[33] T. Kaye, *Unsafe and Unsatisfactory*, pp. 50–51. The allegations of plastic bagging have never been proved.

number of known criminals now believe that the reduction in physical aggression results first from the improved psychological techniques and secondly because the police have realized that a physical assault is counter-productive as this will allow the defence to call medical evidence in support of their claims – although why, if assaults occurred, they did not do so in the past is unclear. Nevertheless, the inquiry found the number of complaints declined significantly after 1986.

As for straightforward brutality to extract a confession, with the arrival of PACE and the requirement for doctors to be called to investigate prisoners' injuries, there is clearly much less today than in the past. Injuries are now only caused in struggles on the way to the police station. If force there must be, then its use must be more subtle.

In one of the more arcane cases since the Police and Criminal Evidence Act 1984 set out the codes of conduct to be observed whilst taking confessions from suspects, ex-DC Susan James told Warwick Crown Court that she had made love with a man she arrested for a credit card fraud, Tony Marren, to get him to grass on his accomplices, David Rowe and David Lowe. Admitting, 'He's a good-looking man – in looks, superficially, yes,' she told the court the love affair had been to build up Marren's trust in her. What she did not realize is that he had been tape-recording their conversations. After the relationship came to light she resigned from the force. Telling the jury her credibility had been partially or even completely destroyed, the judge said her conduct had been a 'gross violation of rules intended to protect arrested persons'.[34]

In December 1992 a case in which it was alleged that Timothy Tindell had hired a contract hitman to kill his second wife, following a bitter and lengthy quarrel over the custody of the child of the marriage, was halted after the court was told that DC David Weatherill, one of the investigating officers, had been having an affair with the wife for a number of months. 'The integrity of the officer in the case was a most important factor and his impartiality is rendered, at the very least, questionable,' said Shaun Spencer QC for the Crown.[35]

Even now not many could put their hand on their heart and

[34] *Daily Mirror*, 24 November 1988.
[35] *The Times*, 15 December 1992.

say they've never gilded the lily. Why do they do it? Says a Chief Inspector, 'The feeling is that the rules of evidence are weighted [against the prosecution] and need help. There's the honest belief that the fellow is guilty and the law needs a bit of help to ensure the right result is achieved. Then there is the person who is innocent and is fitted up. I've never come across the second example but I've come across many examples of the first.'

One of the problems of the police has been the clear-up rate of crime. If it falls too low then the police are clearly not doing their duty. In any event it is likely to be the tip of the iceberg; what criminologists like to call the *chiffre noir*, or the dark number, is the real measure of the amount of crime which has been committed. So the police have taken upon themselves a variety of ways in which the figures can be massaged to produce the result the massager wishes. Techniques vary between forces.

In 1934 a Detective Inspector Morrish was sent to run Croydon division whilst the divisional inspector was off sick. Looking through various registers and record books he became very suspicious of the way crimes were being recorded, so he carried out his own investigation. He concluded that the division's relatively high success rate for crime clearance was thoroughly bogus, because many crimes were being entered up as something else. A woman would have her handbag snatched, but this would be entered in the register as a case of Lost Property. Many other entries were far more ingenious.[36]

Crime on the area could be reduced simply by not recording it. Says a Detective Sergeant of the 1960s, 'When I was a DC if you nicked anyone for drugs it didn't go on the crime book. It was like a flasher – no one ever wanted to know about it.'

In the late 1970s and early 1980s the Kent Police had a particularly attractive way of clearing up crime in their county. According to Chatham-based PC Ronald Walker, who blew the whistle in 1986, Kent detectives were systematically inflating clear-up rates in their own divisions by persuading arrested offenders to confess to non-existent crimes, or to admit to

[36] M. Short, *Inside the Brotherhood*, p. 272.

crimes they had not committed. Prisoners were visited and offered the incentive of a good word over parole. The fiddle, said PC Walker, left more time for 'birds and booze'. One division increased its clear-up rate in 1979 from 24.4 per cent to 69.5 per cent.

The whistle-blowing did him little good. On 19 September 1989, the day Kent Police announced that disciplinary action had been taken against thirty-five of its officers, Walker said he too was facing disciplinary action. He said he had turned down the offer of a job at Maidstone claiming he was sick. 'He has been off sick for nearly four years,' said Paul Condon, then Chief Constable of Kent, who denied the Constable faced disciplinary action but admitted it was an option open. In the inquiry which had resulted from Walker's allegations one Detective Sergeant had been sacked and other officers fined up to £500.[37]

Kent was not alone in its involvement with incorrect crime clear-up rates. Rather more serious was the case of Paul Jarvis who in 1988 admitted his part in 1,510 offences. Here was a godsend for the West Midlands Police. In due course Jarvis turned supergrass and implicated a number of other men, including Valentine Cooke who was convicted in May 1989 of five robberies and one attempted robbery. Fortunately for Cooke and unfortunately for the conviction rate, it was later discovered that of the 1,510 offences earlier admitted by Jarvis more than 200 could not have been committed by him because he was in prison at the time they occurred. Ronald Gail, Gerald Gail and Danny Lynch had their convictions based on the evidence of Jarvis quashed in October 1991; Valentine Cooke was released on 14 January 1992.

Until 1992 this method of clearing undetected crimes appeared still to be widespread. In May 1992 MP Chris Mullin wrote to the Home Secretary calling for the practice of obtaining confessions to unsolved crimes from convicted prisoners to be discontinued. He alleged that the old Kent practice was still up and running throughout parts of the country, pointing to the fact that in 1989, the last year when information was available, forty-four per cent of all crimes in Merseyside were 'solved' through prison interviews, whilst the Met only cleared up one per cent

---

[37] *Daily Telegraph*, 20 September 1989.

in this way. Other forces which relied on the post-conviction confession were West Midlands (thirty-four per cent), Greater Manchester (thirty-three per cent), Cheshire (twenty-five per cent) and North and South Yorkshire (twenty-three and twenty-two per cent respectively). Mr Mullin said:

> The practice is well known – and regarded with much cynicism – by the police and the criminal fraternity. It first came to my attention when I received a letter from a convicted criminal in jail in the south of England saying that he had been visited by two detectives who persuaded him to put his name down for over 300 unsolved crimes, thirty of which had been committed while he was in jail.

Mr Mullin maintained that when John Stevens took over the position of Chief Constable in Northumbria in 1991 he ended the practice. Prior to that, 29.4 per cent of crimes in the area were cleared up by a squad of up to forty officers. Mullin had raised the matter in the House of Commons earlier in May when he asked the Home Secretary to outlaw the practice. Mr Clarke had replied, 'I remember such rumours in the courts many years ago but I am not sure they were substantiated in practice. It is always wise to treat clear-up figures and figures of recorded crime with a certain amount of scepticism.'[38]

Now a number, if not the majority, of forces have put a halt to this method of clearing up their crime statistics.

[38] *Independent*, 25 May 1992.

9

At Work and Play

In his book *The Choirboys*, Joseph Wambaugh presents an entertaining picture of police officers under considerable pressure relaxing at play. Each officer, when in need of rest and recreation, may call a choir practice or group meeting at which all other officers and preferably two cocktail waitress police groupies are present. The meetings end with group sex with one or preferably both of the girls, one of whom is appropriately named Ora-Lee, 'pulling the train'. It is Wambaugh's belief that police at recreation are no different whether they are in London, Los Angeles, Melbourne, Detroit or any other major city. What evidence is there that he is correct?

'We used just to go to the pub. The gay ones pulled the cadets and we pulled the women,' said an ex-Metropolitan PC speaking of the 1980s. In the words of Ecclesiastes, there is nothing new under the sun, certainly not in policing.

I know one or two cases where a policeman would jump into bed with a different woman every night. One instance, when I was a young PC in town – we had one young policeman (he'd been in the navy) and he gave us so much information in the plain clothes section about prostitutes and where the brothels were, we suspected something. This was so good that we recommended him to the boss that he should have a spell in plain clothes and he was actually down in the Superintendent's orders to be posted to the PC section. Round Christmas time, his wife had been to see one sergeant complaining that he hadn't been home over Christmas and

278

this sergeant said, 'Well you know what sailors are – he's been to a party,' and was a bit flippant about it. Really, he should have made more inquiries, because if we were going to be away over night, we had to put in a report before we went. I got a call to a house – the tenant was a foreigner – no dice. The bobby was dead in bed with a prostitute – the gas had been on. This was the party he had got in with and that was how he was able to feed information back.[1]

A letter from a policeman's wife that appeared in *Police Review* encapsulates the problem:

Dave is doing it with WDC Claire from the same station, Rupert is doing it with Josephine, the duty solicitor, and I am reliably informed there are three more in surrounding stations all doing the same thing. I am the wife of Rupert – names have been changed to protect the swine!

If I should go to my local senior officer for help and advice, how do I know he is not getting it from the traffic warden (she already has a reputation)? Or should I go to his wife? But perhaps she gets regular visits from the neighbourhood watch bobby.

If something is not done soon to put a stop to extramarital relationships there could be a wave of deaths of depressed wives by suicide. I would like the officers who are doing it to explain why. What has made them turn away from their wives and family and go with another? How easy does the force make it?

I would like senior officers to voice their opinions. What do they think of it going on all around them? In work time – or using work as an excuse. I think time is running out for me – the new younger woman is too good for me to compete with. After all, she can talk shop – something I am not allowed to be part of. All officers say, when they are at home, that they just want to switch off, but who refuses a drink with the boys, and what do they talk about?

Confused and desperate because I love him so, I fear I have

lost. Please try and help the next person. Surely something has to be done.[2]

Then there is the example of one woman's home being used as a sex-club for Brixton police. So enthralled were they by the woman that officers vied to be members of the 42 Club, named after the number of her house. She had never had trouble with the law until she telephoned Brixton police station two and a half years earlier to lodge a complaint about a street assault on a boyfriend. A Constable called on her, then another, etc. 'I was being woken at all hours of the night by policemen wanting to see me on one excuse or another. Some of them were quite jealous when they heard I was dating a man who was not a policeman. They did all they could to stop me continuing that relationship. They wanted me for themselves, a plaything they could call on whenever they wished.'[3]

History tends to repeat itself and in April 1988 the local police were banned from visiting a Nottingham council house where two young women had been hosting parties. 'When the policemen got to know about us, they just flocked there.' The husband of one of the women said he could cite half the Nottingham police force as co-respondents. One of the women claimed to have had nineteen policemen lovers in four months.

In recent times the spectre of gay sex amongst police officers has reared its loving head. The Met, along with another nine of the forty-three forces in England and Wales, now boasts a gay and lesbian group. In January 1993 in a letter to *Police*, the Police Federation magazine, David Cranmer, an officer of twenty years' standing, extolled the delights of gay sex. He told the readers that since he had come out he had had more sexual contact with gay officers than you could shake a stick at. 'I did not solicit any of those liaisons and most [partners] were married. They regularly admitted unhappiness in their relationships with their wives and said they would probably not have entered into such a state had they not felt obliged to conform.'

It had not always been that way, and of course male

2 *Police Review*, 28 August 1992.
3 *Sunday People*, 31 August 1980.

homosexuality was illegal until 1956. The homosexual officer Harry Daley had difficulties in the force in the 1920s and 1930s, although some officers, ex-Guardsmen, were by no means embarrassed. 'After a time the two men showed off casually with expensive-looking rings, watches and cigarette cases, and by conversing in my hearing let me know they got them from old gentlemen whom they accompanied home. Apparently, what they were not given freely they took for themselves.'[4]

Sex is not the only kind of opportunity for excitement outside the police officer's humdrum working routines. It can come in the form of a punch-up, the clearance of a local pub, and a variety of other forms. Said a Police Constable in 1992, 'Officers were doing crazy things like driving from North-West London to St Albans in their tea breaks. One of them went up in a helicopter. It's to relieve boredom. Even now there's challenges. Go round the North Circular in an hour or go to the seaside and pick up a piece of rock. It's the risk. What happens if you have a crash 70 miles out of your ground?' Well, if you want to go by past experience not a lot.

A similar story is told by an ex-Inspector, referring to the 1970s:

> Doing the books was a well-established Met Police routine in which the senior officer at the station went through all the entries made in the station books (the lost and found property registers, the driving licences produced, persons stopped in the street etc.) since the previous day.
>
> The Chief Inspector's particular fetish was the garage book, in which every car or van at the station logged the time of the beginning and end of each journey, and the individual log books of each car in which more precise details of usage were registered. To him the coincidence of entries in the log and garage books was far more important than the number of crimes committed each day or the number of people arrested.
>
> It was some six months into my acquaintance with the Chief Inspector that I became aware of the reasons for his fixed interest. At a previous station at which he had served, the night duty van driver and some local traffic patrol officers

[4] H. Daley, *This Small Cloud*. p. 85.

had been disciplined for a traditional weekly race to Southend at 2 am. This had gone on for at least twelve months before it became known after the van had crashed well outside the MPD boundary.

According to their defending lawyers, some police officers take to crime to cope with the problem of boredom. PC John Bibby turned to burglary in the 1990s because being a police officer in Leighton Buzzard did not provide the same excitement as serving with the army in the Falkland Islands, Londonderry and Germany. He was jailed at Snaresbrook Crown Court for two and a half years after pleading guilty to ten burglaries whilst on night duty. 'He committed burglaries just for kicks and the sheer excitement of committing crimes,' said Nicholas Browne prosecuting. In a speech in mitigation Alan Mainds said Bibby had found police work extremely boring.

'To understand how police officers see the social world and their role in it – cop culture – is crucial to an analysis of what they do, and their broad political function.[5] This is all the more necessary in understanding corruption in the police. Said a police constable in 1992, 'I was on the Crime Squad for two years. The CID would come on at 6 am, do a couple of warrants and then go and have breakfast. Expenses were cash. Your wife never knew about them. You could eat on duty, drink on duty, fiddle your petrol. The best thing was when you were sent to pick up a prisoner from another nick – you could do all of them.'

Mike McConville, researching for his book *Watching Police, Watching Communities*, undertook a study of the Met, Avon and Somerset, and Gwent Police. He found the similarities between Avon and Somerset and the Met both surprising and striking. 'There was the same macho male culture, a fixation with arrests and the excitement of rushing around. A good dust-up was looked forward to.'

Throughout the history of the police there has been clear evidence of bonding between officers, particularly at the lower levels. It may well have started with the earliest police being Napoleonic War veterans. It may also have been, in part, because of the initial resentment towards these blue locusts

[5] R. Reiner, *The Politics of Police*, p. 85

by the local citizenry. Although traditional historians such as Critchley rosily see the police as being accepted from almost the moment they set off on their first beat, if one accepts Storch's theory, in which he is supported by Brogden, they have never been accepted. As with evidence in the courts, the truth usually lies somewhere in the middle. Probably the predominant image of policing as consensual came within thirty years of the establishment of the various forces.

Resentment there certainly was as the police were gradually foisted on to an unreceptive and often hostile public. Indeed in Colne, Lancashire, the local townsfolk carried out a long-running campaign against the police in the spring and summer of 1840, effectively capturing them so that police supporters had to send for troops from Burnley. The anti-police demonstrators were well versed in cat and mouse tactics. By the time the military arrived it found itself

at a loss for something to do. In fact during the entire history of anti-police resistance in Colne no confrontation with the army ever took place. It was a prominent and intelligent part of the strategy of the resisters never to engage the army, but to wait until they had gone before dealing with the police. On Sunday evening, arguing that calm had prevailed for some days and that the troops required barracks, the army left again. This of course was the signal for the resurgence of anti-police activities.[6]

Grouping within the force was encouraged inadvertently by the arrangements for housing the officers in the equivalent of barracks: 'for in whatever community he lives, and from whatever class he may come, the policeman is something of a social outcast . . . It is a burden which many policemen find difficult to bear. Their isolation, and that of their families, is often accentuated by building police houses in groups on an estate, instead of distributing them in the community.'[7]

[6] There is a full and most entertaining account of this and other early anti-police demonstrations in the provinces in Robert Storch, 'The Plague of Blue Locusts: Police Reform and Popular Resistance in Northern England, 1840–57', *International Review of Social History* and M. Fitzgerald et al, *Crime and Society: Readings in History and Theory*, p. 86.

[7] W. Gay, in C. H. Rolph (ed), *The Police and the Public*, p. 163.

As a result 'the police department has the special property
. . . that within it discretion increases as one moves down
the hierarchy'.[8]

> It is likely that where police are faced with culture shock
> by policing environments to which they are strange, there
> is likely to be a greater tendency to retreat into the cultural
> familiarity of their own organisation. This is considerably
> enforced where police live apart from other communities,
> for example in barracks or enclaves . . . Thus it is that where
> officers are not resident within their policing locations, like
> many others, they have to accommodate two cultures, their
> residential and their occupational.[9]

The nuts and bolts of the discretion theory is that policing
is controlled by the use, by the men on the street, of the
'Ways and Means Act'. This is, in fact, only another way of
expressing the three rules which are required for 'successful'
low-level policing – working, inhibiting, and presentational. It
is the third of these by which an acceptable 'gloss' may be put
on otherwise unacceptable behaviour.[10]

A retired Police Constable, talking of the 1960s, points to
the pressures of group solidarity:

> In those days you knew two obstacles to the honest copper.
> First, whomsoever you went to was just as involved, and
> secondly if anything came of it you were the biggest shit
> in the nick. You might be getting your head kicked in and
> call for assistance and they'd walk backwards.
>
> We were encouraged if we suspected corruption to report
> it to the Yard but you'd still be shown as the informer and
> be on shop door handle nights for the rest of your life.

He is echoed by a Chief Superintendent:

> If you opened your mouth at the wrong time, you didn't stay

---

[8] James Q. Wilson, *Varieties of Police Behaviour*. Other sociologists, notably
Doreen McBarnet, have challenged this view.
[9] J. Alderson, *Law and Disorder*, p. 65.
[10] R. Reiner, *The Politics of Police*, p. 86. His views mirror the findings of the
PSI in 1983.

in the police. Your job would not be worth it. When I was at Peckham I saw an officer transferred from Camberwell because he'd gone and weaseled on an officer taking a few bob from a gas meter in an empty house. He went to East Dulwich, which was a mistake because it's on the same patch. I'm called over to the station and there he is on the floor, blood everywhere. I asked him what happened and he said he fell over. He'd learned his lesson.

Over the years we've all had to keep stumm.

What happened if you did not is told by one Police Constable:

I found a murder weapon, a knife, at a hospital. I called the CID, photographers, duty officer, all the correct people. And then a detective comes down. He was one of those officers who had an alcohol problem. He told me I'd have to change my notebook as to the time I found the knife. The reason was that two of his mates were meant to be on duty and they were on the piss in the police club. I said I couldn't change the notes and next day I reported it. The bloke was disciplined and thrown out. For the next five years the CID at that station wouldn't give me the time of day.

On 1 April 1992 PC Alec Mason was gaoled for thirty months for repeatedly stamping on the head of black motorist Harold Benn on 6 January 1990. Benn had first been breath-tested and when that had proved negative had been arrested on a suspicion (which proved to be unfounded) of driving a stolen car. Eventually Special Constable Georgina Christoforou reported the attack after the case was written up in *City Limits*. 'My decision was regarded by officers at Tooting as grassing. I was given the cold shoulder and have been transferred to another station.'[11]

PC Kevin Lucking, who was charged with falsifying notes and acquitted in the same case, also found he had problems with other officers. After the incident he was attacked and called for help. None came and he was badly beaten. He regarded it as paying the price for going along with the reporting of Mason. A

[11] *Sun*, 2 April 1992.

probationary Constable, Toby Fletcher, was acquitted of assault on Mason but convicted of perverting the course of justice by falsifying notes. He received four months.

Even if the officer merely wishes to distance himself from the group behaviour, it may be difficult. Mike McConville says, 'One officer found the others in his group behaving in an unpleasant manner on a daily basis and his attempt to deal with it was to distance himself from them. That resulted in him being assessed at the end of the year as being negative.'

The corrupting of officers can begin at an early stage. According to reports, two pilot induction schemes with trainee recruits in the Met went disastrously awry. In the first scheme in 1989 recruits were sent to a North London police station. When questioned on their return, they alleged that regular officers had torn up their warrant cards and one member of the group had been held down whilst older officers urinated on him. In the second pilot project in 1991 a trainee patrolling the streets with a senior officer was involved in an incident where the driver of a car drew a gun. Armed officers were called and it turned out that the gun was a replica. The trainee was instructed to lie about his part in the incident, apparently because there might be criticism from the court or exploitation might be made of the involvement of someone with so little experience. The trainee apparently agreed to go along with this because he felt his career would be damaged if he did not.

A senior officer at Hendon commented:

> These incidents are extremely worrying. They suggest that however good the practice and ethics we teach at Hendon, [recruits] may be extremely vulnerable once they come into contact with the service at large. They raise the possibility that we are replicating a cycle of abuse, in which those who start as victims, the abused, in turn copy this kind of behaviour and become abusers themselves.[12]

A study of the way in which recruits are 'socialized' into the police began in the autumn of 1991 at the University of Kent to discover whether there are common factors behind the recruits who are quickly corrupted within the police culture. A second

[12] *Observer*, 15 March 1992.

study was set up with the Evidence Project Implementation Committee (EPIC) looking into the problems faced by the probationer Constable.

McConville sees the process of induction as a speedy one:

> To some extent officers are quickly implicated into marginal or off the books or downright illegal practices. That process is a very important one in understanding how the police achieve solidarity of outlook. If one is attached to another officer or is present when an off the books transaction occurs, a failure to complain or seek corrective action necessarily implicates the officer in the wrongdoing. Not in the sense that they have an obligation but that the failure to complain is an indication that they are willing to access the mores of the group even when they involve illicit practices. It's not a question of major illegality occurring daily, rather it's borderline, trivial transactions, even anti-social behaviour – being rude or provoking civilians into aggression against them – as being a frequent occurence.
>
> In these circumstances a failure to say 'hang on a minute' is seen as condoning and being an active participant in what has occurred.[13]

Fear of the consequences of standing out against group behaviour keeps many officers silent. As C. H. Rolph says:

> So why didn't I, in my twenty-five years' police service, expose it all? Why did I keep quiet? Because I had a wife and family and because my job would have rapidly become untenable – all to no purpose. I would be disbelieved and repudiated by everyone. Many and many a time in the past forty years have I felt tempted to write the fatal article,

[13] McConville is confirming Chesshyre's earlier observations. Describing his time with some new recruits at Hendon he wrote, 'I met them again one night in their section house a few weeks after they had started at Streatham, and I sensed that the barriers were rapidly going up between them and the wider society. They were, one said, already picking up police expressions; a second added, "I prefer anyway sticking to people I know." At night they liked to switch off. "We earn our bread out on the streets," said one, meaning that they resented being asked to perform an off-duty peace-keeping role. They gravitated towards each other in a local pub, up to eighteen of them bunched round the same tables . . . Another shrugged, "There's scrotes everywhere." That was not a word he would have used two weeks earlier.'

which I could have published literally everywhere. I would have been its one and only effective victim.

Some authorities regard the grass-eater, and the man who has once turned his head, as their root problem. It becomes progressively more difficult to break the chain:

> Their great numbers tend to make corruption respectable. They also tend to encourage the code of silence that brands anyone who exposes corruption a traitor. At the time our investigation began any policeman violating the code did so at his own peril . . . The rookie who comes into the department is faced with the situation when it is easier for him to become corrupt than to remain honest.[14]

As officers and some researchers have discovered, acceptance by the group is essential if they are to survive. When Jeremy Gray was researching the *Police and People in London* for the Policy Studies Institute, he was subjected to a series of initiation ceremonies. A simple one was his ability to absorb the details of a violent death and still be able to eat, or at least watch his colleague eat, a bowl of spaghetti bolognese. More difficult was an evening's drinking coupled with trials of strength such as weightlifting and arm-wrestling:

> They were joined by a third PC and JG was taken drinking in a pub until closing time, then in a hotel bar and finally in two clubs, finishing at 6 am. Everyone became fairly drunk, but the police officers tried to remain slightly more sober than JG at all times and kept up a fairly continuous verbal attack. Steve repeated many times that JG could not be trusted, so that he had to keep trying to justify himself. When JG eventually showed some weakness, the PCs suddenly became sympathetic and friendly. They told their Inspector the story of the night out; one was quite remorseful, thinking he had gone too far, 'got out of order' and been too aggressive towards JG. The Inspector thought JG would now be fully accepted by the group, and he turned out to be right.[15]

[14] Knapp Commission, 1972.
[15] D. J. Smith and J. Gray, *Police and People in London*, IV, p. 75.

Later a Detective Sergeant said to him, 'You only get to know a man in drink', adding, 'Now we've had a few drinks I know how far I can trust you.'[16]

The Knapp Commission, which reported in 1972 following the discovery of yet another bout of wholesale police corruption in New York, underlined the sense of isolation and therefore solidarity felt by the police. At the same time it went a long way to destroying the rotten apple theory:

> Feelings of isolation and hostility are experienced by police-men not just in New York but everywhere. To understand these feelings one must appreciate an important charac-teristic of any metropolitan police department, namely an extremely intense group loyalty. When properly under-stood this group loyalty can be used in the fight against corruption. If misunderstood or ignored, it can undermine anti-corruption activities.
>
> Pressures that give rise to this group loyalty include the danger to which policemen are constantly exposed and the hostility they encounter from society at large. Everyone agrees that a policeman's life is a dangerous one, and that his safety, not to mention his life, can depend on his ability to rely on a fellow officer in a moment of crisis. It is less generally realized that the policeman works in a sea of hostility. This is true, not only in high crime areas, but throughout the city. Nobody, whether a burglar or a Sunday morning motorist, likes to have his activities interfered with. As a result, most citizens, at one time or another, regard the police with varying degress of hostility. The policeman feels and naturally often returns this hostility.
>
> Two principal charactistics emerge from this group loyalty: suspicion and hostility directed at any outside interference with the department, and an intense desire to be proud of the department. This mixture of hostility and pride has created what the Commission has found to be the most serious roadblock to a rational attack upon police corruption: a stubborn refusal at all levels of the department to acknowledge that a serious problem exists.

[16] Ibid., p. 83.

The interaction of stubbornness, hostility and pride has given rise to the so-called 'rottten apple' theory. According to this theory, which bordered on official department doctrine, any policeman found to be corrupt must promptly be denounced as a rotten apple in an otherwise clean barrel. It must never be admitted that his individual corruption may be symptomatic of underlying disease.

This doctrine bottomed on two basic premises: first, the morale of the department requires that there be no official recognition of corruption, even though practically all members of the department know it is in truth extensive; second, the department's public image and effectiveness require official denial of the truth.

One underlying factor that keeps being mentioned is the role of booze. From the first day the force marched out, alcohol has been a problem for the police. According to Smith and Gray:

In the case of the CID, it is an integral part of their working lives, whereas among uniform officers it is the focal point of the continued social life of the group outside working hours. A part of the explanation for this emphasis on drinking is that police officers use alcohol as a way of coping with the tension and stress associated with the job. (Both the long hours of boredom and the occasional excitement of police work are causes of stress.) Another part of the explanation is that drinking with members of the working group is charged with a special symbolic meaning for police officers, who need to find colleagues whom they feel they can trust.[17]

In *The English Police* Clive Emsley has documented a number of cases in different areas of the country in which police officers have been disciplined over their abuse of alcohol.[18] The cases start way back. The summer of 1888 was a bad one for George Biggs, a Constable in the Worcestershire Constabulary. He started off by being reduced to a second-class Constable for 'falsifying his duty journal and making untruthful statements to cover the small fault of having overslept himself, which

[17] Ibid., p. 81.
[18] C. Emsley, *The English Police*, p. 221.

he should have acknowledged at once instead of telling lies'. There was worse to come. Biggs had a drink problem and he was constantly on charges throughout the summer until at the end of September he was dismissed.[19]

Six months later Edward Hudspith resigned after having been seen 'asking people in the streets to give him drink and insulting them upon their refusal to do so'. The next year saw the downfall of Owen Thomas, again of the Worcestershire Constabulary. He was on duty at the Bath and West of England Society's Show at Battenhall, Worcester, when he was discovered pilfering the sandwiches and bottles of beer.[20]

And so on . . . In the 1950s and 1960s when the Murder Squad had finished discussing their cases on a Friday afternoon heavy drinking was common on the fifth floor at Scotland Yard. Occasionally drunken fighting would break out amongst these middle-aged king-pin detectives. By the late 1970s Smith and Gray found that the Friday drink was the thing for the CID, as were regular parties to celebrate such events as farewells for long-service officers. Also, they found, CID officers of all ranks often drank in the office, seemingly at all times.[21]

Says a senior managing clerk:

This was a murder and a very bad one – a security guard – and my junior clerk is sent down. He rings me at 4 pm and says 'I'm at Leman Street; it's hot in the kitchen and they won't let me near the front door. Can you pop over and see what you can do?'

As I went in, there was a most disagreeable atmosphere and then the DCI walks in with his hat on the side of his head.

'Hello, Sam boy,' he says, 'what you doing here?' and when I explained, he told the officers in the case to let my boy in. So then the DCI takes me up to his office and asks for two brandies. When an aide brings them he tells him to take them away and get a proper bottle. 'That's for visitors – bring my stuff,' he says and he pours them out. I was emptying half

[19] West Mercia PA Worcestershire Constabulary, Register and Record of Service 1877–83, no. 155.
[20] Ibid., no. 71.
[21] D. J. Smith and J. Gray, *Police and People in London*, IV, p. 82.

mine into the rubber plant; it was shameful really. He was legless by the time we finished chatting.[22]

A Police Constable described his time with the CID:

Lunch was at 11. You were still on duty The uniform could see this and they were resentful. This stopped four to five years ago but they still have a venue which might be, say, a golf club because a lot of them are keen on golf. It's best if it's on your district because there's a better chance of 'after hours' and if you're stopped for a drink drive on your area it'll be one of your uniforms. If you're off your area you'll have to pull strokes.

And then there is the question of racism. 'Is there racism in the police force?' asked Paul Williams and Christopher House in the *Sunday Telegraph*, a newspaper which can generally be relied on to be sympathetic towards the police.[23] They told the story of an officer who was initially required to resign, a punishment later commuted to a fine – 'a heavy sum usually associated with serious crimes such as a bad assault' – for telling two black children 'Fuck off, you black bastards.' There was no complaint by the children, who were either used to such conduct or following the precept that 'defiance on the part of a boy will lead to juvenile court quicker than anything else'.[24] Two friends and colleagues were so appalled that they took the most unusual step of reporting him, said the reporters.

The article went on to suggest that for several years the police service had stood accused of gross racial prejudice with little trial. Evidence, it suggested, had been largely anecdotal until the 'anti-police' riots rather than race riots of 1981 forced the police to acknowledge that, whether or not there was very serious prejudice, there was certainly a very serious breakdown in confidence between the police and ethnic minorities.

In 1979 officers in Brixton were banned from wearing what was considered a racist tie depicting five playing cards, all spades, topped by the Ace. The tie had first appeared in

[22] J. Morton, *Gangland*, p. 232.

[23] *Sunday Telegraph*, 4 November 1984.

[24] Nathan Goldman, *The Differential Selection of Juvenile Offenders for Court Appearances*, p. 106.

the mid-1970s and had the initials LDIVRS in the left top corner of the cards, standing for L Division Robbery Squad. The motif apparently represented a five card straight flush, the 10 through to the Ace, known in card games, said Scotland Yard encouragingly, as 'a fair deal for all'. Despite the ban, officers had been wearing the tie during deteriorating relations in Brixton, the inquiry into the Brixton riots was told.

Lord Scarman, heading that inquiry, had concluded that 'racial prejudice' was a contributory factor to the riots but had decided that there was no institutional racism in the police. The problem, he believed, was confined to a few officers. He admitted that their actions could do incalculable harm.

In fact, said Williams and House in their *Sunday Telegraph* article, the 1983 Policy Studies Institute provided the best unprejudiced account of police prejudice. The result of two years' research, it had found 'racialist language was prominent and pervasive and that many individual officers and also whole groups were preoccupied with ethnic differences'. However, it had also found that this attitude and speech had little impact on relations with the public on the street: 'their relations with black and brown people were often relaxed or friendly . . . the degree of tension . . . was much less than might have been expected.'

Indeed the report found that the police themselves exaggerated the hostility between themselves and the black community and a cultivated 'rhetoric of abuse' was not carried through into actions. In other words, continued Williams and House, 'the behaviour which nearly brought the career of one, unnamed London policeman to an untimely end is the exception, not the rule. And the language of racial prejudice – "sooties", "satchies", "coons" and "wogs" – is more a matter of fashion, part of the vernacular of police sub-culture, than evidence of intentioned, serious prejudice.' Not all would agree with what could be seen as a disingenuous assessment of things.

Two years earlier, at the beginning of 1982, John Fernandes, a black sociologist who had taught at Hendon Police Cadet School since the mid-1970s, had been asked to head a multicultural studies course in the wake of Lord Scarman's recommendation for improved race relations training. Accordingly he asked sixty-two of his students to write essays on blacks in Britain. When he disclosed the results, there was an outcry and allegations of loaded questions and suggestions that the responses were a joke or even perhaps that the papers produced were faked.

Following an internal inquiry doubts as to the authenticity of the essays were finally dispelled. Anonymity to the individual students, sixteen-year-olds straight from school, had been guaranteed. There were no names on the individual papers. One student wrote: 'Blacks in Britain are a pest. They never seem to work at a legal job (except as doctors) but seem to exist off sponging off the welfare state to which decent tax-paying, white, law-abiding citizens like myself contribute.' Another contributed: 'The black people in Britain claim they are British . . . This is just a load of junk . . . If the blacks were deported back to Africa or wherever they came from there would be less unemployment . . . Putting it bluntly: "Kick them out".' There were a dozen essays in similar terms. Almost half the students displayed dislike of black people in offensive terms and the other half were either neutral or positive.

Partly as a result, a human awareness course was taught, covering twenty per cent of the total of 700 lessons. Although only twenty lessons were devoted to race, they did include video reconstructions of racist incidents on which the class was invited to comment, as well as role-play games in which the weaker players could be pushed into a metaphorical corner and during which tempers ran high.

It was not only the cadets who displayed racist tendencies. A survey in the Chapeltown area of Leeds, where West Indians constitute the majority of the population, showed the need for the work being done at Hendon, wrote Peter Taylor:

> The police culture as a whole was fairly critical and unsympathetic towards minorities, particularly West Indians. This was illustrated in the language used to describe and refer to coloured people. Terms ranged from 'the coloureds' to 'our coloured brethren', 'bucks', 'coons' and 'niggers' . . . Officers claimed that, even though not personally prejudiced, they tended to adopt such language and the views it implied because this was one way to be part of the group. This language was therefore presented as being merely one way of emphasizing the group solidarity of the police force . . . Young officers are strongly under pressure to conform, and

thus may speak in racially prejudiced ways in order to feel accepted by their peers.

Taylor in a report for *Panorama* spoke with Les Curtis, chairman of the Police Federation which represents around 120,000 police officers. He asked whether an officer should be dismissed if he called someone 'a nigger':

He was astonished at the suggestion and said it was no different from someone being called a 'cockney' or an Australian using the word 'pommie'. It all depended on the *intent* with which the word was used. The same went for 'black bastard' too. 'It's a common phrase that is used throughout the land,' he said. 'And what about the colour nigger brown? Are we to change those sort of things?'[25]

And what is one to make of this passage written in the 'Policeman on the Dales' style by a retired Met offficer?

Grace, our Nigerian canteen lady, always entered whole-heartedly into the canteen high-jinks. She always was extremely noisy and, if irate, would chase us from the canteen wielding a large knife. I think that, without doubt, our moment of greatest triumph was when two officers from the newly formed Community Relations Department visited the nick. They called into the canteen, impeccably dressed in civilian clothes and bearing the statutory Scotland Yard briefcases. The canteen was fairly crowded and as I sat near the two men, whose sole function was to foster racial awareness in the force, I winked and nodded at Grace. Her large white teeth beamed from her black face. As the men sipped their teas and mumbled together, I suddenly stood up and shouted, 'You black cow, this grub is 'orrible, you'd better bugger off back to Nigeria where you belong.'

'Don't you call me a black cow, you honky bastard,' screamed Grace. She scrambled over the counter and headed hot-foot in my direction, her face contorted with rage.

There was a moment's stunned silence. The troops there,

25 P. Taylor, 'The police and racialism, *Listener*, 21 July 1983.

who knew just what was going to happen, sat still and waited. Grace was leaping about as though demented. We both shouted racial slogans at one another. The community relations men sat for a brief moment, unbelieving and horrified, cups poised. Then, as one, they raced for the canteen door, struggled a little as they became jammed together, and disappeared. Grace and I fell into each other's arms, helpless with laughter. Her eyes were shining, the tears clearly visible running down her cheeks.[26]

Relations between the black community and the police in Hackney had been poor for a generation. An independent inquiry held in 1985 was told of harassment, wrongful arrest, uncivil conduct during raids of people's homes, misuse of stop and search; in fact the whole spectrum of misconduct. Two years before, the local MP had called for a public inquiry into policing in Hackney. The independent inquiry was held following the death on 12 January 1983 of Colin Roach, a young man who blew his head off with an old shotgun in the foyer of Stoke Newington police station. He was not wanted at the time by the police. He had only two minor convictions. There was evidence that he feared 'someone' was out to get him and this was interpreted by part of the black community to mean the police. Relations were so bad that there was a section which genuinely believed that he had been shot by the police. Others believed that whilst the police generically might be capable of doing this, they would not be so foolish – unless this was the most amazing double-bluff – to do it literally on their own doorstep.[27]

The case was a good example of how the authorities mishandled matters. Demonstrations by the community were held throughout January and February, at the end of which the Commission for Racial Equality called for a public inquiry into the policing of Hackney. On 18 April Roach's inquest was opened at the small St Pancras Coroner's Court and was adjourned immediately. The community wanted a venue at

---

[26] D. Brady, *Yankee One and George*, p. 73.
[27] In 1978 in Los Angeles a police officer, Billy McIlvain, was found guilty of kidnapping a Mexican gang leader, taking him to his house and staging a phoney hostage situation until, in his 'escape', McIlvain killed the Mexican. McIlvain received life imprisonment and was released in 1992.

which a substantial number could attend. The coroner refused to change venues and an application was made to the High Court. It ruled that it had no actual power to compel a change of venue but recommended the coroner found one. On 17 June at the much larger Clerkenwell County Court the jury returned a verdict of suicide by an eight to two majority and three days later the jurors wrote to the Home Secretary criticizing the police in their handling of the case. On 12 February 1984 the *Mail on Sunday* announced that the police would not be disciplined and on 9 April the Police Complaints Board informed the juries that the police would not be disciplined. A year later the independent inquiry was launched by Colin Roach's family.

In 1984 there were 680 ethnic minority police officers, a total which had risen in 1985 to 761. By 1987, from a total of 121,500 officers, there were only 948 ethnic police officers in England and Wales. It was that year that a North-West London officer incurred the wrath of community workers. Superintendent Bill Ganley commented that ninety-nine per cent of muggers in Harlesden were black and their victims were split equally between white and Asians. Brent's race relations adviser, Russell Profit, said: 'These comments are most insensitive to the point of being inflammatory. They will only confirm in the minds of young people that the police see them as potential criminals rather than as individuals and that's extremely dangerous for race relations.' An unrepentant Ganley replied, 'I am sick and tired of people who are not involved in this who are trying to pussyfoot around. We have to tell people what the problems are.'[28]

In November 1991 PC Franklyn Asumah, an officer based with the Territorial Support Group at Barnes in West London, settled his claim that for four years he had been subjected to racial abuse; it was an out of court settlement for £20,000. He had alleged that six or seven officers from a total of twenty-two men in the group had been responsible for the abuse for a period of four years from 1987. 'This wasn't an isolated insult, it was a consistent pattern of offensive remarks. It represents a violent insult to the person,' said Michael Day, chairman of the Commission for Racial Equality. 'If the Metropolitan Police are

[28] *Daily Express*, 6 November 1987.

true to their commitment to erase racism from the force then we would expect those responsible to be disciplined.'[29]

But whatever the attitude urban police have towards the Afro-Caribbean community they have a long way to go before they can match that of the New York police, several thousand of whom marched on the City Hall chanting racist obscenities and carrying placards in September 1992. They were protesting against the black mayor, David Dinkins, who had antagonized them by promising an inquiry into the shooting of a Dominican immigrant with a drug conviction, as well as receiving the man's family at his official residence and paying for the body to be flown home. This was seen as 'soft' handling of a law and order issue. He had also promised that there would be a crack-down on brutality to ethnic minority suspects, a commission to investigate police corruption and a plan to introduce an all-civilian board to monitor complaints against the police. The police board received 11,000 complaints in 1990 and 1991 but only eight per cent were proved.[30]

Some see the attitude of the Met to racism as pervasive. 'It's like a golf club. You can join but the members don't seem to want to make you welcome,' said Chris Boothman of the Commission for Racial Equality. A provincial Inspector on secondment described how he 'was in a section house watching that programme about ethnic minority recruits *Black into Blue*. The attitude of the others was that they didn't see blacks as equals. They didn't want them in the force. There was a lovely girl, a scouse who didn't want to be seen as a Bounty Bar in Liverpool, a girl you'd like to bring home to your mother, but she was referred to as a spade by all the PCs there.'

But if the recruits did not understand the finer points of race relations it was hardly surprising. Their elders, seniors and betters were certainly quite capable of putting their big hooves in their mouths in an unguarded moment or two.[31] On 24 May 1984 Inspector Peter Johnson from Durham referred to coloured people as nig-nogs during a debate at the Police Federation conference in Scarborough. 'I was on a working party that was dealing with our coloured brethren, or nig-nogs', he began before he realized what he had said and sat down. Next

[29] *Daily Mail*, 14 November 1991.
[30] *Today*, 30 September 1992.
[31] *Guardian*, 24 May 1984.

day he was saying he did not know how this unfortunate slip of the tongue had occurred. After all he had lectured on racism, telling his recruits to avoid the words coons and niggers. The *Guardian* diarist was not impressed. He thought it was quite easy to understand how it had happened and he recounted a story of what happened at the hotel bar whilst in the company of Merseyside Police Federation delegates the next night: 'A hapless constable was informed over the tannoy his wife wanted to speak with him on the phone. "Your wife's run off with a nigger," cried a colleague. "That's the good news," riposted a colleague, "the bad news is he's a poor nigger."'

In fairness to the Inspector his seniors did not learn from his lesson. The Recorder of London, James Miskin QC, the senior Old Bailey judge, was guilty of a similar offence when speaking at the Worshipful Company of Arbitrators on 21 February 1989. He referred to a case in which a woman claimed she had been approached at a disco by a 'nig-nog' who 'touched her up'. He ended his speech with a comment about murderous Sikhs. Later Sir James apologized for a silly expression he regretted making.

Sometimes, though, it seems that whatever the police may do someone will find fault in their motives. The council-funded Lewisham Action on Policing, set up in 1984, produced a poster three years later urging blacks not to join the police because, it claimed, the police plan to use black recruits to murder other blacks. 'The state want black recruits to carry out police murders. Don't join the police . . . We all know why the authorities want black people in uniform. They think they can hide their racism behind a few black faces.'[32] The cartoon on the poster showed a black policeman shooting a black woman whilst a white officer looks on smugly. The poster seemed to have been specifically designed as a counter to an ethnic minority recruiting campaign which the police were trying to launch at the time. They had limited success. Only nineteen members of the public displayed an interest. Of that number, only six were black and only one black returned the form. As for the Lewisham Action poster, the matter was referred to the Attorney General with a view to a possible prosecution. None was mounted.

[32] *Sunday Times*, 3 May 1987.

When ethnic minority recruits did get on to a force they might have a hard time. A West Indian-born trainee officer resigned from the force and claimed constructive dismissal against West Yorkshire. Nicholas Booth, the first Afro-Caribbean police officer in Bradford, was given the name Toby after the slave in the television series *Roots*. He said that the buttons of his uniform had been sliced off and he had been called a black bastard. For the police, it was claimed that initially he had been rejected by the force because of poor spelling and co-ordination, and that in his probationary period he had made little progress.[33] 'This has to be the most racist, sexist job I've had in thirty years' occupation,' said a white Police Constable in 1992.

It can never be said the hierarchy does not try to instil some sense of comprehension into its force. The *Independent* reported that with 28,000 officers in the Met, of whom 3,758 are women and 570 are from ethnic minorities, a handbook, *Fair Treatment for All*, had been issued. 'Its aim is to tackle lack of knowledge and understanding about the capital's cultural diversity. Officers are to learn that words such as Doris to describe women and spade for black people are now totally unacceptable.'[34]

If ethnic minorities have had a bad time of it in the police, so have women. In 1967 Critchley described their history as a 'depressing one of apathy and prejudice'.[35] For many, it would seem that a quarter of a century later things have improved only marginally. The official line is that since the Sex Discrimination Act 1975 female police officers are treated exactly the same as their male colleagues; but exactly the same may mean different things in different circumstances. Whilst there may be no extra protection for them, so if a male officer goes out alone on foot patrol so will a female officer, all manner of restrictions and hindrances are placed in their way if they seek promotion. And apart from the difficulties they have faced in obtaining advancement in their careers, they have faced considerable problems in their day-to-day existence in what is regarded as the canteen culture.

Twenty-five years after Critchley's description McConville found women police officers undertaking menial tasks in order to

[33] *The Times*, 6 June 1987.
[34] *Independent*, 23 July 1992.
[35] T. A. Critchley, *A History of Police in England and Wales*, p. 215.

ingratiate themselves with individuals whom they saw as setting the standards of the group:

> When I asked why this had occurred, the closest I could get was that the police as a unit were extremely effective at undermining a person's self-esteem before reconstructing it on a group basis. Identity becomes welded into group values and outlooks. This occurs in a very short time on a force. This was very striking in probationary officers. They'd learned the ropes within a matter of weeks of induction.

The other view of policewomen was that of them as 'burglar's dogs' or 'Doreen' cartoon characters in police magazines. The winning entry in the 1979 *Police Review* Christmas card competition showed a large policewoman waiting outside a window holding a piece of mistletoe as the burglar climbed out. His miserable expression was not simply due to his impending arrest. Five years later *Police*, the rival trade magazine, had an eight-foot 'burglar's dog' policewoman towering over Arthur Scargill and lifting two officers off their feet. She was part of a line of officers in a confrontation with miners. The caption read 'Riot training for policewomen is all very well, but we've enough on our hands without having to watch over the weaker sex'.

Rather in the way that women lawyers have been cast in the so-called 'caring roles', doing juvenile, matrimonial and family work, there has been a tendency from the beginning for female officers to be left to deal with juveniles, family disputes and rape victims and to be the harbingers of bad news. Mrs Nott-Bower, the sister-in-law of the then City of London Commissioner, set out the ground rules in 1917:

> . . . the first point is the necessity of having a woman to take statements from women and girls with reference to sexual offences . . . There are other strong reasons for the appointment of women police in work outside the police court: Few people realize the scandalous indecency involved in sending young (male) officers to collect information in such cases as concealment of birth, or abortion, or cases that involve intimate personal investigation . . .
>
> At the present time there are certainly special reasons for desiring the immediate employment of women in the police

force, e.g. . . . the great increase of women workers, many far away from their homes, often obliged to be out late in the evenings, on account of their work or having no other possible time for fresh air, exercise or amusement. These often run into danger and not infrequently come to grief just for the want of the friendly help and counsel of a member of their own sex.[36]

In passing it is interesting to note that it took Roger Graef's documentary television series of the Thames Valley Police in the 1980s before allegations of rape began to be handled routinely by women officers.

The passing of the Sex Discrimination Act 1975 should have cleared away all the barriers which women in the police had to vault in order to compete on equal terms with their male colleagues. But the police, when they put their minds to it, can be as reactionary as the rest of us put together. For a start, a considerable number of Chief Constables, the Superintendents Association and the Police Federation, all called for exemption from the provisions of the Act. The theory may have changed; the practice remained much the same.

Efforts by women to move out of their allotted areas, from which promotion is not a strong prospect, into a position which, if not exactly in the spotlight, is where they have the chance to be observed, have been resisted on a number of grounds, some even more spurious than the others. In 1981 Joan Lock, herself an ex-policewoman, wrote that 'I think it's a shame . . . but the highest female rank in Lancashire Constabulary is chief inspector and she, I believe, is chiefly concerned with *welfare* matters.'[37]

In 1983 WPC Wendy de Launy had passed the necessary driving course to become part of a double-crew traffic patrol. She was then refused permission to share a patrol with a married male colleague. The reason given was that her Chief Superintendent believed the partnership between a married male officer and an attractive and intelligent WPC would create problems. He acknowledged he would not have had the same hesitation if she had looked 'like the back of a bus'. The

---

[36] Quoted in D. May, 'Paying the Price for Equality', *Police Review*, 12 May 1978.
[37] *Police Review*, 17 July 1981.

Equal Opportunities Commission commented, 'Her misfortune is to be both good looking and intelligent, a combination her employers don't seem to be able to contend with.'

It is interesting to note that her 'married male colleague' was subsequently disciplined for giving evidence to the tribunal without the formal approval of the force. This brought down the wrath of the *Guardian* on the head of the Met. The newspaper regarded it as unhealthy that the Met should decide on the right of a key witness to appear without their specific authority, particularly when the witness was to give evidence against their interests.[38]

Apart from sexism and harassment women in the police have always been subject to the quota system. In other words there can never be more than, say, one woman dog handler, or two in the CID, at any one time. WPC Joy Court received substantial compensation for sex discrimination from Derbyshire Police after her efforts to join the detective divison were blocked by a quota system. No more than two women were being allowed to work on any subdivision. Other women had complained but she was the only one prepared to go through with the action.[39]

The old attitude expressed by a senior officer at a CID conference in 1980 has never really died: 'There are three areas where policemen have trouble. They've always existed and I suppose they always will. They are firstly, policewomen; secondly, handling property; and lastly, dealing with children.'[40]

The best interpretation which may be placed on the attitude of some senior officers is misguided paternalism. Young quotes a 1979 memorandum regarding the proposed merger of the male and female police hostels: 'in this age of increasing promiscuity I would expect the divisional commander [in the area] to control the hostel tightly.' Having women in the force seemed generally to conjure up sexual fantasies – 'Our Chief wouldn't allow women in the mounted section because he was afraid there'd be frolicking in the hayloft,' said one now Chief Inspector on a provincial force.

The otherwise generally enlightened Sir Robert Mark also had some strange ideas about the desirability of putting young

[38] *Guardian*, 22 December 1983; *Sunday Times*, 18 December 1983.
[39] *The Times*, 8 April 1992.
[40] Quoted by Malcolm Young in *An Inside Job*, p. 246.

men and women in the same hostel together. This passage from his autobiography encompasses many of the traditional prejudices against female workers generally:

> About this time also I had given way to the blandishments of Henry Hunt, Assistant Commissioner (Personnel and Training), who had long wanted to introduce girls into our (cadet) corps. I was not easily persuaded because recruitment of women police was going well. They are an expensive investment, because, on average, they serve under four years before leaving, usually on marriage, and I was a bit worried at the prospect of 120 nubile young women at Hendon where the cadet school houses 500 young men, healthy, energetic and full of go. With a touch of the Valentines, I inquired acidly if Henry had provided for a professional abortionist to be assigned a police house at Hendon, or was it that recruiting was so bad that we now had to breed our own, as we had already attempted with horses and dogs? Henry bore all this with his usual good humour and was, of course, proved to be right . . . The amusing and encouraging effect, which we did not expect, was the noticeable improvement in the behaviour and manners of the boys. Incidentally, the girls consistently took the major share of academic prizes.[41]

At about the same period Ben Whitaker goes further in his condemnation:

> The restrictions – petty or otherwise – imposed on the off-duty private lives of policemen and women are unknown in virtually any other occupation . . . Policemen are expected to continue to observe a nineteenth-century moral code while daily being vividly aware of its rejection by the rest of society . . . In Portsmouth an unmarried policewoman was put on a charge for kissing a married colleague.[42]

Nor in the 1990s has the situation completely changed. A Roman Catholic policewoman was required by a senior police officer to prove she was practising birth control before he would

[41] R. Mark, *In the Office of Constable*, p. 219.
[42] B. Whitaker, *The Police in Society*, p. 221.

recommend her for CID duties, said Baden Skitt, Chief Constable of Hertfordshire, when he addressed a conference on Equal Opportunities at Bramshill. The Sergeant said that he could not support someone for CID work who could become pregnant and leave. This story had emerged, Skitt said, after a woman colleague held a straw poll amongst fourteen policewomen in his force to assess sexual harassment and discrimination; all fourteen said they had been discriminated against and thirteen said they had suffered harassment. Skitt also told of a WPC who, before she was allowed to join a motorcycle course, had to prove she could lift a 1,000cc machine from its side. No male officers were required to pass that test. A third instance was of a woman officer in the traffic division who applied to take a course for an HGV licence. She was refused several times and was finally told that women officers were not allocated to the course. She took the course privately and passed. She was then instructed to drive the trucks.[43]

The issue of the role of the woman police officer was never fully aired until the case of Alison Halford, who brought a claim against the Merseyside Police Authority over what she saw as a consistent refusal to appoint her to the shortlist of candidates for the position of Chief Constable in another force. It was an action in which the waters became so muddied that no party emerged with the credit or result they had set out to obtain. As with so many police stories – those of Stalker and Lundy are good recent examples – positions are so entrenched that once an attitude is struck for or against one of the protagonists there is little chance of obtaining an unbiased view.

Alison Halford served with the Metropolitan Police for twenty-three years until in 1983 she went to Merseyside as Assistant Chief Constable, a position which for senior officers is frequently regarded as a stepping stone to the rank of Chief Constable, almost invariably with another force. In the next seven years she was turned down for eight promotions and made the shortlist, which is approved by the Home Office, on only two occasions. When she failed to make the shortlist for promotion to Northamptonshire she contacted the Equal Opportunities Commission to assist her. Basically her case was that the three short-listed candidates, all male, had less

43 *The Times*, 25 March 1992.

experience than she did. From then on the dirt started to fly. For a start, a member of the Merseyside Police Authority said it was believed she was a lesbian and she should not have made the appointment to the force in the first place. There was no evidence to support this. Several weeks later she was suspended from duty after swimming in her underwear in a private swimming pool with a junior ranking officer. She had been the senior officer on duty at the time.

Writing of Alison Halford's infamous swim, the police observer and film-maker Roger Graef had this to say:

> [It seems] to reflect one of the three equally unsatisfactory choices open to a woman in the police. She can try to be 'one of the boys'; she can give in to the many sexual advances and be accepted though not respected, as a Martini ('any time, anywhere'); or she can refuse to conform to either stereotype and risk being called a lesbian. Whichever course she adopts she will still be just a 'plonk' in the canteen.[44]

'She was a very good officer ninety-five per cent of the time,' said Jim Sharples, Chief Constable of Merseyside and one of the prime targets of his assistant's complaints. 'It was the five per cent when she showed poor judgment that worried us.'

The voracious tabloid reader was treated to news of leaks from a file kept by the Chief Constable and then to reports from a newspaper that had followed the Assistant Chief Constable to Majorca where she was holidaying with her female housemate. Until the last decade the attitude of the police generally towards anyone suspected, rightly or wrongly, of being a lesbian has been a hostile one. For example, young women officers who have shared flats with their 'cousins' have had their relationship in both senses fully explored.

To the disappointment of many Miss Halford eventually settled her action on what were seen as somewhat unfavourable terms. She had undergone what would have seemed to be the worst part, her examination and cross-examination. She accepted a lump sum payment of £142,600, but not her costs, and an annual pension of more than £35,000, her basic entitlement.

[44] R. Graef in *Daily Telegraph*, 22 July 1992.

In 1991 there were sixty-two complaints to the Equal Opportunities Commission from women officers and Scotland Yard is now facing a string of actions for sexual discrimination. One senior officer responsible for improving the image has himself become the subject of allegations of sexual harassment. The complaints against him relate to a period when he was head of the police youth and community section in Hackney, based in Dalston. A Scotland Yard spokesperson said:

> As far as the officer is concerned, an allegation of sexual harassment is being investigated, although no officer has been suspended.
> The other actions, some of which date back for a considerable period, are not connected with that inquiry. Like any other large employer we do sometimes have allegations of discrimination, and they will all be dealt with through the proper channels.[45]

An Inspector on a provincial force gives this example:

> We had this woman who had seven years' service. She's not a girl to cause problems but she had problems with two officers. They referred to her as the section split arse, among other things. One of them just would not be told. She had a word with the Sergeant and then the DI and nothing happened. At her annual appraisal the Chief Inspector wrote three pages denigrating this woman. That bad appraisal was out of the ordinary. You don't get three pages, more like three lines. Later she made a claim against the officers for sexual harassment. She was moved sections and other officers were very supportive of her rather than of the men. 'I thought she'd got balls,' said one. Anyway she agreed to go to arbitration. She didn't want money, all she wanted was an apology and eventually the officer gave one.
> The only thing that stuck in my throat was that the actual incident had been six months before and she didn't make a formal complaint until after her bad appraisal. I wonder if she made the complaint because of the appraisal or because nothing was being done for her.

[45] *Evening Standard*, 26 October 1992.

Other officers might still see it differently. Says a Chief Inspector on a provincial force:

> Attitudes have changed and things are heading in the right direction but a lot of women maintain they've had a raw deal and I totally disagree. Those with any ability at all have always got on. A lot use the fact that they've been held back to cover their own shortcomings. At the moment a lot of women sergeants are worried about positive discrimination. They don't want to be pushed beyond their abilities.

In January 1993 the *Daily Telegraph* published the preliminary results of a confidential Home Office study of ten forces. The largest of its kind, it involved 1,800 women officers and recommended radical action to stem the problems of sexual harassment of which four out of five of the policewomen in the survey complained. More than 100 female officers had appealed to the pressure group WASH (Women against Sexual Harassment) in 1992, said the newspaper.[46]

One line of thinking is that with more women entering police forces – at just under 16,000 they comprise twelve per cent of the total force – they will both gain in strength and, being supposedly morally superior to their male colleagues, begin, by example, to impose a better course of conduct on them. A counter-argument is the feminist one that power corrupts, or indeed has already corrupted, and women should have nothing to do with it.[47] Moreover, some commentators are doubtful of the potential women have for good influence even if they care to use it. Defendants in the courts speak of women officers as being worse than their male colleagues in their behaviour. says Mike McConville: 'It will take a long time for that [changed behaviour] to occur, because women themselves are victims of the socialization process. In many ways they seek to replicate the characteristics their male colleagues appear to value.'

Rather less frequent than racial and sexual harassment is anti-semitism in the police. In February 1992 dog-handler Nigel Brown, an officer with thirteen years' service behind him, resigned saying that he feared someone would plant drugs on

[46] *Daily Telegraph*, 22 January 1993.
[47] F. Heidensohn, *Women in Control?*

him. He had been told by fellow officers that he would be 'fitted up' unless he quit the force. 'There are senior officers who do not like Jews, and I feel it is time to get out,' said PC Brown.

Brown had recently won his case allowing him the right not to work on Saturdays. He had joined the dog-handling unit in Hyde Park six years earlier and had arranged to switch shifts with another dog-handler so that he could observe the Jewish Sabbath. This had apparently worked well until a new Inspector took charge of the section and ordered PC Brown to stick to the rota which requires officers to work three Saturdays a month. After Brown had won his case, the Metropolitan Police issued an order permitting Jewish officers to have their Sabbath off.

A former Police Constable in the Met commented, 'I think he'd only himself to blame. If he couldn't do the shifts like anyone else then he shouldn't have turned Jewish. It's like those Sikhs and their turbans a bit ago. As for having something planted, I don't believe that. He might have had to endure a few jokes like having the top of his truncheon sawn off but that's all.'

According to an ex-PC, however, anti-semitism was certainly prevalent in his early years in the Blackpool force.

'I was going out with a girl and a senior officer asked if I realized she was Jewish. "I'm half-Jewish," I replied. "You'd never have got the job if we'd known."'

Finally there is the question of just what influence masonry, and for that matter, its lesser known Catholic counterparts such as the Knights of Columbus, has had on the police. Has masonry assisted or impeded promotions, protected criminals, thwarted inquiries? Should, as some say, police officers be banned from becoming masons? Should those serving officers who are masons be required to resign one role or the other? Is masonry, which has been one of the whipping boys of the last 200 and more years, really that influential on the police?

As with all well-organized secret and semi-secret societies, evidence of influence and statistics of membership are hard to come by. Evidence of membership particularly thirty years ago is anecdotal but Brian Hilliard, editor of *Police Review*, researching a book on the Flying Squad, says: 'If you wanted to get into the squad in the sixties you almost certainly had to be a mason whatever other qualities you had. I don't think I've spoken to a CID officer of the period who wasn't a mason.'

Evidence of influence regarding promotion is also anecdotal and can often be attributed to sour grapes. But, like justice being seen to be done is perhaps more important than it being done, so the perception of the influence of freemasonry is perhaps even more important than the actuality. A retired uniform Inspector with the Met recalls of the 1970s:

> In Buggins' way it was my turn to go up. I had the qualifications and the service. Then a younger man started saying openly he'd joined the masons, was attending lodge and so on. The Chief Superintendent was an open freemason. The younger man got the promotion. I put it to the Chief that there had been masonic influence and he replied, 'If you're promoted you won't go any further, but he's got the chance of two or three ranks.' I know that promotion was based on masonry but I can't prove it.

In 1983 Stephen Knight alleged in his book *The Brotherhood* that thirty-eight of the fifty-two police forces in England and Wales had Chief Constables who were masons. Six years later Martin Short in the follow-up, *Inside the Brotherhood*, estimated that twenty per cent of serving police officers were masons. In the intervening years there had been considerable sniping at masonry both from within and outside the force. A handbook for Met police recruits had this to say: 'The discerning officer will probably consider it wise to forgo the pleasure and social advantage in freemasonry so as to enjoy the unreserved regard of all around. One who is already a freemason would also be wise to consider whether he should continue as one.'

The anti-masonry camp had swollen in number principally through two causes. The first was a reaction to the membership of eight officers in the Waterways Lodge whose Master was the master criminal Lennie Gibson, who had been involved in what in 1980 was Britain's biggest robbery, the Essex silver bullion hijacking. Gibson remained a mason after his conviction. At the subsequent Old Bailey trial, police supergrass Mickey Gervaise told the court that freemasons in the police had warned their masonic colleagues of their imminent arrest. As for the officers in the Lodge, four retired from the force whilst Gibson was in prison and two more resigned when he reappeared following his conviction and ten-year sentence. Gibson was eventually expelled from the freemasons in 1989. The second cause was the growing belief that masonry provided another 'firm within a firm' and accordingly was not in keeping with the new, more open policies of the police.

Much of the anti-masonic feeling stemmed from the case of Chief Inspector Brian Woollard, either another of the victims of police bonding in general and freemasonry in particular or, as has often been portrayed by his opponents, an officer whose obsession has proved him to be unreliable. After serving in the Special Branch Woollard had been a detective in the CID with twenty-seven years' service when, in 1981 on a posting to the Fraud Squad as a Chief Inspector, he investigated a complaint which seemed to show deep-rooted masonic influences in the police. After a series of acrimonious discussions with his immediate superior he left the inquiry. Later it was decided there should be no prosecution.

Woollard had then been detailed to work on an allegation of corruption in Islington's works office. His inquiries suggested that there was a masonic link in the allocation of contracts by the authority. Woollard maintains that a very senior member of the staff of the DPP intervened and he was taken off the case. He claims initially that he was asked if he felt under strain and wished to be placed sick. His removal came when he said he wished to carry on. Woollard now believed that there was a masonic link between the man from the DPP and his own superior officers.

For the next decade Woollard conducted a campaign against masonic influence in the police, coupled with an effort to have his grievances remedied. He has had a conspicuous lack of success in the latter but he has conspicuously succeeded in making the public aware of masonry amongst the police.[48]

But, despite the recommendations of the former Commissioner, Sir Kenneth Newman, that officers should not join freemasonry, the Manor of St James', a Lodge formed in 1986 shortly after he made his suggestion, has flourished. Its membership was originally composed of officers, including a number of Commanders and Gilbert Kelland, Assistant Commissioner of Crime, who had served on C division which covered the West

---

[48] There is a very detailed account of Woollard's case in Martin Short's *Inside the Brotherhood*, chapter 12.

End. The name of the Lodge is a pun: manor is the police term for patch or area. This was seen by some as a two-fingered gesture in the overall direction of Sir Kenneth and Scotland Yard, but this was angrily denied in a letter by the Grand Secretary, M.B.S. Higham, who pointed out that plans for its inauguration had been made before the recommendations against freemasonry.[49]

[49] *Independent*, 22 February 1988. The letters column of that day's newspaper carried a letter from a West Country solicitor complaining of malign masonic influences in the law and police over a thirty-year period.

10

Dislike and Distrust

Is the present dislike of the police the fault of the press? After all, whenever there is an inquiry it is generally press-led and the more that appears in the papers the more mud is likely to stick.

In truth the police were not popular from the start. They may, as Critchley says, have been accepted but that is by no means the same as popular. They had, after all, been created to contain the working classes as Britain moved towards an industrial society. St James' was guarded by a watch on St Giles, then an area with a substantial criminal population, and the police certainly were not popular with the inhabitants of that particular rookery. There is also evidence that the middle class regarded them as a nuisance from the beginning and would sometimes urge their coachmen to horsewhip officers as they were trying to clear the way in the London streets. To the middle and upper classes the police were a form of servant, employed to keep the other servants in their place. By giving them some power and discretion, the working classes were required to control their own, often in enterprises which the police themselves favoured such as street bookmaking, on behalf of the middle and upper classes. It was a classic ploy of allowing rats and mice to play together in the cellar so that the gentry could remain undisturbed in the drawing-room upstairs. The rats never had a good relationshp with the mice, who regarded them with fear and hostility.

What turned the middle classes against the police was when they began to be involved with them on something other than a quasi master-servant relationship. It came about at the end of the nineteenth century with the introduction into society of the motor-car. Now, at last, the police had some power and discretion to use against their oppressors. For the first time the middle classes were meeting the police in situations where they could possibly be thought to be in the wrong, and they didn't like it one little bit. The police could have expected no sympathy from the working classes, their then social equals.

At first the police seem to have adopted a *laissez-faire* attitude to the regulation that cars had to be preceded by a man on foot and keep within a limit of four miles per hour. Vehicles were very rare and only owned by the exceedingly rich and powerful. It would be a very foolhardy constable who would go up against such a driver. But as the speed limit was gradually raised, first to ten, then twelve and finally, in 1903, to twenty miles an hour, so the police became more active. In 1901 the *Daily Mail* carried the headline 'Surrey police make war on automobiles'. It quoted the Chief Constable as saying 'I will stop them at any cost.' In their turn motorists complained that the police were not playing the game in a sportsmanlike way, by hiding in ditches or behind hedges.[1]

By 1905 there was something approaching guerrilla warfare, with the police prosecuting AA patrols who warned their members if they were approaching a speed trap. The offence was obstructing the police in the execution of their duties and even today the motorist who flashes his lights to another in warning is at risk. Back in 1905 the AA patrolman adopted the counter-tactic of failing to salute the AA badge-wearer. This was the signal that police were lurking in the vicinity. The struggle continued until 1913 when the police were instructed to construct a speed trap only if the high speed was dangerous.

In 1930, with the speed limit now at thirty miles an hour, it was recognized that antagonism between the police and the middle classes over the motor-car must be calmed and in due course parliament promised the public that there would be more efforts to deal with careless and dangerous driving, with a scheme to promote greater understanding. Introduced in

[1] For a history of relations between the police and the motorist, see *The Golden Milestone, Fifty years of the AA* by David Keir and Bryan Morgan.

1936, this became the so-called courtesy cops scheme for traffic patrol policemen, who operated principally in the North-west and in London and Essex. It lasted until the outbreak of war, after which, with the growth of the motor industry, relations between the police and the motorist grew ever more sour until one senior officer could say that juries refused to convict on police evidence because of their personal experience with the traffic police: 'There's some parts of London where the acquittal rate is so high it can't be true. Some jurors have a hatred of the police. They've had a traffic officer saying they were doing forty-five when they're convinced it was only thirty-five, and by acquitting a villain they've got one back on the police.'[2]

Part of this resentment comes from what the public sees as an 'us' and 'them' situation in which the police, with the assistance of the courts and the Crown Prosecution Service, have reversed the traditional roles. The police are now getting away with things and they, the motoring public, are not.

In 1989 a Chief Superintendent of the Cleveland Police was stopped when driving a two-litre Vauxhall Cavalier at 104 mph. He claimed he was testing it for his force and the local Crown Prosecution Service decided it would not be in the public interest to prosecute. Two years later, in October 1991, a South Wales Police officer was found not guilty of speeding despite having been caught in a speed trap doing 94 mph on the M4 near Swindon. He had been driving a Chief Superintendent and another officer to Twickenham to study crowd control at an England vs France rugby international and he feared he would be late. He based his defence on s87 of the Road Traffic Regulations which provides an exemption for officers and ambulance and fire engine drivers if the observance to the speed limit 'would be likely to hinder the use of the vehicle for the purpose for which it is being used on that occasion'. Under questioning PC Owen admitted that he and his passengers had not only stopped for a second cup of tea but had arrived at Twickenham ninety minutes before the match.

Perhaps it is possible to add that bench of magistrates to those who are unhesitating supporters of the police. Only a few years earlier the then chairman of the Magistrates' Association, Dr Douglas Acres, had said during a programme

2 *Police Review*, 7 February 1986.

on law and order made by Yorkshire Television that he and
the police were on the same side.

More seriously in 1959 an incident had occurred which
showed the extreme volatility of public opinion towards the
police. It was the Podola case. On 13 July German-born
small-time crook and blackmailer Gunther Podola shot and
killed Detective Sergeant Purdy at 105 Onslow Square in
Kensington. Earlier in the month Podola had broken into the
flat of a model, Mrs Verne Schiffman, and stolen jewellery and
some furs but, more importantly, some letters with which he
thought he might blackmail her. Using the name of Fisher and
saying he was a private detective, he telephoned Mrs Schiffman
inviting her to buy back the letters and some tape-recordings.
In turn she telephoned the police. When Podola next called
her, it was traced to a kiosk at South Kensington station.
Two police officers went to arrest him, called out 'OK lad,
we're the police' – at which Podola turned and ran. He was
chased into a block of flats where he was arrested. One of
the officers then went in search of other officers while Purdy
remained on guard.

For an instant Purdy turned away and Podola shot him at
point-blank range. He was chased by a second officer, John
Sandford, but escaped down Onslow Mews and made his way
to the Claremont House Hotel in Queen's Gate where he had a
room. On the afternoon of 16 July police officers broke open the
door of his room. Podola was knocked over a chair and landed
in the fireplace. Unconscious, he was taken to the police station
where he was examined by the divisional surgeon. Hours later,
he was sent to nearby St Stephen's Hospital, drifting in and out
of consciousness.

The public thought the worst. Questions were asked in the
House of Commons. Why, when he had been arrested at
4 pm, was he in the surgeon's room at the police station until
midnight? Jo Grimond, then leader of the Liberal Party, asked
for assurances that Podola had not been chained to a hospital
bed. The public was eager to believe that the police had exacted
retribution for the death of their colleague. A fund for DS
Purdy's widow dried up. A Stevenage solicitor, F. Morris
Williams, was instructed privately by 'a group of individual
private citizens who felt that Podola should be offered legal
help at the earliest opportunity'. Initially Williams was denied

access to Podola because his client was unconscious. Then after mutterings of complaint he was allowed full facilities.

According to Sir Frederick Lawton, Podola's counsel at the subsequent trial and later a Lord Justice of Appeal, some thirty police surrounded the hotel. Twenty minutes after they had entered it they left, and Podola, whom they had arrested, was 'trundled along, boots off, sack over his head, a large policeman on either side'. In the hotel, it was stated, a good deal of blood had been shed. 'Two pillow cases were deeply stained with blood. A coverlet was stained and there was enough blood apparently to seep through on to a mattress and congeal. There was blood spattered on his trousers.'

Three days later in parliament, Lord Stoneham asked the government to:

> institute an inquiry into the circumstances under which Gunther Fritz Podola, who was apparently uninjured when arrested on July 16th, sustained such injuries that, when he appeared at West London Court on July 29th his face was severely contused, with the cheek blackened and with deep purple patches tinged with red for two inches below the eye, and his general condition such that he had to be held up when seated and when walking supported by two officers, dragged his feet slowly.

The Lord Chancellor replied that the Home Secretary denied categorically that Podola had been beaten up in the police station. The case being *sub judice*, he declined to say anything more.

According to the police, when they arrested Podola they rushed suddenly into the room, knowing him to be armed. Podola was hit by the joint impact of a sixteen-and-a-half-stone policeman and the door, and was knocked flying head-first into the fireplace. In hospital it was thought that he had suffered brain damage and that his cerebral injuries could have been caused by a blow from a fist.[3]

Podola's defence was amnesia. If he genuinely could not remember, he could not give instructions to his lawyers and he could not plead guilty or not guilty, so could not be hanged.

[3] C. Franklin, *The Third Degree*, pp. 100–2.

A jury was empanelled to determine whether he was 'fit and sane for trial'. After hearing four doctors for the defence who thought he was genuinely suffering and two for the prosecution who thought that he was faking, and a retirement of three and a half hours, the jury found against Podola. His counsel, Sir Frederick Lawton, was convinced that his client was not faking. Describing this and the incident when the door was broken down, he said:

> It was a fascinating case. It started off with misinformation in the press, because after the the police broke into the room Podola was occupying in Queen's Gate, Kensington, he was carried out on a stretcher. He had to be taken to hospital and was for some time unconscious. The press inferred that he had been struck by the police. He hadn't been. What had happened was that a very large policeman had put his shoulder to the door at the very moment when Podola went to unlatch it.[4]

At the trial proper the defence was at pains to stress that it accepted the medical evidence that Podola had bent down at the exact moment the door was broken down. There was no suggestion of police brutality. The public, however, was not convinced. Anthony Judge, later the editor of *Police*, wrote in his book, *A Man Apart*, 'He had to say it so as not to get the jury's back up.'

The jury this time retired for only thirty-seven minutes. Podola was hanged at Wandsworth Prison on 5 November 1959. 'I have often thought that if the Podola affair had been handled according to the Trenchard maxim [which was embodied in the words "tell the truth – immediately"] things would have been different,' said the former Assistant Commissioner, Sir Ronald Howe. As it was, a great part of the British public could not get from their minds the belief that retribution on a substantial scale had been exacted by the police.

In 1960 C. H. Rolph still found the press bureau at Scotland Yard lacking. It had been established in the early 1930s and had almost immediately received a stinging rebuke by Mr Justice Rigbey Swift at the Old Bailey: 'There has been some mention

---

[4] *New Law Journal*, 30 January 1987.

in this case of a so-called press bureau at Scotland Yard. I do not know what this purports to do, but I have not heard of it before and I do not wish to hear of it again. It sounds to be a most improper idea.' Now Rolph wrote, 'Many a police scandal could be put into perspective today by a machinery for issuing authentic statements to the press and radio in refutation of whipped-up stories like the one about Podola's black eye.'[5]

Many years later a curious letter from David Wells, one of the officers involved in the arrest of Podola, appeared in *Police Review* following an article on the case in January 1987:

> I was present at Podola's arrest (outside the hotel) when Tom Morrisey and Bill Chambers with Mr Vibart arrested Podola. I saw Podola in the station and sat in his cell. Until he saw his solicitor he was absolutely normal in every way. I leave you to draw your own conclusions as to why he suddenly developed amnesia after several hours of normality.

Another reason for the unpopularity of the police in 1959 was possibly the Homicide Act itself. The history of the death penalty in Britain over the years has been a long and troubled one. By the 1950s the death penalty had once been suspended and was now in use in strictly limited circumstances. These included the killing of a policeman. There were two parallel cases in 1959, both involving killings at or near a dance-hall. In one a Terence Cooney had killed another youth and had received life imprisonment. In the second Ronald Marwood had stabbed a police officer who had gone to break up a gang fight outside a dance hall in Islington. 'Why should Marwood die but not Cooney?' asked Charles Curran in the *Empire News*:

> For respect for the police is like respect for the law. Both of them depend ultimately upon public opinion. Without that both of them must fall into disrepute.
>
> Therefore we must get rid of the Homicide Act – because public opinion holds that it is unjust, unfair and conferring a privilege that ought not to exist.
>
> Until we do that we shall see the tide of resentment against the police go on rising in this country.

[5] C. H. Rolph, *The Police and the Public*, p. 192.

Under its pressure more and more citizens will tend to look suspiciously, critically, with hostile eyes, at everything the police do.

Curran's views were expressed in a longer article which quoted Commissioner Sir Joseph Simpson's annual report, saying there was a recession in public respect for the police and the citizen's willingness to cooperate with them.[6]

Perhaps a reason for this is simply that the public recalls the names of the murderers rather than the victims. In the earlier part of his letter, David Wells asked, 'Why, oh why, are cases always known by the murderers and the victims so quickly forgotten?' The names of police killers Bentley, Podola, and Marwood stayed in the public memory far longer than the names of the officers who were killed by them. A great percentage of the present population was not born when in August 1966 Harry Roberts killed three officers, DS Christopher Head, DC David Wombwell and PC David Fox, in Braybrook Street near Wormwood Scrubs to avoid his arrest for being in possession of a stolen car. The names of the officers who were ruthlessly shot down are not known to most of the public but Roberts' name lives on as a heading in books on crime and criminals.

Somehow the police have not been able to keep their triumphs in the public eye as long as their detractors have managed to do with their faults. The police have not, however, been helped by a series of clear miscarriages of justice over the century which have taken years to unravel. The list of cases stretches back to Adolph Beck and Oscar Slater; since the war, Timothy Evans, James Hanratty, Maxwell Confait (one of the few cases known by the name of the victim) and, in Scotland, Patrick Meehan; and in recent years a whole heap: the Birmingham Six, the Maguires, the Guildford Four, Judith Ward, and the non-political but still useful sticks with which to beat the police – the West Midlands cases, Laslo Virag and Stefan Kisko. In some of these cases the errors of the police have been compounded by those of lawyers and the courts but in the public's eye it was not the lawyers who made a mess of things but the police. The 'lilac establishment' – anti-hanging, anti-imprisonment, anti-police – have been much

6 *Empire News*, 26 July 1959.

more vociferous, have had more charismatic proponents and have, often on a much smaller budget, been much more powerful than the police champions.

Resentment has also been built on small, seemingly insignificant things as well as on cases such as that of Marwood. Examples of the former include the watching of clubs for after-hours drinking, often incurring very substantial police expenses in so doing. On 6 September 1955 a case of serving drinks after hours allegedly to Police Inspector Norman Fairman, who had been in the the Stork Club, a fashionable nightclub in Piccadilly, and had run up £86 in two visits, was stopped by Sir Lawrence Dunne, the Bow Street Chief Magistrate.

'The first time the police visited us the bill included seven double gins, a half bottle of German hock, a half bottle of champagne, and several brandies. There was also two complete dinners. The first around midnight was lamb chop. The second at three in the morning was steak, I believe. It was the biggest sum of money spent by one man for some time. The average customer spends £2.10s. in one evening. That gives him a nice meal and a couple of drinks and with luck includes the tip,' said manager William Zygmunt Ofner who had been charged with selling drinks after hours.

The case was stopped after the Inspector had said that he had bought a bottle of champagne but this had not been on the bill. Sir Lawrence said there may be some explanation of this and he was not suggesting the Inspector was lying. A spokesman for the Metropolitan Police said: 'People may feel that nearly £100 spent in one night at a club is a terrible waste of public money. Perhaps it is. But we must carry out our duties and work to the law.'

Here, in the public's view, is the police officer in the role of spoilsport. This is victimless crime which, apparently, the police cannot even manage to supervise properly. Hundreds of pounds in cash and police time are wasted to no real use, runs the argument. Why aren't they out on the streets catching murderers and rapists?

Some years ago there was a sketch on the television programme *That Was the Week that Was* which typified the British attitude towards social status. Three men of greatly varying height went through a routine of 'I am better than he is, but not as good as he is, 'I look down on him but up to him' etc. Because of their origins in the dangerous classes themselves, the police have ranked low in the pecking order of British society. There have been a great number of people to whom they have been required to look up; perhaps, indeed, their deference – the 'Sir' and 'Madam' – is required to the whole population. In consequence, they have developed an attitude towards other groups who command even less status and on whom they can impose their will without interference. For many years this attitude has been accepted and indeed encouraged by society as a whole.

Robert Reiner in *The Politics of the Police* wrote of seven groups of people who could either damage an officer or be damaged by him. What he called 'police property' – known by the police as 'slags' – encompasses a wide and changing group which has been defined elsewhere as a category in which 'the dominant powers of society leave the problems of social control of that category to the police'.[7] Generally, this category includes, in strictly alphabetical order and not exclusively, alcoholics, drug addicts, ethnic minorities, immigrants, the mentally disturbed and prostitutes. Traditionally, society overall has not been particularly interested in monitoring how these groups are managed. Consequently they have been, and still are, subject to harassment, brutality, incivility and a general abuse of power. The language the police use to describe some of the members of these inferior groups – scrotes, prigs who live in 'African villages', scumbags, toe-rags, as well as terms of racial abuse – is indicative of their attitudes.

Prostitutes, for example, are vulnerable on a number of counts. Free sex is one. Nina Lopez-Jones, of the organization, the English Collective of Prostitutes, says:

Prostitute women have to give free sexual services. In one case reported to us recently a prostitute woman has alleged an assault. The DPP has refused to prosecute and the woman is trying to proceed on her own. One of the officers in the case

[7] J. A. Lee, 'Some Structural Aspects of Police Deviance in relations with Minority Groups', in C. Shearing (ed), *Organisational Police Deviance* pp. 53–4.

is sympathetic but now she has told us that his sympathy is because he is getting free sexual service from her.

Historically, prostitutes have also been subject to arrest, forming targets for an easy conviction or a corrupt payment. In the last decade or so, however, they have begun to stand up for themselves, discomforting the police as they do so. In 1982 prostitutes and other women in the King's Cross area occupied the local Holy Cross Church as a protest against police racism and harassment. This section of 'police property' began to fight back and make its position better known. Says Nina Lopez-Jones:

> The police were arresting prostitute women who were known to them but who were not working at the time. We started a legal service in 1982 and the women from Argyle Square used the service. They routinely pleaded guilty. They felt there was no point in fighting. If you appear in the same court after you have had thirty convictions, what chance do you have of getting a fair trial if you plead not guilty? The evidence is they have seen you speak to a guy in a white car. Who is to prove it? It is the word of a 'common prostitute' against the word of a policeman. Magistrates will believe the police more than a jury would and there is no right to jury trial. After a while they [the magistrates] know you.
>
> But once we started the legal service a number of women began to plead not guilty. Then the police started to interfere with the evidence. For example, a woman who had witnessed the false arrest of a friend was giving evidence. Her son lived with her mother. The police went to see her mother and threatened to put the boy in care. They also threatened to arrest the girl's boyfriend as her pimp.
>
> But real pimps were not arrested. During the occupation some pimps were keeping an eye on the church. Why not arrest them? We felt the police and pimps had a shared interest in keeping the women under their control. The police say it is very difficult to prove people are pimps. If women complain about threats, the police say, 'Come back if knee caps are broken.' But when they want to arrest the girls' boyfriends or husbands they have no problem. This is true all over England.

The police will do little or nothing about prostitute women who are raped or assaulted. We have had one complaint from a woman who was assaulted by a client, that she was arrested for loitering and soliciting when she reported it to the police. The man was never arrested.

Now it is going on with condoms. They say they don't search women in the street for condoms but they do search. If you have one or more, you are more likely to be arrested. We are campaigning to get the police to stop this but we have not succeeded yet. They often single out black women for arrest, and lean on the white women to get them to scab on the black women.

They used to park outside our Women's Centre to arrest women who worked in Argyle Square as they left the Centre. That was to prevent them getting their legal rights. We had to get solicitors to come down and escort women away.

One of the problems is that you don't have the right to a jury trial so you are stuck in the magistrates' court.

In recent years the homeless and dispossessed have become another group who, without clout, are subject to the whims and pressures of the police. In 1992 Sat Singh conducted research at an Oxfordshire police station. He says:

The homeless constantly become targets of police coercion. They are viewed as 'toe-rags', 'losers' and 'social security scroungers'. Granting them rights was seen to be laughable because they did not deserve them. I was told that it was outrageous that money had to be spent on feeding them and getting them a doctor.

One man was arrested for sleeping on a park bench. When I suggested to the sergeant [the custody officer] that this was perhaps rather unfair, he replied that it was totally justified: . . . 'he's more than just a blot on the landscape, he's taking up a park bench where members of the public may want to sit . . . Would you want to walk through the park with your wife and kids with the likes of him around?'

Nor has the police attitude towards gays and lesbians been a notedly sympathetic one. The days of illegal homosexuality, when some police officers may have used homosexuals for financial gain, are gone but attitudes change slowly. The staff officer of GALOP, the Gay London Policing Group, says:

> I've been here two and a half years When I joined we weren't speaking to the Met at all. Now things are much better.
>
> Lower down the ranks there is such a wide range of reaction to GALOP which now has a respectable profile. In one case we had a potential murder inquiry in Battersea. There were eyewitnesses not willing to go to the police but who were prepared to talk to GALOP. I contacted the CID at Battersea and suggested we met. The officer in charge of the case ignored my calls for two weeks. He just didn't return them. When at last I did speak to him, telling him I had potential witnesses for him, he said, 'Don't you start telling me how to do my job. I don't want to waste my time with a gay investigating group.'
>
> That's how things can go wrong. There were some threats by me to go public and the matter was then dealt with by a superintendent. The officer in the case retired through ill health. They still feel they have the right to say, 'Fuck off, you disgust me.'
>
> They routinely fabricate evidence. Often when people are caught doing something they will fabricate the evidence to have them doing something else to fit the picture the magistrates expect. People who ring us say I was doing this but the police have added this, that and the other.
>
> I had one case where the allegation was that a man was leaning under the partition wanking off a man sitting on the toilet bowl. When the solicitor for the defence went down to take pictures of the scene he found the man would have had to have a four-foot-long arm or the other one a four-foot-long penis.
>
> At last there does now seem to be less patience even amongst magistrates for this kind of evidence.

The Wages Due Lesbians group confirms the fears of the gay community:

> We find that police don't take violence against gay men and lesbian women seriously. They won't follow up complaints. As a result many of us are put off making genuine complaints.

We also fear we will face violence and even rape from officers. We are targeted because we are independent of men and so are usually poor. We are more likely to find ourselves in hostile situations with the police when we are working as prostitute women or are homeless.

One of the group's *causes célèbres* was the case of PC Swindell who had been on duty as a uniform police officer at Downing Street. He had developed a fetish for bondage coupled with a passion for recording the events. He had graduated from tasteful pictures of young ladies tied up rather prettily around their wrists with pink ribbon to heavy bondage. Finally he had been involved in the death of an eighteen-stone lesbian prostitute who appears to have suffocated in a mask and chains in Swindell's flat. The body was kept by Swindell for some time and eventually dumped by him in Epping Forest, where it was found some time later. He was charged with murder. This was reduced to manslaughter, of which he was convicted. The Court of Appeal quashed the conviction and substituted a conviction of preventing a proper burial. If an eighteen-stone lesbian prostitute had been involved in the death of an officer in similar circumstances would the result have been the same? the group ask rhetorically.

'If you report an attack they'll say, "What does your kind expect?" If you're black or an immigrant into the bargain, then that's double or triple the way they discriminate against you.' In 1989 Nigerian-born Adebola Makanjuola was awarded £8,000 in compensation. She had alleged that a police officer had required her to have sexual relations with him in default of which he would ensure her deportation. PC Sean McCarthy had called at the victim's flat looking for another person. He had then taken the opportunity to deceive Ms Adebola and her boyfriend over their immigration status. McCarthy was never prosecuted and was only dismissed from the police after a hearing instigated by the Police Complaints Authority. Awarding the damages, Mr Justice Henry said that McCarthy had used 'the shadow of his warrant card and the strength of the law for his squalid purposes'.

Members of some of these groups have begun to stand up and fight for themselves. Over the last twenty years there has been a proliferation of support groups for these minority interests and they have achieved considerable publicity for their activities. For example, the English Collective of Prostitutes and it sister group, Women Against Rape, have been notably active. Apart from the occupation of the Holy Cross Church by prostitute women and their supporters, the groups have regularly campaigned against sexual harassment by the police. In 1990 they achieved notoriety when they invaded the Court of Appeal. Lord Justice Tasker Watkins had enraged them when he had allowed an appeal by a PC Anderson who had been convicted of raping a single parent black woman, ruling the case unsafe and unsatisfactory. The Court had ruled that in the summing up insufficient emphasis had been placed on the officer's good character by the trial judge. In another case later that year an officer convicted of raping a woman in a police cell was also cleared by the Court of Appeal, which ruled that the jury had been misled by 'inconsistent and contradictory' evidence.

The women protested that they were not receiving protection from the very people to whom they looked for help. In a survey conducted in 1985 ten women out of 445 who reported being sexually attacked said their assailant was a police officer.

Ethnic minority groups, whose members have suffered at the hands of the police for many years, have started to fight back, often literally. It is, for example, almost inconceivable that if Colin Roach had died in a police station in the early 1960s the community would have banded together to protest as it did and ultimately, when the authorities refused to call a public inquiry, set up its own independent one.

A Chief Inspector on a provincial force who had been seconded to the Met said:

What struck me most forcibly was their use of silly expressions in unguarded moments: 'Doggie-woggie', 'gyppo' and so on. It's very rare in the provinces. If someone does come out with something insensitive they're pulled up by saying, 'You can't say that.' It's almost a catchphrase. If you go to the Met they talk openly about wogs, spades, and expect you not to take offence. They see it as the norm.

The beginning of the 1980s saw a watershed in – some would say disintegration of – police and community relations. The rioting for three nights in Brixton between 10 and 12 April 1981 prompted an immediate inquiry conducted by Lord Scarman. The Brixton riots were followed by further major disorder in Southall, and in areas of the West Midlands, Manchester and Liverpool. The fabric of some of the cities, let alone the breakdown in relations, has yet to be repaired.

One brick in the rebuilding of the emotional fabric was the establishment of the Police Complaints Authority, designed to reform the system of handling complaints against the police. Yet at first it would seem from the statistics of the PCA that racism is not a substantial problem. In 1991, the first year they began to keep statistics about the number of complaints involving racially discriminatory behaviour, only forty-nine were recorded countrywide. Perhaps the reason is that in not even one of the cases were disciplinary charges preferred. All were rejected because of a conflict of, or insufficient, evidence. Complainants simply do not bother in these or many other cases. A London solicitor says:

> You need a good witness, preferably seven, preferably sober and certainly without a criminal record.
>
> Take one case I was involved in. There were three chaps going home. One of them is very merry and a police officer stops him. The third of them is wise and goes home. By the time he's just about indoors, one of the two who stayed behind are in a conflab with the police and an officer has been hurt. Another posse come round to his house. He's in his dressing-gown. No trousers, nothing. 'You're coming down to the nick.' This is on the basis that there has been a fight and the police are not sure who was there. Once the youth is in the van he's punched and kicked. Fortunately for him he'd been seen by neighbours uninjured before the police arrived.
>
> You couldn't even say he'd done anything to warrant it. A police officer had been hurt and the other officers were rowing around for a culprit. It is almost a blueprint for someone being hit.
>
> At the end of a car chase the driver is going to end up being smacked. He doesn't have a prayer. What jury is going to believe him or even be sympathetic?
>
> It goes on a lot because the boys at the sharp end catching

thieves tend to be the young ones. The majority of complaints are against officers aged up to twenty-three who are rarely accompanied by a sergeant.

Another area in which the police have received a bad press over the last two decades has been their handling of demonstrations. Our middle-class grandparents did not demonstrate, our middle-class parents did and it brought them into conflict with the police, which would permanently sour their relations. It is a far cry since those heady days of 1968 when Tony Judge, quoting an Inspector, wrote after the demonstration at the American Embassy that 'we were everyone's friends'. Were they? There is plenty of evidence of brutality in the earlier Ban the Bomb demonstrations.

Lord Kilbracken is quoted as saying of a demonstration in Trafalgar Square:

> I saw a woman in her forties being dragged face downwards by one leg through deep puddles of water at the double from one end of the Square to the other, and then left lying against a wall. Then I saw a group of constables carrying three demonstrators, two of them women, and throw them into the deep water surrounding one of the fountains.[8]

The first demonstration in which a demonstrator was killed came in 1967 in an anti-Vietnam War rally in Red Lion Square, London, not far from what was Coldbath Fields. On 23 April 1979 a demonstrator against a meeting in Southall of the National Front, Blair Peach, was killed, almost certainly by a blow from a police officer. Despite lengthy inquiries no officer was ever charged. Says a London solicitor, 'He was a bit of detritus in the way as they went to cut off the troops. I don't believe any one person could have beaten him to death.'

As the years have passed more and more people who would not normally come into adverse contact with the police have believed that they, or their colleagues, or their children were or would be roughly treated. And, it has to be admitted, the police have not sometimes been helped by the presence of professional strikers, the so-called 'rent-a-mob'. Nor have they been helped

[8] Quoted by Charles Franklin in *The Third Degree*, p. 114.

by the presence of television at the demonstrations and pickets, which has often shown them apparently as the aggressors.

Other kinds of media have also played their part in forming public perceptions of the police. Why are detective stories so fascinating? asked Sir John Woodcock, Chief Inspector of Constabulary, in a speech to the International Police Conference held in London in October 1992:

> There are two reasons, both of considerable significance to the nature of police work and the way in which nature helps or hinders the search for truth.
>
> The first is the connection between normal life and brutal violence; there seems to be a vicarious pleasure in reading about dangers which might, but only just might, touch the life of an ordinary reader. The second is that detective stories happen in an ambience of moral uncertainty; the criminal and the detective appear in a world in which right and wrong are not clear-cut. Tricks and deceptions are used by the detective to catch the murderer, always aided, of course, by the novelist's convenient ability to make the villain leave a vital clue. As readers we are all persuaded, by the high moral end of achieving justice, to overlook the occasional lapse from grace by the detective in the means employed to reach that end.
>
> These two features of detective fiction shed considerable light on the nature of policing. I believe that an everyday proximity to the effects of violence and an everyday experience of competing moral imperatives have a corrosive effect on policing culture, which tends to make officers uninterested in the fine details of procedure.

Later in the speech he addressed the specific problem of perjury. First he quoted the Raymond Chandler novel *The Long Good-bye* in which Philip Marlowe is maltreated by two police officers:

> He points out to them that what they are doing is against the rules. The big fat detective in charge points out to him 'Listen, buddy, there ain't a police force in the world that works within the law book.' That is not true only of America and only in fiction: it has been historically true in Britain.

I see the young men and women who join the police service. Invariably they join out of a sense of idealism, to serve their society. I find it very unlikely that many individuals specifically join so that they can give perjured evidence against fellow citizens and send them to prison.

I don't believe in bad apples. I think that the problem is not one of individual predisposition to wrong doing but of structural – or cultural – failure.

The bad apple theory is convenient but:

How can it be that a guy in his late teens, early 20s will be applying to join the Met Police, will have been vetted for personal character, gone through selection process and then five, ten, fifteen years later some incident comes to the attention of the authorities. He is investigated and comes out of the police force by one end or another and the guy is branded as a bent copper. Now how is it we start off with this rosy-cheeked innocent guy at the outset and he finishes up in that situation? You get comments from senior officers such as 'You'll always get the rotten apple in the barrel' but I would put it this way. You had a perfectly sound apple that was put into a barrel and contracted something.

A former Detective Constable agrees:

I don't think it's that way from the start. It has to be peer influence . . . because that is the way he is going to be accepted, to be considered to be one of them. He might wish to go further and do better than his peers in certain circumstances. Almost every copper that I met in the CID would give a nodding consent to things they knew were going on at their police station, were quite willing to share in the proceeds of any scam that was taking place even if they weren't actively taking part in it. It's much more extensive than the general public would think.

I can say with confidence it had been going on for generations before I learned bit by bit. It's not all shoved at you in a volume: here it is, read it overnight. You just acquire the knowledge as you go along.

Over the years the image of the police has been changed for us by literature, by the cinema and particularly by television. Once, when Mudie's Select and Boots lending libraries were in existence, all literary policemen were courteous, kind to their neighbours and dogs. They may not always have been as bright as the amateur sleuths who solved the crimes but they were always helpful to old ladies crossing a busy road. Now, we would not be surprised if fictional police officers were to help old ladies only halfway across a busy road.

The police officers in Boots and Mudie fiction stemmed from the characters created by Charles Dickens and Wilkie Collins. Dickens, in his police-admiring articles in *Household Words*, did much to popularize them. His Inspector Bucket of the Detective, as he announced himself in *Bleak House*, was modelled on Inspector Field, including that officer's habit of stabbing a fat forefinger out whilst making his points. Wilkie Collins' Sergeant Cuff was modelled on Jonathan Whicher. He had an attribute which must have appealed to his readership – his steely-grey eyes had an unnerving ability 'of looking as if they expected something more from you than you were aware of yourself'. He was also attracted to the rose garden: 'I haven't much time to be fond of anything. But when I have a moment's fondness to bestow, the roses get it.' And there you have it – the world-worn detective in whose hands your safety lies has sacrificed both romance and a settled family for your protection. How could you do less than trust not only him but every detective who ever lived? Particularly if you were in a class of person who was either just learning the benefits of literacy and believed what you saw in print or were an admiring Victorian spinster who probably wished to rescue Cuff from his loneliness which was much the same as your own.

Across the Channel where French detective literature was initially more robust, Gaboriou's astute Lecoq was modelled on Vidocq, one-time thief and one-time head of the Sûreté in Paris. Lecoq, according to *L'Affaire Lerouge*, had had some trouble with the law before he became a police officer. Later his troubles are explained away as a misunderstanding.

From the 1850s there was a steady stream of reminiscences by Scotland Yard officers, then, even more than now, ghosted by hack writers. They purported to be genuine but, at best, there was a great deal of fiction inserted into the pages. In

Recollections of a Detective Police Officer, Detective Waters, the hero, has a wife and daughter who help him solve his cases. Twelve years later *Autobiography of a London Detective*, also by William Russell, has a hero, Henry Clarke, who acknowledges the class structure of Victorian society and the subservient role in which the police officer was placed. In the book he falls in love with Lady Charlotte and believes she returns his affection. She may do but her brothers recognize the real position. One of them is overheard by Clarke as he expresses the hope that the officer was 'not going to make an egregious donkey of himself about Charlotte'.

The one occasion in the police fiction of the time when an officer goes bent is in Israel Zangwill's *The Big Bow Mystery*, a short story written for a newspaper in a fortnight and perhaps showing it. In it a detective cuts the throat of a fellow lodger in a classic 'locked-room' mystery. In fact he is a retired officer who has done this as a means of exposing the inadequacies of Scotland Yard, something over which they triumph. We need not worry. Here indeed is the bad apple, the rogue cop who has been brought to book by those who are there to protect us.

Throughout the so-called golden age of the detective story, deemed to be the 1930s, the reader still had nothing to fear except a certain ineptitude from the police officers. Solving when a crime took place depended, as Raymond Chandler pointed out in *The Simple Art of Murder*, upon the time the butler potted the prize-winning tea-rose begonia or the ingenue flattened on the top note in the 'Bell Song' from *Lakme*. But when there was a fault in the Scotland Yard investigative system there was always Lord Peter Wimsey to sort things out. Meanwhile Scotland Yard had its own hero, Nigel Alleyn – the creation of Ngaio Marsh – well connected, artistic, handsome, to protect our parents from evil-doers who, it seems, were still bent on disposing of boring and argumentative relations in the most complicated way they could devise.

Meanwhile it was still always muffin time at Scotland Yard. This idyllic state of affairs continued well after the war. Even in the so-called tough novels of Peter Cheyney, Gringall, the detective who is the foil to the ace detective, Slim Callaghan, contentedly smokes his pipe and draws pictures of fruit on his blotting paper as the latter unpicks Gringall's carefully constructed case involving yet another will. The prolific writer

John Creasey, writing as J.J. Marric, created a pioneering police procedural series, *Gideon of the Yard*, featuring Commander George Gideon. With, as Julian Symons says, 'very slight attention to sex and his total avoidance of cruelty',[10] the series was enormously popular. Similarly Dell Shannon, in reality Elizabeth Linington, created a series based on the Los Angeles police and a second about Glendale officers.

It was probably Graham Greene who first created a contemporary police officer with family troubles and associated failings with Scobie in *The Heart of the Matter* (1948) but that was in West Africa and so perhaps Scobie, blackmailed because of an association with a young girl, does not count. In *The Police Family* the Niederhoffers have compiled a list of officers with family problems and the price their investigations, and often they themselves, have paid. Of Wambaugh's *The Choirboys* they write: 'The roll call includes alcoholics, sadists, neurotics, deviates and suicides. Their grim marital statistics toll a dirge of repeated divorces and misery.'[11] Gradually we learned that police work had its own pressures and that the Gideons of this world were just a figment of the writer's imagination and, like the retelling of a child's favourite nursery tale, repetition of what we wished to be told.

Innocence was lost, not across the Channel where Maigret kept the peace, but in the United States. It was there we first learned of corrupt policemen and politicians and of tough heroes like Sam Spade and Philip Marlowe who would regard a false arrest by, or a beating from, the cops as all in a day's work. We also learned of the appalling behaviour of the Los Angeles police as portrayed by Joseph Wambaugh and confirmed to us by film clips of the Rodney King case, in which officers seemed to beat a helpless man. Gradually we came to expect such behaviour not only from the bigoted red-necked Southern Baptist officer or drunken girl-chasing Californian policeman but from our own.

The seminal writer who shattered our innocence was G. E. Newman with his *Sir, You Bastard* trilogy of the late-1960s. The novels, which recounted the tale of a corrupt CID officer, always one step ahead of the investigation branch, were roundly

[10] Julian Symons, *Bloody Murder*, p. 205
[11] A. and E. Niederhoffer, *The Police Family*, p. 33. Wambaugh has always maintained that this comic novel is the truest he has ever written.

condemned by the police as inaccurate. Those involved in the law but with less of an axe to grind were amazed at just how accurate they were. 'It was as if everything one's client told one was confirmed,' said one admiring barrister.

Newman's writing had the power to shock and offend. The accuracy of *Sir, You Bastard* and its brothers is now accepted but in late 1992 a television play by Newman in which officers conspired to murder a drug dealer and then had him cremated was met with further howls of disapproval and shouts of inaccuracy. Only time will tell whether Newman, who maintained he obtained his material from interviews with officers, remains one step ahead of the game. Those who doubt his accuracy may care to ponder the following comments by a senior officer from the 1970s:

We had a phone tap going targetting S who was a kind of Mr Big and on it we heard S speaking to a DCS telling him to have a third man X taken out. And by taken out that meant have him killed. S was running this DCS. I went to see a Commander and the matter was reported to the Home Secretary. Eventually there was a compromise. Another officer nicked X saying his papers weren't in order.

But it is through television and the cinema that the changing status of the police officer from that of hero to anti-hero has most clearly reflected the perception of the public. Until the 1940s there was no suggestion on screen that a police officer could be anything but upright. A sheriff in a western perhaps, but that was a representation of history. Television provided a regular diet of courteous hardworking police typified by Jack Webb as Sergeant Friday in *Dragnet*, based on the Los Angeles Police – the wrong suspect before the commercial break, the right one afterwards. In Britain *Dixon of Dock Green*, with George Dixon miraculously restored to life, was happy undemanding Saturday evening entertainment.

Gradually we were weaned from this never-never land where the problem for so long was who stole the marrow which would surely have won first prize at the village fête. *Z-Cars*, the series on Merseyside Police, became popular, followed by the tougher *Softly Softly* and the much more menacing *The*

Sweeney. Perhaps one can trace the ascent of 'realism' in a television series to the October 1968 episode in *Softly Softly* when a Detective Constable beats up a disturbed man who had taken the Constable's daughter for a ride in his car and left her unharmed but badly frightened on a common. Here was an instance of retribution. There was not likely to be any punishment for the offence and so the Constable took matters into his own hands. His actions were approved by his colleagues and he was merely reprimanded by his superior officers.

In the cinema the cracks appeared with such films as *The Asphalt Jungle* and *The Killing*. But this was America. We still had Jack Hawkins of the Yard and Edgar Lustgarten explaining how the Great Potato Marketing Board Fraud had been painstakingly solved. The first we knew of English police corruption on the screen was *The Strange Affair*, a fairly thinly veiled version of the Challenor case. By the time Clint Eastwood's *Dirty Harry* appeared, the floodgates had been opened on both sides of the Atlantic. In the second film, *Magnum Force*, Dirty Harry is obliged to deal with rogue cops who have taken matters into their own hands because the courts cannot deal properly with gangsters. Now, there is seemingly little point in portraying a police officer who acts within what would be regarded as normal police procedure.

Despite the popularity of the Inspector Morse series, the public has been trained by books, films and television into accepting financial corruption and brutality as part of the necessities of police life. As a result our perception of the police has been diminished. And the public has been deprived of its police heroes. There may be the obligatory picture in the newspapers of a wounded officer giving a thumbs up from his or her hospital bed, of a Commissioner sitting with his arm around the patient, but these are not lasting heroes or heroines. Perhaps there never were any except in our imagination but Scotland Yard did its best to cultivate the police star, from Dew, who arrested Crippen, through Greeno, Sharp, Fabian, who had a television series, to du Rose and ending with Tommy Butler and Nipper Read. Indeed the concept of the 'star' was deliberately killed off by the senior police hierarchy after the Great Train Robbery and the Kray case.

Now it is the force as epitomized by the Chief Constable. 'Sharp PR departments promote the image of the force and that of some Chief Constables who are as well known as Wogan.'[12] But they are administrators not crime solvers, which is what we want from our officers.

And solve crime is seemingly not what officers do. When our houses are burgled we expect, but rarely get, a swift response. In fact unless there is an informer or fingerprints match, there is little the police can do, but this negative contact diminishes our respect for and attitude to them.

[12] J. Stalker, *Stalker*, p. 12

11

Where Do We Go from Here?

What then are the motivations for deviance? Bent for oneself is easy. Bent for the job rather less so; and perhaps one cannot be bent for the job without being also bent for oneself – if not in the sense of immediate illicit financial reward then, because of one's arrest and conviction rate, in the sense of the increased rank, pay, status, pension and post-service appointment which will go hand in hand with the successful thief-taker. As has been seen, there is also the possibility of a share in the now considerable reward money which is on offer.

But sociologists and criminologists, let alone historians, would suggest that things are not so simply explained. Police culture has to be set against the tradition of corruption in British life. At the time the police were formed there was corruption in dockyards and with victuallers over supplies for the Napoleonic Wars. There were governors of West Indian islands who, aware of the health hazards, never left the United Kingdom but sent deputies. A lieutenant in Nelson's navy was expected to bribe officials or nothing would be done. There were false musters: a captain would enter the son of a friend or the son of a lord on the books, giving him seatime whilst he was in nappies, so that as soon as he was eighteen he was a lieutenant and at twenty-one a captain. It was against this background, let alone that of the corrupt magistracy and the Runners who earned far more than the new Police Constable, that the New Police, many of whom came from the army and navy, was formed.

Many would argue that it is the occupational culture of policing which condones the bending of the rules and which leads to certain kinds of corruption. Why is this? In the first place, it is suggested that it is the nature of the job itself, the objective of which, despite fine words, posters and campaigns, has in reality for many officers long since ceased to be effective crime prevention and is instead crime detection. And that is what the officer really wants. Says a former Detective Chief Inspector:

> Today we see about seventy-five per cent are uniform officers with about twenty-five per cent CID for all categories of crime work. Far too many uniform officers are employed in unproductive work. We now have a host of special units dealing with non-police work, e.g. juvenile bureaux, domestic disputes, firearms training, race relations, community relations, the so-called crime prevention units, local authority units, liaison with gay and lesbian groups, taxi driver licensing, firearms certificates, admin units, etc. etc. etc. ad nauseam. I believe more police are engaged off the streets than on the streets for crime prevention activities. Therefore the Met has lost sight of its original object, hence deviance in this respect. It is an unwieldy set-up limping along from crisis to crisis, headless and without real direction.

In McConville's study of community policing he found that amongst many officers there was a remarkable lack of enthusiasm for being a community officer. As a result it was the misfit, the older officers approaching retirement, and the women who became community officers instead of 'real' policemen. The street is where the excitement, one of the perks of the job, lies. What many see as real police work includes the thrill of danger. In December 1992 PC Leslie Harrison of the Merseyside force was stabbed in the heart. It was the fourth time she had been injured but, according to newspaper reports, despite pleas by her former policeman boyfriend and one of her parents, she wanted to continue. The possibility of serious injury promotes a high degree of solidarity within the work group – as it does, for example, among firemen and National Hunt jockeys where there is a similar high risk of injury – and encourages bonding.

In turn the bonding can lead to the inclination to cover up. 'Straight' detectives may well know of incidents of dishonesty or violence but because of the close links they have with the offending officer they are less likely to peach on him than people faced with dishonesty in other occupations. In, say, the management of a supermarket there is a positive incentive for a superior to report a colleague or manager who has his sticky fingers in the till or on the shelves.

One view of policing as an activity is that officers have had an extremely difficult task imposed on them by society which has then, by setting arbitrary rules, made it almost impossible to achieve. This encourages recipes for getting the work done in spite of the regulations and constraints besetting them – the old 'Ways and Means Act'. Another argument is that the high degree of solidarity and secrecy which surrounds the occupation makes for ideal conditions to develop short cuts over a period of time.

One major problem is the difficulty of effective front line policing. By the nature of the structure of the organization the top ranks cannot be there when important things are happening and it is hard to effect change if supervisors are not present on the front line. Supervision is difficult when seniors have to rely on written reports. This is something recognized by today's young officers. Says a Police Constable: 'It's only business management above a certain rank. I think you should have a businessman in charge for Chief Superintendent and above. They aren't real policemen anymore. Chief Superintendents could move across. It's paperwork after that.'

Today there are street cops and management cops and although the latter were once on the street themselves they forget – or it is perceived they do – what it was like. Senior officers are divided by the street cop into the butterflies who flit around for promotion and those who will get stuck in. The latter may be inclined to condone rule-bending because they are rooted firmly in the culture of the lower ranks, which makes them liked by the street cop. As a result there is a gulf and consequent antagonism between the groups. Says Mike McConville:

> Senior officers are regarded in such a poor light because they are seen to be involved in betraying the true values of policing and instead to be marketing an untrue but acceptable image of policing in order to satisfy middle-class concerns. They [the canteen officers] see press handouts as telling a lie about what it really means to be a police officer. So far as they are concerned

there are no champions of policing, only apologists.

Another problem facing the senior officer in trying to eradicate corruption is that it is highly likely that he has experienced it at first hand himself in his younger days. Then he may have either participated or, more probably, turned a blind eye. Now he may be at the mercy of his former colleagues. If he leans on them too heavily they have the perfect response and he, because of his higher rank, has more to lose. They may be able to cut a plea bargain by naming him. He may not have a higher-ranking officer to name.

Boiled down, there would seem to be three sociological explanations for police deviance. The first, the sub-culture theory, is that propounded by writers such as Reiner, Punch and Holdaway. A sub-culture is a group inside the host culture. That it has different values from the host group is evident through their expression in deviant behaviour. The sub-culture theory was first used by A. K. Cohen in his study of youth gangs in Chicago but it is easy enough to apply it to the police. For example, some of the 'true' police values are discipline, law, order, integrity, social harmony; the values of the sub-culture or canteen culture are drinking, whoring, excitement, fighting, racism and so on.

The second explanation is that policing is full of strain and contradiction. The police are set very difficult goals to achieve and as a result there is either a ritualistic 'going through the motions' or, because of the constraints and hurdles, a bending of the rules as the only way to achieve the end results; when the rules are changed, then new methods of adapting to them are found. The argument is that, in certain given circumstances, people may either drop out or find new goals. 'I would say we manipulate it [PACE] in a way that doesn't affect it so much. It's about the same. You've got the restraints but you've got the good bits, bad bits; it's about the same I would say. But most police officers adapt it in such a way that it stays the same as it was for us.'[1] Robert Merton's extension of this theory of *anomie* does not apply solely to police officers.[2]

[1] Quoted in M. McConville, *The Case for the Prosecution*, p. 189.
[2] R. K. Merton, 'Anomie and Deviant Behaviour', *Social Theory and Social Structure*. The theory of *anomie* was originally developed by Emile Durkheim in his work *Suicide*, published in 1897. It referred to a situation where there are no social norms to ensure order or where the norms conflict with each other and so social regulation and structure break down, for example after a natural disaster such as an earthquake or war.

The third explanation is the control theory. Policing is inherently very difficult to control. A principal problem is that of providing supervision. Police officers commonly find themselves on their own with a suspect or a member of the public and in this situation they have power, discretion and no supervision, a combination of circumstances which promotes rule bending. Walter Easey, a former officer in the Hong Kong Anti-Corruption Squad, feels that 'opportunities for corruption are greater in policing than in any other work, and this is because of the discretion which is exercised in the public interest; the officer can take action or not, he may make further inquiries or not. There is no sensible way of reviewing this discretion, but it has the potential for corruption.'

A police constable on a provincial force talks of his exercising of discretion with motorists stopped for speeding: 'Attitude, that's what I want. If there's a difference between a summons or an on-the-spot fine, then it's the attitude of the person that's going to count.'[3]

Management, of what are deemed to be punishment centre bureaucracies, is not seen until, in police parlance, the wheel comes off. To avoid punishment, tracks must be covered. This story was told by a Chief Inspector on a provincial force:

We had a PC on the shoplifting squad. He was processing three cases a day. Real hard worker, honest as the day is long. He had some juveniles to be cautioned and he took the kids home, interviewed their parents and wrote it up so they'd get a caution. The third kid's parents were out and so he wrote it up as though he'd interviewed a grandparent. This was corroborated by a policewoman. The notice goes out to the parents to bring the kid in for a caution and the balloon goes up. The PC got nine months.

Now this was a case where he should have been cautioned. He was working without supervision. If he'd had a sergeant in charge of him he'd have had a bollocking and that would have been that.

---

[3] Since the introduction of unit fines by the Criminal Justice Act 1991 the difference between a summons and an on-the-spot fine of £40 can run into several hundred pounds. The opportunity for the officer to use his discretion unfairly is considerable. It is also a new opportunity for corrupt behaviour.

Running parallel with these explanations is the public's attitude (as opposed to respect, *the attitude* to which the Police Constable was referring earlier). A typical police view is that the public does not much care about procedure provided results are achieved and provided that lapses in principle do not become scandals. Until then the police may effectively play by themselves. It is a similar attitude to that towards prison conditions – 'Well, they're only criminals, so why should we worry how they're treated?' Prisoners are, after all, people who haven't earned themselves a particular position of privilege in society.

A further argument is that society doesn't mind too much who gets punished provided somebody does. The rules of conduct are thus reaffirmed and symbolically the job is done. This is the due process model of law and order proposed by the American sociologist, Herbert Packer. However, if too many wrong people are processed and enough fuss is made about it, then in turn it undermines and threatens the state. A counter to this may be seen in certain comments made by the police in relation to well-publicized cases where convictions have been quashed. A whispering campaign goes on to the effect that, whilst there may have been (something which is not admitted anyway) malpractice in relation to obtaining the evidence which led to the conviction, the right people were in the dock. It has been the fault of others, e.g. lawyers, judges, juries, that (a) convictions were obtained and (b) they were subsequently overturned, so leaving the population once more at the mercy of these violent and dangerous people.

Indeed the police are adroit at counter-attack. If your property is stolen or you are assaulted whilst out walking, well then you haven't exercised enough care: your home should have been triple, not merely double locked; no sensible female should walk home alone down that path at night. If the police succeed in instilling this sort of fear, then their achievements in solving crime seem so much the greater. Now that the mystery masked rapist is locked up on remand we may sleep safely in our beds once more. Provided that a gang of burglars has been smashed by the vigilance and ability of the police, we may again leave our windows open on a summer's night. In some ways the police cannot lose. We are made to feel responsible by them for other people's crimes. At the same time we feel anxiety until someone, preferably but not necessarily the correct person, is apprehended, when we can then feel gratitude. And in this behaviour we actively connive with police deviance.

But leaving aside the theory, what in practice can be done? The first point is that we must no longer sit back and allow ourselves to be manipulated so that we do not care who is arrested and convicted provided somebody is (and not of course us). In turning a blind eye when rules are bent to secure a conviction, whether the real criminal suffers the abuse or someone else, we allow corruption to continue.

Former Detective Chief Superintendent John Simmonds, in a paper on corruption delivered to officers in Europe, suggested that it occurred for six reasons: frustration, greed, temptation, coercion, loyalty to colleagues and a mistake in the first instance, requiring criminal acts to cover it. He also suggested the way to recognize it and the way to eradicate it. As with all good schemes his suggestions were simple. It is how they are to be executed that is the problem.

Frustration occurs particularly in the bent for the job syndrome: what officers are doing is for the public good – a view which has been expressed time and again by officers in these pages. Simmonds gives an example of an officer who has to attend court, where he considers an offender is dealt with too leniently. The result is that when an offender is next arrested the frustrated officer exacts a penalty from him which is greater than the court would impose; perhaps he gives him a beating as a punishment. The result is mutually beneficial. The officer has obtained satisfaction and the criminal does not have a further conviction to his name. If caught, the officer will suggest that society has in no way suffered by his actions. Another occasion for frustration is when the officer cannot get a conviction against a defendant whom he 'knows' to be guilty. He may then either manufacture a conviction or – in pre-PACE days – beat the defendant into a confession. An officer on a provincial force remembers:

The very first interview where I was present, I'd been on less than a week and I'd locked someone up. The Duty Crime Control officer came into the cell and said to the man, 'You done this.' He said, 'I haven't.' The officer said, 'You fucking have' and hit him straight in the face. The kid said 'All right, I have' and sat down and made a full and frank admission.

Again if the officer is ever caught he will claim it was for the benefit of society.

Greed is simply bent for self. An expensive girlfriend, a marriage on the rocks, children being educated privately, a mortgage which needs repaying, negative equity in a house, are just some of the reasons why an honest officer may become a corrupt one with or without advice from a more experienced officer. To cure this there has to be adequate, effective supervision. Watch must be kept for those who have high lifestyles or appear to have personal problems. Set against this is the officers' fears that the hint of a failure to cope with a broken marriage, a drinking problem, will destroy their careers. In McConville's research for *Watching Communities, Watching Police*, he encountered officers who said the last thing they would do in their annual assessment would be to disclose a problem. The incentive is to privatize. 'I don't think we found an officer who said the police system would allow him to betray personal weaknesses of any kind.'

Simmonds' next category is temptation: the chance of making a little extra money by not handing in a wallet intact, accepting a small bribe from a criminal, taking goods from an already burgled shop. He again argues that the only way to counter this is supervision.

Coercion, the fourth reason, is, he suggests, the most insidious form of police corruption:

Officers are placed in a position whereby they are suborned by others into corrupt practices. Often there is a basic test to establish the 'strength' of the individual to find out how far he will go. If the individual shows strong character the matter will be laughed off and the core of corrupt officers will be made aware of the individual's position so that they keep clear of him whenever they are embarked upon any shady deals. If he does not react, then after passing the 'initiation' test, further bait is laid down so that he is entrapped. Even though the individual will never be on the insider track he will be used to act as a buffer in the event of any major inquiry and threatened that if the inner track people go down he will also go. Consequently the entrapped officer

will cover up for his corrupt colleagues in order to save his
own neck.

Says Mike McConville, 'When an officer is caught out and
there is nothing which other officers can easily do to rescue
that officer, he will be sacrificed. Everyone knows this. In such
situations if senior officers are not seen to be supporting the
malfeasant officer this is seen as another reason for solidarity
in the ranks as their only protection.'

Coupled with coercion is misguided loyalty and Simmonds
argues that the only way to deal with this is an education process
showing that loyalty should be to the service and the public, and
not to a black sheep. Finally there is the mistake that then has
to be covered up. An early example was the 'refused charge'.
Officers will go to great and often improper lengths to show that
they were right in the first place. Again Simmonds suggests that
education and understanding will minimize this particular form
of corruption.

Mutually advantageous corruption can only exist in a corrupt
culture where the chances of detection are very slight, which
makes police culture potentially an ideal one for corruption to
flourish. The nature of a corrupt act is, from the police point
of view, that it is secretive, of mutual benefit and without a
witness. The deal with a crooked cop and a gangster is one
of mutual support. Both parties are happy. Discovery occurs
for two reasons. First it may emerge incidentally in a quite
different inquiry and secondly, thieves fall out and spill the
beans. Usually the corrupt officer wants too much and the
criminal perceives the scales as balanced too heavily against
his interest: 'At the finish all you was doing was working
for the police to give them the lion's share of what you
was getting.'[4] A slight variation on this is that the criminal
asks for help, can't get it, believes his protector has let him
down and so betrays the police officer to improve his own
condition.

Legal 'reform' is often nothing more than the legitimation of
police practice. Moreover, this has frequently taken place on
the basis that to do otherwise would result in the continuation

---

[4] *Economist*, 7 August 1972.

of illegal police behaviour. Police collaboration in writing up notebooks was made a special exception to the general rule of evidence that witnesses must act independently because, the judges said, the police would otherwise continue to collaborate and then give perjured testimony denying this. Similarly, police were given search powers of a wide nature because the judges acknowledged that the police had assumed these anyway and were likely to continue illegal practices.[5]

> The key to police morality is public respect. If policemen believe they are damned stereotypically, they have little incentive to behave properly – one may as well be hung for a sheep as a goat. Public expectations of police impropriety act not as an impediment to such behaviour but as an excuse for it.[6]

This, of course, reflects a wider corruption culture. In places in the Third World ordinary citizens expect to pay a bribe. If they go out to buy a licence which costs a few pesos or rupees they expect to pay a few on top. On their side officials have low salaries and an expectation of implementing them. This is not the case in countries where there is no corruption culture. Within the corruption culture say in Hong Kong or the Third World, when you are going for a favour you have your money with you. You have already formed the intention. The officer also has the expectation. This was the perceived behaviour in the $5 in the driving licence and in Read's story of the housebreaker, Raymond Jones.

But some officers see any minor misbehaviour as for the good of society generally. A Detective Constable commented of officers' views of themselves in the 1970s:

> Did these guys think they were doing the right thing or did they think they were totally disregarding their function and were out there doing their own thing? I believe that both in that area of how cases were brought to court and in the area of copping [corruption] they rather saw themselves as privateers like Drake and Raleigh. Queen Elizabeth the

[5] M. McConville et al., *The Case for the Prosecution*, p. 178.
[6] C. Taylor, *Forces of Order*, p. 76.

First, she wants her enemies weakened. Given the amount of finance officially, these guys could only do it by making it a self-financing operation and I think that in many cases officers out of their own pockets would spend a great deal of money with no chance of claiming it back.

It had to be funded and in those days policemen's wages wasn't sufficient to fund crime investigation. Police have always been underfunded and the guys, OK, would see themselves as Drake and Raleigh, Drake anyway, as privateers fighting the Queen's enemies. The Queen couldn't afford to pay them adequately and in order to set to sea and pay their crew, provision their ships, they would concentrate on bullion ships from the Spanish fleet. So in a way, as far as corruption goes, let's not see it as this guy wants to finish with a ten-bedroom house in Hertfordshire. Many of the so-called corrupt officers, when people looked into them, their assets wouldn't support an argument they were corrupt. But also if one looked in the back of their diaries over the years one would have found some wonderful cases. And not all swifts by any means.

His attitude and comments are not so different from the more measured tones of Sir John Woodcock speaking of the present day. Sir John blamed the court system for actively encouraging deviance, citing the recording of conversations with suspects. This, he said, allowed officers to believe it was only part of the game. He did not say that the question of independent recollections had been dealt with by the court in the case of Bass. The first ingredient in police deviance, Sir John said, was

a lack of belief in the veracity of some of the rules. The second is an insufficient distance from reality. Police officers see, daily, the effects of violence and crime. They see the scenes shielded from others, the grief that crime causes. Courts have built up defences to this, procedures, rules of evidence, ceremony, distance in place and time. The police officer does not have that distance; he sees what he sees, he hears what he hears, he carries the burden of that knowledge directly. This leads to a belief that he or she 'knows' the truth of what has happened.

The result is malpractice, not out of malice or desire for personal gain, but which begins out of good intention. It is a slippery slope with plenty of handrails to help the descent. Once an officer has lied in one case and got away with it, then he or she feels less compunction another time.[7]

Walter Easey, the former officer with the anti-corruption unit of the Hong Kong Police, believes the *pro bono publico* argument to be a fallacy:

Using information from criminals you are blackmailing to catch lesser fry whilst allowing your contacts to flourish is the operating myth in a corrupt officer's mind; that petty corruption is allowable to catch big criminals. This is a fallacy. If you pay corrupt detectives then the aim is to put your rivals out of business, so you may flourish the better.

Supervision and accountability are essential. Easey continues:

At the top the Commissioner has problems. Institutionally the police are very conservative. For the reforming Commissioner he has five or six years in the post before he reaches the statutory retirement age and this is a very short time to achieve radical reform against what may be considerable resistance. Worse, from his point of view, he inherits the top management team which he did not select and which he cannot replace. He can't act like a businessman and introduce his own tried and packaged team. Of those he inherits some will be all right and some won't. By the time a crusading Commissioner can promote people who think like him into ranks through which he can implement his policies he retires and the cycle recommences.
  Perhaps there should be a clear determination from the top, issuing P45s to people who have done nothing about corruption. That will pass the message down to the rank and file. Command responsibility as there is in the forces hasn't been introduced into police culture. There is no responsibility up the line of command. 'I didn't know.'

[7] Speech to the International Police Conference, London, October 1992.

'It's your job to know.' The top ranks have great power but no accountability.

The problem with that line of thinking is how far to take it. Just how high should have been the head-roll count in *The Times* inquiry? Should, for example, Millen have been required to resign and, if so, what about Brodie? Clearly, a balance would have to be struck but such a scheme would surely concentrate some senior minds.

Amongst others Simon Holdaway has pointed out just how obstructive officers can be when they put their minds to thwarting the good intentions of their superiors. Easey recalls a situation from his days in Hong Kong but which is one which can be applied to any force, anywhere.

One of the obstacles to rooting out police corruption was something I observed. If you get a reforming Chief Superintendent in a division and he starts a crackdown on the CID – random checks, double checking the diaries, stopping contacts with prostitutes and so on – then there is a backlash in the form of a subtle process amounting to covert industrial action. The clear-up rate can be altered administratively by writing up or down crime. Take the following two scenarios. A woman has her handbag snatched in a market and stallholders grab the thief or the thief escapes with her handbag.

The officer in a case where the handbag thief is apprehended can take a statement – which he will write down, don't forget – on the basis that the woman is shaken up, didn't she see something flash, could it have been a knife, she had a lot of money didn't she, can't remember, well had she cashed her giro recently, well how much was that? He's preparing an armed robbery charge.

[In the second scenario], if there's no one in the cells then he can keep the woman waiting and be brusque. Lost your purse or something? Can't waste time. I've got two murders and a rape next door! Dropped it somewhere did you? Well, give the details to the desk sergeant.

So in the first scenario you have a serious crime cleared up and in the second no crime at all revealed so the clear-up rate is looking good. But when you have a reforming Chief

Super the process is reversed and everything is classified. The serious crime rate goes up and, remember, you can't direct a detective to solve a crime any more than you can direct a social worker to care. He or she has to want to. So all losses become theft, and all TWOCs[8] become theft autos or thefts from autos. 'Lost some tapes haven't you? Claim on the insurance.' The result is a massive increase in serious crime and a correspondingly catastrophic drop in clear-up rate. 'No one's talking 'guv', 'no leads', 'you know what it's like with forensic', 'have to write this one off'.

Back at the area headquarters the administration is looking at the twelve boroughs in the division and all are normal except one. Looks as though there's a crime wave, collapse of morale, low arrest rate. The answer is the Detective Chief Superintendent is transferred and everything goes back to normal. In turn he's been punished with a lack of promotion for doing an honest job so he applies for study leave to read for a PhD or he resigns.

It has been said that over the last few years police officers have made a career structure out of informing on their colleagues. Both research and anecdotal evidence show that such behaviour is risky; however it is not a new concept. It appears to have been in operation in Liverpool between the wars: 'The system then was, there was a number of sergeants who had been in the army. There was a number of men who had passed for sergeant's rank, and the only way they could get it was to report another policeman so they could go to the Chief Constable on a discipline charge.'[9]

It was certainly not considered sporting for one officer to spy on another.

A certain bookmaker wrote to Scotland Yard charging a Chief Inspector with blackmailing himself and others in the same industry . . . The charges were quite definite and specific. There is a 'Star Chamber' at the 'Yard' where

---

[8] Taking a vehicle without the consent of the owner. It does not of itself carry a right of trial by jury.
[9] M. Brogden, *On the Mersey Beat*, p. 83.

offences alleged against members of the force are considered 'in camera'. An investigation was at once held by this 'court' into the charges and the nature of the investigation may best be indicated by the following statement made to me by the Chief Inspector in question one night:

'I was returning home rather late. The streets were almost empty. Suddenly I caught sight of a man whose behaviour was most mysterious. He was dodging in and out of front gardens and hiding in doorways. In fact his conduct was so fishy that I kept my eye on him with the intention of "picking him up". He was clearly avoiding me. However by a little manoeuvring I managed to come up with him and took him into custody. I conveyed him to the station and then – what do you think! – he turned out to be a plain clothes police officer from another division! He was watching me! What do you think of that – one officer put on to watch another officer!'

The charge against him proved to be true and was followed by the officer's summary expulsion from the force, in spite of the fact that his term of service had nearly expired, when he would have been due to retire on pension. He was not prosecuted.[10]

In December 1992 the *News of the World* reported details of a plan launched by Greater Manchester Chief Constable David Wilmot and posted on notice boards throughout the county to encourage officers to report on others whom they believed to be involved in corruption. The notice under the heading 'Whistle Blowing' read: 'Occasions may arise when a police officer or a member of support staff become aware of some form of police malpractice. Individuals may feel isolated and established lines of communication may seem inappropriate. Accordingly two hotline extensions have been established at force headquarters.'

The newspaper reported that a police insider said, 'This is not the way to weed out bent coppers. It lends itself to malpractice. This method could be used to settle old scores.' There had been no calls on the hotlines except whistles of derision, a message 'Hitler and Ceaucescu tried this too' and a civilian member of

[10] H. L. Adam, *CID*, p. 31.

staff who wanted to know what she had to do to get herself harassed. Meanwhile Ian Westwood, local chairman of the Police Federation, said, 'Officers are unhappy at this hotline. If people have information they should come out in the open not give it anonymously. I accept people who find corruption need moral courage. But this lends itself to all sorts of abuse.' Instead the *News of the World* itself set up a hot line.[11]

All the whistle blowing down the line may have been humorous for the readers of the *News of the World* but the need for officers to be able to report approaches anonymously is recognized by senior members of the police. Simmonds, referring to coercion and its effect in his paper, said that 'Only education and the opportunity for officers to report approaches anonymously will lay this matter to rest. Equally in the event of an investigation the investigator must be of sufficient calibre to recognize the "inner circle" from the outer circle and be prepared and empowered to offer immunity from prosecution to members of the outer circle.'

According to one former officer in the City of London Police, this is precisely what he had achieved before Operation Countryman swept in:

> If you want to get a seasoned detective you send in seasoned detectives after him. They have to have experience. I broke the detective who would have turned supergrass. He had had £60,000 from the Williams & Glyn's robbery and had given other officers £50 backhanders to protect him and his mates. I was authorized to give him an indemnity against prosecution. Next thing I heard, Countryman went in and just asked for his warrant card. And that was the end of that. I'll never know why they chose the West Country team. They should have had people from somewhere like Greater Manchester or Leeds.

A good example of lack of early guidance comes from a former Flying Squad officer who was himself later investigated but not prosecuted and who later resigned:

This DS in the station I was first sent to had been acquitted

11 *News of the World*, 6 December 1992.

twice at the Old Bailey during and after the war. He was still in the service in 1961 and he used to sit untouched at his desk with an old coat drawn around him. At 10.30 precisely he would lean back and say, 'They've drawed the bolts' and off he would go to the Beehive public house where he would stay until closing time. It was said (with admiration) he was so bent that if he went to a building site break-in he'd have himself a handful of nails. He was a living legend. Corruption is traditional, that's the whole thing.

And again:

Louis was a ticket tout. I was a uniform PC in 1957 and went to Spurs football ground where he was selling tickets outside. I nicked him for pavement obstruction. I took him behind the gate and he nutted me. I did him for assault on police. I took him to Wood Green Magistrates Court in front of the chairman, who was a really hard man. Louis, he pleaded guilty. I was giving his antecedents – he had more form than Arkle – and he was likely to get a carpet for assault when the court inspector got into the witness box beside me and said that Louis was not a bad old boy and it wasn't a very serious assault. I realized then both that Louis was well connected and someone had had a few quid.

Another suggestion for supervision which has been used in New York is the system of checks and balances in the form of an internal audit. One example is random recall statements. An officer from a special unit goes to see a victim of crime some months after the incident and takes a second statement. Court records are checked and the overall picture is reviewed. Another method, again tried in the United States, is the deliberate testing of the honesty of desk officers. A wallet is handed in, drugs are left on the seat of a patrol car, and later checks are made to ensure that the amount of money has been properly recorded or the drugs checked in intact. The price of this sort of check and balance is, however, a high one. The officers begin to feel themselves to be under suspicion and in turn morale is lowered and bonding against the administrators is heightened.

One of the traditional suggestions to cure police corruption is the removal of temptation. With the arrival of the Betting and Gaming Act 1959 the fraudulent prosecution of street bookmakers came to an end. With the Prosecution of Offences Act 1985, which put the conduct of court cases in the hands of the Crown Prosecution Service, the opportunity for the police to 'put in a good word' in return for money was severely curtailed if not totally eliminated. (In fairness, from time to time the 'good word' was genuine or was to assist an informer.)

Brutality is now said to have been eliminated by PACE, the tape-recorder and, the latest cure-all, the provision of television cameras in police stations to supervise not only the interviews but the suspect and his surroundings on a more or less continuous basis, thereby making the police aware of their need for good behaviour. Said a senior detective in 1990:

> I have never personally seen anyone 'fit' a case around a suspect or put a forged signature on their interview notes. But I am also a realist. I would never say that no one has ever been 'verballed', that no policeman has ever given a suspect a set of notes to fit the circumstances, that evidence is never embroidered.
>
> But the cases which are causing all the fuss – the West Midlands and Guildford cases – all belong in the past. There is a distinct gap between the old days and what happens now, both in the rules which govern police practice and in police attitudes as well.
>
> I don't hold with beating or torturing a suspect. It seems to me to destroy what you stand for. When I was a young detective, I wasn't surprised to see someone get a smack around the ear; it was an accepted interview technique. People didn't know their rights then, and didn't question it. You may still get an old-fashioned copper who will still take a swipe at someone, or you get an assault in a confrontation on the street. But an assault in custody does not happen in the modern context. It was once part of police culture, but not now: other policemen won't stand for it.[12]

Yet if the experiments which have been carried out so far are anything on which to base a judgment, police officers soon

12 'A Fair Cop', *New Statesman & Society*, 2 February 1990.

forget the presence of the cameras and revert to behaviour which, according to the senior detective, no longer happens.

In October 1992 PC Alaistair Deakin brought Russell Parker in for questioning to Litchfield police station in the Mid-Staffordshire Police area. The camera in the custody suite should have been switched off but, by mischance, it had been left running and the Constable was filmed slapping Parker across the face with his gloved hand whilst the prisoner was standing quietly with his hands cuffed behind him.

In mitigation it was said that Parker, who had been arrested after a domestic incident with his girlfriend, had kicked Deakin on the side of the head on the way to the police station. 'It is the sort of conduct which more commonly in the past would have been dealt with in the context of police disciplinary proceedings,' said David Twigg, the defence solicitor, tellingly. Deakin was fined £500 and ordered to pay £25 costs.[13]

Perhaps even more serious was the blatant disregard that another West Midlands Police force had for the presence of the cameras and the Code of Practice in PACE set out to protect suspects. The presence of the camera has long been argued as a necessary requirement to avoid malpractice and, just as importantly, the false allegation of malpractice. First came the advocates of the tape-recording and then the advocates of the video. 'If video-recording procedures operate properly, unjustified allegations of malpractice are discouraged, abuse is exposed and third parties can determine later whether interviews with suspects have been fairly conducted or not.'[14]

Mike McConville, together with Yorkshire Television, was allowed access for five weeks to a police station in which video-taping experiments were being introduced. This was done with the full co-operation of the force and all officers involved in the interviews were aware of and agreed to participate in the television filming. The filming was conducted through unobtrusive cameras and microphones, fixed into the station walls and ceilings unaccompanied by any special lighting.

'In front of the camera the official police view was promoted in every particular, both explicitly and implicitly,' wrote McConville. On camera the senior officers asserted faithfulness

13 *Daily Telegraph*, 27 October 1992.
14 John Baldwin in the *Guardian*, 9 December 1991.

to the law and attributed 'sharp practices' to a bygone age ended by PACE. In front of the cameras the position was similar; the officers involved in questioning suspects did so in ways described as consistent with the ethical interviewing principles. Suspects were allowed to give their version of events without harassment or coercive tactics designed to drive them into the case theory of the interviewing officers.

But in two cases, when the police did not believe themselves to be on camera, things changed dramatically. In the first the police officer investigating the case, with a rank of Detective Inspector, was convinced a suspect, Clive, had been responsible for committing a series of burglaries – between two and six o'clock on the night he was arrested. There seems to have been no supporting evidence for this theory and it was important therefore that Clive confessed. This was the police officer treating Clive with dignity and respect:

> I ain't bull-shitting you. I'm gonna charge you with six [offences]. If you want six fucking charges – your barrister ain't got much of a fucking argument at the end of the day. I don't really want to charge you with six fucking charges: I'd rather charge you with a couple and you can have four TICs matters taken [into consideration]. You can rip the fucking four TICs up when you get to court – I don't really give a shit . . . I mean I could really fucking throw it on thick for you.

The second instance followed the same lines but this time required the passive cooperation of the custody officer. Since PACE, the custody officer has been 'the prisoner's friend'. It is his duty to ensure that every time the suspect is questioned the names of those visiting him are recorded, that he is given rest, food, etc. and is not questioned at disorientating hours. On this occasion the interview was not logged and the keys to the cell were merely handed back to the custody officer. The interview, which was also intended to produce a 'deal', included, 'I want an easy life pal. I want to make my fucking life quiet. The easiest way I can do it is the way I want to fucking do it . . .' None of this behaviour was detectable from the official interview.

McConville drew a number of important lessons from 'this short experiment', including the belief that 'where countervailing methods are sufficiently powerful, such as the need to gain convictions or convictions by particular means, the real world belief of police culture – that you cannot do it by the book – easily triumphs over the idealized claim of fidelity to the law.' His experiment also led him to the belief that the introduction of video-taping into interrogations does nothing to prevent off-the-record exchanges between police and suspects or to discourage police rule-breaking in informal settings. Moreover,

> where the police make threats or inducements or strike deals with suspects in private which then lead to a confession in the formal interrogation, the position of a complaining suspect will be weakened rather than strengthened by the supporting video-taped record of the confession because of its apparent ability to recapture reality and because, contrary to the misplaced belief of ordinary people and even of some academics, it is not possible to tell from the video recording whether suspects have been the subject of prior improper pressure.[15]

One of the academics to whom McConville was referring was his erstwhile colleague John Baldwin, who had this to say in riposte: 'Even where improper pressures have been exerted or suspects have been "softened up" in the cells beforehand – things that are unlikely to be explicitly raised in an interview – I would still see it as advantageous to have the formal interview on tape.'[16]

Loyalty, through bonding, misplaced or otherwise, is another bar to research into the police; it is never possible to tell whether the interviewer is being fed the party line. But here are a number of responses of officers who were serving at the end of the 1980s to questions put by Roger Graef about the Holloway Road affair in particular and informing on their colleagues generally. They also throw an interesting sidelight on some extracurricular activities of the police.[17]

> The police made it worse by letting them go. That was a stupid act. The common view is that you do something like

---

[15] M. McConville, 'Videotaping interrogations', *New Law Journal*, 10 July 1992.

[16] J. Baldwin, 'Suspect interviews', *New Law Journal*, 31 July 1992.

[17] All the quotations are from Roger Graef's *Talking Blues*, pp. 234–8.

that, if you go a little bit over the top, then you've got to arrest the buggers. Don't leave them on the street. You've got to arrest them. Everybody thought that what they did was absolutely stupid. There were so many obvious mistakes made – things you learn as a PC just for self-protection. But nobody questions them beating the black kids up. That would be too liberal. *(Met PC, aged twenty-six, seven years' service; formerly with the Special Patrol Group)*

Why did it take so long for Holloway Road to come out? Camaraderie! But there doesn't seem to be much of that at the moment. There used to be. The job's changing. The camaraderie isn't there as much. Perhaps it was a pang of conscience. You get bobbies turning to Christ. We had one here, he said, 'I've turned to God, I'm a born-again Christian.' He resigned, but he said: 'Before I go, I want to clear the air.' He told the Chief Super: 'I'd like to tell you about the various arrests I've made that have been fictional.' All the bobbies were shitting themselves. (*Scottish PC in a large City force, aged twenty-nine, ten years' service*)

The Holloway Road verdict was quite right. I've got no sympathy for them at all. The public won't take any notice of violence against the police while you've got complete idiots like that running around doing it to the public. They'll say, 'What's good for the goose is good for the gander.' It's fair comment. We've let ourselves down.

But life isn't always black and white. For a policeman to use minimum force all the time is very difficult, especially under pressure. Very occasionally someone might snap and people are going to get hit. It's difficult to say, but some slight excesses policemen might cover up because they understand what brings it about. That sounds awfully corrupt. If you've got friends and you know you'll put them in prison for the next five years, it's very difficult. Fortunately, I've never been in that circumstance. (*Met Sergeant, aged thirty-three, twelve years' service*)

If he [the officer who reported the Holloway Road incident] has had a nervous breakdown, that's why. He is a grass. He's got to live with that now. We all stick together and whatever happens happens and we don't tell anybody outside. If that was me, I wouldn't even consider a transfer, I would just leave the fucking force. (*PC aged twenty-six, five years' service*)

People find it very difficult to grass. The villains outside – they don't like a grass. It's the same in here. You can always think: once he's grassed on his mates, who's going to trust him again? It's wrong, but it's human nature. (*Met PC, aged twenty-four, six years' service*)

When you come out of training school there's only one thing on your mind and that's being accepted by your relief. You look out for whatever it is you have to do to be accepted and you do it. It may be looking the other way when a bloke's being hammered. If I lose my rag and get out of order and the other blokes look after me, then I'm going to do the same for them if they do something they shouldn't do.

But I'm not doing bird for anyone else, I can tell you. If it comes to choosing between being loyal to your mates and maybe doing bird, I'd look out for number one. You've got to in this game. (*Met PC, aged twenty-six, three years' service*)

In contrast to that last constable, a former Flying Squad Detective Sergeant, speaking of the end of his career in the 1970s, said: 'When it came down to it, I knew in my heart of hearts if I had to go to prison I would not name anyone. If I'd been done I wouldn't say anything. No way in the world.'

Unsurprisingly, officers are keen to promote a feeling that today's probationers are a different breed who would not stand by and witness violence or dishonesty. Says an Inspector on a provincial force:

I'll give you an example. I was talking to some probationers in the summer of 1992, several of whom had done a bit of training, and one then went out with a tutor Police Constable at a station in an Afro-Caribbean area. The tutor Constable deliberately drove outside a public house, wound down the window and started shouting at the men on the pavement and making gestures. The probationer came back and told his superior at the training school. If you find something totally unacceptable you report it.

What the supervisor at the training school had done is not clear but the Inspector added, 'If I'd been the supervisor I'd have rung up the nick and spoken to the senior officer and said, "You've got a bit of a problem with PC Y."' What was certainly not clear from the story was how PC Y, with what must have been known racist tendencies, was allowed to be a tutor PC in the first place.

Another officer on the same provincial force was not quite so sure about today's probationer's stance towards violence:

> Most of these things are quite marginal. Take violence in charge rooms. Gratuitous violence, I could see the probationer bubbling the officer. But it's the difficult prisoner who has to be put in the van forcibly, taken from the van and put in a cell forcibly. It's then that gauging how much force is necessary is very difficult. I think the majority would complain to their sergeant if they saw undue violence.

This apparently new attitude of probationers was not what McConville found when he was researching *Watching Communities, Watching Police*, in which he observed three widely disparate forces, the Met, Gwent and Avon, and Somerset. 'After a couple of weeks probationer officers had accepted what were portrayed as correct features of police culture.' His researches showed that officers who did not conform to the peer group could find themselves in an untenable position:

> What do you do with an officer who doesn't fit in? You can make someone unwelcome and destroy their morale very quickly. Deliberate talk in the canteen – 'Wasn't the party wonderful on Saturday night?' The officer who wasn't invited quickly realizes he's unwelcome. When jobs are shared no one chooses to work with that officer. He can't stand it and he leaves.
>
> It's schoolboys' clubs. Punishment and triviality are given such magnitude in these relationships.

Loyalty to colleagues is built quickly and the loyal colleague has perhaps the worst of all times when he discovers a fellow officer is dishonest. The man who would go to any proper lengths to bring a criminal to justice will go to the same, but this time dishonest, lengths to prevent his colleague being caught. Sometimes this will be done off his own bat and sometimes he will conform to peer group pressure, fearful of reprisals or ostracism if he does 'shop' his colleague. It is only a complete re-education of the police officers showing their loyalty should be to the service and to society rather than to deviant individuals which will turn around this attitude. For the experience of officers who have grassed, or who have known others who have, does not make for happy reading.

Some see an improvement in the police resulting from a complete separation of the uniform and detective branches and the creation of a National CID. The idea is not new. In 1839 a Royal Commission on County Police advised the formation of a National Police Force with the Met as its nucleus. The concept was rejected and a permissive Act was passed instead which allowed the counties to create their own forces. It was not until 1931, nearly a century later, that a scheme was devised to amalgamate the smaller forces. This modest proposal was resisted at every hand's turn and was seen by many, including the press and Members of Parliament, as a Home Office tyranny. Said Assistant Commissioner Ronald Howe over three decades later:

> In 1965 Scotland Yard will be moving from its old premises to a new site in Victoria, and that should be the occasion for the two branches of the police to become separate, Uniform and Detective. My concern has never been to nationalize the Uniform Branch, but the Criminal Investigation Department, which should be set up with authority and sufficient manpower to be able to take over without delay.
>
> As I have written elsewhere, the Uniform Branch and the CID have different jobs to do. The Uniform Branch works alongside the *public*, dealing with traffic control, patrol activities and crimes in the streets. The CID on the other hand works alongside the *criminal*.

The incidence of crime, particularly robbery with violence, is so high that the formation of a national CID has become imperative. What is needed is a force with central headquarters closely linked, not with the Uniform branch as it is now, but with regional offices of its own to ensure rapid investigation of any serious crime with all its resources.[18]

A quarter of a century later his words are echoed bitterly by a former senior officer who later became a solicitor:

> In the Metropolitan Police Force, there was a grave defect in the leadership and organization. In the main, the senior men were Uniform men, ninety-nine per cent of whom had no CID experience and who were openly jealous of the CID. These men had mainly escaped from general police work to undertake safe jobs in a clerical capacity but called themselves 'administrators', later on 'managers'. Many were eaten up by jealousy of the CID officer and did much to hinder and be awkward. They obtained seats of power oblivious as to the needs of criminal investigators and the public.
>
> I can recall the 1950 to 1975 era. These escapologists from police work decreed that CID had one car for general duties, no cameras, no copiers, very little staff, shoestring budgetry to fight the crime accompanying the expansion of wealth in the UK, with more cars, electronics etc. Our beloved Uniform mandarins had chauffeur-driven cars lying idle from 9 am to 5 pm and from 7 pm till 7 am. They built up armies of admin types but made sure the CID existed on a shoestring. Let me recall a CID taking ten or fifteen crime cases to court in a morning or going to Quarter Sessions and Assizes (later the Crown Court) in a morning and working up to fourteen hours per day to cope. This was the norm for the CID officers.

Cars have always been a power symbol. Says a former Detective Chief Superintendent, 'I always thought he [a senior officer] was a buffoon. Right from Day One. The cars on the squad were changed every three years and we had a red Granada coming. He said, "That's my car. You can have mine", which was a black Princess. He insisted he sat in the front so he could work the radio.'

Remember, however, what happened when the CID in the Met was allowed the autonomy of investigating complaints into its own.

[18] Sir Ronald Howe, *The Story of Scotland Yard*, p. 171.

One source of hope for improvements has been new technology. The use of tape-recorders has been welcomed by
some as a cure-all of police misconduct, although of course
it has not achieved that high ideal. Nevertheless some police
officers are using tape-recorders on their own initiative: about
eight per cent of officers questioned in a survey for the
Royal Commission admitted carrying them, often against
force guidelines. Dr Stephen Moston said, 'It particularly
applies to traffic officers who, when they stop a car, turn
on their tape-recorders in their pockets to prevent subsequent
allegations that they had said something untoward.'[19]

But now the suspects themselves sometimes carry tape-
recorders for their own protection. Two policemen who were
recorded telling an Indian suspect 'It's not your fucking country'
were docked a day's pay. 'I am scared of the police,' said Malkjit
Singh Natt. 'I always carry a tape-recorder because I have been
harassed so many times.' The officer had said that Natt would
have had a worse time in India. 'They'd beat you up or shoot
you. That's what we should do, fucking shoot you.' Natt was
also called a wanker and asked, 'Why don't you go home to
India, Pakistan or wherever you fucking come from, it's not
your fucking country?' Natt had been arrested following a row
with his wife. A police spokesman said, 'These officers have
learned by their experience and regret it deeply.' The papers
were sent to the Director of Public Prosecutions.[20]

Sometimes the police seem to have ignored the possibility that
tape-recorders might be used against them. In the early 1980s a
John Goodwin had been a regular visitor to the Old Bailey, first
as acquitted defendant and later as prosecution witness. He was
charged with the burglary of a bank in Whitechapel in 1982
and on his first trial the jury could not agree. The second was
abandoned when he feigned a heart attack and on the third when
he produced a tape-recording of a detective taking money from
him. The case was stopped. Goodwin had ingeniously placed
the tape-recorder behind the family's Christmas tree and had
recorded what was alleged to be the officers taking bribes. The
detectives were later charged but two were acquitted, one after
putting up the equally ingenious defence that he had taken the

---

[19] *Daily Telegraph*, 12 December 1992.
[20] *Sun*, 4 July 1992.

money but had told the truth so he could not have perverted the course of justice nor committed perjury. The third had his conviction quashed by the Court of Appeal.

Given time, the mandarins of Scotland Yard could show equal ingenuity in defeating awkward technology. The Electrostatic Document Analysis (ESDA) test had been successful – from the point of view of the defendants, that is – in showing that logbooks had been doctored in the Chelsea Headhunters soccer hooligan trial. 'These statements are unreliable,' said Lord Lane, 'and the credit-worthiness of the officers involved in the making of them has been destroyed.' The test was also successfully put to use in the Millwall FC hooligan trial of the same year and in the West Ham 'Inter-City firm'. Now in April 1992 it was discovered that police officers had been instructed to use special log-books that would virtually eliminate their chances of being caught if the notes were later doctored. A plastic backing sheet inserted before writing ensured that no indentations were left and so an ESDA test would prove useless.

Not surprisingly there was something of a legal, if not general, outcry. 'Surveillance books often provided crucial evidence at trials, let alone appeals,' said Michael Mansfield, former chairman of the Bar Anthony Scrivener, and John Hendy, who represented the Tottenham Three in their appeals over their convictions in the Broadwater Farm case. They were in a good position to know that ESDA had played a crucial role in that case. Indeed, admitted Scotland Yard, it was the collapse of the Millwall Football, Tottenham and similar cases which had brought about the review of surveillance operations. The new log-books with their plastic backing sheets had been introduced shortly after the successful appeals; it had taken the legal profession a couple of years to catch up.

It came to light after a London drugs case in which the lawyers had asked to see the surveillance record with a view to ESDA testing. This had proved impossible because of the plastic sheet. Now the aggrieved silks wrote to the Commissioner, Peter Imbert, telling him they were shocked at this innovation. Was it routine? Yes, replied William Taylor, the Met's Assistant Commissioner in charge of specialist operations. The reason for the piece of plastic, he said, ingenuously or ingeniously depending upon your point of view, was that the plastic provided a solid surface on which to write. The same log-book could be used in a number of different cases by insulating one page from another, which prevented information relevant to one case being indented on to a page used in a separate case. Are we all clear now?

A spokeswoman for the Met agreed that this could ruin an ESDA test but suggested that tampering could still be picked up by other forensic tests, on the ink, for example. Anthony Scrivener was not happy: 'ESDA is the only incontrovertible forensic evidence apart from fingerprints. I find it surprising that the police have to adopt any practice which potentially makes it impossible for ESDA to be carried out.'[21]

Once out in the heat of the light the plastic melted: the Met announced the end of the scheme.

Turning to a quite different level, the Police Complaints Authority (PCA) was established in 1984 when, under the Police and Criminal Evidence Act of that year, it replaced the long-discredited Police Complaints Board under which the police investigated the complaints themselves and few complaints were ever found to be substantiated. Says a London solicitor:

> I've only personally been involved with two complaints against the police. One was in relation to an identification parade. The defendant was alleging it had been fixed. Personally I don't think it had, but the statement taken from me by the so-called independent investigation officer was nothing short of fawning. 'You as a very experienced solicitor would have noticed if anything had been amiss, wouldn't you, sir?' The whole idea was exculpation.
>
> The second was when after an acquittal of a client I was asked to withdraw a complaint over the refusal to allow my managing clerk to be present at an interview. I said 'no' and the officers then cautioned my clerk and said he had impersonated a solicitor and that was why he had not been allowed in. This was utter rubbish.

The aim of the PCA part of the Act was to make the system more independent of the police, allowing it more

[21] *Sunday Times*, 5 April 1992.

involvement in running the 'major' investigations concerning death, serious injury, assault and conspiracy. The PCA may (i) choose, or veto the choice of, investigating officers, supervise their inquiries and receive their final report; (ii) monitor the speed and efficiency of the investigation and issue a statement to the Chief Constable saying whether it had been satisfactorily carried out; (iii) receive a Chief Constable's decision upon what action he intends to take as a result of the investigation and, if need be, overturn that decision. It may prefer disciplinary charges itself or refer the case to the DPP for criminal charges. In the event the DPP declines to charge on the grounds there is insufficient evidence, then the PCA may still prefer disciplinary charges.

The public, however, has shown little confidence in the police complaints system. One example of the reasons for this is the case of seventy-five-year-old Kathleen Gibbons who was bundled into a police van whilst supporting the miners' strike by selling the *Yorkshire Miner* outside Collets bookshop in Charing Cross Road. 'I was grabbed by the arms and transported to the van by two officers,' said Mrs Gibbons, 'A third dragged me inside and I ended up on the floor with my knees up in the air. They were all laughing and jeering.' She was taken to West End Central police station where she was held for an hour and a half and then charged with obstructing the highway.

Collets had given her permission to sell newspapers on its patio but police claimed she had obstructed the pavement by extending her arm across it. Mrs Gibbons said the police called her a 'West End tart' and 'an old Commie'. A policewoman accused her of begging.

When the case came for trial the police failed to appear and the magistrate dismissed the charge, awarding her £60 costs. In 1986 she was awarded £1,200 in the County Court for false imprisonment and malicious prosecution. No disciplinary proceedings were taken under the Police Complaints Authority; the Director of Public Prosecutions had already decided not to prosecute. The PCA said: 'The authority is happy with the way the inquiry was carried out and happy with the conclusion that the Metropolitan Police did not have sufficient evidence for disciplining the officers.'[22]

[22] *Independent*, 25 October 1989.

One modern way of countering an allegation of an assault by the police has been to charge the victim. Until the middle to late 1980s, with the tacit approval of the courts, this was a generally successful ploy, although it did not meet with the favour of the criminal fraternity. Says a former bank robber, 'They used to give you a hiding and that was that. Now they give you a hiding and then they charge you.'

Recent years are littered with such cases and the public has tired of having its complaints dismissed. Often, when the defendant has been acquitted, he has in turn sued for damages. Those who have suffered and who brought cases have not been serious criminals. For example, on 28 April 1984 Mr and Mrs Reid of Skelmersdale went out to celebrate Mr Reid getting a job after a long period of unemployment. They were joined by a Mr and Mrs Carr. On their way home around midnight, with Mr Reid driving, they were stopped and Mr Reid was asked to take a roadside breath test. He refused, saying he had done nothing wrong. He was arrested, pushed to the ground and then thrown into the back of the police van with his arm twisted behind him. Mr Carr went to Mr Reid's assistance and he too was put into the van 'with force'. In the van both men were again assaulted and at the station Mr Reid was handcuffed and put in a cell. His head was banged against a wall and he lost consciousness. When he came to in a pool of blood he was asked to give an alcometer reading. It was negative and he was released after spending five hours in the station. The bones on one side of his face were fractured and he spent five days in hospital.

Charges of refusing to give a blood test and assaulting a police officer were brought and, in turn, dismissed by Liverpool Magistrates. At the Liverpool High Court in October 1987 a jury found the men's allegations of assault and false imprisonment proved. Mr Reid received £15,080 in damages and Mr Carr £5,020. The Chief Constable of Lancashire appealed to the Court of Appeal. Before the jury the police had maintained they had done nothing wrong. Now the appeal was to reduce the amount of damages. 'The men had been treated appallingly,' said Sir John Arnold, dismissing the appeal.[23] There is, however, no way that we, the public, know if these officers

23 *The Times*, 21 July 1988.

were disciplined. Indeed, unless the Reids or Carrs made a complaint as well as bringing an action, they will not know officially either.

On 25 September 1992 over £10,000 was paid by the Met to Terry Battenbough. He had been charged with possessing an offensive weapon and acquitted by a jury. In an agreed statement read to the Croydon County Court his solicitor detailed how the officer had given evidence at the trial to the effect:

> He found the flick knife concealed and not easily visible in the plaintiff's breast pocket when he stopped him on February 9 1989. At the trial Mr Battenbough produced the jacket he said he had worn . . . The officer agreed it was similar to that worn by him that evening.
> When the officer demonstrated the position of the knife in the pocket in the course of his evidence, it was plainly difficult to conceal.

No criminal or disciplinary proceedings had been brought against the officer and Battenbough's solicitor Louise Christian said, 'The police complaint was dismissed early on without any real attempt to investigate it. Once again the Met is paying large damages because of the wrongdoing of one of its officers but has not been prepared to do anything to stop the wrongdoing.'[24]

In a review of damages paid out there is a dismal repetition of this sort of case, coupled with the intransigence of the police to admit anything in the faintest way improper has occurred. Less than three weeks later, on 13 October, it was reported that Scotland Yard had agreed to pay Frank Critchlow, founder of the Mangrove Community Association, £50,005 and his court costs to settle his action for false imprisonment, assault and malicious prosecution by police after a drugs raid in Notting Hill in 1988. He had been charged with possessing heroin and cannabis and permitting the supply of heroin and cannabis and other drugs. He was acquitted on all charges by a jury at Knightsbridge Crown Court in June 1989. Nevertheless, when announcing the settlement, counsel Patrick O'Connor told the court that the police still refused to apologize, as they do to this day, denying Critchlow's allegations.

The award meant that by October 1992 the Yard had paid out £347,900 in damages. In all of 1991 it had paid out £471,599. It is a measure of the public acceptance of apparent police malpractice that a single payment of £300 in 1959 was sufficient to bring about a Royal Commission.

One way to restore public confidence would be a change in the complaints procedure. At present the standard of proof is that of the criminal trial: beyond reasonable doubt. There are those who argue that a change will have to be made so that complaints are decided on the balance of probabilities – something that the police argue would be wholly unfair to them. The Police Complaints Authority is arguing for it in lesser cases which would not involve loss of a job or demotion. Walter Easey comments, 'Whenever you have a one-on-one situation with nothing else to support the claim, you can never establish a disciplinary offence to the required standard of proof, which is why you now have a startling increase in civil damage claims.'

Then there are the endless delays. If a complaint is made following an arrest and charge, nothing is done until the defendant is acquitted or convicted. Nor is there any great public confidence in how complaints are routinely investigated. Says a former Assistant Chief Commissioner: 'The officer being investigated expects help from the investigator. I'll give you an example. An Inspector has an allegation to investigate so he speaks with the DC. The questioning gets a bit tight and the DC says, "Listen guv,' whose fucking side are you on?"'

And help was often obtained, certainly in the past. One of the most unfortunate aspects of the insidious corruption rife in the CID was the manner in which allegations against officers were followed up prior to the establishment of A10, a police complaints department. It became regular practice for the officer concerned to be informed immediately of the existence of the allegation in order that he could do whatever was necessary to thwart any serious efforts at investigation.

The rank and file officers could see that there were different standards. As a retired Detective Chief Superintendent said:

'If you investigate a complaint and he [the officer] is working for the good of society, give him a fair crack of the whip. If he's working for himself get him out. I suppose that sums it up.' Nor did complainants know the result of their complaint. One of the things which galled them was the fact that months could pass without their knowing what happened to the officer.

This, however, is one matter which the PCA is changing. The complainant now has the right to attend disciplinary proceedings up to the moment of judgment. He or she is then notified of the result. Why the complainant is effectively ordered out at the moment of truth is not exactly clear. It is rather as if the public gallery was cleared for the jury's verdict.

The next step towards restoring public confidence would be a complete revision of the complaints procedure to refuse permission for officers under investigation to resign on health grounds, so maintaining full pension rights, whilst the investigation is pending. An ex-Assistant Chief Constable remarks:

> Sir Robert Mark always suggested that he was the cleanser of the stables but, in fact, he did as much as anyone to disguise the extent of corruption. In his book *The Office of Constable* he boasts that during his spell as Commissioner some 478 officers resigned in anticipation of disciplinary or criminal proceedings. This allowed many of those who had been steeped in corruption for years to escape by feigning illness and being allowed to resign on full pension.

It is a charge Mark refutes with some vigour. 'I would go so far as to say [allowing resignations] is an essential requirement for cleansing a police force.'[25] In this he is supported by the Police Federation, which argues that whilst an officer may retire before he is suspended, once suspended whilst disciplinary proceedings are in progress he cannot retire. 'There is money to be saved in this way,' says Tony Judge of the Police Federation. 'It is often sensible not to suspend an officer.' It is not a view with which the public at large have much sympathy.

Central to any control of police deviance is the attitude of the courts. The judges have shown that they are willing to deal with financially corrupt officers whilst tolerating a measure of misbehaviour relating to evidence. If all breaches of the PACE codes were to be dealt with by excluding evidence improperly obtained, this would, without doubt, have a salutary effect on the police.

[25] Letter to the author.

At present there is a considerable reduction in the number of cases coming before the magistrates' courts in London. This will have a knock-on effect and the number of cases waiting for jury trials will be greatly reduced in, say, six months' time. The reasons for the reductions are not clear. It may be that with Treasury restraints more people are being cautioned than prosecuted. It may be that the Crown Prosecution Service is refusing to conduct more cases because of lack of evidence. It may be that the police, feeling constrained because of the recent run of Court of Appeal decisions against them, coupled with a growing awareness by defendants and their advisers of the benefits of the right of silence, are not obtaining sufficient evidence to bring charges in the first place.

There is, according to Tony Judge, a change in police attitude, brought on by the constraints of PACE and the prevailing attitude to them:

Police officers began to feel that failure to detect was acceptable to society.

If you have a low conviction rate it is because you stop persuading people whom you know to be guilty to confess – you live with the consequences and you find it doesn't matter very much.

There has been a huge reduction in the business in the courts in London. People believe this is because of the philosophy.

The Lord Chief Justice is amazing if he thinks the civilized conversations between counsel and client before they go into court are the same as interviews with suspects. A suspect is not going to tell you the truth. He is preconditioned to lie. There has to be hectoring and bullying. Of course, they [the officers in Darwell] shouted and repeated the questions. But this outburst by the judges, I think it was the last straw for a lot of people because it showed how divorced they were from the reality of the case. It remains true that the only one to see the criminal in his habitat is the police officer.

When you talk to detectives, you know how they are feeling frustrated.

The twin dangers of this are that the police will slide further into frustration and as a result will take the law into their own hands and administer their own style of extracurricular justice.

One constraint on the police was the establishment in 1985 of the Crown Prosecution Service (CPS), a concept that had been mooted from time to time over the previous 150 years. Before the CPS a number of forces had their own solicitors' departments in or attached to the police station. The Prosecution of Offences Act 1985 quite deliberately removed these departments from what could be seen as too close a relationship. The CPS had to be seen to be independent of pressures and blandishments from officers.

The establishment of the CPS was understandably not popular with the police. In London in particular it took away considerable power from the rank and file officer. It reduced the chances of overtime, pleas bargaining and the day to day opportunity for financial corruption. It also had certain side effects which had not been foreseen. No longer could the officer go to court and follow his case, his arrest, through to acquittal or sentence. This may have been financially wasteful but the officer maintained an interest in his prisoner. Now his case was removed from the officer's hands to become a file in someone else's office.

It also damaged crime prevention. One of the traditional ways in which a detective kept an eye on who was associating with whom was at court. On the day of a court case the public gallery would be packed with friends and well-wishers. It was interesting and valuable for a detective to know just who had come to stand surety for a defendant or who was minding his wife or girlfriend during a remand in custody. With the advent of the CPS this opportunity was gone.

The first few years of the CPS engendered great hostility between the lower- and middle-ranking officers, of whom a great number had many years' service, and what they saw as the inexperienced and often lily-livered young prosecutors in a certainly under-staffed service. It was a time when PACE was also still in its infancy and officers could not, or perhaps would not, understand why charges were dropped by the CPS. Because the police were physically separated from the CPS, often by a considerable distance, there was never the opportunity to explain why decisions had been taken. Relations were at a low ebb as files disappeared, much to the embarrassment of the CPS and the ill-concealed glee of the police. In 1989 things were not that much better and the *Police Review* ran a CPS horror story competition.

One of the great problems of the CPs was and still is that it cannot compel the police to do anything. It may ask time and again but if the officer is 'on nights', 'on weekly leave' or has more pressing business it cannot demand and obtain a piece of crucial evidence. Yet the CPS nevertheless provides a golden opportunity for police regulation and containment. Here is the chance to provide the 'officer class' which Trenchard sought and in which he conspicuously failed. If the Royal Commission recommends that once again there be closer links between police and prosecutor, with the presence of qualified lawyers in the police station, then this could have the effect of reducing deviance of all kinds.

Meanwhile the current fashion in the criminal justice system is the plea bargain. This is a misnomer. It is the sentence bargain. The plea bargain has long been used by officers and prosecutors alike to concentrate the mind of the defendant on the charge. 'If you don't plead guilty to obtaining by deception then I'll have to put a conspiracy to defraud and that means the Bailey,' was a typical suggestion in a cheque fraud case. That was a true plea bargain, as is the acceptance of a plea to a charge of s20 Offences Against the Person Act 1861 in return for the dropping of an s18 charge under the same Act. The s18 charge carries a sentence of life imprisonment, the s20 only five years.

The plea bargain is when the judge, in return for a plea of guilty to a set number of charges, indicates what the sentence will be. There is a tacit understanding at present that a plea of guilty will carry a reduction of between twenty-five and thirty per cent in most cases, but what defendants really wish to know is whether they will walk out to the arms of their loved ones at the end of the morning. Because of a series of deficiencies in the criminal justice system, such as lack of funding, there is now a campaign to allow the plea (i.e. sentence bargain) where the judge will set out the exact sentence he intends to impose for a plea of guilty.

The danger of this is that the police will become further alienated from the court system. Here is an American example of what can happen: 'Six months later, the man who tried to kill Henry Winter with a car agreed to a plea-bargain arrangement with the Brooklyn district attorney's office. The arrangement called for the man to pay a fifty dollar fine.'[26] Although the author does not specifically suggest that the reason for such a deal is that the officer had gone badly crooked, it is implicit that it must have been a contributing factor.

Probably the police can never be successful in fighting crime if they are obliged to stay within the rules, something recognized by Edward Clarke QC defending in the Brighton Detectives case in 1955: 'You do not . . . if you are trying to catch them, follow the Queensberry Rules. You use what methods you can for the purpose of getting the people arrested and punished.'

But systematic deviance can probably be controlled. It should be possible to stamp on the officers who are purely bent for themselves; those who are bent for the job are in a completely different category. As Clarke said, they are expected by us to fight fire with fire, on our behalf.

> The battle of wits which goes on, day in and day out, between the London detective and his quarry is sharp and can be deadly for the unwary and more orthodox detective. Each plots the downfall of the other and each learns the nature of the contest as they develop and mature, either in the ranks of the CID or in those of the criminal network. A professional reputation is to be made on the one hand and large pickings on the other.[27]

With the right of silence being more vigorously observed, the implementation of PACE and the tightening by the courts of the exclusion of evidence in breach of the Codes of Practice, the police are now fighting with what appears to be a hand tied behind their backs. In the past one way to stop deviance has been to remove the temptation, and one way to stop the so-called verbal in the police car on the way to the station or between cell and interview room will be to remove that right of silence. 'The recent sorry trails of overturned verdicts have forced a sudden switch to due process and organized crime has become immeasurably less hazardous.'[28]

---

[26] M. McAlary, *Buddy Boys*, p. 69.
[27] J. Alderson, *Law and Disorder*, p. 176.
[28] John McVicar in *Time Out*, 7 October 1992.

The problem with allowing controlled deviance to fight crime (bent for the public) is that it becomes that much easier to accept and more difficult to control individual deviance (bent for self). In Tony Judge's words:

> I believe the public has lost its sense of innocence about the police without quite understanding why. So it is no longer shocked at the revelation of police malpractice as it used to be.
>
> There is an unspoken understanding on what they can do but they can use legal and extra-legal means to keep the lid on. The more legislation, the more the allegations of malpractice You will end up with a very clean police force but a very ineffective crime fighting force.

C. H. Rolph may have the final comment:

> You ask me how deviance can be contained. I don't think it can. It's universal and endemic. It invades every level of administration and government in every country. If ever 'social ethics' became an educational subject which had a firmer basis than mythological religions, which themselves eat away at the community importance of truth, I mean simply telling the truth, the chances would begin to improve. As it is, lying is an essential instrument of 'law and order'.

Ultimately it is we who will have to decide if that is what we want.

Bibliography

Ackroyd, P., *Dickens* (1990), London (Sinclair Stevenson)

Adam, H. L., *CID Behind the Scenes at Scotland Yard* (1931), London (Sampson Low, Marston & Co)

Alderson, J., *Law and Disorder* (1984), London (Hamish Hamilton)

Ascoli, D., *The Queen's Peace* (1979), London (Hamish Hamilton)

Babington, A., *A House in Bow Street* (1969), London (Macdonald)

Baldwin, J. and McConville, M., *Courts, Prosecution and Conviction* (1981), Oxford (Oxford University Press)

Banton, M., *The Policeman in the Community* (1964), London (Tavistock Publishers)

Barthel, J., *Love or Honour* (1990), London (Piatkus)

Bayley, D. H., *Forces of Order* (1976), California (University of California Press)

Bean, J. P., *The Sheffield Gang Wars* (1987), Sheffield (D & D Publications)

——*Crime in Sheffield* (1981), Sheffield (Sheffield City Libraries)

Beigel, H. and A., *Beneath the Badge* (1977), New York (Harper & Row)

Benyon, J. and Bourn, C., *The Police* (1986), London (Pergamon)

Beveridge, P., *Inside the CID* (1957), London (Evans Brothers)

Birkett, Lord (intro), *The New Newgate Calendar* (1960), London (Folio Society)

Biron, Sir C., *Without Prejudice* (1936), London (Faber and Faber)

Bleackley, H., *The Hangmen of England* (1929), London (Chapman and Hall)

Bottomley, A. K., *Criminology in Focus* (1979), Oxford (Martin Robertson)

Boyle, A., *Trenchard* (1962), London (Collins)

Brady, D., *Yankee One and George* (1984), London (Police Review Publishing Co)

Brogden, M., *The Police: Autonomy and Consent* (1982), London and New York (Academic Press)

——*On the Mersey Beat* (1991) Oxford (OUP)

Brown, A., *Watching the Detectives* (1988), London (Hodder & Stoughton)

Browne, D. G., *The Rise of Scotland Yard* (1956), London (Harrap)

Burnham, M., *The Burnham Report of international jurists in respect to the Broadwater Farm Trials* (1987), London (Broadwater Farm Defence Campaign)

Bunyan, T., *The Political Police in Britain* (1977), London (Quartet Books)

Cain, M., *Society and the Policeman's Role* (1973), London (Routledge)

Campbell, D., *That was Business, This is Personal* (1990), London (Secker & Warburg)

Cater, F. and Tullett, T., *The Sharp End* (1988), London (Bodley Head)

Challenor, H. with Draper, A., *Tanky Challenor* (1990), London (Leo Cooper)

Cherrill, F., *Cherrill of the Yard* (1953), London (Harrap)

Chesshyre, R., *Inside the Police Force* (1989), London (Sidgwick & Jackson)

Chevigny, P., *Police Power* (1969), New York (Pantheon)

Chibnell, S., *Law and Order News* (1977), London (Tavistock Publications)

Chinn, C., *Better betting with a decent feller* (1991), Hemel Hempstead (Harvester Wheatsheaf)

Clayton, R. and Tomlinson, H., *Civil Actions against the Police* (1992), London (Sweet & Maxwell)

Clemente, G. W. with Stevens, K., *The Cops are Robbers* (1989), New York (Avon Books)

Cobb, B., *Critical Years at the Yard* (1956), London (Faber and Faber)

——*Murdered on Duty* (1961), London (W. H. Allen)

Cohen, A. K., *Delinquent Boys: the Culture of the Gang* (1955), Chicago (University of Chicago Press)

Cornish, G., *Cornish of the 'Yard'* (1935), London (Bodley Head)

Cox, B., Shirley, J. and Short, M., *The Fall of Scotland Yard* (1977), Harmondsworth (Penguin)

Critchley, T. A., *A History of Police in England and Wales* (1967), London (Constable)

Daley, H., *This Small Cloud* (1987), London (Weidenfeld & Nicolson)

Daley, R., *Prince of the City* (1979), New York (Houghton Mifflin)

de Castro, J. P., *The Gordon Riots* (1926), Oxford (Oxford University Press)

Devlin, Lord, *The Criminal Prosecution in England* (1960), Oxford (Oxford University Press)

——*The Judge* (1979), Oxford (Oxford University Press)

Du Cann, C. G. L., in Rolph, C. H. (ed), *The Police and the Public* (1962), London (Heinemann)

Dilnot, G., *The Trial of the Detectives* (1928), London (Geoffrey Bles)

Divall, T., *Scallywags and Scoundrels* (1929), London (Ernest Benn)

Emsley, C., *The English Police* (1991), Hemel Hempstead (Harvester Wheatsheaf)

du Rose, J., *Murder was my Business* (1971), London (W. H. Allen)

Fabian, R., *London After Dark* (1954), London (Naldrett Press)

——*Fabian of the Yard* (1955) London (Heirloom Modern World Library)

——*The Anatomy of Crime* (1970), London (Pelham Books)

Fisher, Sir H., *Report of an Inquiry by the Hon Sir Henry Fisher into the circumstances leading to the trial of three persons on charges arising out of the death of Maxwell Confait and the fire at 27 Doggett Road, London SE6* (1977), London (HMSO)

Fitzgerald, M, McLeannan, G. and Pawson, J., *Crime and Society: Readings in History and Theory* (1981), London (Routledge)

Fordham, P., *Inside the Underworld* (1972), London (George Allen & Unwin)

Franklin, C., *The Third Degree* (1970), London (Robert Hale)

Goldman, N., *The Differential Selection of Juvenile Offenders for Court Appearances* (1963), Washington (National Council on Crime and Delinquency)

Graef, R., *Talking Blues* (1989), London (Collins)

Grant, J., *Sketches in London* (1838)

Greeno, E., *War on the Underworld* (1960), London (John Long)

Grigg, M., *The Challenor Case* (1965), London (Penguin)

Gronow, R. H. (ed John Raymond), *The Reminiscences and Recollections of Captain Gronow* (1964), London (Bodley Head)

Heidensohn, F., *Women in Control?* (1992), Oxford (Clarendon)

Hethcrington, Sir T., *Prosecution and the Public Interest* (1989), London (Waterlows)

Hinds, A., *Contempt of Court* (1966), London (Bodley Head)

Holdaway, S., *Inside the British Police Force* (1983), Oxford (Basil Blackwell)

Honeycombe, G., *Adam's Tale* (1974), London (Hutchinson)

Hoskins, P., *No Hiding Place* (no date), London (Daily Express Publications)

——*Two Were Acquitted* (1984), London (Secker & Warburg)

Howe, Sir R., *The Story of Scotland Yard* (1965), London (Arthur Barker)

——*The Pursuit of Crime* (1971), London (Arthur Barker)

Jefferson, T. and Grimshaw, R., *Controlling the Constable* (1984), London (Frederick Muller)

Jennings, A., Lashmar, P. and Simson, V., *Scotland Yard's Cocaine Connection* (1990), London (Jonathan Cape)

Judge, A., *A Man Apart* (1972), London (Arthur Barker)

——, and Reynolds, G. *The Night the Police Went on Strike* (1968), London (Weidenfeld & Nicolson)

Kaye, T., *Unsafe and Unsatisfactory?* (1991), London (Civil Liberties Trust)

Kelland, G., *Crime in London* (1986), London (Bodley Head)

Knapp Commission, *Report on Police Corruption* (1972), New York (George Braziller)

Knight, S., *The Brotherhood* (1983), London (Granada)

Knox, B., *Court of Murder* (1968), London (John Long)

Lang, G., *Mr Justice Avory* (1935), London (Herbert Jenkins)

Laurie, P., *Scotland Yard* (1970), London (Bodley Head)

Lee, J. A., 'Some Structural Aspects of Police Deviance in relations with Minority Groups, in Shearing, C. (ed), *Organisational Police Deviance* (1981), Toronto (Butterworths)

Lee, W. M., *A History of the Police in England* (1901), London (Methuen)

Lieck, A., *Bow Street World* (1935), London (Robert Hale)

Lock, J., *The British Police Woman* (1979), London (Robert Hale)

——*Dreadful Deeds and Awful Murders* (1990), Taunton (Barn Owl Press)

Lustgarten, L., *The Governance of Police* (1986), London (Sweet & Maxwell)

Mark, R., *Policing a Perplexed Society* (1978), London (George Allen & Unwin)

——*In the Office of Constable* (1978), Glasgow (William Collins & Sons)

McAlary, M., *Buddy Boys* (1987), New York (Charter Books)

McConville, M., Sanders, A. and Leng, R., *The Case for the Prosecution* (1991), London (Routledge)

McConville, M., *Watching Communities, Watching Police* (1992), London (Routledge)

McNee, Sir David, *McNee's Law* (1983), London (Collins)

Merton, R. K., 'Anomie and Deviant Behaviour: a discussion and critique', *Social Theory and Social Structure* (1968), New York

Meyrick, K., *Secrets of the 43* (1933), London (John Long)

Millen, E., *Specialist in Crime* (1972), London (George G. Harrap & Co.)

Montgomery Hyde, H., *Norman Birkett* (1964), London (Hamish Hamilton)

Morgan, R. and Smith, D., *Coming to Terms with Policing* (1989), London (Routledge)

Morton, J., *Gangland* (1992), London (Little, Brown)

Napley, Sir D., *Not Without Prejudice* (1982), London (Harrap)

Nisbet, A., *Dickens and Ellen Ternan* (1952), London

Narborough, F., *Murder on My Mind* (1959), London (Alan Wingate)

Neiderhoffer, A. and E., *The Police Family* (1978), Lexington (Lexington Books)

Peto, D., *The Memoirs of Dorothy Olivia Georgiana Peto, OBE* (1970), The Metropolitan Police Historical Advisory Board (unpublished)

Phillips, Sir C. (Chairman), *The Royal Commission on Criminal Procedure* (1981), London (HMSO)

Porter, B., *The Origins of the Vigilant State* (1977), London (Weidenfeld & Nicholson)

——*The Refugee Question in Mid-Victorian Politics* (1979), Cambridge (Cambridge University Press)

——*Plots and Paranoia* (1989), London (Unwin Hyman)

Price, C. and Caplan, J., *The Confait Confessions* (1977), London (Marion Boyars)

Pringle, P., *The Thief Takers* (1958), London (Museum Press)

Punch, M., *Conduct Unbecoming* (1985), London (Tavistock)

Read, L. and Morton, J., *Nipper* (1991), London (Macdonald)

Reiner, R. *The Politics of the Police* (1985), Brighton (Wheatsheaf Books)

Reith, C., *British Police and the Democratic Ideal* (1943) Oxford (OUP)

Richardson, J. F., *The New York Police: Colonial Times to 1901* (1970), Oxford (Oxford University Press)

——*Urban Police in the United States* (1974), New York (Kennikat)

Robbilliard, St J. and McEwan, J., *Police Powers and the Individual* (1986), Oxford (Basil Blackwell)

Rolph, C. H., *The Police and the Public* (1962), London (Heinemann)

Rozenberg, J., *The Case for the Crown* (1987), Wellingborough (Equitation)

Rumbelow, D., *I Spy Blue* (1971), London (Macmillan)

Russell, Earl, *My Life and Adventures* (1923), London

Russell, K., *Complaints against the Police which are Withdrawn* (1986), Leicester (Militak)

Samuel, R., *East End Underworld* (1981), London (Routledge, Kegan Paul)

Seabrook, M., *Coppers* (1990), London (Harrap)

Sherman, L., *Police Corruption* (1974), New York (Anchor Press)

Short, M., *Inside the Brotherhood* (1990), London (Grafton)

——*Lundy* (1991), London (Grafton)

Sillitoe, Sir P., *Cloak without Dagger* (1956), London (Pan)

Skelhorn, Sir N., *Public Prosecutor* (1981), London (Harrap)

Skolnick, J. J. and Bayley, D. H., *The New Blue Line* (1986), New York (Free Press)

Slipper, J., *Slipper of the Yard* (1981), London (Sidgwick & Jackson)

Smith, D. J. and Gray, J., *Police and People in London* (1983), London (Policy Studies Institute)

Smith, R. L., *The Tarnished Badge* (1965) New York (Crowell)

Stalker, J., *Stalker* (1989), London (Penguin)

Stead, P. J., 'Some Notes on Police Corruption: The English Experience', *Police Journal*, January-March 1975

——*The Police of Britain* (1985), London (Macmillan)

Storch, R., 'The Plague of Blue Locusts: Police Reform and Popular Resistance in Northern England 1840–57', *International Review of Social History* 20 (1975)

Symons, J., *Bloody Murder* (1972), London (Faber and Faber)

Taylor, K. with Mumby, K., *The Poisoned Tree* (1990), London (Sidgwick & Jackson)

Taylor, L., *In the Underworld* (1985), London (Unwin Paperbacks)

Thurston, G., *The Clerkenwell Riot* (1967), London (George Allen & Unwin)

Tietjen, A., *Soho* (1956), London (Alan Wingate)

Topping, P., *Topping* (1989), London (Angus & Robertson)

Trodd, A., 'The Policeman and the Lady: Significant Encounters in Mid-Victorian Fiction', *Victorian Studies* (1984), vol 27, no 4

Uildriks, N. and van Mastrigt, H., *Policing Police Violence* (1991), Aberdeen (Aberdeen University Press)

van Laere, E. M. P. and Geerts, R. W. M., 'Deviant Police Behaviour', *Policing* (1985), vol 1, no 3

Vollmer, A., *The Police and Modern Society* (1936), California (California Press)

Waddington, D., *Contemporary issues in public disorder* (1992), London (Routledge)

Wainwright, J., *Wainwright's Beat* (1987), London (Macmillan)

Walsh, D. and Poole, A., *A Dictionary of Criminology* (1983), London (Routledge, Kegan Paul)

Wambaugh, J., *The Blue Knight* (1972), New York (Little, Brown)
——*The Choirboys* (1975), New York (Delacorte)
——*Lines and Shadows* (1984), New York (William Morrow)
Ward, R. and McCormack, R., *Managing Police Corruption* (1987), Chicago (Office of International Criminal Justice)
Waters, W. (*aka* Russell), *Recollections of a Detective Police-Officer* (1856), London (J. and C. Brown)
——*Autobiography of a London Detective* (1864), New York (Dick and Fitzgerald)
Webb, S. and B., *English Local Government: The Parish and the County* (1906), London (Longmans)
Wensley, F., *Detective Days* (1931), London (Cassell & Co)
Westley, William A., *Violence and the Police* (1960), Cambridge (MIT Press)
Whitaker, B. *The Police in Society* (1979), London (Eyre Methuen)
White, W. S., 'Police trickery in inducing confessions', *University of Pennsylvania Law Review* (1979), vol 127, no 3
Wickstead, B., *Gangbuster* (1985), London (Futura)
Wilkinson, L., *Behind the Face of Crime* (1967), London (Muller)
Williams, G., *The Hidden World of Scotland Yard* (1972), London (Hutchinson)
Williams, W. W., *The Life of General Sir Charles Warren* (1941), Oxford (Oxford University Press)
Wilson, James Q., *Varieties of Police Behaviour* (1968) Cambridge (Harvard University Press)
Woffinden, B., *Miscarriages of Justice* (1987), London (Hodder & Stoughton)
Woodiwiss, M., *Crime Crusades and Corruption* (1988), London (Pinter Publishers)
Wyles, L., *A Woman at Scotland Yard* (1952), London (Faber)
Young, M., *An Inside Job* (1991), Oxford (Oxford University Press)

Index